# MILTON AND THE PURITAN DILEMMA

UNIVERSITY OF TORONTO DEPARTMENT OF ENGLISH

STUDIES AND TEXTS, No. 1

# MILTON
## AND THE
# PURITAN DILEMMA
### 1641-1660

BY

ARTHUR E. BARKER

UNIVERSITY OF TORONTO PRESS
TORONTO AND BUFFALO

University of Toronto Press
Toronto and Buffalo
Reprinted 1955, 1964, 1971
Reprinted in paperback 1976
ISBN 0-8020-6306-3
LC 58-3195
Printed in USA

*Ad Patrem*

"*Officium cari taceo commune parentis;*
*Me poscunt maiora. . . .*"

*That which is the only discommodity of speaking in a clear matter, the abundance of argument that presses to be uttered, and the suspense of judgment what to choose, and how in the multitude of reason to be not tedious, is the greatest difficulty which I expect here to meet with.*

TETRACHORDON

*All arts acknowledge that then only we know certainly when we can define; for definition is that which refines the pure essence of things from the circumstance.*

TETRACHORDON

# *Foreword*

THIS study is based upon material embodied in a master's thesis ("Milton and the Struggle for Liberty") presented at the University of Toronto in 1934, and upon material embodied in a doctoral thesis ("Studies in the Background of Milton's Prose") presented at the University of London in 1937. A considerable amount of additional material has since been collected, and the whole has been recast and rewritten. It cannot be regarded as reproducing, even in part, the above theses; yet its publication enables me to record my gratitude to those who have assisted me at its various stages. I owe my thanks to the Provost, the Reverend Dr. F. H. Cosgrave, and to the Corporation of Trinity College, Toronto, for the fellowship upon which the work was begun; to the Imperial Order Daughters of the Empire for an Overseas Scholarship held between 1935 and 1937; to Professor C. J. Sisson of University College, London, for direction, counsel, and many personal kindnesses; to Professor Sir Herbert Grierson for advice and criticism; to Principal M. W. Wallace of University College, Toronto, for his kindly interest in the work from the beginning; to the Department of English of the University of Toronto, and to the committee appointed to help see the volume through the press—Professor A. S. P. Woodhouse and Professor N. J. Endicott of University College, and Professor J. D. Robins of Victoria College; to them, the Reverend Dr. W. C. DePauley, and Mr. Ernest Sirluck for criticizing the manuscript; to Miss Winifred Husbands of University College, London, for generous assistance; to Mrs. A. W. B. Hewitt and the editorial staff of the University of Toronto Press for unflagging patience; to the Librarian of University College, London, for permission to use the Lord Northcliffe Collection; to the Librarians of the British Museum, the Dr. Williams' Library, the Union Theological Seminary, and to the Keeper of the Public Record Office. The extent of my debt to Professor Woodhouse, who has allowed me the unstinted benefit of his knowledge of

Milton and Puritanism from his direction of the original thesis to the publication of this study, cannot here be adequately expressed. It will be obvious to students of seventeenth-century thought and to the readers of my notes. From Dorothy Riley Barker, in the ten years since we began to work together on Milton, I have received much more than the "meet and happy conversation" and "the cheerful help" for which my less fortunate author sought in vain.

ARTHUR BARKER

Trinity College, Toronto,
6 November, 1942.

# *Contents*

# *Introduction*

FEW subjects can be more interesting to the student of literature and of ideas than the development of a great poet's opinions on society. The development of Milton's opinions is especially interesting because of the concentration of his immense energy at a time of national crisis upon questions which are still of fundamental importance, though the terms in which they are expressed have changed. Yet the study of such a subject is attended with serious difficulties, intensified in Milton's case by the unruliness of his energy when he wrote in prose, by the embittered complexity of the disputes he engaged in, and by the deceptive ease with which his statements can be made to seem applicable to present questions. In this analysis of the development of his views during the Puritan revolution I have tried to overcome these difficulties by examining his ideas at each stage in full detail and by interpreting them in the light of the changing climate of opinion among his Puritan associates.

It may be thought that in thus devoting a volume exclusively to his controversial prose works I have lost sight of the fact that his greatness lies in his poetry. That is not the case. Two arguments in defence of a study of this kind may be offered: that a full and exact understanding of Milton's prose is essential to a complete understanding of his great poems, and that the prose is full of interest in itself.

The absurd assumption of the eighteenth century, that the prose and the poetry expressed two strangely incompatible sides of Milton's personality, was the outcome of prejudices—still unhappily apparent in some of his modern critics—which prevented a fully satisfactory estimate of his genius.[1] It is true that his life and works divide themselves into three distinct sections: the years of preparation and the early poems, the period of the revolution and the controversial prose, the post-Restoration years and the three great poems; and it is also true that the revolution diverted his attention for some twenty years from the poetical tasks he contemplated in his youth. But if the prose was a digression, it was nevertheless intimately connected with his literary ambitions; and the energy he devoted to it was fully rewarded—though not in the way he had hoped. If he had not had the stern discipline and the profound experience of which the prose is the record, we should not have had *Paradise Lost*—and it is a romantic fallacy to suppose that we might have had something better.

It is fruitless to speculate on the course Milton's life would have followed had the revolution not occurred; but I do not think that he would have returned from Italy and Greece to compose a triumphant Arthuriad. We read his early poems in the light of his later accomplishments, and rightly find in them suggestions of the spirit and quality of his great works. But throughout them there runs a note of troubled uncertainty. I would not be thought to under-estimate the art of the *Nativity Ode* and *Lycidas*, or the charm of *Comus;* but it is manifestly true—and he was himself aware of it—that his early years were distinguished for their promise rather than for their fulfilment. In my opening chapter I have tried to indicate briefly how his sense of unfulfilment reached a climax after his return from Italy, and how he turned in the prose to a search for the conditions, private and public, which would make possible the fulfilment of his aims. If my reading of the state of his mind in 1640 is in any degree correct, the prose must be regarded not as a mere digression but as a natural and indeed inevitable consequence of his inability at that time to fulfil the poet's function as he saw it.

In his conception the poet was primarily the celebrator of the heroic deeds of great men. For this function learning was essential; but it is difficult to think great thoughts in an academic vacuum, and there is recognizable in the writings of his later youth a sense of the need for a deeper experience of human problems than he as yet possessed. The cloistered poet of Horton set out on his travels in search of it; but he found it in abundance among his countrymen at home.

His late spring was to have after all no true flowering; but it was out of the experience of the revolution that *Paradise Lost* and the later poems ultimately grew. At first sight the break between the prose and the last poems seems even sharper than the digression from the early poems to the prose. But *Paradise Lost* must, I think, have been maturing in his mind at least in the years immediately following his total blindness; and whether or not this was the case, the suddenness of the shock received by his hopes in 1660 must not be exaggerated. It would be difficult to overemphasize the shattering effect of the Restoration upon Milton's confidence; but it should be regarded as the culmination of a process whose significance he was being forced to recognize more and more clearly from 1650 on. The growth of popular royalist sentiment after the execution of Charles I, conclusively demonstrated by the remarkable popularity of *Eikon Basilike*, begot in Milton a deepening sense of bitter impatience with human weakness and hardness of heart. (Indeed, were it not for the absence of explicit evidence, one might date the emergence of this feeling from the scandalized reception of his divorce tracts.) A consequence of this is that in the last decade of the revolution his writings display a combination—unusual in English political thinking—of vigorously radical ideas with cold pessimism. This is the note of *Paradise Lost* and the later poems. In the prose period the mood of these poems was already developing. Moreover, the thought of the later prose is the consequence of Milton's effort to take account of the ill success of the Puritan experiment. The conclusions at which he thus arrived were recorded in his revision of *De Doctrina Christiana* at about the time of the Restoration; and the principles of that treatise (with certain modifications in detail) provided the ideological foundation for *Paradise Lost*. The prose therefore records the transformation of the Horton poet into the immeasurably greater poet of the last poems.

Throughout my study of Milton's thought in the prose I have tried to keep these matters in mind. Yet I have not here attempted to apply the conclusions of my analysis to the great poems. That is a matter itself requiring intense labour and long study. The prose constitutes a unit of Milton's work, by no means unrelated to the other two units but nevertheless complete in itself. I have treated it as such.

This limited subject seems to me in some measure to justify itself, especially at a time when the English-speaking peoples are once more examining their faith and morals with peculiar care. In the eighteenth and nineteenth centuries Milton's opinions had a considerable effect on democratic thought.[2] They have had less influence in the twentieth; but the renewed interest in his life and work (especially among American scholars) seems to indicate that we still have some need of him. In the other camp an attempt has been made to reinterpret his ideas in support of aims altogether opposite to those of critics like Macaulay and Geoffroy.[3] For such an interpretation evidence can be drawn from a part of his thinking: he accepted and defended the dictatorship of Cromwell; he came to distrust the multitude and to desire an oligarchical government. But the effort suffers under the disadvantage which, to a lesser degree, attended the interpretation of those nineteenth-century liberals who regarded him as an advocate of their naturalistic theories of liberty and equality: it requires the suppression of another part of his thinking, and the casting aside of postulates which may now seem to many to have little meaning but which he regarded as axiomatic.

He contended neither for an unrestrained individualism nor for the dictatorship of a political party. He was an unpractical idealist rather than a political thinker; and his theory of society was essentially religious and ethical, not secular and economic. Yet I believe the true influence of his idealism (and of his art) will revive because it is from a faith in the ultimate victory of truth such as he possessed that the human spirit must derive the strength to triumph over its enemies in the twentieth as in the seventeenth century. He wrote of man's destiny with eloquence and profound conviction at a time when the democratic theory of society was receiving its first practical formulation. He recognized its promise, and also some of the dangers which it must overcome if it was not to beget anarchy or be itself overwhelmed by tyranny. His prose records the evolution of his idea of liberty; but it was a liberty to be sought from within rather than from without, and its first essential was self-discipline in accordance with the highest dictates of virtue. That lesson we still need to learn, and he, in some measure, still can teach.

I have not set out, however, to compose a polemical pamphlet of my own, nor to attempt any application of Milton's principles to our problems. I do not mean to emulate Macaulay in extolling Milton—as Professor Liljegren bitingly phrases it—"with the volubility of a merchant marketing cheap goods,"[4] though I am not convinced by the volubility of those who would persuade us that the goods are indeed inferior, or that they came from a storehouse other than we had supposed. Though I refuse the dangerous task of drawing inferences, I may perhaps (with one of Milton's teachers) claim to have "brought my basket of stones, whence the cunning slingers, our Davids, if they please, may choose what they like. . . ."[5]

Milton's age, too, was one of disintegration, when the weakening of accepted principles and the rise of new modes of thought resulted in an intellectual as well as social upheaval. The commotions of the Civil War were, as he perceived, the throes and pangs which accompanied the birth of a new society—not of quite the society he desired, but of one which was to make possible an immense development of human life. Though the Puritan experiment ended in apparent failure, it provided a forcing-ground for ideas which were subsequently to bear their fruit in the slow transformation of the English polity. The successive attempts of one group after another in the Puritan party to effect a new settlement of church and state were not merely the results of a shifting control of power; they were the counterparts of the intellectual efforts of men of divers parties to achieve a synthesis which should replace that swept away by both Renaissance and Reformation, or, if a synthesis were impossible, a segregation which should simplify the problem and release men at once to a free natural and a free spiritual development.

Sir Herbert Grierson has remarked that "it is in Milton's work considered historically and in its entirety that one can contemplate the tremendous character of the forces at work in this troubled age when, simultaneously with, and in part as a consequence of, the reawakening of the mind of man to a full consciousness of his rights to freedom of thought and freedom of imagination, came a requickening of the spirit of Christianity as an other-worldly religion making fresh demands on him for a rigid and meticulous orthodoxy, an even stricter walk with God. . . ."[6] Milton's prose is the record of his effort to develop a theory of liberty, religious, private, and political, which should reconcile these conflicting forces. The future did not belong to those who strove with him to combine freedom of thought and imagination with a strict walk with God, but to those who separated the spiritual and the natural and thereby released the latter to follow its own untrammelled courses, either scientifically according to the prophecy of Bacon, or politically according to the programme of the Levellers. Such a division Milton refused to accept. It seemed to him to release undisciplined forces which might carry with them their own ruin. In order to define the theory which he adopted in its stead, I have considered historically and in its entirety, not the total body of his work, but his work during the revolution.

## 2

The starting point for such a study must be Milton's brief account in the *Defensio Secunda* of 1654 of his activities since the beginning of the revolution.

He opens this by saying that he was induced to return from Italy by "the melancholy tidings from England of the civil war"—the First Bishops' War of 1638—because "I thought it base that I should be travelling . . . abroad while my fellow-citizens were fighting for their liberty at home."[7] Since his leisurely return occupied some nine months, and his first contribution to the struggle did not appear for another two years, he has been charged with a disingenuous attempt to represent himself as having a zeal which he did not possess.[8] Such discrepancies and inconsistencies as this occur throughout the prose. The problem they raise must be dealt with at the outset, for it has been said that his pamphlets exemplify the Machiavellism which the Calvinist could easily justify in terms of God's service.[9] If Milton's statements cannot be accepted as representing his beliefs, if he was guilty of insincerity in recording his actions and of opportunism in the application of arguments, the prose will afford no satisfactory record of his development.

It must be admitted that Milton's accounts of himself are not always perfectly accurate, and that his arguments in the prose are not always obviously consistent; if they were so, this book would never have been written. But it is possible to distinguish inaccuracy and confusion from conscious misrepresentation. It is true that Milton's zeal did not immediately express itself on his return to England. Yet the description of his return is complete; and what it represents is not clumsy misrepresentation but a tendency to foreshorten and to see an ordered pattern where perhaps none existed.

That is also the case with the summary of his prose writings to 1654 which immediately follows in *Defensio Secunda*. Having described the pamphlets of 1641 and 1642 in which he attacked the episcopal government of the church, he observes, "Reflecting therefore that there are in all three species of liberty without which it is scarcely possible to pass any life with comfort, namely, ecclesiastical, domestic or private, and civil; that I had already written on the first species, and saw the magistrates diligently employed about the third, I undertook the domestic, which was the one that remained."[10] He then describes the pamphlets on divorce, freedom of the press, and education, composed between 1643 and 1645, and his writings on civil liberty, beginning with his apology for the execution of King Charles in 1649 and including *Defensio Secunda* itself.

Chronologically and in their subject matter, the pamphlets do fall into three groups, each concerned with a particular aspect of liberty. I have made this grouping the basis for the division of my study, adding a fourth part for the ecclesiastical and political tracts composed in 1659 and 1660, and a fifth for Milton's exposition of the theological principles which governed the theory of liberty developed in the prose. But one must be wary of assuming that the impressive pattern he recognized was the result of conscious planning. Fate had designed it so.

As Milton reviewed his career from the eminence of his *Pro Populo Anglicano Defensio Secunda*, it seemed to possess a striking inevitability; but it was an inevitability which followed the course of events rather than a preconceived pattern. It is not unlikely that Milton observed in 1642, or before, that men exercise themselves in religious, private, and political ways; and he may well have considered that it would be a commendable achievement to set treatises on each beside compositions in the three best poetical forms, tragedy, brief epic, and epic.[11] But he can hardly have perceived at the beginning of the Civil War that the minds of his contemporaries, concentrated in 1641 and 1642 on ecclesiastical reformation, would be agitated in the years following 1643 by the problem of liberty of private conscience, and in those following 1649 by the effort to establish the civil liberty of a commonwealth.

Here again there is foreshortening and over-simplification, but not necessarily conscious misrepresentation. Unlike the Calvinistic deity, Milton's God was essentially reasonable. His ways might be obscure, but Milton could not suppose them to be crooked. Throughout the revolution he possessed an assurance of divine guidance which kept him ever in his Great Taskmaster's eye and issued directly from his sense of inspiration as a poet. Even in his early poems, as I have tried to demonstrate elsewhere, the most characteristic product of that inspiration was an ordered patterning.[12] With his passion for the beauties of decorum and regularity, it is not unnatural that he should have seen his career in retrospect outlined with architectural simplicity. It is the tendency, indeed the function, of the poetic mind to impose patterns upon reality and to figure forth processes as more clearly inevitable than in fact they are.

Yet the student of Milton's developing thought must hesitate to accept the pattern for the reality. There is a pattern in his prose, but it is fluid, not static; and it cannot be recognized in its complexity if the prose is regarded as a series of pronouncements from a fixed and certain point on the three main divisions of liberty. I am unable to share Professor Tillyard's opinion that the pamphlets "express a coherent body of thought which could only have been formed in the meditative period before the Civil War."[13] Milton returned to England with a mind full of literary plans, not of theories of liberty; and the prose seems to me less the expression of ordered ideas than a record of the painful attempt of a sincere but not markedly precise mind to achieve coherence of thought in the midst of social disintegration.

To accept Milton's pattern without reservation is to place upon his activity during the revolution an interpretation which detracts from the achievement of his twenty years of dust and heat. If he could not commend a cloistered virtue, no more could he praise a mind incapable of discovering onward things more remote from its knowledge. Though its broad outlines were fixed by his personality and training, his conception of liberty was in process of development throughout the prose period; and if he did, as I think, arrive at a not inconsistent formulation of his theory of society by 1660, it was only because events had forced him to consider problems of which the Horton poet had been unconscious.

In their admirable studies of Milton, both Professors Hanford and Tillyard have been concerned to dispel the assumption that he "was diverted into prose"; that, but for the events of the revolution, "he would never have written in prose at all"; in short, that the prose was (in Pattison's phrase) "a prostitution of his genius."[14] Professor Hanford would argue that, though they were in part called forth by particular situations, the prose writings were not "merely or even primarily partisan and occasional"; that Milton rather employed the opportunities afforded by the revolution to promote "the ideals which had become part of his thinking as a result of the meditative study of his early years."[15] Undoubtedly (like the earlier Renaissance poets he meant to surpass),

Milton would have found in prose as well as verse a means to "dispose and employ those sums of knowledge and illumination which God had sent him into the world to trade with." The uncontroversial works—the history, the logic, the grammar—demonstrate the truth of this belief. But it by no means follows that, in Professor Tillyard's words, "each fresh occasion in the prose period evoked rather than created ideas in Milton's mind."[16]

Milton was thirty when he returned from his continental tour. His personality, his ideals, and his prejudices were in general fixed. He had acquired a vast sum of knowledge; and the references in his early poetry and prose, and especially (as Professor Hanford has shown) in his *Commonplace Book*, indicate that he had given some consideration to the problems which were subsequently to force themselves on his attention.[17] But that is not to say that he possessed a coherent theory of liberty and society. His early references to church and state are at best merely incidental and at worst merely passionate; his sum of knowledge was, as the *Commonplace Book* itself in part shows, to be immeasurably increased; his ideals and prejudices were to receive in the prose their formulation in thought.

During the revolution his thinking was constantly in process of transformation. In 1641 he accepted certain principles without considering their implications, and expressed them with an assurance which represents rather absence than coherence of thought. Events between 1641 and 1660 forced him continually to reconsider, to readjust, to develop, to enlarge his opinions. In consequence his arguments frequently seem to derive from crass opportunism; Professor Jordan observes that "Milton's thought when considered as a corpus presents perplexing difficulties to the historian"; and Professor Liljegren has been able to assert that even in the last pamphlets his ideas are flatly contradictory.[18] I do not myself believe that there is any argument in the prose which can only be explained by positing insincerity. What at first appeared to me, as to others, obviously contradictory and consequently disingenuous, I have concluded on further study to have been a confusion either in my own mind or in Milton's. Certainly he was no logical thinker. Moreover, he was composing polemical tracts, not philosophical treatises. The habit of the controversialist is to grasp at every argument which comes to hand and to adopt every means to refute the arguments of opponents. This Milton did; but I do not believe him ever to have used an argument which did not seem to him, at the moment, sound, nor to have made use of ideas which were without a relationship to his fundamental and constant convictions. It is of illogicality rather than insincerity that he should be accused.

The illogicality of his thinking is only brought into clearer relief by attempts to construct a pattern through the bringing together of passages from compositions widely separated in time.[19] Milton's opinions underwent a profound change between his first and last pamphlets. It is also increased if one reads into his phrases —the good of the people, natural right, liberty and equality—the modern meanings which they did not have for him. The prose is not the record of an already ordered body of thought, but the record of Milton's efforts to achieve a satisfactory formulation of his ideals in the midst of national disintegration and under the influence of personal experiences, public events, and the opinions of his contemporaries. It is only by analysing his ideas at each successive stage of their expression, by relating them to private and public events, and by interpreting them in the light of contemporary opinion, that one can perceive the developing pattern which they do indeed possess. No man's thought is static, least of all the thought of a man engaged in the effort to guide and to defend a revolution. Milton's thought and the thought of revolutionary Puritanism followed the same intricate courses.

## 3

I have not attempted to write, after Masson, a detailed life of Milton in connection with the history of his time. I have taken account of the experiences—his sense of inspiration, his unfortunate first marriage, his blindness—which modified his thinking because they required to be explained by it; but I have concentrated my attention on his ideas rather than on his total personality. Some degree of misrepresentation has been an inevitable consequence. The apparent contradictions in his arguments arose from his character; the effort to untangle them and to reveal the essential consistency beneath has meant some under-emphasizing of the impatience, the harshness, the intransigience, which produced them. Similarly I have not attempted to provide a complete picture of what Sir Edward Dering termed "a very accusative age."[20] But I have analysed in detail the controversies in which Milton was directly or indirectly involved because they were the forcing-ground of his, as of other men's, thought.

Sir Herbert Grierson has rightly said that "Milton's pamphlets are not to be read as of quite the same kind as those of many of his fellow pamphleteers on either side" since they are distinguished "by the exalted, prophetic tone of one whose vision goes far beyond the demands of the moment."[21] Yet, as Professor Haller has been noting,[22] there were many prophets in those days; and as the prophets of old spoke in the language of Canaan, so Milton spoke in the language (and sometimes with the manners) of his fellow-pamphleteers. His soul was perhaps "like a star, and dwelt apart"; but, in spite of his proud assertion that "my mother bore me a speaker of what God made mine own,"[23] the ideas he applied to the revolution bear a remarkable likeness to those employed by his fellows.

Not that Milton derived all, or most, of his ideas from contemporary arguments. What were their true originals we shall never certainly know. It would require a mind as capacious as his own to follow him through his studies in classical and Christian literature, in history, theology, and poetry; and I have not set out to trace his ideas to their sources (though I have made use of the conclusions of those who have examined his various debts)[24] but to seek analogies and contrasts in the reasoning of his contemporaries which would throw light on his development, the character of his thinking, and its peculiarities. I have concentrated my attention on the many (far more numerous than is commonly supposed) to whom he himself specifically refers in the prose or with whom he can be proved to have been associated; but in order to complete the picture of the immediate background of his thought, I have also drawn on the opinions of men of whose existence he can hardly have been ignorant.

The dominating force in that background was the ideology of Puritanism. As Professor Woodhouse has shown, this rested in its varied manifestations, from the Presbyterians of the right, through the Independents of the centre, to the Sectaries of the left, on "the effort to erect the holy community and to meet, with different degrees of compromise and adjustment, the problem of its conflict with the world."[25] Milton's aim in the prose was the achievement of the holy community as he saw it. It is true that, though he began by supporting those who meant as a first step to replace episcopacy by the presbyterial discipline supposedly prescribed by

God, his idea of the holy community subsequently revealed itself as remarkably radical. But that was also true of many who joined in the attack on the bishops, and who can only be denied the name of Puritan if it is so delimited as virtually to confine it to the Presbyterians.[26] The demand for a reformation which would beget the freedom of a holy community was common to all the Puritan groups; and the successive attempts of these groups to realize their particular interpretations chart the movement of thought between 1641 and 1660 in its main outlines. The general outline of Milton's development conforms to this movement.

Puritanism was not the only force in the intellectual background which affected Milton's thinking. It is a mistake to suppose that the current of thought associated with the Renaissance rather than the Reformation was dammed during the revolution and appeared only in the quiet backwaters of the Cam or the Isis. The two currents crossed not less but more sharply in Milton's "mansion house of liberty"; and their crossing in his prose is a reflection of their crossing in the minds of his contemporaries. As Professor Haller has pointed out,[27] the *Areopagitica* was, apart from its eloquence, no unique phenomenon; nor were its humanistic qualities—its confidence in the powers of man, in human reason, in progress, in a temperate freedom amid profusion—altogether without a place in the thought of his fellow-pamphleteers. In principles such as these a Puritan of the right like Thomas Edwards might see a Satanic design to tempt fallen man to prefer his own corrupt judgment to God's will; but they played a vital part in the naturalistic theory of human society which was developing, along with the sectarian theory of the church, in the minds of Roger Williams, John Goodwin, and the Levellers.

In considering the movement of Puritan thought and of Milton's opinions, one must therefore take account of the rationalism usually associated with the tradition of Christian humanism. Indeed Professor Hanford discerns in the humanism of Milton's early writings "the true source of his later radicalism."[28] But it is nevertheless possible to see, in the disputes which distracted the Puritan party and worked its undoing, a basic pattern of ideas characteristic not only of the right and the centre but even of the sectarians of the left and, with modifications, of the Levellers. The political arguments of these last were, in fact, implicit in the theory of the state propounded by Presbyterians like Samuel Rutherford, and even in the observations of Calvin himself.[29] They underwent reinterpretation and a radical extension; but the association of William Prynne and John Lilburne in the early years of the revolution typifies the connection between conservative and radical Puritanism.

In a not dissimilar way, Milton's association in 1641 and 1642 with the moderate Presbyterians who wrote the Smectymnuan pamphlets, represents his original acceptance of the Puritan presuppositions. As Lilburne became the enemy of Prynne, so Milton eventually condemned the group which included Thomas Young, once his beloved tutor. In both cases the evolution resulted largely from a combination of rationalism and Puritan principles.

The interplay of these two forces is apparent with peculiar intensity, as Sir Herbert Grierson has indicated, throughout Milton's career. It is represented at the outset by the contrast between the two men under whom he is known to have studied as a boy;[30] it was part of the atmosphere of his Cambridge days;[31] it is displayed in the distinctly humanistic quality of his academic exercises, in the violence of his attack on the church in *Lycidas*, in the stern morality which has induced Professor Haller to describe *Comus* (with some exaggeration) as a Puritan sermon.[32] It is no less clear throughout the prose; and one of the tasks of an interpreter should be to estimate the relative effect on Milton's thinking of the humanistic defence and the Puritan condemnation of human nature. Yet England was dominated by Puritan ways of thought during the revolution. That is also true of Milton's thought in the prose; and while I have tried to keep in view the constant influence of humanism, the weight of my emphasis falls inevitably on Puritanism.

It has seemed to me that from his first pamphlet to his last, Milton's thinking developed within the framework of principles which he shared with Thomas Young. His ideas underwent a profound modification; but his view of the revolution, and consequently his theory of human society, expressed itself throughout in terms of the doctrines fundamental to Puritanism—man's Fall, his natural corruption, his regeneration through grace, the peculiar privileges of the elect aristocracy, the Christian liberty of the regenerate. The interpretation of these doctrines at which he finally arrived differed from Young's. But he began by accepting them in their orthodox sense, and he never abandoned them altogether. Humanism had its effect on his reinterpretation; but it is only one of the sources of his radicalism. Another (and perhaps more important) was Puritanism itself, for it also had its radical significance.

The principles I have mentioned were, with varying degrees of emphasis, of first importance in the thinking of Milton's contemporaries—Lilburne and even Hobbes, no less than Rutherford and Cromwell. Though they were originally theological, they were capable of being applied to the problems of the revolution, they could serve the purposes of extremists as well as conservatives, and they provided a means of formulating a theory of liberty and society. In the early seventeenth century, theology still afforded the most acceptable explanation of the facts of experience. Ultimately, therefore, one must turn to Milton's theological opinions for light on his theory. Yet these were not clearly defined until the end of the prose period. For light on his developing opinions one must turn to those of his contemporaries who were striving to solve precisely the problems with which he dealt.

The disputes of the revolution are infinitely complex. One can distinguish certain parties among the opponents of the bishops and the crown, and the outlines of their positions are clear enough. Yet it is not sufficient simply to associate Milton with particular parties. The movement of his thought may be described as a steady shift from the Puritan right to the extreme left; but he belonged to no party, since none had a programme he could regard as wholly satisfactory. Nevertheless he had opinions in common with each party in turn, and it is only by detailed comparison that one can arrive at a clear apprehension of his position. As Lucius Cary, Viscount Falkland once aptly observed, the reader "may well believe me that I take no pleasure in tumbling hard and unpleasant books and making myself giddy with disputing obscure questions";[33] but it has seemed to me that only a thorough consideration of the controversies of the revolution on the church, freedom of conscience, education, the state, and political liberty, would suffice to elucidate the development of Milton's mind in the midst of them.

# *Part I*

## *Reformation and Liberty: the Anti-Episcopal Pamphlets. 1641-1642*

# Chapter I

## Musical Chords

WHEN in August, 1639, Milton returned to England after more than a year of travel on the continent, the forces which had troubled the English church and state increasingly since the accession of James I were gathering themselves for the final conflict. Ahead lay twenty years of exhausting confusion. The effort of Charles and his bishops to impose episcopacy and the English liturgy on Presbyterian Scotland had resulted in the first so-called Bishops' War, of which Milton had heard tidings in Naples; and the King's discomfiture in the Treaty of Berwick had been witnessed with satisfaction by the critics of his personal rule and by the Puritan opponents of episcopacy in England. In the April following Milton's home-coming the Short Parliament met; because of its sympathy with the Scots and its refusal to grant the King subsidies until civil and ecclesiastical grievances were considered, it was dissolved in less than a month. Meanwhile, fighting had broken out again in the north; the Scotch army soon crossed the border; and the King, finding it impossible to raise money, was forced to call a new parliament. On the third of November, 1640, the Long Parliament began its sittings, supported by public opinion and by the Scots in its determination to reduce the power of Archbishop Laud and his fellows and to curtail the abuse of the royal prerogative. With its release from prison of the Puritan pamphleteers, Prynne, Bastwick, and Burton, and its impeachment of Strafford, the momentous issue was joined.

These ominous proceedings were observed by Milton from "a pretty garden-house . . . in Aldersgate Street, at the end of an entry," a dwelling pecüliarly suited to the purposes of a scholarly poet (as his nephew remarks) "by reason of the privacy, besides that there are few streets in London more free from noise than that."[1] In this retreat he "returned with no little delight" to the studies and literary pursuits which had occupied him until his brief excursion abroad, giving some time also to the education of his nephews and "leaving without difficulty the issue of things more especially to God, and to those to whom the people had assigned that department of duty."[2] Until May, 1641, he took no public part in the rising dispute over the reform of the church, but proceeded with his reading and with ambitious plans for a poem, a drama and perhaps an epic.[3]

He had, however, returned from his travels because of the news of what was brewing at home.[4] He had meant to go from Naples to Sicily and Greece, the ultimate source of renaissance culture. Instead he had unhurriedly retraced his steps to Rome and Florence, and made his way through Venice to Geneva, the well-spring of the Puritan desire for reformation. Here he "had daily intercourse with John Diodati, the very learned professor of divinity"; and much of their talk must have turned on the prospects for the further purification of the English church. Thence he journeyed homeward, having turned his back, not without reluctance, on the faded glories of Italy and Greece. Nor was it merely his travels which were thus diverted; the whole course of his career was about to be changed.

There is much in Milton's youth which points towards the twenty years in which he devoted his mature energies almost exclusively to ecclesiastical and political controversy;[5] but of the meaning of these signs he was himself clearly not aware in 1639. Nor was he aware that there was then preparing not only a climax in the national conflict but, in concert with it, the first major crisis in his own development. The singular interest and power of his life and work arise largely from the fact that the elements whose conflict in himself produced his strength found such exact counterparts in the conflicting forces of his day. He wrote for all time because he was so much of his own age; but the full recognition of his place in his age did not come to him until he had tried, and failed, to renew in his quiet garden-house the sweet retired solitude in which throughout his youth he had plumed his feathers and let grow his wings. The ideas and assumptions expressed in his first controversial pamphlets were conditioned by that failure; and it is only by considering the motives which compelled him at length "to transfer the whole force of his mind and industry" from poetry to ecclesiastical reform that one can understand his acceptance in the anti-episcopal tracts of 1641 and 1642 of an attitude of mind by no means wholly consistent with his deepest convictions and subsequently requiring profound modification.

It was not without painful self-examination that Milton determined to "leave a calm and pleasing solitariness, fed with cheerful and confident thoughts, to embark in a troubled sea of noises and hoarse disputes. . . ."[6] In one of his attacks on episcopacy he set down for his reader and for himself an account of the thoughts which had moved him to appear before the full programme of his studies was completed, and in prose. Not vainglory but conscience and the thought of God's strictness in requiring the improvement of talents had compelled him to take a hand in the violent assault on the bishops and to lash the opponents of reformation with righteous zeal. If he withheld his assistance when God seemed, through his special providence for England, to be designing the purification and glorification of her church, he would find himself with no rightful part in her joys if God and good men should work her release from corrupt tyranny, or in her sorrows if wicked men should succeed in oppressing her.[7]

Patriotism and Protestant zeal thus helped to drive him into the controversy. By a typical reaction, both sentiments had been strengthened by his brief contact with papistical and degenerate Italy.[8] But his own account of this experience suggests that the patriotism and zeal of the young traveller's determination to defend his country's religion, were closely connected with his high esteem of himself as an English poet of promise. Behind his entry into the ecclesiastical dispute lay the same personal motive. This is indicated by his inclusion in the account of his thoughts in 1639 and 1640 of a somewhat incongruous discussion of his plans for poetry, of the forms in which he hoped to write, of the broad knowledge and experience required, and especially of that lofty inspiration which the religious poet obtains not "by the invocation of Dame Memory and her siren daughters but by devout prayer to that eternal Spirit who can enrich with all utterance and knowledge. . . ."[9]

Milton's gratuitous covenanting with the reader of his anti-episcopal tract for the fulfilment of his literary designs through the invocation of the heavenly muse was his chief justification for presuming "to meddle with these matters." And his explanation shows that he thought of himself as a dedicated poet who had but temporarily put aside "his garland and singing robes." His principal motive for putting them aside was that he had not yet worn them with the glory to which he aspired. He hoped that the difficulties which had prevented him from doing so might more easily be overcome when the land had "enfranchised herself from this impertinent yoke of prelaty, under whose inquisitorious and tyrannical duncery no free and splendid wit can flourish."[10] The controversialist in Milton was born of the frustration of the poet who seemed to see in the embattled forces in the church and state the public counterparts of the powers contending in his own mind. The zealous and overly optimistic confidence of his assault on episcopacy, and the confusion of mind apparent in his early pamphlets, can be successfully explained only by considering how the view of himself which he had developed in his youth was related to the ecclesiastical controversy.

## 2

Milton's first clear apprehension of the office and the qualifications of the divinely inspired poet is expressed in his ode *On the Morning of Christ's Nativity*, composed near his twenty-first birthday.[11] His facility in verse became apparent very early; but before his nineteenth year his chief compositions were Latin elegies in which he imitated the somewhat artificial but heady sensuousness of Ovid. He delighted in the rich beauty of his model; but he was troubled by suggestions of immorality, and passed in *O Nightingale* and a series of Italian sonnets to a mildly Petrarchan spiritualization of sense. This process of purification was completed by the experience, partly religious, partly literary, recorded in the *Nativity Ode.* In this glorious hymn for the birthday of the incarnate Son of God whose function was to purify man and unite him with the divine, his powers first exercised themselves with full success; for in the harmonious blending of the angels' song with the renewed music of an expectant universe he found a symbol capable of infinitely varied elaboration which could represent both Christ's priest-like function and his own power to join in poetry the beauty of sense and the aspirations of the spirit.

Already, in one of his academic exercises, he had written of the Pythagorean and Platonic music of the spheres that, "if we possessed hearts so pure, so spotless, so snowy, as once Pythagoras had, then indeed would our ears be made to resound . . . with that most delicious music of the revolving stars; then at length, freed from miseries, we should spend our time in peace, blessed and envied even by the Gods."[12] In the *Ode* this Greek symbol of a harmonious nature fused with the idea of Christian regeneration; and thenceforth the music of the spheres, coupled with the angelic song or with the song sung before the Lamb by the virgin saints of *Revelation*, constantly recurred in his verse as the symbol of a divinely inspired yet deliciously beautiful poetry, at once expressing the perfect harmony to which man and nature strive and echoing the spiritual harmony of heaven.[13]

At Cambridge, and afterwards during five years of seclusion at his father's country house, the young Milton set himself to develop the powers requisite for the high calling of such poetry. His independent and energetic self-esteem enabled him to regard himself as a dedicated spirit; and his splendid eloquence and broad love of learning were vitalized by his delight in beauty and his lofty moral idealism. When these powers worked together harmoniously, he wrote at his best. They had done so in the *Nativity Ode* as he contemplated the significance of the Incarnation for man and for himself and elaborated his delightful symbol. They did so again in the most eloquent of his youthful prose writings, the *Seventh Prolusion*, composed some three years after the *Ode* on the eve of his departure from the university, and giving expression to the ideal he had set himself to accomplish. In this noble defence of learning as it supports and is supported by virtue, his energetic desire for the independent experience of knowledge (and by implication of beauty) is perfectly joined with the moral idealism which reinforced his self-esteem. The result is a doctrine perfectly characteristic of the best tradition of Christian humanism. Through his investigation of the workings of the creation, and his study of the records of human experience, the learned man increases his natural powers and his happiness; but these reach towards perfection only if his knowledge is supported by "uprightness of life and blamelessness of character."[14] Knowledge and virtue must be pursued together; for the enrichment of life depends upon the cultivation both of man's natural powers and of the divine spark in him, and in consequence "nothing can be accounted justly among the causes of our happiness, unless it some way takes into consideration both that eternal and this temporal life."[15]

This principle, typically humanistic in its effort to comprehend at once the secular richness of renaissance culture and the spirituality of Christian religion, is the ethical counterpart of the poetical ideal represented by the musical harmony of the *Ode*.

The integration of the natural and the spiritual thus conceived, and the perfecting of the first by the second with the increase not the loss of its peculiar glory, was to be the central aim of Milton's finest work, in prose no less than in poetry; it connoted the potent balance of his special powers. But the mean is always difficult to attain, and even more difficult to preserve. It was especially so in the seventeenth century, dominated in part by an increasingly secular (and cynical) rationalism, in part by the stern other-worldliness of Puritanism. And Milton's powers themselves contained the elements of bitter conflict. Nature, as the *Ode* had said, is "pollute with sinful blame"; and, as the Ovidian elegies seemed to their maturer author to suggest, a passionate love of beauty may be an intoxicating pander to the "wantonness" of "a perverse spirit and a trifling purpose."[16] Because of Milton's abundant energy, the danger from that quarter was ever present —though less threateningly so than he himself supposed. Against it his self-esteem and his moral idealism compelled him to erect barriers; and the barriers sometimes proved to be dams in the way of his eloquence. Already, indeed, in *Elegia Sexta*, written soon after the *Ode*, the humanistic doctrine that the poet himself must be "a true poem; that is, a composition and pattern of the best and honourablest things," is threatening to harden into a cold self-discipline.[17] The poet who would write with high seriousness must preserve the loftiness of his inspiration and the sacredness of his office by repudiating worldly pleasures for spare living, strict purity, and chastity of life. And in the stern dignity of the sonnet *How soon hath Time*—written at a period not far distant from the *Seventh Prolusion* and re-expressing, though in a very different mood, the determination of the *Ode* and of that academic exercise—one can perceive the consequences of the self-criticism induced by this high morality. Indeed, one senses that the inward ripeness which enables more timely-happy spirits to engender their buds and blossoms of beauty is denied to Milton by his very determination to follow, "in strictest measure," whatever lot "the will of heaven" shall design for him, and to write "As ever in my great task-master's eye."

The promise of the *Nativity Ode* and of this sonnet was not soon fulfilled; and Milton sought to overcome whatever was inhibiting his poetical vein not by loosening but by strengthening his self-discipline. He retired to his father's house in Buckinghamshire, setting aside the thought of a career in the church and the inclinations which might make marriage desirable, to pursue a thorough course of study designed as a preparation for the writing of great poetry and as the fulfilment of the ideal of knowledge set forth in his last prolusion.[18] For the associated ideal of virtue and its powers he found support in the romances of chivalry (especially Spenser's), in Plato's mystical doctrine of chastity, and in St. Paul's exhortations to purity;[19] and these confirmed him in the belief that the abilities he desired to possess must be achieved through strict blamelessness of life.

The effects of this conviction are apparent in the writings of the period: in *On Time*, with its triumphant quitting of "all this earthy grossness"; in *Upon the Circumcision*, celebrating the beginning of Christ's satisfaction for humanity's "frail dust"; and in *At a Solemn Music*. In this last the harmonious symbol of the *Ode* is again elaborated, but with a significant addition: to the natural music of the spheres and the heavenly music of the angels, Milton adds "those celestial songs to others inapprehensible, but not to those who were not defiled with women. . . ."[20] In *Comus* more particularly the difficulties attendant on his disciplined self-dedication become clear; for in that delightful though imperfect masque he set out, not only to please his hearers and himself, but to formulate, in terms of the conflict between the virtue personified by the Lady and the perverse lust personified by Comus, his ethical ideal; and the formulation was not accomplished with complete success.

It has recently been demonstrated with convincing fulness that the ethical scheme upon which Milton attempted to construct the action of his masque is perfectly consistent with the ideal symbolized in the *Nativity Ode* and applied to the pursuit of knowledge in the *Seventh Prolusion*.[21] The neo-Platonic speeches of the Elder Brother near the beginning and the Spenserian symbols of the Attendant Spirit's epilogue give expression to a typically humanistic doctrine of ascent from and through nature to grace. Comus would persuade men to repudiate the dictates of the order of grace in favour of "the sensual folly and intemperance" which pervert nature to bestial uses. Virtue, teaches the Elder Brother, spiritualizes the body; it neither perverts nor rejects it. And while the divine grace which supports virtue raises it "higher than the sphery chime," it raises it to a freedom which is not only spiritual but includes a full and legitimate (because well-governed) joy in the beauties and powers of the natural order, through which the

Attendant Spirit rises to his heavenly mansion. Not the repudiating of nature but its perfect because purified use is the doctrine of the masque, as of the *Ode* and the *Prolusion;* and its relationship to Milton's poetical ambition is close. The true poet will accept and use the profuse beauty which nature offers as the material substance of his poetry. But it will not be employed, as by Comus and too often by the Latin elegists, for the satisfaction of sensual desires: through the poet's temperate and chaste virtue, it will provide the means for expressing the highest wisdom and joy attainable on the natural level. And these will be raised above the natural to the spiritual level by the force of the divine inspiration which rewards the poet's chastity. Nor is it fanciful to see a reflection of the poet's aspirations in the mystical powers ascribed to the virgin Lady of the masque, and especially in her song—which ravishes even the ear of Comus—to sweet Echo, "daughter of the sphere," who may be translated to the skies and "give resounding grace to all heaven's harmonies."

But if the masque thus carries on the note of the *Ode* and the *Prolusion* in opposing the ideal integration of nature and spirit to the perverse segregation of them in favour of corrupted nature which Comus would effect, it also carries on the note of stern self-discipline struck by *Elegia Sexta* and *How soon hath Time.* And it is for this reason that it is of the utmost significance in determining the state of mind in which Milton entered the ecclesiastical controversy. For another reply to the "carnal sensuality" of Comus is possible, and another interpretation of the requirements of discipline: not the integration of nature and spirit but their segregation in favour of supervenient grace. Such a reply involves the repudiation, not the perfecting, of nature; and to it Milton was constantly urged by the force of his moral idealism and his fear of fleshly corruption. In *Comus* the scheme of integration seems always on the point of slipping into this much simpler and much colder doctrine; and that is especially true at the dramatic climax of the masque, the debate between the enchanter and the Lady which no one has ever found completely satisfactory.

The note of querulous impatience in the Lady's reply to the arguments of Comus suggests some degree of uncertainty in the mind of the poet as to his ethical principle. Comus strives to overcome her resolution by representing her virtue as an absurd and unlovely extreme. He ridicules the inflexible abstinence which uncompromisingly rejects nature's gifts, and cites the Lady's virginity—with its repudiation of the powers of youth and beauty —as a prime example of this repressive doctrine. In answer to the first part of this attack the Lady develops, with considerable effect, the doctrine of the mean. The extremes of undisciplined indulgence and of rigid abstinence are alike reprehensible; true virtue begins with temperance—the moderate and proportioned use of nature according to reason. But to the second part of the attack she replies with a categorical and cryptic assertion of "the sun-clad power of chastity" and an obscure reference to "the sage and serious doctrine of virginity." What distinction is to be made between these virtues and how they are to be related to temperance she deigns to tell neither Comus—who would perhaps not have understood but is easily convinced—nor us. And she does not indicate, as in the case of abstinence she has clearly indicated, at what point Comus's estimate of virginity is in error. We are left with the uncomfortable feeling that his interpretation of it as a perverse repudiation of powers with which nature has endued the Lady remains unrefuted, not because Comus is inescapably right —his impercipient sophistry has been clearly underlined—but because the Lady is not sure of herself.[22]

Some light is thrown on the difficulty by the discourses of the Elder Brother and the Attendant Spirit. But what they provide is the framework within which the Lady should have presented explicitly the intricate ethical pattern. She prepares her groundwork well in her account of temperance; but she gives over—and the poet with her—when she comes to the centre of the design. She does so, it seems to me, because the centre does not suit perfectly with the frame, and because the poet could not see how to make it suit even imperfectly.

Temperance as the Lady defines it—the right, not the wrong, use of nature—must provide the foundation for an ethical scheme in which nature and spirit are to be joined: either indulgence or abstinence would undermine such an integration at its base. And chastity (as in Spenser's *Faerie Queene*) may be conceived of as a dynamic virtue, rendering temperance positive and finding its fulfilment in the creative joy symbolized by marriage. But in the case of virginity, absolutely considered as here, it is difficult to escape the negative and restrictive implications to which Comus directs our attention and which the Lady does not teach us to avoid. What is immediately suggested is the repudiation of and abstention from nature's gifts.

Behind the doctrine of virginity in *Comus* lies a positive Christian tradition which had a special significance for the young poet who was voluntarily undergoing at Horton a régime of almost monkish rigour. His imagination had been caught by the song of the hundred forty and four thousand of *Revelation* who were not defiled with women; and under the influence of this mystical idea, and of chivalric and neo-Platonic doctrines, virginity became in the masque the symbol of mystical and spiritual powers to be attained on the level of grace. What these powers are, however, the Lady neither clearly explains nor demonstrates; and this is perhaps the source of one's dissatisfaction with the masque: the emphasis throughout falls not on what virginity is but on what it is not, not on what its possessor can positively accomplish but on what she will not do and on what she will prevent others from doing. Our attention is focussed, not merely by Comus but by the Lady herself, upon the negative aspect of virginity on the level of nature instead of on its achievement of a superior good through the sacrifice of an inferior. The hundred forty and four thousand sing for joy at their mystical marriage with the Lamb. Of this there is just an echo in the Attendant Spirit's epilogue; but the Lady neither says nor does anything to suggest that there is a correspondingly positive end to her virginal repudiation.

But even if the Lady had answered the second part of Comus's attack in these terms, there would still remain for her the necessity of showing the relationship between temperance and chastity and between temperance and virginity. For the first, Spenser had provided an excellent example; but the second would have offered some difficulty since virginity is inevitably presented in the masque not merely as a symbol of powers attained on the level of grace but as a condition to be rigorously maintained on the level of nature. This difficulty the later Milton will avoid by preserving the doctrines of temperance and chastity but discarding the doctrine of virginity: marriage, he will say, is not to be called a defilement. But the Lady makes no such concession; nor does she explain how the temperate use of nature's gifts is to be reconciled with virginity's refusal to employ nature's powers. It would be absurd to assert that such a reconciliation is impossible; but it remains significant that *Comus* does not show how it is to be accomplished. For the poet is preoccupied with discipline rather than with the fruits of discipline; and this preoccupation tends to transform the humanistic theory of disciplined activity springing from temperance and chastity into the very doctrine of unyielding and negative restraint scornfully represented in Comus's association of virginity with "lean and sallow abstinence." What Comus describes is the segregation of nature and grace which the Puritan would make in order to repudiate the former in favour of the latter. It is the Lady's failure to refute the restrictive implication in the case of virginity as well as in the case of temperance which leaves the reader (in spite of the Elder Brother and the Attendant Spirit) with an uneasy impression that the ethical doctrine of the masque, "clad in complete steel," thwarts the poet in the full and free exercise of his powers; for her failure is the consequence of Milton's inability to prevent his moral idealism and his fear of corruption from inhibiting his delight in nature and from producing the restrictive ethic characteristic of Puritanism.[23]

*Comus* is not an ethical disquisition; it is a work of art, with special beauties and with special limitations arising from its genre and circumstances which should not be ignored. But even when these have been taken into account, there remains at the centre precisely the dilemma which faced Milton as poet. How can the ideal integration of nature and spirit be translated into action without sacrificing the proper glories of either of its elements to the demands of the other? If the claims of nature are allowed to overwhelm those of grace, the poetry may possess beauty of a sort but not the lofty dignity of great poetry; if the dictates of the spirit involve the repudiation of nature, the poet is cut off from the living beauty of the world of men. This dilemma is not successfully solved in *Comus*, for as Milton gathers his strength to avoid the first danger, he is on the point of running headlong into the second. That is one, perhaps the chief, reason why the masque does not possess the composition and pattern of the *Ode*. And the sense that it did not properly fulfil the promise of that poem may explain the author's disinclination to publish it, and the deprecatory lines from Virgil which he prefixed to it when it was published without his name by a friend.[24]

The connection of the *Comus* problem with Milton's anti-episcopal activity is indicated by *Lycidas* (1637), of which he saw fit to observe in 1645 that it foretold "the ruin of our corrupted clergy."[25] The opening lines of the elegy give expression to the feeling of uncertainty and unpreparedness recognizable in the masque; but partly because the death of Edward King provided a less intractable correlative and partly because of his masterly handling of the pastoral genre, Milton dealt more successfully with his theme.[26] Yet the first question suggested by King's untimely death is the question posed by the enchanter: were it not better to enjoy the natural pleasures offered by Amaryllis and Neaera? And the shepherd-poet's decision "to scorn delights and live laborious days," in the hope not of earthly fame (which is illusory) but of heavenly fame, repeats, though less harshly, the determination of the Lady. The same appeal from the order of nature to the order of grace is made in answer to the second problem suggested by King's death, the frustration of the true shepherd-priest by the corruption of a worldly church: the two-handed engine of divine justice stands ready to punish the carnality of those who prey upon religion. Moreover Lycidas achieves the reward to which Milton looked as the justification of his self-discipline: he enjoys in heaven the fulfilment of his functions as poet-priest, joining in "the unexpressive nuptial song" of the saints in *Revelation*. A final link between these ideas and the prose is provided by the *Epitaphium Damonis*, in which Milton's dead friend, Diodati, is represented as taking his part in the immortal marriage song of heaven because of the virginity of his stainless youth.[27]

The *Epitaphium Damonis* was composed after Milton's return from Italy, probably in 1639. It not only suggests, in its account of the apotheosis of Diodati, the continuance in Milton's mind of the theory of strict self-discipline expressed in *Comus* and *Lycidas;* it also provides a lengthy account of the national epic, an Arthuriad already described in the poem addressed in Italy to Manso, upon which Milton was striving vainly to work in his pretty garden-house.[28] In spite of his self-discipline his ambition remained unfulfilled; so far as we know, his efforts to begin his great poem met with no success whatsoever. It was to explain this failure, not so much to his reader as to himself, that he included in his account of his entry into the ecclesiastical controversy the description of his literary plans which we have examined. What is more important for our purposes, it was because the purification of the church promised to provide the means whereby he might at last achieve his desired inspiration that he took a hand in the dispute. The association of the two questions in *Lycidas*—the discipline and aim of the poet, the state of the church—did not result merely from the fact that King was the author of a few undistinguished poems and had taken holy orders; it sprang from Milton's inability to find, in the spiritual life of a nation dominated by a clergy whose "lean and flashy songs Grate on their scrannel pipes of wretched straw," any genuine assistance in the solution of the problem, unsuccessfully treated in *Comus*, which required to be resolved for the harmonious release of his full powers.

## 3

In the ecclesiastical dispute between the bishops and the Puritans he dimly perceived the counterpart of his own conflict. Episcopacy assumed in his eyes the lineaments of Comus; it was the public manifestation of the perversions of carnal sensuality against which he had striven in favour of high seriousness. The reformed discipline of the Puritan church similarly assumed the aspect of the virgin Lady, possessed of transcendent spiritual powers. Its triumph over episcopacy corresponded to the triumph of chastity over lust; and like the triumph of the Lady—and of Lycidas and Damon—it seemed to promise the fulfilment of his spiritual aspirations and their expression in divine song.

The association of episcopacy with Comus is suggested by the nature of Milton's attack on it. The violent scurrility of his vituperation—far more violent than anything discoverable in the writings of his fellow pamphleteers—arose from the fact that he was releasing his zeal not merely against an ecclesiastical institution but against the corrupting enemy of his youthful ambitions. The bishops and their supporters are "a tyrannical crew and corporation of imposters," ambitious for "worldly glory and immoderate wealth," for "the pride and gluttony of their own backs and bellies . . ., their unctuous and epicurean paunches," and possessed only of a "temporal, earthly, and corporeal spirituality."[29] Because they fear "the plain field of Scripture," they retire into the confusion of antiquity, like Comus in "the perplext paths" of his enchanted wood: "they seek the dark, the bushy, the tangled forest, they would embosk; they feel themselves struck in the transparent streams of divine truth, they would plunge and tumble, and they think to lie hid in the foul weeds and muddy waters, where no plummet can reach the bottom."[30] Their chief support comes from those libertines who, like the followers of Comus, hate all discipline because they are dominated not by reason but by "lust and licentiousness."[31] Their policy is "to turn the inward power and purity of the Gospel into the outward carnality of the Law," and to establish "the old pomp and glory of the flesh" which is Jewish, pagan, and papistical.[32]

Milton's contrast between the degeneration of religion which has resulted from the forces animating the bishops and its purification as designed by the Puritans exactly parallels the Elder Brother's contrast between the imbruting of the spirit by lust and the spiritualizing of the body by virtue. In the primitive church, with its "spiritual height and temper of purity," the ceremonial circumstances of time and place "were purified by the affections of the regenerate soul," and faith did not need "the weak and fallible office of the senses." But the "grossness and blindness" which begot traditions and a "foul and sudden corruption," caused religion "to backslide one way into the Jewish beggary of old cast rudiments, and stumble forward another way into the new-vomited paganism of sensual idolatry. . . ." The consequence of this imbruting of the spiritual is that "the soul, by this means of over-bodying herself, given up justly to fleshly delights, bated her wing apace downward, and finding the ease she had from her visible and sensuous colleague the body in the performance of religious duties, her pinions now broken and flagging, shifted off from herself the labour of high soaring any more, forgot her heavenly flight. . . ."[33] These are the phrases in which Milton spoke of his muse and of the dangers that, as poet, he strove to avoid.

The reformation was to reverse this process and to restore the church to the purity and spirituality of her primitive discipline by removing the "wanton tresses" with which the prelates had overlaid her "chaste and modest veil," and by preparing her for her union with Christ as "a pure unspotted virgin."[34] Thus, it seemed to Milton, would be renewed those "musical chords" of discipline which beget perfection: for "certainly discipline is not only the removal of disorder, but if any visible shape can be given to divine things, the very visible shape and image of virtue, whereby she is not only seen in the regular gestures and motions of her heavenly paces as she walks, but also makes the harmony of her voice audible to mortal ears."[35]

The echo of *Comus* and of the symbols in which Milton's ambition expressed itself is too obvious here to require comment; but not only did the process of ecclesiastical purification seem to parallel the ideal process of his own self-discipline; its completion seemed to promise the exalted atmosphere in which he might at last fulfil his ambition. In his enthusiasm he thought of it as the prelude to the Second Coming, when at last man should be united eternally with the divine; and he looked forward expectantly to the enjoyment on earth of something like the apotheosis of Lycidas. He called upon the Lord to perfect his glorious acts, and promised that, when the Millenium was accomplished and "all thy saints address their voices of joy and triumph to thee," then "he that now for haste snatches up a plain ungarnished thank-offering . . . may . . . perhaps take up a harp and sing thee an elaborate song to generations."[36] It was in this mood of expectant zeal that he concluded his first anti-episcopal pamphlet:

> Then amidst the hymns and hallelujahs of saints some one may perhaps be heard offering at high strains in new and lofty measures to sing and celebrate thy divine mercies and marvellous judgments in this land throughout all ages; whereby this great and warlike nation, instructed and inured to the fervent and continual practice of truth and righteousness, and casting far from her the rags of her old vices, may press on hard to that high and happy emulation to be found the soberest, wisest, and most Christian people at that day when thou, the eternal and shortly expected King, shalt open the clouds to judge the several kingdoms of the world. . . .[37]

Such a song, "to God's glory by the honour and instruction of my country," would have been the fulfilment of Milton's hopes for a national and religious epic.[38] The Puritan reformation promised to raise him to that exalted power which would enable him to celebrate both the natural and the spiritual glories of his country. But this epic was destined never to be written.

The enthusiastic belief that the completion of England's reformation would bring with it the long-sought release of his poetical powers swept Milton into the ecclesiastical controversy. It precipitated his hitherto disconnected thoughts on the condition of the church; and it led him, as we shall see, to accept and to express with uncritical zeal the Puritan theory of church discipline and the view of human nature it necessarily implied. But the implications of that view were those of the Lady's virginity in *Comus*. For the time being Milton accepted them; he was soon to discover that they were essentially negative and restrictive, and that they promised not the release but the further frustration of his powers. They met the dangerous temptations of Comus and episcopacy not by an ideal integration of the claims of nature and grace but by a segregation which denied the claims of nature. In the anti-episcopal tracts Milton too was to cry, "Open your eyes to the light of grace, a better guide than nature."[39] But that solution of the problem could not finally satisfy him. It did not solve the dilemma which confronted the poet, for it implied the repudiation of his energetic love of beauty and his independent self-esteem. Nor did it solve to his satisfaction the corresponding and, for him, intimately connected dilemma which immediately confronted Puritanism when episcopacy was overthrown: how to reconcile the liberty which man claims as his right by the dignity of his nature and as the source of his earthly happiness with that divinely-revealed truth of the spirit upon which ecclesiastical reformation must be founded and through which man must seek his eternal happiness.

## Chapter II

# The One Right Discipline

IN his retrospective account of his first pamphlets in *Defensio Secunda*, Milton half-unconsciously pointed to the dilemma which occupied a central place in Puritan thought throughout the revolution—the problem of the relationship between the reformation of the church and the establishment of liberty. The Puritan demand for church government after the manner of the "other reformed churches . . . and above all by the word of God," led him to compose his attacks on episcopacy because it suggested "that men were in the right way to liberty; that, if discipline originating in religion continued its course to the morals and institutions of the commonwealth, they were proceeding in a direct line from such beginnings, from such steps, to the deliverance of the whole life of mortal man from slavery."[1]

Like the pamphlet activity which it describes, this statement of 1654 rests upon the fundamental assumption that reformation according to the word of God and true liberty are inseparable. It was an assumption from which Milton never departed; it was taken for granted by his Puritan contemporaries from Robert Baillie to John Lilburne. But its significance obviously depends on the interpretation and the relative importance of its terms. If the eye is fixed on reformation, the liberty which follows will be of a particular kind, to be exercised only within the limits of reform; if the eye is fixed on liberty, the reformation demanded will be of a kind calculated to permit the liberty desired. So long as the terms remained indefinite, as they were in the early 1640's, Puritanism exhibited a remarkable degree of unanimity. John Lilburne enthusiastically distributed the pamphlets of William Prynne; and Milton wrote as the associate of the Smectymnuans. But the removal of antichristian episcopacy meant the end of unanimity. In its larger aspects, the history of Puritanism between

1643 and 1660 is the history of conflicting efforts to find definitions of reformation and of liberty which would make possible the achievement of both. Puritanism failed to find an acceptable solution; the liberty demanded by the left destroyed the reformation desired by the right, and the reformation desired by the right denied the liberty demanded by the left. But Puritanism continued to think in terms of true liberty and reformation according to the word of God. When Roger Williams demanded the reformation of the church in Massachusetts in order to allow liberty of conscience, his Congregational opponents replied that under their church polity true liberty was fully exercised and only licence restrained.[2]

The development of Milton's thought in the prose is the development of his attempt to find for this problem a solution which satisfied the exigences of his time and his own personal needs. In 1654, when he wrote the words quoted above, he was still attempting to find suitable definitions; in 1641 he was so convinced of the truth of the assumption as to be scarcely aware that definitions were necessary.

In the end he was to achieve, for himself if not for his country, something like a solution; its outlines are discernible in the early pamphlets since it ultimately depended on his own personality and since this particular problem is but one aspect of a much more fundamental problem. It is but the translation into terms of public policy of the problem of the relationship between God's will and free will, righteousness and unrestrained activity, fate and individual responsibility. It may be regarded, moreover, as the fundamental problem of a personality distinguished at once for great pride and vigorous independence. The anti-episcopal pamphlets inevitably express the convictions which were to condition Milton's ultimate solution of the Puritan dilemma. But the solution itself is not presented because, under the stress of immediate necessity, the convictions are imperfectly formulated, and because in Milton's mind the conflict is as yet unresolved. One recognizes the materials, but the pattern is obscure.

Since he is chiefly concerned at this stage with the destruction of episcopacy as the essential preliminary, rather than with the achievement of reformation and the establishment of liberty, it is vain to attempt to discover from the early pamphlets precisely the kind of reformation or precisely the kind of liberty he had in view. If (while remembering the spirit which begot them) one sets aside the examples of episcopal corruption marshalled from history, the patristic learning displayed in the repudiation of the Fathers, the vituperation and the zealous eloquence directed against the prelates, the residuum of positive thinking is seen to be remarkably small. That is why Milton was honoured by but two replies, both of them anonymous.[3]

Such ideas as are expressed in these pamphlets, though potentially of enormous importance, remain undeveloped and imperfectly related. They group themselves about three convictions, of which the first and second alone receive adequate expression for reasons which are obvious considering the nature of the controversy: the conviction that a pattern of church government is immutably laid down in Scripture; the conviction that the individual Christian, though a layman, possesses a peculiar dignity; and the conviction that the human reason, rightly guided, is the image of God in us yet remaining. The first is the fundamental axiom of the Puritan reformers; out of the second and third is to be fashioned a theory of liberty.

## 2

From Cartwright and Browne to Edwards and Burton, the Puritans had emphatically asserted that a particular government had been divinely instituted for the church of Christ no less than for the Jews, and that to disregard the institution was to ignore divine ordinance and establish Antichrist. This assertion is an extension of the Protestant insistence on the exclusive authority of Scripture; but as presented by the Puritans it becomes a practical expression of the Calvinistic belief that corrupt humanity must submit itself unquestioningly to the immutable will of God. If such a conviction is logically maintained and if the institution is regarded as extending even to the minutiae of discipline, the inevitable result must be the establishment of a fixed and defensive orthodoxy, as in Geneva and Massachusetts; and this orthodoxy will set definite limits to the exercise of liberty.

The position is superbly outlined for refutation in the third book of Hooker's *Ecclesiastical Politie;* in his day the issue was clear-cut.[4] Cartwright's attack on episcopacy was consistently based on the divine prescription of presbyterial government; Hooker argued with equal consistency from a belief in the ability and the right of the human reason, assisted by God and guided by the general principles set forth in Scripture, to evolve a system capable of fulfilling the divine purpose while meeting the requirements of changing human societies.

The success of Puritanism in 1642 was largely due to the enthusiastic and unanimous definiteness with which it expressed its fundamental conviction that episcopacy was not the divinely ordained discipline. And the force of that argument on the seventeenth-century mind is indicated by the fact that episcopal apologists like Bishop Hall, deserting the philosophical defence of Hooker, attempted to take their stand on the vantage-ground of the Puritans and to resist the attack by a counter-appeal to the divine right of episcopacy.

The dispute between Hall and those Puritan ministers who, under Thomas Young's leadership, signed themselves "Smectymnuus," is typical of the ecclesiastical controversy.[5] The issue is no longer clear-cut. Hall derives a "supply of accessory strength . . . from the light of nature and the rules of just policy,"[6] but his principal emphasis is on the argument which Hooker had specifically repudiated, on the scriptural and patristic evidence for episcopacy as the divine discipline.[7] The apostles "were through the guidance of God's spirit in the acts of their function inerrable"; "if the foundations [of episcopacy] were laid by Christ and the walls built up by his apostles, the fabric can be no less than divine"; consequently, episcopacy "is not only an holy and lawful but a divine institution, and therefore cannot be abdicated without a manifest violation of God's ordinance."[8]

The Smectymnuans, with others of their party, were not slow to comment on the change of front involved in this defence;[9] but their attack on episcopacy develops from the same principle. "There is in the word of God an exact form of government set down," and in it "all true ministers of the Gospel are of equal power and authority."[10] Consequently the appeal to human reason and experience is altogether invalid: "you must renounce that government which is merely human and ecclesiastical, be the authority of it never so venerable, if it stand in competition with that which may plead a *jus divinum*."[11]

Conducted in these terms, the argument reduces itself to the blank opposing of biblical interpretations and the citation of a cloud of patristic witnesses. Through this labyrinth it is fortunately unnecessary to follow the combatants. But when one turns to Milton's writings in these early years of the revolution, they are seen to be dominated by precisely the same unproductive conviction. His thundering eloquence and his exegetical, patristic, and historical evidence, serve to support this fundamental, and yet ultimately untenable thesis, that Scripture provides an exact form of church discipline to which the nation must perforce submit.

The sentiment which begot Milton's attack on the Fathers in his first and second pamphlets is perfectly expressed by his quotation from Cyprian's seventy-fourth epistle: "What obstinacy, what presumption is this to prefer human tradition before divine ordinance!"[12] The Fathers themselves, according to Milton's reading, "sent all comers to the Scriptures as all-sufficient"; and if they themselves emphasize the "absolute sufficiency and supremacy inviolable" of God's word, clearly in reformation it is necessary to go beyond tradition and make "the Gospel our rule and oracle."[13] Even traditions derived from the most primitive times are of no significance; not the reported acts of the apostles, but "what they writ, was of firm decree to all future ages."[14]

If the testimony of history and tradition cannot be permitted to oppose the establishment of the "church government that is appointed in the Gospel," much less can the argument from present convenience. In a large part of his first pamphlet Milton is concerned to show that the reformed discipline is perfectly compatible with monarchy, an argument which will subsequently require attention. It is of secondary importance; the primary argument is more radical. To maintain, with Hall, that "no form of church government is agreeable to monarchy but that of bishops," is to imply that "the form of church discipline must be minted and modelled out to secular pretences." But the reformed system is "taught in the word of God." "If, therefore, the constitution of the church be already set down by divine prescript . . . , then can she not be a handmaid to wait on civil commodities and respects. . . ."[15] If the defenders of prelacy are right in maintaining that "episcopacy is now so weaved into the common law" that the latter cannot stand without the former, "in God's name let it weave out again; let not human quillets keep back divine authority!"[16]

Whatever may be the consequences, humanity must submit, like the Jews, to the divine edict. And if reasons are demanded for the reformed system, "the first and greatest . . . we may securely . . . affirm to be because we find it so ordained and set out to us by the appointment of God in the Scriptures."[17] In the third and most carefully composed of his anti-episcopal tracts, Milton continually returns to this argument. In fact, in examining "the reason of church government," he reiterates yet more definitely (if that were possible) the Smectymnuan assertion that *jus divinum* over-rides all human judgment. His purpose is to demonstrate "of what excellence and necessity . . . church discipline is, how beyond the faculty of man to frame, and how dangerous to be left to man's invention, who would be every foot turning it to sinister ends; how properly also it is the work of God as father and of Christ as husband of the church. . . ." As God "gave to David for Solomon, not only a pattern and model for the temple, but a direction for the courses of the priests and Levites and for all the work of their service," so when he meant to reform the Christian church, he "never intended to leave the government thereof . . . to be patched afterwards and varnished over with the devices and embellishings of man's imagination." "God hath still reserved to himself the right of enacting church government"; and man has no power to change "the decrees of God that are immutable."[18]

Milton's fundamental argument for reformation is thus typically Puritan. He sees the history of the church not as the record of the rational development of divine principles but as "so many dark ages" of foul corruption.[19] "The bright and blissful reformation (by divine power) struck through the black and settled night of ignorance and antichristian tyranny";[20] and this divine intervention is to result in the re-establishment of the discipline revealed in Scripture as the will of God. Such a view of events depends, as the pamphlets make abundantly clear, on the complete acceptance of the harsh Calvinistic doctrine of the corruption and powerlessness of man.

Milton's attitude could be paralleled in innumerable Puritan pamphlets. One statement must suffice for illustration (chosen because of the light it throws upon subsequent developments in Milton's thinking), the statement of the Scotch Presbyterian, Robert Baillie:

> If the reformation of episcopacy be intended, we must not take our rule and pattern from ancient and primitive times, but from the first times and from the very beginning; as Christ in the matter of divorcement did not speak of David's, or Abraham's, or Lamech's times, but of Adam's, saying "but in the beginning it was not so," so must we in the matter of this divorcement ascend not to the times of Augustine, or Cyprian, or

Ignatius, but to the times of Christ and the apostles and to the first institution of the ministry at the beginning. . . .[21]

When Milton wrote his divorce pamphlets he was conscious of the force of this analogy; he had also become aware of the intricate difficulties involved in the Puritan assertion of a divinely instituted discipline. He gave no indication of being aware of them when he wrote the anti-episcopal pamphlets; in his confident enthusiasm for the work of reformation, he had, like the Smectymnuans, no patience with those who questioned this fundamental assumption.

That in itself indicates the gulf which separated his thinking at this time from the philosophical rationalism of Hooker. At one point, in fact, he turns specifically against Hooker himself and adopts the arguments outlined for refutation in *Of the Lawes of Ecclesiastical Politie*.[22] At other times he turns his denunciation upon those moderates, especially in Parliament, who without being sympathetic to Laudian episcopacy, felt that there was little to choose between one divine right and another. In a sense, men like Lucius Cary, Viscount Falkland, and Lord George Digby were attempting to carry into Parliament the arguments of Hooker and, more particularly, the rational opportunism of Bacon. Milton was familiar with their views and with Bacon's writings on ecclesiastical affairs; but, like his Puritan associates, he was deaf to their warnings. They had the note of "carnal reason" when what was needed was not moderation but righteous zeal, the speedy vehemence of the reforming kings of Judah. In the present case, even more certainly than in the case of *Comus*, the judicious policy of avoiding the danger of one extreme in the process of attacking the other seemed fallacious: "for if it be found that those two extremes be vice and virtue, falsehood and truth, the greater extremity of virtue and superlative truth we run into, the more virtuous and the more wise we become; and he that, flying from degenerate and traditional corruption, fears to shoot himself too far into the meeting embraces of a divinely warranted reformation, had better not have run at all."[23]

Such agreement as there is between Milton's views on the church and Bacon's arises from Milton's approval of Bacon's criticism of episcopal shortcomings. A not insignificant disagreement is indicated by his silent ignoring of Bacon's remarks on Puritanism.[24] Though he was not averse to reformation, the fundamental Puritan argument seemed to Bacon altogether false. "The substance of doctrine is immutable and so are the general rules of government," but it is a mistake to assert that "there should be but one form of discipline in all churches, and that imposed by a necessity of a command and prescript out of the word of God."[25] To this Puritan argument he would answer, "*Conveniamus in eo quod convenit, non in eo quod receptum est;* let us agree in this with every church, to do what is convenient for the estate of itself, and not in particular customs."[26] For in his politic view, the whole Puritan "manner of handling the Scriptures" was infinitely dangerous: "while they seek express Scripture for everything, and . . . have in a manner deprived themselves and the church of a special help and support by embasing the authority of the Fathers, they resort to naked examples, conceited inferences, and forced allusions, such as do bring ruin to all certainty of religion."[27] These words were prophetic; but they did not impress Milton, though Bacon's criticism might have been applied to his own pamphlets. He did not ignore the efforts of the parliamentary moderates to preserve a balance between extremes; he denounced them.

In the debates in the Commons in 1641, Falkland and his associates followed Bacon in attacking both the abuses of episcopacy and the inflexibility of Puritanism.[28] Like Milton, Falkland thought the influence of the bishops tended towards political tyranny; but he would have preserved a limited episcopacy on grounds of policy, for he was not disposed to substitute for one discipline claiming divine right another which might, like the Scotch, prove equally unmanageable: "to *jure divino* the Scotch ecclesiastical government pretends, to meet when they please, to treat of what they please, to excommunicate whom they please, even parliaments themselves, so far are they from receiving either rules or punishments from them."[29]

On the day following Falkland's speech, Lord George Digby repeated these arguments with greater force.[30] Like Falkland, Digby saw in the City Petition then under debate, with its demand for the divinely ordained government of presbyters, the hint of tyranny to come. But his counsels of prudence and moderation fell on deaf ears. Milton had read Digby's speech, and in the last pages of his first pamphlet he took notice of the parliamentary moderates and of the dangers which "the sluggish and timorous politician thinks he sees." His first answer to their arguments is a demand for the "divinely-warranted reformation," for "the most needful constitution of the one right discipline."[31]

In 1641 and 1642 Milton supported the Smectymnuans, not merely out of sympathy with their leader, Thomas Young, but because he shared their essential convictions, founded on the fundamental Puritan assumption. There is, in fact, scarcely a single idea in his early pamphlets which cannot be found in the Smectymnuan writings; and it is no flight of fancy to suppose that he derived his principles, in the first instance at least, from his former tutor.

The only distinctions one can make between Milton's thinking at this time and the thinking of Puritans like Young are distinctions of emphasis. They are, of course, significant of future developments, for out of them Milton was to evolve ideas which would make him the opponent of Young's party. But for the time being his agreement with Young was apparently complete. That was possible because, while the general convictions of Puritanism were being expressed with repetitive definiteness, the utmost confusion prevailed as to their detailed implications. What the one right discipline implied, it was the appointed task of the Westminster Assembly to determine. Already in 1641 and 1642, Scotchmen like Baillie had very definite ideas on the subject and were proposing their own church as the proper model for the English. Englishmen like Young had considered the subject deeply, and were able to outline in general the system they desired. But the reformed churches abroad offered not one but several patterns, and among English Puritans there was an infinite variety of opinion.[32]

These diverse interpretations, already apparent among the Puritan exiles in Holland, were the rocks on which English Puritanism was to founder. The confusion is reflected in Milton's early pamphlets. He was not, like Young, specifically concerned with the organization of the church; what he hoped to leave "so written to after times, as they should not willingly let it die," was not a controversial tract on church government. He was certain that episcopacy was the source of ecclesiastical corruption, and that there existed "one right discipline" with an equality of ministers instead of a prelatical hierarchy; but he had not troubled to go much beyond that point. He demanded reformation; but he had not yet attempted to define it precisely.

## 3

There was justification for Bishop Hall's exasperated assertion that the Puritan pamphleteers sounded chiefly "the Babylonish note . . . : 'Down with it! down with it even to the ground!' "[33] If his defence of episcopacy was inept, his remarks on the proposed reformation were to the point: "Who sees not that the wood whereof it is framed is so green that it warps every way? Plainly, the sworn men to this exotical government are not agreed of their verdict; an exquisite form they would fain have, but where it is or what it should be, they accord not. . . . Fain would I know whether they can ring this peal without jars!"[34] The jars were before long to become deafening; but, for the time being, righteous zeal united the opponents of Antichrist. For, as Nathaniel Fiennes said in answer to Digby's cautious doubts, episcopacy was clearly "a deviation or aberration from the prescript of divine rule; and though it be not easy to find what that is in all particulars, yet it is not hard to say what it is not."[35]

That statement perfectly expresses the mood of Milton's anti-episcopal pamphlets. When one considers the confusion of opinion of which the dissenting members in the Westminster Assembly were subsequently to remind the orthodox majority, it is not surprising that he offered no clear exposition of the one right discipline.[36] The references to details of government scattered throughout the pamphlets do not amount to a coherent system. They do not necessarily indicate that Milton had in mind a discipline precisely modelled on Scotch Presbyterianism. The Scots were already urging their English allies to adopt their polity; but the English were in general content to appeal to the Scotch example with the "other reformed churches," and to reserve judgment. It was only after the establishment of the Assembly that the influence of its Scotch advisers grew predominant and the differences among the English became sharply apparent.

The individualism which was more characteristic of England than of Scotland in the sixteenth century had already affected English Puritanism before the revolution. The Separatist movement which began with Robert Browne was not an isolated phenomenon; it was an extreme expression of the independence which appeared more moderately in the Congregationalism expounded by such eminent English divines as William Ames, called by Thomas Young "learned Ames of pious memory."[37] The influence of this liberal but not extreme Puritanism is apparent in the Smectymnuans and in Milton.

With its emphasis on the particular congregations as autonomous bodies and its desire for their voluntary association into a Church of England, Congregationalism provided a Puritan *via media* between the strict regulation of the church by a superior assembly and the centrifugal effect of Separatism. This desirable balance was difficult to attain. In practice the system foundered on the problem of reformation and liberty; for it inevitably slipped either towards orthodox strictness or towards radical individualism.[38] But in the early 1640's, it was still possible to be optimistically theoretical, and to hope for God's guidance along the treacherously narrow path between ecclesiastical tyranny and the disintegration of the church. This was the desire of both the Smectymnuans and Milton, though subsequently he was to follow one of the courses open to English Puritanism, and they the other.[39]

Milton agreed with Young and his Puritan colleagues that unity (unattainable through episcopacy) was a desirable and inevitable result of true reformation. The idea of an undivided church arose naturally from the belief in the one right discipline which was to be accepted as God's will by the English people, ever kept "under the special indulgent eye of his providence."[40] Thus when Hall asserted that only episcopacy could prevent schism, they replied in similar terms. The Smectymnuans asked "how it comes to pass that in England there is such an increase of popery, superstition, Arminianism, and all profaneness, more than in other churches?"[41] And Milton likewise maintained that episcopacy begets instead of preventing disunity: "So far was it from removing schism that, if schism parted the congregations before, now it rent and mangled, now it raged."[42]

It is true that the Apostle said that divisions would come; but neither Milton nor his associates chose to meet the episcopal argument by maintaining their desirability. They believed that the one right discipline would prevent them; the reform of church government would serve to keep intact (as episcopacy had not) the purity of doctrine achieved by the original reformation.[43] Since the sects existing in England were the result of episcopal tyranny, Milton could call them "but the throes and pangs that go before the birth of reformation." When "truth has the upper hand and the reformation is perfected," then these "many fond errors and fanatic opinions . . . will easily be rid out of the way or kept so low as that they shall be only the exercise of our knowledge, not the disturbance or interruption of our faith."[44] Reformation would not beget "a rabble of sects"; instead "a unanimous multitude of good protestants will then join to the church, which now . . . stand separated."[45]

Neither Milton nor the Smectymnuans proposed that this desirable unanimity should be achieved through pressure of authority from above in the Laudian manner. It was to be the spontaneous result of the voluntary co-operation of all good Christians associated in their respective congregations. There would be a Church of England, but it would not produce the forced conformity of the episcopal hierarchy. The Gospel discipline was less centralized. There would be a national synod; but, as the Smectymnuans told Hall, it was more proper to speak of "the churches of England" than of "the Church of England."[46]

In their view, as in Milton's, the particular congregations provided an essential foundation. According to him, they should associate to form such councils as were convened by the apostles—the true method of preventing schism. "Of such a council as this, every parochial consistory is a right homogeneous and constituting part, being in itself as it were a little synod, and towards a general assembly moving upon her own basis in an even and firm progression, as those smaller squares in battle unite in one great cube, the main phalanx, an emblem of truth and steadfastness."[47] Because it refused thus to root itself in the congregations, episcopacy was a kind of ambitious and monarchical pyramid which did not conduce "to perfection or unity."

It is significant that Milton nowhere gives an account of the powers of the general assembly here mentioned. When he writes of the details of government, as of church censure, it is always in terms of "the parochial consistory." Hall had noted the tendency of English Puritanism to emphasize the particular congregation as the unit of discipline, and commented in scathing terms on the (to him) absurd and dangerous consequence of it, the increased importance of the laymen in church government.[48] Neither the Congregationalists nor the more extreme Separatists had precisely determined the extent to which the laity should take part in the actual administration of a particular church.[49] But they agreed that a congregation must be a kind of mixed polity, partaking of the virtues of monarchy, aristocracy, and democracy: Christ is king, and the minister and elders are a spiritual aristocracy under him, executing in his name a power conferred upon them by the believers who voluntarily associate to form the congregation.[50] The theoretical analogy with the English monarchy was a popular illustration; and Milton employed it in demonstrating the desirability for England of the reformed system. As the members of parliament are elected by the people to have cognizance under the king of civil affairs, so in a reformed church "the godliest, the wisest, the learnedest ministers in their several charges, have the instructing and disciplining of God's people, by whose full and free election they are consecrated to that holy and equal aristocracy."[51]

Milton's belief in the power which belongs rightfully to the laity is characteristic of a large section of English Puritanism. There is in fact little practical difference between his demands and those of the Smectymnuans. When he insists on the "voice of the people to be had ever in episcopal elections," he is repeating (with much the same authorities) precisely the contrast between primitive and modern bishops already developed by these Puritan ministers.[52] When he argues that true church censure is executed by the minister, assisted by "a certain number of grave and faithful brethren," and that "the whole body of the church is interested in the work of discipline," he is echoing their complaint against the manner in which "our bishops have invaded the right and power of presbyters and people in church censures."[53] Indeed, the Smectymnuans devoted an entire section of their *Answer* to defending against Hall "the joint power of these seniors, with the clergy, in ecclesiastical affairs, that by their wisdom and care peace might be settled in the church; for which cause these seniors are called ecclesiastical men, and yet they are distinguished from clergymen."[54]

The general framework of Milton's idea of reformation in the early pamphlets is thus agreeable to the principles of orthodox English Puritanism, as represented by five ministers who were to be members of the Assembly. The insistence on the one right discipline prescribed in Scripture, the argument for equality in the ministerial aristocracy, the tendency to emphasize the particular congregation, the desire for unity and for singleness in doctrine, the assertion of the layman's right to a share in church government, these are common to Milton and Young at this time. The Puritanism represented by Young dominates Milton's thinking;

yet there are differences between them which are big with significance for the future.

The fact that the Smectymnuans were ministers and Milton a layman is obvious but important; for it led in their pamphlets to an emphasis on the aristocratical element in the one right discipline, and in his to an equal emphasis on the democratical. The dispute between Hall and the Smectymnuans centred upon the superiority of the bishops to the rest of the clergy;[55] though this most obvious aspect of reform occupied Milton's attention throughout the anti-episcopal pamphlets, the centre of his argument lay elsewhere.

The Smectymnuan point of view is made clear by a comment on Hall's assertion that church government must be aristocratical: "Our present church government is not aristocratical but monarchical. . . . If it were aristocratical, then ought every minister to be a member of that aristocracy, for certainly no man will account the minister *de plebe;* in the judgment not only of the ancient Fathers but of reason itself, none can be accounted *pleb* but the laics, seeing that every minister is elected *optimatum* and is one of a thousand. . . ."[56] This distinction between clergy and laity is curiously expressed in the Smectymnuan criticism of the liturgy. When they argue against set forms of prayer, they contemplate freedom only for the ministers: "the ability to offer up the people's wants to God in prayer is part of the ministerial office." Indeed, it is partly because of the responses that they object to the Prayer Book. "Whereas the minister by the Scriptures is the people's mouth to God, this book prescribes responsories to be said by the people, some of which . . . are made to be so essential to the prayer as that all which the minister saith is no prayer without them, as in the Litany."[57]

For the time being Milton accepted this distinction; but he did so with certain reservations. As yet he did not contemplate a church in which there should be no ministerial order; but it is already possible to discern the feelings which were to lead him in that direction. With every Puritan pamphleteer of the day, he launched his main attack on episcopacy from the scriptural identification of bishop and priest; but he carried his detestation of the monarchical government of the prelates farther than the Smectymnuans, for he thought of reform as a transformation of the whole church rather than a change in the ministerial body. It seemed to him, as to Sir Henry Vane, that the church was undergoing a kind of regeneration, not the purification merely of its form of government, but the renewal of its primitive simplicity.[58]

In 1641 he considered the institution of episcopacy the sole cause of the church's degeneration: "it is still episcopacy that before all our eyes, worsens and slugs the most learned and seeming religious of our ministers."[59] His attack on episcopal corruption, its pride, its wealth, its excessive power, is conducted in terms which constantly echo the Smectymnuan denunciations. But they did not look, as he did, for a return to the simple poverty of the primitive ministry:

For our parts, we are so far from envying the gracious munificence of pious princes in collating honourable maintenance upon the ministers of Christ, that we believe that, even by God's own ordinance, double honour is due unto them, and that, by how much the ministry of the Gospel is more honourable than that of the Law, by so much the more ought all that embrace the Gospel to be careful to provide that the ministers of the Gospel might not only live but maintain hospitality according to the rule of the Gospel.[60]

This is much less exacting than Milton's ideal: "a true pastor of Christ's sending hath this especial mark, that for greatest labours and greatest merits in the church, he requires either nothing, if he could so subsist, or a very common and reasonable supply of human necessaries."[61] Against this standard Young himself was shortly to be measured, and found wanting.[62]

This difference of opinion is made strikingly clear by their divergent estimates of Constantine. In the eyes of the Smectymnuans, he is "admired Constantine, that great promover and patron of the peace of the Christian church." He is "pious, religious Constantine"; and though they condemn, with Milton, the episcopal "attendance upon civil and secular affairs" which resulted from his identification of church and state, they nevertheless regard his acts as examples of "the gracious disposition of princes towards Christian religion."[63]

Milton, on the contrary, traces back to the emperor the two great banes of the church, the corruption of the clergy by riches and worldliness, and the confusion of the secular and religious spheres. He devotes several pages in *Of Reformation* to demonstrating why it is impossible to receive any light from "the dim taper of this emperor's age that had such need of snuffing."[64] Through his introduction of ceremonies, fasts, and feasts, his building of stately churches, and his giving "great riches and promotion" to bishops, Constantine becomes a symbol of the degeneration of Christianity and particularly of the ministry. In an ominous passage, Milton turns upon the clergy themselves: "They extol Constantine because he extolled them, as our home-bred monks in their histories blanch the kings their benefactors and brand those that went about to be their correctors. If he had curbed the growing pride, avarice, and luxury of the clergy, then every page of his story should have swelled with his faults. . . ."[65] The reference here is to the defenders of episcopacy, and especially to Hall; but it could already apply to the Smectymnuans.

There is no parallel in their writings for Milton's repeated and stormy outbursts against "the ignoble hucksterage of piddling tithes" and the "brood of flattering and time-serving priests" in general.[66] They were less extreme both in their attack on episcopacy and in their idea of reformation. Milton's zealous hatred of prelatical corruption carried him beyond the mere equality of presbyters to the simplicity of the Gospel ministry. It carried him yet further; his vigorous attack on ministerial corruption is but the obverse of his belief in the privileges of the laity. The transition is indicated by a passage in which he measures present abuses against primitive purity:

> Thus then did the spirit of unity and meekness inspire and animate every joint and sinew of the mystical body; but now the gravest and worthiest minister, a true bishop of his fold, shall be reviled and ruffled by an insulting and only canon-wise prelate, as if he were some slight paltry companion; and the people of God, redeemed and washed with Christ's blood, and dignified with so many glorious titles of saints and sons in the Gospel, are now no better reputed than impure ethnics and lay dogs; stones and pillars and crucifixes have now the honour and the alms due to Christ's living members; the table of communion, now become a table of separation, stands like an exalted platform upon the brow of the quire, fortified with bulwark and barricado to keep off the profane touch of the laics, whilst the obscene and surfeited priest scruples not to paw and mammock the sacramental bread as familiarly as his tavern biscuit.[67]

According to the Smectymnuans, "none can be accounted *pleb* but the laics"; according to Milton, "all Christians ought to know that the title of clergy St. Peter gave to all God's people."[68] In spite of their agreement on the rightful functions of the laity in government, it is necessary to look beyond Young for a spirit comparable to that in which Milton's demands are made. Its source lies in his own experience; it finds its formulation in terms which are Puritan, but characteristic of the extreme rather than the orthodox.

## Chapter III

# Admirable and Heavenly Privileges

THE opening pages of Milton's first pamphlet constitute a preface to the anti-episcopal tracts. He sketches in them his attitude towards the movement of reformation; he also gives expression to his belief in the peculiar pride which ought to be characteristic of every Christian. The "foul and sudden corruption" which befell the church in early times, made religion an external formality, so that the soul, "given up to fleshly delights, bated her wing apace downward." Consequently, "to all the duties of evangelical grace, instead of the adoptive and cheerful boldness which our new alliance with God requires, came servile and thrall-like fear."

These words express the basis upon which Milton associates reformation with liberty. Sensual corruption begets tyranny and servility. The reformation, at once spiritual, ethical, and disciplinary, is to sweep away "the piebald frippery and ostentation of ceremonies." With them is to go the false humility, the "servile crouchings," which subordinate the Christian soul to things. "The quickening power of the Spirit" will beget not humility but independent pride, exercised in those "many admirable and heavenly privileges reached out to us in the Gospel," the rightful possession of the "coheirs of the happy covenant," sealed with "the seal of filial grace." Peter's "unseasonable humility" when Christ came to wash his feet, was indeed "arrogant and stiff-necked."[1]

This assertion of the need for "cheerful and adoptive boldness," this pride in the dignity of election and regeneration, sounds as an undertone throughout Milton's attack on episcopacy and defence of the one right discipline. It serves to add vigour to his support of the Smectymnuan demand for reformation; and he does not as yet suspect that his sense of Christian pride is incompatible with their idea of the true church. But it is from this source that the subsequent divergence arises.

If Milton was content to assist the Smectymnuans in the achievement of the "holy and equal aristocracy" of the ministers, he was nevertheless not unaware that from that aristocracy he was himself technically excluded. His insistence on the equality of all Christians, lay as well as clerical, was very largely the expression of his own self-esteem. It was not merely that he felt himself to have been "church-outed by the prelates."[2] The sense of his own worth had a more positive source. For if he was not ordained to God's service in the sight of men, he felt himself, as he said in the *Nativity Ode*, "toucht with hallow'd fire" as was the prophet Isaiah. To this divine quality of true poetical inspiration he referred again, as we have seen, in *The Reason of Church Government.*[3] Such inspiration represented, for him, the inner light, the spiritual illumination, which the Puritans associated with grace. His conception of inspiration, and his theory of the literature which it should produce, condition to no small degree the interpretation of Christian theology which he was eventually to evolve. He entered the controversial arena on the side of Puritanism because the reformation of the church seemed to promise the long-sought fulfilment of his powers; but the view of reformation he adopted was modified by his high view of his poetical function.

If Origen, while yet a layman, could teach and expound Scripture publicly, the same privilege might well be accorded a learned Christian poet, particularly at a time of reformation when God seemed to be pouring out his grace more abundantly on all men.[4] Ordination is merely an outward sign. "It creates nothing, it confers nothing; it is the inward calling of God that makes a minister, and his own painful study and diligence that manures and improves his ministerial gifts. In the primitive times, many before ever they received ordination from the apostles, had done the church noble service, as Apollos and others."[5] So likewise would Milton in the return of the church to its primitive purity; and to justify his presumption he offered an account of his literary plans.[6]

But if his enthusiastic expression of the Christian's dignity came ultimately from his sense of special calling as a poet, the terms in which he formulated the conviction were commonplaces of Puritan theology, discoverable even in the writings of Young, though more effectively employed by less orthodox Puritans.

They are summed up in the Protestant doctrine of Christian liberty.

There is little theology in the anti-episcopal pamphlets; Milton will find it necessary to examine the details of Christian doctrine only when he turns to the question of divorce. Since at this time he appeals only in general terms to Christian liberty, discussion of the doctrine itself may be reserved for later examination. It is the appeal which is here significant; for it was not made by the Smectymnuans. They were content to argue from the divine prescript, and they continued to think of the church as a corporate body having a definite discipline and laws. To appeal for reformation on the ground of Christian liberty is to think of the church, not merely as a corporate body, but as a body composed of individuals each equally possessing Christian privileges. This was more characteristic of those extremists, like Henry Burton, who were shortly to be ranged against the Puritan orthodoxy represented by Young and his colleagues.

Burton and his followers were already demanding in 1641 a reformation along the lines of the Separatism so eminently expounded earlier in the century by John Robinson in exile at Leyden.[7] Like Milton and the Smectymnuans, Burton emphasized the Puritan opposition between "will-worship devised by men" and the rule prescribed by God, "who hath done all exactly; he hath been as exact a law giver in the New Testament as in the Old."[8] But he also emphasized, far more than the Smectymnuans, the difference between those two laws. The Mosaic Law was a captivity from which Christians are freed by the Gospel. This is the basis of the doctrine of Christian liberty, whereby Christians are released from God's former commands in worship, and also from human ordinances: "This shows you to have no part in Christ, so long as you are subject to human ordinances; for Christ's death hath abolished all ordinances of the Law, which were of God's ordaining; much more the ordinances of men in the worship of God. To set up those things and to let the conscience lie under bondage, this is a great captivity."[9]

Every Puritan would have agreed substantially with the first part of this statement; but the preoccupation with the individual conscience suggested by the last sentence is the root of the Separatist view of church government. Burton's words were directed specifically against the human ordinances of episcopacy. They were capable of broader application. They received it when the Presbyterians seemed about to insist upon an interpretation of God's rule contrary to Burton's, and therefore in his eyes no less merely human than episcopacy.

The disintegration of Puritanism resulted from this difference of opinion; for it produced the controversy over freedom of conscience which made impossible the establishment of Presbyterian government. If there was disagreement as to the interpretation of the divine prescript for the church, to what authority were the parties to appeal? The Presbyterians appealed to the Assembly (in which they commanded a majority) set up by the Parliament to interpret God's will. But for those who differed from the opinion of the Assembly, the ultimate appeal could only be beyond this human authority to the individual consciences of those who possessed Christian liberty. A logical conclusion of this appeal is the belief, at which Milton eventually arrived, that a true church may consist of one Christian.

In 1641, Burton was already appealing to Christian liberty against the enforced establishment of a national church to replace episcopacy. The Separatist system of church government was based, not on the nation, but on particular congregations formed by the voluntary association of true believers. A national church must include the "ignorant and profane"; a true church "consists of none but such as are visible living members of Christ . . . and visible saints under him." Consequently reformation means the destruction of national churches:

> Christ's voice must first be heard to call forth his sheep and to gather them into his flocks and folds. For *ecclesia*, the church, is properly a congregation of believers called out from the rest of the world. For so saith the Lord, 2 *Cor*. 16. 17, "Come out from among them and be ye separate, and touch not the unclean and I will receive you." A strange speech, "and be ye separate." Surely God's people must be separatists from the world and from false churches, to become a pure and holy people unto the Lord.[10]

This theory of church government is a not illogical result of the Calvinistic doctrine of particular election; the particular congregation is a visible expression of the equal aristocracy of grace. And it is only for the visible saints that Burton makes his appeal; they alone can claim Christian liberty. The Parliament (which must certainly have an eye to God's will) may very well organize a national church for the ignorant and profane; but the living members of Christ must be allowed the enjoyment of "Christian liberty in the true use of such ordinances and of such independent church government as Christ, the only law giver of his church and lord of the conscience, hath left unto us in his word."[11]

The peculiar limitations of this Separatist appeal to Christian liberty are made clear in the answer of one of Burton's followers, Mistress Katherine Chidley, to the Presbyterian objections of Thomas Edwards.[12] She denies that the Separatists are demanding freedom of church association for those whom they regard as unregenerate; such are to be left to a kind of missionary effort directed by the secular authorities.[13] And when Edwards asserts that if, by the granting of Separatist demands, "the door of toleration should be but a little opened, there would be a great crowding by all sorts to enter in at it" and consequently "many errors and novelties broached and so greater contentions and breeches amongst us," his opponent replies that "the toleration of the maintenance of heresy and schism is not the toleration that we plead for."[14] The Separatists demanded, in fact, only liberty for themselves: "that which we desire is liberty of conscience to practise God's true worship," and that this worship "may be set up in the kingdom by those that understand what it is, and that by the sufferance of the governors."[15] Christian liberty is simply the fulfilling of God's will by his elect: "The saints are called to liberty, but not a liberty to sin, . . . but to be freed from the yoke of bondage which is the tyranny of tyrannical government of the canon laws, either of Rome or England."[16] Their liberty is only "to practise God's true worship," divinely and specifically prescribed in Scripture.

Though Christian liberty was limited to the elect and defined by God's will, it nevertheless became an assertion of individual right when it was opposed in this way to the dictates of a national authority. The privileges of the individual lay saint are heavily emphasized by Mistress Chidley (whose zeal for them was perhaps increased by her sex). If "all the Lord's people are made kings and priests to God," the organization of the church, the selection of ministers, the execution of discipline, are offices belonging to them rather than to an Assembly appointed by an all-too-human Parliament.

All these things are well allowed of us, for who hath a greater measure of the Spirit than believers? and who hath more skill than he that hath been trained up in the school of Christ and hath learned this lesson, to be obedient to his master, Christ, in keeping of all his commands? and who hath greater authority upon the earth than they that are visible saints? and what makes men visible saints if not the manifestation of their obedience to God, the Father, and Christ, his Son, in practice of all his ordinances.[17]

Theoretically, this argument fuses reformation and liberty in the idea of Christian liberty; but the Separatists displayed a confident and optimistic simplicity in their attempt to persuade the Presbyterians and the profane of its validity. They never doubted that they were themselves visible saints; but their definition of a visible saint depended on a particular interpretation of the divine ordinances for church government. They were never able to convince the Presbyterians that this was the correct interpretation; nor were they ever able to discover how the ignorant were to be prevented from asserting the same privileges as were claimed for the saints. The task of separating the good wheat from the tares had finally to be reserved for the angels; the effort to achieve Christian liberty without permitting the maintenance of heresy and schism resulted in twenty years of increasing confusion. There was, as Roger Williams perceived, no middle path between submission to human authority and complete religious liberty. To that extent Edwards was right: the appeal to Christian liberty set open the door of toleration. If, as one pamphleteer remarked, "God's people, as well as worldlings, have their times to fish in troubled waters,"[18] those not of that privileged order could hardly be prevented from making the best of the same opportunity. But these developments lay in the future; for the time being the Separatists could afford to be theoretically positive though unconsciously unpractical. Their argument from Christian liberty was at least consistently developed; and their simplicity is less remarkable than the optimistic confusion of mind which permitted the ally of the Smectymnuans to employ precisely the same argument.

Milton's confidence in the reformation was broader than Burton's or Mistress Chidley's. They were content to speak for a relatively small group of Separatists; he thought of the nation at large. His enthusiasm for reform, his hatred of episcopacy, his belief in the destiny of England, his trust in the abundant grace of God, prevented him from making in 1641 the discriminations subsequently forced upon him by events. If he was more liberal than the Smectymnuans, he was as yet less extreme than the Separatists. He saw no need for a sharp distinction between the saints and the rest of the nation. He transferred his sense of

Christian dignity to the laity as a whole, demanding for them something of the liberty required by Burton for the elect, and applying to them in general the enthusiastic phrases reserved by the Separatists for the chosen of God.

His ill-defined appeal to Christian liberty in the anti-episcopal pamphlets arose largely from his deep belief in the essential inwardness of Christian religion and from his complete acceptance of the Protestant assertion of the direct relationship between the individual soul and God. In his eyes, the reformation meant not merely a return to the forms of godly government but a sweeping away of the human barriers which prevented man from approaching his Creator as the veil of the temple had prevented him from approaching the Holy of Holies. The Gospel "is the straightest and the clearest covenant can be made between God and man, we being now his adopted sons."[19] It is chiefly in this that it differs from the old dispensation and begets Christian liberty.

When the need arises, Milton is capable of appealing, with Young, to the example of the Mosaic Law;[20] but he is more ready to assert, with Burton, that Christ's death has abolished both the ordinances and the spirit of the Law. When episcopal apologists draw a parallel between the Jewish and Gospel priesthoods, he demonstrates their error by showing that "the Gospel is the end and fulfilling of the Law, our liberty from the bondage of the Law." "The children of the promise, the heirs of liberty and grace," are not to be brought under a government modelled on the old dispensation. That would be "a cancelling of that birthright and immunity which Christ hath purchased for us with his blood." It would be to "turn the inward power and purity of the Gospel into the outward carnality of the Law."[21]

Milton at this time believes that there should be "a ministry set apart to teach and discipline the church"; but under the Gospel there can be no priestly caste. For, as John Robinson had said (echoing the phrases of Luther), "the oil of gladness" with which Christ is annointed by the Father, "runneth down to the skirts of his clothing, perfuming with the sweetness of the Saviour every member of the Body, and so makes every one of them severally kings and priests, and all jointly a kingly priesthood or communion of kings, priests and prophets."[22]

Milton's attack on episcopacy as tyrannous, like Mistress Chidley's defence of the laity against clerical domination, is inspired by this conception of the joint priesthood of all believers.

When he writes of the functions of the laity in church government, it is in terms more familiar to the Separatists than to the Smectymnuans. In discussing church censure, for example, he is moved to an eloquence more enthusiastic than Young's by his sense of the "pious and just honouring" of himself which is characteristic of one who "holds himself in reverence and due esteem both for the dignity of God's image upon him and for the price of his redemption which he thinks is visibly marked upon his forehead."[23]

> . . . [W]hen every good Christian, thoroughly acquainted with all those glorious privileges of sanctification and adoption which render him more sacred than any dedicated altar or element, shall be restored to his right in the church and not excluded from such place of spiritual government as his Christian abilities and his approved good life in the eye and testimony of the church shall prefer him to, this and nothing sooner will open his eyes to a wise and true valuation of himself, which is so requisite and high a point of Christianity. . . . Then would the congregation of the Lord soon recover the true likeness and visage of what she is indeed, a holy generation, a royal priesthood, a saintly communion, the household and city of God.[24]

In his trust in God's promise "to pour out such abundance of knowledge upon all sorts of men in the times of the Gospel," Milton thus goes beyond the hopes of the Smectymnuans.[25] When he demands "that freedom which is the chief prerogative of the Gospel," the "liberties and lawful titles of God's freeborn church," he is demanding something more than the mere reorganization of the national church government.[26] He is thinking less of reformation than of a national regeneration; and "the saints are called to liberty. . . ."

Milton's task in the prose is the definition of this liberty; and the doctrine of Christian liberty will constitute a prime element in its formulation. It will serve to express his sense of particular calling as a Christian poet; and that fact will make his interpretation of the doctrine the measure of his divergence not only from orthodox Puritanism but ultimately from the Separatists themselves.

## 2

The radical consequences of Milton's assertion of Christian liberty did not make themselves explicitly felt in his early pamphlets, largely because he was swept away by the idea of a national regeneration which would dedicate England to God. It seemed to him that the whole people, under parliamentary leadership, was rising against Antichrist. His broad enthusiasm helped to modify another conception involved in the Separatists' denial of the right of the representatives of the whole people to legislate for the elect servants of God, the belief that the worldly power of civil authority and the spiritual power of the church must be distinguished.

The question of the relationship between church and state had a profound importance in the development of the theory of toleration; it will subsequently require close attention. In 1641 and 1642 it was of urgent importance to the Puritans because of the episcopal appeal to Caesar and the employment of Caesar's power to support episcopal policy. The Puritans asserted with one accord that the secular employment of ministers was contrary to the spirituality of the Gospel; that the bishops were (in the words of the Smectymnuans) "fallen from spiritual felicity and infected with secular smoke"; and that their increasing temporal power made them an evil influence in the state.[27] This denunciation led inevitably to their exclusion from the House of Lords in February, 1642. They were moreover denounced by the Puritans for the civil jurisdiction which they exercised in the ecclesiastical courts. Such a temporal jurisdiction was likewise contrary to the Gospel. "The spiritual is over our consciences, the temporal but over our purses," said the Smectymnuans. The episcopal confusion of powers was therefore dangerous to the church as well as to the state.[28]

This attack on the use of the civil sword in ecclesiastical censures was carried further by those who desired a church composed exclusively of visible saints voluntarily associated. Since the church is a mystical body, argued William Bradshaw, it "neither hath nor ought to have any power in the least degree over the bodies, lives, goods, or liberty of any person whatsoever."[29] It deals with men's souls; it must leave "their bodies to the sword and power of the civil magistrate." Hence "no ecclesiastical minister ought to exercise or accept of any civil, public jurisdiction and authority, but ought to be employed in spiritual offices and duties to that congregation over which he is set." And hence "the spiritual keys of the church . . . are not to be put to this use, to lock up the crowns, swords, or sceptres of princes and civil states, or the civil rights, prerogatives, and immunities of civil subjects in the things of this life, or to use them as picklocks to open withal men's treasuries and coffers, or as keys of prisons to shut up the bodies of men; for . . . such a power and authority ecclesiastical is fit only for the Antichrist of Rome. . . ."[30]

Milton expresses precisely these views in the anti-episcopal pamphlets. He attacks the episcopal lust for "secular high office and employment," and demonstrates, in the manner of the Smectymnuans, the harm to the state which has resulted.[31] He denies that ecclesiastical officers can claim any civil jurisdiction, and denounces the episcopal courts "where bribery and corruption solicits, paltering the free and moneyless power of discipline with a carnal satisfaction by the purse."[32] And he elaborates at length the distinction, only suggested by the prudent Smectymnuans but drawn out by Congregationalists and Separatists, between spiritual and temporal power.

If that distinction is valid, it follows that the functions of magistrate and minister must be separated.[33] "The magistrate hath only to deal with the outward part, I mean not of the body alone, but of the mind in all her outward acts, which in Scripture is called the outward man." His proper business is with the external effects of sin and corruption. "His general end is the outward peace and welfare of the commonwealth and civil happiness in this life. His particular end in every man is, by the infliction of pain, damage, and disgrace, that the senses and common perceivance might carry this message to the soul within, that it is neither easeful, profitable, nor praiseworthy in this life to do evil."[34]

Though civil punishment may carry this lesson to the soul, the magistrate's weapons cannot affect the soul itself, or touch "the inward bed of corruption." "Therefore God, to the intent of further healing man's depraved mind, to this power of the magistrate which contents itself with the restraint of evil-doing in the external man, added that which we call censure, to purge it and remove it clean out of the inmost soul." This "office of preserving in healthful constitution the inner man" is the function of the church, and the means to be employed in it are wholly spiritual.[35] The minister and officers of a church (Milton is thinking of a particular congregation) can employ no temporal remedies or punishments, not "imprisonment, or pecuniary mulct, . . . stripes, or bonds, or disinheritance," but only "fatherly admonishment and Christian rebuke" and finally "the dreadful sponge of excommunication."[36]

In addition to the exaggerated Puritan emphasis on the spirituality of Christian religion, the motives underlying this distinction between the powers of magistrate and minister were twofold: on the one hand it provided a defence against the episcopal punishment meted out to Puritan "martyrs" like Prynne, Burton, and Bastwick; on the other it met the need for conclusively demonstrating that the reformed discipline carried no threat to the authority of the civil magistrate. Both motives are apparent in Milton's writings as in the writings of the Congregationalists and Separatists.[37] The point against episcopacy was well taken; and the attempt to reassure the King and Parliament was well advised. But the distinction as made in Milton's early pamphlets and by the Separatists themselves (not to speak of the Smectymnuans) had a specious simplicity.

The denial of civil power to ecclesiastical authorities was an important step towards toleration; but in itself it no more effectively solved the problem of the relationship between church and state than the English denial of such power to the pope. It remained to ask what interest the state could rightfully claim in matters of religion. Robert Greville, Lord Brooke (whose liberal rationalism and Separatist sympathies were far more marked than Milton's in these years), made precisely the Separatist distinction. He asserted that "the churches' utmost compulsive power . . . is but expulsion or excommunication," and that one who dissents from a church's determination cannot be punished with "fine, imprisonment, loss of member or life, except his dissent in practice hath necessarily with it a destructive influence unto the state also and body politic."[38] Clearly it is of the utmost importance to a theory of toleration to define "destructive influence" in practice. This Brooke does not attempt. Similarly, Milton's distinction, apparently so definite, rests upon a division which he himself seems to have felt vaguely unsatisfactory.[39] The church is to deal with the mind; the magistrate with "the mind in all her outward acts." It follows that, though the church cannot employ temporal punishments, the magistrate may nevertheless concern himself with such outward acts as express religious convictions. If the distinction between ecclesiastical and secular power is to have significance for the state (as well as for the church), what is needed is a distinction not merely between the mind and outward acts, but between acts properly religious and acts properly civil. Milton does not (even as ambiguously as Brooke) offer this distinction in the anti-episcopal pamphlets. That is why the future author of the

*Areopagitica* can in 1642 advise the civil magistrate to take into his care "the managing of our public sports and festival pastimes."[40]

Nor is his advice confined to these trivialities. The whole matter of the distinction between church and state was in fact complicated by the Puritan appeal, not it is true to Caesar, but to the temporal power of Parliament. According to Sir Henry Vane, the Long Parliament had "been called, continued, preserved, and secured by the immediate finger of God" for the work of reformation; Thomas Young told the members that God had made them "the ministers of his glory"; in Milton's view they were "the mediators of this his new covenant which he offers us to renew."[41]

If Scripture indubitably revealed the pattern of one right discipline, to what extent must the secular representatives of the nation ensure its establishment and defend it when established? If they were to make war upon antichristian episcopacy and mediate the new covenant, were they to continue to wield the civil sword against God's enemies, even though the church must content itself with flourishing the sword of faith? To this question, Burton's argument might have supplied a sufficient answer had the saints been recognizably visible. That not being the case, it remained for Erastians in Parliament like John Selden, for the Presbyterians in the Assembly, for the Independents and sectaries without, for Cromwell, the Levellers, and Roger Williams, to offer each an answer. In 1641, even the Congregationalists were in a state of some confusion; for while they denied civil power to the congregation and its ministers, they nevertheless asserted (with the bishops before their faces and the suspicions of the civil authorities in their minds) that all ecclesiastical officers, however high, should be punishable by the civil power, "not only for common crimes, but even for the abuse of the ecclesiastical offices" and offences against "ecclesiastical laws."[42]

With reference to his early pamphlets, Milton wrote in *Defensio Secunda*, "I had endeavoured from my youth, before all things, not to be ignorant of what was law, whether divine or human."[43] In 1641 and 1642 he was certain that "jurisdictive power in the church there ought to be none at all"; and that the church is not, as Constantine made it, "a vine in this respect because . . . she cannot subsist without clasping about the elm of worldly strength and felicity, as if the heavenly city could not support itself without the props and buttresses of secular authority."[44] But, as events were soon to show, the distinction required much more study than he had yet given it.

Nevertheless, this emphatic though partial distinction, and the appeal to Christian liberty with which it is coupled, represent differences in emphasis which indicate that his association with men like Thomas Young rested upon a superficial identity of opinion and purpose. They suggest a deeper sympathy with the Separatist attitude. His enunciation of these principles in the early pamphlets is enthusiastic but confused; clarity of definition will come only as the result of his own urgent problems and the problems of the Puritan experiment.

As his confidence in the nation diminishes, he will sound the note of separation with increasing vigour. Yet his initial confidence in the English people represents a conviction which will serve to modify his conception of Christian liberty. There are assumptions in the early pamphlets which to some extent already distinguish him from the Separatists as well as from the Smectymnuans. Christian liberty is properly the prerogative of God's chosen saints; but that "pious and just honouring" of oneself arises, not merely from a consciousness of the mark of redemption, but also from a sense of "the dignity of God's image," the mark of man's original creation.[45] That dignity is proper to man as man, to man as a reasonable creature.

# Chapter IV

## That Intellectual Ray

CONSIDERING the tone on the one hand of Milton's academic prolusions and on the other of his *Areopagitica*, it is remarkable that "the godlike power and force of the mind" receive in the anti-episcopal pamphlets such very scant attention.[1] If there is little in his Cambridge exercises which suggests the arguments of his writings ten years later, there is little in his first pamphlets which suggests the spirit of his eloquent defence of "free reasoning." What he has to say of the dignity of the human reason is significant; it is also significant that he did not say more. Explanations for his silence are not far to seek.

In the dispute over liberty of conscience which reached its height between 1643 and 1647, the appeal to the sovereign rights of the individual reason was to constitute an argument even more disruptive in its implications than the appeal to Christian liberty. If Christian liberty is the possession of the individual saint through election and God's peculiar grace, the faculty of reason by which man at his creation was distinguished from the beasts provides every individual with a natural right. The significance of the toleration controversy lies in the combination and confusion of these prerogatives in the writings of the opponents of Presbyterianism.

The association of the two arguments was already being suggested (though not developed) by Burton. The "new Jesuitical doctrine of blind obedience" taught by the prelates, seemed to him an offence against the power of understanding as well as against God's commands. "We must therefore so obey God in the first place, by guiding ourselves according to his word, as no command of man prevail with us to cross that. It is for beasts without reason to yield a blind obedience to their masters; but men are of another stamp, who have not only reason but religion to be the rule of their actions."[2] Reason is, of course, subordinate to religion and God's precepts; and the extremists will subsequently have to determine what limits are to be set to its activity, and how the errors inevitably arising through human frailty are to be curtailed. Ultimately freedom of reason will altogether supersede the Christian liberty demanded by Burton. But this statement indicates the manner in which they might be associated.[3]

The appeal to reason also found a place in the arguments of the Smectymnuans. It formed for them, as for Hall, a "supply of accessory strength," especially with regard to tradition and custom, in which the judgments of human reason are perpetuated. When Hall appealed to "the light of nature and the rules of just policy," the Smectymnuans replied in kind: "It is evident that these things, which to former ages have seemed necessary and beneficial, may to succeeding generations prove not necessary but noxious, not beneficial but burthensome. And then the same light of nature and the same rules of just policy that did at first command the establishment of them, may and will persuade their abolishment."[4]

In such statements the Smectymnuans were balancing Hall's appeal to Cartwright's principles by a counter-appeal to ideas more characteristic of Hooker. And at first sight their argument from reason may appear to involve inconsistency. Their chief contention is not for something designated by the light of nature or human reason, but for those divine ordinances to which things human must inevitably give place. If scriptural precept has the clarity and authority claimed for it by the Smectymnuans, such considerations have no significance.

It was possible for them (and for Milton) to resort to arguments of this kind, not because they accepted Hooker's rationalistic theory of the constitution of church government, but because they regarded episcopacy as established by human instead of divine laws, as a human invention unsuccessfully designed for the prevention of schism. Criticism based on the light of nature and the rules of just policy might properly be applied to such an institution. It exemplified that tendency of custom to beget error upon which Hooker himself had commented.[5] Hence the Smectymnuans find Cyprian's statements much to their purpose: "It is a good observation of Cyprian that Christ said, *Ego sum via, veritas, et vita*, not *Ego sum consuetudo;* and that *consuetudo sine veritate est vetustas erroris;* Christ is truth and not custom, and custom without truth is a mouldy error. . . ."[6]

In *Of Reformation* Milton repeated the Smectymnuan argument and the references to Cyprian.[7] His initial intention was, like theirs, to demonstrate the ineffectiveness of human reason and custom as opposed to divine prescript, not to propound Hooker's theory of church government. His vigorous attack on patristic tradition was not made in favour of the free activities of the experimental reason; as Hooker observed, the rejection of traditional authority was a direct consequence of the doctrine of divine institution.[8] Milton agreed precisely with the assertion of his Puritan associates that "one grain of Scripture is of more efficacy and esteem than whole volumes of human testimonies."[9] To human tradition and human reason he opposed, in Cyprian's phrase, that "which is revealed for the better by the Holy Ghost."[10]

Throughout the anti-episcopal pamphlets his emphasis is consequently not upon the prerogatives of the human reason but upon the deficiencies of that blunted instrument, "the gross, distorted apprehension of decayed mankind."[11] The processes of his thought were in due course to invalidate for him many of the doctrines emphatically asserted by Calvinism; but the doctrine of original sin, of the corruption of human nature in all its faculties, was not only a constant conviction but one without which he could not have faced the problems presented with increasing urgency by his time. To regard him as having, at any point in his thinking, an essential affinity with nineteenth-century naturalism, is to destroy the very core of his thought. In the early pamphlets, human depravity serves to explain the existence of episcopacy; it is supported by a logic as specious as Comus's. Milton's attack on "this rare device of man's brain . . . preferred before the ordinance of God," thus involves a contrast between "the weak mightiness of man's reasoning" and "the mighty weakness of the Gospel."[12] And it leads him to express a view of human nature which, associated as it was with a belief in God's immutable decrees for the church, might very well have provided the foundation for an attitude not unlike that of the inveterate anti-rationalist and opponent of toleration, Thomas Edwards. In 1641, Milton is impressed, not by the powers of the human reason, but by the consistent perversity with which throughout its recorded history it has preferred corrupt and antichristian error to divinely revealed and prescribed truth.

For truth . . . hath this unhappiness fatal to her, ere she can come to the trial and inspection of the understanding: being to pass through many little wards and limits of the several affections and desires, she cannot shift it but must put on such colours and attires as those pathetic handmaids of the soul please to lead her in to their queen; and if she find so much favour with them, they let her pass in her own likeness; if not, they bring her into the presence habited and coloured like a falsehood. And contrary, when any falsehood comes that way, if they like the error she brings, they are so artful to counterfeit the very shape and visage of truth that, the understanding not being able to discern the fucus which these enchantresses with such cunning have laid upon the features sometimes of truth, sometimes of falsehood interchangeably, sentences for the most part one for the other at the first blush, according to the subtle imposture of these sensual mistresses that keep the ports and passages between her and the object.[13]

This fanciful account of the weakness of the understanding serves to demonstrate the necessity for accepting the divine prescripts and repudiating human judgment. And the argument is repeated in the last of the anti-episcopal pamphlets, with reference to "the corrupt mass of Adam" and "sin original," when Milton deplores the "dim glass" of human affections "which in this frail mansion of flesh are ever unequally tempered, pushing forward to error and keeping back from truth oft-times the best of men."[14]

This sense of human frailty, of the corruption of human nature and the depravity of man's understanding, was to lead Thomas Young and his associates to seek certainty in the authoritative interpretation of the divine commands provided by the Westminster Assembly. The only alternative seemed to them the confusion of error in which the Father of Lies delights. Many of the Presbyterians were in fact to become far more anti-rationalist than Calvin had been. The extreme is represented by Edwards' violent denunciations of those who hold that "faith is not the guide of reason, but reason the guide of faith."[15]

There was little in Milton's early pamphlets to indicate that he was not to follow a similar course. But the rationalism of the *Areopagitica* is connected with the anti-rationalism of the ecclesiastical pamphlets through the divorce tracts; for Puritanism was capable of finding a place in its thought for the human reason without destroying the conception of divine prescript. Once the divine ordinances had been recognized, reason could supply an "accessory strength." And further, there were obviously questions (less important than the constitution of the church) upon which the divine will was obscure, perhaps not directly expressed at all.

With one such question, the observation of the Sabbath, Thomas Young had dealt in his *Dies Dominica*.

There is no divine prescript in the New Testament for the keeping of the Lord's day. Consequently Young's argument for its observance is based on a logic somewhat different from that which supports the Smectymnuan demand for the one right discipline. The law of the Jewish Sabbath provides him with an important analogy; but his chief arguments are derived from the testimony of "the reverend, ancient Fathers" about the practice of the apostles and the early Christians, and from the dictates of "our own reason" on the propriety of setting aside one day wholly to God's worship. "Not only reason itself, but the consent of all good men and learned" confirms his desire for a proper observance.[16]

In such matters as this, Young could recognize the function of the human reason without lessening his belief in the immutable authority of those divine ordinances which (in his view) clearly defined the essentials of doctrine and discipline. And it was through the consideration of subjects of this kind that the argument from reason effected an entry into the Puritan and Calvinistic system, and ultimately destroyed it. In matters about which no definite divine revelation has been made human judgment must determine by the light of God's word. It remained to be decided whether the judgment to be accepted was that of an authority like the Assembly or of the individual alone. And it is at this point that an alliance could be effected between the radicals who demanded Christian liberty and those who demanded freedom for men as reasonable creatures. Such matters, so ran the argument of those who desired toleration, are "indifferent" since God has issued no specific commands about them and they may be either good or bad according to circumstances. Determination concerning them should be left to the individual conscience, though no such freedom can be claimed for it where the divine prescript is apparent.

The question of things indifferent formed the thin edge of a wedge which split the Puritan group. It had already been employed against episcopacy. It was the contention of episcopal apologists that liturgical and administrative matters concerned only indifferent things not covered by positive scriptural commands or prohibitions, and that dissenters ought peaceably to submit to the required uniformity in them since no offence against conscience could be involved.[17] The Puritans replied to this argument that, if such matters were by nature indifferent (an assumption in itself questionable), then episcopacy could not claim to be executing divine authority concerning them, and ought consequently to leave the decision to the consciences of believers. In controversy, this argument from conscience was inevitably confused with the appeal to divine prescript against episcopal government; and in the attempted reconstruction of the church, the Westminster Assembly adopted precisely the prelatical position on indifferent things. But the attack on episcopacy provided the Independents with a weapon which could be used as effectively against the Assembly as against the Star Chamber; and from things indifferent the opponents of orthodoxy passed on to complete freedom of conscience.

Milton's break with the group represented by the Assembly originated in a particular application of this theory of indifferency. But in the anti-episcopal pamphlets, it is accorded only three brief references. In the opening paragraph of his first pamphlet, he refers incidentally to the mistake of "attributing purity or impurity to things indifferent"; and later, while describing the harmful effect of episcopacy on the kingdom, he mentions those who have fled to "the savage deserts of America" because "their conscience could not assent to things which the bishops thought indifferent." He goes on, "What more binding than conscience? what more free than indifferency? Cruel then must that indifferency needs be that shall violate the strict necessity of conscience, merciless and inhuman that free choice and liberty that shall break asunder the bonds of religion."[18]

The third reference occurs in his last anti-episcopal pamphlet when he praises the Parliament for its liberation of "the inward persuasion," an achievement far greater than that of those ancient worthies who delivered men merely from outward tyranny:

They set at liberty nations and cities of men, good and bad mixed together; but these . . . called out of darkness and bonds the elect martyrs and witnesses of the Redeemer. They restored the body to ease and wealth; but these, the oppressed conscience to that freedom which is the chief prerogative of the Gospel, taking off those cruel burdens imposed not by necessity . . . but laid upon our necks by the strange wilfulness and wantonness of a needless and jolly persecutor called Indifference.[19]

These isolated references express a conviction which was to have an important place in the development of Milton's thought. In both cases indifference is connected with liberty, specifically in the second with the Christian liberty of God's elect. Milton is demanding liberty of conscience in indifferent things. But he makes no attempt to define the nature either of that liberty or of indifference. Nor does he suggest the connection, subsequently of paramount importance, between indifferency and the activity of the human reason. The matter is, for the time being, of merely incidental importance in the effort to establish the one right discipline.

## 2

The limitations of Milton's thought on this subject in 1641 and 1642 are indicated by the writings of a man for whom he was to have the most profound admiration, Robert Greville, Lord Brooke.[20] Something of the spirit of Sidney's age lived on in the nephew and heir of Fulke Greville; his personality, and his death while leading a parliamentary force against the Close at Lichfield in the spring of 1643, made him one of those heroes who might have been celebrated in Milton's unwritten national epic. But the praise of Milton's reference to this "right noble and pious lord" in the *Areopagitica* is more than a tribute to a romantic parliamentary hero. The *Discourse opening the Nature of . . . Episcopacie* which Brooke had published in November, 1641, displays a mind of much subtlety and force from whose findings Milton appears to have derived considerable enlightenment.[21]

Brooke combined Puritan principles with a liberality of tone unusual in the controversy over episcopacy, and he brought to the dispute a clarity of mind which was beyond the Smectymnuans and as yet unachieved by Milton. His example serves, in part at least, to account for the qualities which distinguish the *Areopagitica* from the anti-episcopal pamphlets. If he did not provide Milton with new ideas, he seems to have reminded him of the significance of principles lying temporarily dormant in his mind. More than that, Brooke sketched out the lines of the controversy over liberty of conscience in which Milton was to find himself involved as a result of his unfortunate marriage.

Brooke's discourse is remarkable for its association of the Separatist appeal to the dignity of the saints with the rationalist's appeal to the dignity of the reason. His argument against episcopacy (largely borrowed indeed from the Smectymnuans) is based on the usual contrast between the divine institution and ineffectual human inventions.[22] His sympathies are, more definitely than Milton's, with the Separatists. He repeats their argument that, because "the flock of Christ is styled by the Spirit of Christ an holy priesthood, a royal people," the government of the church should be controlled by the members of "democratical" congregations.[23] He thus, with Burton, adds the privileges of saintship to the argument from divine institution; and his eloquent appeal for tolerance in religious disputes arises largely from his sympathy with those who believe "that God promised to pour out his Spirit upon all flesh, all believers."[24]

But such ideas do not provide the principal basis for the theory of liberty of conscience which he develops from his discussion of "the nature of indifferency" and the function of reason.

Brooke devotes not a few incidental references but two long and well-argued chapters to indifferent things. His consideration begins with the argument, shared with Milton and the Puritans in general, that the episcopal interpretation of indifferency is tyrannical; it ends with an assertion of the sovereign right of the individual conscience or reason. In his opinion, one is bound always "to do what is best, or at least on exactest search seems best"; and the conclusion must be based on "the dictates of right reason." It must be assumed that right reason will always dictate what is best to be done in any particular case of conscience; otherwise all certainty would be destroyed and it would have to be concluded that, "whenever reason does happen to dictate right, it is but by chance or some fancy of its own, not by any certain constant rule taken from the nature of things rightly stated in such and such circumstances." Such a conclusion would mean that men are "under reason as under a most corrupt judge that will follow no constant rule, founded on the nature of things, but only his own humour, which will give very different judgments on the very same, or like cases, in all circumstances."[25]

If right reason is the ultimate rule, to argue either that "we are not bound to follow right reason's dictates," or that "we are not bound to ask right reason what it will dictate, but may do hand over head, as they speak, without any dictate of reason right or wrong," becomes in Brooke's opinion "very strange doctrine." It implies that "all my acts may be irrational and not sinful, a strange tenet, and sure a case never to be found but in a distracted man." It is not necessary "to stay disputing for some hours or days" before every "common action": that would "turn all practice into bare and nice speculation." But it is necessary, "if there rise but the least scruple, . . . to discuss it till reason rectified dictate the action lawful and best to be done, and till this dictate, the act must be suspended."

Two possible actions—"suppose to marry or not to marry"—cannot be equally good; one must be the better. Right reason must determine which is to be preferred. "And if right reason have not or cannot determine me to which side soever I incline and rest, I sin; because I act unreasonably, being determined by humour, fancy, passion, a wilful will and not right reason, the candle of God, which he hath lighted in man, lest man groping in the darkness should stumble and fall."[26]

The phrase from *Proverbs* 20. 27, so full of meaning for Christian rationalists like Whichcote,[27] comes easily to Brooke's lips. It represents the difference in emphasis which distinguishes his view of reformation from the view of the Smectymnuans, and even of Burton. It would be difficult to find a parallel for his admirably succinct exposition of the principle of right reason in any of the Puritan pamphlets of the day. And applied to the question of indifferency, his confidence in right reason leads directly to the doctrine of freedom of conscience which Milton will not for years so clearly enunciate.

According to Brooke, what is called indifference lies not so much in things or actions themselves as in our apprehensions, nothing being either good or bad but thinking makes it so. "Nothing is indifferent *in re, in se;* but to our understandings some things seem so for want of a good light."[28] The light is provided for each individual by the candle of the Lord.

If this is so, the church can claim no power to make any one thing indifferent, nor even (ominous statement) "to determine what is indifferent." If "all indifference comes only from the darkness of our understanding . . . , it then lies not in the power of all other men living to determine what seems indifferent to one man's understanding, since he may perhaps not see what they all see, *& e contrario.*" The church may attempt to decide which of two extremes is preferable, though this must be done warily and according to the "constant law" of right reason. But between the right of the individual to judge and the power of the church to attempt determinations, there can be no conflict; first, because right reason should lead both to the same conclusion, and secondly, because in a difference of opinion, the individual can only listen to what seems to him right reason.

The individual is bound to "give passive obedience" even when he thinks the church mistaken, but not active obedience since that would involve him in sin. He must not make "a rent, schism, faction that may fire church and state"; but on the other hand the church must not force him to accept its decisions. For what is "lawful and necessary to one that sees it so," may appear unlawful to another. "In this case I conceive no power on earth ought to force my practice more than my judgment."[29]

The plea for liberty and tolerance, with which Brooke's pamphlet ends and to which Milton referred in the *Areopagitica*, is thus something more than the expression of a gentle spirit.[30] It is based upon an argument which undermines not only episcopacy but also the position of those who were already opposing the Separatists. Brooke's rationalism leads him, indeed, beyond the restricted appeal to the Christian liberty of the saints, to an assertion of the right of the individual conscience or reason to judge not merely in indifferent things but as to what things are indifferent. Complete freedom of conscience is the inescapable result.

This, in brief, is the argument which the extremists (with Milton among them) were to direct against the Assembly. More needed to be said than Brooke could say; many of his assertions demand further explanation. What, for example, is the significance of the phrase "right reason," and how does it differ (if at all) from reason? "Who shall tell us what is *recta ratio?*" asks Brooke; "I answer, '*Recta ratio.*' "[31] If that is so, clearly every man's reason is his own right reason, and it will be difficult to find any other acceptable standard of measurement. If Brooke had survived he would undoubtedly have attempted a fuller answer to such questions as this. But these deficiencies do not detract from the force of his argument; they serve rather to make more pointedly effective the confidence in reason which he had already expressed in his highly metaphysical treatise, *The Nature of Truth*.

Reason is for Brooke a "ray of the divine nature, warming and enlivening the creature, conforming it to the likeness of the Creator."[32] Of "that intellectual ray which God hath planted in us," Milton also speaks in *Of Reformation*. In terms common among the Christian rationalists, but familiar also to the champions of divine prescription, he has been asserting the clarity of Scripture in things "most necessary to be known." That clarity is partly the result of the "extraordinary effusion of God's spirit upon every age and sex," partly of the injustice which would be involved if God required strict obedience to ambiguous commands, and largely of the fact that his commands are inevitably such as can be understood by rectified reason.

> The very essence of truth is plainness and brightness; the darkness and crookedness is our own. The wisdom of God created understanding fit and proportionable to truth, the object and end of it, as the eye to the thing visible. If our understanding have a film of ignorance over it, or be blear with gazing on false glisterings, what is that to truth? If we will but purge with sovereign eye-salve that intellectual ray . . . , we would believe the Scriptures protesting their own plainness. . . .[33]

Brooke's conviction that "the understanding and truth can be but one," is a conviction that Milton shares. It was to serve him in good stead in the midst of later problems; and he returns to it for a moment in the opening pages of *The Reason of Church Government.* There he points out, with a reference to Plato, that as it is neither generous nor wise to publish human laws without explaining their reasons, so it is with things divine. If Moses carefully instructed the Jews in the reason of their church government, "how much more ought the members of the church under the Gospel seek to inform their understanding in the reason of that government which the church claims to have over them, especially for that the church hath in her immediate care those inner parts and affections of the mind where the seat of reason is, having power to examine our spiritual knowledge and to demand from us in God's behalf a service entirely reasonable."[34]

These statements are significant; it is also significant that in the anti-episcopal pamphlets the ideas which they suggest remained undeveloped. Though Milton probably knew Brooke's pamphlet before he wrote *The Reason of Church Government,* there is nothing to show that he recognized the profound significance of the question of indifferency and its connection with that intellectual ray. Moreover, both the passages quoted above are immediately followed by pages of argument asserting, against the claims of human intelligence, the Smectymnuan conception of an unquestionable divine prescription for the church. This is not inconsistency; in his confident enthusiasm Milton simply omits the important links in a chain of reasoning subsequently to be hammered out. For the time being he is more impressed by the effects of the film of ignorance, so apparent in the supporters of episcopacy, than by the brightness of the intellectual ray. He is more concerned to demonstrate the plainness and authority of divine ordinance than the capacities of that human reason to whose mistaken findings episcopacy appealed for support. He will shortly discover that such arguments serve not merely to destroy episcopacy but almost inevitably to turn presbyter into old priest writ large.

There is, however, at least one passage in the anti-episcopal pamphlets which, considered with Milton's references to the intellectual ray, suggests the course he was to follow in his divorce pamphlets. The second section of the Smectymnuan *Answer* is devoted to an attack on *The Book of Common Prayer* and the imposition of set forms. If there is no need to compel ministers to read the homilies, there is no need to compel them to use an authorized liturgy. "Why should the free liberty of using or not using a liturgy breed more confusion than the free liberty of reading or not reading homilies, especially when ministers shall teach people not to condemn one another in things indifferent?"[35]

Hall had admitted that no scriptural prescript commanded a liturgy, and had justified the Prayer Book by appealing to the decisions of the councils. Milton replied that he would "take counsel of that which counselled them, reason; and . . . I shall be bold to say that reason is the gift of God in one man as well as in a thousand." The councils had instituted the liturgy in an attempt to prevent heresy and diversity. "What," asked Milton, "if reason, now illustrated by the word of God, shall be able to produce a better prevention . . .?"[36]

Since there are no specific divine decrees concerning the liturgy, it becomes like the Sabbath a subject for the activity of the human judgment guided by God's word. It is a thing indifferent, upon which the reason of one man may determine as effectively and as freely as the combined reason of many. This statement shadows forth Milton's argument on divorce and his opposition to the opinion of the Assembly on that question. The violence of his attack on episcopacy had blinded him to the conflict between liberty and reformation and to the repressive implications of Puritanism. But personal experience of its restrictiveness was to make him strive anew for the integration of nature and grace, with reason as the mediator.

# *Part II*

## *Liberty and Conscience: the Divorce Tracts, Areopagitica, Of Education. 1643-1645*

## *Chapter V*

# *Closing up Truth to Truth*

IN *Defensio Secunda* Milton wrote that, when the bishops had been overthrown, he began to consider how he could "contribute to the progress of real and substantial liberty." He turned his thoughts to the second of the "three species" of liberty, the domestic or private; "as this also appeared to be threefold, namely, whether the affair of marriage was rightly managed, whether the education of children was properly conducted, whether lastly we were to be allowed freedom of opinion," he composed his pamphlets on divorce, *Of Education*, and the *Areopagitica*.[1]

The processes of thought which issued in this second group of pamphlets were actually somewhat less consciously directed than this account would suggest. The brief tractate on education, a by-product of the tutoring of his nephews and other youths, was written with some reluctance at the request of the versatile reformer, Samuel Hartlib. The *Areopagitica*, though expressing convictions long held, was an answer to the Presbyterian condemnation which, to Milton's evident surprise, greeted the publication of his first pamphlet on divorce. The divorce pamphlets themselves, in spite of some earlier evidences of a superficial interest in the subject, were a direct result of his unfortunate union with Mary Powell. If Milton's uncritical acceptance of the Puritan point of view in the anti-episcopal pamphlets requires explanation in terms of his failure to fulfil his literary ambition, the change of front which becomes apparent in these compositions requires explanation in terms of the re-examination of himself to which he was compelled by his matrimonial mistake and its consequences.

Precisely what occurred in his mind in the late spring of 1642 we shall probably never know. The account set down more than fifty years later by his nephew remains perfectly expressive of our perplexity: "About Whitsuntide it was, or a little after, that he took a journey into the country, nobody about him certainly knowing the reason, or that it was any more than a journey of recreation; after a month's stay, home he returns a married man that went out a bachelor, his wife being Mary, the eldest daughter of Mr. Richard Powell, then a Justice of Peace, of Forest Hill, near Shotover in Oxfordshire. . . ."[2] There is in these remarks a suggestion of impetuosity which is even more definite in the observation of another early biographer that "he in a month's time (according to his practice of not wasting that precious talent) courted, married, and brought home" his wife; and it is clear from the sequel that his choice had been made with insufficient judgment.

The determination to marry is itself of some significance. As we have seen, the young Milton's preoccupation with self-discipline led him towards a strict view of chastity and, at times, to an identification of that virtue with virginity. But his vitality made the full acceptance of a doctrine of celibacy impossible. Already in entries in the *Commonplace Book* which probably belong to a period well before 1642, he was considering arguments for the legitimacy of marriage for the clergy;[3] the subject was prominent in Protestant thought, but its application to himself is unmistakable. And in the *Apology against . . . A Modest Confutation*, published some two months before his marriage, he ended the account of his youthful concern for chastity (a refutation of the charge of incontinence) with the significant observation that the description of the virgins who sing before the Lamb as "not defiled with women" must be taken to mean that they were guiltless of fornication, "for marriage must not be called a defilement."[4]

With his early biographers, we may suppose that Milton's consideration of marriage was the natural result of his maturity and of his acquisition of an establishment of his own after his return from Italy. In itself it indicates a modification of his earlier views. But what was of profound importance for the development of his thought was the fact that the decision was most unhappily executed; for whatever may have been the motives for his marriage with Mary Powell, its consequences must immediately have suggested to him that he had allowed himself to be misled by those natural inclinations whose perversion had been represented by Comus.

The romantic suggestion has sometimes been made that Milton fell violently in love with Mary and was swept headlong into his marriage by passion. If it was so, he never in his life performed a less characteristic action. But there is little reason for believing that this was the case. What is clearly apparent is that he knew less of women and of Mary than would, under the circumstances, have been desirable, and that, having made up his mind to marry, he paid too little attention to what he did know of her. He was acquainted with her father, for that gentleman owed him £500 under a bond drawn up by the elder Milton in 1627; and he can hardly have been ignorant of Powell's sympathy with the bishops and with the King, whose headquarters were shortly to be established at Oxford.[5] The implications of these factors the bridegroom seems to have ignored. Nor does he appear to have been moved to serious contemplation by the fact that he had no previous acquaintanceship, not to say intimacy, with Powell's family. A wise man will look to the mother of his prospective wife for some indication of the kind of domesticity he may expect to enjoy with the daughter. It is a fact, hitherto unnoticed, that before the time of his marriage Milton was not acquainted with his mother-in-law.[6] If he did not know Mistress Anne Powell before the spring of 1642, it is unlikely that he was any better acquainted with Mary, who was living under her eye. In consequence of his failure to consider sufficiently the character of his bride and the circumstances of her family, he brought back to London a young woman of sixteen or seventeen who, "after having been used to a great house, and much company and joviality," could hardly be counted on to value the charms of his "philosophical life,"[7] whose family's opinions in the national dispute were contrary to his own, and whose father owed him a sum of money which he was quite incapable of paying. When Mary, having returned to Forest Hill after a month of married life, refused to come again to her husband in London at the time appointed, Milton must have inquired with profound dismay into the state of mind which had led him to ignore these facts.

It is not uncharitable, and it is certainly instructive, to consider what view would probably have been taken of such a situation by the author of *Comus*, *Lycidas*, and the anti-episcopal tracts, if it had been hypothetically proposed to him in 1641. He might have offered such charitable observations on human frailty and the incapacity of innocence to defend itself at all points against the world as now occur in the divorce pamphlets.[8] But he would certainly have added, I think, that such an experience must be the consequence of the triviality of a mind insufficiently guided, restrained, and protected by virtue, and that the reformed church should provide the spiritual discipline by which alone such mistakes could be prevented. As we shall see, the weight of emphasis in the divorce argument by no means falls on such ideas. The burden of that argument is not the prevention of mistakes through discipline but the freedom of divorce necessary if their unhappy consequences are to be avoided; and the argument is supported, not by the citation of the inflexible decrees of divine authority and the condemnation of the weakness of degenerate humanity, but by an insistence on the infinite mercy of divine charity and a defence of the legitimate (if frail) inclinations of human nature.

This change of direction was the consequence of Milton's need to reconcile his thinking with the demands of his own personality. His self-esteem had suffered a blow of the utmost severity, and he had been forced to recognize his own humanity. Though he never cites his own case, the emotional frustration and dismay which resulted from Mary's unsuitability and desertion find indirect expression in passages too well known to require quotation here.[9] If his self-esteem was to be revived, his mistake must be excused and the natural inclinations leading to it must be justified, and more, must find a legitimate means for fulfilment. It is not therefore upon disciplined virtue that the weight of his discussion falls—though, as we shall find, that note is continued in a modified form; it falls rather on the blamelessness of natural inclinations which may lead to mistakes but are not in themselves vicious, and it demands the freedom of their fulfilment that must necessarily be accorded if man's life is not to be a frustrated and ignoble bondage.

Yet if the direction of Milton's thought changes in the second group of pamphlets, his attack on the orthodox view of divorce follows, at least in the beginning, the pattern of his attack on episcopacy. According to the received opinion, divorce (or rather separation *a mensa et thoro*) could be granted only on the ground of adultery, and did not include the right to remarry.[10] Milton's biographers are at one in insisting that Mary had done him no dishonour, and that he at no time supposed that she had; and there is no reason whatever for believing that their difficulty arose from her refusal to consummate the marriage.[11] It arose from a temperamental incompatibility which pointedly expressed itself in the difference between the Powells' view of the war and Milton's; and the echo of this difference is undoubtedly to be heard in his remark in *Defensio Secunda* that a consideration of divorce was particularly necessary "when man and wife were often the fiercest enemies, he being at home with his children, while she, the mother of the family, was in the camp of the enemy, threatening slaughter and destruction to her husband."[12] The consistent argument of the divorce tracts is therefore that "indisposition, unfitness, or contrariety of mind, arising from a cause in nature unchangeable," provide a sounder reason for divorce than frigidity or adultery; and Milton's attack is directed against "the bondage of canon law" which would make a physical offence of greater moment than spiritual or intellectual offences.[13] The canon law is naturally associated with the papistical tradition of the episcopal hierarchy; and in its attention to bodily rather than spiritual or intellectual needs is discerned the carnality which the anti-episcopal pamphlets had represented as characteristic of prelacy. Especially in *The Doctrine and Discipline of Divorce*, this sensual perversity is taken as exemplifying the alliance of episcopacy with the licentiousness which it would foster for its own tyrannous purposes; and the question is proposed as "seasonable to be now thought on in the reformation intended" because it is "the hope of good men that those irregular and unspiritual courts have spun their utmost date in this land, and some better course must now be constituted."[14]

At the outset, Milton's effort to overcome the difficulty created by the royalist Powells thus fuses with his hatred of episcopacy. Yet his argument involved factors which combined to prevent it from preserving the anti-episcopal pattern. For the doctrine and discipline of divorce there existed no such clear scriptural prescript as had seemed to define church government. But Puritanism had accepted the canonical view of Christ's precept. The refutation of this view therefore required an appeal to the dictates not merely of Scripture but of reason; and Milton seems to have supposed that, as the reason of one man prevented a council from denying marriage to the clergy—an example he had cited against Hall's arguments for the liturgy—so his reason might set to rights a question hitherto misunderstood. Again, divorce in his view was a matter upon whose legitimacy only the individual conscience could judge. The centre of reference in the divorce tracts therefore shifts from the revealed will of God to the rights of the particular believer. It was because of the implications of these factors that Milton's argument met with severe condemnation from the Presbyterians whose struggle for reformation he had supported; and even if they had not been operative upon his thought, this condemnation would have prevented him from repeating the pattern of his earlier pamphlets.

Even before his marriage, according to his early biographers, he had been convinced "upon full consideration and reading good authors" of the "lawfulness and expedience of divorce." His own problem led him to express his opinion, and "to fortify himself with arguments."[15] That fortifying was the beginning of a transformation in his thought and theology. He was aware of the delicacy of the question, and regarded himself as a pioneer. Consequently it was "with severe industry and examination" that he "set down every period," and only "at length" that he published.[16] But the deep thought required by the nature of the subject was made doubly necessary by the reception of his first tract. Mary's desertion must have been itself less shattering than the discovery that he was being attacked by the Presbyterians, in the pulpit and in the press, as an "impudent" exponent of licentious doctrines perfectly representative of "the late dangerous increase of many anabaptistical, antinomian, heretical, atheistical opinions."[17]

Instead of being at one with the best part of the nation, he now discovered himself practically alone. It had not been difficult to throw off prelatical attacks as the voice of Antichrist; it was not so easy to set aside the condemnation of the Assembly in which sat his Smectymnuan friends. He had unwittingly exchanged "an immortality of fame" for "a world of disesteem." His sonnets "on the detraction which followed upon my writing certain treatises" show that he was hurt as well as angered; and in his counter-attack on Prynne there is a note of pained surprise.[18] It was as if the Attendant Spirit had come to the defence of the Lady with further arguments against Comus, only to discover to his amazement that his views, no less than the tempter's, were abhorrent to her.

If the unfortunate outcome of his marriage forced Milton to take thought with himself, these attacks forced him to reconsider his view of reformation. It became essential to his self-esteem, not merely to deal with the Powells and the carnality of canon law, but also to oppose the cold restrictiveness of the Puritan ethic as it appeared in its extreme form among the Presbyterians. Whereas in his first pamphlets he had been attacking episcopacy alone, he now found himself involved in a war on two fronts; and this situation, added to the personal problem created by his own mistaken judgment, urged him back towards the central position from which his attack on prelacy had swept him, towards the balance expressed in the

*Nativity Ode* and the *Seventh Prolusion* and overturned in the anti-episcopal tracts. Mary was responsible for the first edition of *The Doctrine and Discipline of Divorce*; Milton's scandalized Presbyterian critics were the cause of the fortifying arguments which transformed the principles of that slim pamphlet into the eloquent assertion of a liberty both Christian and human in the *Areopagitica* and *Tetrachordon*. For Milton's experiences in 1642 and 1643 demanded a reconsideration of the claims of nature and their reconciliation with the claims of the spirit. In his first pamphlets he had too easily set aside the claims of the first, and too uncritically accepted the orthodox Puritan view of the second. Now the privileges of the individual Christian—first in divorce, but by implication in other matters as well—together with the dictates of reason and the irrepressible demands of nature, operated to modify his view of reformation and to develop his theory of real and substantial liberty.

Within the Puritan group itself a not dissimilar process was under way; and in spite of his preoccupation with a particular problem, Milton was profoundly influenced by the development and application of ideas which it involved. The first edition of *The Doctrine and Discipline of Divorce* appeared precisely a month after the meetings of the Westminster Assembly had begun. The Separatists were already agitating for a limited toleration; but it was only after the signing of the Covenant on September 21, and after instructions had been received from the Parliament on October 12, 1643, that the Assembly began the discussion of church government which was to lead immediately to dispute and in January to an open break between the Presbyterians and the five Independent or Congregationalist members who then published *An Apologeticall Narration*, an appeal not only to Parliament but to public opinion.

Milton was singularly without interest in the controversy over the details of church government; but he was immediately involved in the dispute over conscience, because his treatment of divorce made it a representative case of conscience. His opinions on divorce were associated by the Presbyterians with such arguments for toleration as those in Roger Williams' *The Bloudy Tenent of Persecution*.[19] When the enlarged edition of his tract appeared in February, 1644, the dissent of the Independents was already occupying public attention; and the marks of its influence are apparent in this new edition and in the pamphlets which followed.

## 2

It is sometimes said that Milton approached the divorce problem with the confidence of an unpractical idealist. He was, in fact, far more practical in his argument on divorce than he had been in his argument on reformation. As his first anti-episcopal pamphlet had opened with an account of the corruption of religion arising from man's depravity, so he begins his first divorce tract (and subsequently his first political pamphlet) with a reference to the inherent evil of the fallen human heart. The reasoning of the author of *Paradise Lost* always starts from the fact of the Fall. Human depravity has an important bearing on Milton's view of divorce itself; but its first service is to explain, as in the ecclesiastical pamphlets, why a mistaken view of God's will has arisen. "For though it were granted us by divine indulgence to be exempt from all that can be harmful to us from without, yet the perverseness of our folly is so bent, that we should never lin hammering out of our own hearts, as it were out of flint, the seeds and sparkles of new misery to ourselves . . . ; and no marvel if out of our own hearts, for they are evil. . . ."[20]

The Fall serves once more to demonstrate the danger of trusting to the supposed wisdom enshrined in canons and precepts and handed down in traditions. This is the mood in which Milton began the new address, "To the Parliament of England with the Assembly," which he prefixed to the second edition of his tract. "Of all teachers and masters that have ever taught," custom joined with error has "drawn the most disciples after him, both in religion and in manners." Indeed, all truth and wisdom would at length be lost, "were it not that God, rather than man, once in many ages calls together the prudent and religious councils of men, deputed to repress the encroachments and to work off the inveterate blots and obscurities wrought upon our minds by the subtle insinuating of error and custom. . . ."[21]

To what extent the Assembly could be considered such a council, Milton was perhaps already wondering. But he regarded the reform of divorce as part of "this general labour of reformation." He had agreed with men like Robert Baillie that church government must be patterned on the original model presented by Scripture; he begins his argument on marriage and divorce with an appeal beyond tradition to the original expression of God's will and purpose, "those words of God in the institution promising a meet help against loneliness."[22] Here as elsewhere "the infallible grounds of Scripture" must be the guide and rule.[23]

But for reasons inherent in the very nature of the problem, what is opposed in the divorce pamphlets to the error of human judgment and tradition is not precisely what was opposed to it in the anti-episcopal pamphlets. The importance of Milton's consideration of divorce in the development of his thought lies primarily in this fact. It was possible roundly to assert that Scripture clearly outlined a form of church government which did not include diocesan bishops, and (though the details were perhaps obscure) flatly to oppose this divine institution to antichristian tradition. It was possible to assert that the judgment of decayed mankind could have no part in determining the form of government, and that even the regenerate could demand only liberty to establish the one right discipline. Divorce was a matter of a very different kind: first, because the Scriptures taken literally appeared to show an absolute contradiction between God's will revealed in the Mosaic Law and Christ's statement to the Pharisees;[24] secondly, because the dissolution of marriage (a contract between two human beings, not like church government part of a covenant between God and man) must depend on the free choice of the two individuals concerned.

The case for presbytery had seemed to Milton perfectly clear; he had asserted that we must "believe the Scriptures protesting their own plainness and brightness." When he wrote these words he can hardly have contemplated devoting to four places of Scripture the hundred pages of his *Tetrachordon*. In 1643 he was not yet prepared to ask whether the manifest confusion of Scripture perhaps made it after all a not infallible guide. But he was not at all disposed to accept the seeming contradiction between the plain statements of Moses and Christ. He found it impossible to believe that God could contradict himself, or that the opinion on divorce at which he had arrived could be contrary to the divine will. Consequently, instead of opposing the plain truth of Scripture to custom, he had now to reinterpret the precept on which custom seemed firmly to base itself, and by sheer ratiocination to reconcile Christ's statement with what seemed to him the sense of the Mosaic Law and the original institution. This task required something more than "reason illustrated by the word of God." It was necessary to explain the word of God and defeat custom through "the industry of free reasoning."[25] If Milton's thought on divorce possesses a new firmness as a result of his private struggle with passion and depression, it also reveals the effects of the necessity, imposed on him by his subject, of thinking less zealously and more logically.

The painful exegetical labours of the first divorce tract led directly to the *Areopagitica*. The scriptural difficulty could only be removed by challenging the interpretations of "the extreme literalist," and by insisting that "all places of Scripture, wherein just reason of doubt arises from the letter, are to be expounded by considering upon what occasion everything is set down and by comparing other texts."[26] It is true that Milton shared the Protestant dislike of "petty disputations" and "empty quibbles" in the application of Scripture, and that the proposed method of exegesis bears a striking resemblance to the method Hooker had been denounced for employing with regard to St. Paul's directions to Timothy.[27] But it now appears that "there is scarce any one saying in the Gospel but must be read with limitations and distinctions to be rightly understood," and therefore that the Scriptures require "a skilful and laborious gatherer."[28]

The defence of free reasoning in the divorce tracts recalls the suggestion in the anti-episcopal pamphlets that a layman might justifiably imitate Origen.[29] That right is boldly asserted in Milton's advice to the Assembly in 1644: "Let the statutes of God be turned over, be scanned anew, and considered, not altogether by the narrow intellectuals of quotationists and commonplacers, but (as was the ancient right of councils) by men of what liberal profession soever, of eminent spirit and breeding, joined with a diffuse and various knowledge of divine and human things. . . ."[30]

The scriptural difficulty modified Milton's approach to divine prescription and led to his attack on the Assembly's attempt to erect its authority on the principle of one right discipline. The fact that, in his view, divorce was a matter of conscience, not of prescript, set him among those who were demanding religious liberty. His initial difference of opinion with the orthodox rests upon this point rather than in the heretical interpretation of particular doctrines. They believed that, whatever Moses might have permitted the Israelites because of their incorrigible hardness of heart, Christ had positively prohibited divorce except for fornication. He believed that Christ's words did not have the force of divine command but were conditional, and that particular decisions were left, as by Moses, to the individual.

This does not mean that Milton was denying the immutable authority of divine prescript in essential matters of doctrine and discipline. Marriage and divorce are matters of choice, and so things indifferent. The prohibition of divorce is part of the antichristian tyranny of presenting "things indifferent" under the "banners of sin."[31] It was left by the Mosaic Law "to a man's own arbitrament, to be determined between God and his own conscience," because God's purpose was "to command or to allow something just and honest, or indifferent."[32] It involves a merely human relationship; and though a Christian will act in it according to righteousness, Christ's statement is misinterpreted by those who regard divorce as in itself an unrighteous act. As one may refrain from marriage without sin, so one may divorce without sin.[33] Christ's prohibition concerns not divorce but unrighteous divorce. Interpreted in the light of the Mosaic permission, it is seen to be simply a warning to the unrighteous Pharisees that determinations in this indifferent matter must be, as in all things, according to righteousness.[34] And since, except in the case of fornication, only the individual's conscience can determine whether the desire for divorce arises from sinful motives, the decision must rest with him. To the divorce problem Milton thus applies Brooke's theory of indifferency. Brooke had instanced "suppose to marry or not to marry";[35] Milton adds, as it were, "to divorce or not to divorce."

This view of the problem arises from his conviction that a true marriage is a union of minds, not merely of bodies. If "that rational burning" must first be satisfied, it follows that incompatibility is a greater reason for divorce than fornication.[36] Further, fornication is an outward act capable of proof; to incompatibilty the inward man only can testify. Hence it is that Milton expresses a theory of marriage and divorce precisely analogous to the theory of faith and freedom of conscience propounded by the opponents of the Assembly.

The end of marriage, as Milton defines it, cannot be achieved through constraint. Consequently, patience in the face of difficulties can only be "exhorted," not "enjoined"; for "lamented experience daily teaches us the bitter and vain fruits of this our presumption, forcing men in a thing wherein we are not able to judge either of their strength or of their sufferance."[37] Such unjust austerity arises "neither from Scripture or reason," but from the "letter-bound servility of the canon doctors."[38] For obviously no court, ecclesiastical or civil, can successfully remove "the unaccountable and secret reasons of disaffection between man and wife."[39] If such a disaffection exists, the parties are to be left free to dissolve their contract, not forced to maintain it; "to interpose a jurisdictive power upon the inward and irremediable disposition of man, to command love and sympathy, to forbid dislike against the guiltless instinct of nature, is not within the province of any law to reach. . . ."[40]

This in brief is Milton's case for divorce according to conscience; and if faith and religion are substituted for love and marriage, what results is substantially the position of the *Areopagitica*. That pamphlet appeared on November 24, 1644, four months after the second divorce tract—the translation from Bucer—and not quite four months before the publication of the last two divorce tracts. It is not a digression but the product of Milton's divorce argument; and it serves to indicate the intimate connection between that argument and the toleration controversy

## 3

The *Areopagitica* was a defence of those who could bring "a helpful hand to the slow-moving reformation which we labour under" because truth had spoken to them "before others."[41] Among these was to be numbered the author of *The Doctrine and Discipline of Divorce*, to whom the new *Ordinance for Printing* of June 14, 1643, seemed a disastrous renunciation of assistance. From the point of view of the Presbyterians, the restraint of printing through ministerial licensers served as a necessary protection for the reformation, now no longer attacking but entrenching itself through the Assembly and Parliament. It provided a barrier against the counter-attacks of the routed prelatists and against the clamouring extremists who threatened to undermine the one right discipline before it could be established. Milton's attack on the ordinance consequently indicates the extent to which his view of reformation had been clarified and transformed as a result of the condemnation of his opinions on divorce.

The anti-episcopal pamphlets had called for a reformation not "slow-moving" but "speedy and vehement." By 1644, Milton had come to see that it was not to be happily completed merely by "the unfrocking of a priest, the unmitring of a bishop, and the removing him from off the presbyterian shoulders"; for his own experience of Presbyterian reaction seemed to show that there were deeper sources of "this working mystery of ignorance and ecclesiastical thraldom which under new shapes and disguises begins afresh to grow upon us."[42] Apparently Christ is not after all "ready at the door"; nor will it avail to think in terms of "Atlantic and Utopian polities which never can be drawn into use."[43] The world is at best a place of mingled good and evil, the New Jerusalem a heavenly city. Reformation is not to be achieved at a blow and immediately upon the downfall of Babylon. Though it may be plain that episcopacy is antichristian, truth is not everywhere so imperatively obvious. It requires laborious and skilful gatherers, and even they may discover that their labours do not immediately persuade.

In Milton's second group of pamphlets the emphasis is not on reformation and divine prescript but on liberty and free reasoning. Instead of a rebuilding according to the clearly revealed pattern, reformation becomes a progressive search for truth. Thanks is to be given "for that great measure of truth" already enjoyed; but it is not to be taken for granted (as apparently by the Assembly) that "we are to pitch our tent here, and have attained the utmost prospect of reformation that the mortal glass wherein we contemplate can show us, till we come to beatific vision. . . ."[44] In the anti-episcopal pamphlets the cloudiness of that glass had served to explain the corrupt stubbornness of episcopacy, and to demonstrate the necessity for setting divine prescript above depraved human wisdom. It now serves to demonstrate the danger of mistaking human error for divine truth, and to prove the need for unrestricted discussion of doubtful matters. Christ brought truth back to the world, and it is revealed in Scripture; but man is not yet in full possession of the truth revealed.

> Truth indeed came once into the world with her divine master, and was a perfect shape most glorious to look on; but when he ascended and his apostles after him were laid asleep, then straight arose a wicked race of deceivers who, as that story goes of the Egyptian Typhon with his conspirators, how they dealt with the good Osiris, took the virgin Truth, hewed her lovely form into a thousand pieces, and scattered them to the four winds. From that time ever since, the sad friends of Truth, such as durst appear, imitating the careful search that Isis made for the mangled body of Osiris, went up and down gathering up limb by limb still as they could find them. We have not yet found them all, Lords and Commons, nor ever shall do till her master's second coming; he shall bring together every joint and member, and shall mould them into an immortal feature of loveliness and perfection.[45]

The divinely perfect truth of the Gospel, its sudden corruption, the return of perfection with the second coming, these ideas had found a place in the anti-episcopal pamphlets. But when Digby and Falkland had urged moderation because of man's uncertainty and the dangers of the appeal to *jus divinum*, Milton had proclaimed the certainty of the one right discipline.

The *Areopagitica* marks a significant change in the emphasis of his thought. Scripture remains for him the revelation of the divine will. But in 1641 he had thought of history as the record of the church's progressive degeneracy, and of the downfall of episcopacy as the effect of a sudden divine intervention, the prelude perhaps to the second coming. He now thinks of the future as a progression from truth to truth which will terminate only when the divine pattern is at length completely imparted to man at Christ's return. He begins to look, not backward with the orthodox Puritans to the express command of God, but forward. To that extent he becomes less the reformer than the revolutionary, especially since the achievement of the perfect pattern—though finally possible only with divine assistance—requires the human activity of "free reasoning."

This development in Milton's thinking reflects a similar development in English Puritanism. The idea of the progressiveness of reformation and the search for truth was profoundly important in the toleration controversy because it made possible a theory of liberty without destroying the fundamental assumption that all ultimate truth was enshrined, though obscurely, in Scripture. It naturally found its fullest expression among those who had progressed through the successive stages on the road from Anglicanism to Separatism. Thus John Robinson was reported to have urged the Pilgrim Fathers in his farewell sermon "to follow him no further than he followed Christ; and if God should reveal anything to us by any other instrument of his, to be as ready to receive it as ever we were to receive any truth by his ministry. For he was very confident the Lord had more truth and light yet to break forth out of his Holy Word."[46]

Even the moderate Congregationalists in the Assembly shared this expectancy and offered it as an excuse for their inability to accept the Presbyterian system proposed. The Gospel discipline seemed to them "to lie in a middle way" between Presbyterianism and Separatism; and in their *Apologeticall Narration* they were bold enough to assert that "the Calvinian reformed churches" themselves stood in need "of further reforming."[47] They protested their agreement in doctrine with their brethren in the Assembly; but in discipline they wished to proceed as before its establishment, when "for all such cases wherein we saw not a clear resolution from Scripture, example, or direction, we still professedly suspended until God should give us further light. . . ."[48]

Those who were yet less orthodox hastened to draw out the

implications of the refusal "to make our present judgment and practice a binding law unto ourselves for the future." If new light was anticipated, the restraint of those who differed in any degree from received opinion might prove an offence against the Lord instead of a bulwark against error. Thus Roger Williams, looking forward to "a new light of Scripture yet to shine," condemned the "locks and bars" of the licensers as impediments to the breaking forth of "any other light but what their hemisphere affords."[49] Henry Robinson demanded freedom of conscience because "God is pleased only to discover the Gospel to us by piecemeals as we become worthy and capable of the mysteries and truth thereof."[50] And it became a fixed principle among the opponents of strict Presbyterianism that true Christians "count not themselves perfect but stand ready to receive further light, yea, from the meanest of the brethren."[51]

Orthodox Puritanism replied to this new threat from within the gates precisely as it had answered the prelatical opponents of reformation. It appealed against human error to what Baillie had termed "the plain truth of Scripture, obvious to everyone who desireth to know."[52] Just as Baillie had argued against the supporters of episcopacy that "in the matters of the Kingdom of Christ, the head and monarch of his church, . . . we have no power to dispense, or to decline to the right hand or to the left," so Thomas Edwards now asserted that the permission of error was incompatible with reformation according to Scripture: "a toleration is against the nature of reformation, a reformation and a toleration are diametrically opposite; the commands of God given in his word for reformation, with the examples of reforming governors, civil and ecclesiastical, do not admit of toleration."[53] It seemed to the Presbyterians that the suspended judgment of the dissenters undermined the authority, not merely of the Assembly, but of God's word itself. It implied that "the government and way of the church visible is so uncertain and doubtful as that little or none may be positively laid down and concluded as *jure divino*."[54]

The Presbyterians were not asserting much more than Milton had asserted in his first pamphlets. But for them divine prescript had ceased to be a basis for attack and had become a bulwark of defence. God's will had triumphed; the rule of the Gospel had supplanted Antichrist; and the orthodox Puritans refused to proceed further along the treacherous path which led through Independency to Separatism and the sects. It seemed to them that this path wound back to Egypt; whether they were right or not, time was to tell. But the Presbyterian attitude appeared to the more extreme Puritans, from the Narrators to Roger Williams, to involve, not a safeguard against human depravity, but the substitution of one human tradition and authority for another. It substituted Calvin and the early reformers for the Fathers, and the Assembly for councils and synods. John Robinson had deplored this tendency to establish a new orthodoxy on the authority of the original leaders: "though they were precious shining lights in their time, yet God had not revealed his whole will to them."[55] Now the Independents warned the Assembly that "to eke out what was defective in our light in matters divine with human prudence" constituted "the fatal error to reformation."[56]

Milton was altogether without interest in the dispute over the details of discipline. He was so fully occupied with his particular problem that he could regard this most important public matter only with impatience. When he urged the Assembly, in the new edition of his divorce pamphlet, "to scan anew" God's law on such points as he was agitating, he asserted that "to expedite these knots were worthy a learned and memorable synod, while our enemies expect to see the expectation of the church tired out with dependencies and independencies, how they will compound, and in what calends."[57] Even in his own contribution to the toleration controversy, he displays once more a desire to avoid the troublesome details of government. Irritation has replaced the enthusiasm of the early pamphlets; and it is still impossible to discover his precise opinions on the one right discipline. He was not averse to Congregationalism: "We stumble and are impatient at the least dividing of one visible congregation from another, though it be not in fundamentals." But he had no clear sense of what was involved in the debate and regarded it as comparatively unimportant: "He who hears what praying there is for light and clear knowledge would think of other matters to be constituted beyond the discipline of Geneva, framed and fabrict already to our hands."[58]

Yet he had himself appeared as the vessel of new and unorthodox light; and his consideration of divorce led him to express precisely the arguments employed in the church controversy by those who suspected the discipline of Geneva. What the Presbyterians asserted of those who would not accept the orthodox constitution of the church could be applied to him. When William Prynne described the disturbing appearance of "prodigious, new, wandering, blazing stars and firebrands, styling themselves new lights, firing our church and state,"[59] he included the author of *The Doctrine and Discipline of Divorce* in that galaxy. Consequently Milton's reply to his critics is, like the Independents', an assertion of the need for "the reforming of reformation itself."[60] "We have looked so long upon the blaze that Zuinglius and Calvin have beaconed up to us, that we are stark blind." But "the light which we have gained was given us, not to be ever staring on, but by it to discover onward things more remote from our knowledge." "For such is the order of God's enlightening his church, to dispense and deal out by degrees his beam, so as our earthly eyes may best sustain it."[61] In these statements Milton disposes of the reformation desired by Thomas Young and the Assembly.

The *Areopagitica* is thus a defence of those who were engaged in activities like Milton's own. He is still convinced that "the favour and the love of heaven [is] in a peculiar manner propitious and propending towards us," that "God is decreeing to begin some new and great period in his church. . . ."[62] Consequently his enthusiastic optimism once more expresses itself in the general application of the terms of saintship: "For now the time seems come wherein Moses, the great prophet, may sit in heaven rejoicing to see that memorable and glorious wish of his fulfilled, when not only our seventy elders but all the Lord's people are become prophets."[63] In such statements the divorce pamphlets and the *Areopagitica* carry on his earlier insistence on "the admirable and heavenly privileges" of the saints. They also (and more significantly) extend his appeal to that other principle of liberty more fully enunciated by Brooke, for the beam which God dispenses is "that intellectual ray," and its product is the activity of "free reasoning."

# Chapter VI

## The Voice of Reason

MILTON'S defence of the sects in the *Areopagitica* marks his break with the orthodox Puritanism represented by the Assembly. It seemed to him that the Temple of the Lord was not being fashioned at Westminster but would rise through the "spiritual architecture" of what the uninspired regarded as "fantastic terrors of sects and schisms." He no longer explained that these were the unhappy but inevitable effects of misgovernment. They testified to "the earnest and zealous thirst after knowledge and understanding which God hath stirred up in this city." Unity was desirable, but a unity of spirit rather than of doctrine: "perfection consists in this, that out of many moderate varieties and brotherly dissimilitudes that are not vastly disproportional, arises the goodly and graceful symmetry that commends the whole pile and structure."[1]

Milton's denunciation of the Presbyterians resulted from their desire to "suppress all this flowery crop of knowledge and new light sprung up and yet springing daily in this city."[2] But even in the *Areopagitica* it is clear that the new light he sought was somewhat different from the new light which inspired the meteoric careers of those leaders of the sects who were making enthusiasm triumphant.[3] His sympathy with the left wing of Puritanism was real; but as his support of the Smectymnuans resulted from common opposition to episcopacy, so his defence of the sects arose from common opposition to Presbyterianism, not from an identity of fundamental principles. The first divorce pamphlet was offered to "the choicest and learnedest"; the *Areopagitica* is less a defence of the sects than of learning and learned men.[4] Milton rejoiced in the spectacle of the people "disputing, reasoning, reading, inventing, even to a rarity and admiration, things not before discoursed or written of"; but he spoke especially for "all those who had prepared their minds and studies above the vulgar pitch."[5]

It is not without significance that the *Areopagitica* contains proportionately more references than any of the other controversial tracts (except *Of Education*) to those pagan writers "with whom is bound up the life of human learning," that the Parliament is urged "to imitate the old and elegant humanity of Greece," that Adam and Psyche are mentioned in the same breath.[6] It had not yet occurred to Milton to separate the Renaissance from the Reformation: "divine and human learning" were together "raked out of the embers of forgotten tongues."[7] And the incipient anti-clericalism of the early pamphlets emerged fully in the *Areopagitica* because the licensing ordinance was an offence against "the free and ingenuous sort of such as evidently were born to study and love learning for itself," men "whom God hath fitted for the special use of these times with eminent and ample gifts, and those perhaps neither among the priests nor among the pharisees. . . ."[8]

Milton's sense of particular calling distinguishes him not only from the Smectymnuans but from their more radical Puritan brethren. He thought of divine inspiration in terms of heavenly light; but he never had the profoundly-moving religious experience, the sense of mystical rebirth and miraculous enlightenment, at once supernatural in its origins and enrapturing in its effects, which provided the Puritan extremists with their energetic and fiery zeal. He often employed the phrases in which the saints described their conversion; but to the Calvinistic doctrines in which (despite Calvin) it found perfect expression—the doctrines of predestination, of special election, of free grace triumphing over human depravity, of the perseverance of the saints—to these he gave an interpretation which answered his own peculiar needs. The typical experience of the Bedford tinker was not for him.[9] He never in any sense regarded himself as "the chief of sinners"; nor did he arrive, after a long agony of helpless self-condemnation and self-torture, at a time when suddenly he received refreshment, assurance, and illumination, and heard the sound of voices rushing upon him with the noise of a wind from heaven. He was never the helpless and passive recipient of divine assistance; such support came to him from the studious summoning up of "all his reason and deliberation."[10] The voices which heartened him employed no mystical utterance; they spoke in the phrases of divine philosophy and with the ordered rhythms of classical poetry. The light which broke forth, God-given though it was, was never blindingly mysterious; it was that intellectual ray, the candle of the Lord.

It is this experience, not the experience of sectarianism, which inspires Milton's assertion that "he who destroys a good book, kills reason itself, kills the image of God, as it were, in the eye," and "strikes at the ethereal and fifth essence, the breath of reason. . . ."[11] And in his appeal to Parliament to obey "the voice of reason from what quarter soever it be heard speaking," one recognizes the echo, not of Thomas Young's Puritanism, but of Alexander Gill's belief in "common reason rightly guided" as "the image of God in us yet remaining."[12]

The opposition to his divorce argument and the general course of events forced Milton to recognize in 1644 what he had refused to recognize when it was pointed out by the moderate rationalists two years before, that protection was necessary against the tyranny of Puritanism's one right discipline as well as against the tyranny of Antichrist. He sought protection where Hooker and the Christian rationalists had sought it, in the sovereignty of the reason; the liberty which he demanded in the *Areopagitica* resembled the liberty they had striven to defend.[13]

The men, like John Hales and William Chillingworth, who made up at Lord Falkland's house a *convivium philosophicum*, had perceived more clearly than the Puritans, or than the Milton of 1641 and 1642, the inevitable consequence of the Protestant appeal to Scripture against ecclesiastical authority. They met the Roman assertion that it meant confusion, not by proposing the establishment of a new authority, but by announcing their confidence in the mercy of God and in the findings of "reason illuminated by revelation out of the written word."[14] This is the burden of Chillingworth's defence of the religion of Protestants. They did not believe (as his Roman antagonist appeared to assert) that men were to be given over to reason guided only "by principles of nature," by prejudices and popular errors, to come to their beliefs by chance. They were to follow "right reason, grounded on divine revelation and common notions written by God in the hearts of all men, and deducing, according to the never-failing rules of logic, consequent deductions from them. . . ."[15]

In the anti-episcopal pamphlets Milton had chosen with the Puritans to regard such arguments as the elevation of depraved humanity above the plain command of God. But Chillingworth and Falkland could see no opposition between reason and the divine will. Reason was for them, as for Hooker, the primary instrument through which divine grace exercised its influence. Falkland had maintained long before Milton that God demanded "a reasonable service" and "a reasonable faith"; but his conclusions had been somewhat different from those of Milton's fourth pamphlet on the one right discipline.[16] He believed that the interpretation of Scripture by reason provided the only solution for the problem presented by Rome and Geneva, and in 1641 by Laud and the Puritans.[17] But he protested against the assumption that this rationalism detracted from divine authority and grace: "When I speak thus of finding the truth by reason, I intend not to exclude the grace of God, which I doubt not . . . is ready to concur to our instruction as the sun is to our sight, if we by wilful winking choose not to make, not it, but ourselves guilty of our blindness. . . . Yet when I speak of God's grace, I mean not that it infuseth a knowledge without reason, but works by it as by its minister, and dispels those mists of passion which do wrap up truth from our understandings."[18]

When Milton spoke of the intellectual ray in *Of Reformation*, he expressed precisely Falkland's conviction; but it is difficult to distinguish zeal from passion, and his hatred of ecclesiastical corruption swept him away into attacks on moderate rationalism. It required the events of 1643 to bring out the implications of his belief that man's understanding was proportionable to truth if he would purge it of the effects of sin. In the early pamphlets the emphasis falls on reason's depravity; in the *Areopagitica* it is thrown where Falkland placed it, on reason's potentialities.

The conclusions of the *Areopagitica* are those at which the Christian rationalists had long since arrived. Chillingworth's enunciation of the principle of right reason carried with it a recognition of the right of every man "to judge for himself with the judgment of discretion."[19] Falkland maintained that a man's belief must be his own, not one accepted from authority;[20] and consequently that it was "not to choose by reason, and Scripture, and tradition received by reason" that made a heretic, but "to choose an opinion which will make most either for the chooser's lust, or power, or fame. . . ."[21] Hales had likewise argued that heresy "is an act of the will, not of reason, and is indeed a lie, not a mistake."[22] And both maintained that "it is the unity of the Spirit in the bond of peace, not identity of conceit, which the Holy Ghost requires at the hands of Christians."[23] The way of salvation, said Falkland, "is seeking truth impartially and obeying diligently what is found sincerely, and he who treads this way, though he miss of truth, shall not miss of his favour who is the Father of it. . . ."[24]

This is substantially the argument of the *Areopagitica*. The immediate inspiration of its rationalism is probably to be found in Lord Brooke's pamphlet rather than in the writings of Chillingworth, Hales, and Falkland.[25] But Milton's tribute to the dead parliamentary leader marks his recognition of the need for the reasonable and charitable moderation expounded by both Falkland and Brooke in the House. The Civil War offers no more painful illustration of the tragedy of human kind than their deaths on opposing sides. In temperament and in thought they were brothers, not opponents in arms; but they were caught in a mist of passion from which death (in Falkland's case through suicidal recklessness) provided an escape. For Milton a yet more dispiriting fate was reserved. He was to learn through hard experience something of their tolerance. It was to be long before he could express Falkland's view of the tender mercy of the Father of truth. He found it difficult, even when chastened by defeat, to consider for a moment that he might himself be wrong. But in 1644 the shock of his matrimonial mistake and the condemnation of his divorce tract brought him to something like their position. The centre of his argument in the pamphlets on divorce and in the *Areopagitica* is the conviction that when God gave Adam reason, "he gave him freedom to choose, for reason is but choosing."[26] From that conviction arises his defence of active freedom in faith and virtue, and his appeal for "a little forbearance of one another, and some grain of charity. . . ."[27]

The pamphlets written between 1643 and 1645 constitute Milton's most emphatic demand for liberty. The *Areopagitica* contains significant reservations; but what one remembers is the assertion that "liberty . . . is the nurse of all great wits."[28] In his first divorce tract Milton argued that "God delights not to make a drudge of virtue, whose actions must be all elective and unconstrained."[29] In the *Areopagitica* he maintained, with a reference to Plato, that freedom was only to be governed by "the rules of temperance," by the "unwritten, or at least unconstraining laws of virtuous education, religious and civil nurture."[30] In *Tetrachordon*, in a passage which applies to religion as well as to marriage, he argued that God "hates all feigning and formality where there should be all faith and sincereness."[31] It is in sincerity of endeavour that salvation lies rather than in submission to precepts. "A man may be a heretic in the truth; and if he believes things only because his pastor says so or the Assembly so determine, without knowing other reason, though his belief be true, yet the very truth he holds becomes his heresy."[32] To assume the authority over man represented by the licensing ordinance is contrary to divine purpose: "God uses not to captivate under a perpetual childhood of prescription, but trusts him with the gift of reason to be his own chooser. . . .."[33] In that statement the Christian rationalist elevates individual liberty above reformation. And it is at this point that one recognizes the full effect on Milton's thought of the events of 1642 and 1643. For, if this doctrine rejects the restrictive ethic whereby the Puritan of the extreme right would deny the full and free use of nature's gifts, it also rejects the perverse and undisciplined indulgence offered by Comus. The temperance which is guided in its legitimate use of nature's abundance by laws received through reason from the order of grace is firmly established as the basis for that integration of spirit and nature which *Comus* had failed to represent with complete success.

## 2

The appeal to the example of Isocrates, the presentation of Athens as an admirable pattern, the references to the classical learning of the early Christians, the allusions to Plato, Bacon, and "our sage and serious poet Spenser," the praise of free and heroic activity, the echoes from the tradition of Erasmus and Hooker, all these give the *Areopagitica* the tone of a humanistic document. One is reminded of the Milton of the *Nativity Ode* and the academic exercises rather than of the antagonist of episcopacy. But one is also reminded, if only by Brooke, that a liberal rationalism was not incompatible with principles essentially characteristic of Puritanism.

The divorce pamphlets and the *Areopagitica* lose something of their significance in the development of Milton's thought if only the opposition between an anti-rationalistic Puritanism and a rationalistic Humanism is recognized in their controversial background. Milton's insistence on the sovereignty of reason does not represent simply a return to earlier loyalties; it reflects developments within the ranks of those who regarded episcopacy as unscriptural and an arm of Antichrist.

It is necessary to distinguish degrees of rationalism among the Puritans. One extreme is represented by Thomas Edwards' repeated denunciations of those who believed "that right reason is the rule of faith,"[34] that "faith is not the guide of reason but reason the guide of faith, nor is a man to believe anything in Scripture further than he sees reason to induce him."[35] But Calvin himself was no stubborn anti-rationalist;[36] and Edwards represents not Puritanism but the right wing which sought to establish a new orthodoxy through the Assembly. Against this group the *Areopagitica* is directed; but its fundamental arguments had already been employed by the left wing of the Puritan party.

This opposition had a history which dated from the early years of the Puritan movement.[37] It is best represented in the pre-revolutionary period by John Robinson, who was a liberal rationalist as well as pastor of the Pilgrim Fathers and most eminent of the Separatist ministers. He believed that "divine authority is to sway with us above all reason" because "reason teacheth that God is both to be believed and obeyed in the things for which man can see no reason."[38] But if he would have agreed with Edwards to that extent, he was no more able than Falkland to discern a contradiction between grace and reason. The faith which comes with grace is to be set above reason, but not over against it. The effect of grace is not the opposition of the spiritual and the human; it is the unity of the whole creature: "for these three, faith, reason, and sense, being all God's works in man, cannot be contrary in their use, one to another; neither can anything be true in one which is false in another but use order and perfect it; reason sense, and faith both sense and reason. . . . Sweet is the harmony of all the powers and parts both of the soul and body of a sanctified person."[39] To this statement Christian rationalists from Hooker to Benjamin Whichcote could have subscribed.

Robinson's idea of sanctification provides the basis for an assertion of liberty of conscience. Eighteen years before Chillingworth had defended the legitimate authority of reason against Roman claims, Robinson was defending it against the ambitions of the Presbyterians: "What are consequences regulated by the Word, which sanctifieth all creatures, 1 *Tim.* 4. 4, 5, but that sanctified use of reason? and will any reasonable man deny the use and discourse of reason."[40] It followed for him, as for the rationalists, that "the meanest man's reason, specially in matters of faith and obedience to God, is to be preferred before all authority of all men." Men must "live by their own faith" as they must see with their own eyes; for "God, who hath made two great lights for the bodily eye, hath also made two great lights for the eye of the mind: the one, the Scriptures for her supernatural light, and the other, reason for her natural light. And indeed only these two are a man's own; and so is not the authority of other men."[41]

This argument is typical of the early Separatists. The individualism which begot the discipline of particular congregations found support in the natural liberty which belongs to reasonable creatures as well as in the Christian liberty of the saints. When the theoretical differences between the right and the left became of urgent practical importance, the left appealed to both of Robinson's lights. Few of the Assembly's opponents in 1644 desired to sacrifice divine authority and the light of grace; but at the same time they insisted with one accord that "there is no medium between an implicit faith and that which a man's own judgment and understanding lead him to."[42] They argued that it was impossible to impose a uniformity of faith when "the Spirit himself waits and violates not the liberty of the reasonable soul by superseding the faculties thereof, but approves truth to the understanding and moves the will without violence, with a rational force."[43]

This was the argument of John Goodwin, whose name was to be linked with Milton's in circumstances unforeseen in 1644.[44] Next to Roger Williams, he was perhaps the most notorious of the Assembly's opponents. He borrowed many of Williams' arguments; but his demand for freedom of conscience differs from Williams' precisely as does Milton's. He was vigorously Separatist in his theory of church government, and suspiciously Arminian in his theory of justification.[45] While Milton was insisting on the one right discipline, Goodwin was expounding "many shall run to and fro" as indicating that many "shall discourse and beat out the secrets of God in the Scriptures with more liberty and freedom of judgment and understanding, and traverse much ground to and again . . .; 'and knowledge' by this means 'shall be increased.' "[46] It seemed to him that the destruction of the Great Whore "by Christians of inferior rank and quality," prophesied in *Revelation* 18, could hardly be accomplished "except the judgments and consciences of men should be loosened and set at liberty. . . ."[47]

In pamphlets written in 1644 and 1645, he marshalled most of the arguments that could be produced for toleration. He insisted on the privileges of the saints;[48] and though willing (like Burton) to see the national church reformed under Presbyterian discipline, asserted the superiority of Congregationalism because "that way which shall be able to out-reason, not that which shall out-club all other ways, will at last exalt unity and be at last exalted by gathering all other ways unto it."[49] He repeated Williams' arguments to prove that the powers of church and state must be distinguished, and that "prisons and swords are not church officers."[50] He pointed out that "God reveals more and more of the Gospel every day in a fuller and clearer manner"; and, since he does so chiefly through individuals, maintained that "the determination of a council or of the major part of a council against any way, doctrine or practice, is no demonstrative or sufficient proof for any wise man to rest or build upon."[51] And because God "regards no man's zeal without knowledge, though it should pitch and fasten upon things never so agreeable to his will," he repeatedly asserted "that reason ought to be every man's leader, guide, and director in his faith or about what he is or ought to believe, and that no man ought to leap with his faith till he hath looked with his reason and discovered what is meet to be believed. . . ."[52]

If Milton's *Areopagitica* is set against a background thick with arguments such as these, it is not difficult to understand why what is now his best-known prose work seemed to fall still-born from the press. It is remarkable that his eloquent defence of learning received no public attention;[53] but the London of 1644, in danger from the royalist forces and torn by passionate controversy, had no time for Attic periods, especially when their essential arguments (including the appeal to the sovereignty of the individual reason) were the common property of the Assembly's opponents. Moreover, the *Areopagitica* dealt chiefly with a minor aspect of the great public controversy, the point at which the efforts of the Presbyterians to establish an orthodoxy touched most nearly the author of *The Doctrine and Discipline of Divorce.* It represented no party; it offered no solution for the pressing ecclesiastical problem. Its author announced that the question of discipline upon which the public eye was focussed was of comparatively little importance.

## 3

A further possible explanation for the *Areopagitica's* failure to attract attention is more significant for the development of Milton's thought. In spite of the radical tone of its arguments, the denunciation of censorship, the attack on the Presbyterians, and the plea for forbearance, the extent of the freedom Milton demands remains uncertainly restricted. His readers would have observed that his arguments were much less extreme than those with which complete liberty of conscience was asserted by Roger Williams, lately come from Rhode Island to obtain a charter for his new colony.[54]

Williams' arguments for religious liberty in *The Bloudy Tenent of Persecution* represent the last degree in a series which begins with the Assembly. Each extreme offered a logical escape from the dilemma presented by the incompatibility of liberty and reformation. The Assembly sacrificed liberty to the idea of the holy community. Williams sacrificed national reformation to the freedom without which true righteousness seemed to him impossible. Yet both conclusions were consistent with Puritan principles. Williams never ceased to think of true religion in strictly Calvinistic terms; but he saw the holy community as altogether spiritual, and founded a civil state with liberty of conscience as its corner-stone. He could do so because he had formulated more clearly than others in his time a "principle of segregation" which cut through the mutual recriminations of Presbyterians and Independents in England.[55]

The toleration controversy between 1643 and 1645 never escaped altogether from differences about the definition of the one right discipline. It was difficult for men who thought in terms of revealed truth to accept unreservedly the diversity which accompanies religious freedom; and the controversy resolved itself into the assertion by each side that the other attempted to substitute human for divine authority. Goodwin and his fellows maintained that the Assembly endeavoured to supplant the authority of God in the individual conscience by a human authority dependent on the state. Thomas Edwards argued, with prophetic fear, that toleration was the "last plot and design" by which Satan "would undermine and frustrate the whole work of reformation." If reformation meant the sweeping away of human corruptions in favour of the divine discipline, it appeared to Edwards that to tolerate differences meant compounding with error:

> This general toleration throws down all at once; it overthrows the Scriptures in that it allows a liberty of denying the Scriptures to be the word of God, in that it sets up the conscience above the Scriptures, making every man's conscience, even the polluted, defiled, seared consciences, the rule of faith and holiness before the pure and unerring word of God, crying out that men must do according to their consciences but never speaking of going according to the word of God; yea, setting up men's fancies, humours, factions, lusts, under the name of conscience, above the word of God, which is to set up the creature, yea, the corrupted, defiled creature, above God, and to make man's conscience greater than God, whereas God is greater than men's consciences, 1 *John* 3. 20.[56]

This statement perfectly expresses the Presbyterian position. The conscience must submit to the plain word of God, and its refusal indicates a wilfulness which ought to be corrected by the church and the state. The church, in the words of Baillie, possesses power to "declare the mind of God in all questions of religion with such authority as obliges to receive their just sentences"; and, asserted Edwards, it is the duty of magistrates who call themselves Christians to defend this divine truth.[57]

The question of conscience really hung on this last assertion. If the Christian magistrate must defend God's word as interpreted by the church, he may perhaps tolerate degrees of difference within limits, but he can never permit the complete religious liberty which would involve freedom to deny that there is any word of God at all. At this point Williams sowed his dragon's teeth, for he said that the magistrate, even if a Christian, had as magistrate nothing to do with matters of religion.

Williams boldly took the step at which nearly every other Puritan stumbled. He not only denied secular power to the church, he also denied spiritual interests to the state.[58] This meant little more than the extension of principles expressed by the early reformers; but (as a later chapter will show) Williams substituted radical democracy for the political conservatism of Luther and Calvin, and avoided the misinterpretation of St. Augustine which prematurely brought the holy community down from heaven and established it at Geneva.

It is significant that, whatever may be their political importance, the claims of the reason play only a small part in Williams' defence of free conscience. They would have confused the issue as he saw it, and might have prevented him (as ultimately they prevented Milton and Goodwin) from arriving at a theory of complete religious liberty. For him no less than for the Presbyterians, faith is the gift of God, not the achievement of reason; and the basis of his argument is the conviction that Christian religion is essentially spiritual. In his constant "expectation of light to come which we are not now able to comprehend," he sought a supernatural rather than an intellectual illumination.[59]

Williams accepted in its strictest form the doctrine of predestination which the rationalists (including Goodwin and subsequently Milton) found incompatible with confidence in human reason. He believed that the saint was elected according to God's incomprehensible will: "the Lord himself knows who are his, and his foundation remaineth sure; his elect or chosen cannot perish or be finally deceived."[60] But if they cannot be finally deceived, it is not because their faith is an intellectual achievement: "faith is that gift which proceeds alone from the Father of Lights, *Phill.* 1. 29; and till he pleases to make his light arise and open the eyes of blind sinners, their souls shall lie fast asleep. . . ."[61]

What Williams recognized with perfect clarity was that, if *only* God knows who are his and gives them faith, the holy community must be a mystical fellowship, and the acceptance of particular doctrines by the intellect can provide no test of membership. He observed that if the magistrate was to be called upon to apply such a test, the ultimate judgment of divine truth must rest with the state, not the church, since the magistrate alone can determine what interpretation he will defend. This seemed to him truly the subjection of divine authority to human; and he escaped from the vicious circle by asserting that the spheres of grace and of nature, the religious and the secular, were altogether distinct, and consequently that the magistrate's power extended only to civil peace.[62]

This segregation of the spiritual and the secular is founded on the Calvinistic distinction between man as naturally depraved and man as spiritually regenerate. Because the distinction between nature and spirit exists within the individual himself, he must be considered "in reference to God" and "in civil respects."[63] In reference to God he is either regenerate or unregenerate. The regenerate constitute Christ's mystical kingdom, of which particular congregations are the earthly types. Such voluntary associations derive from Christ the power to root the weeds out of their own spiritual gardens by church censure and excommunication. But to the magistrate they have only the relation of a private corporation.[64] In civil respects, their members and the unregenerate are equal, and together they claim from the magistrate their rights as men.[65] In reference to God, the regenerate are a spiritual aristocracy of brethren in Christ; but in their natural capacity they remain on a level with their unregenerate fellows.

It is from the agreement of men in their natural capacity that the magistrate's power is derived. And since natural power derived in part from the unregenerate cannot justly be exercised over the spiritual activities of the regenerate, the Erastians err in arguing that church government should be established by the state.[66] On the other hand, the type of Christ's kingdom being the particular congregation, it is equally a mistake to impose a national religion on regenerate and unregenerate alike. "As the lily is amongst thorns, so is Christ's love amongst the daughters; and as the apple-tree among the trees of the forest, so is her beloved among the sons; so great a difference is there between the church in a city or country, and the civil state, city, or country in which it is."[67] Consequently the Congregationalists in Massachusetts were at fault in attempting to establish a theocracy by excluding all but church members from civil rights, and the Assembly was at fault in urging Parliament to compel all Englishmen to become members of a Presbyterian Church of England.

Both in the old world and the new, the orthodox defended the refusal of toleration by appealing to the practice of God's chosen people, an example which Milton's patriotism brought constantly to his mind.[68] They argued that, in addition to his civil responsibilities, the Christian magistrate must defend true religion and restrain heresy because, by inheritance from the Jewish, he was "*custos utriusque tabulae*."[69] The church exercised its proper power in censuring a heretic; the magistrate proceeded against him because he endangered the civil peace of the Christian state. Williams replied that the polity of the Jews was an earthly type of Christ's heavenly kingdom which was abolished by his sacrifice, to be replaced by the particular congregation wherein the "corporal killing of the Law" became "spiritual killing by excommunication."[70] With the abrogation of the old law, the religious power of the Jewish magistrate ceased; henceforth all magistrates, whether Christian or heathen, possessed only a natural power to govern according to the consent of the people and the law of nature.[71]

Consequently Williams argued, not that the magistrate ought to exercise forbearance or tolerate differences of opinion, but that he is bound to allow complete freedom in religion. He must defend the civil rights, not merely of varieties of true Christians, but of "Jews, Turks, antichristians, pagans," even of papists, "upon good assurance given of civil obedience to the civil state."[72] Such rights include freedom in religious association and the expression of religious opinions.

The Presbyterians and Congregationalists alike denied that their churches endeavoured to control the conscience through carnal weapons; they dealt spiritually with the inward man, the magistrate with the outward. They maintained further that what they wished to see restrained was the wilful denial of God's plain precepts which showed the conscience to be defiled and Christian liberty forfeited. And they protested that they called upon the magistrate only to defend those fundamentals upon which God's word was clear, that he had no power "to make what laws he please either in restraining from or constraining to the use of things indifferent."[73] These distinctions seemed to Williams sophistical. He recognized the necessity of freedom of action as well as of conscience in religion. He observed that God's plain precepts might be variously interpreted. And he saw that indifference provided an ambiguous reservation which might permit a degree of liberty but equally denied it beyond the received definition of fundamentals.[74] He avoided disputes over definitions of doctrine and discipline simply by denying the magistrate any power over things religious, fundamental or indifferent. The church is God's enclosed garden; but the world is the devil's wilderness where good wheat and tares flourish and decay together.[75]

Milton never recognized with Williams' clarity the segregation of nature and grace which provided a solution of the difficulty presented by reformation and liberty. Even in his most liberal moments he tended to insert reservations where Williams made distinctions. It is for this reason that Williams' opinions merit the attention devoted to them here. Because they embody a radical theory of religious liberty founded on Puritan principles, they provide a standard against which Milton's opinions may be measured. Each of Williams' arguments appears at some point in Milton's prose; but he never reached Williams' theory of religious liberty. The principles which prevented him from doing so lie at the centre of his thought and are to be discerned even in the arguments of the *Areopagitica* and the divorce pamphlets. They were fundamental to his view of himself, and especially to his theory of his function as poet.

## 4

Milton's failure to arrive at a doctrine of complete religious liberty is not peculiar to him. It is typical of the group which constituted a centre party between the Presbyterians on the right and the extreme sectaries on the left.[76] The principle of segregation became of major importance in the religious (and the political) controversies of the revolution; but few applied it with Williams' logical and effective simplicity. It was possible to hew out of the virgin forests of Rhode Island a state incorporating "such liberty of conscience" as this idea justified;[77] but it was impossible, even with its logic, to sever the Gordian knot of political, economic, and social complications in England.

Even those who appropriated or had themselves developed the argument hesitated to pronounce for the freedom demanded by Williams. Henry Robinson asked, like Cromwell at a later date, "May not papists and Brownists as lawfully serve their king and country as those thundering legions of primitive Christians did the heathen emperors?"[78] But Cromwell was to find it perplexingly difficult to draw the line between religious opinion and disservice to the Christian state; and Robinson hastened to assure his readers that he did not desire the toleration of papists. Williams recognized the political danger of popery, and made civil obedience a condition of religious freedom. Robinson added to this familiar protest the spiritual argument. Papists submit to a spiritual tyranny, and cannot be tolerated "by reason of their idolatry."[79] This represents a confusion of principles of which Williams was never guilty.

Even John Goodwin fell into the same snare. He excluded papists from toleration, not only because "their very principles oppose the secular power," but because "they differ in fundamentals and are properly another religion."[80] If, as Goodwin had argued with Williams as a guide,[81] matters of religion are beyond the magistrate's jurisdiction, it is difficult to see what fundamentals have to do with toleration. And Goodwin took another step away from *The Bloudy Tenent* when he admitted with Mistress Chidley that the Parliament might reform the national church as it pleased, though it ought to tolerate in their minor differences the "so inconsiderable" number of those who adhered to the Congregational way.[82]

At yet another remove from Williams was the author of *The Ancient Bounds, or Liberty of Conscience*. He agreed that the magistrate's province embraced "all vicious and scandalous practices, contrary to the light of nature or manifest good of societies."[83] But his distinction between church and state entangled itself in the relationship between the law of nature and true religion. He thought it wrong to argue that "errors of manifest scandal and danger to men's souls and consciences, as Arianism, Socinianism, Familism, etc., ought not to be restrained by the Christian magistrate, and the assertors and maintainers of them interdicted under penalties the divulging or spreading of them by public preaching or printing. . . ."[84] It seemed to him that "to preserve the acknowledged truth from being scandalized and corrupted is a work of love and charity, which the magistrate's arm is requisite and must extend itself unto. . . ."[85]

This concern for acknowledged truth set between *An Apologeticall Narration* and *The Bloudy Tenent* a wider gulf than there was between the Narrators and their Presbyterian brethren in the Assembly. They protested that they agreed perfectly with the Presbyterians in doctrine, and desired only "the allowance of a latitude to some lesser differences with peaceableness."[86] They pointed out that their opinion of heresy and its treatment was precisely that of the Assembly, and that their disagreements in church discipline did not involve "the received principles of Christianity."[87] They were in matters which might be regarded as indifferent.

What point in this scale is occupied by Milton's "speech for the liberty of unlicensed printing"? With Robinson, Goodwin, and *The Ancient Bounds*, he appealed to the sovereignty of reason, the binding power of conscience, the inwardness and progressiveness of faith. But in spite of his noble eloquence, he hesitated with them at Williams' demand for absolute religious liberty. His arguments, like theirs, make the demand seem inevitable; but he could not accept the full implications of Williams' segregation, nor the tolerant latitudinarianism of pure Christian rationalism, because his mind was still dominated by the need for defending acknowledged truth in religion. The *Areopagitica* is a vigorous pronouncement on individual liberty; but it is not a pronouncement from a fixed point on which Milton had always stood and was always to stand. It is a pronouncement from a point on the line of development between the opinions of Thomas Young and those of Roger Williams, though the final position of the founder of Rhode Island was in fact never to be reached by the defender of the English Commonwealth.

Behind the demand for liberty of conscience voiced by the Assembly's opponents lay the question of church discipline. It was difficult to escape from the confining belief that reformation must result in the erection of the one right discipline (whether presbyterial or congregational) ordained by God; but an escape was provided by the door of lesser differences cautiously opened by the Narrators and impossible to close thereafter. Behind the *Areopagitica* lay the argument of the divorce pamphlets for individual liberty in the determination of what Milton defined as a thing indifferent. His pamphlet on the press was specifically concerned with a similar question; and in spite of the principles which seemed to carry him beyond the point at issue, the purpose of his argument was to demonstrate that "the law must needs be frivolous which goes about to restrain things uncertainly and yet equally working to good and to evil."[88]

Whether or not he still believed in the need for the one right discipline, he still believed that there existed a body of fundamental and undeniable truth which must be preserved. If we are to discover onward things more remote from our knowledge, it does not follow that we are to permit the light we already have to be extinguished. Consequently, with Robinson and Goodwin, he denies toleration to papists on religious as well as civil grounds: "I mean not tolerated popery and open superstition which, as it extirpates all religions and civil supremacies, so itself should be extirpate. . . ."[89] Like the author of *The Ancient Bounds*, he is certain that what "is impious or evil absolutely, either against faith or manners, no law can possibly permit that intends not to unlaw itself . . .";[90] Williams would have omitted "faith." Like the Narrators, it is for "moderate varieties and brotherly dissimilitudes that are not vastly disproportional" that Milton solicits toleration and forbearance: "those neighbouring differences, or rather indifferences, are what I speak of, whether in some point of doctrine or of discipline. . . ."[91] If the reservation implied by this plea be remembered, no surprise need be occasioned by Milton's attitude towards "malignant books" or his subsequent activities on behalf of the Council of State.[92]

Whatever may be the apparent force of the arguments in the *Areopagitica*, the reservations are unequivocal. Freedom must be permitted in those things concerning which there is no positive command or prohibition from God, and in which the balance of good and evil can be determined only by the individual conscience. It is in the knowledge of such matters that faith will progress, just as the author of *The Doctrine and Discipline of Divorce* has arrived, in spite of centuries of misunderstanding, at the true interpretation of the divine will in that respect. Restraint at such points is unwarranted because right decisions can be arrived at only through reason and experience. It is here, not with regard to fundamentals, that the experimental reason finds its place in Milton's thought. Adam was given reason by which to choose in his original perfection; "law and compulsion" are not to tyrannize over his fallen sons in "those things which heretofore were governed only by exhortation."[93] "Without the knowledge of evil," there can be no wisdom of choice where God's will has not been declared.[94] "Good and evil we know in the field of this world grow up together almost inseparably. . . . And perhaps this is that doom which Adam fell into of knowing good and evil; that is to say, of knowing good by evil."[95] The sense of this doom might have led Milton to a doctrine of religious liberty; it would have done so had he not been convinced that, while good and evil are *almost* inseparable, the distinction has in some cases been plainly indicated by divine revelation.

Milton's liberty is theoretically limited at yet another point. It is not for licence that he pleads, but for a freedom which the good man will exercise according to "the rules of temperance" exemplified by that Spenserian knight whose virtue is sometimes less Aristotelian temperance than Puritan renunciation.[96] In the *Areopagitica* the ideal is translated into more significant terms, for Milton protests especially against the "tradition of crowding free consciences and Christian liberties into canons and precepts of men."[97] Williams disposed of the distinction between conscience and conscience truly free, liberty and Christian liberty in matters of religion. Milton cannot praise "a fugitive and cloistered virtue," for "that which purifies us is trial, and trial is by what is contrary";[98] but what he is defending is the Christian liberty of purity. Restraint in things indifferent denies the exercise of that freedom indicated by the "remarkable saying" of St. Paul, "to the pure all things are pure. . . ."[99] To them there can be no danger from evil or from the truth which has more shapes than one: "What else is all that rank of things indifferent wherein truth may be on this side or on the other without being unlike herself? What but a vain shadow else is the abolition of 'those ordinances, that handwriting nailed to the cross'? What great purchase is this Christian liberty which Paul so often boasts of? His doctrine is that he who eats or eats not, regards a day or regards it not, may do either to the Lord."[100] The *Areopagitica* and the divorce pamphlets apply this principle to one who reads or reads not, divorces a wife or divorces not.

The *Areopagitica* is a magnificently eloquent appeal for a particular kind of liberty, for Christian liberty in indifferent things. The adjectives involve significant reservations. What are the precise limits the *Areopagitica* only suggests, and further definition will depend largely on the course of events. But that there were limits was as clear to Milton as to the author of *The Ancient Bounds*, who pertinently remarked, "Moses permitted divorce to the Jews, notwithstanding the hardness of their hearts; so must this liberty be granted to men (within certain bounds) though it may be abused to wanton opinions more than were to be wished."[101] Further light on Milton's idea of Christian liberty must be sought in his discussion of that Mosaic permission.

## Chapter VII

# Christian and Human Liberty

THE divorce problem imposed on Milton a valuable discipline; it forced him to define more clearly his essential principles. His tracts on this subject are consequently more than exercises in textual juggling, for the complicated exegesis which makes them less readable than the *Areopagitica* is necessary to a formulation of his views on the laws which govern the individual's relation to his fellows and to God. In *The Doctrine and Discipline* and *Tetrachordon*, his theology becomes more philosophical and less merely controversial than at any other point in his pamphleteering; and the argument of these carefully written works is in fact more significant in the development of his mind than his somewhat rhetorical declamations on the press. They are the first in a series of justifications; and if the echoes of his domestic misfortune are later to be heard in the mutual recriminations of Adam and Eve in their shame, *The Doctrine* and *Tetrachordon* present as it were a preliminary sketch of the philosophical and theological background of his epic.

By March, 1645, he had neither completely nor consistently formulated his theory of liberty; but the fundamental pattern was firmly outlined as a consequence of the nature of the divorce problem. Since in his opinion marriage and divorce were improperly made matters of ecclesiastical concern through a misinterpretation of the divine will expressed in the Old Testament and the New, it was necessary to argue the question in terms of God's law and Gospel liberty. Since marriage was designed to satisfy the natural needs of spirit and body, it was necessary to demonstrate the justice of divorce in terms of the law of nature and the innate dignity of man. The argument thus involves two sets of principles, independent of each other yet capable of intimate relationship. Williams' segregation of the spiritual and the natural kept these principles distinct.

It is their confused relationship which makes the *Areopagitica* ambiguous in comparison with *The Bloudy Tenent.* But the argument of the divorce tracts leads to a combination which makes possible at once a demand for liberty and a condemnation of licence.

One of the results of Milton's careful revision of his argument for the second edition of *The Doctrine and Discipline* and his more extensive rewriting of it for *Tetrachordon* was the progressive definition of the Christian liberty to which he had appealed positively but indefinitely in the anti-episcopal pamphlets.[1] Indeed it is only in the light of that definition that the significance of his appeal to the principle in the *Areopagitica* becomes apparent.

Other opponents of ecclesiastical authority were making controversial use of this theological doctrine. It had a precise meaning for the trained theologian, and became a radically useful weapon only in proportion as its orthodox definition was blurred. Though its consequences might be differently estimated, it clearly meant in general that the Gospel brings with it freedom of conscience. Hence Christian liberty was constantly demanded even by those who did not share Mistress Chidley's enthusiastic assurance of saintship.

In her eyes it was a liberty restricted to the visible saints, God's elect; and it was associated with the idea of the one right discipline because it extended only to the right to establish God's positive ordinances. This, somewhat less rigidly, is the liberty desired by the Independent authors of *An Apologeticall Narration* when they plead for "the enjoyment of the ordinances of Christ, which are our portions as we are Christians."[2] This appeal might include not merely the demand for the freedom of a particular group—in effect, the aristocracy of grace—but also the denial of similar freedom to other groups. Thus one pamphleteer used the phrase in his title to indicate the contrast between the righteous freedom he desired and the unbridled liberty he condemned with the Presbyterians: he composed *A Paraenetick . . . for* (*not loose but*) *Christian Libertie.*[3]

But when the moderate author of *The Ancient Bounds* asked the Parliament not "to shut the door of Christian liberty that was first opened to us by your means,"[4] he was pleading for something which, in spite of his moderation and the efforts of Parliament, really meant the breaking down of the door altogether. In the hands of the extreme pamphleteers, Christian liberty is transformed into a freedom which knows no bounds. Because there was no agreement as to what constituted the one right discipline, it inevitably followed that each must be allowed to set himself under what seemed to him the Gospel ordinance. And because it was impossible to determine who were elect and so properly possessed of Christian liberty, it followed ultimately that the same individual liberty must be accorded all men, at least all men living under the Gospel, no matter what the peculiarities of their doctrine and discipline. Thus Henry Robinson inquired "whether it be not a greater infringement of Christian liberty and propriety to have burdens and impositions laid upon the conscience, whereby a poor soul lives in hateful bondage upon earth and subjects itself to perpetual torments in hell hereafter . . .?"[5] And William Walwyn (subsequently an associate of the Levellers) argued that, in spite of the confidence of the divines and in view of the diversity of opinion, "it is but meet that they should decree only for themselves and such as are of their own mind, and allow Christian liberty to all their brethren to follow that way which shall seem to them most agreeable to truth."[6]

Milton's treatment of Christian liberty exactly parallels this contemporary development. From being a demand for the right to constitute the Gospel discipline, it becomes a demand for the freedom of the individual conscience from human ordinances. The bounds of such a liberty are practically incapable of definition, and the doctrine consequently becomes a revolutionary principle whose potentialities extend beyond the limits of church discipline.

Among orthodox divines, the doctrine had no such implications. For Calvin and Luther it had a definite theological significance and precise limitations.[7] If the limitations were removed, it might become revolutionary; if they were preserved, it might (as in Massachusetts[8]) become an instrument of reaction. It is for this reason that the principle is of essential importance in the development of Milton's thought.

In the divorce pamphlets and the *Areopagitica*, Milton's emphasis falls on liberty rather than on its limitations; but he felt that, though he was "taxed of novelties and strange producements," his doctrinal arguments were not in themselves unorthodox.[9] Certainly the differences between his interpretation of Christian liberty and Calvin's are not on the surface of striking consequence. This is particularly true of the first edition of *The Doctrine and Discipline*; in *Tetrachordon* the implications of the argument are more apparent.

With Luther's commentary on *Galatians* and his letter *Concerning Christian Liberty*, Calvin's chapter on the doctrine in the *Institutes* provided the source for orthodox opinion. Theologically the two treatments differ very little, though it is possible to distinguish between the effects on English Puritanism of Luther's mystical enthusiasm and Calvin's legalistic logic.[10] The *Institutes* fixes the meaning of the doctrine with exactness.[11] Christian liberty consists of three parts: (1) "The consciences of the faithful, when the assurance of their justification before God is to be sought, may raise and advance themselves above the Law, and forget the whole righteousness of the Law." This is the most obvious aspect of Christian liberty: the law of works is abrogated by the gospel of faith, and Christians are freed from the impositions of the Mosaic Law, though the moral part of the Law is still in force, and teaches, exhorts, and urges to good. (2) Christian consciences "obey the Law, not as compelled by the necessity of the Law, but being free from the yoke of the Law itself, of their own accord they obey the will of God." Depraved mankind is manifestly incapable of fulfilling the law of righteousness; but the elect, freed from the necessity by Christ's vicarious suffering, "cheerfully and alertly" follow God's guidance in the Law as the spontaneous result of grace. (3) "We be bound with no conscience before God of outward things which are by themselves indifferent, but that we may indifferently sometime use them and sometime leave them unused." All things concerning which there is no gospel prohibition are sanctified to the Christian's use.[12]

Calvin was careful to point out that Christian liberty cannot permit error or be used as "a cloak" for lust, that it "is in all the parts of it a spiritual thing," and that it is perverted by those who "think that there is no liberty but that which is used before men." Luther similarly remarked that "Christian liberty is a very spiritual thing which the carnal man doth not understand," and that "Christ hath made us free, not from an earthly bondage, but from God's everlasting wrath."[13] Yet Calvin had also written that, because believers, "having received such prerogative of liberty . . ., have by the benefit of Christ obtained this, that they be not entangled with any snares of observations in those things in which the Lord willed that they should be at liberty, we conclude that they are exempt from all power of men."[14] The significance of this statement obviously depends on the interpretation of "those things." Calvin's limitations make Christian liberty in effect simply a definition of the spiritual relationship between the elect soul and God; but the Puritan extremists were to extend its implications to produce a radical doctrine of liberty to be exercised in the world. Through the breaking down of the orthodox reservations by authors who were not theologians but pamphleteering controversialists, Christian liberty ceased to be an exclusively spiritual privilege possessed before God, and became a liberty to be used not only before men but in spite of human authority, ecclesiastical or civil.[15]

In general, that is the significance of Milton's interpretation of the doctrine. But Goodwin, Robinson, the author of *The Ancient Bounds*, and their fellows, centred their demand for liberty of conscience on church discipline, a subject concerning which the enemies of episcopacy were loath to admit that there was no divine prescript binding Christians. Milton was chiefly concerned with a matter he considered indifferent. Because he regarded divorce as one of those things in which the Lord willed men to be at liberty, it was with the third of Calvin's parts of liberty that he was at first chiefly concerned. His original difference of opinion with the orthodox lay in his belief that divorce came under that heading. Consequently it is in the application rather than in the essential doctrines that his argument is heretical. He observed that none of those who inveighed against his conclusion deigned to attack the doctrinal reasoning behind it. He in fact believed that he was simply applying the statements of orthodox divines to a specific case: they "leave their own mature positions like the eggs of an ostrich in the dust; I do but lay them in the sun. Their own pregnancies hatch the truth. . . ."[16] But the truth by which Milton would make man free developed peculiar characteristics, largely because of difficulties encountered in the hatching.

## 2

Milton's interpretation of Christian liberty is given a curious twist, which at first sight seems to direct it away from the radical attitude and towards the orthodox, by the relationship between the Mosaic divorce law and Christ's statement. According to the received opinion the Gospel abrogated the ceremonial and civil law of Moses, but the moral law, including the decalogue, remained in force for Christians and served as the rule for magistrates as well as the church.[17] In proportion as the Mosaic Law is regarded as having been totally abrogated, the radical potentialities of Christian liberty increase. In *De Doctrina Christiana*, Milton was to assert that "the entire Mosaic Law was abolished," just as Williams had argued that the whole Law was fulfilled by Christ's sacrifice and abrogated in favour of the law of faith.[18] But Milton arrived at this conclusion by a strange route, for it was of the utmost importance to his divorce argument to prove that Christ could not have repudiated the Mosaic divorce law.

His divorce pamphlets involve two lines of attack on the accepted opinion. He first attempts to refute the usual interpretation of Christ's statement by arguing that divorce cannot in itself be sinful, because it was permitted in the Law, the expression of God's eternal will, which Christ did not come to abrogate.[19] He then argues, from a different quarter, that it is the nature of the Gospel to permit a greater, not a lesser, degree of freedom than the Law.

The insistence of the first argument on the Law as the revelation whereby God communicates his ordinances to man has an obvious analogy with the assertion of the anti-episcopal pamphlets that God has prescribed a discipline for the Gospel church as he had for the Jewish—a prescription which presumably takes the place of the ceremonial law, the moral law remaining. Like the earlier assertion, it is also intimately connected with the habitual appeal to first institutions, in this case the original institution of marriage. The Mosaic divorce law is the necessary consequence of God's purpose in the institution; if the end of marriage is not achieved, there must be freedom to divorce.[20]

But the general principles which support the refutation of the accepted view are more significant than their application to the immediate problem. It cannot be true that *Deuteronomy* 24. 1, 2, permitted divorce for "hardness of heart" in the sense of sin, because God could not permit sin "in his Law, the perfect rule of his own will and our most edified conscience."[21] The received opinion makes God the author of sin "more than anything objected by the Jesuits or Arminians against predestination."[22] The purpose of the Law was "that sin might be made abundantly manifest to be heinous and displeasing to God that so his offered grace might be the more esteemed."[23] If God had permitted the Jews to sin in divorcing, he would have at once permitted and condemned, "saying in general, 'Do this and live,' and yet deceiving and damning underhand with unsound and hollow permissions. . . ."[24] This is impossible; nor can God allow sin by dispensation, for he is "a most pure essence, the just avenger of sin, neither can he make that cease to be a sin which is in itself injust and impure, as all divorces, they say, were which were not for adultery."[25]

So much would have sufficed to indicate that on orthodox grounds divorce for causes other than adultery cannot in itself be sinful; but Milton does not restrain his argument to the specific subject. The reasoning from the Law rests on the assumption, suggested but not developed in *The Reason of Church Government*, that God's revealed prescripts are necessarily in accordance with the unchanging principles of right reason.

The hidden ways of his providence we adore and search not; but the Law is his revealed will, his complete, his evident and certain will. Herein he appears to us as it were in human shape, enters into covenant with us, swears to keep it, binds himself like a just law giver to his own prescriptions, gives himself to be understood by men, judges and is judged, measures and is commensurate to right reason.[26]

This view of the Law as expressing, at least in its moral part, the eternal and unabolishable principles of right reason is similar to the view taken by orthodox divines like William Ames.[27] It is because it expresses these principles that the moral law is unabrogated and still binds Christians.

Moreover, in *The Doctrine and Discipline* and more largely in *Tetrachordon*, Milton supports his contention that divorce is not sinful by arguing from the nature not merely of the Mosaic Law but of law in general. Sin "cannot consist with rule," and though laws may bear "with imperfection for a time," it is impossible to "make that lawful which is lawless," to legalize vice and error. "For what less indignity were this, than as if justice herself . . . instead of conquering should compound and treat with sin, her eternal adversary and rebel, upon ignoble terms?" Law cannot moderate sin, which "is always in excess"; it is impossible "to put a girdle about that chaos"; and the end of all law, as of God's law in particular, must be to root out sin altogether.[28]

In its main outlines, this reminds one of the arguments by which Edwards proved the impossibility of toleration. It throws light on the reservations of the *Areopagitica* and will also help to explain some apparent inconsistencies in Milton's political theory and his later opinions on conscience. It is because of the impossibility of girdling that chaos that, whatever may be the temporary consequences, he always demands not liberty but Christian liberty.

But it is already possible in the divorce pamphlets to distinguish a difference between the orthodox view and Milton's idea of the continuance of the moral law and of Christian liberty. Christ's statement must not be interpreted as a repudiation of the Mosaic permission because it is "absurd to imagine that the covenant of grace should reform the exact and perfect law of works, eternal and immutable," or to "talk of Christ's abolishing any judicial law of his great father, except in some circumstances which are Judaical rather than judicial, and need no abolishing but cease of themselves. . . ."[29] It follows that "whatever else in the political law of more special relation to the Jews might cease to us, yet that of those precepts concerning divorce not one of them was repealed by the doctrine of Christ."[30] But if divorce is still to be permitted under the Gospel, it is not simply through the Mosaic code that it is authorized. Christ's saying is to be so interpreted "as not to contradict the least part of moral religion that God hath formerly commended. . . ."[31] It was Christ's office to maintain, not the Mosaic code, but the law "grounded on moral reason" and "that unabolishable equity which it conveys to us."[32] Milton's argument rests, not on the particular Mosaic formulation, but on the eternal morality and equity which lay behind the law ceremonial, political, judicial, and moral; and it is this, not the Mosaic formulation, which still binds under the Gospel.

This somewhat subtle distinction has an important effect on Milton's second line of attack, the appeal to Christian liberty proper. The premises of this argument are to be found in Calvin's interpretation of the doctrine, but the consequence of Milton's handling is the assertion of personal liberty not merely in the indifferent matter of divorce but from all external authority.

So far was Christ from introducing a new morality that his function was to release believers from the bondage of the Law. As Calvin suggests under the first part of Christian liberty, "the Law ever was of works and the Gospel ever was of grace."[33] The new dispensation, says Milton, does not "impose new righteousness upon works" but remits "the old by faith without works."[34] The only new command introduced by Christ was "the infinite enlargement of charity."[35] He came to remove "the bondage not the liberty of any divine law."[36] While the Law was "rigid and peremptory," the Gospel is "considerate and tender."[37] Consequently Christ cannot have meant to prohibit divorce to Christians, for if "the Law will afford no reason why the Jew should be more gently dealt with than the Christian, then surely the Gospel can afford as little why the Christian should be less gently dealt with than the Jew."[38]

This charity is not something exercised by God only; it requires men to permit freedom to their fellows in the solution of such problems as the one under discussion. Moreover, as Calvin's second part suggests, Christian liberty means spontaneous obedience, not obedience under compulsion. This is a principle which applies beyond the sphere of indifference. Christian liberty is to be exercised in divorce because marriage is one of the things in which Christ, like Moses, wished believers to be free from human authority. But the fact that he "spake only to the conscience," disavowing compulsion, even the compulsion of the Mosaic Law, is something which defines not only the Christian's freedom in things indifferent but the very meaning of the Gospel.[39]

It is in pushing Christian liberty beyond the indifferent thing which is his immediate objective that Milton becomes unorthodox and arrives at his reinterpretation of that doctrine especially in *Tetrachordon*. The old dispensation imposed ordinances on the outward man, "punctually prescribing written law"; the Gospel offers salvation through faith, "guiding by the inward spirit."[40] What the Christian voluntarily obeys is not the formulation of the moral law in external impositions, but the eternal principles rendered clear in his heart by the Spirit. As Milton indicates in expounding "So God created man in his own image," this means a freedom not confined to indifferent things:

> It is enough determined that [by] this image of God wherein man was created is meant wisdom, purity, justice, and rule over all creatures. All which, being lost in Adam, was recovered with gain by the merits of Christ. For albeit our first parent had lordship over sea, and land, and air, yet there was a law without him as a guard set over him. But Christ, having "cancelled the handwriting of ordinances which was against us," *Col.* 2. 14, and interpreted the fulfilling of all through charity, hath in that respect set us over law, in the free custody of his love, and left us victorious under the guidance of his living Spirit, not under the dead letter; to follow that which most edifies, most aids and furthers a religious life, makes us holiest and likest to his immortal image, not that which makes us most conformable and captive to civil and subordinate precepts. . . .[41]

This is an assertion of Christian liberty in its fullest sense. It is "by the rules of nature and eternal righteousness, which no written law extinguishes and the Gospel least of all," that Christ's saying must be interpreted and the Christian governed. It is promised that "the law of Christ shall be written in our hearts."[42] Hence the freedom of the Christian is yet greater than Adam's, for he is not subjected even to such an external law as the prohibition concerning the tree. He is freed from the restrictions of the dead letter, whether of the Mosaic Law or of civil and human precepts, to live according to the guidance of the law of conscience which, under the Gospel, is substituted by the Spirit for external law.

Subsequently, especially in *De Doctrina Christiana*, Milton will formulate this position more clearly. But in March, 1645, he has already arrived at the interpretation of Christian liberty, as radical as Calvin's is reactionary, which will find a place in his later writings both on church and state. It is an interpretation which results in extreme Christian individualism. Milton's assertion of Christian liberty in divorce leads him ultimately to the repudiation of all human authority at which the opponents of Presbyterianism arrived through their assertion of Christian liberty in church discipline.

Moreover, as the demand for toleration enlarged the doctrine to include the individual's relationship to his fellow men as well as the soul's relationship to God, so Milton's demand for divorce according to conscience involved the extension of the principle from the spiritual to the natural sphere. Marriage was instituted to satisfy natural needs; and "wherefore serves our happy redemption and the liberty we have in Christ but to deliver us from calamitous yokes, not to be lived under without the endangerment of our souls, and to restore us in some competent measure to a right in every good thing, both of this life and the other."[43] Christian liberty is not to be used as a cloak for lust; but it is not merely "a spiritual matter." It has human as well as spiritual consequences.

## 3

Milton's anti-episcopal pamphlets were chiefly attacks on the presumption of decayed mankind; the chastening experience of 1642 reminded him of his humanity. He turned from the marriage of Christ with his church to focus his attention on a specifically human problem. The divorce tracts are significant in the development of his mind, not only because the ecclesiastical side of the case required the definition of Christian liberty, but because its natural elements invited the consideration of principles excluded from the demand for the one right discipline. Human quillets were not to keep back the divine prescription for the church; but human necessities in marriage and divorce are not to be thwarted by a misunderstood prohibition.

This fact leads to the presentation of arguments which will be carried over into Milton's political pamphlets. If divorce according to conscience is a privilege included in Christian liberty, it is also a right to be claimed under the law of nature. At this point the demands of Christian and of natural liberty are practically identical; and it would have required a mind far more precisely logical than Milton's to have kept the two principles distinct in controversial pamphlets on the particular subject with which he was concerned.

But his association of these arguments is similar to the confusion in the toleration controversy of the privilege of the saints and man's natural right as a reasonable creature—a confusion which was profoundly important in the development of political thinking during the Commonwealth. The reader of the *Areopagitica* who recognized the arguments from Christian liberty and reason as the common property of the pamphleteers for toleration would not have been surprised at the justification of divorce in terms of nature.

John Goodwin demanded indulgence for Congregationalism not only through Christian liberty but because of "that natural right we have in the kingdom as well as the Presbyterians, that cries out for it. . . ."[44] Samuel Richardson was to ask "whether it be not a natural law for every man that liveth to worship that which he thinketh is God, and as he thinketh he ought to worship . . . ?"[45] And the author of *The Ancient Bounds* remarked (as if echoing Roger Williams) that "the immunity and impunity of differing opinions in religions, as in relation to the civil magistrate, may seem to be a principle in nature, founded upon the light of reason, seeing many of the ingenuous heathen practised it. . . ."[46]

The ultimate source of these appeals and of Milton's argument was the humanistic thought of the Renaissance;[47] but the principles lay ready to hand in the arguments employed by Presbyterians and parliamentarians to justify resistance to the King. Milton himself points the analogy when he offers, in replying to Herbert Palmer's attack on his first divorce pamphlet, to "make good the same opinion which I there maintain, by inevitable consequences drawn parallel from his own principal arguments in that of *Scripture and Reason*. . . ."[48]

*Scripture and Reason Pleaded for Defensive Armes* was an answer by several divines to Henry Ferne's royalist pamphlet, *The Resolving of Conscience . . . , Whether . . . Subjects may take Arms and resist?* Though by no means the best parliamentary apology, it presents the usual arguments from Scripture and parliamentary political theory.[49] The latter provides the "principal arguments" Milton had in mind. They are not a source for his ideas in the divorce tracts; but they offer an analogy which indicates how closely his thinking reflected contemporary movements. The principles by which *Scripture and Reason* justified defensive arms were the principles by which he justified divorce.

The anonymous divines argued that civil government, being "moral," must be viewed in the light of eternal justice and according to the end proposed in it. The end of the state is the good of men in society—*salus populi suprema lex*; and the conflict between the King and Parliament should be judged in accordance with this principle.[50] Though governments are God's ordinance, men are not bound to submit to them if the end is not achieved; "marriage is God's institution and ordinance, and more originally than government political, and necessary for increase, yet all are not bound to marry but for their own good and comfort, and so of others, and advancing God's glory in both."[51]

This is precisely Milton's argument, though he would add that men are not bound to remain married but for their own good and comfort. "Every command, given with a reason, binds our obedience no otherwise than that reason holds"; and because the end proposed in God's original institution of marriage was clearly the good of man, it cannot be contrary to his will to terminate the relationship when that is not achieved.[52]

It is true that this is to dissolve a covenant made between two persons, and we have been told that covenants are to be kept. But the answer to this is indicated by the argument which meets the royalist assertion that defensive arms are a forswearing of allegiance. *Scripture and Reason* maintained that "certainly a free people, and in their right wits, never meant to enslave themselves to the wills and lusts of those they chose their princes."[53] Consequently a king must "consent to the first conditions or covenant"; and because "he that is free (as all men are by nature . . .) becomes not subject *de jure* till his consent, agreement, or election makes him so, and to no more than his consent reaches, explicitly or implicitly," there remains if the conditions are not fulfilled a "natural right" to resist, to exercise "the natural liberty that all have to be no further subject than God hath commanded or themselves consented with God's consent."[54] Similarly John Goodwin wrote in a pamphlet approved by the divines that, "supposing they be but reasonable men that have conferred the power upon a king, it cannot be thought or once imagined that they should give a power out of themselves against themselves, a power to injure or to wrong either them or their posterity."[55] And the Scotch Presbyterian, Samuel Rutherford, defended Parliament on the ground that "there be no mutual contract made upon certain conditions, but if the conditions be not fulfilled, the party injured is loosed from the contract."[56]

Milton applied the same reasoning to marriage. "For all sense and equity reclaims that any law or covenant, how solemn and strait soever, either between God and man, or man and man, though of God's joining, should bind against a prime and principal scope of its own institution, and of both or either party covenanting. . . ."[57] And in a passage added to the enlarged edition of *The Doctrine and Discipline*, he pointed to the parallel with the civil contract:

He who marries intends as little to conspire his own ruin as he that swears allegiance; and as a whole people is in proportion to an ill government, so is one man to an ill marriage. If they, against any authority, covenant, or statute, may by the sovereign edict of charity save not only their lives but honest liberties from unworthy bondage, as well may he against any private covenant, which he never entered to his own mischief, redeem himself from unsupportable disturbances to honest peace and just contentment.[58]

Because Milton was willing in 1644 to leave civil liberty to the magistrate, from whom "it drew sufficient attention,"[59] discussion of the political significance of this statement may be reserved for a later chapter. But, as the phrase "either between God and man or man and man" suggests, the principle involved is not restrained in the divorce tracts to marriage. Milton's mind sweeps out from the centre of discussion in ever-widening circles, and each argument is supported by increasingly broader applications. As Christian liberty was not confined to its exercise in an indifferent thing, so the idea that the good of man must be the end and rule is not confined to human relationships. That principle found little place in the anti-episcopal pamphlets. It could reasonably be assumed (since even Bodin had admitted it) that the reformed government would conduce to civil good; but since God had prescribed one right discipline, moderating arguments from considerations human and civil could be thrown out of court. In the divorce pamphlets, on the contrary, man's good becomes the fundamental rule not merely for human but for divine law. Here again the consequence is the freeing of the individual from external control.

Nothing, it would seem, could be more made for God and his worship than the Lord's day; and the author of the anti-episcopal pamphlets had berated the bishops for commending its defilement with sports. "Yet, when the good of man comes into the scales, we hear the voice of infinite goodness and benignity, that 'Sabbath was made for man, not man for Sabbath.'"[60] So with marriage: "to enjoin the indissoluble keeping of a marriage found unfit, against the good of man, both soul and body, . . . is to make an idol of marriage, to advance it above the worship of God and the good of man."[61]

If Milton had confined this principle to marriage, his argument (though not its application) would have been in conformity with Calvin's statement that indifferent things are sanctified to the Christian's use. But when man's good, like Christian liberty, is pushed beyond such matters as divorce, the distinction between things divinely commanded and things indifferent disappears altogether. The argument is driven forward to a conclusion which has the broadest possible application: "no ordinance, human or from heaven, can bind against the good of man."[62] Charity does not only permit the free use of things indifferent; it "turns and winds the dictate of every positive command, and shapes it to the good of man."[63] Nor is it only his spiritual or eternal good that is designed; "the general end of every ordinance, of every severest, every divinest, even of the Sabbath, is the good of man; yea, his temporal good not excluded."[64]

Compared with his reasoning on the church, Milton's divorce argument thus involves a remarkable shift in the centre of his thinking. The basic principle of divine prescription is replaced by the basic principle of human good, temporal as well as spiritual. If the zealous author of the anti-episcopal pamphlets suggests the young Milton attacking Comus, the divorce pamphlets remind one that he had written, "Nothing can be recounted justly among the causes of our happiness unless in some way it takes into consideration both that eternal life and this temporal life."[65]

The orthodox may well have wondered at the monstrous brood hatched out of their mature positions. To make man's good the rule of divine prescript seems certainly to set the creature above God. If God's will is to be interpreted according to human good, and if only the individual is capable of judging what is his good, little room is left for external authority, even of God's explicit law. But the germ of the argument is in *Scripture and Reason*: "In nature, the safety of the universe is the fundamental of the elements, and the power and inclination of each creature towards his preservation."[66] Hence, Milton argued, man has the right to ignore the letter of divine law (as David with the shewbread and Hezekiah with the Passover)[67] when his good is in question: "Men of most renowned virtue have sometimes by transgression most truly kept the law, and wisest magistrates have permitted and dispensed it, while they looked not peevishly at the letter but with a greater spirit at the good of mankind, if always not written in the characters of the law, yet engraven in the heart of man by a divine impression."[68]

Christian liberty and the good of man thus produce the same consequence: for the plain immutability of divine prescription which overthrew episcopacy is substituted the law written in the heart not only by the Spirit but by nature.

## 4

If God's laws are designed to achieve the temporal and spiritual good of man, they must operate in accordance with man's nature. If a man finds in marriage "neither fit help nor tolerable society, what thing more natural, more original and first in nature than to depart from that which is irksome . . .?"[69] In the original institution, God considered the natural desire of man for conjugal companionship; in the Mosaic Law, he "bids us nothing more than is the first and most innocent lesson of nature, to turn away peaceably from what afflicts and hazards our destruction. . . ."[70] Having instituted marriage, he necessarily provided for divorce because his ways "are equal, easy, and not burdensome; nor do they ever cross the just and reasonable desires of men, nor involve this our portion of mortal life into a necessity of sadness and malcontent by laws commanding over the unreducible antipathies of nature. . . ."[71]

Milton thus turns from the revealed will of God to "the fundamental law-book of nature which Moses never thwarts but reverences."[72] The Mosaic Law itself commands us "to force nothing against sympathy and natural order";[73] and this prohibition is equally a part of the Gospel's charity. Whatever else it may do, "the power of regeneration itself never alters" the basic properties of man's nature.[74] Therefore it would be "against plain equity" to interpret Christ's saying to the Pharisees "without care to preserve those his fundamental and superior laws of nature and charity," those "rules of nature and eternal righteousness, which no written law extinguishes, and the Gospel least of all."[75]

God's revealed will is thus not only "commensurate to right reason" but to the nature of man as man:

> God indeed in some ways of his providence is high and secret past finding out, but in the delivery and execution of his law, especially in the managing of a duty so daily and so familiar as this is whereof we reason, hath plain enough revealed himself, and requires the observance thereof not otherwise than to the law of nature and of equity imprinted in us seems correspondent.[76]

The eternal morality and equity underlying the Mosaic Law and made plain by the Spirit in the hearts of believers is, it appears, intimately related to the law of nature. The right of judgment Milton demands for the individual is thus both Christian and natural. It is a part of the liberty of the Gospel and is "engraven in blameless nature."[77] In fact it is "so clear in nature and reason" that divorce was left to conscience "not only among the Jews but in every wise nation."[78] That "God and the law of all nations" so leave it is abundantly demonstrated in "that noble volume written by our learned Selden, *Of the Law of Nature and Nations*."[79]

Milton was soon to discover that the appeal to natural right is fraught with danger; in demanding liberty one may succeed only in "introducing licence."[80] The objection that might be raised on that ground is partly met in the divorce pamphlets; but such was the complexity of his problem and the uncertainty of his thought that he did not clearly recognize the necessity for distinguishing between the two possible meanings of "nature."

He perceived that, because the institution of marriage occurred before and the law of divorce after the Fall of man, it might be argued that Christ pointed to the perfection of the first as the standard for Christians while condemning the second as fit only for the unregenerate. "Ay, but, saith Paraeus, there is a greater portion of spirit poured upon the Gospel, which requires from us perfecter obedience."[81] Milton turns this objection into an ingenious argument for his own case; but in doing so he runs uncomfortably close to the wind.

The fact that the Gospel can introduce a standard of morality no higher than the eternal principles expressed by the Law solves this difficulty in part. But Milton is not content to rest in that. Though God cannot have compounded in his Law with hardness of heart in the sense of "a stubborn resolution to do evil," it is obvious that both under the Law and the Gospel he gave merciful consideration to hardness of heart in the sense of "infirmity and imperfection" even in good men.[82] Had man remained perfect there could hardly have been an ill marriage. Since he is imperfect, God takes into account not only the natural desires implanted in all men through Adam but also the weakness of judgment consequent on the Fall which may appear even in the good. He ordains a means by which they may avoid the unforeseen results of their innocent mistakes and escape the injuries which the stubborn hardness of another's heart may inflict on them.[83]

It is clearly impossible to take as a pattern a time when man was "much more perfect in himself."[84] It will "best behoove our soberness to follow rather what moral Sinai prescribes equal to our strength than fondly to think within our strength all that lost Paradise relates."[85] Obviously, then, the "sympathy and natural order" with which the Mosaic Law accorded was not simply the order of perfect nature; it included in its consideration the weakness (though not the sinfulness) of fallen nature. Under the Gospel "the nature of man is still as weak"; and though the Gospel "exhorts to highest perfection," its charity "bears with weakest infirmity more than the Law."[86] Therefore, while it is no more capable of compounding with sin than the Law, it cannot purpose "to root up our natural affections and disaffections, moving to and fro even in wisest men upon just and necessary reasons."[87] Consequently, in referring the Pharisees (who had "taken a liberty which the Law gave not") to the perfection of Paradise, Christ cannot have meant to remove "the particular and natural reason of the Law," nor "thereby to oblige our performance to that whereto the Law never enjoined the fallen nature of man. . . ."[88]

Even if he had understood the distinction between sin and natural weakness, Edwards would certainly have regarded this reasoning as setting, not merely the creature, but "the corrupted, defiled creature above God." According to Milton's argument, fallen man need "perform the strict imposition" of God's commands only according to his strength, for "needful and safe allowances" are made to accommodate his "fallen condition."[89]

Thus Milton introduces an additional appeal to the law of nations and especially to the Justinian code. He seems to have discerned the force of this argument only after reading Selden's *De Jure Naturali & Gentium*. It makes its appearance only in the second edition of *The Doctrine and Discipline*, and does not receive full expression until *Tetrachordon*. There he argues that, because of "the imperfection and decay of man from original righteousness," God "suffered not divorce only but all that which by civilians is termed the 'secondary law of nature and of nations.'" That sufferance covers a multitude of weaknesses:

> He suffered his own people to waste and spoil and slay by war, to lead captives, to be some masters, some servants, some to be princes, others to be subjects; he suffered propriety to divide all things by several possession, trade and commerce, not without usury; in his commonwealth some to be undeservedly rich, others to be undeservingly poor. All which, till hardness

of heart came in, was most unjust; whenas prime nature made us all equal, made us equal coheirs by common right and dominion over all creatures. In the same manner, and for the same cause, he suffered divorce as well as marriage, our imperfect and degenerate condition of necessity requiring this law among the rest, as a remedy against intolerable wrong and servitude above the patience of man to bear.[90]

It seemed to Milton as stupid to deny divorce as it would be to abolish juridical law, civil power, and the whole law of nations. It is clear from *Colossians* that seeking one's right by law through magistrates is the result of hardness of heart; but he would not follow the Mennonites in rejecting magistracy and legal processes.[91] It is clear that, had man remained upright, all things would have been in common; but he would not agree with the Diggers that such a community is possible now.[92]

In the beginning, had man continued perfect, it had been just that all things should have remained as they began to Adam and Eve. But after that the sons of men grew violent and injurious, it altered the lore of justice, and put the government of things into a new frame. While man and woman were both perfect, each to other, there needed no divorce; but when they both degenerated to imperfection . . . then law more justly did permit the alienating of that evil which mistake made proper than it did the appropriating of that good which nature at first made common. . . . The Gospel indeed, tending ever to that which is perfectest, aimed at the restorement of all things as they were in the beginning; and therefore all things were in common to those primitive Christians in the *Acts*. . . . But who will be the man shall introduce this kind of commonwealth, as Christianity now goes?[93]

This is a remarkable statement. Milton's zeal for the purity of Christian religion has been somewhat modified by the events of the three years since the publication of the last anti-episcopal pamphlet. He has come to recognize that the reformation cannot be sudden; more than that, he has had proof of his own infirmity and imperfection. So far is he from discounting the significance of the Fall that, here at least, the idealist gives place to the realist. The divorce problem and its attendant difficulties not only lead him to remark on the impossibility of Atlantic and Utopian polities, but to justify liberty in terms of fallen nature. He is in process of learning the lesson enforced on him repeatedly in the prose period, that Christ's kingdom is not after all of this world. And apparently not virtue alone is free.

It is a little difficult to see how this reasoning is consistent with Milton's emphatic assertion of Christian liberty and his constant protest against licence. The appeals in *Tetrachordon* to the eternal law, the Mosaic Law, the law written in the heart, the law of blameless nature, and the secondary law of nature, provide perhaps the best example of the lack of coherence in his thought. Only one thing is positively clear: that each permits the kind of divorce for which he contends. But the divorce tracts are significant in the evolution of his thinking for what they leave obscure as well as for their development of definitions.

It seemed to Milton that to be weak was miserable, doing or suffering. He seldom admitted weakness in himself, nor did he find it easy to excuse it in others. If he learned to compound with it, he could never bring himself to justify it intellectually. Charity (of a kind) remained for him the rule of Christ; but his view of law became more stern in proportion as reformation gave way before the demand for a liberty even more extreme than his own. He came increasingly to recognize the bounds of liberty, and to distinguish between Christian and unrighteous liberty. If his political thinking is not to be regarded as inconsistent, the grounds for that distinction must be discoverable in the divorce pamphlets.

Whatever may be said of human imperfection and Gospel charity, the law of fallen human nature is clearly an impossible foundation for Christian liberty. Even after Milton's extension of Calvin's interpretation, the source of Christian liberty remains the law of the Spirit in the hearts of believers, while the secondary law of nature applies to men in general. Consequently the appeal to the example "of the noblest and wisest commonwealths, guided by the clearest light of human knowledge,"[94] must be regarded as a subsidiary argument. It provides the basis upon which the state must accord freedom of divorce to all men, believing and unbelieving. It is impossible for the magistrate to judge the motions of the affections and disaffections whether in the regenerate or unregenerate.[95] All men may therefore equally claim a natural right in divorce according to the secondary law of nature.

But that law is incompatible with the Gospel, which tends to restore things to their original perfection. Moreover, it can hardly be by this imperfect law that we are to interpret Christ's statement, for we have been bidden to "measure it by the rules of nature and eternal righteousness, which no written law extinguishes, and the Gospel least of all."[96] It is therefore with the primary not the secondary law of nature that the Gospel accords, a fact which is made clearer by the discussion of law in an author Milton was reading at this time.

William Ames (whose doctrine was perfectly orthodox though

his discipline was not) explains that the law of prime nature and the Mosaic Law in its moral aspect are different expressions of "the Law Eternal." "Natural law is the same which usually is called eternal law; but it is called eternal in relation to God, as it is from eternity in him; it is called natural as it is ingrafted in the nature of man by the God of nature."[97] It is to this law that Milton refers when he says that originally "all that was natural or moral was engraven" in Adam's breast "without external constitutions or edicts."[98]

But after the Fall, according to Ames, the law "writ in the hearts of all men by nature" became obscure. This is the source of the secondary law of nature, an imperfect expression of the original law of nature. And because of this obscurity a new promulgation of the eternal law was necessary through Moses: "ever since the corruption of our nature, such is the blindness of our understanding, and perverseness of our will, and disorder of our affections, that there are only some relics of that law [of nature] remaining in our hearts, like to some dim, aged picture, and therefore by the voice and power of God it ought to be renewed as with a fresh pencil."[99] Similarly Milton remarks that "there are left some remains of God's image in man as he is merely man"; and he would agree with Ames that "all the precepts of the moral law are out of the law of nature."[100] But, though the "moral reason" of the law can never be abolished, he would not agree with Ames' statement that, because of the consequences of the Fall, this unchanging morality can now be found only "in the written law of God."[101] Under the Gospel there is a second fresh pencilling of the eternal law by the Spirit in the hearts of believers, a renewing of the law originally engraven in Adam's breast.

This law of the Christian conscience provides the foundation for the liberty which is Milton's real concern. The fact that to the pure all things are pure is as important in *Tetrachordon* as in the *Areopagitica*.[102] Because a wise man "can gather gold out of the drossiest volume," while "a fool will be a fool with the best book, yea, or without book," there seemed to him no reason why "we should deprive a wise man of any advantage to his wisdom while we seek to restrain from a fool that which being restrained will be no hindrance to his folly."[103] It is thus freedom of reading for the wise and good that he demands, since "God sure esteems the growth and completing of one virtuous person more than the restraint of ten vicious."[104] The divorce tracts are in the same way primarily concerned with the freedom of good men. Moses' law was open to abuse by the evil; but this "he held it better to suffer as by accident, where it could not be detected, rather than good men should lose their just and lawful privilege of remedy."[105] It was this abuse that Christ rebuked in the Pharisees, not the privilege designed for "good men principally";[106] "for it was seasonable that they should hear their own unbounded licence rebuked, but not seasonable for them to hear a good man's requisite liberty explained."[107]

Two kinds of liberty which must be distinguished are thus involved in both the *Areopagitica* and the divorce tracts. One is the liberty which all men equally may claim under the secondary law of nature. It must be suffered as a consequence of the Fall. The other is the liberty which all men would have possessed had Adam remained upright but which is now to be claimed only by good men and believers. This is true natural liberty, the right only of those who will act in accordance with that perfect law which is being cleared in their hearts by the Spirit and is the basis of Christian liberty as Milton has defined it. And it is at this point that Milton differs from Roger Williams. To a certain extent, Williams' distinction between the spheres of nature and grace may seem to be operating here; but Milton's distinction is really between fallen nature and nature rectified, and he is in process of integrating, not of segregating, the true liberty of nature and the liberty of grace.

## 5

One of the most important effects of Milton's consideration of divorce was the bridging of the gap which in Puritan thought separated man as Christian from man as man. Because divorce concerns an essentially human problem, his humanistic tendencies come in to right the balance which the too-positive Puritanism of his earlier pamphlets threatened to upset. The divorce pamphlets, the *Areopagitica* and *Of Education* form a group not only in time but because each contributes to Milton's definition of Christian liberty, "domestic or private."

*Of Education* serves to clarify the differences between Milton's thought and the tendencies of both the right and left wings of Puritanism. It would be untrue to say that Puritanism was necessarily obscurantist in its attitude towards human learning; Thomas Young first introduced Milton to the pleasures of classical poetry.[108] But the distinction between nature and grace implicit in Calvinistic theology accounts in part for Thomas Edwards' suspicion of human reason and for the theory of education as essentially secular in its purposes which was characteristic of the Puritan extremists.

The segregation of grace and nature has an obvious analogy with the Baconian distinction between theology and philosophy. The effect in both cases was not simply to set the spiritual on a plane apart but to free the secular for development according to its own laws. And if faith was the gift of God, not the achievement of the mind, education could possess no real religious and spiritual value, a conclusion which sectarians such as Samuel How, a cobbler, were already setting forth.[109]

The same Samuel Hartlib whose "earnest entreaties" evoked Milton's markedly humanistic tractate also received a letter on education from William Petty who followed "the great Lord Verulam" in emphasizing "real and experimental learning," the practical arts and sciences, and the teaching of useful trades.[110] Petty was no Puritan; but his view of education was shared by Williams, who relegated it along with magistracy to the sphere of nature. He could "honour schools for tongues and arts"; but "for any depending of the church of Christ upon such schools, I find not a tittle in the testament of Jesus Christ."[111]

Milton's attacks on "the scholastic grossness" of the universities in the academic exercises, the anti-episcopal pamphlets, and *Of Education*, remind one of both the Puritan and Baconian attacks on corrupt and unpractical teaching.[112] But his denunciations arise from a humanistic sense of the contrast between the learning of "barbarous ages" and "the old and elegant humanity of Greece."[113] The spiritual and the natural are not separated but combined in his theory of education; for classical and Christian learning are together raked out of the embers of forgotten tongues, and one of the chief things to be inculcated is "what religious, what glorious and magnificent use might be made of poetry both in divine and human things."[114] The end of learning is not merely utilitarian. It fulfils a function in the natural sphere by fitting "a man to perform justly, skilfully, and magnanimously, all the offices, both private and public, of peace and war."[115] But it can only do so by achieving its primary end, which is "to repair the ruins of our first parents by regaining to know God aright, and out of that knowledge to love him, to imitate him, to be like him, as we may the nearest by possessing our souls of true virtue which, being united to the heavenly grace of faith, makes up the highest perfection."[116]

The end of education is, then, the renewal of the unconstraining laws of virtue, and the achievement through obedience to them of both human dignity and Christian liberty. As the system of education is designed not for the multitude but for "our noble and generous youth," so Christian liberty belongs to the aristocracy of the wise and good. In the *Areopagitica* and the divorce pamphlets that reservation is obscured by the nature of the activities in which liberty is demanded. Williams perceived that Christian liberty provided an unsure foundation for freedom of conscience because of the impossibility of recognizing with certainty the saints who could claim it. Like Milton's, his chief concern is always for them; but if their liberty is to be preserved, the same freedom must be extended equally to all men and claimed from the magistrate as a natural right, not as a special privilege. In the same way Milton observed that freedom in reading and divorce must be extended to all men, though the evil were to be suffered in the liberty natural to all fallen men, while the good exercised a liberty at once Christian and truly human.

Milton was in fact incapable of making the Calvinistic distinction between the natural and the spiritual in the personality of man which was essential to Williams. That intellectual ray guided his footsteps through this life as well as towards the next. For a full explanation of his view of human nature, one must wait till *De Doctrina Christiana*. But it is abundantly clear from the divorce pamphlets that, because what was lost in Adam "was recovered with gain by the merits of Christ," the Christian is both naturally and spiritually free. Like the author of *The Ancient Bounds*, he believed that men possess a liberty "as they are men and reasonable creatures, who are born with this privilege and prerogative, to be led forth always under the conduct of their own reason; which liberty is much enlarged by being Christians. . . ."[117]

It seemed to Milton as he began his last divorce tract that, though man was created in God's image, "nothing nowadays is more degenerately forgotten than the true dignity of man, almost in every respect. . . ." But an explanation of this disregard occurred to him immediately: "if we consider that just and natural privileges men neither can rightly seek, nor dare fully claim, unless they be allied to inward goodness and steadfast knowledge, and that the want of this quells them to a servile sense of their own conscious unworthiness, it may save the wondering why in this age many are so opposite both to human and to Christian liberty. . . ."[118] That consideration, with its firm basing of natural privileges on virtue and its integration of nature and grace, also serves to explain in large measure the peculiarities of Milton's political theory.

## *Part III*

# *Liberty and Justice: the Political Pamphlets. 1649-1654*

# Chapter VIII

## The End and Good of the Monarchy

THE author of *Regii Sanguinis Clamor Ad Coelum* wrote more truly than he knew when he said that Milton "passed from the severing of marriages to the divorce of kingdoms."[1] Though almost four years separated *The Tenure of Kings and Magistrates* from *Tetrachordon*, the political pamphlets did in fact apply to a larger field the ideas developed in the divorce tracts.[2]

Milton chose to regard the writings between 1649 and 1654 as his contribution to the achievement of civil liberty; and it is true that he wrote nothing specifically on this last of the three species "till the King, pronounced an enemy by the Parliament and vanquished in war, was arraigned as a captive before judges, and condemned to lose his head."[3] But his opinions in these years must be approached in the light of the general principles defined in the earlier pamphlets and especially of his incidental remarks on the state.

It has been suggested that the evolution of his political thinking was altogether due to events, not to the development of principles.[4] This is true of the machinery he advocated at each successive crisis; and it is also true that his arguments in defence of the regicides appear somewhat incoherent and inconsistent. But he himself regarded the proposed measures as temporary; and, though the course of events conditioned his attitude, one can discern an underlying consistency in the development of his political theory if one remembers that from 1641 on (whatever the immediate situation) he looked forward with constant hope, if diminishing expectation, to the establishment of a perfect community according to the principles of true religion.

Neither the systematic detachment of *Leviathan* nor the logical consistency of *The Bloudy Tenent* is discoverable in his political pamphlets. But neither Hobbes nor Williams represents the dominant tone of political theory in the early seventeenth century. The student of Milton is under an obligation from which he cannot escape with those whose interest is centred on modern ideologies: he must interpret the principles of Milton's political writings, not in terms of causes which have established or may establish themselves, but in terms of a cause whose loss in 1660 marked the final crisis in the development of Milton's opinions. If his political theory is considered in its place in the total evolution of his thinking and with reference to the climate of opinion under the Commonwealth, it is possible at once to estimate the impact of events upon his permanent convictions and to observe the progressive definition of his fundamental ideas.

One of the basic convictions which he shared with the majority of his contemporaries was that civil good was only to be achieved through "discipline originating in religion."[5] He differed from many of them in his definition of the terms in that axiom; but religion was always for him "the best part of our liberty," and its ultimate source.[6] In the political pamphlets themselves, it is the religious issue which forms the centre of the argument; and his theological treatise, like Calvin's, considers political theory as an integral part of Christian doctrine. He could think of the state as distinct from the church, but he could not think of it without reference to Christianity. He did not regard a theocracy after the model of Geneva or Massachusetts as either desirable or possible "as Christianity now goes"; but with those who wished to see England moulded into a holy community, he shared ideas which are basic in the Puritan view of the state. This is abundantly clear in the early pamphlets, where his general attitude towards reformation is typically Puritan and he eagerly anticipates the coming of "the eternal and shortly expected king" who was to settle "peace in the church and righteous judgment in the kingdom."[7]

## 2

In the Smectymnuan controversy with Hall, there occurred a peculiar passage of arms. Pushing the divine institution of episcopacy to its limits, Hall had remarked that, "if antiquity may be the rule, the civil polity hath sometimes varied, the sacred never; and if original authority may carry it, that came from arbitrary imposers, this from men inspired. . . ."[8] The notion is not extraordinary, and as *A Modest Confutation* was to remind Milton, had been expressed in much the same words by Bacon.[9] But the condition of Puritan thought on the state is typified by the righteous indignation with which those who insisted on the one right discipline (with Milton among them) hastened to denounce the pride which elevated episcopacy above the power of the crown.[10]

Hall sought to escape the consequences of his observation through a counter-attack. He reminded the Smectymnuans, with a reference to Buchanan, that "they are your better friends" who argue that "kings, princes, and governors, have their authority from the people, and upon occasion they may take it away again as men revoke their proxies. . . ."[11] Unfortunately, Milton's associates did not reply to this innuendo; but it is clear from their pamphlets that they were uncomfortably aware of the common impression that radical political views accompanied the demand for reformation, for they are careful to repudiate them.

Such a repudiation was characteristic of English Puritans before the revolution. Their civil aims were limited to the persuasion of the King that reformation was necessary; and even when the conflict between the King and Parliament was transferred to the field, the right wing of the party did its best to avoid recognizing the King's situation and the connection between reformation and revolution by directing its attacks against the evil counsellors who had seduced the royal ear. As Hall suggested, experience had made the Scots less hesitant; but the activities under the Commonwealth of staunch parliamentarians like Prynne are consistent at least in the fact that, while they had sought theory and precedent to support parliamentary opposition, they never supposed that the King could be deprived of his royal authority. In the 1640's those whom the Smectymnuans represented refused to believe that political upheaval must inevitably follow reformation. Indeed, they argued, as we have seen, that reformation could come, as in Judah, only through civil authority, and further that the Gospel discipline was so far from being dangerous to the magistrate that it would immeasurably strengthen him.

These opinions were not confined to Cartwright and the English Presbyterians; they were held even by those Congregationalists and Separatists who denied that the church could be coterminous with the nation and include the unregenerate. It is true that in their impatience some attempted "reformation without tarrying for any"; but they did so because it was wilfully denied by the magistrate, not because they believed him to be without the rightful power to reform if he would.[12] Even those who preferred expatriation to Antichrist maintained that it was the magistrate's office and duty to purify the church.

Bradshaw and Ames combined their belief in Scripture as "the sole canon and rule" for the church with the idea that the magistrate "should have supreme power" in both civil and ecclesiastical affairs and should protect the churches "by his civil sword and authority."[13] Bradshaw specifically denied in *A Protestation of the Kings Supremacie* that Puritans wished to release the church from royal power. He said that reformation must come through "civil public persons," and that while believers ought to endeavour to persuade the civil authorities to reform, it was unlawful to set up even "the true worship and service of God" against "the will of the magistrate and state."[14] John Robinson was yet clearer than Bradshaw on the impossibility of a national church; he protested that, whatever might be the duty of subjects, the magistrate could not lawfully use his power "against the laws, doctrines, and religion of Christ." But if he believed that the state might not support a false church, he nevertheless maintained that it both might and must exercise its power "for the furtherance of Christ's kingdom and laws."[15]

Underlying the political theory of Puritanism one recognizes the principle of absolute divine institution; it is the Christian magistrate's duty to establish the one right discipline. This is the centre of the political thinking of Luther and Calvin, though in practice it reduced itself to *cujus regio, ejus religio*. Calvin's aim is always at once to preserve the power of the magistrate and to prevent the establishment of Antichrist. And though it was possible (as Milton discovered) to produce the opinions of orthodox divines in defence of revolution, the right of resistance was strictly limited by Calvin to commands incompatible with obedience to God, "to whose will the desires of all kings ought to be subject, to whose decrees all their commandments ought to yield. . . . "[16] The potentialities of that right were obviously proportionate to the interpretation of God's will; but the limitation remained theoretically in force even among the extremest Puritans, and they were willing to appeal to it when the need arose.

In the early 1640's the Smectymnuans and Hall were here, as elsewhere, on opposite sides of a vicious circle. Neither wished to destroy the magistrate's control over the church; but both argued that his power must be exercised according to divine institution. Before 1640 the only escape open to the Puritan lay in the establishment in New England of a magistrate theoretically subordinate to the crown, yet willing dutifully to employ his power according to the particular Puritan interpretation of the one right discipline.[17] After 1640, each section of religious opinion conferred theoretical sovereignty on that power which accepted its version of true religion—the prelatists on the King and the Oxford Parliament, the Presbyterians on the King (momentarily misled) and the London Parliament, the Independents at first on the parliamentary group which became the Rump and then on Cromwell, the extreme sectaries on Cromwell and the Army, and then on the Army alone as representing the people, the Fifth Monarchists on the saints or in effect themselves.

It would of course be altogether untrue to say that this was the only factor in the political disputes of the Civil War and Commonwealth; but it explains the intimate connection between reformation and the state which existed throughout the period in the minds of all but those few whose interests were exclusively civil, like Selden and Henry Marten, or who achieved a sharp theoretical distinction between grace and nature, like Roger Williams. Moreover, it not only provides a pattern for the political conflict seen from the religious view-point, but is essential to an understanding of the development of Milton's political theory: he was in search of a sovereign power which would ensure the establishment and protection of true religion as he saw it. His theory of sovereignty changed according to the turn of events as King and Parliament, Parliament, Rump, Cromwell, Army, successively proved themselves unwilling to share his views; his view of true religion itself suffered change for the same and other reasons; but this principle remained constant in his politics from 1641 on.

The general political ideas incidentally expressed in the early pamphlets are those of moderate Puritanism. Civil no less than ecclesiastical liberty according to God's will finds its place in Milton's thinking at this time; but he is at one with the Smectymnuans in placing the emphasis on reformation rather than on freedom. It is in fact remarkable that he should have had so little to say of the political situation, though it is not difficult to discern the movement of his sympathies between May, 1641, and March, 1642. In his first pamphlet he refers only obliquely to the dispute between the King and Parliament, and speaks in the highest terms of the royal dignity; in his fourth pamphlet he emphasizes the efforts of the prelates to seduce the King with "false doctrine, to engage his power for them"; in his fifth pamphlet, he avoids attacking the King but writes a glowing eulogy of Parliament.[18] Yet there is very little in the political references of these pamphlets which reflects the attempts of parliamentarians like Henry Parker and William Prynne to work out the theoretical basis for opposition to the King.[19] Milton is at this time interested only in the general bearing of political theory on reformation.

His most obvious belief is that reformation must come through the civil power—through the King (willingly or unwillingly) in Parliament, and that this will bring about the restoration of the kingdom. Just as divine and human learning were revived together, so the Parliament is to revive both church and state. God had reserved for them, said Thomas Young, "the reforming of the church" and "the repairing of the shattered commonwealth."[20] He chose them, said Milton, "to be the reformers of the church and the restorers of the commonwealth."[21]

As we have seen, that belief modifies Milton's distinction between the functions of church and state. Clearly the church cannot claim the civil power of the state, nor the state claim the spiritual power of the church; but their purposes and duties are related, for the state must exercise its civil power for the establishment and protection of the one right discipline and, if need be, reform its laws in accordance with divine prescription.

There is consequently nothing in Milton's theoretical distinction between the interest of the church in the inward man and of the state in "the mind in all her outward acts" which could not have been accepted in the Massachusetts theocracy.[22] Experience was to convince him that a clearer distinction was necessary if the one right discipline was to purge the church of ungodly tyranny. But one will search in vain in the early 1640's for the theoretical amputation which Williams performed in *The Bloudy Tenent*.[23] To achieve his segregation of the spiritual and the natural is to deliver the church from the power of the unregenerate; but it may also be said to deliver the state over to the assaults of the devil.

That was a consequence from which even Lord Brooke drew back. Like Milton, he attacked episcopacy as "monstrously compounded of different, yea, opposite offices, and those the greatest, ecclesiastical and civil";[24] but the theory of religious liberty which he erected on the principle of indifference did not prevent him from believing that the Christian magistrate was *custos utriusque tabulae*, the heir of the Jewish at least in that respect. "Church and state government differ as much as the sexes. Yet there may be an happy union, both keeping their bounds whilst the husband has the supremacy. So there may be between the church and state a sweet harmony, the state having committed to it the custody of the ten commandments and yet the church preserving to herself her rights."[25]

This assumption, with the desire for that difficult harmony, is apparent in Milton's early pamphlets. His appeal to Parliament is not merely the result of fortuitous circumstances; it represents a basic Puritan principle. Moreover, at the outset he protests with Bradshaw that the king's supremacy is not in question. When the church is reformed, "the king may still retain the same supremacy in the assemblies as in the parliament; here he can do nothing alone against the common law, and there neither alone or with consent against the Scriptures."[26] The common limitation upon the exercise of civil power is operating here in the usual way for the church and significantly, through the analogy between God's law and civil law, also for the state. Upon the meaning he gives to this limitation the subsequent development of Milton's politics will largely depend; but for the time being he is content to indicate the desirable harmony and to assure his readers that the king "wears an authority of God's giving, and ought to be obeyed as his vice-regent."[27]

It is episcopacy, in Milton's opinion, not Puritanism, which undermines "the towering and steadfast height" of the "royal dignity."[28] But the king is "God's vicar, and therefore to rule by God's laws." He must "betake himself to the Old and New Testament, and receive direction from them how to administer both church and commonwealth."[29] If he rules according to that direction and the laws of the land, and for "the maintenance of the common good"—not according to the prelatical advice which begets lawless tyranny—then will be preserved "the holy covenant of union and marriage between the king and his realm."[30]

These are ominous statements; but in 1641 and 1642 Milton had not yet had occasion to consider the dissolution of marriage covenants, and nowhere in the anti-episcopal pamphlets does he indicate what steps are to be taken if Charles stubbornly refuses to govern according to God's and the nation's laws as the Puritans and Parliament see them. His political theory remains undeveloped, though certain basic principles are clear. The king must govern with parliament for the good of the people and according to laws human and divine; and it is his duty as a Christian magistrate to fulfil his function by establishing true religion.

## 3

Milton's linking of commonwealth and church in the act of reformation after the manner of Protestant political theory is intimately connected with the opinions on civil liberty expressed in the early pamphlets. Those opinions could hardly be described as radical; for just as he reflects the received principles of Puritanism in insisting on the fundamental relationship between church and state, so he denies with the Smectymnuans that reformation necessarily involves political upheaval, that "no bishop" means "no king."

If the Puritans were to persuade the civil magistrate to reform, it was necessary to convince him that his authority would not be endangered. Thus Bradshaw was careful to demonstrate that "the laws, orders, and ecclesiastical jurisdiction of the visible churches of Christ, if they be lawful and warrantable by the word of God, are no ways repugnant to any civil state whatsoever, whether monarchical, aristocratical or democratical."[31] Instead they "tend to the further establishing and advancing of the right and prerogatives of all and every of them."[32] Conversely, he asserted, antichristian government, by going "beyond the limits and confines that Christ in his word hath prescribed," causes the "civil authority of secular princes to decay."[33] The real danger to civil polities lies in episcopacy, for English Puritans "renounce and abhor from their souls all such ecclesiastical jurisdiction and policy that is any way repugnant and derogatory to any of them, specially to the monarchical state, which they acknowledge to be the best for this kingdom."[34]

Calvin had set the seal of orthodox approval on Aristotle's opinion that a "mixed polity" was the ideal government; and as Sir Thomas Smith had said, the English monarchy seemed to fit that pattern.[35] Consequently both Ames and John Robinson could justify Congregationalism, without casting aspersions on the civil authority, by demonstrating that it "is altogether monarchical in respect of Christ, the king; but as touching the visible and vicarious administration of it, it is of a mixt nature, partly as it were aristocratical, and partly as it were democratical."[36] As has already been indicated, the Congregationalists and Separatists were never altogether clear as to the power of the democratical part. Lord Brooke suggests the political potentialities of the analogy;[37] but it was possible to employ it in refuting the charge of radicalism. The

Separatist Henry Ainsworth declared that "for popular government, we hold it not, we approve it not; for if the multitude govern, then who shall be governed?"[38] And John Cotton echoed the sentiment from Massachusetts: "Democracy I do not conceive that ever God did ordain as a fit government either for church or commonwealth. If the people be governors, who shall be governed?"[39]

The political radicalism which one associates with the congregational discipline had not yet had an opportunity to develop in England; nor had it as yet developed in Milton's mind. When in *Of Reformation* he wished to show the harmlessness of the reformed discipline, it was to the common analogy that he turned, with a reference to Sir Thomas Smith.[40] Nothing is "more baneful to monarchy than a popular commotion, for the dissolution of monarchy slides aptest into a democracy"—a prospect unpleasing in 1641 to the future defender of the regicides.[41] He believes that "there is no civil government . . . more divinely and harmoniously tuned, more equally balanced" than England's, partaking as it does of "a certain mixture and temperament."[42]

Because of its nature, the one right discipline thus constitutes no danger to civil authority. It is on the contrary advantageous. Milton is prepared to assert that civil considerations may not keep back the divine authority on which his attention is concentrated; but that is an argument to be used only in an extremity. The fact is that the true discipline is "helpful to all political estates indifferently."[43] The effect of reformation will be to render "the people more conscionable, quiet and easy to be governed," so that "the civil magistrate may, with far less toil and difficulty and far more ease and delight, steer the tall and goodly vessel of the commonwealth."[44]

In spite of the difference between their jurisdictions, the reform of the church and the welfare of the state cannot be considered separately. They are, as Henry Jacob said, "distinct and clearly severed the one from the other, albeit each doth aid and succor the other."[45] Hence Milton's attack on the bishops is twofold. Their corruption of the church and fostering of schism has its counterpart in their influence on the state. They encroach upon the rights of the magistrate and divert the civil wealth to their own uses; they would, like the pope, subordinate royal to episcopal power; they stir up civil broils, as history shows, to further their ends; in brief, they would transform the monarchy into a tyranny, the "dissolution of law," which means government by "private will" and ends either in slavish obedience or lawless chaos.[46]

The most obvious significance of this attack is the one which naturally receives increasing emphasis in Milton's first series of pamphlets, the defence of the civil liberty the bishops would persuade the King to destroy. Like the parliamentarians, he appeals to "our Great Charter," and looks for the restoration of freedom as the result of reformation: "for the property of truth is, where she is publicly taught, to unyoke and set free the minds and spirits of a nation first from the thraldom of sin and superstition, after which all honest and legal freedom of civil life cannot be long absent."[47]

But there is another side of the matter which is equally emphasized: honest and legal freedom is conditional on reformation. What is to be achieved is not simply release from wilful and lawless tyranny, but the substitution for it of the right civil as well as ecclesiastical discipline. "There is not that thing in the world of more grave and urgent importance throughout the whole life of man, than is discipline." It is "not only the removal of disorder, but . . . the very visible shape and image of virtue."[48] Consequently Milton contemplates with satisfaction the replacing of the prelatical design to corrupt the nation (typified by the desecration of the Lord's day) by the disciplinary efforts of a magistracy which will take into its care, "not only the deciding of our contentious law cases and brawls, but the managing of our public sports and festival pastimes. . . ."[49]

Virtue is the best school of liberty; and what is demanded in the early pamphlets is the moral reformation both of the ministry and the state. For "liberty consists in manly and honest labours, in sobriety and rigorous honour to the marriage-bed . . .; and when the people slacken, and fall to looseness and riot, then do they as much as if they laid down their necks for some wild tyrant to get up and ride."[50] Moreover such virtue is inseparable from reformation: "they who seek to corrupt our religion are the same that would enthral our civil liberty"; and religion and "native liberty" are "two things God hath inseparably knit together."[51]

The general framework of Milton's political thinking in the early pamphlets, like the general framework of his view of reformation, is thus representatively Puritan. The next twenty years will leave that framework intact. Milton's political theory will never be that of "a modern politician," because it is always in terms not of commonwealths but of "Christian commonwealths" that he thinks. The purpose of civil government, as of education, "is to train up a nation in true wisdom and virtue, and that which springs from thence, magnanimity . . . , and that which is our beginning, regeneration, and happiest end, likeness to God, which in one word we call godliness. . . ." In fact, "a commonwealth ought to be but as one huge Christian personage," for as Aristotle taught simply "from the principles of reason," the happiness of the individual and the state spring from the same sources.[52]

Consequently, "that which is good and agreeable to monarchy will appear soonest to be so by being good and agreeable to the true welfare of every Christian; and that which can be justly proved hurtful and offensive to every true Christian will be evinced to be alike hurtful to monarchy; for God forbid that we should separate and distinguish the end and good of a monarch from the end and good of the monarchy, or of that from Christianity."[53] Milton's political principles will be developed and moulded by the course of events which transforms his opinion of monarchy; but, whatever may be said of the divorce of kingdoms, he will never be able to accept a theory of the state which severs it from the true service of God. "*Inter religionem et rempub. divortium esse non potest.*"[54]

# Chapter IX

# Free by Nature

THE development of Milton's political opinions between 1642 and 1649 cannot be traced in detail. The divorce tracts indicate the general movement of mind which eventually issued in his theory of political liberty; but his writings before 1649 contain remarkably few references to the theories of civil rights being developed by the parliamentarians, by more extreme divines like John Goodwin, and by the Levellers in the early stages of their activity.[1] That he was not without some interest in these matters is indicated by the comment he made on the analogy between marriage and allegiance used in *Scripture and Reason* and other parliamentary apologies.[2] But his advice to the Parliament involved the application of general principles only to the particular problems of the press and divorce, not to its constitutional dispute with the King. Those principles at once developed the convictions of his earlier tracts and pointed on towards his political writings; but it was only under the pressure of the events which culminated in the execution of Charles I in January, 1649, that his political theory became explicit. From March, 1645, until that time, he published no prose, and there is only scanty evidence of his thinking.[3] Reasons for this silence are not difficult to discover. It was a period of bewildering confusion both in the nation and in his own household.

The united front which Puritanism had presented to episcopacy steadily disintegrated as the toleration controversy proceeded towards an impasse. The Presbyterians, supported by the Scots, at first commanded a majority, and early in 1645 Parliament accepted their church system. But after the fall of Oxford in June, 1646, the influence of Cromwell and the Independents increased, and the efforts of the Presbyterians to apply their discipline were frustrated. Sectarianism flourished, especially in the Army; and along with it—largely in consequence of the attempts of the Presbyterian block in

Parliament to proscribe not only Anglicanism but the Puritan sects—there rapidly developed the radical political theory expounded with great vigour by the Levellers. The future of the nation hung in the balance while the Independent leaders in the Army and Parliament determined how far towards the ecclesiastical and political left their opposition to royalism and Presbyterianism required them to go. In the great debate between the Independents and the Levellers in the General Council of the Army at Putney in October, 1647, Cromwell and his associates emphasized the anarchical implications of radicalism. But by the spring of 1648 the increasing royalism of the Presbyterians and the Scots, and the stubborn refusal of the King to come to a composition, had driven them to the extreme courses for which the way was cleared by the defeat of the Scots in the Second Civil War (May to August, 1648).

On the significance of these developments Milton expressed at the time no recorded opinion. He must have been aware of them; for Leveller propaganda attracted wide public attention, and Milton's subsequent reviews of the course of the revolution—as for instance in *Eikonoklastes*—show that he was familiar with and sympathetic to the Independent position. The intermittent attacks on his divorce opinions, which begot the two sonnets probably written in 1646 and 1647, aligned him with the opponents of the Presbyterians; and in 1646, at the time of the attempt to discipline the sects, he wrote *On the New Forcers of Conscience*, with its indictment of "new presbyter" as "but old priest writ large." But the distress of mind consequent on the reception of his divorce tracts, and the realization that the destruction of episcopacy had produced uncontrollable chaos instead of the holy community, seem to have prevented him from developing any well-considered comment on the situation. He was wearying of the continued and apparently unending disputes. In April, 1648, he translated a series of psalms. Their chief burden is the nation's loss of divine guidance. And the sonnet addressed to Fairfax at the siege of Colchester in August, 1648, is less a paean of joy at military victory than a weary demand for the establishment of faith and peace.

This public confusion was accompanied by private difficulties no less distressing. In 1645 he was reconciled to Mary; but the domestic comfort he might now have expected was destroyed by the overcrowding of his house with pupils and relatives. His father had come to him from the house of his royalist brother, Christopher, after the fall of Reading in 1643; Christopher himself soon followed.

On the fall of Oxford, Mary's family took refuge with him. Daughters were born to him in 1646 and 1648. Both Christopher and Powell were involved in complicated legal proceedings arising from the confiscation of their estates; and in 1647 Milton himself was involved in a case in Chancery as a result of his financial relationship with Powell.[4] It is not difficult to understand why Milton wrote in a letter of April 21, 1647, of "very frequent grievings over my own lot" begotten by the fact that "those whom the mere necessity of neighbourhood, or something else of a useless kind, has closely conjoined with me, whether by accident or by the tie of law, they are the persons, though in no other respect commendable, who sit daily in my company, weary me, nay, by heaven, all but plague me to death. . . ."[5]

Yet to the difficulties in the way of thought and composition created by the chaotic state of the nation and the confusion of his household, one even more distressing fact must be added. Sometime shortly after the end of 1644, he began to feel his sight "getting weak and dull." His eyes were painful when he sat down to read in the morning; "not long after, a darkness coming over the left part of my eye . . . , removed from my vision all objects situated on that side."[6] The weakness which had been with him from youth was beginning the destruction of his sight; and though he was not to be completely blind until 1652, it would be difficult to exaggerate the effect which his pain and distress must have had on his thinking during these eight years. In some degree at least, the obscurity of his political argument in the pamphlets written between 1649 and 1652 must be ascribed to this affliction. What effect it had upon his spirits during the interval in his writing can be judged from the psalms of 1648. Two of these express, according to his reading, a personal, not a national despair; and it is clear from the peculiarities of his translation that what oppressed him was the sense of encompassing darkness both physical and spiritual.[7]

With this accumulation of fact, there is no need to speculate about the state of his mind between *Tetrachordon* and his first political pamphlet. He turned in distaste and weariness from public controversy among those who "bawl for freedom in their senseless mood" but repudiate truth because it is "licence they mean when they cry liberty." And he attempted to take up again the pursuits he had set aside in 1641. But the "still time when there shall be no chiding,"[8] to which even then he had been looking for the fulfilment of his ambitions, had not yet come. It was hardly possible to write an Arthuriad in the England of 1645 to 1648; and he began his *History of Britain* instead, partly at least in commutation of the design.[9] He may also have worked upon his theological treatise; but any satisfying literary accomplishment was impossible. At the end of 1645 he published his *Poems . . . both English and Latin.* The volume contained few pieces composed after 1641. It would seem that he offered it in partial fulfilment of his "covenant with the knowing reader," made four years earlier. But his great poem was still to write; and he seems to have been at a loss for inspiration. "What safe retirement for literary leisure," he asked in April, 1647, "could you suppose given one among so many battles of a civil war, slaughters, flights, seizures of goods?"[10] And in the Latin ode written to the librarian of the Bodleian about the volume of 1645, he complained of the conditions which oppressed his "sterile brain":

> My one prayer is that some god, or some one born of a god, pitying the worth that our race had in ancient times—if only we have rendered atonement in full measure for our sins of earlier days, for our ease made degenerate by soft luxury—, may some god, I say, sweep away the godless uprisings of fellow-citizens [against citizens], and, by his holy power, bring back once more life-giving pursuits, and the Muses, now without their proper seats, banished now from well nigh every nook and corner of the land of England's sons, and may that god stab through and through, with darts from Apollo's quiver, the birds that threaten us with loathly talons, and may he drive away Phineus's brood far, far away from the streams of Pegasus.[11]

Clearly, the expectations of 1641, both public and private, had been frustrated. The successful assault upon episcopacy had not produced, either in the nation or in Milton, the spiritual conditions requisite for the composition of great poetry. Nor was there any certain promise that they would be achieved amid the fruitless bickerings of the Puritan parties. But with the conclusion of the Second Civil War and the rise to power of Cromwell and the Independents, the revolution seemed about to make a new and determined effort. Because of his stubborn adherence to episcopacy and his negotiations with the Presbyterians and the Scots, Charles came more and more to seem the chief hindrance to a settlement. And when the Independent chiefs determined to take the momentous step of expelling the Presbyterians from Parliament and bringing the King to trial, it must have seemed to Milton that God had heard the prayer of his servants and that the way was preparing for the fulfilment of the nation's destiny, and his own. For a brief period the high hopes of the early pamphlets revived. To episcopacy and apostate Presbyterianism, Charles was now added as a symbol of the licentious and wilful degeneracy which begets tyranny in both church and state. And in a mood of enthusiastic expectancy Milton prepared his *Tenure of Kings and Magistrates.*

The argument in defence of the right of a people "free by nature" to depose and punish a tyrant and to establish a commonwealth[12]—first presented in that pamphlet, and repeated in subsequent pamphlets with changes in emphasis and clarifications—was intimately related at every point to his reasoning on the law and liberty of divorce. Much of the apparent confusion of his political argument is in fact dispersed if one remembers from the outset that, in spite of his appeal to the secondary law of nature in the divorce tracts, he had there asserted that even civil law cannot properly compound with sin, for its function is "to restrain it by using all means to root it out."[13] If that is the case, the magistrate's eye must be fixed on absolute truth and justice; and he must not "surrender up his approbation, against law and his own judgment, to the obstinacy of his herd."[14] Moreover, commonwealths decay "when men cease to do according to the inward and uncompelled notions of virtue, caring only to live by the outward constraint of law."[15] It is therefore the magistrate's duty to induce his people to live according to the laws of justice written in the heart.

Nearly the whole of Milton's political theory, as it was expressed in the pamphlets written under the pressure of the Commonwealth's difficulties, is implicit in these general statements. But it had yet to be developed. Its development was not without embarrassing complications, and its pattern is not immediately obvious. There were, moreover, implications in the argument of the divorce tracts which had to be reconsidered.

The demand in 1645 for the equal freedom of all men in divorcing and reading might have been the prelude to a demand for a similar liberty and equality in the state. Up to a point it is; and to that extent Milton agreed with those somewhat confused prophets, the Levellers. Their opinions had developed under similar circumstances, and like them Milton looked more and more to the Army for a solution. But the Army could variously represent the people, or Cromwell, or the saints; and the chief practical difficulty Milton encountered in his defences was his uncertainty as to which of these he was defending. His first choice depended partly on events, largely on convictions which he shared with contemporaries other than the Levellers. The adjective "Christian" was always at his hand to modify, if necessary, the substantive "liberty"; and there was a distinction to be made between choice in things indifferent and things fundamental. It was his interpretation of "those unwritten or at least unconstraining laws" which finally determined the extent of his agreement with those who were developing the theory of democracy. The appeal to the sovereignty of the individual judgment in 1645 took him part of the way along the road which led to declarations of right and independence; but he left it at a crucial point to attempt a hill more difficult.

Yet the general development of his mind conformed to the movement of which the Levellers were an extreme example. The sources of the political ideas of the Commonwealth lie beyond the scope of this study, in the writings of the early reformers and especially of the renaissance philosophers who developed the concept of natural law which they had inherited from Roman jurisprudence.[16] To these last Milton himself owed a debt not yet completely estimated.[17] But important as are those sources and Milton's private studies in them, it is the development during the revolution of a theory of natural and political freedom by analogy with the Puritan (and especially Congregationalist) idea of church discipline and saintship, which throws the clearest light on the movement of his opinions.

The disintegration resulting from the Civil War and the disagreements of the Puritan groups, hastened the extension of Protestant theory and invited attempts at the practical application of democratic and even communistic systems. Had the war not occurred, such systems would have developed eventually: the principle of equality had already found a place in Utopian dreams. Their rapid emergence was largely due to the necessity for reconstructing both church and state. The debates on ecclesiastical discipline prepared the way for debates on the civil constitution; the dispute over conscience provided principles capable of political application when it appeared that religious necessarily required the addition of civil liberty.

To under-estimate the intimate connection between religious and political ideas is to miss the homogeneity of the seventeenth-century mind and of Milton's, and to sacrifice a valuable source of illumination. He was not alone in approaching the civil from the ecclesiastical problem, and his political opinions were conditioned, as were those of most of his contemporaries, by religious principles. Even Lilburne, the arch-priest of seventeenth-century democracy, began his career of martyrdom by being punished for anti-prelatical agitation, and proclaimed from the pillory in Westminster not so much that he was naturally free as that he was one of God's saints.[18]

## 2

It is difficult to discover to what extent there had developed among English Puritans before the Civil War a more radical political theory than was set forth by moderate parliamentarians like Henry Parker.[19] What evidence there is comes chiefly from those who were willing to believe the worst of reformers. Hall had a wary eye on the example provided by the Scots divines and the seditious opinions of Buchanan.[20] Others pointed to the German "Anabaptists," and prophesied that "what rule soever our wise and pious Parliament shall fit, it will not set bounds to the unquiet spirit of a lawless generation which is now crying out, 'Let Christ rule!' because they would have no rule."[21] The "Lysimachus Nicanor" whose "defaming invectives" evoked retorts from Milton,[22] assured the loyal that, in their subversive belief in the right of a people to resist and murder its king, Puritans were indistinguishable from Jesuits.[23] But these warnings were not fully justified until the activities of the royalist armies and the Presbyterian Assembly combined to produce a radical extension of Puritan and parliamentary thought.

One writer at least recognized in 1641 the political potentialities of the Puritan view of church discipline; in fact Sir Thomas Aston indicated the process which was to result in the arguments both of the democratic Levellers and the communistic Diggers. He perceived that the power of censure and excommunication claimed for congregations of believers even by the Smectymnuans, less conservatively by Milton, and especially by the Separatists, could be transferred by analogy to the secular sphere.

A dangerous doctrine, if once grounded in vulgar apprehensions! These, possessed with an opinion of an equal interest in the power of the keys of the church . . . , will much more plausibly embrace the suggestion of a parity in the sway of the state, as better suiting their capacities. It will be somewhat difficult to possess the common people that we are all sprung from the tribe of Levi; but the old seditious argument will be obvious to them, that we are all sons of Adam, born free. Some of them say the Gospel hath made them free. And law once subverted, it will appear good equity to such chancellors to share the earth equally. They will plead Scripture for it, that we should all live by the sweat of our brows, *Genesis* 3. 19. They will tell us that in Egypt we were all fellow brick-makers; and it is no novelty in the stories of this state that such artificers have levelled the palaces of nobles and squared out the dimensions of the gentry and law givers according to the rule of their reason.[24]

Aston's prophecy was abundantly fulfilled in the theories developed by John Lilburne and Gerrard Winstanley from man's liberty in Adam and the Gospel, and from the rules of Scripture and reason; and these principles, though not the extreme conclusions they could be made to support, had their place in Milton's political thinking, as we shall see.

Milton's interest in the details of church government suddenly subsided after 1642; but Aston's analogy between congregational discipline and political radicalism throws at least an indirect light on the pattern of his political theory because of its significance for Leveller doctrine. It is possible to perceive an almost exact parallel between the democratic theory of self-government and the theory of the self-governing congregation composed of believers who are equally prophets, priests, and kings in Christ.[25]

Basic in the congregational system was the doctrine of Christian liberty, interpreted as a right of the individual believer to judge for himself, to associate with like-minded brethren in the formation of a church, to elect church-officers, and to share in ecclesiastical affairs. Such an association was usually expressed in a covenant or declaration of faith subscribed by the members, though this legalistic formality was repudiated by the more extreme sectaries; and the congregation was governed, under the fundamental laws of God revealed in Scripture and written in the hearts of believers, by the ministers and elders whose authority had come from Christ through the members.[26]

The translation of this system into political terms was attended by complexities both practical and theoretical; and one may doubt whether many in the seventeenth century were fully conscious of its significance. But the effect of the analogy is abundantly shown in the writings of the Levellers and in the debates in the General Council of the Army in 1647.[27] Its chief points are obvious. The priesthood of all believers became the natural equality of all men; Christian liberty, the natural liberty and right of every individual to consent to and share in the government under which he lives; the church covenant, a social contract or agreement of the people; God's law, the law of nature expressed in the fundamental laws of the constitution according to which the executive governs by the authority received from the people or its representatives.

Only some of the elements in this analogy were developed by Milton; his omissions and reservations are the measure of the difference between his political conclusions and the Levellers'. But one can recognize in Henry Burton's observation that in a true church "the power of discipline is not left to one man but indeed to the whole congregation," a source both of the Leveller demand for government by the people and of Milton's attack, in defence of tyrannicide, on the assumption that a king is the absolute ruler of his people and "they all in one body inferior to him single."[28] In both cases ideas appropriate to the religious sphere were transferred to the political through the medium of the appeal to conscience.

As the consequences of reform were prophesied by the prelatists, so the consequences of toleration were prophesied by the Presbyterians. Thomas Case assured the Commons in 1647 that, if liberty were granted the sectaries, "they may in good time come to know also (there be them that are instructing them in these principles too) that it is their birthright to be freed from the power of parliaments and from the power of kings, and to take up arms against both where they shall not vote and act according to their humours. Liberty of conscience, falsely so called, may in good time improve itself into liberty of estates, and liberty of houses, and liberty of wives, and in a word, liberty of perdition of souls and bodies."[29] Case was thinking particularly of the Levellers, but also by the way of the scandalous Divorcers; and the problem he posed had ultimately to be faced not only by the Assembly and Parliament but by Cromwell and Milton himself. If the individual was to be accorded freedom to judge in faith and divorce according to inward laws, within what bounds was his sovereign conscience to be allowed to undermine the authority of powers supposedly sovereign in the state?

Milton's solution of that problem was the definition of civil liberty developed in the political pamphlets. In the first of them especially, it seems remarkably similar to the definition offered by the Levellers; and it was so for reasons which are suggested by the pamphlet to which *The Tenure of Kings and Magistrates* was an answer. Milton claimed for his discussion of tyrannicide a detachment which it did not altogether possess, for he was refuting the arguments of certain Presbyterian ministers in *A serious and faithful Representation* addressed "to the General and his Council of War" on the day preceding the King's trial.[30] This was partly an answer to the Council's invitation to join "in consultation about matters of religion," partly a protest against the Army's "unwarrantable courses" in purging Parliament and bringing the King to trial;[31] and its significance here lies in the fact that the ministers saw the desire for toleration and the new political developments as two aspects of the same subversive movement. Both matters, they told the Council, are "out of your sphere"; for the Army was taking into its unauthorized hands the interpretation of both divine and civil law.

The authors of the *Representation* were striving to defend reformation according to divine prescript by supporting legal sovereignty against those—and they would have included here the Council, the Levellers, and Milton—who seemed to demand a lawless freedom. Whatever might be said of the right of resistance by properly authorized magistrates, neither divine nor natural law appeared to them to warrant action, "without any colour of legal authority," by "a multitude of private persons, though they have strength in their hands to effect it."[32] Both the Army's "intent of framing and contriving a new model . . . of the laws and government," and of allowing "a total impunity and universal toleration of all religions," were "manifestly opposite to . . . the duty and obedience which by the laws of God and man" were due to authority in church and state.[33] They arose in fact from trust in depraved human judgment rather than in divine prescript and civil law. "Nor is it safe to be guided by impulses of spirit or pretended impressions in your hearts without or against God's written word; for by this means the temptations of Satan and the motions of God's Spirit will be put in equal balance."[34]

This linking of the religious and the political underlines their intimate connection in the minds of those who feared ecclesiastical and civil tyranny. The question at issue between the Presbyterians and their opponents in 1649, as in 1644, was the question of law and conscience. Here again one discerns a close parallel between the civil and religious problem. The ministers, who were defending the right of Parliament to treat with the King against the Army's determination to punish him, looked to Parliament for an authoritative interpretation of the law of the land as they looked to the Assembly for an authoritative interpretation of Scripture. Those who had denied the authority of the Assembly in favour of conscience were now defending the Army's action against both Parliament and King by analogous arguments.

Just as the Puritans had been led by the bishops' claims to declare the supremacy of Scripture, and by religious dissension to assert the Assembly's interpretative authority, so the Parliament had been led by the King's claims to declare the supremacy of law, and by civil dissension its own authority to interpret it. The Assembly acted as the official conscience of the nation; the Parliament (in Pym's words) stood "to the body politic as the rational faculties of the soul to a man."[35] In both cases the alternative was anarchy. But when the Assembly's decisions differed from the convictions of the sects, and the parliamentary majority's from the desires of the Army, both claims took on the appearance of a new tyranny from which escape was provided only by an appeal to higher laws—the laws written in the hearts and minds of believers and men by the Spirit and nature.

It was by this appeal (complicated by appeals to the written law of the land) that Milton sought to prove "that it is lawful . . . for any who have the power to call to account a tyrant."[36] It was also the centre of the Leveller argument in favour of political liberty and equality. His argument from the law of nature, natural liberty and right, in defence of the King's punishment through the power of the Army and with a parliamentary approval obtained only by force, is similar to their argument for democratic government, largely because his was the product of his reasoning on conscience and divorce, theirs of the toleration controversy.

## 3

The principal ground upon which the defenders of the regicides based their justification of the extra-legal processes through which the King was executed was the axiom, already employed by the parliamentarians, that the state was an instrument designed to achieve the good of the people. That the supreme political dictate of the law of nature is "the public and common benefit and good of the community of men,"[37] is, for example, the central argument of John Goodwin's *Right and Might well met*, published six weeks before *The Tenure*, and one of the earliest and ablest defences of the proceedings which led to the trial of the King. This is also the central principle of Milton's justification of tyrannicide; the execution was in accordance with the law "which God himself and nature hath appointed: that all things for the safety of the commonwealth should be deemed lawful and righteous."[38] As Goodwin's argument was in a natural sequence with his earlier defence of the Parliament and of toleration, so Milton's is the political application of the argument developed in the divorce tracts, that the end of all law, whether divine or human, is the good of man. In order to demonstrate the significance of that rule for divorce, he had argued from the original institution of marriage (as before from the original institution of the church); in the political pamphlets he returned for the same reason to "the original institution of commonwealths."[39]

The main outlines of this hypothetical institution, ultimately derived from classical theory, were generally accepted by Milton's contemporaries. The Presbyterians, Parker, and the Levellers, believed with him that after the Fall men perceived that unrestrained violence meant common destruction and so "agreed by common league to bind each other from mutual injury"; that because "no faith in all was found sufficiently binding," they deemed it necessary to establish "some authority that might restrain by force and punishment what was violated against common right"; and that because of the failings of magistrates, they limited the power of authority by laws and counsellors. They would have agreed, too, with his conclusion: that "the power of kings and magistrates is nothing else but what is derivative, transferred, and committed to them in trust from the people to the common good of them all, in whom the power yet remains fundamentally and cannot be taken from them without a violation of their natural birthright. . . ."[40]

But disagreement arose on the steps which could be taken if a magistrate proved tyrannous. Thomas Hobbes argued that a return to primitive violence—infinitely worse than any tyranny—could only be avoided if the sovereign's power was absolute and irrevocable; there could be no lawful resistance, for resistance meant a return to lawlessness.[41] Parker and the Presbyterians shared this view in part. They wished to avoid the dangers both of "unbounded prerogative" and of "excessive liberty," and sought to do so by balancing the parliament's against the king's authority. They argued that through parliament alone "the people may assume its own power to do itself right without disturbance"; that the people had "entrusted their protection into the king's hands irrevocably," and that he could not be disciplined or deposed "by any private persons."[42] They thus divided the sovereign power, but denied a right of resistance in the people themselves.

With the Levellers, Milton somewhat hesitatingly and confusedly took another step. He recognized the dangers of excessive liberty and clung to the fiction of parliamentary authority for the King's punishment; his attention remained fixed on the execution rather than on the tyranny of the Long Parliament which had come for the Levellers to be as detestable as the King's. But he also perceived that Parliament alone would never have executed the King without pressure from the Army. Consequently his search for justifying arguments went beyond the parliamentary position to the basic law of nature and the people's rights under it. Because "the safety of the people, not the safety of a tyrant, is the supreme law," he concluded that "when the public good requires it, that power which the people had entrusted to another for the public safety may for the same reason, and without violation of right or law, be recalled by the people unto itself."[43] Nor was this a right to be exercised merely in the case of apparent tyranny: "since the king or magistrate holds his authority of the people, both originally and naturally for their good in the first place and not his own, then may the people, as oft as they shall judge it for the best, either choose him or reject him, retain him or depose him. . . , merely by the liberty and right of free-born men to be governed as seems to them best." This right of the people to alter the government "as they shall judge most conducing to the public good," seemed to Milton "that indeed in which all civil liberty is rooted."[44]

It seemed so also to the Levellers; and their insistence on it was to create for Milton and the Commonwealth a very serious embarrassment. They had already carried the transference of final sovereignty beyond the farthest point Milton was ever to reach, for they had invoked the people's rights not only against Charles but against the Parliament which they had begun by supporting. That shift in emphasis took place in 1645, not long after the publication of *Tetrachordon*. It resulted partly from the temporary ascendancy of the Presbyterians in the Commons, more especially from the imprisonment of John Lilburne from July to October for anti-parliamentary speeches. One could illustrate it from his writings, but it seems first to have been suggested by his associate, William Walwyn.[45] In January, 1645, Walwyn was writing of the English government (much after Milton's manner in *Of Reformation*) as "of all others . . . the most excellent," parliament being "the supreme power" and "the only makers of law," to whom "the king is accountable" with all other magistrates.[46] By October he was insisting on the power of the people over parliament rather than of parliament over the king, for "most parliament men are to learn what is the just power of a parliament, what the parliament may do, and what the parliament itself may not do." It had become in Walwyn's eyes "that tyrannous court"; its members appeared to believe that they "have power over all our lives, estates and liberties, to dispose of them at their pleasure, whether for our good or hurt," and that their actions "are bound to no rules, nor bounded by any limits." Parliament's pretensions were thus exactly those of Charles; Walwyn met them by arguing that as the king is accountable to parliament, so parliament is accountable to the people. Its authority "is a power entrusted by the people . . . for their good, safety and freedom"; and though it makes laws, its powers are limited by its function and by "the universal rules of common equity and justice."[47]

The burden was quickly taken up by other Leveller pamphleteers. In July, 1646, *A Remonstrance of Many Thousand Citizens* (probably composed by Richard Overton) attacked the Parliament for not fulfilling its function, announced the sovereignty of the people, and proclaimed their right to repudiate all former acts not according to the fundamental equity of natural law: "Ye were chosen to work our deliverances and to estate us in natural and just liberties, agreeable to reason and common equity; for whatever our forefathers were, or whatever they did or suffered or were enforced to yield unto, we are the men of the present age, and ought to be absolutely free from all kinds of exorbitancies, molestations, or arbitrary power. . . ."[48]

The Levellers were working out the ultimate and revolutionary end of the doctrines derived by their parliamentary predecessors from the law of nature and the people's good. Lilburne could quote Parker to support his case;[49] and in *The Tenure* Milton could likewise say of *Scripture and Reason Pleaded for Defensive Armes* that, though its Presbyterian authors "disclaim utterly the deposing of kings . . . , both the Scripture and the reasons which they use draw consequences after them which without their bidding conclude it lawful."[50] Some of these consequences had already been indicated in the divorce tracts; *The Tenure* handled them, much after the Leveller fashion, in defence of tyrannicide.

Milton's chief argument in justification of the King's execution was thus drawn from the same sources as the Leveller argument for popular sovereignty. The legality of the trial might be defended at some pains by an appeal to the parliamentary authority through which the Court of Justice was established, and even by an appeal to the authority deputed to the Army by Parliament.[51] But its final justification was provided by "that general and primary law" which, according "to the will of God, to nature, and to reason," made the people's good the supreme law of the state.[52] It might be objected that "the Parliament and military Council do what they do without precedent";[53] but it was Milton's argument here, as in the divorce tracts, that all laws and precedents must give way before the rule which defines their essential end and is taught by "nature and right reason."[54]

Parliamentarians like Prynne preferred the documentary evidence of the past. Milton had already repudiated tradition and custom in favour of free reasoning. Like the Levellers, he now argued that men were not "to have their hands bound by laws in force, or the supposition of more piety and wisdom in their ancestors."[55] "That is not always best which is most regular to written law. Great worthies heretofore, by disobeying law, oft-times have saved the commonwealth; and the law afterward by firm decree hath approved that planetary motion, that unblamable exorbitancy in them."[56] As Christ's saying to the Pharisees required interpretation according to reason, so for the achievement of the good of the people, reason is "a better evidence than rolls and records" because it is "the best arbitrator, and the law of law itself."[57]

This defence of the execution on the ground that "the law is right reason above all else,"[58] is clearly an extension of the argument employed in 1645. But it was not peculiar to Milton; others had developed it in the toleration controversy, and it was being applied to the political situation by Goodwin and, with even more radical deductions, by the Levellers. Goodwin had argued in *Right and Might* that "the laws of nature and of common equity are the foundation of all laws . . . , and whatsoever venditateth itself under the name or notion of a law, being built besides this foundation, wanteth the essence and true nature of a law, and so can be but equivocally such."[59] And he too had defended the Army's actions on the ground that "the law of nature, necessity, and of love to their country, . . . being the law of God himself written in the fleshly tables of men's hearts, hath an authoritative jurisdiction over all human laws and constitutions whatsoever, a prerogative right of power to overrule them and to suspend their obliging influences in all cases appropriate to itself."[60] But it is in the Levellers that one discovers the profound significance of this theory and the problems which it produced.

Goodwin's law written in the fleshly tables of men's hearts is of course simply the law of nature; and it must be distinguished from the law written only in the hearts of true believers by the Holy Spirit. It is the law of reason not of faith. But that theoretical distinction was difficult to preserve, especially when reason and faith, natural and spiritual law, were together involved in the dispute over the rights of conscience. The phrases appropriate to the one were readily transferable to the other; and their transference, either by analogy or identification, is especially the mark of radical Puritan thought. The fundamental rule to which the Levellers appealed was much more than the mere natural law of self-preservation. The true law of England, according to Lilburne, was "the perfection of reason, consisting of lawful and reasonable customs, received and approved by the people, and of old constitutions and modern acts of parliament made by the estates of the kingdom; but only such as are agreeable to the law eternal and natural, and not contrary to the word of God; for whatsoever laws, usages, and customs, not thus qualified, are not the law of the land, nor are to be observed and obeyed by the people, being contrary to their birthrights and freedoms. . . ."[61]

Most of the King's opponents (and some of his supporters) would have subscribed to the first part of this statement; but it includes an assertion of the right of disobedience from which the parliamentarians recoiled as the Presbyterians recoiled from the doctrine of free conscience; for it left the determination of what was lawful, not to authority, but to the judgments of the people.

The relationship between this appeal to unwritten natural law and the appeal of the sectaries to the law of the Spirit is illustrated by the Leveller attack both on the ministry and upon "black coats" of a different kind, the lawyers eminently represented by Milton's "marginal Prynne."[62] What was said of the Gospel's plainness in the argument against the interpretative authority of the ministry and in favour of liberty of conscience, could also be said of the law of the land. Walwyn told Prynne that it would have been "a proper work for him, a Christian lawyer in a time of reformation," to have demonstrated "how improper it is that our laws be written in an unknown language, that a plain man cannot understand so much as a writ without the help of counsel."[63] Lilburne inquired whether, "seeing the Parliament hath taken care that the Bible shall be in English that so laymen (as they call them) may read it as well as the clergy, ought they not also to be careful that all the binding law in England be in English, that so every freeman may read it as well as lawyers?"[64] There seemed to him little difference between lawyers and popish clergy; and he indicated the significance of this double attack in a statement which goes to the root of Leveller theory: "The law taken abstract from its original reason and end is made a shell without a kernel, a shadow without a substance, and a body without a soul. It is the execution of laws according to their equity and reason which, as I may say, is the spirit that gives life to authority. The letter kills."[65]

This is an application to politics of the legal reasoning behind the doctrine of Christian liberty developed in the toleration controversy. The author of the divorce tracts could have accepted it with few reservations. And the obstructiveness of parliamentary lawyers like Prynne (added to his private legal difficulties) made him, with Lilburne, impatient with those who contested "for privileges, customs, forms, and that old entanglement of iniquity, their gibberish laws."[66] Indeed, it led him to observe that Parliament "would have had more regard for the people, and for the cause of Christianity," if it had "abolished more of the laws as well as more of the pettifogging lawyers."[67] And with the Levellers he appealed to first principles to justify "great actions above the form of law and custom"; for, as even the heathen recognized, tyrannicide was "just by nature ere any law mentioned it."[68]

## 4

The appeal to the law of reason and nature in Milton's political pamphlets supports a further argument—which also has its parallel in the divorce tracts—in favour of the right of a people to depose its ruler. The covenant between a king and his people is governed, like the marriage contract, by conditions; and if the good which is the end of the covenant is not attained, it ceases to be binding. All covenants and contracts "are ever made according to the present state of persons and of things, and have ever the more general laws of nature and reason included in them, though not expressed."[69] A people is therefore justified in renouncing its allegiance to a ruler who seeks his own rather than the public good; for his authority "was by the people first given him conditionally, in law and under law, and under oath also, for the kingdom's good, and not otherwise."[70] Indeed on this point the *Defensio* echoes the phrasing of *The Doctrine and Discipline of Divorce*: "Certainly, if no people in their right wits ever gave power over themselves either to a king or to any magistrates for any other purpose than the common good of all, there can be no reason why, for exactly the inverse purpose, to prevent the utter ruin of them all, they may not take back again the power they gave. . . ."[71]

The chief objection that could be alleged against this argument was the difficulty of perceiving what limits could be imposed on the excessive liberty which might be claimed through it. Samuel Rutherford had set upon it the seal of Presbyterian approval: "There be no mutual contract made upon certain conditions, but if the conditions be not fulfilled the party injured is loosed from the contract."[72] But the Presbyterians had attempted to limit its implications through the authority of parliament and law. If that restriction were removed there would remain no rule but private judgment. Indeed, it was Thomas Hobbes' opinion that the unconditional preservation of the original civil contract would alone preserve all other civil contracts; the only alternative was the lawless condition of nature in which every man's judgment is his own law.[73]

Because of the Leveller appeal to the spirit of the law of nature, that prospect had already in 1647 troubled the minds of the Army leaders (though subsequently they thought good to go part of the way themselves). In the debates in the General Council of the Army at Putney on the *Agreement of the People*, which the Army Levellers were somewhat prematurely proposing as a new basis for government, the first objection raised by Cromwell and Commissary-General Ireton concerned the importance of examining the previous engagements of the Army to the Parliament and the King before debating the desirability of the *Agreement*'s momentous scheme. The Leveller reply to this objection—voiced by John Wildman of London—was that if an engagement "were not just, it doth not oblige the persons, if it be an oath itself."[74] The debate immediately resolved itself into a heated argument on the rights and wrongs of covenant-breaking and the dangers of repudiating established authority.

Ireton (supported by Cromwell) pointed out that this principle would "take away all commonwealth" by undermining the authority of law;[75] that what was in dispute was not the right of conscience to determine "what is sinful before God," but "the foundation of justice between man and man";[76] that the basis of civil right was that men "should keep covenant one with another";[77] that the appeal to abstract justice would mean an anarchy of private judgment:[78] "And therefore, when I hear men speak of laying aside all engagements to consider only that wild or vast notion of what in every man's conception is just or unjust, I am afraid and do tremble at the boundless and endless consequences of it."[79]

To these arguments, Colonel Thomas Rainborough replied that "every honest man is bound in duty to God and his conscience" before he is bound by engagements.[80] Wildman added the objection that "in case a parliament, as a true parliament, doth anything unjustly, if we be engaged to submit to the laws that they shall make, though they make an unjust law, though they make an unrighteous law, yet we must swear obedience." He demanded that the engagements and the *Agreement* should be judged on the contrary according to the principles laid down in the Army's own *Representation*, "such principles of right and freedom, and the laws of nature and nations, whereby men were to preserve themselves though the persons to whom authority belonged should fail in it. . . ."[81] And the climax of the dispute was reached when Robert Everard (the Agent of Cromwell's regiment) announced, "Whatsoever hopes or obligations I should be bound unto, if afterwards God should reveal himself, I would break it speedily, if it were an hundred a day. . . ."[82]

These statements illustrate the effect of the transference from the religious to the civil sphere of the right of private judgment according to unwritten and inward laws. As their sectarian brethren repudiated the authority of the church, of tradition, and finally of the letter of Scripture itself, in favour of the inner light of the Spirit, so the Levellers repudiated established authority, history, and recorded law. They too could quote chapter and verse from the law when it served to formulate their inner promptings; but they looked beyond the letter to the light of reason for fundamental equity, and thereby created in the civil sphere a problem analogous to that which faced the Assembly.[83]

That problem was not solved at Putney; nor was its solution made easier when, two years later, the leaders of the Army and their apologists were forced to adopt, at least partially, the Leveller position. It was by such arguments as Wildman had formulated that Goodwin and Milton sought to justify the Army leaders and a minority in Parliament in taking the law against the King into their own hands. Milton appealed to the "very principles of nature," to the "unwritten law of common right, so engraven in the hearts of our ancestors . . . as that it needed not enrolling"; and argued that "if any law or custom be contrary to the law of God or of nature, or in fine, to reason, it shall not be held a valid law."[84] Goodwin likewise asserted that "men by the tenure of their very lives and beings, which they hold of the God of nature, stand bound to obey the law of nature, and that against all other obligations and bonds whatsoever; yea, the truth is that all other obligations cease in presence of these, all laws, covenants, and engagements besides, being homagers unto it."[85] Goodwin sought to avoid the anarchical implications of this argument by declaring that "it is no such great matter of difficulty, clearly to discern and judge of such emerging necessities (at least of many of them) which are authorized by God with a prerogative interest of suspending human laws." But he (and Milton) had yet to face with the Commonwealth the problem of determining how that principle was to be prevented from justifying the subjection of law and authority to the right of mere judgment, individual or collective, which had emerged from the dispute over conscience.[86] As Filmer observed in commenting on Milton's argument, "If any man may be judge, what law is contrary to God's will, or to nature, or to reason, it will soon bring in confusion. . . ."[87]

The right of free judgment according to nature, in things human as well as divine, had been the proved conclusion of *Tetrachordon*. In the argument of that pamphlet (whatever its theoretical distinctions) the privileges of Christian had merged with those of human liberty to support the demand for the natural right of all men equally to break the marriage contract according to conscience. In *The Tenure* (and elsewhere in the political pamphlets) Milton applied similar arguments to the political problem in order to prove the natural right of a people to break its contract with a ruler. That right clearly applies equally to all; and to that extent the development of his thinking conforms to the movement of ideas which produced the demand for liberty and equality, the inevitable consequence of the Leveller appeal to the law of nature written in all men's hearts.

In the divorce tracts, the argument from natural right seemed—in effect though not in intention—to overwhelm the argument from Christian liberty; in the Levellers' argument for freedom of conscience, it did so altogether. Complete religious liberty became a corner-stone of their political system; and the right originally demanded for Christians alone became for them the natural right of all men, and thereby lost its spiritual conditions. This translation of the one into terms of the other is illustrated by a passage in Overton's *Arrow Against All Tyrants*, which may be set beside the comment of Lilburne on the spirit of the law, already quoted:

> by natural birth all men are equally . . . born to like propriety, liberty and freedom; and as we are delivered of God by the hand of nature into this world, everyone with a natural innate freedom and propriety . . . , even so are we to live, everyone equally . . . to enjoy his birthright and privilege, even all whereof God by nature hath made him free . . .; every man by nature

> being a king, priest, and prophet in his own natural circuit and compass, whereof no second may partake but by deputation, commission, and free consent from him whose right and freedom it is.[88]

As Professor Woodhouse has observed, "This is virtually a statement of the doctrines of Christian liberty and equality with *man* written over the word 'believer,' and *nature* written over the word 'grace.'"[89] The equal privileges of the saints, as spiritually prophets, priests, and kings, have become the equal privileges of all men as naturally reasonable creatures; and Christian liberty is indistinguishable from natural liberty.

Overton's arrow was aimed at civil as well as religious tyrants; and his statement provided a basis for political as well as religious freedom. At Putney the idea issued in the demand for a theoretically universal suffrage; and when Cromwell and Ireton raised objections against this revolutionary change, Colonel Rainborough observed that "the main cause why Almighty God gave men reason, it was that they should make use of that reason, and that they should improve it for that end and purpose that God gave it them." The argument had been made familiar in the dispute over church discipline; but Rainborough and his Leveller associates concluded from it "that every man born in England cannot, ought not, neither by the law of God nor the law of nature, to be exempted from the choice of those who are to make laws for him to live under. . . ."[90] This was the ultimate deduction from "the principles and maxims of just government" cited by Wildman.[91]

Milton's appeal to similar principles carried with it an apparently similar deduction. As the denial of freedom in divorce and in reading seemed to him against human dignity, so to affirm that a ruler was the absolute lord of his people seemed "a kind of treason against the dignity of mankind." A hereditary ruler should not be allowed to transform a nation "from the nature and condition of men born free into natural, hereditary, and successive slaves."[92] Because "all mankind" is made "after the image of God," there exists "a rational sovereignty and freedom of will in every man" which a tyrant unlawfully denies when he attempts to "captivate and make useless that natural freedom" by making "his reason the sovereign of that sovereignty." Nor could it be argued from the origin of government (as by Salmasius and Hobbes) that men hold their "natural freedom by mere gift" from their rulers.[93] Though men are bound to render unto Caesar what is his, they are not bound to render up the liberty which is theirs through God's gift of reason:

> Our liberty is not Caesar's, nay, but God's own birthday gift to us; and to render unto any Caesar you like this which we got not from him were an action most foul, most unworthy the origin of man. If one should look upon the countenance of a man, and inquire whose image was that, would not any one answer at once that it was God's? Being then God's own, that is, free in very truth, and consequently to be rendered to none but God, surely we cannot without sin and sacrilege the greatest deliver ourselves over in slavery to Caesar, to a man, that is, and what is more, to an unjust man, a wicked man, a tyrant.[94]

This assertion of human dignity reminds one of Overton's. Aristotle had said that "among likes and equals it is neither profitable nor just that anyone should be lord and master over the rest." Milton cited his opinion, and asserted—in a phrase that Lilburne could have approved—that "all the citizens alike should have an equal right to be free. . . ."[95]

But that statement occurred in his defence in 1654 of a government regarded by the Levellers as no less tyrannous than Charles or the Long Parliament. With them he had derived from the ecclesiastical dispute arguments for the people's good according to the supreme law of nature, and for a natural liberty and equality; but these did not exhaust the principles of political applicability which that dispute provided. The congregational discipline, the theory of free conscience, the doctrine of Christian liberty, involved distinctions and reservations, ignored by the Levellers, but no less capable of application to the state than the liberating principles which they adopted and transformed.

Though in Milton's eyes, truth political (like every other variety) "among mortal men is always in her progress,"[96] there was for him, as for the Presbyterians, a point in the progression from reformation to liberty beyond which it seemed impossible to go without sacrificing truth and righteousness to a wilful and depraved freedom. Aristotle himself had assumed that an equitable distribution of rights involved not an even division but their apportionment according to merit. Merit, in a slightly different sense, depended for the Puritan upon the acceptance of divine truth, not upon merely natural and degenerate reason. And liberty, in Milton's mind, was inseparable from wisdom and virtue, not the mere prerogative of men simply as men. He was to be forced to define this conviction more precisely by the swiftly moving events of the Commonwealth and Protectorate, and to make clear the qualifications required for the exercise of an equal right to freedom.

# Chapter X

## The Good of the People

THROUGHOUT *Eikonoklastes* and the defences Milton continued to justify the King's execution by asserting the natural right of a people to freedom; but the agitations of Royalists, Presbyterians, Levellers, and Fifth Monarchists forced him to recognize that the Commonwealth and Protectorate were the work merely of a small though powerful party. The disintegration of the Puritan front was not altogether ignored in *The Tenure*; yet if there were some apostates, Milton could still persuade himself that the acts of the Independent Rump and the triumphant parliamentary Army were approved by the people. He was reluctant to set aside the vision of the "right pious, right honest, and right hardy nation" which seemed to have roused itself "like a strong man after sleep"[1] for the extraordinary tasks of 1649. But the vision was dissipated by the alarming popularity of *Eikon Basilike, The Portraiture of His Sacred Majesty in His Solitudes and Sufferings*. The confident enthusiasm of *The Tenure* gave place in *Eikonoklastes* to diatribes against the "besotted and degenerate baseness" of "an ungrateful and perverse generation."[2]

*The Tenure* was a defence not merely of tyrannicide but of the Independent leaders who had brought Charles to trial. In March, 1649, a month after the appearance of that pamphlet, Milton had been appointed Secretary for Foreign Tongues to the Council of State of the newly established Commonwealth. Thenceforward the enemies of the state became, even more definitely, his own enemies; and if the dead King assumed the aspect of Comus, the masses who cherished his memory became "a rout of monsters." The unbelievable success of *Eikon Basilike* demonstrated "what a miserable, credulous, deluded thing that creature is which is called the vulgar," "an inconstant, irrational, and image-doting rabble . . . , like a credulous and hapless herd, begotten to servility, and enchanted with these popular institutes of tyranny." It showed how carnal were the minds of most Englishmen, "prone oft-times not to a religious only but a civil kind of idolatry, in idolizing their kings, though never more mistaken in the object of their worship. . . ."[3]

Milton's official reply to the King's Book thus marked a shift in the emphasis of his political thinking which was to be made yet clearer in his answer to the charge of Salmasius—already indeed formulated by the Levellers—that "the great change throughout three kingdoms was brought about by a small minority in one of them."[4] This charge, it became increasingly clear, was perfectly just. The Commonwealth was established by a determined few, while the rest of the nation was paralysed by the confusion and troubled by the falling off of trade. *Eikon Basilike* provided a focal point for the sentimental attachment to the royal house and to episcopacy which had been reviving during the King's imprisonment. But for Milton the cause of the few was identified with the divine will and with himself.

The chief factor in the development of his thought to 1660 is therefore his attempt to meet the realities of the political situation, and to solve the problem of justifying an unpopular government in terms of the people's good. This required a rewriting of the theory of *The Tenure*, and left in the defences what appear to be flagrant inconsistencies. But these were less the product of insincerity than of hasty composition and confused thinking; for the revision of *The Tenure's* appeal to natural right meant no repudiation of the basic principles of that pamphlet.

Milton may have been altogether wrong in his judgment of what was right and necessary in these difficult circumstances. That is not here in question. But if he had no shred of patience with gainsayers, and drove forward with harsh stubbornness to an unhappy conclusion, the course of his life and of his arguments in their totality abundantly supports his claim to have "written nothing which I was not persuaded at the time, and am still persuaded, was right and true, and pleasing to God. . . ."[5] There was, in fact, little in his later political thinking for which *Tetrachordon* had not prepared the way. Though he wrote of past events rather than of new designs, it is consequently less true to say that he clumsily adjusted his ideas to fit the facts than that events seemed to him to confirm his assumptions and forced him to clarify his position on questions too confidently left undetermined. The student of his thought must attempt to explain, in the light of contemporary opinion and the general development of his mind, how he was able sincerely to regard as consistent arguments which to most readers appear contradictory and against his own position.[6]

In the *Defensio* and the *Defensio Secunda* Milton was, by his own admission, the apologist less of the English people than of the Independents of the Parliament and Army, who alone "knew from first to last how to be true to their cause, and what use to make of their victory."[7] That party consisted chiefly of "the middle sort,"[8] not only in wealth but in religious and political convictions; and in general Milton's thinking between 1649 and 1654 conforms to this mean between the Puritan extremes. It is difficult to define the limits of a middle group—especially when it contains such heterogeneous elements as were provided by the authors of *An Apologeticall Narration* and other ministers who shared their views, John Goodwin, the members left in Parliament after the ejection of those who opposed the execution, and the higher officers of the Army; but the Independents clearly occupied a position between the Presbyterians and old parliamentarians (who aimed at ecclesiastical reform according to Scripture and civil according to written law) and the sectaries and Levellers (who demanded for the individual the utmost freedom of judgment in religion and politics).[9] They attempted to combine the ideals of reformation and liberty. They opposed the tyranny of national episcopacy and presbytery, believing Congregationalism to be the Gospel discipline; but if they desired a measure of toleration and could sympathize with the sects, they were suspicious of enthusiasts and free-thinkers, and wished to set bounds to religious liberty. They opposed the tyranny of the crown, and were more radical than Presbyterian parliamentarians like Prynne; but if they executed Charles to achieve liberty (and as a last resort), they clung to the established power of a Parliament representing chiefly the middle class, and resisted the too-subversive demands of the less-privileged, formulated by the Levellers, and of the scarcely articulate proletariat, voiced by the Diggers.

The objectives of this centre party shifted with the course of events—towards the left when the King and the Presbyterians in Parliament proved obstinate, towards the right when these were defeated and it remained to establish a settlement. Milton's opinions moved in the same manner; and his confusion as to the organs of real sovereignty reflects the difficulties encountered by the Independents in their effort to erect a Commonwealth which should achieve liberty and the people's good without undoing the work of the Army. "Through the judgment of God upon the nation all authority hath been broken to pieces, or at least . . . it hath been uncertain where the supreme authority hath been," said Wildman.[10] In a sense more complete than Milton liked to admit, the tyrannical setting at naught of law had prompted a return to the lawlessness of force according to the natural principle which "of old taught men from force and violence to betake themselves to law."[11] In this chaos—interpreted by Hobbes and the Levellers as a return to lawless nature—Milton sought with others for a sovereignty; and his simultaneous assertions of the right and authority of the people, Parliament, the Rump, the Army, and finally of Cromwell, are less satisfactorily explained by the fallaciously simple charge of insincerity than by the manifest confusion of affairs and opinions which surrounded him and destroyed the party he defended.

It is impossible to trace here the succession of events between 1649 and 1654; but it is necessary to summarize Milton's statements on the organs of legal power in order to define his chief problem and explain his reasoning on it. In the pamphlets written before Cromwell's dissolution of the House (April 20, 1653), he defended the King's execution as an act of the people through Parliament, arguing that by the laws of England every member was the King's "fit peer and judge," and that "the whole people" was "virtually in Parliament."[12] He took no account of the Leveller complaint that Parliament as then elected actually represented a small part of the nation; it never occurred to him to question the established political right of the middle classes. He assumed—with the old parliamentarians—that "citizens" meant the propertied, that they were "the people" in a political sense, and legally stood for the nation as a whole. He echoed Pym in observing that law in England was "public reason, the enacted reason of a parliament";[13] and when he argued that the people was superior to the king and might revoke its delegated power, he was thinking not of the multitude but, like Parker, of the parliamentary representatives of the citizens.[14] He is consequently able to affirm that Charles was brought to justice legally and in accordance with the opinion of Calvin and other Protestant divines "that to do justice on a lawless king is to a private man unlawful, to an inferior magistrate lawful. . . ."[15]

It is natural that the superiority of the people's representatives should be the theme of the chapters in *Eikonoklastes* reviewing the disputes of the earlier years of the war.[16] The affirmation is less plausible with reference to the unrepresentative body remaining after the defection of the Royalists, the exclusion of the Presbyterians by Pride's Purge (December 6, 1648), and the resolution against the power of the House of Peers (January 4, 1649).[17] With the Independents—Cromwell and Ireton among them—Milton clung as long as possible (and beyond) to the authority of Parliament as guardian of the people's good. He accepted the purged Parliament's claim to represent the nation and to exercise "supreme power," and argued that "to exclude and seize upon impeached members" for opposing the King's trial did not diminish the sovereignty of the House.[18] Those members were "conspiring and bandying against the public good, which to the other part appearing, and with the power they had, not resisting had been a manifest desertion of their trust and duty."[19] Until the *Defensio* he simply avoided the troublesome objection that "of the three estates there remains only a small number, and they 'the dregs and scum of the House of Commons.'" A parliament is, after all, "no more than the supreme and general council of a nation, consisting of whomsoever chosen and assembled for the public good"; and since (assuming the King's execution to be for the public good) the remnant could be taken to conform to that broad definition, it was still possible to affirm that the people did justice on the King.[20]

This affirmation was complicated by the fact that the Army alone provided what power the Parliament now possessed, and by the disagreements between the members, the higher officers, and a part of the soldiery, which arose when their unanimous designs against the King had been fulfilled.[21] With Goodwin and others, Milton justified the Army's interference on the ground that its forces were "enlisted and embodied for the express purpose of being the defenders of the laws, the guardians of justice in martial uniform, the champions of the church."[22] Its power was delegated by the people through Parliament; it could moreover claim with some truth to be now more representative than the House. And finally there was always an appeal open to higher though unwritten laws. *The Tenure* offered a defence of the unprecedented actions of "the Parliament and military Council" by appealing beyond legal authority to such laws; and in *Eikonoklastes*, Milton appeared rather as an Army apologist than as a parliamentarian when he commended the seizure of the King at Holmby by Cornet Joyce, and the expulsion from the House of those who wished to disband the Army without its arrears of pay.[23] But it is the *Defensio* which is primarily a justification of the Army's courses.

Though the power of Parliament is there reasserted, the King's execution is defended as approved by "the whole Army and a great part of the people"; those who opposed the Army's desires—being "under the thumb of a certain number of seditious ministers"—are denounced as traitors to the cause; and the Army is praised for its coercive advances on London and Westminster: "It being in our power by their means to keep the liberty, the safety of our state, do you think all ought to have been surrendered and betrayed by negligence and folly?"[24] Not only did "the sounder part of the House, finding themselves and the commonwealth betrayed, implore the aid of the Army, valiant and ever faithful to the commonwealth"; the Army itself, when the people's representatives failed, exercised a just and necessary power: "our soldiers showed better judgment than our senators, and saved the commonwealth by their arms when the others by their votes had almost ruined it."[25]

In Milton's view the Court of Justice and the Council of State which virtually governed the Commonwealth were thus legally established by the delegated authority of the House and the power of the parliamentary Army.[26] Out of that establishment grew the situation which prevailed when he composed his *Defensio Secunda*, a justification at once of the King's execution, the Independent Commonwealth, and Cromwell's Protectorate. Here he first squarely faced the issue between the House and the nation: "Was the nod of the people to be waited for, on which to hang the issue of counsels so important?" If the Parliament, having accepted sovereign power, "had been compelled again to refer, I do not say to the people (for though invested with this power, they are themselves the people) but to the multitude, who from feeling their own ignorance had before referred everything to them—what would have been the end of this referring forward and backward?" Moreover, what if the multitude "had demanded that Charles should be restored to the kingdom?"[27] In the face of that possibility (now admitted), Milton's right of a people free by nature clearly becomes the right of a small parliamentary minority, entrusted with the care of the people's good and supported by military power.

But by the time of writing, even that organ of sovereignty had proved a broken reed. With the support of the greater part of the Army, and in the face of opposition from the remainder, Cromwell had dissolved the Long Parliament, and then its select but short-lived successor, the Nominated Parliament.[28]

> Perceiving that delays were artfully contrived; that everyone was more attentive to his private interest than to the interest of the public; that the people complained that they were disappointed in their expectations and circumvented by the power of a few; you put an end to their arbitrary authority, which they, though so often advised to it, had refused to do. A new parliament is called; the privilege of voting is allowed to those only to whom it was proper to allow it; the elected meet; do nothing; and having harassed one another for a while with their dissensions and altercations, and most of them being of opinion that they were unfit persons, and not equal to undertakings of such magnitude, they dissolve themselves. Cromwell, we are deserted; you alone remain; the sovereign authority of the state is returned into your hands, and subsists only in you. . . .[29]

The authority of the Rump had become in Milton's opinion an arbitrary tyranny; and the power naturally in the people had produced, not the fully representative parliament demanded by the Levellers, but first an ineffective House chosen through the authority of the Council, and then once more—this time with Milton's approval—"the sovereign power" of a single individual.

The development of Milton's political thinking was conditioned by the necessity of justifying the changes in the organs of effective sovereignty indicated above. Because his theories were governed by the incomprehensible logic of events, the result was a web of arguments in which it is difficult to distinguish the particular strands. The successive events requiring justification begot varying levels of reasoning; and the crossing of arguments from natural law and right, the people's good, the law of the land, the authority of Parliament, the power of the Army, justice, and necessity, produced a tangle which, as Hobbes rightly observed, is not redeemed even by Milton's magnificent Latin periods.

From that tangle no distinct pattern emerged until the swift events of 1659 imposed the discipline of despair; but it is nevertheless possible to discover its developing outlines in the political pamphlets. The situation was capable of explanation—was indeed in part receiving it from others—according to the principles Milton had developed before the execution of the King. Natural right and the good of the people were as essential to his political argument in 1654 as natural liberty and the good of man had been to his divorce argument. But they required to be modified by other principles, already defined in 1645, if he was to reconcile them with the situation that presented itself and so to justify what he firmly believed were developments "which God in his stupendous providence had pre-ordained should be exhibited among this people. . . . "[30]

## 2

In the seventeenth century the convenient identification of the people's good with the people's will was established in the minds of but a few. One must recognize the theoretical difference between a right to liberty according to the judgment of a majority of the individuals constituting a nation and a right according to the unchanging rules of justice. Parliament's struggle with the King served as a forcing-ground for democratic theory; but only the Levellers assumed that the people as a whole were capable of determining their own good, and that it was consequently to be achieved through a government, limited by the fundamental laws of nature to which all would agree, and chosen by the whole people (temporarily excepting those who had supported regal tyranny).[31] They denounced the Long Parliament and Rump as unrepresentative; and though Cromwell fulfilled one of their purposes when he dissolved that self-perpetuating body, the Protectorate seemed to them to put England into new and even less acceptable chains.[32] They were therefore able to co-operate against it with the Presbyterians and Royalists—who did in fact (though the Levellers ultimately deplored it) represent what will the majority of the people can be said to have possessed.[33]

The Independent opponents of the Levellers met their arguments not by denying the good of the people but by maintaining that it was not so to be achieved. The principles of this denial are clearly indicated in the Putney debates. The first (and least abstract) of these was an appeal to the constituted rights of property, endangered by the demand for a theoretically universal suffrage since the electorate consisted in general of possessors of at least a forty-shilling freehold. The Levellers desired no "dividing of the land by telling of noses";[34] but it was difficult to see how the implications of their reasoning could be avoided. In answer to Rainborough's assertion that even the poorest had a right to the political influence of his reason, Ireton said, "Give me leave to tell you that if you make this the rule . . . you must fly for refuge to an absolute natural right, and you must deny all civil right. . . ." It seemed to him and to Cromwell that "the consequence of this rule tends to anarchy, must end in anarchy; for where is there any bound or limit set . . .?"[35] If all, merely as men, were to possess a right to elect representatives, they might also claim by nature "the same freedom to anything that anyone doth account himself to have any propriety in."[36] The result would be not the good of the commonwealth but its disintegration.

Ireton's defence of the "fundamental part of the civil constitution" which restricted the franchise, indicates the contrast between the Leveller appeal to first principles and the Independent effort to preserve as far as possible the foundation of legal rights derived from the past.[37] His protest that civil rights were based, not on abstract laws of God or nature, but on established laws and engagements, reminds one of Hobbes;[38] it also suggests Milton's argument from the established rights of parliament. And Ireton's conviction that the good of all was to be achieved only through representatives elected by those who were truly the people in a civil sense—those possessing "the permanent interest in the land"—is reflected in Milton's assertion that among the middle sort "the wisest and most skilful in affairs are generally found."[39] The rights of property must have influenced the thinking of the son of the successful Bread Street scrivener. But they play little part in his theoretical justification of events; and though Ireton's economic objections suggest motives unrecognized by Milton, Cromwell's warnings in religious terms are here more illuminating.

Just as he disliked "that heady way of . . . every man making himself a minister and preacher" and sought to preserve (though without presbyterial tyranny) a public church and ministry, so Cromwell was suspicious of the Leveller appeal to the political sovereignty of every man's reason.[40] In their programme he saw the promise of "an absolute desolation of the nation," not only because of the threat to established right, but because he questioned whether, desirable as it might be, "the spirits and temper of the people of this nation are prepared to receive and to go along with it." He was himself one of Milton's worthies, ready to repudiate the letter in favour of higher principles, and he could sympathize—perhaps more than the cautious Ireton—with appeals to laws written in the heart. He shared with the Levellers (and with Milton) the conviction that "our best way to judge" is by "the law written within us, which is the law of the Spirit of God, the mind of God, the mind of Christ." But, Calvinist as he was, he did not share the optimistic assumption of the Levellers that all men possessed by nature a light sufficient for the difficult work in hand. In words which recall the Presbyterian protest against free conscience, he told them that "we are very apt, all of us, to call that faith that perhaps may be but carnal imagination and carnal reasonings."[41]

Cromwell's warnings suggest the limits of, and the intimate connection between, the Independent theories of religious and political liberty. As the Presbyterians protested that freedom to run into error mistaken for truth was not for the good of men's souls, so Cromwell warned the Levellers that a similar political freedom would lead to the perdition of their bodies. The natural reason and will of all men was in his opinion no trustworthy guide for public policy. Certainly, the people's good is the supreme law; but, he exclaimed, "That's the question: what's for their good, not what pleases them!"[42]

The exclamation throws light on the establishment of the Protectorate—a paternal tyranny designed to achieve the nation's good—and on the opinions of the Secretary for Foreign Tongues. Milton likewise believed that the people's good (as he saw it), not their will, was of paramount importance; and he was convinced that its achievement depended on submission, not to the dictates of unenlightened reason, but to the eternal laws of justice which most men have not the capacity to perceive. Clearly there was in all men a "natural freedom of will" which withstood the King's attempt to impose his own mere will on the nation; but it did not appear that all men enjoyed a natural freedom which could be translated into a civil right simply by substituting the will of all for the will of the King. Men in general could be said to possess a natural freedom only in the restricted sense which made unjust the tyranny of one man's will, their equal; but *The Tenure* said not that all men *are* born free but that "all men naturally *were* born free" until the consequences of "Adam's transgression" deprived them of their privileges.[43]

This was a conclusion borne in on Milton's mind by the events following the King's execution; but it introduced into his thinking no new principle. The significance of the Fall as the source of human error and corruption was not obscured even by the optimism which suggested in the early years of the revolution that God was pouring out his grace more abundantly on every age and sex; nor is that consideration absent from the argument for freedom in the *Areopagitica* and the divorce pamphlets, though the confident tone of the first and the radical conclusion of the second represent the minimizing of its practical importance. But the course of events, the disintegration of the Puritan group, the stubborn religious convictions of a large part of the people, and their evident sympathy for the King, seemed to indicate a depraved hardness of heart, a wilful rejection of enlightenment, which could not be ignored even by one who possessed an ineradicable confidence in the dignity of human nature and in the destiny of England.

Had the Commonwealth met with popular approval, Milton would have had less to say of the "ignorance and perverseness" which appeared "national and universal" and made those "who adhere to wisdom and truth . . . seem a sect or faction."[44] But without ignoring the self-righteous assurance which he shared with most of his contemporaries, it is possible to recognize in the defences not Machiavellian hypocrisy but the painful effort of a noble mind to avoid a conclusion forced upon it by the course of history. The explanation provided by natural depravity required not so much a new departure as a righting of the balance of Milton's thought which was always being disturbed by his enthusiasm for an unattainable freedom. It occupied, moreover, an essential place in the theory of the evolution of states generally accepted by his contemporaries.

## 3

There was little singularity in Hobbes' idea that man naturally lived "in that condition which is called War, and such a war as is of every man against every man," and that he escaped only by establishing civil governments.[45] Said Parker, "Man being depraved by the Fall of Adam grew so untame and uncivil a creature that the law of God written in his breast was not sufficient to restrain him from mischief or to make him sociable."[46] Hence, as Milton agreed, men had to impose on themselves by covenant an external law and authority supported by public force: "Without magistrates and civil government there can be no commonwealth, no human society, no living in the world."[47]

The idea of natural equality was an accepted part of this hypothesis, though its consequences were variously interpreted. The Presbyterian Rutherford expressed the usual Puritan view when he said, "Every man by nature is a free man born," and proceeded to reply to those who would defend kingly power in terms of natural inequality and because men "are now under sin and so under bondage for sin," that kings share sin "equally with all other men by nature."[48] That is substantially the view of Hobbes: "all men equally are by nature free," for in the depraved state of natural warfare every man is a law unto himself and follows the dictates of his own will and passion.[49]

The Levellers merely applied this principle of equality without taking account of the depravity which, both Rutherford and Hobbes agreed, it was the function of civil governments to restrain. They spoke of the natural man, as we have seen, in the terms reserved by the Puritan for the regenerate in whom sin had been spiritually overcome. When Lilburne argued that Adam and Eve, created by God after his own image, were "the earthly original fountain . . . of all and every particular and individual man and woman . . . in the world since, who are and were by nature all equal and alike in power, dignity, authority, and majesty," he simply ignored the Fall altogether.[50]

Like Paine and the eighteenth-century radicals who inherited their creed, the Levellers repudiated the past as the product of human corruption and assured themselves that the destruction of its institutions would mark the dawning of an age of reason whose light all men would soon come to recognize. The ultimate sources of this assurance lay in the religious beliefs which contributed to the Puritan revolution. But because they were never in power, the Levellers never found it necessary to explain the continuance of darkness in terms other than the perpetuated tyranny of the powers that were; they did not need to avail themselves of the more fundamental explanations provided by Christian doctrine. They could continue, while ignoring the doubts and difficulties suggested by practical politicians like Cromwell, to assert "that all government is in the free consent of the people," that all men are naturally and politically equal, and that final sovereignty lies in the will of the people exercised according to fundamental principles of justice.[51]

At the other extreme stood those who recognized a natural equality of all men but denied the people's right to exercise its will politically. It was to that position that the Presbyterians retreated when the revolution escaped from their control; but its clearest exposition is given by Hobbes, whose conclusions are based on principles recognizably similar to the Levellers', but with materialistic pessimism substituted for their naturalistic idealism.

The natural liberty and equality which Hobbes defined could not be translated into civil right because it meant anarchy; "every man has a right to everything," to exercise his power for his own good and others' harm according to his own reason.[52] In the condition of mere nature, "private appetite is the measure of good and evil," and the result is constant war.[53] From this situation Hobbes could see no escape to security except through the establishment of a civil government which would "reduce all their wills . . . to one will" (whether of a single person or an assembly). That sovereign will becomes the final measure of law, which is simply the "manifestation of the will of him that commandeth" with authority. For the wills and appetites of natural men are substituted the civil "will and appetite of the state."[54]

That will ought, Hobbes admitted, to accord with the laws of God and nature; but since no absolute expression of the law of nature is discoverable, and no complete agreement can be reached concerning either its principles or the dictates of God's revealed law, the sovereign will must be the measure of itself; there can be no appeal beyond it, and no lawful resistance to it because its repudiation inevitably means a return to the anarchy of nature.[55]

Hobbes was careful to make it clear that a return to the state of nature through revolution could lead to the establishment of a new sovereign power either by conquest or tacit consent.[56] The Levellers continually agitated for an agreement of the people, a new social contract, to provide the foundation for such a new polity. Milton likewise argued that tyranny, being lawless force, begot a state of lawless force. The difference between Hobbes and the Levellers lay in his attribution of sovereignty to the will of the governors and their attribution of it to the will of the people. Milton stood between them because of his repudiation of the factor common to both. Justice, not will, seemed to him the necessary basis of true sovereignty. It was, said the sceptical Hobbes, "another error of Aristotle's politics that in a well-ordered commonwealth not men should govern but the laws."[57] It was precisely his retention of that doctrine—a variation of the principle opposed to episcopacy in the early pamphlets and reasserted in the divorce tracts—which differentiated Milton's theory both from the absolutism of Hobbes and the democratic radicalism of the Levellers: men established governments "that so man, of whose failing they had proof, might no more rule over them, but law and reason, abstracted as much as might be from personal errors and frailties."[58]

To the right common to all men Milton appealed in defence of tyrannicide just as he had appealed to it in defence of free divorce. Because all men, though fallen, were naturally equal, a king might not claim to impose his mere will on his subjects. Tyrannicide was therefore justified—as the heathen clearly perceived and history abundantly proved—by the law of nature and nations, which taught that the end of the state was the good of the people. But, if it might thus be regarded as an act of the people, it was the law, not their will, which justified it.

Moreover, "what nature and right reason dictates, is best ascertained from the practice not of most nations but of the wisest."[59] Among the heathen the chief of these were the Greeks and Romans, whose understanding of the obscured law of nature was less imperfect than that of other pagan nations, and upon whose history and literature Milton freely drew. But a better example was provided by God's own people, governed directly by him under a new law which rewrote for them the obscured principles of prime nature.[60]

Behind the reasoning of the political pamphlets one perceives the theory of law developed in 1645. There is a secondary law of nature and nations, applicable to all men in their fallen estate, but most clearly perceived by the best nations, in whom it approaches right reason; there is a perfect law of nature, unrecognized by men in their fallen estate, but specially rewritten for the Jews in the Mosaic Law; that perfect law was given by God at the Creation as the natural expression of right reason and the eternal law. Like divorce, tyrannicide is justified by each of these, but its most authoritative justification is its consonance with the last.

The principle that no law, whether of God or man, can justly contradict the eternal law thus has profound significance for Milton's political thought. Rutherford argued against the sovereignty of the King's will that "only God's will, not the creature's will, can be the cause why things are good and just."[61] Hobbes' sovereign is simply the product of his application in a crude political form of the Calvinistic conception of a divinity ruling by power and will.[62] Even Lilburne, champion of fundamental laws, laid it down that God alone "is circumscribed, governed, and limited by no rules, but doth all things merely and only by his sovereign will and unlimited good pleasure."[63] But the author of the divorce tracts was convinced that even the will of God himself could not make an unlawful act lawful or a lawful unlawful. He commands things only in accordance with his own right reason, which is the rule of justice: "It was not because God commanded it that it was right and lawful to kill a tyrant, but it was because it was right and lawful that God commanded it."[64]

What applied to tyrannicide applied also to the government to be substituted for tyranny. It seemed to Milton that the will of a majority of the people might no less certainly result in tyranny than the will of a king—and the growing desire for a restoration convinced him that it could be a tyranny producing the same results. He believed that the breaking of the social contract by a tyrant returned power to the people; but he did not believe that a people might justly exercise its power against its own good. It is true that "the same form of government is not equally fitting for all nations, or for the same nation at all times"; and that to take from a people "their power to choose what government they wish takes that indeed in which all civil liberty is rooted." But, while God permitted the Jews in accordance with the law of nature to change their commonwealth into a kingdom, he did so with this provision, "so they were justly governed."[65] And though all nations do not perceive what is just with equal clarity, each nation ought to establish as just a government as possible; for "justice is the only true sovereign and supreme majesty upon earth."[66]

## 4

The task of the Commonwealth, as Milton saw it, was thus the establishment of a government conforming as nearly as possible to the justice of absolute law. The imperfection of things human seemed to Hobbes to make such a task impossible; but it was also the aim of the Levellers. *The Agreement of the People* was designed to codify the fundamental laws of nature which the government might not transgress. But the Levellers ignored altogether the imperfection which in Hobbes bulked so largely. He believed that virtually no agreement on fundamental laws was possible, apart from submission to the supreme will of a sovereign; Overton could make the laws "engraven in the tables of the heart by the finger of God in creation," the basis of an appeal to the people at large.[67] Milton and the Independents disagreed with both; they believed that justice must govern, but that the Leveller argument opened the way for the lawless rule of carnal will.[68]

The relationship between the Levellers and Independents is exactly illustrated by the reappearance in the Putney debates and in pamphlet controversies at this time of the vexatious problem of submission which had previously occupied the Parliamentarians and Royalists.[69] Milton's interpretation of such scriptural admonitions to submit as *Romans* 13 and 1 *Peter* 2, in a manner which justified resistance to the King but condemned resistance to the powers he approved, has been cited as an example of his unscrupulous casuistry.[70] But if his reasoning was unpractical, it was not without consistency; and the handling of these texts by the Independents emphasizes their reluctance to swing altogether to the left in their theory of revolution.

Of the ministers associated with the middle party none was more radical in opinion than John Goodwin. He wrote able expositions of the right of resistance, defending the Parliament and Army; and in some respects he belonged rather among the sectaries than among the Independents, for his theory of conscience (already mentioned) is scarcely distinguishable from Roger Williams'.[71] Yet in the series of pamphlets in which he defended the King's execution and the government of the Commonwealth and Protectorate, he repeatedly argued for submission from *Romans* 13. That did not mean that he had changed his interpretation since his composition of *Anti-Cavalierisme.*

Goodwin justified the expulsion of the Presbyterian members and the execution of the King by appealing, like Milton, to "the light of nature and that sense of equity and of what is reasonable, planted in man by God."[72] He also appealed to "the reason or end of the law, the soul of the law," to defend the Commonwealth and Protectorate against the subversive efforts of Royalists, Levellers, and Fifth Monarchists.[73] It might be true that these governments were not established according to "the letter of the law"; but if it was just for the remnant of the Parliament and the Army to try the King "in order to the people's good" though "contrary to the letter and outside of the law," it was also just to erect a government for the people's good according to the law of nature, though contrary to the letter and their wills.[74]

To such a government, argued Goodwin, the apostles recommended submission; for his constant interpretation of their precepts was, not that they justified wilful resistance or (with Hobbes) commanded unconditional submission, but "that there is no subjection commanded by God unto any higher powers, further or otherwise than they act or quit themselves in due order or proportion to the good of men."[75] All men, "collectively taken in their respective communities," are "naturally free," and a people may thus resist tyrants; but that principle does not necessarily mean—as the Royalists attempted to show in order to undermine it—that individuals may refuse submission to a "lawfully established" government "so far as it is lawful."[76] Hence Goodwin's citation of *Romans* 13 against the opponents of the Commonwealth and Protectorate: these seemed to him—whether mistakenly or correctly is not here in question—powers "ordained by God" for the people's good and the continuance of that justice, invoked in the execution of the King, which is "absolutely and essentially necessary to the preservation and well-being of the body politic."[77]

This is precisely the reasoning implicit (though not explicit) in Milton's handling of these admonitions. When Salmasius accused the regicides of ignoring St. Paul's command to submit "to the powers that be," Milton observed—in a passage suggesting Hobbes' convenient judgment—that the royalist interpretation would prove equally well "that the power that now is in England is ordained of God, and that all Englishmen within the confines of the Commonwealth are bound to submit to it."[78] But he repudiated the argument from mere dominance. Even *The Tenure* attached to resistance the condition of injustice; the admonitions were not explained away but interpreted to be "understood of lawful and just power."[79] *Eikonoklastes* observed that "neither God nor nature put civil power in the hands of any whomsoever but to a lawful end, and commands our obedience to the authority of law only. . . ."[80] And this is the argument repeated in the third chapter of the *Defensio* as a justification of the King's execution and, by implication, of the Commonwealth, a lawful power established (in Milton's view) "for the punishment of evil-doers, and for the praise of them that do well." "Who but the wicked denies, who but the wicked refuses, willingly to submit to such a power or its minister?"[81] Under the pressing circumstances and considering the chaotic alternative, it was also possible (though with reservations) to regard Cromwell as the temporary minister of such a power.[82]

Clearly the reasoning of Hobbes, if one can be content with his stark realism, is a more adequate explanation of human experience even in our own day. Goodwin and Milton strove unsuccessfully to make their experience fit an ideal pattern. One recognizes in their reasoning a resurgence (in a modified form) of the orthodox Protestant doctrine of resistance only to magistrates transgressing fundamental law, and of Calvin's gloss upon 1 *Corinthians* 7. 13, "that we should not yield ourselves in thraldom to obey the perverse desires of men. . . ."[83] And one observes that in the 1650's the Independents were striving to substitute for the rule of imperfect human will the just power which had been their objective before the execution.

The Independent political theory was more radical than the Presbyterian, less so than the Leveller; and because it sought the mean between extremes, it more easily foundered on the practical difficulties clearly recognized by Hobbes. The law of nature was "of all laws the most obscure"; justice is not the basis of power but power is the basis of justice; the only logical alternative to unconditional submission is that men should obey or disobey "as in their private judgments they shall see fit."[84] If "right reason is not existent," and if no convincing expression of the absolute justice of the perfect law of nature is discoverable, it is difficult to conceive of any final authority either for government or for resistance but will; and that will must triumph which possesses the strongest power. Milton and his Independent associates never succeeded in discovering the machinery which would make that painful conclusion avoidable.

But if this might prove to be the lesson of experience, there seemed available in the 1650's an alternative explanation of events, and an applicable (though as yet imperfect) rule of justice, in the Christian doctrines ignored by Hobbes and transformed almost beyond recognition by the Levellers. One discerns in Milton's political thinking a resumption of the idea of an absolute law which had formed the centre of his attack on episcopacy and whose restrictive implications had seemed to disappear in the reasoning of the divorce tracts. "Justice is but truth in our practice";[85] and it is only by the truth that men are made free.

In spite of the apparent implications of his argument for freedom of conscience, he was in 1649 still able to attack the King's comments on the *Solemn League and Covenant* for "intimating as if 'what were lawful according to the word of God' were no otherwise so than as every man fancied to himself."[86] With "law of nature" substituted for "word of God," that was exactly his reply to those who complained that government was not according to the people's will. "Justice and victory," he had said in *The Tenure*, are "the only warrants through all ages, next under immediate revelation, to exercise supreme power."[87] It seemed to him, as to Goodwin, that in 1654 right and might were still well met—and with the seal of a revelation only less than immediate.

## Chapter XI

# Real and Substantial Liberty

MILTON'S belief in the justice of the Commonwealth issued in the demand "not that our cause should be judged of by the event but the event by the cause." Yet he could cite its success as an additional testimony, "for to the wicked God hath denounced ill success in all they take in hand."[1] He perceived that the appeal to "the high and secret judgments of God" might be two-edged; and he could say in reply to the King that "most men are too apt, and commonly the worst of men, so to interpret and expound the judgments of God and all other events of Providence or chance as makes most to the justifying of their own cause. . . ."[2]

But he might have said of the King what Cromwell said of Sir Henry Vane: "I pray he make not too little, nor I too much, of outward dispensations."[3] If Milton was suspicious of appeals to Providence when they did not coincide with his convictions, he was yet with Cromwell "one of those whose heart God hath drawn out to wait for some extraordinary dispensations, according to those promises that he hath held forth of things to be accomplished in the later times."[4] In December, 1648, the Army marched on London, "there to follow Providence as God shall clear our way."[5] It found, in Milton's opinion, "a path not dark but bright, and by his guidance shown and opened to us."[6]

"The powerful and miraculous might of God's manifest arm" confirmed Milton's belief in the justice of the King's execution.[7] The ability to wield that "sword of God"—"whether ordinary, or if that fail, extraordinary"—was of divine origin.[8] And the fact that "the hand of God appeared so evidently on our side"[9] also went to prove that the events which followed, though they might be contrary to the people's desires, were also according to the divine will.

But Milton's argument from events cannot be considered without reference to his belief that God was incapable of willing anything contrary to the eternal principles expressed in the law of nature. In the divorce tracts that belief permitted the interpretation of divine prescript according to the dictates of nature; in the political pamphlets it permitted the divine law to limit the rights deducible from nature. Even the heathen ascribed their ancient laws to divine authorship; and it is axiomatic that "the law of God does exactly agree with the law of nature."[10] If it was "never the intent of nature, whose works are . . . regular," that men should hold their liberty merely at the arbitrary pleasure of a ruler, it was therefore "never the intent of God, whose ways are just and equal."[11] It also follows that a just and natural liberty can be only such as the laws of God permit.

A similar association of divine and natural law was characteristic of the radicals who opposed the Commonwealth. Overton constantly cited the law of right reason whose "perfection and fullness is only in God."[12] Lilburne's frequent imprisonments by the Parliament and Council were no less works of the Beast than his punishment by the bishops. They were unjust equally by "the law of God, the law of nature . . . , the law of the heathen Romans, and the known law of the land." The two last were in his view applicable but supernumerary; their example held only when consistent with the two first. "No government can be just or durable but what is founded and established upon the principles of right reason, common and universal justice, equity and conscience. . . ." This is the law of nature. But it is also the law of God: "All men whatsoever must and ought to be ruled by the law of God, which is in a great part engraven in nature and demonstrated by reason. . . ."[13]

The communistic Diggers, who carried the levelling principle a step farther, cited a similar law, not merely engraven in nature but renewed by the Spirit of the Gospel. Gerrard Winstanley declared "a full commonwealth's government, according to the rule of righteousness which is God's word," to be such a community of nature as prevailed while Adam governed by the law "so clearly written in the hearts of his people." Carrying over to the economic sphere the mystical doctrines of the Familists and Quakers, he explained that the "inward law" was a law of universal spiritual love which was to destroy "that letter at this day which kills true freedom"; and that it did not depend "upon the will of any particular man or men, for it is sealed in the spirit of mankind, and is called the Light or Son of righteousness and peace." "The true ancient law of God is a covenant of peace to whole mankind; this sets the earth free to all;

this unites both Jew and Gentile alike into one brotherhood, and rejects none; this makes Christ's garment whole again, and makes the kingdoms of the earth to become commonwealths again. It is the inward power of right understanding which is the true law. . . ."[14] This statement illustrates the ultimate consequence of the identification of the laws natural and divine, written in men's hearts by the Creation and the Gospel.

In the Levellers and Diggers one perceives a tendency to employ some of the implications of Christian theology while ignoring others—a tendency which eventually led to the substitution of humanitarian naturalism for an ethical and spiritual discipline. The seventeenth-century radicals minimized the significance not only of the Fall and original sin but also—by a necessary consequence—of regeneration and grace, especially as interpreted by Calvinism. Their political application of theological arguments is too confused to permit of positive generalizations and accurate distinctions; but both the Levellers and the Diggers tended to obscure the distinction between the regenerate and the unregenerate, and between the perfect law of God and of prime nature and the imperfect law of degenerate nature. The rationalistic and democratic Levellers confused the perfect law, written in men's hearts at the Creation, with the natural law imperfectly perceived by men after the Fall. The mystical and communistic Diggers—and especially their leader, Winstanley, in whose thought the idea of a spiritual illumination begetting the law of love occupied the place of the Levellers' common reason—demanded the establishment of a polity founded on the law of the Spirit which they identified with the original law of nature. Both groups were seeking the general political application of a law which should be recognized by and applicable to all men without distinction, though the Levellers emphasized the natural equality of all men and ignored the superior claims of the regenerate, while the Diggers emphasized the community of spiritual righteousness and (in their Utopian fervour) minimized the intractableness of the unregenerate.

Milton's divorce argument had involved the same kind of confusion in its appeals to the laws of God, of Moses and of the Gospel, of perfect and of imperfect nature. And this variety of sanction appears again in the political pamphlets. But the distinction between the perfect law of God and of prime nature and the imperfect law of degenerate nature was reinforced for him by the distinction between the regenerate and unregenerate, which seemed to become more, not less, evident as the revolution proceeded. He might in the 1650's have quoted himself against Lilburne and Winstanley: "Who will be the man shall introduce this kind of commonwealth as Christianity now goes?" He must have shared the opinion of the Diggers which was expressed by one of the journals supporting the Independents' political plans: "The men seemed to be of sober life and conversation, and say their rule is to do unto others as they would be done unto. But the grand question is whether they do not take the consequent for the matter or substance, for as men fell before the curse came, so must it follow that (before the earth) man should be restored to the first estate in Adam, and propriety is but the consequent effect of the first offence."[15]

Milton firmly believed with the radicals that the spirit of eternal justice, the foundation of laws divine or natural, should be the rule of civil law. But whatever might be said of man's obligation to recognize it, events seemed to show that the principle was not in fact written in all men's hearts. Increasing royalist sympathy and continued opposition to the Commonwealth served to reinforce for him the exclusive implications of Christian doctrine, ignored by the radicals, but discernible in his reasoning in 1645 in spite of his extreme conclusion.

The justice of the King's execution ought in his opinion to have been apparent to "any man's reason, either natural or rectified";[16] but it became clear that most Englishmen were incapable of recognizing its consonance even with the secondary law of fallen nature which all should be able to perceive, and much less capable of recognizing its consonance with the law whose perfection was obscured by the Fall. It was possible to say, in justifying the execution as an act for the good of the people, that "under the word people we comprehend all our citizens";[17] but it was apparent that all were not fitted to share in the establishment of a government conforming as far as possible to the absolute justice of God's and nature's law. Though the benefits must accrue to all, the task was properly undertaken by the better and sounder part.[18]

Ireton told the Levellers at Putney that the consequence of trusting to "that wild and vast notion of what in every man's conception is just or unjust" would be, not the achievement of liberty, but the destruction of civil rights. More than that, he argued that the effect of an unrestricted suffrage would be to put liberty "into the hands of those men that will give it away when they have it."[19] Though he thought in terms of established civil rights less than

Ireton, that was Milton's view. It was impossible to trust the government of the commonwealth to men "who have never learnt what law means, what reason, what is right or wrong, lawful or unlawful"; for the result would be the loss of the justice and liberty so dearly won.[20]

As we have seen, the equal right which all men possess by nature is in Milton's opinion a right to be governed justly. But, though it is true that all men once were born free, and that all men ought by nature to be free, it is also true that bad men are "all naturally servile." Their natural equality is what Hobbes regarded as the only natural right; and Milton would have agreed with him that its necessary consequence is government by arbitrary will, though for a slightly different reason. They "love not freedom but licence, which never hath more scope or more indulgence than under tyrants."[21] Those who desired, "after such a fair deliverance as this," to restore the monarchy, therefore showed themselves "to be by nature slaves and arrant beasts, not fit for that liberty which they cried out and bellowed for."[22] The mastering of reason by "sense and humour" which had led the King to tyranny, seemed to Milton also to prevail among the throng "of vulgar and irrational men."[23]

Conversely, "none can love freedom heartily but good men";[24] and only they can achieve it. "I confess there are but few, and those men of great wisdom and courage, that are either desirous of liberty or capable of using it. For the greatest part of the world prefers just masters—masters, observe, but just ones."[25] Implicit in this statement is the whole of Milton's defence of the Commonwealth; the few who are wise and good "deservedly bring under the yoke" those who unnaturally prefer tyrannous masters.[26]

Their right to do so seemed to Milton to lie in the fact that they alone could recognize the essential principles of justice. Most men are manifestly not governed by reason but "give up their understanding to a double tyranny of custom from without and blind affection from within."[27] The justice by which the King was executed could be perceived only by "the uprighter sort" of the magistrates "and of the people, though in number less by many, in whom faction least hath prevailed above the law of nature and right reason. . . ."[28] These justifiably established the Commonwealth; "for there is nothing more agreeable to nature, nothing more just, nothing more useful or more for the interest of man, than that the less should yield to the greater, not number to number, but virtue to virtue and counsel to counsel." And since the foolish and wicked ought not to command the wise and good, "they that take the government out of such men's hands act quite according to the law of nature."[29]

What Milton developed was thus the argument already employed by Goodwin in defence of the Army and, with a different application, by the Presbyterians in defence of the Assembly: as one "who, either through imbecility or derangement of mind, cannot manage his own affairs, is not left at his own disposal," so those among the people who were incapable of recognizing their own good were subjected to the rule of those who could.[30] Hence the people could be said to have done "whatever the better, that is, the sounder part of the legislature did, in which the true power of the people resided"; and "if the majority of the legislature should choose to be slaves or to set the government to sale, ought not the minority to prevent this and keep their liberty, if it be in their power?"[31] This is according to the law of God and nature which teaches that government is to be, not according to the will or the good of all men indiscriminately, but "above all else according to the safety and welfare of good men."[32]

In *Tetrachordon* Milton had observed that "just and natural privileges men neither can rightly seek, nor dare fully claim, unless they be allied to inward goodness and steadfast knowledge."[33] His reasoning on events between 1649 and 1654 is simply a reapplication, with certain variations, of that principle. What distinguishes his theory from the Levellers' is his consistent differentiation between the good and the evil, produced from the ethical to the political sphere, and between the natural freedom from injustice which all may claim equally and the right to liberty which only the good can exercise because only they have in themselves its sources. True liberty springs "from piety, justice, temperance, in fine from real virtue . . ."; the absence of these begets slavery.[34]

For know, that you may not feel resentment or be able to blame anybody but yourselves, know that to be free is precisely the same thing as to be pious, wise, just and temperate, careful of one's own, abstinent from what is another's, and thence, in fine, magnanimous and brave; so to be the opposite of these is the same thing as to be a slave; and by the wonted judgment, and as it were by the just retribution of God, it comes to pass that the nation which has been incapable of governing and ordering itself, and has delivered itself up to the slavery of its own lusts, is itself delivered over, against its will, to other masters; and whether it will or no, is compelled to serve.[35]

This view of the situation in the 1650's is simply the obverse of the view taken in the anti-episcopal pamphlets. Tyranny and corruption are inseparable; for as it is in the interest of a tyrant to corrupt his people, so a corrupted people naturally produces a tyranny. But it is not a repudiation of the principles developed in the *Areopagitica* and the divorce tracts; indeed in *Defensio Secunda* Milton twice reaffirmed his confidence in their findings.[36] They dealt with a specific department of liberty which required peculiar treatment.

The pamphlets on private or domestic liberty defended the freedom necessary in indifferent things, "uncertainly and yet equally working to good and to evil," concerning which a proper determination was possible only according to the laws written in the consciences of good men.[37] Because no absolute rule was apparent for such matters, it was necessary to assure the liberty of good men by extending the same freedom even to those who, through hardness of heart, would judge according to private will and lust instead of the laws of good conscience. But for Milton there could be no extension of that argument to support a demand for universally equal political rights. The political pamphlets did not deal with indifferent things but with matters fundamental to the preservation of true liberty and determinable only according to the principles of absolute justice. These cannot be assigned, along with private liberty, to those who have not learned "to obey right reason, to be masters of yourselves." "It does not suit, it does not fall to the lot of such men to be free"; for they would destroy the just liberty which by nature belongs to the wise and good.[38]

In the 1650's Milton had to face a practical problem whose delicacy one is forced to recognize almost daily, the problem of establishing and preserving liberty without on the one hand destroying justice or on the other releasing in unrestrained activity forces whose consequence is the destruction of liberty itself. For that problem he never found a practical and wholly satisfactory solution; nor has one been found yet. He sought it first through the Commonwealth; but the Parliament proved unable or unwilling to erect the necessary machinery. He sought it next through Cromwell; and the too-fulsome adulation of *Defensio Secunda* was clearly addressed to his own mind as well as to the enemies of England, for the weight of his advice is the measure of his doubts. Cromwell had triumphed over himself before he triumphed over tyranny; and he had repudiated (however unwillingly) the title of king. He seemed to combine strength with virtue, and the favour of God with wisdom, and to have not his own but the public benefit at heart. Since anarchy appeared the only alternative, it was not difficult to believe that, while the tyranny of a wilful king is contrary to human dignity, "there is nothing in human society more pleasing to God, or more agreeable to reason, that there is nothing more just in the state, nothing more useful, than that the most worthy should possess the sovereign power."[39]

But Cromwell in turn proved incapable of translating his sovereign power into a rule of right reason for the benefit of those naturally free and equal in Milton's sense. If it seemed impossible to preserve justice and at the same time to found civil rights upon the natural equality of all men which the Levellers recognized, it seemed no less impossible to achieve justice by founding civil rights on the natural superiority of the wise and good. The ideal had been before men's eyes since the days of the Greeks; but across its path lay an insuperable obstacle, which provided Filmer, the most sensible contemporary critic of Milton's political theory, with his chief objection: "If the sounder, the better and the uprighter part have the power of the people, how shall we know or who shall judge who they be?"[40] The consequences of this difficulty were witheringly indicated by Hobbes: "who hath that eminency of virtue above others, and who is so stupid as not to govern himself, shall never be agreed upon amongst men."

> I know that Aristotle in the first book of his *Politics*, for a foundation of his doctrine, maketh men by nature, some more worthy to command, meaning the wiser sort (such as he thought himself to be for his philosophy), others to serve (meaning those that had strong bodies but were not philosophers as he), as if master and servant were not introduced by consent of men, but by difference of wit; which is not only against reason, but also against experience. For there are very few so foolish that had not rather govern themselves than be governed by others; nor when the wise in their own conceit contend by force with them who distrust their own wisdom, do they always, or often, or almost at any time get the victory. If nature therefore have made men equal, that equality is to be acknowledged; or if nature have made men unequal, yet because men that think themselves equal will not enter into conditions of peace but upon equal terms, such equality must be admitted. And therefore for the ninth law of nature I put this, *That every man acknowledge other for his equal by nature.* The breach of this precept is pride.[41]

The applicability of these observations to Milton hardly needs to be stressed. But he would have replied that a just evaluation of oneself is more desirable than unseasonable and stiff-necked humility. And he would have offered a similar answer to Hobbes' sceptical view of right reason: "for want of a right reason constituted by nature . . . , when men that think themselves wiser than all others clamour and demand right reason for judge, yet seek no more but that things should be determined by no other men's reason but their own, it is as intolerable in the society of men as it is in play after trump is turned to use for trump on every occasion that suit whereof they have most in their hand."[42] In Milton's view of human nature, right reason must inevitably be the product of "real and sincere devotion to God and man, not an idle and wordy, but an efficacious and operative devotion. . . ."[43]

## 2

If Milton was a supporter of the Protectorate, he was also one of its critics. He never supposed that it was possible to preserve justice without preserving the liberty which was equally a product of truth. In 1654 he still desired a pure and free church; in the teeth of Cromwell's ecclesiastical policy, he demanded that the ministers should be deprived of civil support in power and tithes.[44] He still believed that freedom of divorce was necessary if public was to be erected on private freedom; in spite of reprehension, he reviewed the argument of his pamphlets—though he regretted their being "written in the vernacular."[45] He still perceived that the development of liberty required the progress of truth, and that this necessitated free inquiry and publication; apparently with no sense of irony, he denounced "those who never fancy themselves free unless they deprive others of their freedom, who labour at nothing with so much zeal and earnestness as to enchain not the bodies only but the consciences of their brethren, and to introduce into church and state the worst of tyrannies—the tyranny of their own mis-shapen customs and opinions."[46] And he feared that the Protector would mistakenly introduce "a multiplicity of laws," the effect of which would inevitably be the undue restraint of liberty.[47]

But if his advice to Cromwell and the review of his prose writing in *Defensio Secunda* thus stood as a reaffirmation of his pleas for freedom, they also reaffirmed the conditions upon which alone it was attainable and the limitations which are implied even in the most extreme passages of his prose. If "liberty is the most excellent thing to form and increase virtue," it is conversely true that vice is the greatest hindrance to liberty. "Real and substantial liberty . . . is to be sought for not from without but within, and is to be obtained principally . . . by the just regulation and proper conduct of life."[48]

Cromwell is therefore advised to "introduce fewer laws than you abrogate old ones," and to avoid such laws "as would bring the good and bad under the same yoke, or such as, while they provide against the knavery of the unprincipled, should at the same time prohibit what to honest men should be free from all restraint. . . ."[49] The good must be left to the governance of the laws written in the heart; it is the evil, in whom the effects of the Fall are most apparent, who chiefly require the restraint of external law and authority. Yet provision must be made for the development in good men of spiritual and ethical principles.[50] To this end, the state must make "a better provision for the education and morals of youth"; here it will discriminate between "the teachable and unteachable, the diligent and idle."[51] And since the first requisite for liberty is "to be pious," it must have an eye to religion; here it will discriminate between the true and the false.[52]

In this view of the state one discerns the operation of two distinct though closely related influences—classical thought and Christian doctrine. The pernicious effect of the idea of liberty developed by Aristotle and Cicero moved Hobbes to observe that "there was never anything so dearly bought as these western parts have bought the learning of the Greek and Latin tongues,"[53] an opinion which partly accounts for the fact that Milton "did not like him at all."[54] Milton's debt to classical thinking cannot here be accorded the attention it merits; partly through the medium of renaissance political theory, largely through his own reading, he derived from it immense support for his principles. The most obvious instances may be mentioned. He had already in his first pamphlet cited Aristotle's praise of "universal justice" and his opinion that "what the grounds and causes are of single happiness to one man, the same ye shall find them to a whole state."[55] In the *Areopagitica* Plato's "unwritten or at least unconstraining laws of virtuous education, religious and civil nurture," in the divorce tracts Cicero's philosophy of law, had found important applications.[56] In the political pamphlets, Aristotle—"whom we commonly allow for one of the best interpreters of nature and morality"—contributed heavily to the definition of tyranny and even to the elucidation of the apostolic admonitions;[57] "the divine Plato" lent his weight to the supreme authority of justice;[58] and Cicero's "light of truth and wisdom" showed that law "is no other than right reason, derived from the command of the gods, enjoining whatever is virtuous, and forbidding the contrary."[59]

Clearly Milton's theory of just government by the wise and good had roots in the classical ideal. But his interpretation of that ideal was conditioned by the Protestant, even Puritan, doctrine which it helped to transform. Classical theory did not alone provide for him the principle of divine justice and the distinction between the naturally good and evil; it lent a modifying weight to the Puritan principle of divine prescript and the distinction between regenerate and unregenerate. In Milton's hands the rule of the wise and good became, in fact, indistinguishable from the rule of the illuminated and righteous.

He was radical but not democratic because he was at once a Puritan and a Christian humanist.[60] If the humanistic ideal had not provided at once an incentive and a check, he might either have occupied the Presbyterian position with Thomas Young, or have followed the Levellers—and Roger Williams—in the extension of Puritan thinking which fostered naturalism. It is significant that John Goodwin, to whose thought Milton's bears the closest parallel not merely at one point but throughout the revolution, was similarly Arminian in his theology and humanistic in his scholarship without ever departing altogether from the Puritan fold.[61] Both remained Independent to the last, and there was a singular fitness in the linking of their names in the closing act of the experiment. The Presbyterians (and Hobbes) could become royalists, and Williams and Lilburne—both Calvinistic in their purely theological opinions—could move forward towards an ultimate political extreme, because the strictly Puritan view of the spiritual was compatible with a view of the natural leading either to authoritarianism or to democracy. But while rationalism—as the discussion of the toleration controversy has shown—had a profound effect on the development of the Puritan extremists, the idealistic rationalism of the Christian humanists was compatible neither with a completely optimistic nor a completely pessimistic view of humanity in its natural sphere.

In Milton's political theory one perceives once more the basic contrast between his thinking and the thinking of the Puritan radicals. They reproduced more sharply (and yet with different consequences) the segregation of the spiritual and the natural whose reactionary possibilities are apparent in the opinions of Calvin and Luther. In Lilburne and more clearly in Roger Williams, this principle of segregation permitted an argument (unconfused by identifications) which accorded equally to all men in the natural sphere privileges analogous to those accorded equally to the saints, even by the orthodox, in the spiritual sphere.[62]

The significance of Williams' thinking for the problem of conscience has already been indicated; it has precisely the same significance for the political problem. The achievement of complete religious liberty required in his opinion both the denial of civil power to the church and the denial of an interest in religion to the state. The state, he argued, is not without a divine sanction; but it is a natural, not a religious, sanction, and it is derived from the law of nature, not from a spiritual law. The law of nature which governs human societies came from God; indeed it can be related to the Second Table of the Decalogue. The First Table—"the law of worship"—was specifically given to the Jews as the rule of their religion. The Second specially codified for them "the law of nature, the law moral and civil," and this Table is imitable by other states according to their condition.[63] But the whole Law, given "peculiarly" to the Jews, was abrogated when they ceased to be God's peculiar people; its authority no longer binds any man or society. The place of the First Table has been taken by the new law of the Spirit peculiar to God's elect; the place of the Second by the natural law which applies to all men in their fallen state, and to the regenerate in their natural capacity. This last has no necessary connection with the Spirit, for its principles are discoverable by "carnal and natural judgments" without special revelation.[64] That fact is the basis of civil equality.

Upon this law alone Williams erected his theory of a state which must restrict itself to the relationships between men as men, ignoring their relationship with God and the spiritual distinction between mere men and Christians. Because all men are capable of discerning the natural law which is its rule, it is a state democratically governed according to the will of the people. Not only does power reside theoretically in them, but they must be free to erect "what form of government seems to them most meet for their civil condition," and the rulers can claim only such power as the people "consenting and agreeing shall betrust them with."[65] "All lawful magistrates in the world, both before the coming of Christ Jesus and since (excepting those unparalleled, typical magistrates of the church of Israel) are but derivatives and agents, immediately derived and employed as eyes and hands, serving for the good of the whole. Hence they have and can have no more power than fundamentally lies in the bodies or fountains themselves, which power, might, or authority is not religious, Christian, &c., but natural, human, and civil."[66]

These principles seemed to Williams "as true and lawful in those nations, cities, kingdoms, &c., which never heard of the true God, nor his holy Son, Jesus, as in any part of the world beside where the name of Jesus is most taken up."[67] The law of nature applies to this world only, and the end of the state is a welfare "merely and essentially civil and human."[68] The spiritual and everlasting good of Christians is the exclusive province of the church. Upon that province natural men must not be allowed to obtrude their corruption; conversely, the saints must not press for a recognition (in the civil sphere) of their peculiar privileges. In *Romans* 13, St. Paul handles only "the duties of the saints in the careful observation of the Second Table in their civil conversation or walking towards men, and speaks not at all of any point or matter of the First Table concerning the kingdom of the Lord Jesus."[69]

This does not mean that the state is unconcerned with morality. Like the Second Table, the law of nature is a moral law; and the welfare of a community cannot be achieved without reference to the conduct of its citizens.[70] But it will be achieved without reference to faith, which is a spiritual gift of God. True faith will, of course, contribute to morality (and hence indirectly to the good of the state); but "few men either come to or are ordained unto" faith, and "a subject, a magistrate, may be a good subject, a good magistrate," without it. It is necessary to apprehend, "in their distinct kinds," not only the organs of religion and civil society but their respective products. "Civil and moral goodness" is not to be confused with righteousness; where it exists it is "commendable and beautiful, though godliness, which is infinitely more beautiful, be wanting, and which is only proper to the Christian state, the commonweal of Israel, the true Church, the holy nation. . . ."[71]

The segregation of the spiritual and the natural spheres was thus a principle which Williams applied consistently at every point in his thinking. Because of it he could preach the liberty and equality of believers in the spiritual sphere, and—by exact analogy across the gulf of separation—the liberty and equality of all men in the natural sphere. And it was his completely logical acceptance of the Calvinistic view of faith which made this possible. He was radical in his theory of both church and state because he drove to an extreme the difference which separates faith and reason, "spirit and flesh," "the church and the world, and the spiritual and civil state."[72]

Paradoxical as it may appear, the foundation of his political radicalism was his contempt for a world "dead in sin." With reference to the territorial disputes of the colonies, he remarked that it was monstrous "that professors of God and one mediator, of an eternal life and that this is like a dream, should not be content with those vast and large tracts. . . ." "Alas, sir, in calm midnight thoughts, what are these leaves and flowers, and smoke and shadow, and dreams of earthly nothings about which we poor fools and children, as David saith, disquiet ourselves in vain? Alas! what is all the scuffling of this world for . . . generally but for greater dishes and bowls of porridge . . .?"[73]

When these words were written in 1670, Milton could unreservedly have echoed their sentiment. But in the 1650's his midnight thoughts must have been of a different kind, ultimately because the distinction between spirit and flesh was one which he could not fully accept. When he wrote in 1654 that "those things only are great which either make this life of ours happy, or at least comfortable and agreeable as far as is consistent with honesty, or which lead to another and a happier life," he might have echoed even more accurately the phrasing of his Seventh Prolusion.[74] He was capable of drawing a sharp distinction between the naturally evil and the good; but, because he could not allow himself to believe that the struggling elements within himself were ultimately irreconcilable, he was incapable of tearing the natural from the spiritual. What he sought was a just commonwealth which might enable men to achieve the integration of powers he himself sometimes enjoyed in the composition of his poems when the report of his senses and the inspiration of the Spirit fused to produce harmonious verse. For this reason, in the years of the revolution at least, he was (as Sir Herbert Grierson has said) "less immediately concerned with how to gain heaven than with the making of a new earth by the spirit of the philosophy of Christ. . . ."[75]

But that characteristically humanistic aim had the peculiar effect of making acceptable to him precisely those deductions from Puritan doctrine rejected by the Calvinistic Williams. "The instance of Geneva" Williams utterly repudiated.[76] Milton could say in 1655—with mental reservations but by no means complete inaccuracy: "I am in the constant habit . . . both of thinking and speaking highly of the city of Geneva. I admire, first, its worship and study of a purer religion; and my admiration of the republic is scarcely less high. . . ."[77]

The contrast which we have noted in their views of education is thus reproduced, with increased complexity, in their views of the state. The end of society for Milton was "either Christian or at least human."[78] That was the proper order; and because of his convictions and the force of circumstances, he was no more capable of dissociating the two in his later pamphlets than in *Of Reformation*. The purpose of the revolution was not, for him, primarily political; it was to destroy Antichrist. The end of the Commonwealth was not merely the establishment of civil liberty; it was the preservation of true religion. The urgent practical problems which the founder of Rhode Island could ignore reinforced principles which Milton hesitated to discard.

If "Christ's Kingdom could not be set up without pulling down" the kingdom of Charles,[79] it seemed clear that civil liberty could not be preserved without reference to Christianity. In the course of events Milton found evidence not only for the inseparability of tyranny and corruption but for the banding together of "tyranny and superstition," "the combination between tyranny and false religion."[80] It never occurred to him to suppose that one could separate justice from virtue, and virtue from true religion. Hence "tyrants, by a kind of natural instinct, both hate and fear none more than the true church and saints of God as the most dangerous enemies and subverters of monarchy, though indeed of tyranny . . .; whereof no likelier cause can be alleged but that they well discerned the mind and principles of most devout and zealous men, and indeed the very discipline of church, tending to the dissolution of all tyranny."[81]

The discussion of Milton's views on the relationship between church and state will best be deferred to a later chapter, since a reasoned exposition of the fundamental beliefs underlying his political theory is not to be found in the political pamphlets but only in his theological treatise. But it is clear that for him there could be no separation between true reformation and freedom. Their connection explains the profound importance of his political appeal not merely to natural but to Christian liberty.

## 3

The analogy between the congregational discipline and political democracy, to whose dangerous implications Hall and Aston had drawn attention, served the purposes both of the Levellers and of

Milton. But whereas it remained merely an analogy for Williams and the Levellers, Milton's parallel between the power of churches "to bring indifferently both king and peasant under the utmost rigour of their canons and censures ecclesiastical," and the power of a people to bring both under the civil sword, was something more: "justice and religion are from the same God. . . ."[82] To perceive the perfect law of nature is to possess the principles of civil justice; to perceive the perfect law of God is to possess true religion; to perceive the necessity of acting in accordance with the eternal law which is the source of both, is to possess true liberty. But that perception is reserved for those in whose hearts the obscurity caused by the Fall is being progressively cleared by the action of the Spirit.

The theory developed in 1645 thus finds its political application. It is Milton's firm retention of the doctrine not merely of the Fall but of Regeneration, with something of the exclusive and particular significance it had for the true Calvinist, which distinguishes his thinking from Overton's naturalism and Winstanley's mysticism; and it is his transference of that doctrine to the natural sphere which distinguishes his politics from Williams' on the one hand and Hobbes' on the other. If all men by nature are equally dead in sin, a case can be made out either for democracy or dictatorship. If in some the ruins of our first parents have been repaired, then all are not by nature equal, for some are in a state of unregenerate and others of regenerate nature.

The application of that distinction to the civil sphere made possible an association of Christian and natural privileges which supported the ideal of government by the wise and good. Overton's opinions demonstrate the manner in which the privileges of believers could be transformed into natural rights; but the gulf of separation could be crossed in another direction. The Independent author of *The Ancient Bounds* recognized the distinction between Christ's natural and spiritual kingdoms, but observed that "they agree in one common subject-matter, man and societies of men, though under a diverse consideration."

And not only man in society, but every man individually is an epitome either of one only or of both these dominions; of one only, so every natural man (who is in a natural consideration called *microcosmus*, an epitome of the world) in whose conscience God hath his throne, ruling him by the light of nature to a civil outward good and end; of both, so every believer who, besides this natural conscience and rule, hath an enlightened conscience, carrying a more bright and lively stamp of the kingly place and power of the

Lord Jesus, swaying him by the light of faith or Scripture; and such a man may be called *microchristus*, the epitome of Christ mystical.[83]

It seemed to this author (as has already been shown) that the merely natural man could claim, within limits, a right to freedom of conscience, but that such a right belonged even more to those who lived under *both* dominions. The natural liberty of men is "much enlarged by being Christians." That is Milton's assumption in the political pamphlets. Men are free "either as citizens or as Christians."[84] Those who are free in both capacities have, it appears, a right superior to the right of those who can claim freedom only in the first.

Milton's political theory thus exemplifies, not the analogy between the separated spheres of nature and grace, but the direct application of Christian liberty to human affairs which both Williams and Calvin repudiated. When he wrote of the natural right of a people to freedom from tyranny, he thought of a right which belonged even to men in a state of degenerate nature, such a right as must be accorded even the hard of heart in divorce. But when he wrote of the natural liberty which is the end of just government, he was thinking of a liberty of which the unregenerate were incapable, such a liberty as the good man will exercise in availing himself of divorce. That is a liberty possessed only by those whose nature is regenerate.

Tyrants seemed to Milton to hate true Christians "for that their doctrine seems much to favour two things to them so dreadful, liberty and equality."[85] It not only favoured, it begot them. Christ died to free his chosen from more than their bondage to sin. Even the old law—"though it taught slavery in some sense"—"set God's people free"; that is much more true of the Gospel, "heavenly promulgation of liberty."[86] The *Magnificat* prophesied the cutting down of tyrants;[87] in his comment on the princes of the gentiles—"it shall not be so among you"—Christ showed that civil domination and Christianity were incompatible, and told Christians "what manner of law concerning officials and the civil power he desired should be set up among them."[88] Though he himself submitted to tyranny, it was—as St. Paul, 1 *Corinthians* 7.31, showed—for the achievement "not only of evangelical but also of civil liberty."[89] Neither in the church nor in the state are Christians to be servants of men, for their allegiance is to Christ himself. They are required to submit, but only to just governors, and "as free."[90]

The argument that the Gospel is not "to be understood of inward liberty only, to the exclusion of civil liberty,"[91] at once prevented the handing over of the state to depraved nature which seemed a consequence of Williams' argument, and provided an answer to the orthodox fear that the power of magistrates would be undermined "by interposing pretences of Christian liberty against their authority and so turning it into libertinism."[92] The inward sources of Christian liberty express themselves in an external liberty which is not licence. The doctrine thus made available a defence both of the execution of Charles and of the oligarchical Commonwealth. When the Independents were charged with Anabaptism, Milton could reply that "if we would call things by their right names, equality in the state is not Anabaptism, but democracy, a thing far more ancient; and as established in the church, is the discipline of the apostles."[93] The Gospel discipline supplied both a pattern and its bounds, for equality in the church is the exclusive privilege of regenerate Christians, and equality in the state—recognized by the ancient pagans as the natural right of the wise and good—is perfected by Christian doctrine. The Commonwealth was established for the liberty and good of men, and "as much as the nature of the thing will bear, for their equality."[94] It was this virtual identification of natural with spiritual equality which enabled Milton to meet the demands of the Levellers with an exhortation to the people "to fear God and work righteousness."[95]

So far as he followed the Levellers and Williams in translating Christian into natural privileges, Milton was radical; so far as he refused to accept the segregation of the spiritual and the natural he was restrictive. He could agree with Williams up to a point; but he could also have answered negatively (though with reservations) the query of the Presbyterian Edwards: "Whether the commanding men by the power of laws to do their duties, to do the things which God requires of them, with the using outward means to work them to it when unwilling, be unlawful for the magistrate and against Christian liberty, yea or no?"[96] He differed from Edwards in his interpretation of what was required—especially in the church—and he refused to concede the magistrate a compulsive as well as a restrictive power in religion; but because justice was from God and could be recognized in its perfection only by those in whose hearts the law had been renewed, Christian liberty remained for him the measure of true freedom. And since he believed with Ireton that "men as men are corrupt and will be so," he thought it the magistrate's duty to prevent them from destroying true freedom and establishing—in Luther's phrase—"that liberty wherein the devil hath made them free."[97]

That belief seemed abundantly supported by the events of the 1650's. More than that, they served to confirm rather than to weaken the exclusive reservations attached to Puritan doctrine. Most men seemed wilfully to reject the design of Providence; so, for the execution of his decrees, "it has pleased God to choose such men as he chooses to be made partakers of the light of the Gospel."[98] These "he hath selected as the sole remainder, after all these changes and commotions, to stand upright and steadfast in his cause. . . ."[99] It seemed to Milton that God's purpose included both church and state; clearly it may be concluded that he "would have the same reformation made in the commonwealth as in the church, especially if it has been put to the proof that the assigning of infallibility and omnipotency to man is the identical cause of all the evils in both."[100] In Milton's mind that was more than a mere analogy: the function of the revolution was to achieve civil liberty through the inward laws of true religion. It was, indeed, to prepare for the setting up of God's kingdom on earth, with its final establishment of the rule of grace in the sphere of nature.

## Chapter XII

# That Only Just and Rightful Kingdom

THE Leveller doctrines represent but one of the possible extensions of Puritan thought which created embarrassment for the Commonwealth and Protectorate. They depended either upon the naturalistic weakening of dogma which is only partially apparent in Milton's thinking, or upon the strict segregation of the spiritual and the natural which he could not finally accept. But it was possible to arrive at a radical position by courses other than these; and—Presbyterians and Royalists apart—the chief threat to Cromwell's rule actually came from the Fifth Monarchists, who occupied with the Levellers the Puritan left wing yet rejected the equality of nature.[1]

The doctrine of Christian liberty played as important a part in their millenarianism as it did in the theories of the Levellers. They also applied it to the natural as well as to the civil sphere; but they applied it directly and retained its original distinctions. In a sermon published in 1642 as *The Peasants Price of Spirituall Liberty*, Nathaniel Homes preached church reformation in terms of a "God-given liberty" consisting of two parts, "first, personal, of body, state, and condition; secondly, spiritual, of soul and worship":

> . . . these put together are a right platform of Christian's purchased liberty; viz., the partition wall is down, all are subjects to Christ's kingdom, all brethren; no longer slaves, so much as civilly. And ecclesiastically, all needless ceremonies, superstitions, and human inventions are put down. And so Christians are no longer subject to those rudiments of the world of which St. Paul speaks, *Colos.* 2, no longer to live in subjection to such ordinances as these—Touch not, taste not, handle not, after the commandments of men. . . .[2]

This is precisely the liberating principle applied by Milton in the anti-episcopal pamphlets, in the tracts on conscience, and even civilly.

But, like Milton in the early 1640's, Homes was chiefly concerned to deal with those "unworthy spirits, who prescribe antiquity, to prefer a sordid condition before a God-given liberty," and who "plead custom for servility." These, he said, God would fill "with the filth and foul of their own ways," if they would not "conceive what is spiritual liberty, nor receive it, but resolve against it."[3]

> Such persons as these, that will not understand the excellency of their liberty but stand out against it with custom, naturalize themselves into a liberty-loathing or despising complexion. So that, as the great philosopher said, "Some are servants by nature, foolish, passive, silly in regard of governing others; but in regard of subjection to be governed, they are *instrumenta rationala*, they have reason enough to work according to the direction of another." So these men by corrupt custom are fitted to be led by the stream of times, and the examples of corrupt men, and the rotten principles of blind guides. There is that power, or rather tyranny, of a vain conversation received by tradition, that nothing but a redemption, and that by the blood of Christ, will fetch a man off. . . .[4]

The great philosopher is, of course, Aristotle; and the ideas are those expressed by Milton ten years later. They were also essential to the millenarian description of "the new world or the new reformed church," which Homes published in 1651.[5]

In Milton's political pamphlets a similar association of Christian liberty with the Kingdom of Christ was almost inevitable; nor is it at all remarkable that the idea of the Kingdom as an earthly state formed a permanent element in his thought. In the words of Hanserd Knollys, "although this may seem to be strange, yet heretofore it hath not been accounted so."[6] To disregard that conception would be to ignore one of the chief sources of seventeenth-century idealism. It lent itself easily to fanaticism; but it was by no means contemptible, and its attraction was not felt by the ignorant alone. The great Joseph Mede of Milton's own college had treated the prophecies concerning it in his *Clavis Apocalyptica*, a volume which met with profound admiration from men of all sorts.[7]

Imaginations, already prepared by Mede and other commentators, were deeply stirred by the early events of the revolution. The mood in which Milton wrote his first pamphlets was not unlike that in which Hanserd Knollys preached in 1641 a sermon called *A Glimpse of Sions Glory*. Both thought that "God is beginning to stir in the world"; both somewhat presumptuously declared it "the work of the day to give God no rest till he sets up Jerusalem as the praise of the whole world"; both believed that God was illuminating even the unlearned—though Knollys was somewhat more emphatic on the function of those "of the meaner rank"; both looked for the light to "grow brighter and brighter till that time, which is the great design of God for his glory to all eternity"—when "Antichrist is down, Babylon fallen, then comes in Jesus Christ reigning gloriously. . . ."[8]

The effect of such a vision of the New Jerusalem is recognizable, among much else, in Milton's early view of the revolution. As we have seen, it was specifically recorded, with an eloquence which is the testimony of sincere enthusiasm, in the passage in *Of Reformation* in which he envisaged for himself, when the work of reformation should be completed and "the eternal and shortly-expected King" should appear, a kind of earthly counterpart of the apotheoses described in his elegies.[9] And in *Animadversions* this enthusiastic expectancy became yet more importunate: "Come forth out of thy royal chambers, O Prince of all the kings of the earth! put on the visible robes of thy imperial majesty, take up that unlimited sceptre which thy Almighty Father hath bequeathed thee; for now the voice of thy bride calls thee; and all creatures sigh to be renewed."[10]

As the revolution progressed, Milton's confidence diminished; but if he lost his faith in the English people and his sense of the imminence of Christ's coming, the idea of the Kingdom remained fixed in his mind. In the pamphlets of the second group, there is discernible a growing disillusionment, arising partly from personal difficulties, partly from the futility of "casting pearl to hogs."[11] In the *Areopagitica* he sadly observed: "To sequester out of the world into Atlantic and Utopian polities which never can be drawn into use, will not mend our condition; but to ordain wisely as in this world of evil, in the midst whereof God hath placed us unavoidably."[12] That conviction pervades the political pamphlets; but the passage requires exact interpretation. The *Areopagitica* and the divorce tracts deal with perplexing human problems, left by God to the conscience and not to be solved according to the unpractical rules of the impossible republics of Plato, More, or Bacon, designed by mere men and dependent upon a perfection not to be achieved by human powers alone. but beside such statements, one must set the convictions which throw them into relief. Though the time has not yet come, the ultimate end of the Gospel is to restore all things to their primitive perfection. "As . . . the state of man now is," good and evil, truth and falsehood, grow up together almost inseparably; yet truth is always in her progress towards the time when, at "her Master's second coming, he shall bring together every joint and member, and shall mould them into an immortal feature of loveliness and perfection."[13]

Even in the years of his first disillusionment, the Kingdom thus provided Milton with a definite point of reference in the future and a focus for his idealism; and his hopes were ready to be revived. Their disappointment in the years of the Assembly's dominance was something which he shared with men like Knollys. Millenarianism suffered an eclipse as the war dragged on amid conflicting counsels. But it flamed up once more under the influence of the New Model Army and with the trial of the King. The erection of the High Court of Justice seemed to many the establishment of the throne of the Ancient of Days; the events which followed appeared the beginning of the fulfilment of the prophecies.[14] By that renewal of enthusiastic expectancy Milton did not remain untouched.

2

In the writings of the Secretary for Foreign Tongues one will hardly discover much of the fanatical zeal for overturning which characterized the activities of Fifth Monarchists under the Commonwealth and Protectorate. He cannot have approved the obscure and fantastic plots of the Lord's people nor the inflammatory sermons which moved the authorities to imprison the prophets in spite of their protests that the weapons they employed were spiritual only.[15] Milton was not in that sense an "Anabaptist": he felt that safety lay in submission to a government founded in justice and designed, however imperfectly, to preserve it.

Yet in the desire for justice there lay a source of dissatisfaction with the Protectorate. There can be no doubt of Milton's admiration for the Cromwell who led the victorious parliamentary armies; but his official connection with Cromwell's government—a connection which became less close after his complete loss of sight in 1652—should not be permitted to obscure his suspicion of the continued rule of a single person wielding all but regal power. His five years' silence between 1654 and 1659—broken only by the purely personal diatribe of the *Defensio Pro Se*—is not without its significance.[16] The warnings offered in *Defensio Secunda* had not in fact been heeded.

When that pamphlet was written in 1654, the Millenarians were in complete disrepute because of the dismal failure of the Nominated Parliament. The calling of this body was in part a fulfilment of their desires. It was an assembly of godly men, chosen by the Council from lists sent up by the Congregational churches in each county, so that, as Milton put it, the privilege of voting was "allowed to those only to whom it was proper to allow it."[17] Cromwell told it in his opening speech that it was assembled by a higher than human power: "I say, you are called with a high call; and why should we be afraid to say or think that this way may be the door to usher in things that God hath promised and prophesied of, and set the hearts of his people to wait for and expect? . . . Indeed I do think something is at the door."[18] In Milton's brief reference to this unsuccessful assembly, one can recognize the disappointment of just such an expectation; and that deduction is supported by the nature of his advice to Cromwell. The abolition of tithes, the confirming of religious liberty, the separation of the church from the state, the reform and reduction of laws, were precisely the aims of the extremists in the Nominated Parliament whose vigorous opposition to the purposes of the more moderate members resulted in its dissolution.[19] They were, moreover, aims coupled not with the dangerous principle of natural equality but with the principle of rule by good men.

While Milton was no Fifth Monarchist, he was far more sympathetic to their millenarian ideas than to the naturalistic tendencies implicit in Levelling. The reign of Christ might itself be impossible to establish, as Christianity then went; but its desirability is an underlying motive in the political pamphlets, for it provided an ideal pattern of government by the wise and good. Indeed, the idea of the Kingdom itself received support from the imperfect testimony of the ancients. The Platonic Socrates had said: "In heaven there is laid up a pattern of such a city, which he who desires may behold, and beholding may govern himself accordingly. But whether there exists or ever will exist such a city, is no matter; for he will live after the manner of that city, having nothing to do with any other."[20]

Milton not only believed in the existence of such a heavenly pattern but was certain that it would eventually find its fulfilment on earth in the Kingdom of Christ which would be the Gospel counterpart of the polity of God's peculiar people, the Jews. The motives which supported the application of Christian liberty in the natural and civil spheres also confirmed the idea of an earthly as well as a heavenly Kingdom. The spiritualization of sense necessarily draws with it, in some degree, the materializing of spirit; and this view of the Kingdom was consequently one of the few beliefs which Milton shared with Hobbes.

One of the most curious products of Hobbes' materialistic philosophy was his positive assertion that divines were mistaken in speaking of "the Kingdom of God" as if it meant either "eternal felicity after this life, in the highest heaven, which they also call the Kingdom of Glory," or, metaphorically, "sanctification, which they term the Kingdom of Grace."[21] In his opinion it could mean only an earthly kingdom, and most properly the commonwealth of Israel, "instituted (by the consent of those which were to be subject thereto) for their civil government, and the regulating their behaviour, not only towards God their King, but also towards one another in point of justice and towards other nations in peace and war." That state came to an end when the Jews rebelliously chose a human king; but its restoration, in another form, was promised by the Gospel, and to pray, "Thy Kingdom come," meant in Hobbes' view to pray for the time "when Christ shall come in majesty to judge the world and actually to govern his own people," not in heaven but in the "eternal life on earth" which Adam forfeited and Christ regained.[22]

The effect of this interpretation is to shut man off eternally from heaven in a Paradise capable of explanation in terms of matter in motion. The more usual reading was that Christ would reign, either personally or through his saints, for a thousand years, after which the old earth and heaven would pass away. But it was essential to Hobbes' political scheme to avoid the implications which might be drawn from the Kingdom, and to his materialism to keep it earthly. He therefore argued that it was "not of this world," but of the new world which would not come "till the general resurrection." It could therefore have no more effect on existing institutions than had Christ's own ministry: "The Kingdom he claimed was to be in another world, he taught all men to obey in the meantime them that sate in Moses' seat, he allowed them to give Caesar his tribute, and refused to take upon himself to be a judge. How then could his words or actions be seditious, or tend to the overthrow of their civil government?"[23]

This reasoning is at once an illustration of the importance attached to Christ's Kingdom by the seventeenth-century mind (even when sceptical), and of the peculiar workings of the principle of segregation. The spiritual can hardly be said to have existed for Hobbes at all; but when he was forced to recognize it, he first reduced it as much as might be to material terms, and then separated it from the secular. In his reasoning the segregation of the spiritual and the secular (though not of civil and ecclesiastical organizations) prevented the patterning of human societies on God's Kingdom, in either of its expressions, exactly as it did in Roger Williams.

Hobbes observed that to seek sanction for civil sovereignty from a power higher than itself was to undermine it since men would not agree on the sense of divine dictates; Williams saw that to deduce civil power from a higher than natural source must lead to persecution for religious opinions other than those officially accepted. For different reasons, both consequently repudiated the model provided by the commonwealth of God's peculiar people and by the Kingdom to come. In Hobbes' view the first would be restored only by the second in another, though material, world; in Williams' view, the first was an earthly type, not of an earthly kingdom, but only of Christ's spiritual Kingdom, the church, now existing in the world but at the last to be perfected spiritually: "The state of the land of Israel . . . is proved figurative and ceremonial, and no pattern nor precedent for any kingdom or civil state in the world to follow."[24]

So long as the institutions of Israel were regarded as merely (in Williams' words) "types and figures of a spiritual land, spiritual people, and spiritual worship under Christ,"[25] neither the polity of God's people nor Christ's coming Kingdom could have a direct effect on the theories of democracy or of unconditional sovereignty which might be deduced from natural law according to the particular interpretation adopted. But where the principle of segregation did not operate with the decisiveness it has in Williams, there was possible an appeal to Jewish precedent and to the final reign of godliness. For the orthodox Puritan the Old Testament always remained the record of divinely sanctioned law; but Puritans of the left found it no less difficult to abandon the authoritative model provided by God's own commonwealth, especially when they regarded the Civil War as essentially a battle with Antichrist. William Aspinwall simply gave more positive expression to an assumption common both to the right and the left when, in describing the Fifth Monarchy, he said of the Jewish polity, "Though the laws be few and brief, yet they are perfect and sufficient, and so large as the wisdom of God judged needful for regulating judgment in all ages and nations; for no action or case doth, or possibly can, fall out in this or other nations . . . but the like did, or possibly might, fall out in Israel."[26]

The divorce tracts are the record of the conflict in Milton's mind between the divine authority of the Mosaic Law and the legalistic restrictiveness of the old dispensation which was to be contrasted with the spiritual freedom of the new. He at length determined with Williams for the complete abrogation of the old law in favour of the law written by the Spirit in the hearts of believers. That conception remained fixed in his thinking; it provided a basis for his theory of liberty, and issued politically in the demand for the abrogation of laws which might restrict the freedom of the good. Yet Scripture remained for him the measure, in some sense, of the law of the Spirit; and the Jewish polity remained a model divinely sanctioned. The Jews provided a precedent for the Commonwealth since its case was one which had fallen out among them.

Some of the restrictive consequences of taking Israel for a model could be avoided by arguing that the relevant laws were no more than a particular codification of the law of nature. This was Williams' interpretation of the Second Table;[27] Lilburne went yet further, saying that the precepts even of the First Table recorded conclusions which might be based on natural reason;[28] and the Independent Ireton observed that "there are some things of perpetual and natural right, that the Scripture of the Old Testament doth hold forth, wherein it does bear a clear witness to that light that every man hath left in him by nature, if he were not depraved by lust."[29] Clearly the significance of this idea of the consonance between Jewish law and the law of nature will depend on the importance attached to Ireton's conditional clause. It has already been shown that events impressed upon Milton the necessity of that condition; and its effect is apparent in his appeal to Jewish precedent in defence of the Commonwealth. Even though it serves to demonstrate what is naturally just, and is therefore supported by a host of examples from the practice of the best heathen nations, it nevertheless remains a precedent of peculiar authority; for the perfect law of nature, obscured through the Fall, must be most clearly indicated through the laws which God gave to his peculiar people and through his approbation or disapprobation of their actions.

The history of Israel seemed to Milton to offer weighty examples of the "ways of kings which God himself so much condemns," and more especially of the dangers of kingship itself.[30] Monarchy was clearly not in itself contrary to the law of nature, for God permitted his people to exercise their natural right in changing their government from a commonwealth under him to a kingdom. But the change met with his displeasure; and he warned them through Samuel that, while a commonwealth prevented tyranny, kings were prone to it: "A commonwealth . . . in the opinion of God was, under human conditions, a more perfect form of government than a monarchy, and more useful for his own people; for he himself set up this government and could hardly be prevailed withal a great while after, and at their own importunate desire, to let them change it into a monarchy."[31]

It seemed to Milton, with his deep conviction of God's special providence for England, that the events of 1649 constituted a reversal of this unfortunate act. In executing the King and establishing a "reformed commonwealth," the English were erecting a government according to the model provided by God for his chosen people, and were themselves demonstrating their right to that title. They might justifiably hope "that, as God was heretofore angry with the Jews who rejected him and his form of government to choose a king, . . . he will bless us, and be propitious to us, who reject a king to make him only our leader and supreme governor, in the conformity, as near as may be, of his own ancient government. . . ."[32]

That hope was coupled in Milton's mind with the revived confidence which he shared with those of his contemporaries who believed that "something is at the door."

## 3

Though the Jewish commonwealth provided a model, it had not itself been permanent; what "happened even to the ancient Romans after they had become effeminate and unnerved through luxury," happened also to God's own people.[33] Such a calamity could only be prevented from occurring in England through the establishment of settled government by good men. That was a programme which recommended itself to men of all sorts. Even the Levellers would have excluded from the exercise of their natural and equal right—though only for seven years—those who had supported the King; and even for them the Army in general stood as the representative of "the good party."[34] But their scheme involved theoretically the inclusion of the whole people in the direction of government, at least in the future; and there could be no doubt that this would mean the speedy ruin of the unpopular Commonwealth. Government by good men seemed a safer way; and though the active Millenarians, from whom that design received its clearest definition, were few in number, they voiced a criticism of the Protectorate which was echoed even by those who were less certain that Christ would shortly appear.

The programme of government by the good—or alternatively, the saints—had been clearly set forth in a petition presented to the Council of Officers in February, 1649, as a countercheck to the *Agreement* being pushed by the Levellers.[35] The petitioners warned against taking "the dim light of nature for our law when God hath given the light of the Scriptures, a better law," and against "the setting up of a mere natural and worldly government, like that of heathen Rome and Athens. . . ." What was needed to replace the now-fallen monarchy of Charles was a government which would achieve the permanent good of all men by being conformable to the rule of Christ through his saints; "which done, we doubt not but God shall have much glory, the godly party shall be comforted, natural men (enjoying their estates) will be at rest also and much satisfied; and this commonwealth will be exalted to be both an habitation of justice and mountain of holiness, even such a people as God will bless. . . ."[36]

That desirable condition was to be achieved, so the petitioners thought, through the methods subsequently employed in a modified form for the selection of the Nominated Parliament. The members of the Congregational churches were to elect "such as are to sit in general assemblies or church-parliaments . . . , and those elected, to sit there as Christ's officers and the churches' representatives, and to determine all things by the Word, as that law that God will exalt alone and make honourable." The privileges of the saints were thus to be translated into civil privileges; the churches were to become the kingdom, and the kingdom the church; and while natural men enjoyed the benefits of such a government, they were also to be evangelized so that when they "are converted and the Son of God makes them free, they may enjoy the former freedoms with the rest of the saints." Thus would be established a godly government, "monarchical, as when Christ, the Head and King, appears visibly, or parliamentary, as in the meantime, when Christ's officers and the churches' representatives rule."[37]

If this visionary scheme proved a miserable failure when a partial attempt was made to put it in practice, it was nevertheless based on principles not unacceptable to the middle party. In the early years of the Commonwealth, Independent divines like John Owen and Thomas Goodwin preached of the Fifth Monarchy and read in events "the hand of the Lord" and such "shakings of the heavens of the nations" as presaged their transformation into "the Kingdoms of our Lord Jesus."[38] Milton could likewise accept the idea in principle. It was based on an interpretation of Christian liberty in large measure similar to his; its end was government in accordance with divine justice through the rule of good men; it was modelled not only on the commonwealth of the Jews but on Christ's Kingdom. And in the rising up of the nation against Antichrist and the execution of the King, he also read the fulfilment of prophecies.

Kings seemed to him to fear true Christians, not only because their doctrine taught liberty and equality, but "because they are the children of that Kingdom which, as ancient prophecies have foretold, shall in the end break to pieces and dissolve all their great power and dominion."[39] Clearly, the good party in England had "a warrant from God to judge wicked kings, for God has conferred this very honour upon his saints, *Psalm* 149, that while they celebrate the praises of Christ their own King, yet as for the kings of the heathen (and such, according to the Gospel, are all tyrants), 'they shall bind them with chains . . . to execute upon them the judgment written . . . .' "[40] "Therefore 'to bind their kings in chains, and their nobles with links of iron,' is an honour belonging to his saints; not to build Babel (which was Nimrod's work, the first king, and the beginning of his kingdom was Babel), but to destroy it, especially that spiritual Babel; and first to overcome those European kings which receive their power, not from God, but from the beast, and are counted no better than his ten horns."[41]

It is significant that, while Milton's appeals to the law of nature are balanced by his specific condemnation of equal civil rights, such distinctly millenarian passages as these are not balanced by any condemnation of Fifth Monarchism in the political pamphlets. It is also significant that there are no such passages, and no references either to Christ's Kingdom or to God's opinion of the Israelites' desire for a king, in *Defensio Secunda*.[42] The idea of the Kingdom did not pass from Milton's mind: it appears once more in subsequent pamphlets. Yet if he could entertain millenarian notions, he seems to have recognized, like the Independent divines, the danger of anarchy which they threatened to introduce when, the Nominated Parliament having failed, Cromwell turned from the rule of the good to seek another settlement and so qualified himself, according to the Millenarians, for the title of "Little Horn."[43]

After the establishment of the Protectorate the Independents did their best to undo the effects of their own preaching and to defend the government against Fifth Monarchist attacks.[44] Among others John Goodwin offered tranquillizing arguments. In the 1640's he had thought "the time of God's preordination and purpose for the downfall of Antichrist" was drawing near; and he had made it an argument for freedom of conscience that "the commonalties of Christians . . . shall be most active and have the principal hand in executing the judgments of God upon the Whore."[45] But by 1646, he was censuring such "unpolitic Christians" as would cast off both ecclesiastical and civil discipline altogether, "to catch at the spiritual privileges of New Jerusalem before it comes down from heaven," and who suppose that "they should or might anticipate that other great privilege of the heavenly city . . . , freedom from magistracy, by a present ejecting of this ordinance out of the world."[46] Seven years later he was defending the Commonwealth against all its opponents as ordained by God, and especially against the Fifth Monarchists who would overturn it and so hasten the Kingdom. He reminded them that "the Epocha," the time "wherein that Great Jubilee of the Monarchy they speak of shall begin, is unchangeably, unalterably, unremovably fixed by God," so that "no human endeavours or contributions towards such a thing are anyways available to accelerate or hasten this period of time, nor (on the other hand) any human oppositions or obstructions or unworthy actings of men anyways able to retard or set it back."[47]

Though Milton did not specifically condemn the Millenarians (even when defending Cromwell), and though he retained his sense of the revolution as a crusade against Antichrist, he would probably have accepted this pacifying argument. But a recognition of the fact that the time of Christ's coming was not to be changed by human acts did not destroy the significance of his Kingdom as a model for commonwealths under which men might await it. As Thomas Collier told the Army at Putney in 1647, in a sermon called *A Discovery of the New Creation*, not only is it God's design "to exalt righteousness" but "truly prudent policy calls for righteousness and the undoing of burdens. . . ."[48]

Collier's sermon suggests the outline of the pattern of thought, not explicitly recorded in Milton's political pamphlets, but alone capable of bringing into order all the ideas which are there expressed.[49] His view of the new creation was neither materialistic nor inflammatory; on the contrary, it represents the admirable spirituality which Puritanism was capable of producing when its harshness was modified by an essentially Christian idealism. He did not believe that the creation of a new heaven and a new earth meant that Christ would come to reign personally as monarch, but that he would "come in the Spirit and have a glorious kingdom in the spirits of his people. . . . The Kingdom of God is within you." That belief he based not merely on Scripture but on "experimental truth," on the living experience of good men; for this kingdom seemed to him to depend, not merely on God's might, but on the "renovation or renewing of the mind: an internal and spiritual change, a transformation out of the nature of the first, into the nature of the second, Adam."[50] It arose therefore from the spiritual condition of individual men, and it brought with it the renovation of the will through perfect knowledge of God and of the "spiritual liberty in Christ" which frees from "all spiritual enemies, sin, law, condemnation," and from subjection "to men in the things of God." Its product was therefore first a new church—"new in respect of ministry, not in the letter but in the spirit . . .; that is, in the wisdom and power of that law in the Spirit which will deliver saints from fleshly actings into the glorious liberty of spiritual actings, that they shall no more act from a legal principle to a law without them, but from a principle of light, life, liberty, and power within them."[51] And it produced, secondly, a new earth and a renovation of magistracy. It meant that magistrates must be "such as are acquainted with, and have an interest in, the righteous God." "This is the great work that God hath to effect in the latter days of the Gospel, to reduce magisterial power to its primitive institution, that you may see (*Rom.* 13.1), 'there is no power but is ordained of God, and it is ordained for the punishment of them that do evil, but for the praise of them that do well.' Although this end hath been a long time lost, yet now God will reduce it to this institution."[52] That is precisely the end Milton thought the Commonwealth was to achieve through the government of the wise and good who had the true law in their hearts and so possessed the knowledge of real liberty.

## 4

The pattern of ideas suggested by Collier is more completely illustrated in the writings of Sir Henry Vane, who was in Milton's opinion "young in years, but in sage counsel old."[53] Though he was suspected of intriguing with the Fifth Monarchists, Vane was never closely associated with their schemes. Indeed, in the years immediately following the King's execution, he strove to preserve the power of the Parliament against the Army and Cromwell. When it was dissolved he went into retirement, refused a seat in the Nominated Parliament, and was at length imprisoned by the Protector in 1656.[54] But as his despondency increased with the failure of the Commonwealth, he turned to the religious thoughts which had been in his mind throughout his career, especially to the idea of the regeneration of things human which had seemed to him to be under way in the opening years of the revolution;[55] and the coming Kingdom, conceived much after Collier's manner but with greater subtlety, became for him of profound importance.

The elaborate exposition of Christian doctrine which he published in 1655, *The Retired Mans Meditations*, cannot be examined in detail here. But Milton almost certainly read it, and his political thinking—especially in its relationship to his theological opinions—is illuminated by Vane's consideration of magistracy. That is especially true of Vane's rendering of the idea of human progress, to whose development Puritanism greatly contributed.[56] Briefly, his view of the Commonwealth's task was that it must establish a godly government which would grow towards the perfect Kingdom to come eventually on earth.

Like Williams, Vane associated magistracy in its degenerate state with the kingdom of Satan; it was part of the rule of Antichrist for "oppressing and keeping under the dear saints and holy ones of the true and living God." But it had also to be considered "in its primitive constitution and right exercise, wherein it is not only capable of serving to a higher end, but must, through the restitution that all things are to be brought forth in at the last, be made actually instrumental unto the holy designs and glorious interest of Christ and his people, as his earthly throne, wherein he will sit and rule the nations as with a rod of iron. . . ."[57]

Vane thus not only looked back to the original and perfect institution of government but forward to the restoration of its perfection. He did not associate it, as did Milton, solely with the consequences of the Fall; and he did not share the antinomian opinion that government would never have been instituted if man had remained upright, and that it would be unnecessary when he was restored to his original condition. The function of government seemed to him not merely to restrain but to protect and support:

We are not to conceive, as most are apt to do, that man in his innocent state and sinless nature stood in no need of this office of magistracy; for it is not only useful to restrain from unrighteousness and disorder occasioned by sin

> and the Fall, but also to conserve and maintain men in the good order and right disposition of things wherein by their creation they were placed, in a preventing way unto disorder and danger that lust threatens and is ready to introduce upon man in his mutable righteous and holy state. And in this way of exercise it will be upheld by Christ during his reign on earth the thousand years when, with the whole creature, it shall be restored from the bondage of corruption into the glorious liberty of the sons of God, and be made subservient to the interest of the right heirs of salvation. . . .[58]

Because Milton regarded magistracy and law chiefly as the product of the depravity they were to restrain, and sought to free the regenerate from all external compulsion, there is a real difference between his theory and Vane's. Yet he could have agreed with this view of the state as a necessary instrument for preserving and fostering the principles from which true liberty springs.[59]

Those principles depended in Milton's view upon the spiritual and moral condition of individuals. That was also Vane's opinion, no less than Collier's; and for that reason political theory found its place in his theological meditations. There is no theology in Milton's political pamphlets; but he too was engaged in the preparation of a doctrinal treatise, and Vane's reasoning suggests the relationship of Milton's politics to his theology, for both viewed the political problem in the light of regeneration through Christ, from whom "all natural as well as spiritual good doth flow."[60]

Though Vane knew

> Both spiritual power and civil, what each means,
> What severs each,

and recognized "the two distinct branches and administrations" of Christ's government of men, he could not fully accept the consequences which Williams drew from the principle of segregation, for Christ was not only "the giver of the Holy Ghost," but also the "restorer of pure, uncorrupt nature."[61] He believed that if Adam had not fallen, he would have been lifted up into a spiritual state "sure, immovable, and fixed."[62] Such a glorification seemed to him now the final end of salvation through Christ. But the process necessarily involved also a restoration of the natural man to the perfection from which he fell, and with it the regeneration of human society. This was obscurely shadowed forth in Israel; but through regeneration God's chosen are "enabled to sing both the song of Moses and of the Lamb in perfect harmony, and to do the will of God in earth as it is done in heaven."[63]

In its spiritual aspect, regeneration thus meant for Vane a process of transformation from the natural into the "new-creature state" which unfallen Adam would have attained in due time but which is now finally attained only at the resurrection. In its natural aspect, it meant the repairing of the ruins of our first parents, and a renewal of "the light and manifestation of God's mind and will" which man at his creation possessed as the "law within him, called in Scripture, the candle of the Lord." That light man lost through not preserving himself "in the sinless state wherein he was created." It may still be partially discerned by all men through "a common enlightening when they receive their beings." It was revealed in a peculiar manner to God's chosen people. It is more fully apprehended by those who have received "the knowledge of Jesus Christ . . . through the ministry of the written word." But it is recognized in its perfection only by such as possess the mystical light of the divine love, and with it "the light of pure nature and right reason, fixed and made incorruptible through faith and regeneration, whereby the former frailty and leaking of the vessel is perfectly cured. . . ."[64]

Milton was working his way towards a similar view of regeneration in the treatise which was to become his *De Doctrina Christiana*; it had already been roughly worked out in the divorce tracts. And its significance here is indicated by the fact that the stages of enlightenment had for Vane their counterparts in administrations among men. If Adam had remained upright, magistracy would have existed in its natural perfection. Since man fell, the heathen live under governments in accordance with the imperfect law of nature, improved—as among the Greeks and Romans—so far as is possible by the exercise of fallen reason alone. The Mosaic Law was a "heightening of civil magistracy into a suitableness unto the divine service of this worldly sanctuary"; but it gave the Israelites a government only according to the letter expressly revealed by God and not again to be reproduced, though to revive it "many attempts have been made." Under the Gospel there are two administrations, the church which is spiritual, and magistracy which is natural. And these must develop towards the final administration, the Kingdom of Christ in which the saints will not only enjoy their spiritual privileges but have the "charge and office of administering natural right and justice."[65]

Vane's theological speculations have been described as the weakness of a strong man; a similar opinion has been expressed concerning Milton's.[66] But while one may doubt the truth of Vane's theological conclusions, it is impossible to understand without reference to them the full significance of the advice which he offered the nation under Cromwell. The mystical opinions of the speculator could be translated only imperfectly by the politician into practical propositions; but the criticism of the Protectorate and the scheme of settlement presented in Vane's *Healing Question propounded* were nevertheless the products of his meditations in retirement.[67]

Vane agreed with Goodwin in believing that, if "the saints should sit down in faith and patience," Christ's Kingdom would be established "in his due time."[68] But he also believed that the "pure state of magistracy" in its primitive and final perfection was at least in part "capable to be brought into its exercise and practice." Through human frailty there would be imperfections; but men should look for further light, and listen to those who are "sincere to Christ in longing after his coming, to set up even magistracy itself in the purity of its use and exercise."[69]

Though the time was immovably fixed, there was "a duty of the day, a generation work . . . which calls upon us to use all lawful and righteous means that are afforded by the good hand of God . . . whereby to make way for and to be hasting unto the coming of that day of God. . . ." Therefore, "once we have well considered what rule Christ himself, if he were on earth, would exercise over men . . . , we ought . . . to be as near this in our practice as possibly we may. . . ."[70]

Towards the end of his speculative consideration of magistracy, Vane wrote that an effort should be made to bring government into conformity with "its first institution and original pattern . . . upon the principles of natural right and just," so that "the ordinances and institutions of God may become also the ordinances and statutes of men, established in a free and natural way of common consent. . . ."[71] *A Healing Question propounded* was an expansion of this statement and an attempt to outline the machinery which might achieve such an aim. Vane's recommendations were echoed in Milton's later pamphlets. That fact is explained by the similarity between their views of the end to which the Commonwealth must be directed; and Vane's opinion of the Protectorate also suggests the thoughts which must have been in Milton's mind after 1654.

Cromwell's government seemed to Vane neither an attempt to erect the ordinance of God nor established in accordance with natural justice; and it is because those offences amounted ultimately in his eyes to the same thing that he provides the best final comment on Milton's political thinking. He regarded Cromwell as Milton had regarded Charles, for the Protector had chosen to impose on the nation the rule of his arbitrary will. Instead of the settlement expected, "private and selfish interest" had caused "a great interruption."[72] That was "the first rise and step to tyranny"; for it introduced "the highest imposition and bondage upon the whole body, in compelling all the parts . . . to serve and obey, as their sovereign rule and supreme authority, the arbitrary will and judgment of those that bring themselves into rule by the power of the sword. . . ."[73]

The Protectorate thus reproduced in the civil sphere man's original mistake. Adam had been given the choice either of trusting to his own guidance, or of distrusting his wisdom as insufficient and his will as mutable, and so depending on the guidance of "his natural Head, Lord, and Sovereign."[74] England had been given a like choice; and its subjection to human will rather than to divine guidance accounted for its continued distractions.

These were to be healed, thought Vane, only through an effort to establish government according to the law of nature; and this would be achieved only through the free exercise of the people's natural right "to set up meet persons in the place of supreme judicature . . . , for the rule and government under which they shall live . . . , and through the orderly exercise of such measure of wisdom and counsel as the Lord in this way shall please to give unto them, to shape and form all subordinate actings and administrations of rule and government, so as shall answer the public good and safety of the whole."[75] Only through the recognition of this natural right would the good of the commonwealth be achieved. "The sword never can, nor is it to be expected ever will, do this, whilst the sovereignty is admitted and placed anywhere else than in the whole body of the people that have adhered to this cause and by them to be derived unto their successive representatives, as the most equal and impartial judicature for the effecting thereof."[76]

In Vane's programme one recognizes the influences of such principles as were pressed by the Levellers. A convention elected according to natural right was to draw up the fundamentals of government (including freedom of conscience), and then to make way for a representative legislature and an executive body—preferably "a standing council of state elected for life."[77] Yet not dissimilar recommendations had been made by the Millenarians; and Milton had employed the arguments from nature. Behind Vane's limitation of the privilege of election to "the good party," to "the adherents to this cause," one perceives something more than the necessity of discrimination which the Levellers were willing temporarily to recognize.[78]

Like them, Vane was striving to bring theory into line with practical necessity; but the theory behind *A Healing Question* was the theory developed in his *Meditations*. For practical purposes the good party consisted of such as had supported the revolution. But in theory it consisted of "those that, by the growing light of these times, have been taught and led forth in their experiences to look above and beyond the letter, form, and outward circumstances of government, into the inward reason and spirit thereof, herein only to fix and terminate."[79] According to the *Meditations*, these can only be the regenerate.

Vane was aware that the results of his proposals might be other than those he desired.[80] But the arbitrary rule of the Protector's will was unbearable; and he trusted that reliance on God's guidance would lead to the proper exercise of true natural right. God had taken courses "to fit and prepare a choice and selected number of the people unto this work"; and Vane believed that he "will pour out so abundantly of his spirit upon his people, attending on him in righteous ways, and will also so move their hearts to choose persons bearing his image unto the magistracy, that a more glorious product may spring up out of this than at first we can expect, to the setting up of the Lord himself as chief judge and law giver amongst us."[81]

Vane's writings exemplify the association of the natural with the spiritual—and consequently of natural with divine law, of human with Christian liberty, of perfect magistracy with the Kingdom of Christ—which provides the pattern demanded by the arguments of Milton's political pamphlets. That is not to suggest that Vane and Milton agreed in every particular; but Milton's commendation of Vane was a recognition, not, as in the sonnets to Fairfax and Cromwell, of triumphs in arms, but of a similarity in ideas.[82] Milton shared in Vane's belief that through the exercise of just liberty the nation's troubles would "prove as shadows, ready to flee away before the morning brightness of Christ's heavenly appearance and second coming, to the bringing in of that Kingdom of his that shall never be moved."[83] And he was convinced that through the modelling of magistracy on its primitive and final perfection, "good men and God's own people might not despair of being taught by God, and enabled through his power, to grow up to that wherein, like faithful servants unto Christ, they might receive encouragement from their Lord at his coming and finding them so doing, with their loins girt and lamps burning, ready to receive him at his second appearance."[84]

That had been Milton's hope as he wrote the early pamphlets. In spite of disillusionments and the perplexing events surrounding him, it was still in his mind when he wrote the political pamphlets; and though the unsettled state of the Commonwealth made him feel, like Goodwin, that the efforts of the Fifth Monarchists to anticipate the Kingdom would lead to further chaos, the ideal pattern nevertheless remained for him, as for Vane, a fixed point of reference. As the 1650's moved towards their close, the enthusiasm of *The Tenure* diminished, and Milton must have shared Vane's increasing conviction that the time of Christ's coming was yet far distant.[85] But in his retirement in blindness, while Cromwell's rule was proving once more the futility of trusting to human power and judgment, he too turned to theological meditations in which the Kingdom had an essential place, though he was to break his silence only after Cromwell's death, and it was to be long before his speculations saw the light of day.

He was no less conscious than Vane of the imperfections of the government which had replaced monarchy: "Our constitution is what the dissensions of our time will permit, not such as were to be desired, but such as the persistent strife of wicked citizens will suffer it to be."[86] But its purpose was nevertheless the establishment of the eternal justice which is the rule of nature and the right of true human dignity. Such a purpose could not be achieved through the arbitrary will of one man, nor through the arbitrary wills of men in whom the light of nature was obscured by lust, but only through the wisdom and goodness of men who had the Kingdom within them because its laws were written in their hearts. The Royalists might argue that regal sovereignty was modelled on God's sovereignty; but "who is worthy to hold on earth a power that shall resemble the divine power, save one who, as he far excells other men, is even in wisdom and goodness likest unto God? and such a person . . . none can be but the Son of God we wait for."[87]

Meanwhile, acknowledging the mighty support of God's manifest arm and the divine guidance apparent in the triumph of his cause, the English must strive to establish and perfect a government in which God alone would rule through good men. They must fix their eyes on "that only just and rightful kingdom" under "our immortal

King," "our only King, the Root of David, . . . whose kingdom is eternal righteousness," in which their "happiness and final hopes are laid up" and which they "pray incessantly may come soon."[88] Christ alone is king. "We acknowledge him, we rejoice, and we pray that he will come as soon as may be; for he is worthy, nor is there any that is like unto him or that can follow him."[89] When that prayer should be answered, and the imperfections of things human finally removed, there would no longer be any inconsistency in appealing at once to Christian and to natural liberty, for both would be fulfilled.

5

Milton's political pamphlets are the not altogether successful attempt of an idealist, who was neither a systematic philosopher nor a practical politician, and whose perplexity was increased by the shock of blindness, to read in the chaotic events of revolution a pattern which would justify both the ways of God and of men. Through the Commonwealth he sought at once the achievement of liberty and the establishment of justice. The one he recognized as the natural right of man as a reasonable creature, the other as the law divinely given for his good. Those principles he found developed in classical theory; but the relationship between the arguments with which he supported now one and now the other in the face of distracting counsels, can be completely understood only if his thinking is seen against the fundamental pattern provided by Puritanism.

The balance between liberty and justice as it appeared in his political writings was a modification of the precarious balance between Christian liberty and reformation according to divine prescript. The natural right which he would make the foundation of civil society was the earthly expression of that condition of goodness and enlightenment whose other-worldly expression was the spiritual liberty of the Gospel. The natural justice he thought the basis of all civil law was the earthly expression of the right reason which was the spiritual law of God's own being. But as that law was perceived only imperfectly by man in his degenerate state, so men in that state were capable of exercising only a natural right limited by laws imposed from without. The full privileges of human dignity could be claimed only by those whose nature had been restored to its primitive perfection through the divine grace which renewed the original and inward law and added to natural the privileges of Christian liberty.

But the translation of that right into practical terms in a world torn by the strife of wicked men could be but imperfect. It would enjoy its complete fulfilment only with the setting up of the Kingdom ruled by Christ, which would restore human society to the perfection prevented by Adam's Fall. Yet if the good of man, both temporal and spiritual, was meanwhile to be achieved, it could only be so in a commonwealth modelled as far as possible on this divine pattern. The end of the revolution as Milton saw it was therefore the realization of the ideal not simply of a perfectly natural but of a holy community, which in a variety of forms was the purpose of the several groups of Puritans.[90]

That ideal proved impossible of achievement, for the balance between reformation and liberty could not be preserved at any point. But Milton could have asserted with Vane in 1662 that "this Cause . . . was the cause of God, and for the promoting of the Kingdom of his dear Son, Jesus Christ, wherein is comprehended our liberties and duties, both as men and as Christians."[91] Like Vane he recognized the hand of God in the work, and believed that God had chosen special instruments for its prosecution. And it seemed to him that the people's rejection of the just liberty which was offered was a rejection of God's own purposes and "against your very destiny."[92]

# *Part IV*

# *The Spirit and Liberty: the Final Pamphlets 1659-1660*

# Chapter XIII

## A Far Surpassing Light

TO the revised edition of the *Defensio* in 1658, Milton added a statement of his satisfaction with a performance beneficial not only to England "but even to men of whatever nation, and to the cause of Christendom above all," concluding with the assurance "that I am pursuing after yet greater things if my strength suffice (nay, it will if God grant), and for their sake meanwhile am taking thought and studying to make ready."[1] Among those greater things is to be numbered the epic he must already have been contemplating; but the chief place in his mind was then occupied by the work he addressed "to all who profess the Christian faith throughout the world," and described as "my best and richest possession"—his *De Doctrina Christiana*.[2]

If the immediate effect of his blindness was a feeling of impotence, his retirement from public activity in the comparative peace of the Protectorate afforded an opportunity, frequently desired during fifteen years, for an undisturbed reconsideration of his opinions.[3] The divorce tracts and the political pamphlets had handled problems which necessitated a modification of his ideas; and in the late 1650's he was engaged in taking stock of his position and preparing to make up his "true account." His beliefs in 1645 had been reasonably clear; and though his conclusions might be unusual, he could still regard his principles as fundamentally orthodox, and unhesitatingly condemn particular heresies either specifically or by implication.[4] But in 1654, the confusion of events and the hurry of business had perplexed his thinking. It is possible to discern the pattern of his thought in the political pamphlets, through reference to the divorce argument and the theories of his contemporaries, only when it is recognized that such a supply is made necessary by the bewildered and disordered reasoning with which he strove to express his convictions and to meet the shifting situation.

Even when due weight is given to the nature of his subject and to his tendency to approach it in the light of renaissance thought, a singular paucity of doctrinal arguments and condemnations of heresy is apparent in the political writings. And that is not true of theological concepts alone; appeals to first principles become progressively fewer in each pamphlet. All of Milton's controversial prose works were evoked by particular events; but that was especially the case with those forming the third group. Among them only *The Tenure* can be described as a discussion of political theory, and even it had reference to a specific event and was a refutation of a particular pamphlet. *Eikonoklastes* and the *Defensio* are page-by-page confutations of individual works. That is also the case with the two subsequent defences; but *Defensio Secunda* is even more a generalized apology for events and persons—especially for Milton himself—than an exposition of principles; and the *Defensio Pro Se* suggests a desire to avoid the consideration of principles, for in it ideas give place altogether to masses of vituperation and contemptuous wit.

There is a sharp contrast between the defences and the two pamphlets on the church which Milton published in 1659.[5] *Of Civil power in Ecclesiastical causes* and *The likeliest means to remove Hirelings out of the church* deal with specific problems of ecclesiastical organization which are less interesting than matters of state, and their English wholly lacks the magnificence of the Latin of the defences. But they are more closely and exactly reasoned than anything Milton had written since *Tetrachordon*; and they are more concise than even that work.[6] They indicate a new certainty, for in writing them Milton was more clearly aware of his position and especially of the doctrinal peculiarities to which his reasoning and experience had led him. They were in fact the product of "more maturity and longer study,"[7] more precisely, of the reconsideration of his thought required by the revision of the theological treatise casually begun in the 1640's. Their subjects and arguments occupied important places in *De Doctrina Christiana*—shortly, so Milton hoped, to be published; they dealt with matters essential to the well-being of Christians, and ought "therefore to have been written in the common language of Christendom" rather than addressed to the English alone.[8] They contain references—subsequently to be noted—to the work chiefly engaging Milton's attention, and are not merely incidental products of his meditations but brief treatments, prompted by events, of considerations involved in the larger ordering of his thought. They thus reduce to its simplest form, but not without reference to fundamental principles, the view of the church to which the attempt at reformation had led him.

The political pamphlets composed on the eve of the Restoration afford a similar account of his view of the state.[9] These also were the product of longer study, and had their relationship, though less intimately, to his theological treatise. But as he was composing them, the structure of the Commonwealth was tumbling thunderously about his ears; and they were consequently more hurriedly written and less closely reasoned than the ecclesiastical tracts. Yet they are concise since necessity reduced their arguments to the barest essentials. The pattern discernible in the earlier political writings stands revealed in them, and they provide a distinct account of his theory of civil society.

The pamphlets of 1659 and 1660 thus enable the student of Milton's development since 1641 to estimate exactly its extent. *De Doctrina Christiana* supplies a full discussion of the first principles—not always clearly defined in the controversial prose—which governed the development of his opinions and were modified to support his position at the end of the prose period.

The defences of a free church and a free commonwealth, with the systematic exposition of Christian doctrine, constitute an almost complete expression of the opinions on society at which Milton had arrived after twenty years of active, and sometimes feverish, thought. They have been said to make up his nearest approach to the description of a Utopia.[10] That is a not unacceptable view of them, so long as one remembers his increasingly painful consciousness of the inevitable imperfection of things human. The final ecclesiastical and political pamphlets expound what is necessary to be done, in Milton's opinion, as Christianity now goes; *De Doctrina Christiana* makes it clear that the Utopia of which he constantly thought had been lost with man's expulsion from Paradise, to be regained for men in society only through the establishment of Christ's Kingdom.

## 2

In the ecclesiastical pamphlets on conscience and tithes, Milton dealt with the two closely-related aspects of the central problem of the relationship between church and state which had agitated the minds of his contemporaries from the beginning of the revolution. Since 1642 he had offered no reasoned argument on the church. In the pamphlets of 1643-1645, he had been impatient with the disputes on ecclesiastical organization; but in the years between the formal acceptance of Presbyterianism by Parliament and the establishment of the Protectorate, he had frequently given brief expression to his feelings on the subject.

The events which disposed an exasperated House to pass the ordinance of March 5, 1646, for the establishment of the Presbyterian system, produced the sonnet *On the New Forcers of Conscience* with its complimentary reference to the Independents in the Assembly and its attack on the chief Presbyterian pamphleteers who desired "to force our consciences that Christ set free."[11] In May, 1652, the *Proposals* of the Committee for the Propagation of the Gospel (appointed by the Rump and dominated by moderate Independents) for the establishment of state-regulated congregationalism with a limited toleration, evoked the sonnet condemning those who were "threatening to bind our souls with secular chains," and imploring Cromwell (a member of the Committee) to

> Help us to save free conscience from the paw
> Of hireling wolves whose gospel is their maw.[12]

And the sonnet to Vane, in July of the same year, referred not only to the war with the Dutch, then in progress, but to this problem of settling "the bounds of either sword."[13]

Moreover, though the political pamphlets included no specific consideration of the church, incidental references suggest the manner in which the course of events had partly confirmed, partly modified, the opinions of the anti-episcopal tracts. Milton had reaffirmed the conviction, developed in the pamphlets of 1643-1645, that religion, when "not voluntary, becomes a sin."[14] His increasing dislike of the Scots, and the political defection of the English Presbyterians, deepened his suspicion of their discipline; and he had renounced the authority not only of the Fathers but even of reformed precedent.[15] Like those who were defending conscience against the Assembly, he had come more consistently to take the view that the church was not to be thought of as a geographical unit but as composed of particular congregations.[16] He had emphasized more heavily the exclusively spiritual nature of church discipline, and the distinction between ecclesiastical and civil power;[17] and he had asserted that the church could exercise only spiritual censure within the congregation, and that the magistrate should confine himself to civil questions.[18] Finally, in *Defensio Secunda*, he had denounced those who "in a savage rage" would compel agreement "with the sword," and who "struggle tooth and nail in defence of tithes."[19]

The advice offered Cromwell in 1654, to which reference has already been made, thus arose from Milton's firm belief in the necessity for separating the ecclesiastical and civil organizations in order to preserve spiritual freedom. And although there had been no place in the political pamphlets for a rehearsal of arguments supporting this principle, it is the conclusion of his reasoning in 1659. From that fact one can deduce his opinion of the ecclesiastical policy of the Protectorate.

In spite of Cromwell's remarkably patient tolerance, his efforts to achieve a religious settlement which would satisfy all the Puritan parties and so contribute to civil peace, constituted a rejection of Milton's advice; for ecclesiastically his government was dominated by the moderate Independents whose position, a little to the left of liberal Presbyterianism, seemed to provide the surest means to satisfaction because of its centrality. But the final collapse of Presbyterianism with the defeat of the Scots in the Second Civil War, resulted in a dissolution of the effective alliance formed against the Assembly by the Independent centre and the sectarian left. The Independent swing to the right in politics had its religious counterpart in the efforts of moderates like John Owen to meet the liberal Presbyterians in an agreement on a state church and a limited toleration which would stem the flood of heresy let loose by the controversy over conscience and by Parliament's disinclination to implement the Assembly's recommendations.[20]

The position of the conservative Independents had been outlined in their *Apologeticall Narration* of 1643 and in succeeding pamphlets.[21] They had been driven somewhat to the left by the Assembly's obstinacy and the enthusiasm of their allies; but when they offered proposals for an ecclesiastical settlement, first in 1652 on the eve of the Protectorate, and again in 1658 on the morrow of Cromwell's death, they repeated substantially their original demands, designed equally to establish reformation and to procure a limited freedom.

In spite of their earlier opposition to the Assembly, the Independents justified a limited use of civil power in religion in *The Humble Proposals . . . for the . . . Propagation of the Gospel* drawn up by the Committee appointed by the House early in 1652, and again in the *Declaration* issued after their conference at the Savoy in 1658. They were now occupying the defensive position surrendered by the

Presbyterians, and their recommendations were based only on a more liberal interpretation of the principles expressed in the *Westminster Confession.* They believed that the magistrate must be a nursing father to the church; and consequently proposed the establishment of congregationalism as the national discipline, with a ministry supported by tithes or some other civil maintenance, and commissioners appointed by parliament to approve or dismiss ministers. And though they denied that the churches themselves could exercise material power, they proposed toleration outside the establishment only for such as accepted the fundamentals of Christian religion—the doctrines of the Trinity, the Incarnation, justification by faith, the necessity of forsaking sin, the Resurrection, the Scriptures as the only certain revelation of the divine will, and the necessity of worship.[22]

With certain liberalizing variations, this was the system adopted by the government of the Protectorate both in the *Instrument of Government* in 1654 and in the *Humble Petition and Advice* in 1657. There was to be a national church, without a supreme assembly but with committees of Triers and Ejectors to supervise a ministry supported by tithes, until "a provision less subject to scruple and contention, and more certain," could be devised; and there was to be toleration for "such as profess faith in God by Jesus Christ (though differing in judgment from the doctrine, worship, or discipline publicly held forth), . . . so as they abuse not this liberty to the civil injury of others, and to the actual disturbance of the public peace on their parts; provided this liberty be not extended to popery or prelacy, nor to such as, under the profession of Christ, hold forth and practise licentiousness."[23]

The continuous efforts of the conservatives to define more exactly the limits of toleration and the fundamentals of belief, and of the extremists to achieve a freedom even greater than the Protector would allow, cannot be considered here.[24] But in the disputes over the establishment are still to be distinguished the levels in the theory of toleration which were apparent in 1644 and 1645. Presbyterians like Prynne were still demanding the establishment of a strict system, with civil maintenance and no toleration.[25] Moderate Independents like Owen and Thomas Goodwin were reasonably satisfied, though they desired more precise limitations to freedom.[26] Even some of those who, like the Baptist Samuel Richardson, had vigorously attacked the Assembly for restraining conscience, were defending the Protector's policy as the broadest compatible with peace.[27] But more extreme Independents like John Goodwin denounced his partial subjection of the church to the state as a source of future danger.[28] And the sectarians of the left wing—among them the Levellers, the extremer Baptists, the Fifth Monarchists, and Roger Williams, lately come once more from Rhode Island to have a hand in redressing the balance of both worlds—clamoured for free conscience, the abolition of all civil maintenance, and the complete severance of the ecclesiastical from the civil organization.[29]

Because of Cromwell's comparative tolerance and the administrative connivance which permitted an uncertain and illegal but broad freedom to the sectaries (and even to Anglicans, Roman Catholics, and Jews), the centre of the ecclesiastical dispute had shifted from freedom of conscience to freedom from state-imposed tithes; but the one involved the other since both concerned the right of the church to claim support from the magistrate, and his authority to exercise civil power in religious matters on its behalf. The controversy had subsided somewhat with the decline of Presbyterian influence and the appearance of pressing political problems after the execution of the King; but it continued intermittently throughout the Protectorate. The question of tithes, agitated from time to time during the early years of the revolution, became intensified in 1652 and 1653, when the Rump and, after it, the Nominated Parliament attempted to settle the church, and again from 1657 to 1659, during the Protector's last parliament, the brief sitting of Richard's, and the early months of the restored Rump.[30] In the midst of the first, Milton composed the sonnets to Cromwell and Vane. In the intervening years he had offered only incidental comments; and since 1654—though others were attacking the Protector's policy with Williams and Goodwin—he had remained silent in the encompassing darkness. But the second outburst of controversy was the occasion of the two pamphlets on the church. By implication they condemned Cromwell's policy; they were refutations of the arguments for an establishment advanced by Prynne and the Presbyterians, and by the *Proposals* of the Independents;[31] and they presented the view of the church held by the Puritans of the extreme left.

## 3

Much of Milton's reasoning in 1659 was a repetition of ideas already employed in the anti-episcopal tracts; but it now supported a theory of the church much more like Williams' than like the Smectymnuans'. Indeed, his reasoning on conscience closely paralleled the argument of *The Bloudy Tenent*, and on tithes, of *The*

*Hireling Ministry.* The course of events had convinced him that no peaceful settlement could be achieved until the ecclesiastical and the political were rigorously separated, and therefore he now presented the prime argument of sectarianism with much more clarity than in 1645: "then both commonwealth and religion will at length, if ever, flourish in Christendom, when either they who govern discern between civil and religious, or they only who so discern shall be admitted to govern. Till then nothing but troubles, persecutions, commotions can be expected; the inward decay of true religion among ourselves, and the utter overthrow at last by a common enemy."[32]

The efforts of the Presbyterians, and then the Independents, to achieve the establishment of their versions of the one right discipline, had taught him to abandon at least partially that interpretation of divine precept, to reject the magistrate's assistance, and to conclude with the sectarian critics of Independency that discipline was "not so plainly expressed as to leave the conscientious without dispute and difference thereupon, nor so collected into one book as to convince that God now under the Gospel so exactly enjoined church government as he did under the Law."[33] He could agree that "Independency" described "the true freedom of Christian doctrine and church discipline subject to no superior judge but God only";[34] but he believed that "independence and state-hire in religion can never consist long or certainly together," since civil authorities less sympathetic to liberty will support only those who agree with them, and "any law against conscience is alike in force against any conscience," perhaps to be cited in future even against those who erect it.[35]

Milton's final position was thus, not that the civil power must overthrow disciplines contrary to Scripture and establish the right, but that it must secure freedom from the tyranny of error for those who were moved to submit themselves to the divinely authorized government. This was substantially the argument rehearsed by Burton in 1642, and the similarity has its significance. He had not abandoned the idea of divine institution; but he had come to emphasize both its authority and its requisite freedom, and he had adopted without reservation the theory of independent and voluntary congregations. In its larger sense, the church "is the whole people of God"; it is "universal, not tied to nation, diocese, or parish, but consisting of many particular churches complete in themselves, gathered not by compulsion or the accident of dwelling nigh together, but by free consent choosing both their particular church and their church officers"; and these congregations can exercise discipline "on them only who have willingly joined themselves in that covenant of union."[36]

This theory of gathered churches—common to the Puritans of the left, and written into the programmes of Baptists, Levellers, and Millenarians—was a product of the individualism which issued from a complete acceptance of the Protestant doctrine of the direct relationship between the soul and God and the essential spirituality of Christian religion. In Milton's last ecclesiastical writings the convictions which had modified the position of Young in the early tracts received their full weight, to an extent even greater than in the pamphlets on conscience. He rejected both tithes and the restraint of conscience, and indeed all civil control of the churches, on the ground that religion is exclusively the spiritual concern of the individual.

The four reasons produced against the exercise of civil power in ecclesiastical causes—that Scripture is the only rule of faith, that the magistrate has no right of religious judgment, that in claiming it he violates the privileges of the Gospel, that such ends as he may propose cannot thus be achieved—were merely variations of this basic principle. "First it cannot be denied, being the main foundation of our protestant religion, that we of these ages, having no other divine rule or authority from without us warrantable to one another as a common ground but the Holy Scripture, and no other within us but the illumination of the Holy Spirit so interpreting that Scripture as warrantable only to ourselves and to such whose consciences we can so persuade, can have no other ground in matters of religion but only from the Scriptures."[37]

The emphasis on Scripture here is more than the argument of the early pamphlets concerning its authority, for to that has been added the positive assertion that it can be interpreted only according to the divine illumination within the believer, so that "no man or body of men in these times can be the infallible judges or determiners in matters of religion to any other men's consciences but their own." The original protestation against the imperial edicts of Charles V is thus firmly extended to its extreme to deny, not only tradition and patristic testimony, but all external authority whatsoever, in favour of the full right of individual religious judgment: "neither traditions, councils, nor canons of any visible church, much less edicts of any magistrate or civil session, but the Scripture only can be the final judge or rule in matters of religion, and that only in the conscience of every Christian to himself."[38]

That principle, somewhat less definitely stated, had its place in the early pamphlets. It was indeed (as has already been remarked) generally accepted in theory even by the Puritans of the right, and by Hobbes. Both A. S. and Rutherford admitted that punishment could not correct the conscience since faith and election depended on God alone; and Hobbes (with his eye on Rome rather than on Puritanism) had observed that "conscience is not subject to compulsion or constraint" and that "faith is the gift of God, which man can neither give, nor take away by promise of rewards, or menaces of torture."[39] But the Presbyterians argued that God's truth and glory must be defended against false teachings and irreligious actions arising from corrupt consciences; and Hobbes had denied civil power to the church only to make the civil sovereign absolutely supreme in religious as in secular matters.[40]

At this point *Of Civil Power* marks an advance even beyond the assertions of the *Areopagitica*, for it defines "matters of religion" in a way which includes not merely the inward man and things indifferent but outward acts and fundamentals: "such things as belong chiefly to the knowledge and service of God, and are either above the reach and light of nature without revelation from above, and therefore liable to be variously understood by human reason, or such things as are enjoined or forbidden by divine precept, which else by the light of reason would seem indifferent to be done or not done, and so likewise must needs appear to every man as the precept is understood."[41] Men must not be molested either "for belief or practice in religion according to this conscientious persuasion"; both doctrine and discipline are the proper concern of the church alone, which "deals only with the inward man and his actions, which are all spiritual and to outward force not liable"; things indifferent (as the Savoy *Declaration* had said) may not "for that very cause by the magistrate be commanded"; but further, even the revealed fundamentals must be left to conscience since divine prescript may be variously interpreted.[42]

In thus defining matters of conscience, Milton went beyond Independency and appeared to adopt the position set forth by those who demanded complete religious liberty, notably by Williams in *The Bloudy Tenent*. Such beliefs and actions as flow "from the work of divine grace" upon the will and understanding,[43] were to be distinguished from those governed merely by the light of nature. And the pamphlets of 1659 made that the basis of a further distinction, not clearly applied in the writings of 1641 and 1645, but essential to the theory of religious liberty.

Milton once more defined the interest and power of the church as wholly spiritual. "We read not that Christ ever exercised force but once, and that was to drive prophane ones out of his temple, not to force them in. . . ."[44] The church's extremest power is therefore spiritual censure, which "proceeds only to a separation from the rest, proceeds never to any corporal enforcement or forfeiture of money."[45] It cannot employ any further measures against those who are excommunicate, nor can it take action against those not voluntarily under its rule. The seduction of believers by false prophets is to be prevented only "by fit and proper means ordained in church discipline; by instant and powerful demonstration to the contrary; by opposing truth to error, no unequal match. . . ."[46] To employ force in matters ecclesiastical "is no service to Christ or his kingdom, but rather a disparagement, and degrades it from a divine and spiritual kingdom to a kingdom of this world, which he denies it to be. . . ."[47]

This definition does not differ materially from the assertions of the early pamphlets; but to it Milton now added a definition of the sphere and power of the magistrate which confined him to civil and excluded him from religious things. If the church cannot employ force against error, much less can he; for he has no rule of judgment beyond that possessed by every Christian, and so "cannot infallibly determine to the conscience without convincement"; and his power is of a kind altogether different from that to which believers willingly submit themselves in congregations.[48] "To distinguish rightly between civil power and ecclesiastical" is essential to the proper ordering of both church and state.[49] "Christ hath a government of his own, sufficient of itself to all his ends and purposes in governing his church"; and the magistrate is therefore not to make himself "supreme lord or pope of the church as far as his civil jurisdiction stretches, and all the ministers of God therein, his ministers or curates," for that is "to rule by civil power things to be ruled only by spiritual." It is true that his power is from God; that is proved by *Romans* 13. But "many are the ministers of God, and their offices no less different than many; none more different than state and church government"; and what God has severed man may not join.[50]

Milton's reasoning in *Of Civil Power* is almost an abstract of the arguments (already discussed) which Williams and Goodwin repeated in their writings under the Protectorate. Like them, he had forsaken reformation in favour of liberty and virtually sacrificed absolute and revealed truth to uncontrolled individualism in religion. If religion is "our belief and practice depending upon God only"—or more precisely on the individual's reading of the light within him—it follows that there can be no discrimination against men for religious opinions or their absence, for "force neither instructs in religion nor begets repentance or amendment of life, but on the contrary hardness of heart, formality, hypocrisy, and . . . every way increase of sin."[51] There can consequently be in religion no imposition of external discipline or external authority, whether ecclesiastical or civil.[52]

By the argument for voluntary belief and church association, proving that "the settlement of religion belongs only to each particular church by persuasive and spiritual means within itself," and that "every true Christian . . . hath the word of God before him, the promised Holy Spirit, and the mind of Christ within him," Milton thus disposed, like Williams, of Presbyterians, Independents, and Erastians alike, and took his place, without reservations, among the Puritan extremists.[53]

## 4

Against tithes he produced precisely the same argument. They symbolized the corruption of Christianity by worldliness which set in even before Constantine; indeed any form of civil maintenance for the clergy seemed bound to "suspend the church wholly upon the state, and turn her ministers into state pensioners."[54] He recognized with Williams that "for the magistrate in person of a nursing father to make the church his mere ward . . . and so by his examinant committees to circumscribe her free election of ministers," inevitably meant that he could subject her "to his political drifts or conceived opinions by mastering her revenue." This was to erect over her a head other than Christ, "a human on a heavenly, a carnal on a spiritual, a political head on an ecclesiastical body."[55] Here again the separation of the spiritual and the secular operated with radical consequences: "if Christ the master hath professed his kingdom to be not of this world, it suits not with that profession either in him or his ministers to claim temporal right from spiritual respects."[56]

By his view of the ministry, even more than by his view of conscience, Milton now associated himself with the sectaries of the left, for he denounced not only civil maintenance but any supervision (outside the particular congregation) which would formally distinguish the ministry from the laity. The anti-clerical tendencies of the early pamphlets reach their final conclusion in his description of gathered churches, taught by a ministry dependent on alms and its own secular occupations for support, and reproducing the evangelical conditions recorded in the *Acts*. Congregations in cities will support their own ministers; and for the gathering of churches in the country-side and among the poor, other ministers will engage in "itinerary preaching," supported by gifts and the contributions of richer churches. When they have gathered a church and taught it for a year or two "all the points of religion necessary to salvation," they will create elders to teach and govern, and pass on elsewhere, leaving the flock "to meet and edify one another whether in church or chapel, or . . . in a house or barn."[57] Thus the Gospel will be spread as in the beginning, with no forced maintenance from the state; for if no other support should be available, the true preacher will live, like St. Paul, by the work of his own hands.[58]

Like his argument for free conscience, Milton's contentions in *The Likeliest Means* depend upon the spiritual quality of faith, and further on the equality of all believers. Here also the principles expressed in the early pamphlets are pushed to the extreme conclusions already reached by the sects. As William Dell had argued the need "to make void the distinction of clergy and laity among Christians," since "all Christians, through the baptism of the Spirit, are made priests alike unto God, and every one hath right and power alike to speak the word," so Milton said that there would be no danger from hirelings "if Christians would but know their own dignity, their liberty, their adoption, and let it not be wondered if I say, their spiritual priesthood, whereby they have all equally access to any ministerial function whenever called by their own abilities and the church, though they never came near commencement or university."[59] A "distinct order," accepted in 1642, is now completely rejected in favour of a ministry given by God and chosen by the churches "out of all sorts and orders of men; for the Gospel makes no difference from the magistrate himself to the meanest artificer, if God evidently favour him with spiritual gifts, as he can easily and oft hath done. . . ."[60] Moreover, because "the inward sense of his calling and spiritual ability" is alone sufficient to make a minister, even the qualifications whereby Origen was justified in preaching though unordained, are now utterly repudiated.[61]

The plainness of the Gospel which served in the anti-episcopal tracts to prove the evident necessity for the erection of the one right discipline, now shows that virtually no discipline is necessary, and that no supervision of ministerial qualifications is justified. Because the Scriptures are "translated into every vulgar tongue, as being held, in main matters of belief and salvation, plain and easy to the poorest," and because "such no less than their teachers have the Spirit to guide them in all truth," little training is required for preaching.[62] Consequently, the attack on hirelings is coupled, as in the early pamphlets, with an attack on corrupt and unnecessary learning, and especially on "those theological disputations" in the universities which "perplex and leaven pure doctrine with scholastical trash."[63] "It is a fond error . . . to think that the university makes a minister of the Gospel";[64] "to speak freely, it were much better there were not one divine in the university; no school divinity known, the idle sophistry of monks, the canker of religion; and that they who intended to be ministers were trained up in the church only, by the Scripture, and in the original languages thereof at school; without fetching the compass of other arts and sciences, more than what they can well learn at secondary leisure and at home."[65]

This is in part a repetition of the contempt for scholasticism which the younger Milton shared with the Christian rationalists. Falkland had said that "in the Scripture . . . all that is necessary is clear"; Chillingworth had made its plainness his chief argument against Rome, and had condemned those who spent "an age in weaving and unweaving subtle cobwebs, fitter to catch flies than souls"; Taylor had observed that "God had made the way to heaven plain and simple, and what was necessary did lie open" until "the easy commandment" was "wrapped up in uneasy learning."[66] Cudworth had told the Parliament in 1647 that "the way to heaven that Christ has taught us is plain and easy," though spiritual truths require "a divine light within, to irradiate and shine upon them."[67]

But Cudworth had also urged Parliament "to promote ingenious learning, and cast a favourable influence upon it." "I mean not that only which furnisheth the pulpit, which you seem to be very mindful of, but that which is more remote from such popular use, in the several kinds of it, which yet are all of them, both very subservient to religion and useful to the commonwealth"; for "these raised improvements of our natural understandings may be as well subservient and subordinate to a divine light in our minds as the natural use of these outward creatures here below to the life of God in our hearts."[68] Milton's recommendations on the contrary repudiate the evaluation of learning expressed in the *Areopagitica* and *Of Education*, and strangely reflect the sectarian demand for a wholly practical education and for a ministry dependent, not on learning, which "is but the tradition of men," but on the inner light.[69]

The educational controversy had increased in intensity, like the dispute over tithes with which it was closely associated, in 1653 and again in 1657 and 1659.[70] The contamination of spiritual truth by worldliness of which state-maintenance was the most obvious form, could be discerned in the university requirements which subjected the clergy to a training in human and, what was worse, philosophical learning. Under the Protectorate, the rejection of human traditions and the attack on Aristotelianism thus combined to produce violent criticisms of established educational institutions from the pens of sectarian reformers, like William Dell and John Webster, who joined a materialistic and utilitarian theory of human knowledge with the sectarian emphasis on the exclusively spiritual quality of faith.

Webster could quote Bacon to distinguish natural from spiritual truth.[71] He argued that "the whole Scripture was given that man might be brought to the full and absolute abnegation of all his wit, reason, will, desires, strength, wisdom, righteousness, and all human glory and excellencies whatsoever," and at the same time that education should be made practical and experimental in order to achieve "good, politic, useful and profitable" ends. He maintained that, because spiritual knowledge was "merely the fruit of grace" and unattainable "by the wit, power, and industry of man," it was impossible to teach more than the letter of Scriptural languages, which kills without "the true original tongue, the language of the heavenly Canaan," the voice of the Spirit alone.[72] Dell likewise demanded the establishment of practical schools in every city; and emphasized the spiritual capacities of plain and unlearned men, on the ground that "there needs nothing to the ministry of the New Testament but only God's pouring out his spirit," and that the Gospel "is not only contrary to the philosophical divinity of the schools and university, and the common carnal religion of the nation, but doth also reprove and condemn them."[73]

Roger Williams had once more given expression to this sectarian distinction between learning and spiritual enlightenment in *The Hireling Ministry*. He had said that "natural and unspiritual" men, however learned, cannot perceive "the things of God"; and that "no man ever did nor ever shall truly go forth to convert the nations, nor to prophesy in the present state of witnesses against Antichrist, but by the gracious inspiration and instigation of the Holy Spirit of God. . . ."[74] While he did not deny that "human learning and the knowledge of languages and good arts are excellent, and excel outward gifts as far as light excels darkness, and therefore that schools of human learning ought to be maintained in a due way and cherished," he nevertheless asserted that "they will be found to be none of Christ's." Not those "seminaries of hirelings and mystical merchants," but "the churches and assemblies of the saints" are "the only schools of the prophets appointed by Christ Jesus."[75]

Milton's argument in *The Likeliest Means* reproduced this point of view exactly. Though he was careful to remark that he did not speak "in contempt of learning" or dispute what the university might "conduce to other arts and sciences,"[76] the emphatic assertion that men have equally "the Spirit to guide them in all truth" takes the place of his view of education as primarily designed to repair the ruins of our first parents; and the principle of segregation as applied by the sectaries is now employed to refute those who defend tithes because they think "the knowledge of Christian religion harder than any other art or science to attain."[77]

In Milton's opinion it is "far easier, both of itself, and in regard of God's assisting spirit, not particularly promised us to the attainment of any other knowledge, but of this only. . . ." Those who first preached the Gospel, and like them the first reformers, were "otherwise unlearned men." Such "spiritual knowledge and sanctity of life" as they possessed are therefore sufficient for the ministry. In 1659, for the first but not for the last time, St. Paul is quoted to show that God "never sent us for ministers to the schools of philosophy, but rather bids us beware of such 'vain deceit,' *Col.* 2. 8."[78]

Milton now deems necessary for Christianity only such learning as "may as easily and less chargeably be had in any private house"—like his own—as at the university. But "the land would be soon better civilized" if the state diverted the funds improperly given to the church, "to erect in greater number all over the land schools and competent libraries to those schools, where languages and arts may be taught free together"; "those public foundations may be so instituted as the youth therein may be at once brought up to a competence of learning and to an honest trade; and the hours of teaching so ordered as their study may be no hindrance to their labour or other calling." Thus a spiritual ministry would arise, unhindered by worldly considerations; for while it is counted "the reproach of this age that tradesmen preach the Gospel," it would be well if ministers "were all tradesmen; they would not then so many of them, for want of another trade, make a trade of their preaching. . . ."[79]

In these opinions one recognizes echoes both of the proposals of empiricists like Petty and of the complaints of those who demanded spiritual freedom and considered Independent, no less than Presbyterian, churches to be without the true mark, the preaching of God's word only: "For judge you, had they the Spirit of God as they pretend, would they need, as they do, when they have resolved to speak to you from a text of Scripture, to go sit in their studies three or four days together turning over those authors that have written thereupon and beating their own brains to find out the meaning and true intent thereof? No certainly; had they the Spirit of God, it would in an instant, in the twinkling of an eye, inform them the meaning of his own writings."[80] It might have been observed of Milton's pamphlets, as of this sectarian attack, "It seems there are church-Levellers as well as state."[81] He likewise believed that, besides the illumination of the Spirit, few helps were necessary "to make more easy the attainment of Christian religion by the meanest: the entire Scripture translated into English with plenty of notes; and somewhere or other, I trust, may be found some wholesome body of divinity, as they call it, without school terms and metaphysical notions, which have obscured rather than explained our religion, and made it seem difficult without cause."[82]

On just such a body of divinity he was himself at work in his retirement.[83] That fact suggests one of the causes of the view of religion presented in the pamphlets of 1659; for he was not only, as in the anti-episcopal tracts, a layman engaged in doctrinal studies, but he was peculiarly dependent on "an inward and far surpassing light."[84]

## 5

The account of his blindness which Milton offered in *Defensio Secunda* in refutation of the gibes of detractors was composed by one only recently afflicted and still half-inclined merely to stand and wait. The insistence on divine guidance with which this defence opens, and the repeated assurance that "I neither believe nor have found that God is angry," clearly resulted from his need to free himself from a sense of heaven's desertion. It would be difficult to exaggerate the dispiriting effect of blindness in middle age on one "devoted even from a child to the more humanizing studies."[85] Milton overcame despondency; but he could do so only by fixing the eye of his mind on the divine spark within himself. "Why, in truth," he wrote in 1657, "should I not bear gently the deprivation of sight, when I may hope that it is not so much lost as revoked and retracted inwards, for the sharpening rather than the blunting of my mental edge?"[86]

His accomplishments after 1652 were courageously magnificent; but he was dependent for the materials of thought upon memory and the mechanical assistance of others. At its chief entrance, wisdom was quite shut out; the book of knowledge had become a universal blank, the works of men and nature expunged and razed. From the inconvenient assistance of others he freed himself as much as possible, and utterly rejected the support of human testimony; memory spoke with a voice like that of the eternal Spirit, who sends his seraphim to touch with hallowed fire the lips of whom he pleases. The pamphlets of 1659 heavily emphasize Scripture and the Spirit as the only sources of faith because Milton himself had necessarily turned in the reconsideration of his thought to God's word illuminated by the celestial light.

The intensification of convictions apparent throughout his prose, and the similarity between his conclusions and the tenets of the extreme sectaries, arose from that fact of his experience. If he never underwent precisely the spiritual conversion on which the Puritan extremists based their mystical doctrines, he did have an experience which deepened the feeling of inspiration he enjoyed in the composition of his poems. The complete rejection of merely human wisdom in things spiritual to which Williams came in the isolation of colonial America, and the Bedford tinker because learning had been denied him, Milton finally adopted in the solitude of physical darkness. The view of Christian religion presented in 1659 was a defence of the illumination, now for him of exclusive significance, of which he had written thirty years before in describing the announcement of the Nativity "as well to the shepherds of Bethlehem by angels, as to the eastern wise men by that star. . . ."[87]

Yet if the sense of inspiration was the source of Milton's sublime independence, it carried with it a conviction of special calling which begot his lofty pride and issued in reservations yet to be considered. The arguments of the last ecclesiastical pamphlets constitute a demand for unrestricted liberty (especially in *Of Civil Power*) and for complete equality (especially in *The Likeliest Means*) in matters of religion. The ideas which had in the anti-episcopal pamphlets the effect of liberalizing Young's position were now pushed to an ultimate extreme; but it is nevertheless true that the conclusions which suggest Williams were yet modified by restraining limitations. The liberty and equality of which Milton wrote were Gospel privileges belonging to Christians, not to all men; and the levelling process was still confined within certain bounds.

# *Chapter XIV*

## *Of Christian Liberty*

IN the debates of the Council of Officers at Whitehall in December, 1648, on the reserve in religion to be included in the *Agreement of the People,* Colonel Sir Hardress Waller observed in exasperation "that it was the question, it is the question, and it will be the question to the ending of the world, whether the magistrate have any power at all in matters of religion, and what that power is."[1] In spite of their apparent lucidity, Milton's last ecclesiastical pamphlets provide for that enigma an answer no more conclusive than was reached in the Whitehall dispute which ranged the Levellers and sectaries against the moderate Independents.[2]

The exact significance of his recommendations can be determined only in the light of the arguments which support them. First in importance among these is the argument from the abrogation of the Jewish Law which had a minor place in the anti-episcopal tracts, occupied the centre of his reasoning on divorce, and was now applied to tithes and to conscience. Among both the orthodox and the unorthodox, this was the chief ground of the theological concept which Milton designates as the subject of his two pamphlets: "Of civil liberty I have written heretofore by the appointment and not without the approbation of civil power; of Christian liberty I write now. . . ."[3]

The distinction between the old and the new dispensations developed in *Tetrachordon* is precisely defined in 1659:

> The state of religion under the Gospel is far differing from what it was under the Law: then was the state of rigour, childhood, bondage, and works, to all which force was not unbefitting; now is the state of grace, manhood, freedom, and faith, to all which belongs willingness and reason, not force; the Law was then written on tables of stone, and to be performed according to the letter, willingly or unwillingly; the Gospel, our new covenant, upon the heart of every believer, to be interpreted only by the sense of charity and inward persuasion; the Law had no distinct government or governors of

church and commonwealth, but the priests and Levites judged in all causes, not ecclesiastical only but civil . . . , which under the Gospel is forbidden to all church ministers. . . .[4]

In this contrast is implicit the whole of Milton's view of the Christian church and its relation to the magistrate.

Its application to a system of maintenance modelled on the Jewish and defended by appeals to Mosaic example, is self-evident. According to Milton's reasoning, tithes were part of the ceremonial law, admitted by all to be abrogated under the Gospel. Whereas the Law commanded their payment, God left the maintenance of the Christian ministry "to charity and Christian freedom," according to "that difference which he hath manifestly put between those his two great dispensations."[5] In this respect the difference lies chiefly in the contrast between the Mosaic orders of priesthood and the Gospel ministry of presbyters and deacons; and more especially in the fact that "the priesthood of Aaron typified a better reality . . . , signifying the Christian true and holy priesthood, to offer up spiritual sacrifice." Under the ceremonial law the Israelites were a mere laity; but Christians are "now under Christ a royal priesthood . . . , as we are coheirs, kings, and priests with him, a priest for ever after the order or manner of Melchisedec."[6]

Given Milton's view of the church, this argument—and with it the assertion that Christ "hath freed us by our union with himself from all compulsive tributes and taxes in his church"[7]—is perfectly appropriate. That the labourer should be rewarded is "of moral and perpetual right"; but the ceremonial example of Moses is not therefore to be made the ground of civil compulsion in a church which consists exclusively of voluntary members. To force maintenance from those who have willingly joined, or to prevent them from supporting ministers of their choice, is to deny the voluntary nature of their association and "to violate Christian liberty." To force maintenance from those who have not willingly joined, or to support out of public funds ministers not chosen by the people, is clearly unjust. Tithes therefore "can stand neither with the people's right nor with Christian liberty."[8]

Milton thus consistently applied to the question of maintenance, which properly concerned Christians alone, the principle of the segregation of the spiritual and the natural, the contrast between the Law and the Gospel, and the argument from Christian liberty. That contrast was also his chief argument in *Of Civil Power*; and it is here that his thinking must be submitted to a rigorous test. As

Williams perceived, the argument from the abrogation of the Law and from Christian liberty is not sufficient for a theory of full religious freedom without the unrestricted application of the principle of segregation.

The Whitehall debates provide an excellent illustration of this fact and of the complexity of Milton's subject; for in the course of that dispute over the magistrate's power and duty in religion, the several problems to be solved by a theory of religious freedom were sharply posed. All those present—moderate Independents, Levellers, and divines sympathetic to sectarianism—believed with Ireton that the magistrate could not "bind men's judgments," that "he hath not power to conclude your inward, but only your outward man."[9] Yet agreement on the extent of his power over actions foundered on the interpretation of "matters of religion," the definition of "civil and natural," and the difference between compulsive, restrictive, and defensive power.[10] Each of these problems is involved in *Of Civil Power*, and each had an intimate connection with the relationship between the Law and the Gospel.

Ireton introduced this relationship to the consideration of the Whitehall conference by citing Israel as a proper model for the Commonwealth. He did not produce it, like the Presbyterians, in defence of a compulsive power in the magistrate through which men should be forced to accept the rulings of an established church; but he argued that, as the Jewish magistrate was commanded to restrain from false worship even those who were not Jews (though being careful not to force them into the Jewish church), so the Christian magistrate must restrain erroneous and sinful outward acts of religion, though refraining from attempts to compel to true: "it hath been the practice of magistrates in all the time of the Old Testament, till the coming of Christ in the flesh, to restrain such things"; "and therefore what was a rule of duty to them . . . should be a rule and duty of magistrates now."[11]

This argument had been presented continuously (with more or less liberal variations) in the pamphlets of moderate divines like Owen and Milton's former Smectymnuan colleague, Stephen Marshall; it was supported at Whitehall by the Independent Philip Nye.[12] But to those on the left it seemed to differ little from the position set forth in the twenty-third chapter of the *Westminster Confession*;[13] for even when it was limited to the restraint of actions contrary to the fundamentals of Christian religion, it accorded the magistrate a right of judgment and a disciplinary power which might be used against the sectaries and might produce another religious tyranny.

In the Whitehall dispute John Goodwin met it by the arguments already illustrated from the writings of Roger Williams. He pointed out that "the magistracy of the Old Testament was appointed, instituted and directed by God himself," while "the magistracy under the Gospel is chosen by men, and they are vested with that power which they have from men." They can consequently act only in human matters, the power of the Jewish magistrate in religion being reproduced by the spiritual power of the church alone; for "the land of Canaan, and indeed all things in it, . . . was typical . . . of the churches of Christ under the Gospel, of the purity of them and holiness of them."[14]

Goodwin was supported in this by Wildman and the Levellers, by the radical divines, and by Thomas Collier, who said that the magistrate might meddle with matters of religion if he "hath his power from divine institution, and so hath his power from God and not from the Agreement of the People"; but that he must in fact allow complete religious freedom, even to idolatry, because "the law of the Jews is not binding to us under the Gospel."[15] He might claim a right, said other radicals, to interpose "between man and man . . . ; but as between God and man he hath not"; and therefore he must not "restrain men professing their consciences before God, while they walk orderly according to civil peace and honesty."[16] As *The Leveller* of 1659 put it, he might not concern himself with either "the inward truth of men's religion" or with their worship, but only with outward acts of morality, influenced, it is true, by faith, but "plainly evil without the divine light of truths that are only revealed."[17]

That distinction is included in Milton's definition of religion in *Of Civil Power*; indeed, all the sectarian arguments are represented in that tract. With Williams, he now repudiated the example of the reforming kings of Judah; for Moses "did all by immediate divine direction," and the Jewish rulers "might have recourse . . . to divine inspiration, which our magistrates under the Gospel have not." They might enforce obedience to "that national and strict enjoined worship of God," since they "had a commonwealth by him delivered them, incorporated with a national church, exercised more in bodily than in spiritual worship, so as that the church might be called a commonwealth and the whole commonwealth a church; nothing of which can be said of Christianity. . . ."[18]

That institution typified the spiritual church, and came to an end with Christ. Therefore the magistrate could no longer claim to be "*custos utriusque tabulae*, keeper of both tables"; for, argued Milton, no matter to what degree the first (concerning God) and the second (concerning one's neighbour) are morally binding to Christians, they "give magistrates no authority to force either."[19] Their sphere is limited to "civil and moral things, the settling of things just, things honest, . . . and the repressing of their contraries determinable by the common light of nature."[20] To go beyond that limit might be to "force the Holy Ghost, and against that wise forewarning of Gamaliel, fight against God."[21]

Up to this point Milton's arguments are those of the Puritan left; and they support a theory of religious liberty broader than that of moderate Independency or of his own early pamphlets. The conscience is altogether free; and the civil power cannot deal with outward acts not defined by the light of nature. Included in this category are such indifferent things as marriage (and presumably divorce), the particular day to be set aside for worship, and the amount to be contributed for the maintenance of the ministry.[22] These involve moral duties, best performed according to religion, which were governed under Moses by external laws now abrogated in favour of the free dictates of conscience according to laws written in the heart. But the reservation also included the very fundamentals of Christian doctrine, revealed by God only; for the rules, either of faith or morals, implied by Christianity, must arise from the inward spirit which cannot be forced.

Such a view should have produced a theory of complete religious liberty. Whether it did or not depended, not only on the definition of Christianity, but on the interpretation of "civil and moral" and of "nature."

## 2

Like the sectaries, Milton had come to recognize the insuperable difficulties in the way of achieving a definition of divine truth which would be acceptable to all: "the church itself cannot, much less the state, settle or impose one tittle of religion upon our obedience implicit, but can only recommend or propound it to our free and conscientious examination. . . ."[23] If God's revelation was thus capable of various interpretations according to individual conscience, the problem of heresy, which had agitated the minds of the Independents hardly less than of the Presbyterians, immediately ceased to exist; for it is difficult to see how heresy can be defined if truth is indefinable.

Presbyterians like Thomas Edwards had maintained that, because "ministers and synods in their interpretations and decisions going according to the word of God which is infallible, judge infallibly," any contrary opinion was heretical, and could not be tolerated.[24] The Independents at the Savoy, though declaring that conscience could not be forced, had defined the Christian fundamentals and asserted that the magistrate must be careful "that men of corrupt minds and conversations do not licentiously publish and divulge blasphemy and errors in their own nature, subverting the faith and inevitably destroying the souls of them that receive them."[25]

Both accepted such a definition of heresy as was offered by the great Congregationalist, Ames:

> To make a man a heretic . . . , it is required: 1. that he be such an one as makes some profession of Christianity. . . . 2. It is required secondly that the error which he holds be not only contrary to the doctrine which is contained in the Scriptures, but that it be contrary to that doctrine which belongs to the sum and substance of faith and manners. . . . 3. It is required thirdly that the error which he holds be joined with stubbornness and obstinacy. . . . Such an one is to be accounted stubborn as, when the truth is not only manifestly revealed in Scripture but is also sufficiently propounded and manifested unto him, yet doth so adhere to his error that he either opposeth himself to the plain Scripture and will not, through the naughtiness of his mind, perceive the sense of it, for he is obstinate which is not ready to captivate all his understanding and reason unto the Scripture.[26]

In the orthodox sense a heretic was thus one who wilfully refused to accept what was assumed to be the plain teaching of Scripture on fundamentals.

With both the *Westminster Confession* and the *Savoy Declaration* in mind, Milton disposed of this basis for compulsion by asserting that heresy in the Greek "is no word of evil note, meaning only the choice or following of any opinion, good or bad, in religion or any other learning; and thus not only in heathen authors, but in the New Testament itself without censure or blame." It signified "choice only of one opinion before another, which may be without discord," so long as persecution does not force divisions.[27]

This was substantially the view taken by the radicals. Williams perceived that the orthodox definition—whether in old or new England—meant a perpetuation of ecclesiastical tyranny; and he therefore argued from 1 *Timothy* 1. 4, that "this Greek word 'heretic' is no more in true English . . . than an obstinate and wilful person in the church of Crete striving and contending about those unprofitable questions and genealogies," not one who conscientiously differs from the received interpretation of fundamentals.[28] Goodwin likewise asked (with reference to the proposed ordinance of 1646 for preventing the spread of heresy[29]), "The Scriptures not having clearly determined or defined what is erroneous or heretical in many (if not in the most) of the particulars mentioned in the said ordinance, who, or of what capacity or interest, ought they to be that are meet to be constituted judges or determiners of such cases and questions? . . . Or who have any power or authority from God to appoint judges in such cases as they please?"[30]

Among the radicals, this view of divine truth and of heresy merely as differing opinion on matters for which no absolute definition was available, together with the belief in the Spirit as the exclusive source of faith and in the sole responsibility of the individual conscience, produced a demand for absolute religious freedom. Goodwin denied that either church or magistrate could employ "any degree of severity against blasphemers, seducers, heretics, erroneous persons . . . simply as such"; and in his later pamphlets echoed Williams' assertion of liberty for all men, whatever their beliefs, for Jews, pagans, Turks, and papists.[31]

In *Of Civil Power*, Milton approached this position; but he did not quite reach it. There is a second definition of heresy which is more limited than the first and requires careful analysis. It introduced the boundary of truth beyond which Milton was not prepared to go: "In apostolic times therefore, ere the Scripture was written, heresy was a doctrine maintained against the doctrine by them delivered; which in these times can be no otherwise defined than a doctrine maintained against the light, which we now only have, of the Scripture."[32] Only one external rule remains by which the dictates of conscience are to be recognized as from the Spirit, for as Calvin had said, "he will have us to know him by the image of himself which he hath printed in the Scripture";[33] but the existence of that check has important consequences for Milton's theory of religious liberty.

This definition of heresy was clearly more advanced than the orthodox opinion, for it left the authoritative interpretation of Scripture neither to an ecclesiastical synod (as with the Presbyterians) nor to the civil power (as with Hobbes), but to the individual alone:

Seeing therefore that no man, no synod, no session of men, though called the church, can judge definitively the sense of Scripture to another man's conscience, which is well known to be a general maxim of the Protestant religion, it follows plainly that he who holds in religion that belief or those opinions which to his conscience and utmost understanding appear with most evidence or probability in the Scripture, though to others he seem erroneous, can no more be justly censured for a heretic than his censurers.[34]

Consequently, perhaps with an eye to the several licensing ordinances of the Commonwealth and Protectorate and the disputes over them,[35] Milton asserted that among Protestants "nothing can with more conscience, more equity, nothing more protestantly can be permitted than a free and lawful debate at all times, by writing, conference or disputation, of what opinion soever, disputable by Scripture. . . ."[36]

Yet the emphasis here is upon the general maxim of Protestantism; those who do not accept it remain heretics: "He then who to his best apprehension follows the Scripture, though against any point of doctrine by the whole church received, is not the heretic; but he who follows the church against his conscience and persuasion grounded on the Scripture," who "maintains traditions or opinions not probable by Scripture," or who "holds opinions in religion professedly from tradition or his own inventions and not from Scripture."[37]

Even to these heretics Milton applied the extreme sectarian argument at one point in *Of Civil Power*. As Sprigge (a radical Independent) averred at Whitehall, no provision should "be made to prevent heresies in the world besides that same which is . . . the only means of suppressing and eradicating them, and that is the breaking forth of him who is the truth, the breaking forth of Christ, in the minds and spirits of men."[38] Milton asserted that, though heretics were civilly punished under the Law, "in the Gospel such are punished by excommunication only," and their errors are met by "that dreadful awe and spiritual efficacy which the apostle hath expressed so highly to be in church discipline."[39] Indeed, that such a man is "not always punishable by the magistrate unless he do evil against a civil law, properly so called, hath been already proved without need of repetition."[40]

This is the most radical statement in *Of Civil Power*. The contention was proved in the opening pages of the tract, in the Whitehall debates, and in the writings of the sectaries, by the separation of church and state, the segregation of the spiritual and the natural, and the limitation of the magistrate to matters determinable by the light of nature. But if each of those principles was rigidly applied, the magistrate was automatically excluded from all religious questions; and the definition of heresy in any terms became at once superfluous.

Milton's reiterated assertion that heresy is belief against conscience guided by Scripture indicates a preoccupation with problems from which Williams and Goodwin had managed to escape. His definition is precisely that employed by Chillingworth to defend the religion of Protestants against papists:

> Let all men believe the Scripture and that only, and endeavour to believe it in the true sense, and require no more of others; and they shall find this not only a better but the only means to suppress heresy and restore unity. . . . For he that believes Scripture sincerely and endeavours to believe it in the true sense, cannot possibly be a heretic; and if no more than this were required of any man to make him capable of the church's communion, then all men so qualified, though they were different in opinion, yet notwithstanding any such difference, must of necessity be one in communion.[41]

This was the basis of the latitudinarian theory of a church which should remain Christian yet exclude none who could be called Christian. The similarity between it and Milton's definition is significant; for in both cases the belief in Scripture provided the single fundamental which must be accepted if the privileges of communion were to be enjoyed. In Milton it was the condition, not simply of liberty, but of Christian liberty; and this single requirement stood in the way of a complete theory of religious freedom, less tyrannously but no less certainly than the fundamentals of the Independents. It prevented him from applying the principle of segregation as consistently to conscience as to tithes.

## 3

As Ireton was disturbed at Putney by the Leveller appeal to an absolute natural right, so he was troubled at Whitehall by the demand of the sectaries, not merely for freedom of conscience, but for an unrestricted liberty in religion. It seemed to him that their reasoning would "necessarily debar any kind of restraint on anything that any man will call religion," and that it would leave the wicked free "to practise idolatry, to practise atheism, and anything that is against the light of God."[42] He believed, with Nye, that in determining the magistrate's power it was necessary to distinguish between the true and the false, and to deprive him of force only in "those things that are truly religious."[43]

That the state might not persecute true religion but ought not to compound with manifest error had been the constant argument of both Presbyterians and Independents. They differed only in their views on the limits of fundamental truth. Even John Goodwin retained something of this preoccupation with right belief in his earlier pamphlets on conscience; for in 1646 he denied legal toleration to Jews, Socinians, and papists.[44] Though he insisted that only spiritual weapons were efficacious against errors of faith, and distinguished sharply between ecclesiastical and civil power, he nevertheless exemplified in 1645 the original Separatist habit of thinking in terms of revealed truth and the one right discipline. He then argued that, though the church should not "condescend and be compelled by politicians," it was to the state's advantage "to give all accommodation and honour unto it." "The truth is that the government of Christ's kingdom in a civil state will never do any great thing for it, except it first receive accommodation from it. The truth knows no compliance, but only with those who submit to it."[45]

By 1648, experience had convinced Goodwin of the dangers of this view; by the 1650's he had adopted (though for peculiar reasons) the full consequences of the arguments rehearsed by Williams in *The Bloudy Tenent.* Like him, Milton had been progressively closing up truth to truth, and had passed beyond the Independent defence of doctrinal fundamentals. But the one fundamental remained immovably fixed in his reasoning. Whatever might be the limits of the magistrate's power, it was still his duty "to assert only the true Protestant Christian religion, as it is contained in the Holy Scripture."[46]

The argument of the pamphlets of 1659 was based exclusively on the "true fundamental principles of the Gospel."[47] They required the distinction between ecclesiastical and civil power, the separation of church and state, and the denial of compulsive power to the magistrate. But they did not beget an equal liberty for all men; for though Milton presents the separation of the ecclesiastical and the civil in its sharpest form, the segregation of the spiritual and the natural is undermined in his reasoning because at certain points the interests of church and state overlap, and because his concern is with true religion, not religion, with the Christian magistrate, not the magistrate, and with Christian liberty, not liberty.

He commended the Commonwealth Council of State for "so well

joining religion with civil prudence, and yet so well distinguishing the different power of either."[48] While he insisted on the need for the second part of this policy, he could not accept a view of human society which would dispense with the first, and so set not merely God's people but the irreligious free. He recognized the danger which impelled the Independents at Whitehall to seek justifications for a restrictive, though not a compulsive, power in the magistrate.

The Independents found support not merely in the example of Israel but in the law of nature codified particularly for the Jews with a perfection unattainable by fallen man in general. Calvin had said that, though the Jewish ceremonial and civil laws were abrogated, "the moral law, . . . contained in two chief points, of which the one commandeth to worship God with pure faith and godliness, and the other to embrace men with unfeigned love, is the true and eternal rule of righteousness prescribed to the men of all ages and times that will . . . frame their life to the will of God," because it was a divine promulgation "of the natural law, and of that conscience which is engraven of God in the minds of men."[49]

In these terms Ireton defended the right of magistrates to restrain the corrupt from false worship. It is true that they are not now under divine direction; but they are bound to govern according to the law of nature, and if they are Christians, according to the scriptural account of it. They must prevent the breaking of the first four commandments, for "those are things against which there is a testimony in the light of nature, and consequently they are things that men as men are in some capacity to judge of, unless they are perverted—indeed, a man perverted in his own lusts cannot judge of anything, even matters of common honesty." The Jewish magistrates acted in this respect, not simply under divine direction, but "as magistrates having an authority civil or natural"; and though the judicial laws are abrogated, "yet there are some things of perpetual and natural right that the Scripture of the Old Testament doth hold forth." Consequently, "for those things themselves for which they had a perpetual ground in relation of the duty to God, a perpetual rule by the law written in men's hearts, and a perpetual testimony left in man by nature, and so consequently for those things whereof the ground of duty towards God is not changed—for those things I account that what was sin before is sin still, what was sin to practise before remains sin still, what was the duty of a magistrate to restrain before remains his duty to restrain still."[50]

The radicals themselves had sometimes argued that the substance of the commandments was apprehensible in the light of nature; but Wildman met Ireton's reasoning by asserting, not only that without revelation it was difficult to conclude more than that there was a First Being, but that "if a man consider that there is a will of the Supreme Cause, it is an hard thing for him by the light of nature to conceive how there can be any sin committed; and therefore the magistrate cannot easily determine what sins are against the light of nature, and what not."[51] That opinion was eventually to destroy not only the religious power of magistrates but the whole conception of society as governed by the laws of morality. Few in the seventeenth century were prepared to go so far; yet Goodwin denied that Ireton's reasoning justified restrictive power in religion on the ground that, though "men are capable by the light of nature to conceive that there is a God, yet to conceive this in a right and true manner, it is in the profundities, in the remotest part, amongst those conclusions which lie farthest off from the presence of men. . . ."[52]

He had come to see, with Williams, that, if "the best oracles that magistrates and judges have to direct them in doubtful cases about matters of religion, are men of very fallible judgments,"[53] it would only be possible to prevent the persecution of unrecognized truth by completely removing religion, Christian or otherwise, from the supervision of the state. Since the state was to punish "such evil doers only who sin against the clear light and law of nature," he could pertinently inquire "whether the office and work of the civil magistrate, as such, be not entire within itself and consisting within its own appropriate bounds and limits, so that nothing more accrues to him by way of duty in his office by his being Christian, nor is anything which is matter of duty unto him as a magistrate diminished or taken off from him by his being, or turning, pagan?"[54]

Milton was likewise concerned to prevent matters of religion from being brought (in Vane's phrase) "before the judgment seats of men."[55] He had written his first controversial pamphlets in order to demonstrate the necessity of submission to God's will rather than fallible human judgment; and the definition of religion in his tract on conscience included a reassertion of the liberty demanded by *Tetrachordon*: "Whence I here mean by conscience or religion, that full persuasion whereby we are assured that our belief and practice, as far as we are able to apprehend and probably make appear, is according to the will of God and his Holy Spirit within us, which we ought to follow much rather than any law of man, as not only his word everywhere bids us, but the very dictate of reason tells us: *Acts* 4. 19, 'whether it be right in the sight of God to hearken to you more than to God, judge ye.' "[56] But if he was concerned to prevent the tyranny of human judgment, he was still intent on making the will of God prevail, and still, as in the political pamphlets, wary of making way instead for the wills of corrupt men. Reason dictates that men must follow the fallible opinions neither of other men nor themselves, but the eternal law revealed by the light of the Spirit.

The principal statement in *Of Civil Power* on the source of the magistrate's duty is by no means lucid, partly, no doubt, because it comes at the end of a pamphlet for whose brevity—"not exceeding a small manual"—Milton apologized, and largely because the complex problem of the Mosaic Law was to be more elaborately treated elsewhere. But the statement requires careful interpretation in the light of contemporary opinion, for it is only thus that one can see how he was able to employ all the arguments of the sectaries, and yet to deny the complete liberty in religion which they advocated.

That there can be no place then left for the magistrate or his force in the settlement of religion, by appointing either what we shall believe in divine things or practise in religious (neither of which things are in the power of man either to perform himself or to enable others) I persuade me in the Christian ingenuity of all religious men, the more they examine seriously, the more they will find clearly to be true; and find how false and deceivable that common saying is, which is so much relied upon, that the Christian magistrate is *custos utriusque tabulae*, keeper of both tables; unless is meant by keeper the defender only; neither can that maxim be maintained by any proof or argument which hath not in this discourse first or last been refuted. For the two tables, or ten commandments, teach our duty to God and our neighbour from the love of both; give magistrates no authority to force either; they seek that from the judicial law, though on false grounds, especially in the first table, as I have shown; and both in first and second execute that authority for the most part not according to God's judicial laws but their own. As for civil crimes and of the outward man, which all are not, no not of those against the second table, as that of coveting; in them what power they have, they had from the beginning, long before Moses or the two tables were in being. And whether they be not now as little in being to be kept by any Christian as they are two legal tables, remains yet as undecided, as it is sure they never were yet delivered to the keeping of any Christian magistrate. But of these things perhaps more some other time; what may serve the present hath been above discoursed sufficiently out of the Scriptures. . . .[57]

Milton here firmly denies that the Christian magistrate can be justified in forcing men, either in their relationships to God or to other men, in virtue of the two tables given specifically to the Jewish but to no other magistrate. Those tables were moral; to justify their imposition, it is necessary to cite the judicial law of the Jews, which cannot apply since it has been abrogated. But the magistrate does not need mistakenly to derive his power over the outward man from Moses. The crimes mentioned in the table which concerns one's neighbour are not all crimes which can come within his cognizance: coveting is a sin of the inward man, over which the magistrate can have no control since he cannot discern it. Yet the magistrate will enforce the substance of the second table (as Williams had implied[58]); and though he cannot compel men to love their neighbours, he will prevent their harming them according to the power which all magistrates have, and had even before the Jews received their special laws, the power which comes from the law of nature.

Those special laws were imposed on the Jews by God from without. They cannot be so imposed on any other people without divine command. As legal tables they are therefore now no more in being than they were before Moses, when all men lived under the law of nature alone. To what extent, and in what manner, Christians are bound to observe them as moral laws is (as these pages have frequently indicated) not yet agreed upon among Christians. Of that Milton already had more to say. He had said more in *Tetrachordon*; and he knew that he was to say more—if indeed he had not already done so—on another occasion, in the twenty-sixth and twenty-seventh chapters of the first book of *De Doctrina Christiana*. He was concerned in *Of Civil Power*, not with the responsibilities of individual Christians, but with the duties of magistrates; and he had already sufficiently proved that they derived their power and interest from nature only, and so could not compel men to live in accordance with the Jewish law.

But if the Christian magistrate is not, in the Jewish and Presbyterian sense, the keeper of both tables, he is at least their defender; and Milton here makes no distinction between the two tables. The magistrate will defend the second, according to the civil power which he naturally possesses, by preventing wicked men from harming their neighbours; he will defend the first, in the same manner, by preventing wicked men from dishonouring God.

With compulsive power in religion, Milton would have nothing to do; it was contrary to the spirit of the Gospel which required faith and charity within. But he nevertheless retained, like Ireton, the belief that the magistrate should exercise a restraining power; and he did so on precisely the grounds produced in 1645 by the author of *The Ancient Bounds.* That Independent had insisted on the magistrate's exclusively natural power; but he had not confined him to matters of the second table:

He may enter the vault even of those abominations of the first table . . . so far as nature carries the candle before him. Therefore it seems to me that polytheism and atheistical doctrines (which are sins against the first table and commandment), and idolatry (which is against the second commandment), such as may be convinced by natural light, or the letter of the command where the Scriptures are received, as the worshipping of images, and the breaden-god, the grossest idolatry of all:—these, so far forth as they break out and discover themselves, ought to be restrained, exploded by the Christian magistrate; for 'tis that which a heathen's light should not tolerate, nature carrying so far (*Rom.* 1). And also blasphemy (which is against the third commandment, and is a common nuisance to mankind), and the insolent profanation of the Lord's day (though the keeping of it be not obvious to nature's light) ought not to be suffered by the Christian magistrate.[59]

Moreover, it seemed to this author that "the duty of a Christian magistrate is somewhat more than of another magistrate," beyond the civil protection which he owes all men; "a Christian magistrate owes something more to the truth he professes, and to those that profess the same with him; which duty of his differs only in degree, not in kind, from the duty of another Christian that is no magistrate. For it is the duty of every Christian to improve every talent and advantage entrusted with him, for the honour of Christ and good of the body to the utmost in a lawful way."[60]

That is almost precisely Milton's position in *Of Civil Power.* The Christian magistrate's duty included, not only the settling of justice according to the common light of nature, but "the defence of things religious settled by the churches within themselves."[61] They can prosecute their work by spiritual means without the aid of civil compulsion; but this is "much easier under the defensive favour only of a Christian magistrate," and the separation of powers "yet disproves not that a Christian commonwealth may defend itself against outward force in the cause of religion as well as in any other, though Christ himself, coming purposely to die for us, would not be so defended."[62] The English magistrates are therefore exhorted to act in "the defence of true religion and our civil rights."[63]

In these statements Milton revealed the preoccupations which still differentiated his thinking from Williams'; for Williams had pointed out that to make the magistrate "the reformer of the church, the suppressor of schismatics and heretics, the protector and defender of the church," was inevitably "to make him the judge of the true and false church, judge of what is truth and what error, who is schismatical and who heretical."[64] Goodwin and he had therefore desired to prevent the magistrate from restraining even blasphemy and idolatry.[65]

Milton was still attempting to distinguish the true from the false, "matters of conscience and religion . . . from blasphemy and heresy, the one being such properly as is despiteful, the other such as stands not to the rule of Scripture, and so both of them not matters of religion, but rather against it. . . ."[66] In this respect his position had not changed since 1649, when, in reply to complaints, he had said that the Commonwealth would "not tolerate the free exercise of any religion which shall be found absolutely contrary to sound doctrine or the power of godliness," so that "if any be found among us declared atheists, malicious enemies of God and Christ, the Parliament . . . professes not to tolerate such, but with all befitting endeavours to suppress them."[67]

In 1659 he observed that blasphemy originally meant "any slander, any malicious or evil speaking, whether against God or man or anything to good belonging." But he added that "blasphemy or evil speaking against God maliciously, is far from conscience in religion"; and he referred to "that prudent and well deliberated Act, August 9, 1650, where the Parliament defines blasphemy against God, as far as it is a crime belonging to civil judicature."[68] That Act was passed by a coalition of moderate Presbyterians and Independents, and though it was more liberal than previous acts and avoided the definition of fundamentals, it was directed specifically against the sectaries of the extreme left.[69]

Idolatry likewise seemed to Milton obviously intolerable; for "who knows it not to be evidently against all Scripture both of the Old and the New Testament, and therefore a true heresy, or rather an impiety; wherein a right conscience can have naught to do; and the works thereof so manifest that a magistrate can hardly err in prohibiting and quite removing at least the public and scandalous use thereof."[70] To the Puritan mind it was practically indistinguishable from popery; Milton therefore denied freedom also to Roman Catholics.

Popery provided the severest test for seventeenth-century theories of religious liberty. The political dangers which were foremost in men's minds were not without their foundations; even Williams was careful to note that, while papists should be tolerated along with Jews, Turks, and pagans, they must first give assurance of civil obedience.[71] That was one of Milton's conditions; but not his single condition. In 1649 he had said that there was no "more blasphemous, not opinion, but whole religion, than popery, plunged into idolatrous and ceremonial superstition, the very death of all true religion."[72] In defining heresy in 1659, he remarked that the true heretic, "for aught I know, is the papist only." The reasons which he gave against tolerating popery were therefore threefold: it was politically dangerous; it threatened to introduce persecution; it was not itself a true religion. "Their religion the more considered, the less can be acknowledged a religion, but a Roman principality rather, endeavouring to keep up her old universal dominion under a new name and mere shadow of a catholic religion; being indeed more rightly named a catholic heresy against the Scripture; supported mainly by a civil and, except in Rome, by a foreign power; justly therefore to be suspected, not tolerated by the magistrate of another country." It was, he observed, "for just reason of state more than of religion" that papists should be prohibited freedom. But a further comment throws a flood of light upon his thinking: "Besides, of an implicit faith, which they profess, the conscience also becomes implicit; and so by voluntary servitude to man's law, forfeits her Christian liberty. Who then can plead for such a conscience, as being implicitly enthralled to man instead of God, almost becomes no conscience, as the will not free, becomes no will?"[73]

The exclusion of those who refuse to accept Scripture, interpreted by conscience according to the light of the Spirit, as the sole rule of true religion, of those who deny Christianity, of those who submit to an external rule or would impose one, of those who are idolaters, heretics (according to Milton's definition), or blasphemers (according to Parliament's definition), virtually limited freedom of religious practice to the centre party of Puritanism. Less strictly interpreted, Milton's reasoning confined it to "all those diversified sects, who yet were all Protestants, one religion, though many opinions." "No Protestant therefore of what sect soever following Scripture only, which is the common sect wherein they all agree, and the granted rule of every man's conscience to himself, ought, by the common doctrine of Protestants, to be forced or molested for religion."[74] So long as they avoided blasphemy, this would have included all the sects on the Puritan left. It would also have included both Anglicans and Presbyterians, but only if they surrendered their theories of a national church imposing conformity; for the duty of a Christian magistrate "is not to constrain or to repress religion, probable by Scripture, but the violators and persecutors thereof."[75] He must preserve the rights of true conscience, and therefore the freedom of the true religion which alone begets Christian liberty.

## 4

At the end, as at the beginning, of the revolution, Milton found it impossible to separate the good of the state from Christianity, or from the good of every true Christian. The moderate Congregationalism which in 1641 had been almost indistinguishable from Thomas Young's moderate Presbyterianism, had been transformed into a theory of the church which was altogether sectarian and, more than that, individualistic; for if submission to the spiritual discipline of a particular congregation was to be wholly voluntary, it followed that individual Christians might remain in communion with the universal church without being associated with any congregation. Nevertheless, though he had reduced the Christian fundamentals to a minimum, Milton could have agreed with Nye that "the things of God" are "of public good and public concernment";[76] and though he had arrived at a more radical interpretation of divine prescript, he could still have subscribed to Calvin's assertions "that no policy can be happily framed unless the first care be of godliness, and that those laws be preposterous which, neglecting the right of God, do provide only for men." With Calvin he still believed it the duty of a Christian magistrate to see "that the true religion which is contained in the law of God, be not openly and with public sacrileges freely broken and defiled."[77]

That did not mean that he regarded the power of the Christian magistrate as more than natural or civil; but, under the law of nature, the responsibilities of Christian magistrates seemed to him greater than those of non-Christian magistrates precisely as the privileges of Christians seemed greater than those of mere men. The sectaries of the left maintained with Vane that religious, like political liberty, was to be claimed "upon the grounds of natural right."[78] It is significant that *Of Civil Power* contains not a single reference to the rights of men merely as men.

Vane had argued for religious liberty for all men on the ground that "unto this freedom the nations of the world have right and title by the purchase of Christ's blood, who by virtue of his death and resurrection is become the sole lord and ruler in and over the conscience. . . ."[79] Milton would have agreed that, because the Gospel was a wholly spiritual dispensation, this liberty belonged equally to all men. But he did not extend the same liberty of outward action to all men; that freedom he reserved for acts of true religion.

He recognized that it was impossible effectively to influence the conscience by means other than spiritual; it was therefore the province of the church, not of the state.[80] But the magistrate was prevented from dealing with irreligious consciences simply because they were not in his power. Cromwell had said, with reference to the Roman Catholics of Ireland, "I meddle not with any man's conscience. But if by liberty of conscience, you mean a liberty to exercise the Mass, I judge it best to exercise plain dealing and to let you know where the Parliament of England have power, that will not be allowed of. As for the people, what thoughts they have in matters of religion in their own breasts I cannot reach, but shall think it my duty, if they walk honestly and peaceably, not to cause them in the least to suffer for the same."[81]

In 1649 Milton had delivered precisely the same opinion: "it can be no way proved that the Parliament hath countenanced popery or papists, but have everywhere broken their temporal power, thrown down their public superstitions, and confined them to the bare enjoyment of that which is not in our reach, their consciences. . . ."[82] According to the Covenant, Parliament lent its aid to the suppression of heresy and error; but it necessarily left their effective eradication to the spiritual ministrations of the church, since it could deal only with the outward man: "for the conscience, we must have patience till it be within our verge."[83]

In *Of Civil Power* this distinction between outward and inward corruptness was still operative. Milton believed with *The Leveller* that because "all true religion in men is founded upon the inward consent of their understandings and hearts to the truths revealed . . ., no man can compel another to be religious, or by force or terror constrain the people to be of the true religion."[84] As he had argued that the true end of marriage would not be achieved by compelling the preservation of its outward form, so he now maintained that "to compel outward profession, which they will say perhaps ought to be compelled though inward religion cannot, is to compel hypocrisy, not to advance religion. . . ."[85]

The magistrate may propose three ends for religious compulsion: "first, the glory of God; next either the spiritual good of them whom he forces, or the temporal punishment of their scandal to others." But, under the Gospel, God cannot be glorified by an unwilling and hypocritical service; the spiritual good of men can be achieved only through faith, not by works; and believers can be protected from infection only by spiritual means.

To compel therefore the profane to things holy in his profaneness is all one under the Gospel as to have compelled the unclean to sacrifice in his uncleanness under the Law.... For if by the apostle, *Rom.* 12. 1, we are beseeched ... to present our bodies a living sacrifice, holy, acceptable to God, which is our reasonable service or worship, then is no man to be forced by the compulsive laws of men to present his body a dead sacrifice, and so under the Gospel most unholy and unacceptable, because it is his unreasonable service, that is to say, not only unwilling but unconscionable.[86]

Yet if Milton refused the Christian magistrate compulsive power over the consciences and outward acts of the profane, he nevertheless accorded him a restraining power over the outward acts already discussed. He did so because he continued to distinguish between acts of true and false religion, and because his argument was primarily designed to defend the freedom, not of all men, but of the truly conscientious. The chief reason why magistrates must be wary of exercising their power in matters of religion is that thereby "the way lies ready open to them hereafter who may be so minded to take away by little and little that liberty which Christ and his Gospel, not any magistrate, hath right to give...."[87] It was with those who could claim this liberty that Milton was concerned; for the rights of others he would not bother to argue:

But grant it belonging any way to the magistrate that profane and licentious persons omit not the performance of holy duties, which in them were odious to God even under the Law, much more now under the Gospel; yet ought his care, both as a magistrate and a Christian, to be much more that conscience be not inwardly violated than that licence in these things be made outwardly conformable; since his part is undoubtedly as a Christian, which puts him upon this office much more than as a magistrate, in all respects to have more care of the conscientious than of the profane; and not for their sakes to take away (while they pretend to give) or to diminish the rightful liberty of religious consciences.[88]

In 1644 Goodwin had observed that it was the duty of Christian magistrates not to "impose anything upon the people of God," but "to provide for the immunity and peace of the saints within their jurisdictions, to protect them against all injuries and violence of men," and to do "whatsoever maketh for the benefit, safety, and honour of the whole community and society of persons fearing God within the limits of their jurisdiction, without the pressure or just grievance of others."[89] At Whitehall Ireton strove to preserve both the perpetual rule of right and the freedom of "men that are members and servants of Jesus Christ."[90] In 1659 Milton's aim was likewise the preservation of "the fundamental privilege of the Gospel, the new birthright of every true believer, Christian liberty."[91]

In *Of Civil Power* he once more defined that doctrine, substantially as in *Tetrachordon*, though with more precision and a fuller citation of biblical texts. It was a privilege that "sets us free not only from the bondage of those ceremonies, but also from the forcible imposition of those circumstances, place and time in the worship of God, which, though by him commanded in the old Law, yet in respect of that verity and freedom which is evangelical, St. Paul comprehends . . . under one and the same contemptuous name of weak and beggarly rudiments. . . ." It freed believers therefore from all externals, which, having in themselves no morality, were alike indifferent. It freed them from all outward rules, from "what was once the service of God," and even more from "what now is but the service of men," "blotting out ordinances written by God himself, much more those so boldly written over again by men, ordinances which were against us, that is, against our frailty, much more those which are against our conscience."[92]

Moreover, Christ not only gave "this gift as a special privilege and excellence of the free Gospel above the servile Law, but strictly also hath commanded us to keep it and enjoy it."

It will therefore not misbecome the meanest Christian to put in mind Christian magistrates, and so much the more freely by how much the more they desire to be thought Christian (for they will be thereby, as they ought to be in these things, the more our brethren and the less our lords) that they meddle not rashly with Christian liberty, the birthright and outward testimony of our adoption; lest while they little think it, nay, think they do God service, they themselves like the sons of that bondwoman be found persecuting them who are freeborn of the Spirit; and by a sacrilege of not the least aggravation, bereaving them of that sacred liberty which our Saviour with his own blood purchased for them.[93]

The purpose of Williams' argument had been the full achievement of this same privilege; but he had perceived (and Goodwin after him) that it could only be achieved for the saints if similar privileges were accorded the unregenerate. Milton discerned that fact in part. As he had maintained in the divorce tracts that even the hard of heart must be permitted liberty in order to procure the requisite liberty of good men, so he observed in *Of Civil Power* that "those pretended consequences of licence and confusion" were produced by men "whose severity would be wiser than divine wisdom . . . ; as if God without them when he gave us this liberty knew not of the worst which these men in their arrogance pretend will follow; yet knowing all their worst, he gave us this liberty as by him judged best."[94] Yet the political pamphlets had involved a distinction between the liberty of all men and the rights of the good; and that distinction remained in the last ecclesiastical pamphlets because "the right of Christian and evangelic liberty" was, by definition, "unseparable from Christian religion," and the peculiar privilege of true believers: "2 *Cor.* 3. 17, where the Spirit of the Lord is, there is liberty."[95]

Milton therefore required full liberty in religion only for those whose belief and practice was "not wilful but conscientious."[96] The consciences of others could not be molested; and, within the limits indicated, they might claim freedom of action. But they could neither claim full liberty nor be compelled by the magistrate, for "if we turn again to those weak and beggarly rudiments, we are not free; yea, though willingly and with a misguided conscience we desire to be in bondage to them; how much more then if unwillingly and against our conscience?"[97]

In the pamphlets of 1659, Milton occupied a position which was well towards the Puritan left. His view of Christian religion, of church association, and of the ministry, was scarcely distinguishable from that of the extreme sectaries. But he differed from them in setting bounds to religious liberty, and in applying one fundamental test to discriminate between those who must be accorded full, and those who might claim only partial, liberty. His interpretation was radical; but his preoccupation with true religion meant that his reasoning reproduced the basic Puritan pattern recognizable in the thought of the Presbyterians and the Independents in spite of their divergent deductions. As a consequence of that preoccupation, he allowed the Christian magistrate a defensive and a restrictive power in religion which the sectaries denied him. He therefore differed from them not so much in his view of the church as in his view of the state. He did so because he could not pass, with Williams, Goodwin, and the Levellers, beyond Puritanism to a naturalism involving the strict segregation of the spiritual and the natural.

The view of a spiritual ministry presented by *The Likeliest Means* clearly issued from Milton's effort, in blindness, to revise his *De Doctrina Christiana*. The careful account in *Of Civil Power* of the true believer who is not a heretic, is an exact description of the author of that work, for it expressed opinions distinctly unorthodox. His reasoning in both pamphlets was the product of experience which confirmed the beliefs he shared with the Puritan extremists. But there were elements in his experience which he did not share with them; and these prevented him from accepting their view of nature.

In spite of his repudiation of learning, the inner light remained for him that intellectual ray; and he could not accept Williams' theory of equal liberty, even in religion, because he could not accept the view of human nature which Calvinism produced at either its reactionary or radical extreme. In this he differed from sectarians like Dell, who said, "Neither doth man's sense or reason understand the things of the Spirit . . . ,"[98] and from those Quakers to whom he has frequently been compared. He would have agreed with Robert Barclay that "the testimony of the Spirit is that alone by which the true knowledge of God hath been, is, and can only be revealed. . . ." But he could not have subscribed to the Quakers' belief that the Spirit spoke a language which the reason could not comprehend: "That man, as he is a rational creature, hath reason as a natural faculty of his soul, we deny not; for this is a property natural and essential to him, by which he can know and learn many arts and sciences beyond what any other animal can do by the mere animal principle. Neither do we deny that by this rational principle man may apprehend in his brain and in the notion a knowledge of God and spiritual things; yet, that not being the right organ . . ., it cannot profit him towards salvation, but rather hindereth."[99] Milton on the contrary believed that, while spiritual truths could not be understood by fallen man without "the illumination of the Holy Spirit," God "gives us reason also, *Gal.* 6. 4, 5."[100] In 1659 the Gospel remained for him not only freely spiritual but "our free, elective, and rational worship."[101]

The theory of religious liberty, its extent and limits, which Milton presented in his last ecclesiastical pamphlets, necessarily depended upon the theory of spiritual regeneration he was already developing, according to his own experience, in the pages of his theological treatise. But even his small manual on civil power affords a glimpse of that theory sufficient to account for his conclusions.

> What evangelic religion is, is told in two words, faith and charity, or belief and practice. That both these flow either the one from the understanding, the other from the will, or both jointly from both, once indeed naturally free, but now only as they are regenerate and wrought on by divine grace, is in

> part evident to common sense and principles unquestioned, the rest by Scripture. . . . If then both our belief and practice, which comprehend our whole religion, flow from faculties of the inward man, free and unconstrainable of themselves by nature, and our practice not only from faculties endued with freedom, but from love and charity besides, incapable of force, and all these things by transgression lost, but renewed and regenerated in us by the power and gift of God alone, how can such religion as this admit of force from man . . . ?[102]

According to Milton's interpretation, the extent of the religious liberty which a Christian magistrate might permit and men might claim depended on the regeneration of the natural faculties of the individual. This explains why his pamphlet does not present the sectarian argument from natural right. His view of Christianity permitted no strict segregation of the spiritual and the natural; natural right, in its true sense, was therefore included in Christian liberty. The full implications of this theory become apparent in his last political writings.

# Chapter XV

## The Main End of Government

IT was under the violent pressure of events that Milton composed the letters and pamphlets of the months immediately preceding the Restoration of Charles II and the final defeat of the effort to establish the holy community.[1] Since 1655 he had been living in comparative retirement because of his blindness; and if we are to judge from the tone of his *Letter to a Friend* of October 20, 1659, he remained undisturbed by the confusion which followed Oliver's death until this unknown person (perhaps Vane) acquainted him with "these dangerous ruptures" and urged him "to consider more intensely thereon than hitherto I have been wont. . . ."[2] Even then it was too late to stem the rushing tide upon which Charles was returning from his travels. Vane and Lambert were overcome by it; and the blind and retired secretary, who had been quietly devoting himself to his scholarly and theological studies, found it difficult even to comprehend its confused drift. But the main direction was clear; it was towards a restoration of the monarchy, "which the inconsiderate multitude are now so mad upon. . . ."[3]

Against this tide of madness Milton strove to erect a barrier—a crazy structure hastily raised from the debris of the crumbling republic, weakly supported by appeals to the past and the future, and founded on an idealism which could hardly withstand the terribly weakening force of facts. He was never at ease with details of organization; and, interesting to the political historian as are some of the proposals he offered in 1660, they are made the more inconsistent and disordered by the frustration which gives his writing a tone unusually shrill. The forces of injustice, tyranny, lust, and greed, against which he had confidently unleashed his zeal in 1641, were again triumphing, with what danger to the servants of the true God could easily be imagined. For Milton himself less was in store than he feared;[4] but for the leaders of his cause there was certain death, and for the cause itself defeat and infamy. As he sat in darkness in his house in Petty France, now two years bereft of his late espoused saint, seldom visited by his comrades, and urged by his friends to remove himself while there was time, he was overcome by a sense of God's desertion yet greater than had attacked him in the hour of his blindness; for he witnessed the blotting out not now of physical light but of that abundant light poured out by divine power for the regeneration of the English people.

As expositions of political theory the last pamphlets are consequently even less satisfactory than the writings of 1649-1654. By comparison, the argument of the two pamphlets of 1659 is coolly abstract. Milton's Utopia never rose above chaos. But if all the old contradictions are here intensified, the very pressure of events forced a simplification. The main outlines of the structure are recognizable, and the basic convictions are defined with the boldness and the harshness of despair. The urgency of the situation left no time for logic; but it compelled Milton to draw out the full implications both of his defence of the Commonwealth and of his argument for Christian liberty.

The two fundamentals on which he insisted throughout these months were that government should not be by a single person, king or military dictator, and that freedom of conscience should be established and tithes abolished.[5] His chief practical proposal was that these should be achieved through the remnant of the Long Parliament—the Rump—purged of dissenting voices, enlarged through restricted elections, and perpetuated in power. All his other recommendations—for the decentralization of government, a council of state, the reform of legal procedure, the establishment of schools—were subservient to this policy. Its absurdity is the measure of his hopelessness; but it was not altogether unpractical. It was indeed virtually the course Vane had urged throughout the Commonwealth,[6] and the Rump would now have adopted it if it could. More important for our purposes, it was in the circumstances the logical outcome of Milton's thought. In the midst of anarchy it was just possible to believe that the Rump might be made to stand for the government of the wise and good.

The obvious folly of such a belief requires no comment. The contradiction between this view and the approval of Oliver's dissolution of Parliament expressed in *Defensio Secunda* is to be explained by the Protector's failure to follow Milton's advice about the church. As the "Address" of *The Likeliest Means* shows, he hoped that the Rump (restored by the Army officers May 7, 1659, after the dissolution of Richard's Parliament) would proceed to complete the reformation. In spite of its fruitless debates and the timorous ecclesiastical policy with which (against Vane's wishes) it tried to placate the Independents, its second expulsion by the Army (October 13) seemed to Milton "most illegal and scandalous."[7] The Parliament was, it is true, "famous, though not harmless"; and it might be thought "well dissolved, as not complying fully to grant liberty of conscience and the necessary consequence thereof, the removal of forced maintenance from ministers."[8] But its expulsion left the nation "in anarchy," and Milton was no more able than Vane and the officers to propose a solution.[9] Consequently he greeted with full approval the return once more (December 26) of "our old patriots, the first assertors of our religious and civil rights";[10] and, hoping that they had at last learnt their lesson, he proceeded to support their effort to keep themselves in power by proposing "that a former act of their own be reinforced, whereby they sit indissolubly, and that they and all henceforth to be chosen into the Parliament do retain their places during life, unless by particular faults they deserve removal."[11] He made the same proposal in the first edition of *The Readie & Easie Way to Establish A Free Commonwealth*, after the Rump had issued writs for elections to fill up its numbers. But the readmission of the excluded Presbyterian members by Monck's direction in February, and their decision for a full and free parliament, removed the one prop of his plan, and left him in the second edition of his pamphlet to invite the parliament then being elected to make way for a perpetual senate instead of for the King.[12]

Up to a point, this support of the Rump arose from the sense of insecurity which moved the Army officers to restore it a second time because they were "desirous, like drowning men, to lay hold of anything that had the least appearance of civil authority. . . ."[13] But the situation was too desperate to permit of more than gestures towards legality; and the introspection which issued in the doctrine of the Spirit in Milton's tracts of 1659 caused him to consider the political problem according to principles higher and less definable than human laws afforded. He might term the expulsion of the Rump illegal, and refer to the Act of May 10, 1641, against the dissolution of the Parliament; but the rights he sought were those of a Christian commonwealth, not the legal and constitutional rights of Englishmen. The appeal of *Eikonoklastes* to rolls and records and the ancient English constitution is scarcely echoed in the last pamphlets. Legality had a foundation at once more positive and more abstract. For Milton meant the Rump, by a metamorphosis that would have been miraculous, to transform itself into an instrument through which good men might govern according to the absolute justice of the pure law of nature.

But the divine intervention for which he cried in the last sentences of *The Readie and Easie Way* was not forthcoming; the people of England had already rejected it. The shrillness of the last pamphlets is the effect of the terrible realization that those who should have been God's chosen people were determined to league themselves with the forces of antichristian tyranny in church and state. The high vision of 1641 and the *Areopagitica*, clouded by the controversies of the late 1640's, had been restored after the execution of Charles and given new expression in the epic defence of the English people; but it vanished in the despair of 1660. The most positive element in the first pamphlets was hatred of the carnal corruption of episcopacy; the most positive element in the last is hatred of tyranny, made more violent by disgust with the "epidemic madness . . . of a misguided and abused multitude," the "strange degenerate contagion suddenly spread among us, fitted and prepared for new slavery. . . ."[14] The Rump was to be perpetuated not only to prevent the rule of a single person but to prevent the people from exercising its will for monarchy.

Yet, if the popular clamour for the King shattered what remained of Milton's confidence in the English people, the remnants of his belief in human dignity are still apparent in the arguments against tyranny which he carried over to the last pamphlets from *The Tenure* and the defences. He told the royalist preacher, Matthew Griffith, as he had told Salmasius, that "if a people be put to war with their king for his misgovernment and overcome him, the power is then undoubtedly in their own hands how they will be governed."[15] He asserted once more that this choice, by a free people or their representatives, "is so essential to their freedom that longer than they have it, they are not free."[16] In reviewing the course of the revolution, much as in the *Defensio*, he roundly stated that the Parliament "knew the people of England to be a free people, themselves the representers of that freedom"; and, with a momentary reminiscence of the *Areopagitica*, he said that the demonstrations after the execution of the King manifested "a spirit in this nation no less noble and well fitted to the liberty of a commonwealth than in the ancient Greeks and Romans."[17] He demanded the return of the Rump because "no government is like to continue unless founded on the public authority and consent of the people, which is the parliament"; and he set it down as axiomatic that "the ground and basis of every just and free government (since men have smarted so oft for committing all to one person) is a general council of ablest men, chosen by the people to consult of public affairs from time to time for the common good."[18]

As Roger L'Estrange and others of Milton's critics before and since have pointed out, these statements seem to sort strangely with the exclusion of the madly royalist multitude from any share in the government and the proposal of a perpetual senate beyond their control.[19] Here again are the contradictions of the earlier pamphlets—the unreconciled claims of parliament, Rump, people, justice—now become sharper since the will of people and King had coalesced and since the real enemy was not so much the King as the people itself. But again it is possible, not only to explain the contradictions in terms of confusion of mind intensified by despair, but to discover the basic principles which make these statements ideally consistent and the fundamental convictions to which Milton was driven both by his personality and by events. The statements quoted, like the contentions of Vane's *Healing Question* which they seem to echo,[20] are the product of an idealism which refuses to be quenched even in the hour of defeat; and the principles by which they can be made consistent with a recognition of the facts of human society are now more clearly—though not even now precisely—defined.

What, one has again to inquire, is meant by "people," by "liberty," by "ablest men," and by "the common good"? If one is to do justice to Milton, one must frame one's answers, not in terms of modern democratic theory, but in terms of the Puritan idealism whose positive expression is given in the tracts of 1659 on religious liberty. Those tracts present an interpretation of Christian liberty as radical as any; but in the last pamphlets Milton is not so much attacking tyranny as making a last and desperate stand in defence of the righteous freedom which belongs to those few who are God's faithful servants. His emphasis therefore falls not on the rights of men but on the qualifications required for the exercise of true liberty; and in his definition of them one hears echoes of the bitter controversy between the radicals of the Spirit and the radicals of nature in the midst of which the Puritan party finally disintegrated.

## 2

As we have seen, each stage in the revolution was marked by a further breaking up of the offensive alliance against episcopacy formed by the Puritan groups in 1641. The establishment of the Assembly set the Independents and the sectaries of the left against the Presbyterians; the policy of the Protectorate set the sectaries against the Independents; and in the anarchy after Cromwell's death the divergences between the parties of the left, already apparent under the Protectorate, became acute. While Milton was composing his last pamphlets, the old disputes between the parties were continuing, with the Presbyterians aligning themselves in desperation with the Royalists, and the Independents searching for an army leader to replace Oliver.[21] But their oft-repeated arguments throw less light on Milton's opinions than the new disputes among the radicals.

One hesitates to put a girdle about the chaos of the Puritan left; but it has already become apparent that the radicalism which developed during the revolution produced two distinguishable types of opinion. Both were individualistic, and both demanded freedom of conscience; and they were capable of a temporary alliance with the Independents and with each other. But their differences were fundamental. On the one hand were the Levellers and those who with them, whether through the progressive secularization of their thought or (as in the case of Williams) through the application of the principle which segregated the natural and political from the spiritual and ecclesiastical, developed a radical theory of the church and a democratic theory of the state based on the natural liberty and equality of all men. On the other hand were those who, because their thought remained essentially religious and because they could not accept the segregation of the natural and the spiritual, developed an equally radical theory of the church but transferred to their theory of the state the rights and privileges of the saints.[22]

Under the Protectorate these groups were kept in check and in alliance by the strong hand of Oliver.[23] But with the return of the Rump each began to urge anew the adoption of its policy. Among those who desired, if not the actual rule of the saints, at least a commonwealth patterned on Christ's Kingdom, the most articulate were a group called by their opponents "the Vanists" because they pressed for the adoption of the proposals made in *A Healing Question propounded.*[24] The Levellers as a party had ceased to exist; but their place had been taken by James Harrington and his followers, who recommended the adoption of the democratic system of government described in *The Commonwealth of Oceana* which Harrington had dedicated to the Protector in 1656.[25] Much light is thrown on Milton's position by his relationship to these two groups; for, though he stood as ever alone, his opinion of Harrington, his deepest convictions, and the desperate situation, aligned him with the Vanists.

Milton was certainly familiar with Harrington's elaborate system. According to Aubrey, "Mr Cyriak Skinner, an ingenious young gentleman, scholar to John Milton," acted as chairman of the Rota Club whose public discussions of Oceana attracted much attention in 1659. Andrew Marvell, Milton's friend and associate in the secretaryship, was one of Harrington's intimates.[26] And in both editions of *The Readie and Easie Way*, Milton considered Harrington's system of rotation, whereby a third part of the senate of Oceana was changed annually.[27] It seemed a possible means of satisfying those who might be ambitious to have a part in the government of Milton's commonwealth; but, Milton observed, "I could wish that this wheel . . . in the state . . . might be avoided, as having too much affinity with the wheel of fortune."[28]

This remark succinctly expresses a fundamental difference of opinion. Milton desired the stability of absolute justice; Harrington's wheel was turned not only by fortune but by the fickle will of the people.

Such similarities as there are between their views merely serve to emphasize this difference. Both desired a commonwealth, sought to avoid the tyranny of a single will, and denounced government by men instead of laws. Milton must have approved Harrington's criticism of Hobbes: "If the liberty of man consist in the empire of his reason, the absence whereof would betray him into the bondage of his passions, then the liberty of a commonwealth consisteth in the empire of her laws, the absence whereof would betray her unto the lust of tyrants; and these I conceive to be the principles upon which Aristotle and Livy (injuriously accused by *Leviathan* for not writing out of nature) have grounded their assertion that a commonwealth is an empire of laws and not of men."[29] The analogy had been constantly in Milton's mind since the divorce tracts; but its meaning was different for him because the empire of reason required the assistance of a divine grace in which the sceptical Harrington had no faith.

Harrington was in fact as suspicious of abstract principles as

Hobbes. His commonwealth was an elaborate system of checks and balances—a limiting agrarian law, the division of the people into tribes and classes, a senate proposing and a representative assembly passing laws, the system of rotation, the ballot—whereby he meant to prevent the self-interested tyranny of one or a few and the anarchical consequences of the Leveller system.[30] By law he meant simply the "orders" of Oceana for the organized expression of "the will of the whole people" which alone could define "the public interest, which is no other than common right and justice."[31] He had, it is true, little faith in the good sense of the people without organization; but he argued that " 'Give us good orders and they will make us good men,' is the maxim of a legislator, and the most infallible in the politics."[32]

Harrington had thus taken over the fundamental Leveller doctrine of popular sovereignty and provided it with machinery through which it might function.[33] But Milton had no faith in artificial and mechanical checks on original sin; and he disliked Oceana for two reasons which, though at first sight contradictory, take one to the centre of his thinking in the last pamphlets: first, because it gave dangerous privileges where none were due, and secondly, because it restricted true liberty.

A considerable part of the second edition of *The Readie and Easie Way* is devoted to arguments in favour of Milton's perpetual senate and against such a representative assembly as Oceana required. Milton observed that "this annual rotation, as is lately propounded, requires also another popular assembly upward of a thousand, with answerable rotation," and that this body was bound to be "troublesome and chargeable."[34] He who had defended the English right to frequent parliaments in *Eikonoklastes* had now come to believe that popular assemblies "are much likelier continually to unsettle rather than settle a free government," and that this was demonstrated by history. There were popular checks on the senates of Athens, Sparta, and Rome; "but the event tells us that these remedies either little availed the people, or brought them to such a licentious and unbridled democracy as in fine ruined themselves with their own excessive power."[35]

We may pass over this strange reading of history, for what Milton had really in mind was the experience of the past twenty years in England, during which a succession of more or less representative assemblies had served only to bring the country to its present pass. The failure to establish a commonwealth could "be ascribed with most reason to the frequent interruptions and dissolutions which the Parliament hath had, partly from the impatient or disaffected people, partly from some ambitious leaders in the Army. . . ."[36] And if Milton was concerned, with Harrington, to prevent the latter danger, he was even more concerned to put an end to the former by making the Rump perpetual. An assembly representative of the people would destroy the commonwealth; for they were "running headlong again with full stream wilfully and obstinately into the same bondage."[37]

This objection to Oceana shows the depth of Milton's disillusionment. The other objection arose from his stubborn belief in true liberty. Harrington's system limited the freedom of good men by a multiplicity of laws more complex than those Cromwell had been asked to simplify; Milton's proposals were not so encumbered:

> The way propounded is plain, easy, and open before us; without intricacies, without the introducement of new or obsolete forms, or terms, or exotic models, ideas that would manacle the native liberty of mankind, turning all virtue into prescription, servitude, and necessity, to the great impairing and frustrating of Christian liberty; . . . this way lies free and smooth . . . , invents no new incumbrances, requires no perilous, no injurious alteration or circumscription of men's lands and properties, secure that . . . no man or number of men can attain to such wealth or vast possession as will need the hedge of an Agrarian law. . . .[38]

In the rejection of Harrington's limitation of private property, one hears the voice of the London scrivener's son; but the collocation of native and Christian liberty, and the insistence on a free and active virtue, echo the *Areopagitica* and the tracts of 1659. Harrington's liberty was defined by elaborate external laws, designed to nullify the effects of natural corruption: "Where the security is in the persons, the government makes good men evil; where the security is in the form, the government makes evil men good."[39] But Milton's liberty was to be had only from within through a nullification of sin which made external law and force unnecessary.

The political significance of this nullification had indeed already been indicated in the "Address" of *The Likeliest Means*, with reference to a Harringtonian petition of July 6, 1659. There Milton had said that, until true religion should be freed from hirelings and Christian liberty fully established, "no model of a commonwealth will prove successful or undisturbed. . . ."[40] The system of Oceana was the product of secular and sceptical reasoning; but Milton believed "that then both commonwealth and religion will at length, if ever, flourish in Christendom, when either they who govern discern between civil and religious, or they only who so discern shall be admitted to govern."[41] But, as we have seen from the tracts of 1659, the course of the revolution had abundantly convinced Milton that such discernment primarily required the acceptance of true spiritual religion. It was government by men so enlightened, not by popular orders, that he desired in 1660; but there has never been found a ready and easy way to achieve it.

### 3

Milton's repudiation of Oceana in favour of a commonwealth founded upon spiritual and ethical principles is typical of Puritanism. In spite of the failure of every effort to translate such principles into political terms, it was still the ideal of the holy community which animated those who refused to accept defeat. The Presbyterians and Independents had exhausted themselves; but in the months following the fall of Richard there appeared a host of theocratic proposals of varying degrees of liberality.[42] Of these perhaps the most significant was the moderate Richard Baxter's *A Holy Commonwealth, or Political Aphorisms, Opening The true Principles of Government* (July, 1659). The author gave over in despair, and published his work unfinished.

Baxter's work demonstrates not only the bankruptcy of Puritanism but the reasons for its inability to compound with facts. His book was written at Harrington's invitation and as a criticism of Oceana. It arrived at no practical counter-proposals; only the objections to Oceana are explicit. And these are substantially the objections expressed by Milton and by Harrington's two chief opponents among the Vanists—a strangely assorted pair—John Rogers, the Fifth Monarchist imprisoned by Cromwell with Vane in Carisbrook Castle in 1656, and Henry Stubbe, who owed his university education to Vane, and held a post in the Bodleian until he was dismissed in 1659 for his attacks on the ministry.[43]

In spite of differences among themselves, Baxter and the Vanists agreed with Milton in distrusting Harrington's system. Baxter argued that "it is not the model but the better men that must do most," for "it is no mere frame or model of a government that will make happy a commonwealth . . . so much as . . . men of prudence and the fear of God."[44] Rogers said, "Nor can we trust that maxim of his, 'Give us good orders, and they will make us good men,' so much as give us good men and they will make us good orders, and government with God's blessing."[45] And this sentiment was strongly reinforced by the evident temper of the people.

Harrington was aware that his equal suffrage might mean a restored monarchy; but he viewed the possibility with equanimity, and argued according to his principles that an oligarchy was as bad as any regal tyranny and that a commonwealth must give equal rights to all its citizens without distinction of parties. Even the Royalist, "for having opposed a commonwealth . . ., can neither be justly for that cause excluded from his full and equal share in the government, nor prudently for this, that a commonwealth consisting of a party will be in perpetual labour of her own destruction; . . . if you will be trampling, they will fight for liberty, though for monarchy, and you for tyranny, though under the name of a commonwealth."[46]

The case could not have been more truly stated; but even so, Harrington's opponents were convinced that "the ignorant and ungodly rabble" were "utterly unfit for sovereignty," and that "all this stir of the republicans is but to make the seed of the Serpent to be the sovereign rulers of the earth; when God hath promised that the kingdoms of the world shall become Christ's kingdoms, these men would have them to be the Babels of Satan, the seat of confusion, and the enemies of Christ to reign through the earth."[47]

It was natural that the opponents of monarchy should be afraid of the Harringtonian demand that "the parliament or supreme authority of England be chosen by the people to represent them with as much equality as may be."[48] Even *Lilburns Ghost*—appearing, it is true, in a somewhat questionable shape—made like Milton a distinction, reserving the right of suffrage to those who had served the cause of liberty by money or arms; "for in this case, those only ought to be reckoned the people, the rest having by a traitorous engagement, compliance, neutrality, or apostasy, endeavoured to destroy the people, and by consequence have forfeited their rights and membership of free people...."[49] This had been Vane's argument in *A Healing Question*; and in Millenarian pamphlets and petitions of 1659 and 1660, the note is even stronger, for it is supported by the appeal to righteousness. *The Fifth Monarchy*, quoted Millenarian passages from Presbyterians, Independents, Cromwell, Army officers, and parliamentary declarations, denounced all these for their apostasy, and demanded a commonwealth according to Christ's law and "that the people most read and best practisers of this excellent and perfect law be chosen out to the administration thereof under Christ, in opposition to the ignorant, profane and scandalous, and all, both old and new malignants, that have visibly opposed him. . . ." *The Declaration and Proclamation of the Army of God* revived the scheme proposed before the calling of the Little, or Nominated, Parliament: "Elections not to be by a confused rabble, nor yet by a more corrupt sheriff, but to be chosen or at least approved by the several congregations. . . ."[50]

But the difficulty of distinguishing the free from the malignant, the profane from the saints, was even greater now than it had been after the execution of the King. And though moderates like Baxter might oppose the rule of Satan and desire the rule of Christ, they joined with Harrington in attacking the extremists like Rogers who thought that something like the rule of the saints should be established. The last months of the experiment were diversified by a bitter three-cornered controversy in which Baxter and Harrington argued with one another and joined in attacking Rogers for desiring an oligarchy of the saints, and Stubbe for wanting "a select senate for life consisting of Independents, Anabaptists, Fifth Monarchy Men, and Quakers."[51]

This controversy perfectly represents the final collapse of the revolutionary alliance between moderate Puritanism, the sects, and the new secular spirit of democracy. Milton seems to refer to it, and to recognize its dangerous significance, when he says in his *Letter* of October, 1659, "And whether the civil government be an annual democracy or a perpetual aristocracy is not to me a consideration for the extremities we are in. . . ."[52] He soon came to take a different view, for an aristocracy exercising its power through a perpetual senate seemed the only way to preserve the liberty of a Christian commonwealth against the King and the people.

There is certainly nothing unique in Milton's bitter denial of rights to the English people in general; and though the tone is harsher because of the approaching "lent of servitude," the reasons he gave for it are the same as those set forth in the defences. The review of the course of the revolution with which *The Readie and Easie Way* begins is chiefly designed to show that it was the work of a few and that "the best affected also and best principled of the people stood not numbering or computing on which side were most voices in Parliament, but on which side appeared to them most reason, most safety. . . ."[53] As "a greater number might be corrupt within the walls of Parliament," so a greater number might be, and in his opinion now obviously were, corrupt without. As in 1649, but more urgently, it was clear "that most voices ought not always to prevail where main matters are in question: if others hence will pretend to disturb all councils, what is that to them who pretend not, but are in real danger. . . ."[54] The logic of the revolution showed the way in the present crisis:

They who past reason and recovery are devoted to kingship, perhaps will answer that a greater part by far of the nation will have it so. . . . I reply that this greatest part have, both in reason and the trial of just battle, lost the right of their election what the government shall be; of them who have not lost that right, whether they for kingship be the greater number, who can certainly determine? Suppose they be; yet of freedom they partake all alike, one main end of government; which if the greater part value not but will degenerately forgo, is it just or reasonable that most voices against the main end of government should enslave the less number that would be free? More just it is doubtless, if it come to force, that a less number compel a greater to retain, which can be no wrong to them, their liberty, than that a greater number for the pleasure of their baseness compel a less most injuriously to be their fellow slaves. They who seek nothing but their own just liberty have always right to win it and to keep it, whenever they have power, be the voices never so numerous that oppose it.[55]

Under the pressure of events the appeal to the ancient rights of Englishmen has altogether given way to an appeal, not quite to naked force, but to force and a justice recognized by few of Milton's countrymen. The frustration of a great idealism is a painful spectacle; and it would be a bold man who should sit in judgment on this pitiful declaration of failure in which strength and weakness, determination and despair, hope and fear, are so inextricably combined. One may taunt Milton, like the royalist author of *The Censure of the Rota*, with believing that "liberty is safer under an arbitrary unlimited power by virtue of the name 'Commonwealth' than under any other government, how just or restrained soever, if it be but called kingship," and exclaim with him, "I wondered most of all at what politic crack in any man's skull the imagination could enter of securing liberty under an oligarchy, seized of the government for term of life, which was never yet seen in the world."[56] But having recognized the critical position to which Milton has been brought, the student of his thought will turn to inquire how the convictions which inspired the *Areopagitica* and the tracts of 1659 could be made to support this repressive programme, and how they supported his stubborn confidence in himself and his God in the hour of defeat.

From this appeal to the force of a few—a force which Milton could scarcely have hoped to find available except through an act of God[57]—it is apparent that he had lost confidence not merely in the nation in general but in the majority of his own party. But he had not lost faith in the rightness of his cause. His argument is the political counterpart of the harsh Puritan belief in the duty and privilege of the righteous to impose the divine will on the unregenerate mass. It is also the product of his refusal to believe that no such high standard existed and that Hobbes' secular mere will and pleasure must be the rule of right. "God hath yet his remnant, and hath not quenched the spirit of liberty among us. . . ."[58]

The distinction Milton is making—so unpalatable to the modern mind—is still the distinction of the *Defensio* between an absolute justice and the will of corrupt mankind. It was the belief in such a justice and in its ultimate triumph in the hearts of men, that supported Vane on the scaffold, and his followers in their losing struggle against what seemed to them the disastrous principle of popular sovereignty.

To Rogers as to Milton it seemed that Harrington's model involved the primary error of "not laying justice in the foundations of the commonwealth, but planting it upon the whole multitude and community. . . ." Following *A Healing Question*, he argued for "discriminating good and bad, adherents and delinquents, sound and unsound, according to the nature, reason and righteousness of our cause, and indeed the best forms of all commonwealths," on the ground that "not the spirit of the people . . . but the spirit of God, of Christ, of his people in parliament and adherents to the cause is the fittest for the government of the commonwealth."[59] This is the typically Millenarian design. Rogers' congregation had once invited Cromwell to put the government in the hands of seventy godly men, chosen by prayer; and it was a government modelled in this way on Israel that he now hoped to see the Rump produce. But his Millenarianism had been somewhat tempered by experience and modified by his association with Vane. He found support for his argument not only in the Spirit but in his Aristotle: "3 lib. *Polit.* c. 7, *Bonos & aequos dominari oportet, autoritatem que habere omnium* . . . , the good, just, and faithful ought to govern, and others to be excluded that are insane and insuitable to the weal of the public."[60]

Rogers' associate in the defence of Vane arrived at a similar conclusion by a different route. Stubbe did not altogether disapprove of Harrington's system. He replied to Baxter's warning against "democratical politicians" that "democratical government . . . was the government of Christian assemblies till the people were deprived of their votes, and . . . was the government of Israel instituted by God himself." But, as we have seen, this example could be used either to support the full democracy of the Levellers or Harrington,[61] or, as by the sectarian supporters of the Nominated Parliament, to justify the limited and exclusive equality of church members. Stubbe was no Millenarian; but because of the situation in 1660, because of his admiration for Vane, and because of his liking for the aristocracies of Greece and Rome, he wished to see the Oceanic model "limited to the good people which have adhered to the Good Old Cause." He argued that political rights should be restricted to "the honest and faithful party, leaving the residue so much liberty as they are now capable of, or may prove hereafter," for he thought "that the universality of this nation is not to be trusted with liberty at present, that an equal commonwealth is that whereunto we ought and may prudently grow, but which we cannot at once fabric without running an extraordinary hazard of being again enslaved."[62]

Stubbe never clearly outlined his system; but in one way or another "the select senate, whose name hath amazed some and exasperated others," was essential to it. He said in reply to Harrington that a representative body, "regulated according to his own model, may choose ill"; and, following Vane, that a power must be "constituted for the preservation of fundamental liberties against a popular assembly."[63] It seemed to him that "the commonwealth of Israel may herein, as in other causes, become our pattern"; and that "the history of Lacedemon is a plea for optimacy."[64] And to these precedents he added arguments from the law of nature. All men are "by nature free, and equally free from an over-ruling magisterial power"; and "when a government is broken, all men are cast into their natural freedom." But when a new government is established, it is necessary to discriminate: "When there is any such intention in any number of men, and it be certain, or highly probable, that others who either live intermixed with them, or joining unto them, will oppose or subvert the government which they are going to establish, it is lawful, and an act of self-defence, to subject such persons or parties, so far to depress them as there is danger of their prejudicing the government intended."[65]

The significance of these disordered arguments of the Millenarian and the librarian does not lie merely in their support of a programme not unlike Milton's in purpose. They show how the two sources of his idealism could be united in defence of the proposals of Vane's *Healing Question.* The same combination is still present in *The Readie and Easie Way*, operating to sustain the hope of the *Defensio* for a Christian commonwealth which should equal and surpass the achievements of the ancients. The civilization of Greece and Rome still provides a pattern of excellence to be imitated. "The old Athenian commonwealth, reputed the first and ancientest place of civility in all Greece," is still an example.[66] But because of the stubborn hardness of heart of the English, this ideal is hardened into the likeness of the more than Spartan rigour of the commonwealth of Israel.

In the face of the defection of the English people, Milton's contempt for the weakness of worldly-minded degeneracy congeals into a harsh bitterness. The King and the madly monarchical people take on the aspect of Comus and his riotous and unruly crew. "Free commonwealths have been ever counted fittest and properest for civil, virtuous, and industrious nations, abounding with prudent men worthy to govern; monarchy fittest to curb degenerate, corrupt, idle, proud, luxurious people."[67] Those who desire "basely and besottedly to run their necks again into the yoke which they have broken," who would "prostitute religion and liberty to the vain and groundless apprehension that nothing but kingship can restore trade, . . . will bring us soon . . . to those calamities which attend always and unavoidably on luxury. . . ."[68] Such are "worthy indeed themselves, whatsoever they be, to be forever slaves," and it is against all justice that they should be permitted to drag "that part of the nation which consents not with them . . . into the same bondage."[69]

In the fate that is prepared for them, one recognizes the cold temper of the Lady; and yet there remains in the last pamphlets, in spite of disillusionment, the ideal of a fully and freely developed humanity exercising itself in a strong and virtuous liberty which *Comus* imperfectly and the *Areopagitica* abundantly expressed. Behind the arguments from man's natural right and dignity which these pamphlets still produce there lies the dying hope for a society of men free in their wisdom and goodness. *The Readie and Easie Way* is not merely a design for the repression of Milton's opponents, but a plan for those who were, he still hoped, "reserved . . . by divine providence to a better end." He recognized the potential tyranny in his scheme; but he hoped that it might be prevented from becoming "an oligarchy or faction of a few." If the well-affected choose men "who may be found infallibly constant to those two conditions forenamed, full liberty of conscience and the abjuration of monarchy," then the "well-ordered committees of their faithful adherents in every county may give this government the resemblance and effects of a perfect democracy."[70] This is Milton's version of equal liberty among the good party. But further, once liberty is thus established, those who are excluded from it may be brought to deserve its privileges. To preserve the commonwealth it will be necessary, as the *Declaration* proposed, "to well-qualify and refine elections, not committing all to the noise and shouting of a rude multitude, but permitting only those of them who are rightly qualified to nominate as many as they will." But it will also be necessary "to make the people fittest to choose, and the chosen fittest to govern" by mending "our corrupt and faulty education, to teach the people faith not without virtue, temperance, modesty, sobriety, parsimony, justice; not to admire wealth or honour; to hate turbulence and ambition; to place everyone his private welfare and happiness in the public peace, liberty, and safety."[71]

It is remarkable that in the midst of disaster Milton should retain his faith in the power of education not merely to convey knowledge but to inculcate the principles of virtue. It is the more remarkable that, after expressing in the tracts of 1659 a view of education which, as we have seen, is very close to the view of those sectaries who had no belief in its power to lead the mind to faith, he should here include the teaching of faith among its functions. But, as we also saw, no matter how nearly Milton might approach the sectarian view, there always remained in his mind the conviction that faith is an achievement of the developing reason, and that virtue is only to be achieved through faith. In spite of the frustration of 1660, he continues to trust not only in the power but in the progress of truth. Terrible as his renunciation of the English people is, that belief sustains him, and will sustain him in his last years. With Vane and Rogers he yet believed in the process whereby "the kingdoms of the world shall become the kingdoms of our Lord and of his Christ."[72] And, like Stubbe, he was convinced that to prevent the nation from "treading back again with lost labour all our happy steps in the progress of reformation" was essential if the way was to be kept open for an advance towards "a free government, though for the present not obtained."[73]

Milton's confidence in the divine truth and efficacy of Christian religion is stronger, not weaker, in 1660. The motive of his strange programme is the hope that thereby "we shall retain the best part of our liberty, which is our religion, and the civil part will be from those who defer us much more easily recovered, being neither so subtle nor so awful as a king enthroned."[74] Since the government of his commonwealth, according to the principles developed in *Of Civil Power*, would have repudiated compulsive (though exercising a limited degree of restrictive) power in religion, and since it would have avoided the imposition of a multiplicity of laws and permitted unlicensed discussion, even the unregenerate would presumably have enjoyed under it a large measure of freedom from state control—as the hard of heart were to be permitted freedom of divorce to ensure the good man's righteous privilege. Yet in order to preserve the Christian liberty defined in 1659, he is willing to sacrifice all but the shadow of political liberty. For he has reached the point in the progress from reformation to liberty beyond which he cannot go; and like the Puritans of the centre and right, he can solve the dilemma only by sacrificing liberty to gain the truth which ought to free.

## 4

Stubbe was close to the truth when he said of the disputes in the last months of the interregnum, "I do verily believe that the quarrel was toleration or no toleration, rather than monarchy and the Stuartian interest."[75] Harrington's penetrating intelligence went to the centre of the question when he said, in reply to Baxter's party on the one hand and to Stubbe and Rogers on the other, that "one main exception which the prelatical and presbyterian sects have against popular government is that as to religion it will trust every man unto his own liberty; and that only for which the rest of the religious sects apprehend popular government is that the spirit of the nation . . . is not to be trusted with liberty of conscience in that it is inclining to persecute for religion."[76]

Harrington meant to have the best of both arguments. Like the Levellers he insisted on freedom of conscience as a fundamental political right: "Where civil liberty is entire, it includes liberty of conscience. Where liberty of conscience is entire, it includes civil liberty."[77] But Oceana was nothing if not comprehensive; and because he distinguished two sorts of conscience, the one private, the other public, he also provided for a state church through a Council of Religion which was to administer the ecclesiastical endowments, and to keep the peace in religious matters.

He argued that the known doctrines of Christian religion should support the national conscience, and that liberty should be preserved for difference of opinion and further light. But the truth is that his mind was entirely secular and sceptical, and he could make these concessions to both sides since he was completely free from the Puritan preoccupation with an absolute and revealed truth.

Baxter and the Vanists approved in Harrington's model those provisions which suited with their particular views of revelation. Baxter still maintained, though with moderation, the Presbyterian and Independent position. He approved of Oceana's state church, but condemned its freedom of conscience on the ground that it would destroy not only the church but the principles on which a Christian commonwealth must be founded. Rogers and Stubbe, on the other hand, repudiated the state church and argued for the freedom of conscience required by *A Healing Question*. Stubbe, who quoted "the excellent Mr. J. Milton" on Constantine's corruption of Christianity, stated the case succinctly when he said that it was "not such a religion the speculative part of which was clearly manifested unto all," but one whose doctrines were "not to be proved by natural reason and common principles, but pure revelation which is delivered in the Scripture . . . , and for the full explanation whereof tradition is no way conducible, but only the Spirit guiding those that are not reprobate unto all knowledge."[78]

This is precisely the argument of *Of Civil Power*; and it is made to prove the error of compulsion by the state just as Milton's was.

But, as Harrington said, Rogers and Stubbe could not couple this religious liberty with full civil liberty because the popular will was clearly for a restoration, not merely of the monarchy, but of episcopacy, and such a restoration would mean, as the event proved, the loss of the freedom of conscience which the revolution had achieved. It was for this reason that Rogers sought for something like the rule of the saints who believed in the spiritual revelation, and Stubbe proposed his select senate made up of those groups who depended upon it.

Milton found himself in exactly the same position. Whatever may be the political repressiveness of *The Readie and Easie Way*, it involves no retreat from the principles developed in the radical tracts of 1659. In contending that "this liberty of conscience, which above all other things ought to be to all men dearest and most precious, no government [is] more inclinable not only to favour but to protect than a free commonwealth," he referred back to their argument; and, in the first edition of the pamphlet, briefly repeated it.

> And in my judgment, civil states would do much better, and remove the cause of much hindrance and disturbance in public affairs, . . . if they would not meddle at all with ecclesiastical matters, which are both of a quite different nature from their cognizance, and have their proper laws . . . with such coercive power as belongs to them. . . . If there were no meddling with church matters in state councils, there would not be such faction in choosing members of parliament, while everyone strives to choose him whom he takes to be of his religion, and every faction hath the plea of God's cause. Ambitious leaders of the armies would then have no hypocritical pretences so ready to hand to contest with parliaments, yea to dissolve them and make way to their own tyrannical designs; in sum, I verily suppose there would be then no more pretending to a Fifth Monarchy of the saints; but much peace and tranquillity would follow. . . .[79]

This is a profoundly significant passage; and its significance is increased by the fact that it was removed from the second edition of *The Readie and Easie Way.*

As it stands in the first edition, this ascription of the troubles of the Commonwealth—including Cromwell's rule—to the Puritan preoccupation with the truth of Christian religion and the desire not only of the right but of the extreme left to make the state the instrument of true reformation, emphasizes those arguments for the complete separation of church and state, the ecclesiastical and the civil, in which the tracts of 1659 so closely approximate the contentions which Williams developed from his strict segregation of the spiritual and the natural. It seems to invalidate the thesis of the preceding chapter—that ultimately this segregation was impossible for Milton.

It was deleted, not because Milton ceased to believe that true spiritual religion must, from its very quality, be free of state control and independent of secular force, but because the practical political situation in 1660 seemed to demonstrate conclusively that the state must be so constituted as to provide for the defence of true spiritual religion, and that in consequence (while true religion must remain free, and church and state therefore separate) the strict segregation of the spiritual and natural was not only undesirable but impossible.

The effect of the omission of this passage in the second edition is to throw a heavier emphasis on what followed it in the first, the argument that the restoration of monarchy will mean the restoration of episcopacy, and that this will mean loss of liberty not only to the sects but even to the "new royalized Presbyterians." This argument was, indeed, substantially enlarged in the second edition.[80] There remains, of course, the demand for freedom of conscience not for all men but for such as "profess their faith and worship by the Scriptures only";[81] but with Stubbe and Rogers, Milton has been forced to argue that this liberty can only be preserved if the civil government is restricted to those who believe in it. We have already perceived that Milton's need to reconcile the instincts of his own nature with his sense of divine goodness made the principle of segregation invalid for him. But even if he had been capable of adopting it, the events of 1660 would have prevented him, as they prevented Rogers and Stubbe. For it seemed clear that only those who depended on the freedom of the Spirit could be allowed to govern since only they would repudiate the misuse of civil power which is contrary to true Christian religion.

Even more explicitly than the tracts of 1659, the last pamphlets insist on the duty of the truly Christian magistrate to leave "both maintenance of ministers and all matters ecclesiastical to the church in her several congregations," and at the same time "to defend religion from outward violence."[82] But, as Williams had said, this latter duty required the magistrate to determine what religion was to be so defended. To avoid the danger from a magistracy determining wrongly, Milton and the Vanists are demanding in 1660—what each of the Puritan groups had demanded in its turn—that the magistrates shall be only such as already recognize the religion which is true.

Even the Millenarian Rogers was reluctantly forced to reinterpret Vane's *Healing Question* in this light. In commenting on Vane's pamphlet, Baxter pertinently inquired how, if liberty of conscience was to be granted to all men indiscriminately, popery was to be prevented from invading England once more, and what provision was to be made against those who would subvert both religion and the commonwealth, if the magistrate was to be forbidden to act against them. Rogers replied that the *Healing Question* concerned itself "only about the magistrate not compelling or imposing in the matters of God, not about this restraining of papists and infidels," and added: "I dare not positively affirm that the civil magistrate is not to intermeddle in matters of religion; for it is his duty to provide for and encourage the faithful preachers and professors of the Gospel, and to be a nursing father to the church of Christ; but how far the magistrate is to proceed in suppressing erroneous doctrines and where the bounds are to be set beyond which he is not to go, I suppose a wiser man than Mr. Baxter cannot easily determine."[83] This indeed is a melancholy conclusion to twenty years of heated argument and determined effort. But the conflicting claims of reformation and liberty could not in fact be reconciled. And those who were incapable of believing that Christian truth could have no direct influence on the daily lives of men, who were reluctant to hand the state over to Satan either by accepting Williams' segregation or by resting in exhaustion in the scepticism of Harrington, were ultimately forced to escape from the dilemma by resorting to civil power.

Milton could warn the Parliament in 1660 to beware lest "the abandoning of all those whom they call sectaries . . . be a wilful rejection of their own chief strength and interest in the freedom of all Protestant religion, under what abusive name soever calumniated"; but because monarchy and episcopacy "are individual," he could not, even if he had wished, have distinguished the end and good of the true Christian from the end and good of the true Christian commonwealth.[84] He was forced to unite them by "the reluctance, I may say the antipathy, which is in all kings against Presbyterian and Independent discipline; for they hear the Gospel speaking much of liberty; a word which monarchy and her bishops both fear and hate, but a free commonwealth both favours and promotes."[85]

It is the reinforcing of this conviction by events that explains the difference between the view of education taken in 1659 and the proposals of the last pamphlets. The return to the humanistic confidence of *Of Education* is only partial; but it is a return, for education is to perform both a religious and a civil function. The commonwealth cannot force its citizens to accept the religion of the Spirit; but it will defend the church which can persuade them to it, and it will support this persuasion through "the liberty to erect schools in every city and town . . . , whereby the land will become more civilized. . . ."[86] But to be civilized it was necessary, in Milton's view, to be Christian. In these schools "their children may be bred up in their own sight to all learning and noble education, not in grammar only, but in all liberal arts and exercises. This would soon spread much more knowledge and civility, yea religion, through all parts of the land. . . ."[87] Thus will be produced citizens capable of exercising their civil privileges in the achievement of that good, both human and spiritual, which is defined by the law of absolute justice recognized by the enlightened, and by them alone.

## 5

It was enough for Harrington that Oceana provided the machinery whereby the people's will might define the good of the commonwealth. But, because of the popular desire for the King, Milton's last pamphlets express even more firmly than the defences the conviction that the good of the commonwealth cannot be defined by the imperfect will either of one or many but only in accordance with the absolute and divine law. Like the Vanists, he would have agreed with Baxter that "the happiest commonwealth is that which most attaineth the ends of government and society, which are the public good, especially in matters of everlasting concernment and the pleasing of God, the absolute Lord and King of all."[88]

Baxter perfectly expressed the aim common to all the Puritan groups when he said that "in a divine commonwealth the laws of God, in nature and Scripture, must be taken for the principal laws, which no rulers can dispense with." And in the course of his effort to describe the Christian Utopia, he inevitably turned to the problem of defining these laws which we have seen Milton struggling to solve in the divorce tracts and the political pamphlets:

> Though the Law of Moses as such oblige us not, yet the matter of it under another form may oblige; that is, the Moral Law still bindeth us, both as the law of nature and of the Redeemer; and the reasons of the laws commonly called Political . . . do still bind, so far as, our case agreeing with theirs, we can perceive in those laws how God would have such a case determined. If God's laws keep not the pre-eminency, his government is rejected. . . . All the world have the law of nature; Christians also have the law of grace, and the law of nature in the most legible characters. These are to be the principal statutes for the government of the commonwealth; and man's laws should subserve them.[89]

It is Milton's full acceptance of this idea which begets the repeated citation in the last pamphlets of the experience of the Israelites "who much against the will of God had sought a king and rejected a commonwealth wherein they might have lived happily under the reign of God only, their king."[90]

But between the moderate and extreme Puritans there remained in 1660 that unhappy and fundamental difference of opinion on the interpretation of the divine law which had begun the frustrating of the experiment in godly government in 1643. It seemed to men like Baxter that the sectaries ignored the authority of scriptural revelation to follow their own wilful fancies; it seemed to the sectaries that the moderates interpreted the letter of revelation according to their own corrupt devices.

By 1659 Baxter and his group were indeed in a sad case. They found themselves between the devil of democracy and the raging sea of sectarian enthusiasm; and every plan for imposing the divine law on the nation had failed. If Baxter disliked Oceana because it did not admit the existence of such a law, he also disliked the Vanists because they pretended to "the inward warrant of justice and righteousness."[91] Such a warrant was inconclusive. "The rule of righteousness is without us in the laws; and there can be no such thing as an inward righteousness which is contrary to that outward law, the Rule of Righteousness, because that conformity is its essential form."[92] Yet the definition of that outward rule was difficult. Like his predecessors, Baxter sought for the foundations of his holy commonwealth in statutes and precedents and acts of parliament. But the revolution had undermined their authority; and because he could find no other authoritative prescription but the laws of the Jewish state, he had to content himself with arguing, "Let so much of God's own law be owned, as is still undoubtedly in force."[93]

This desire to establish the holy commonwealth in England by putting in force the Mosaic Law, duly modified, constantly appears in the pamphlets of these last months. Thus *The Fifth Monarchy* asked "that the laws of this great King, as they are recorded in the Old and New Testaments, remaining in force, be the declared laws of this nation."[94] And John Eliot, writing from the theocratic peace of New England, argued that the state should not be formed according to human wisdom since "the sufficiency and perfection of Scripture" provided the most perfect pattern.

> The particular form of government which is approved of God, instituted by Moses among the sons of Israel, and profitable to be received by any nation or people who reverence the command of God and tremble at his word, is this: that they choose unto themselves rulers of thousands, of hundreds, of fifties, of tens, who shall govern according to the pure and holy, righteous, perfect, and good law of God, written in the Scriptures of the Old and New Testaments.[95]

This theory of what Baxter called "holy theocratical government," based on the written law of Scripture, is the political counterpart of the Puritan idea of the one right discipline. But just as the sectaries had revolted against the imposition of an external ecclesiastical discipline, developing the argument from Christian liberty and the abrogation of the Mosaic Law into a theory of the sovereign individual conscience, so they rejected this copying of the external Mosaic code for the state. *The Declaration . . . of the Army of God* thus required "God's laws to be enthroned, but not the Jews'."[96] And when Rogers cited "the laws, word, and spirit of God, of nature," he meant the laws written in the hearts of the redeemed.[97]

Milton's hope was for a commonwealth based on a similar law. The relationship between the arguments of *The Readie and Easie Way* and the beliefs of the sectaries was in fact dimly recognized by the Presbyterian author of the longest answer to them. *The Dignity of Kingship Asserted* is a laborious and slow-moving review of the revolution, designed to show the illegality of the Independents' political actions. "G. S." indicated the centre of the question between the right and the left when he observed that the King's enemies seemed averse to "having any laws at all," and proceeded to underline (with a reference to the divorce tracts) the antinomian implications of Milton's political opinions: "Truly, Mr. Milton, however you palliate things, I believe verily there lies the knot that troubles you, there your shoe pinches. I find generally such Christian Libertines, as your writings show you to be one of, come at last to throw off all external, coercive, or binding laws, and desire only to be governed by the laws within them, which in truth is a spirit of lawlessness. To this your doctrine of divorce seems to incline. . . ."[98]

The difference between this view of the case and Milton's conception of an absolute law of justice in the hearts of the good need not again be emphasized. But the conception is fundamental to the argument of his last pamphlets. He may point to the example of the Jews and refer to the legal rights of parliament; but these appeals are secondary to the appeal to the law of nature, and the law of nature is virtually identified with the law of the Spirit. Thus in justifying the unprecedented acts of the revolution, he argues that those who desired a just liberty were

> therefore not bound by any statute of preceding parliaments, but by the law of nature only, which is the only law of laws truly and properly to all mankind fundamental, the beginning and the end of all government; to which no parliament or people that will throughly reform, but may and must have recourse; as they had and must yet have in church reformation (if they throughly intend it) to evangelic rules, not to ecclesiastical canons, though never so ancient, so ratified and established in the land by statutes, which for the most part are mere positive laws, neither natural nor moral, and so by any parliament for just and serious considerations, without scruple to be at any time repealed.[99]

This distinction between mere positive and therefore accidental laws and the permanent natural and moral law involves the transference from the ecclesiastical and private to the political sphere of the argument of the divorce pamphlets and the tracts of 1659. Their arguments proved the right of the good man to divorce according to his rectified conscience and of the true Christian to religious liberty in accordance with the illumination of the Spirit. In both cases a consequence was the permission of a degree of liberty to the hard of heart and the erroneous. But in the political sphere, such is the practical necessity of preserving the good man's liberty, that privileges must be restricted to those who recognize the permanent natural and moral law.

And the relationship between civil reform according to the law of nature and church reform according to the law of Scripture and the Spirit is in Milton's mind something more than an analogy. He told the royalist Griffith that "no law can be fundamental but that which is grounded on the light of nature or right reason, commonly called moral law. . . ."[100] But, as we have seen, an effect of the spiritual illumination of the true believer was, according to the tracts of 1659, the renewing of the original moral law of nature in the heart. It follows that only those who possess this illumination are capable of perceiving that absolute justice which defines the good of man and upon which the truly Christian commonwealth must be founded.

It is only in *De Doctrina Christiana*, as we shall see, that this identification of the law of the Spirit and the law of nature is fully developed. But its presence in Milton's mind as he composed the last pamphlets explains why they contain no appeal to the secondary, or imperfect, law of nature, partially apprehended by all men through reason. This is the law of the heathen commonwealths, carried to its highest level by the ancients. But as the Jewish commonwealth which surpassed them had a written law revealed by God himself, so the Christian commonwealth which should surpass both has the revealed spiritual law as its guide. It is for this reason that Milton emphasizes the depravity of those who desire the King, for they do not recognize the divine justice which the King and his bishops would overthrow. And it is for this reason that he demands a perpetual senate—perpetual since the moral law is perpetual—which should be composed, so far as may be, of men whose natures have been regenerated by the Spirit.

Harrington argued that, "as the natural body of a Christian or saint can be no other for the frame than such as has been the natural body of an Israelite or of a heathen, so the political bodies or civil governments of Christians or saints can be no other, for the frame, than such as have been the political bodies or civil governments of the Israelites or of the heathens."[101] But this application of the principle of segregation by the secular sceptic absolutely contradicted

Milton's view of the effects of regeneration. It also contradicted the views of the Millenarian Rogers.

We have seen how among the Levellers the freedom of conscience claimed as a Christian liberty by the Separatists was transformed by a process of secularization or of segregation into the democratic theory of natural political rights. In the writings of Rogers in the last months of the experiment one can see the Millenarian counterpart of this process taking place and producing an argument for natural political rights limited to those who possess Christian liberty. The very pressure of events, the popular will, the danger of losing freedom of conscience, forced Rogers to bridge the gap—still not completely bridged in *A Healing Question*—between nature and the spirit. What he demands for the good party is "our rights and liberties, both as Christians and men (or in matters of conscience and in civil things) declared and contended for . . . , conquered and maintained; of a legitimate and full grown conception, founded in the laws, word, and spirit of God, of nature, and of the reason and wisdom in this nation. . . ." Collected together and fused in this statement are all the radical principles of the revolution; but they are limited to those who have adhered to the cause, and so have proved themselves true Christians and possessed of "that natural right, freedom and liberty, which Christ hath purchased by his blood."[102] As we have seen, Overton wrote man over "believer" and nature over "grace" in translating the doctrine of Christian liberty and equality into political terms; Rogers renews the original draught.

In this ascription of regained natural rights to Christ's sacrifice for believers is expressed a fusion of the principles of "the mere commonwealths man" with those of "the rigid Fifth Monarchy Man."[103] A similar, though not identical, fusion is apparent in Milton's last pamphlets, for the events of 1659 and 1660 confirmed him in the tendency to regard human and Christian liberty as two expressions of the spiritual and ethical condition of the regenerate man. Whereas Harrington, Baxter, and the Royalists now joined against the sects to maintain, like the author of *Saintship No Ground of Soveraignty*, that civil government "belongs to men not as they are Christians but as they are men, and is a consequent not of our spiritual but of our natural birth,"[104] Milton finds himself, because of the ethical preoccupation of the humanist and the spiritual preoccupation of the Puritan, joining with the Millenarian Rogers to defend both the religious and the political liberty of true Christians.

As monarchy means "the destruction of true religion and civil liberty," so a free commonwealth on the contrary has been "not only held by wisest men in all ages the noblest, the manliest, the equalest, the justest government, the most agreeable to all due liberty and proportioned equality, both human, civil, and Christian, most cherishing to virtue and true religion, but also (I may say it with greatest probability) plainly commended or rather enjoined by our Saviour himself to all Christians, not without remarkable disallowance and the brand of gentilism upon kingship."[105]

It is, of course, to Christ's words to the sons of Zebedee, already cited in the *Defensio*, that Milton here refers. But his deductions have a fulness not found in the earlier political writings. As all the radical motives of the revolution are gathered in the statement of Rogers, so in this very similar statement are gathered the aims which have animated Milton. His commonwealth is to achieve the noble manliness and virtue which inspired the ancient philosophers; but because human, civil, and Christian liberty are for him inseparable, it must also achieve the true religion upon which they are properly founded, and it therefore possesses not merely the sanction but the authority of Christ himself. In *The Readie and Easie Way*, the argument of the divorce tracts that Christ came to free his servants for the enjoyment of every good thing not only of the other life but of this, issues finally in the flat assertion that here "he speaks of civil government."[106]

As the author of *The Censure of the Rota* pointed out, this assertion flatly contradicts the argument used by Milton, as by the sectaries, against the exercise of temporal power by the church: "For if the text which you quote . . . be to be understood of civil government, and to infer a commonwealth . . . and not to be meant of his spiritual reign, of which he was then speaking . . . , you must prove that he erected a republic of his apostles and that, notwithstanding the Scripture everywhere calls his government the Kingdom of Heaven, it ought to be corrected and rendered the Commonwealth of Heaven or rather the Commonwealth of this World. . . ."[107] But that was precisely the end to which Milton had been driven by the course of the revolution which clearly demonstrated the unsoundness of the strict principle of segregation. Limited as it was by his stern sense of right and duty, and frustrated by the defection of his countrymen, Milton's radical and ethical individualism was compelled to arrive at a transference of rights from the religious to the secular sphere similar to the transference which characterized the thinking of the Puritan radicals.

The "liberty and proportioned equality" which his commonwealth supports is the political expression of the liberty and equality of those who are prophets, priests, and kings in Christ.[108] The democratic aims of the Levellers and Harrington have their place in his scheme as in Rogers'; his ideal is "a frugal and self-governing democraty or commonwealth . . . , thriving in the joint providence and counsel of many industrious equals," and affording the "civil rights and advancements of every person according to his merit."[109] But such is the manifest effect of original sin unredeemed that this freedom and equality must be made to depend on the spiritual merit which is the possession of the elect through Christ. The author of *The Censure* was closer to the truth than he knew when he told Milton that "the Fifth Monarchy Men . . . would have been admirable for your purpose if they had but dreamt of a fifth free state."[110] And Roger L'Estrange uncharitably and unwittingly went to the root of the matter when he said of Milton's reference to the happiness of the Jews "under the reign of God only, their king": "This expression doubtfully implies you a Millenary. Do you then really expect to see Christ reigning upon earth, even with those very eyes you lost (as 'tis reported) with staring too long and too saucily upon the portraiture of his viceregent, to break the image. . . ?"[111]

One can still clearly recognize in the proposals and arguments of the last pamphlets not only the influence of the example of those ancient commonwealths whose achievement was the inspiration of so much of Milton's thinking but also the influence of the Platonic search for that ideal city whose pattern is laid up in heaven and which should be ruled by the wise and the good according to the ideal laws of nature. One can see also in Milton's theory of proportioned equality the influence of that intelligent discrimination on which the Aristotelian theory was erected. But in the last pamphlets these influences are profoundly modified by the events which made it seem clear that only the assistance of divine power could enable fallen man to gain what the Greeks had been unable to achieve. Milton's humanistic idealism remains vital; and it is his rationalistic interpretation of Christian regeneration which makes him still suspicious of the irrational enthusiasm of the illiterate saints. But his humanism is nevertheless fused with and qualified by the sectarian idea of the rule of Christ through the Spirit in the hearts of the regenerate.

Zebedee's sons were perhaps mistaken in thinking that the Kingdom "was to be ere long upon earth"; but if "the Kingdom of

Christ, our common king and lord, is hid to this world," and so provides kings with no warrant to set themselves up as his viceregents, yet the pattern of the Kingdom's laws, both spiritual and natural, is being cleared in the hearts of believers by the Spirit, and it is their duty and privilege to strive for a commonwealth modelled, though imperfectly, on it.[112] If the groundwork of the commonwealth is laid in such principles, the details "may be referred to time, so we be still going on by degrees to perfection."[113] The return of monarchy means the undoing of the reformation's progress in the achievement of religious, private, and also political liberty; but if the ready and easy way is taken,

there can be no cause alleged why peace, justice, plentiful trade and all prosperity should not thereupon ensue throughout the whole land, with as much assurance as can be of human things, that they shall so continue (if God favour us and our wilful sins provoke him not) even to the coming of our true and rightful and only to be expected King, only worthy as he is our only Saviour, the Messiah, the Christ, the only heir of his eternal father, the only by him anointed and ordained since the work of our redemption finished, Universal Lord of all mankind.[114]

But the wilful sins of the English people prevented this happy consummation of the Puritan experiment. And the last paragraph of *The Readie and Easie Way*, added in the second edition and therefore Milton's final comment on the revolution, is a despairing cry for God's assistance in the establishment of liberty: "Thus much I should perhaps have said, though I were sure I should have spoken only to trees and stones; and had none to cry to but with the prophet, O Earth, earth, earth! to tell the very soil itself what her perverse inhabitants are deaf to. Nay, though what I have spoke should happen (which thou suffer not who didst create mankind free; nor thou next who didst redeem us from being servants of men) to be the last words of our expiring liberty."[115] In that parenthetical appeal to the Creator of natural freedom and to the Redeemer of both spiritual and natural freedom is expressed the very centre of Milton's thought on liberty.

On the eve of the Restoration which finally defeated the effort to establish the holy community in church and state, Milton must have shared in the disillusionment which made Baxter bring suddenly to an end, with "Meditations and Lamentations," his account of the Holy Commonwealth: "God is not the God of confusion, but of order. Wonderful! whence then are all the woeful disorders of the world!"[116] The effort of will and the resilient idealism whereby

Milton overcame this disastrous conclusion are already represented in the prose, though they now needed to be themselves regenerated. The justification of the ways of God to men depends not merely on the recognition of man's hardness of heart, but on the existence of that fit audience though few whose wisdom and goodness, illumination and righteousness, should have issued in the establishment of the holy commonwealth. Even though "the effects of wisdom are so little seen among us,"[117] Milton's faith in its power remained to the end.

# *Part V*

# *Principles of Liberty: De Doctrina Christiana*

# Chapter XVI

## Knowledge in the Making

THROUGHOUT his controversial prose, in the pamphlets on political, no less than in those on religious and personal problems, the basic principles of Milton's thought were provided by Christian doctrine. Christian theology was not for him of merely academic interest; nor did it concern only an unreal world separated from the present by death. It served to bring into ordered significance the lessons of a life full of intense experience. This experience resulted in a modification of the orthodox pattern at many points; but the explanation he sought at the end of the prose period found its formulation in terms of the doctrines accepted by him from his teachers in youth and generally received by his contemporaries as defining the conditions of human existence.

Hobbes, and others for whom theology had ceased to have any real significance, sought explanations elsewhere. Milton could have agreed with his assertions that "the true and perspicuous explication of the elements of laws natural and politic . . . dependeth upon the knowledge of what is human nature"; and that the prime rule for the investigator is "*Nosce teipsum*, Read thyself."[1] Yet he would have said of Hobbes' explication that it left out of account some of the essential facts of human experience, explained by Christian doctrine and exemplified by the course of the Puritan revolution itself. The doctrines of man's Fall and Regeneration were essential to Milton's understanding of human nature because they served to explain why twenty years of effort ended in confusion, and to define the objective which with God's abundant help ought to have been achieved.

The reformation of human society, ecclesiastical, domestic, and political, was designed to enable men to repair their original ruins and to exercise the Christian liberty which regeneration begot. That definition of its purpose was the product of Milton's reading both of events and of himself. Christian liberty, as he interpreted it, defined the ideal of a personality of which the chief characteristic was a proud independence, increased by blindness, and issuing at once in an assertion of individual freedom and in a sense of superiority to the generality of men. The doctrine caught up into itself the virtue of temperance, and was extended to include activity in the order of nature as well as in the order of grace. It therefore served to express that integration of the natural and the spiritual through which, in Milton's view, his powers as poet must fulfil their harmonious function.

For both personal and public reasons, Christian liberty was therefore the central theme of Milton's prose. From 1641 to 1660 his attention was concentrated on the search for institutions which would make possible the exercise of this peculiar privilege in its three aspects, religious, private, and civil, without at the same time releasing the unregulated activity of licence. Yet the full significance of the doctrine was not clearly apprehended from the outset. The prose is the record of the progressive development and definition of its implications. Since it gave expression to what was basic in his personality, all of Milton's ideas, without exception, had ultimately to relate themselves to this concept. But its significance became apparent only in the light of events; and the progressive definition of the implications of his first statements was conditioned by the course of the revolution and by the terms in which contemporary opinion expressed itself.

With this concept as centre, it is possible to discern behind Milton's controversial writings the development of a not incoherent pattern of thought. The prose itself is not coherent; nor was the pattern static; for it was the product of living experience amid violently conflicting opinions. But as one recognizes in Puritans of whatever degree of orthodoxy, not a unity but a continuity of thought,[2] so one recognizes in Milton's reasoning a continuity of development within a fundamental pattern for which Christian liberty provided the focal point.

The continuous line of development which linked *Of Reformation* with *The Readie and Easie Way* was parallel to the line which joined the Puritans of the right to those of the left. In fact, Milton's thinking followed almost exactly the course which is defined by the shift of revolutionary dominance from Presbyterianism through the parties of the centre, to the extremes of sectarianism. As that progression reached its end in the last months of 1659 and the early months of 1660, so Milton reached and defined in the pamphlets of the closing months of the Puritan experiment what is, for the purposes of this study, his extreme position. His exposition of the basic principles supporting that position was to have been offered, as the fruit of long study and mature experience, in the theological treatise which he was then bringing to completion.

*De Doctrina Christiana* had been in process of composition since the beginning of the revolution. Shortly after his return from Italy and establishment in London in 1640, Milton had begun "a tractate which he thought fit to collect from the ablest of divines who had written of that subject, Amesius, Wollebius, etc.; viz., A perfect System of Divinity. . . ."[3] The task of studying first "a few of the shorter systems of divines," then "some of the more copious theological treatises," must have occupied him at intervals throughout the prose period.[4] The results of his investigation are apparent in his pamphlets on the church and, much more strikingly, in the subtle doctrinal reasoning of his divorce tracts. In the four years between *Tetrachordon* and *The Tenure*, his chief undertaking was the *History of Britain*;[5] but theology must also have occupied his attention until the press of official business and the composition of his defences put an end to systematic study for the time being. When he was excused in 1655 from the routine of his secretaryship as a consequence of his blindness, he returned to "the framing a body of divinity out of the Bible";[6] and by 1658 his work was sufficiently advanced to warrant the promise which concluded his revised *Defensio*. The ecclesiastical pamphlets of 1659 handled briefly matters more largely canvassed in its chapters. If 1660 had seen the establishment of a commonwealth having as one of its fundamentals "liberty of conscience to all professing Scripture to be the rule of their faith and worship," the treatise would shortly have appeared. But it was destined to remain unpublished for almost two hundred years.

The extant manuscript of *De Doctrina Christiana*—partly recopied after his death, partly written out under his direction, with minor revisions in a number of hands—represents substantially his opinions at the time of the Restoration.[7] His classing of scriptural passages "under certain heads" had been transformed by his efforts to "ascertain for myself the several points of my religious belief" into an elaborate disquisition, "useful in establishing my faith or assisting my memory," which required to be fairly transcribed for the purpose of publication.[8] The process had led him to conclusions "which will at once be seen to differ from certain received opinions";[9] and if his Theological Index, and the original manuscripts of his treatise with their revisions, had survived, it would have been possible to trace the stages in his interpretation of Christian doctrine by which he arrived at the distinctly heretical positions of his final treatise.

Those stages would certainly have been found to correspond with the steps marked by the reasoning of his controversial pamphlets; and the most significant factor would have been the transformation of the conservative version of Christian liberty into the doctrine which provided the basis for his final pamphlets on church and state, and which is now fully expounded in the twenty-sixth and twenty-seventh chapters of *De Doctrina Christiana*, Book I. But even without the lost evidence, the process can be deduced with a high degree of accuracy from the prose itself; for the problems with which the prose dealt were the immediate causes of the transformation.

## 2

In the anti-episcopal pamphlets of 1641 and 1642, Milton appeared to be perfectly orthodox. His intimate connection with Thomas Young and the Smectymnuans, his reproduction of many of their arguments, his general acceptance of their view of the church and of reformation, associated him with the moderate English Puritanism which tended to modify strict Scotch Presbyterianism in the direction of the Congregationalism expounded by William Ames. His chief purpose in these pamphlets was to assist in the overthrowing of episcopacy, a discipline erected according to the imperfect judgment of decayed mankind, and in the establishment, through the power of Parliament, of the one right discipline ordained by God for the Gospel no less certainly than the Law was ordained for the Jews. The basic Puritan demand for reformation according to absolute scriptural precept was therefore the dominant note in his argument; his doctrinal reasoning depended on this postulate, and was indistinguishable from orthodox Puritan opinion.[10]

Because human reason was corrupted by original sin, it was necessary to subdue politic considerations to divine prescript and to submit to the scriptural revelation of God's will. The Jewish priesthood could not provide a legitimate model for episcopal discipline, since the ceremonial laws governing the Jewish polity were abrogated by the Gospel; but the spiritual discipline of the Christian church, without bodily ceremonies yet organized under the orders of presbyters, deacons, and elders, had been instituted in a manner so clear that the civil power could not refuse to establish it without wilfully contradicting God's command. The Christian liberty of which Milton wrote was therefore in its practical applications precisely the liberty of which orthodox Calvinists wrote. It freed the Christian from fallible human judgments in the service of God, and from the impositions of the former covenant with the Jews, for submission to God's revealed will and to the rules prescribed for the Gospel.[11]

Milton was not as yet aware of the problems which were to arise from this view of reformation as interpreted by the Westminster Assembly. But they were already being indicated by the more radical Puritans whose uncompromising reading of the Protestant doctrine of grace fostered religious individualism and begot the theory of a church composed exclusively of the professedly converted associated in particular congregations. In Milton's pamphlets, convictions similar to theirs were being partially expressed; and these served to modify his acceptance of Young's position and to prepare for the subsequent development of his thought.

The nascent anti-clericalism which issued in his violent attacks on episcopal corruption was primarily the result of his being a learned layman who thought of himself as an inspired Christian poet. Because of this sense of particular calling, his independent temper expressed itself in two convictions, already contributing to the sectarian individualism which was to wreck the Assembly's plan of national reformation. The first and more obvious of these was the insistence on the dignity of all believers as equally prophets, priests, and kings, an idea intimately connected with the Protestant view of the direct relationship between the individual soul and God, confirmed by Milton's opinion of himself, intensified by the belief that for the work of reformation God was pouring out abundant grace on every age and sex, and essential to the arguments of Henry Burton and the Separatists.[12] The second was the rationalism temporarily suppressed by the denunciation of human judgment in favour of divine prescript, but issuing in the belief that God's will was not unreasonable, and capable of associating itself with the Separatist view of the believer and the church to produce the assertion of the sovereignty of the individual conscience which is exemplified by Lord Brooke's development of the problem of indifference.[13]

In the thought of the radicals, these principles broadened the significance of Christian liberty without destroying the theoretical conditions which limited it to the elect and bound it to divine prescript. Milton's development of the doctrine was foreshadowed, along with the dispute which was to split the Puritan party, in the Separatist demand for Christian liberty from human and civil impositions to submit themselves to the one right discipline as they interpreted it, and in Brooke's appeal for tolerance and the prerogative of individual judgment according to right reason.

The pamphlets on private liberty between 1643 and 1645 record the process by which this development took place in Milton's mind as a direct consequence of his personal difficulty, his attempt to solve the divorce problem, and his difference of opinion with the orthodox Assembly. His own misfortune resulted in the assertion of individual liberty in a matter indifferent (according to his definition) because neither commanded nor prohibited in Scripture but permitted according to the judgment of conscience. His effort to reinterpret the biblical statements on divorce begot his defence of free reasoning in doubtful questions. The nature of his problem, and the condemnation of the orthodox, made necessary an elaborate analysis of the doctrine of Christian liberty.[14]

Beginning with orthodox conceptions—the abrogation of the ceremonial and judicial laws of the Jews, the spiritually liberating effect of faith, the conscientious freedom of the believer in things in themselves indifferent—he ended by arguing that the rewriting of the moral law by the Spirit in the hearts of Christians, and their spontaneous efforts to determine conscientiously in accordance with this new revelation, virtually freed them from the external imposition of all written law.[15] The individualistic consequences of this view were intensified by the fact that his problem concerned, not the relationship between God and man, but a natural relationship between two human beings. Marriage was to satisfy spiritual and bodily needs in man's temporal estate; divorce was to make possible his release from a contract whose end was not fulfilled. Milton's rehandling of the doctrine of Christian liberty therefore involved its practical application in the natural rather than the spiritual sphere.[16] It was possible for him to regard his particular application as justified by the orthodox view of Christian liberty in things indifferent; but the effect of the problems discussed in this second group of pamphlets was to divert his attention from the need for submission to the one right discipline, and to concentrate it upon the right of the individual Christian, free from the tyranny of human dominance, to seek, according to the reasonable laws of God and nature, the spiritual and temporal good which is the end of all law.

Such an individual right was denied by the Assembly's view of reformation as requiring unconditional submission to divine prescript and by the argument that its decisions on matters of indifference must be imposed on the national church. Milton's reasoning between 1643 and 1645 aligned itself with the reasoning of those who, opposing the attempt of the Puritan right to establish its version of the prescribed discipline, asserted (with varying degrees of emphasis from the Independents, through John Goodwin, to Roger Williams) liberty of conscience as first a Christian, then a natural, right. The tendencies which had partially distinguished Milton's original position from Young's were emphasized in his development with the radicals of a theory of liberty according to rights, both spiritual and reasonable, derived from divine and natural law. This theory was capable, in his case as in theirs, of an application to questions of wider significance than the indifferent matters originally involved in their assertions on ecclesiastical discipline and conscientious belief, and his on conscientious divorce and the free publication of opinions. It was to receive its further development in the disputes over the political settlement.

Because of the danger to the progress of truth in doubtful matters, and because only the individual conscience, not any authority, was capable of determining whether divorce was justified, the *Areopagitica* and the divorce tracts demanded unrestricted liberty for all men. Yet they contained important reservations. The *Areopagitica*'s eloquent defence of the activity of the human reason implied a broad intellectual freedom; but it nevertheless assumed the applicability of the typically Independent distinction between doctrinal or disciplinary fundamentals and things doubtful or indifferent.[17] The divorce tracts argued, like Williams on conscience, that an equal freedom must be permitted to all in order to achieve the just liberty of good men; but divorce was by definition a thing indifferent. Moreover, Milton's attention in both cases was focused, not on individual liberty, but on the requisite liberty of the good individual who, as a believer accepting the fundamentals of Christianity, would act spontaneously in accordance with the laws of morality, renewed by the Spirit in his heart. Because such a Christian would choose according to the reasonable laws governing his spiritual and temporal good, he would be free from the enforced imposition of their external expressions, whether human or divine, to progress actively in repairing the ruins of our first parents, and in achieving the good life in the present with salvation hereafter. The wicked, on the contrary, would be free only within bounds, and only to increase the hardness of their hearts. This distinction associated Milton rather with the moderates than with the radicals who demanded freedom as the natural right of all men as men; and it was likewise capable of a broader application.[18]

The *Areopagitica* and *Tetrachordon* expressed Milton's most extreme interpretation of Christian liberty and its consequences. They were attacks on the repressive policy of the Assembly; and they were written while his confidence in the powers and destiny of the English people, led by God and supported by his grace, was as yet scarcely diminished. Much of that confidence was carried over to his first political tracts; the execution of the King promised to begin the firm establishment of liberty. But the difficulties of the Commonwealth forced him to assume a defensive rather than offensive attitude; and his compositions between 1649 and 1660 reverse rather than reproduce the process by which the radicalism of 1645 had emerged from the reforming zeal of 1641. His thought continued to develop, with the privileges of Christian liberty as its central theme and the assertion of its implications in the natural sphere as its chief end; but events made necessary the more exact statement of the conditions on which alone it could be exercised, and of its difference from the liberty which was not Christian but corrupt.

In *The Tenure* (and in the other political tracts where they reproduced its arguments) he transferred his theory of natural liberty according to the good of man from a matter of private and indifferent significance to a subject of public importance. The processes of his thought here were similar to those by which the Levellers, under Lilburne and Overton, evolved a democratic theory of liberty and equality from the dispute over conscience. Like them, he applied to civil society the principles associated with Christian liberty in the things of God; but he also carried over into the political sphere the reservations expressed, though not emphasized, in his writings on conscience.[19]

Because all men as men possessed a natural right to freedom from the tyranny of depraved human will which must do them harm, the revolution was to be justified in terms of the good of all. But it did not follow that the good of the people was to be achieved merely by erecting the corrupt wills of humanity in general as the rule for the state. Man's temporal good was only to be achieved in accordance with the law of nature, imperfectly apprehended by all men, but corresponding in its perfection to the moral and reasonable law of God.[20] Government according to such laws was possible only through submission to the just rule of the wise and good, who recognized them within themselves. In the political tracts the distinction between the good and the wicked therefore operated in a manner which denied an equal right to all men. True natural freedom could be exercised only by those who had the moral law restored to its original clarity in their hearts. Under their rule, all would possess a larger degree of liberty than could be had under tyrants; but to preserve the rightful liberty of good men, and hence the true good of the whole, the exercise of full political privileges must be restricted to the good.[21]

The problems of the Commonwealth consequently led Milton to condemn the undiscriminating appeal to natural right, and to take up his position with the political Independents represented by Ireton, even to accept (with reservations) the rule of Cromwell. But his reasoning had its ultimate parallel elsewhere, not among the extremists who, like the Levellers and Williams, asserted full natural liberty in the secular sphere and full Christian liberty in the spiritual sphere, but among those who, like Vane and the Millenarians, proposed as the model the kingdom of Christ under the rule of his saints, and transferred the privileges of Christian liberty to the secular sphere while preserving at the same time the distinction between regenerate and unregenerate which limited its proper application to the elect. Their reasoning provided the Puritan counterpart of the conception of a natural aristocracy, and the ideal of government by the wise and good, which Milton derived from the classical theorists.[22]

The effect of his reasoning in both the second and third groups of pamphlets was thus the virtual identification of Christian with true natural liberty, and their differentiation from the liberty which might be allowed or denied depraved humanity according to particular circumstances. Of the final group of pamphlets, those on the church reapplied the principles of the divorce tracts to achieve a conclusion similar to *Tetrachordon*'s, though involving broader issues; those on the state reapplied the arguments of the political pamphlets under conditions which necessitated the full acceptance of their implications.

In the last ecclesiastical tracts, Milton demanded an almost unrestricted freedom in matters of conscience and religion, fundamental or indifferent, for all men, regenerate or unregenerate.[23] Yet his insistence on one fundamental—Scripture as the external test of the Spirit's teaching—carried with it a distinction between true and false religion, and consequently between legitimate and illegitimate religious liberty. Although all men were necessarily free in conscience, and must be free because of the spirituality of Christian religion from the imposition of outward forms of confession and worship either by church or state, his real concern was still with the good men and true believers who could claim the full privileges of Christian liberty as he now defined them.[24]

Largely because of the blindness which cut him off from the chief source of human wisdom and forced him to concentrate his attention on the light of the Spirit within, Milton's final view of Christian faith was scarcely distinguishable from that of the sectaries on the extreme left of the Puritan group; and his interpretation of Christian liberty as depending solely on the inner light, and as releasing the believer from all outward rules whatsoever, human or divine, save for the Scriptures, pushed it to its utmost bounds.[25] But his radical religious individualism did not destroy the conviction that man's temporal as well as spiritual good could only be achieved through true religion; and his separation of civil and ecclesiastical power did not prevent him from arguing that the Christian magistrate must exercise, in defence of Christian liberty and the true faith from which alone it sprang, the power which is naturally his under the moral laws of nature more perfectly apprehended by Christians than by other men.

He conceded the Christian magistrate a defensive and restrictive power in religion denied by those radicals who, like the Levellers and Williams, had escaped from the framework of Puritan thought (without necessarily rejecting the typically Calvinistic view of Christian faith), and had developed in the natural sphere the theory of the equal rights of all men as men. He did not demand complete liberty of religion for all men of whatever creed; for though his position was more extreme than the Independents', like them he required the Christian magistrate to preserve the conditions under which alone true freedom could be exercised and to prevent evil men, who would endanger Christian liberty or openly attack the fundamentals of true religion as he defined them, from abusing the freedom necessarily accorded to all.[26]

The last ecclesiastical pamphlets thus associated Milton with the Puritan radicals by defining more sharply Christian liberty and the necessary liberty of all men in matters of conscience and religion. The final political pamphlets more clearly illustrated the application of Christian liberty in the political sphere and the necessity of denying equal privileges to the wicked. True freedom in religion was the chief end to be achieved by Milton's commonwealth. This end, and the civil good of men, could only be attained in a state governed in accordance with the law which is the natural counterpart of the law revealed by the Spirit and Scripture. Such a government was to be established, not by making the depraved will of the people the sovereign authority as in Harrington's system, but through an aristocracy composed of those having the law restored in their hearts and able truly to claim the privileges of Christian liberty. Though it could not be established in its perfection until Christ's second coming, a Christian commonwealth must be progressively modelled on the pattern of his kingdom. The good must therefore assert their legitimate freedom as men and Christians, and impose on the evil the external forms which accord with true natural freedom, though the evil are incapable of exercising it and would prefer slavery under superstition and corrupt will.[27]

Milton's final view both of the church and the state therefore found its closest parallel in the theories of the Millenarians. His ideal remained the Holy Community, in a temporal sense, which was the chief distinguishing mark of Puritan thought. His retention of that ideal, and its necessary consequence, a belief in a fundamental rule which would distinguish true from false religion, kept his thinking within the basic Puritan pattern, variously manifested in the *Westminster Confession*, the Savoy *Declaration*, and the aims of the Millenarians. His interpretation of the ideal, and of the Christian liberty associated with it, swung steadily to the left as the revolution proceeded, until he arrived at the position of the Puritan extremists. This radical development principally involved an extension of the individualistic significance of the doctrine of Christian liberty. Like the sectarian radicals, Milton transferred its privileges from the spiritual to the natural sphere; like the Millenarians, he preserved the conditions which restricted its privileges to the aristocracy of grace. This restriction distinguished him from Williams; for he could not apply the principle of segregation which confined the spiritual privileges of Christian liberty to the elect, but permitted the equal exercise of natural liberty to all men without discrimination.[28]

It is incumbent upon the student of Milton's thought between 1641 and 1660 to attempt an explanation, first, of his movement to the extreme Puritan left, secondly, of his refusal to proceed farther in the line of development with Williams, Goodwin, and the Levellers. One explanation is to be sought in his reading of the events of the revolution and in his personal experiences during its course. But his reading of events depended in the last analysis on his interpretation of what is human nature; and his interpretation of human nature depended ultimately on his reading of his own personality. Both issued in the doctrine of regeneration, expounded in *De Doctrina Christiana* as the revolution drew to its close, to provide the basis for the positions of his last pamphlets. In that exposition of his principles an explanation must now be sought.

# Chapter XVII

## Of Christian Doctrine

MILTON engaged in his study of Christian doctrine principally because "it is only to the individual faith of each that the Deity has opened the way of eternal salvation." Yet a second motive was provided by the fact that a true faith must contribute to "earthly comforts," since "nothing else can so effectually rescue the lives and minds of men from those two detestable curses, slavery and superstition. . . .'"

It is neither necessary nor possible to offer here anything like a complete examination of his theological opinions; attention must be concentrated only on those beliefs which had a direct bearing on the second of these two motives, the religious and political liberty of the individual. The peculiarities of his ontology and cosmology were not without their relationship to his views on this more worldly subject; but they are of essential importance in the study rather of his last poems than of the thought of his middle years. What is essential to the theory of church and state then developed, and repeated in *De Doctrina Christiana*, is his view of man's Fall and Regeneration. The extent to which his interpretation of these doctrines agreed with and differed from the orthodox interpretation is at once a measure and an explanation of his radicalism and its limits.

He could not accept the typically Puritan view of man's condition in its totality; but he did accept, without substantial variations, the Calvinistic doctrine of man's original corruption. At no point in the prose did the significance of the Fall slip from his mind; and it was abundantly confirmed by his experience of an apparently fruitless revolution in which the efforts of God and good men were frustrated by the depravity of the greater part of the people.

His opinion of the powers of fallen and unregenerate man was no whit higher than Calvin's. Both believed that in his perfection

Adam's will was completely submissive to his reason, and his reason exactly conformable to God's; but that the result of his disobeying "the special command" imposed on him as (in Calvin's phrase) "a trial of obedience," was the obscuring of "that rule of conscience which is innate and engraven upon the mind of man," and the loss of the perfect freedom of will which came from its full acceptance.[2]

"No works whatever were required of Adam" in his original state; he performed them spontaneously since he "was made in the image of God" and therefore "had the whole law of nature so implanted and innate in him that he needed no precept to enforce its observance."[3] But "as a test of fidelity," he was set under a precept which concerned "an act in its own nature indifferent."[4] Milton believed that, like the institution of marriage, this was what Ames defined as a positive command, a precept not part of natural law, but "added to the natural by some special revelation of God."[5]

Adam's transgression therefore consisted in exercising his freedom of will in choosing to disobey a single precept concerning a matter otherwise indifferent. But this disobedience included every conceivable sin, and was "a transgression of the whole law."[6] For that "innate righteousness, wherein man in the beginning lived unto God," there was consequently substituted in Adam and all his posterity "an innate propensity to sin."[7]

The fact that Milton would not allow man's original corruption to be complete does not in itself break down the significance of the Fall, nor is it a justification of the powers of fallen humanity. That "some remnants of the divine image still exist in us, not wholly extinguished," was a perfectly orthodox assumption; and he was merely echoing Calvin and Ames when he said that "these vestiges of original excellence are visible, first in the understanding," since "the gift of reason has been implanted in all," and secondly in the fact that freedom of will is not "entirely destroyed," since it can determine in "things indifferent, whether natural or civil," and is "not altogether inefficient in respect of good works, or at any rate of good endeavours."[8] Hence it is that "almost all mankind profess some desire of virtue, and turn with abhorrence from some of the more atrocious crimes."[9]

Calvin had likewise said that reason "could not be altogether destroyed," that "the wit of man, how much soever it be perverted and fallen from the first integrity, is yet still clothed and garnished with excellent gifts of God" which reveal themselves in his love of truth;[10] and further that men possess "a natural desire of good" and retain in some degree "the faculty of willing."[11] Ames had declared—in phrases which may well have been the originals of Milton's—that "the remainders of God's image . . . appear both in the understanding and the will"; that in all men "that have the use of reason," they appear in some knowledge of good and evil; that "a certain inclination unto good" is therefore "found in all in some measure, whence also it is that at least the shadows of virtues are allowed and embraced by all"; and that there is consequently in all men a "restraining power" which "pertaineth to the will together with the understanding, whereby excess of sin is restrained in most, so that even sinners abhor the committing of many gross sins. . . ."[12]

But the orthodox Puritan would not allow that this remnant of power in the will and understanding was of itself of any efficacy towards salvation. Though man may discern even what is best "by right reason," he is, according to Calvin, incapable of willing it; he retains the faculty of willing, but it is "inclined and hasteth to sin": for "man, since he is corrupted, sinneth indeed willingly and not against his will nor compelled, by a most bent affection of mind, and not by violent compulsion, by motion of his own lust, and not by foreign constraint; but yet of such perverseness of nature as he is, he cannot but be moved and driven to evil."[13] Because of this corruption, it is only through God's grace that he can achieve salvation. That was also Milton's opinion.

Whatever relics of God's image might remain, Milton believed that "the whole man becomes polluted" in the Fall.[14] Its chief result in his eyes was "the death of the spirit" heavily emphasized by Calvinism.

> This death consists, first, in the loss, or at least in the obscuration to a great extent of that right reason which enabled man to discern the chief good, and in which consisted as it were the life of the understanding. . . . It consists, secondly, in that deprivation of righteousness and liberty to do good, and in that slavish subjection to sin and the devil, which constitutes, as it were, the death of the will. . . . All have committed sin in Adam; therefore all are born servants of sin.[15]

In Milton's view, no less than in Calvin's, the consequence of the Fall was complete corruption, "the death of the spiritual life"; nor did he express a higher estimate of the efficacy of the remnants. Reason may be not altogether inefficient; "but its power is so small and insignificant as merely to deprive us of all excuse for inaction, without affording any subject for boasting."[16]

Both at the beginning and the end of the prose period, Milton's conception of the Fall and its effects on human nature was precisely that of orthodox Puritanism. To minimize its significance for his thought is to destroy one of his fixed points of reference. Though fallen humanity, even without the grace of God, could assert a dignity arising from the remnants of his image which could justly prevent its enslavement to the mere will of a tyrant, yet its corrupt propensity to evil prevented it from asserting or achieving any other liberty than the liberty to sin.

Man's depravity provided Milton in 1641 with a principal reason for the establishment of the one right discipline. It provided him in 1660 with his principal reason for denying complete and equal liberty in religion and the state. His firm retention of this part ot the Puritan view of human nature helps to explain the preoccupations which continued in the last pamphlets to link him with Puritans of the centre and even of the right, and also his refusal to follow the Levellers in their naturalistic justification of the freedom of all men merely as men. But it does not afford an explanation of the radicalism which distinguished him from orthodox Puritans; for that one must proceed to his theory of regeneration.

## 2

The most striking difference between the orthodox theory of the way in which man's Fall was offset and Milton's theory is his rejection of the Calvinistic doctrine of predestination. He could not accept the idea, retained by Roger Williams no less definitely than by William Prynne, that out of his mere good pleasure and his secret will, and because all men were indiscriminately worthy of eternal damnation through their natural corruption, God from eternity arbitrarily predestined some to election, accepting Christ's imputed righteousness as their justification, and reprobated the rest to a just damnation.[17]

This doctrine contradicted both Milton's conception of the nature of God and his view of human nature. His reinterpretation of the process of election after the Arminian fashion represents the influence of the forces which drove him to oppose the Puritan right. But it is possible to exaggerate the significance of this reinterpretation; it had no real effect on his view of unregenerate men.

In its crude form, the doctrine of predestination necessarily involved what seemed to Milton to be an altogether unjust and unmerciful condemnation of the reprobate. It made man's spiritual fortunes depend on an arbitrary determination of the divine will. If grace was given to some and not to others according to God's pleasure, it seemed to follow that those to whom grace was refused were predestined to sin and then punished for the sin from which they were forbidden to escape: if God "inclines the will of man to moral good or evil, according to his own pleasure, and then rewards the good, and punishes the wicked, the course of equity seems to be disturbed. . . ."[18]

Milton's first motive in rejecting the orthodox interpretation therefore arose from his view of God as perfectly just, reasonable, and merciful, and consequently incapable of condemning man merely according to pleasure. The Calvinist justified God's ways by asserting that man sins voluntarily, through the bias of his corrupt nature, necessarily, but not by compulsion. Milton could not accept this paradox: "What can be imagined more absurd than a necessity which does not necessitate, and a will without volition?"[19] The orthodox explained that since all men are inescapably corrupt, those who are condemned are justly condemned, and those who are elected to salvation are saved only through God's free mercy and choice. Milton argued that "since God has so plainly declared that predestination is the effect of his mercy, and love, and grace, and wisdom in Christ, it is to these qualities that we ought to attribute it, and not, as is generally done, to his absolute and secret will. . . ."[20]

Further, God frequently declares "that he desires not the death of anyone but the salvation of all; that he hates nothing that he has made; and that he has omitted nothing which might suffice for universal salvation." It seemed to Milton to follow that Christ must have died for men in general, so that the Scripture "offers salvation and eternal life equally to all."[21] The Calvinist agreed that Christ's sacrifice would have sufficed for all men, had God so willed it; but he added that predestination limited its efficacy to those particularly chosen.[22] But Milton's view of the divine nature required that none should be wilfully and unmercifully excluded from the possibility of salvation; and he therefore maintained that "calling," the first step in the process of regeneration, meant an offering to all men of grace "at least sufficient for attaining knowledge of the truth and final salvation."[23]

According to Milton's reading, predestination to salvation was therefore general and conditional, not particular and absolute. "None are predestinated or elected irrespectively . . . ; Peter is not elected as Peter, or John as John": but only upon their fulfilment of the condition required by God, and made possible by the offering of at least sufficient grace, that they should "believe and continue in the faith."[24] If this grace is rejected by men, their damnation is justified by their own wilfulness, not by God's arbitrary determination. In order to justify God's ways, Milton thus ascribed to all men the freedom of will necessary to an acceptance or rejection of God's offered grace: "There can be no doubt that for the purpose of vindicating the justice of God, especially in his calling of mankind, it is much better to allow to man (whether as a remnant of his primitive state, or as restored through the operation of the grace whereby he is called) some portion of free will in respect of good works, or at least of good endeavours. . . ."[25]

In spite of his interpretation of the Fall, Milton's view of the condition of men in general therefore differed from the orthodox Puritan view in that he did not restrict the possibility of salvation to a few specifically chosen by God, but extended it to all. It is impossible to fix the time at which this reinterpretation began to develop in his mind; but it is clear that it was in his defence of the freedom of man's will in divorce that he first came into collision with the uncompromising Puritan attitude towards human nature. It is true that he defined divorce as a thing indifferent; but the problem forced him to attack the structure of Puritan theology at many points, and opened the door leading to Arminianism because it involved the whole question of man's relationship to God's purposes.[26] It did for Milton what the dispute over conscience did for John Goodwin.

Goodwin's Arminian tendencies were apparent very early in his career; but he strove to keep his speculations within bounds, until his doubts having been intensified by the Assembly's policy, he proceeded to develop, in *The Divine Authority Of The Scriptures Asserted* of 1648, and in a series of subsequent pamphlets of which the most striking was *The Pagans Debt, and Dowry* of 1651, a view of predestination closely similar to Milton's as outlined above, though with a heavier emphasis on such as were ignorant of the Scriptures.[27] To the Arminian arguments for a general and conditional predestination, he added arguments which were already contributing to the theory of natural, as distinct from revealed religion.

His estimate of natural reason had changed since the Whitehall Debates; in 1651, he observed that his "apprehensions concerning the light of nature, carefully preserved, prudently managed, and industriously improved and employed, run very high."[28] He insisted, as Milton after him, that "the Scriptures in several places . . . plainly insinuate a capacity in the heathen, yea, in all men by the light of nature . . . , by such a regular and rational process of discourse . . . to attain or make out this evangelical conclusion, that some mediator, some atonement or other, hath been made and accepted by God for the sins of men."[29] He therefore concluded that "all the world, even those . . . that have not the letter of the Gospel, have yet sufficient means of believing granted unto them."[30]

In his exposition of Christian doctrine, Milton had naturally less to say of those to whom Christianity was unknown. But he observed that "all are called," even "those who have never heard the name of Christ and who believe only in God"; and that this explained how "many, both Jews and others, who lived before Christ, and many also who have lived since his time, but to whom he has never been revealed, should be saved by faith in God alone. . . ."[31] Such statements broke down the limits imposed on Christian faith and divine grace by the exclusiveness of orthodox theology. They suggest not only Goodwin's development but the Christian rationalism illustrated in the philosophical exposition of the Apostles' Creed by Milton's early teacher, Alexander Gill;[32] and the liberalizing of Christian doctrine which they represent must be fully appreciated. But it must not be misinterpreted or exaggerated; for neither in Goodwin nor in Milton did this view imply any justification of the ways of unregenerate men.[33]

Goodwin's high apprehensions are to be associated with the tendency which had already produced the thought of Herbert of Cherbury, and after the Restoration was to beget the naturalism which had its full flowering in the eighteenth century. But he was concerned to demonstrate the pagan's debt as well as his dowry; and the argument from nature had for him a special purpose which included neither the breaking down of the distinction between the regenerate and the unregenerate nor the assertion of universal redemption. To argue that God has left men "destitute of all power to do what he requires of them," seemed to him to impugn God's justice and mercy; yet he did not assume that, having the power, all men would "believe and turn to him," and so be regenerated by divine grace.[34]

Goodwin's argument from nature was intended to undermine "the high-Presbyterian spirit" of intolerance;[35] it was also meant to bring the pagan within the Christian scheme of salvation and damnation. If those who had not heard of Christ could discover through natural reason the necessity for a redeemer, they could justly be damned for not believing on him; though they have not the Gospel (in this broader sense), "the want of the letter or oral preaching of it unto them doth not excuse them from sin in their non-believing of it...."[36] The "law of nature," according to Goodwin, performed for the pagan exactly the same function as the Law of Moses for the Jews; it "bindeth men unto what is unpossible," and therefore demonstrates their need of divine grace through an atonement.[37] Milton likewise remarked that "to those who are not yet regenerate, the law of nature has the same obligatory force, and is intended to serve the same purposes, as the Law of Moses to the Israelites."[38] And he would have agreed completely with Goodwin's assertion that "no man since the Fall ever yet did or ever will believe unto salvation, but only by the special assistance of the special grace of God."[39] Whether they have heard of the Gospel or no, men are saved only "through the sole merits of Christ";[40] those who are saved, whether pagans or Christians, are those who have fulfilled the condition required for salvation, and having taken the first step in accepting their "calling," are given the grace which effects their regeneration.

Whatever may be the result for the regenerate of the rejection of Calvinistic predestination in Milton and Goodwin, its results for the unregenerate are scarcely perceptible, and when they are so, wholly negative. Since faith is the result of the voluntary acceptance of God's general call, no basis for salvation through persecution can remain. Hence the argument in Milton's *Of Civil Power* against the magistrate's compulsion in outward acts of religion. But the only liberty that accrues to fallen man as such through this argument is the liberty of will by which he may either accept the call or irretrievably damn himself to the eternal torment, the texts concerning which are marshalled with relentless severity in the last chapter of *De Doctrina Christiana*, Book I. Man's freedom in this initial choice serves to justify God in meting out punishment to those who wilfully reject him; but it does not provide the many who are thus wilful with a subject for boasting: "such as refuse to believe are left without excuse."

These remain, not merely damned, but without any real enlightenment of the understanding or rehabilitation of the will since this can only follow their acceptance of grace. As Goodwin said, "when men shall turn their backs upon that 'candle of the Lord'... which by the hand of Christ is lighted in every man's soul," then God "suspends the influence of his former blessing" and "curseth that tree of light within them," and this "in process of his most just severity and indignation."[41] The revolution had taught Milton, moreover, that this was the fate of most men; "they which believe are few."[42] His controversial pamphlets sufficiently declare his acceptance of Calvin's conclusion (though not of his explanation) that, "if it be the pleasure of God that this treasure of understanding be laid up in store for his children, it is no marvel, nor unlikely, that in the common multitude of men is seen such ignorance and dulness."[43]

In spite of Milton's rejection of the doctrine of particular election, the Puritan view of the unregenerate thus remained with him practically intact. It offered an explanation of the conviction, which 1660 made for him inescapable, that "liberty hath a sharp and double edge, fit only to be handled by just and virtuous men; to bad and dissolute, it becomes a mischief unwieldy in their own hands. . . ."[44]

## 3

Milton's view of the condition of virtuous, and therefore regenerate, men was his second reason for dissatisfaction with the doctrine of particular election. It provided what is here the most significant motive for his disagreement with orthodox Puritanism. What is true throughout the controversial prose, both in the pamphlets on divorce and those on the state no less than in those on true religious liberty, is also true of the treatise he addressed, not to humanity, but "to all the churches of Christ." His real concern is not with men in general but with good men.

It remained his fixed principle that humanity must be governed so "that good men may enjoy the freedom which they merit, and the bad the curb which they need";[45] and his chief difficulty with the Puritan doctrine of election and regeneration was "that it would entirely take away from human affairs all liberty of action, all endeavour and desire to do right."[46] If man is to be regarded as acting under a necessity consequent on God's will, "his liberty must be wholly annihilated," and not merely the liberty of the evil but of the good.[47] To that part of the orthodox theory which described the evil as the slaves of sin, Milton had no objection. But the doctrine of particular election seemed to him to redeem men from that slavery, not to make them free, but only to enslave them to God's inscrutable and arbitrary will. Not only were the evil damned through no responsibility of their own, but the elect were saved in spite of themselves.

As in the divorce tracts and the final pamphlets, so in *De Doctrina Christiana* the assertion of the liberty of good men involved the allowance of a degree of liberty to all men. There either remains in fallen man or is universally offered, a freedom sufficient for the acceptance of the initial calling. But to mistake this shadow for the substance is to miss the most significant distinction in Milton's thought. The "efficient grace" which results in regeneration is reserved for those who accept the call; and only the regenerate are accorded a liberty which is real and substantial.

It is therefore in his theory of the process of regeneration and of the Christian liberty which it begets that the ideas which distinguish him from orthodox Puritanism are to be seen most clearly. The problem is by no means a simple one; it involves the most delicate points of Christian doctrine, and can be treated here only inadequately. Yet it is abundantly plain in the controversial prose that Milton escaped from the repressive attitude towards humanity which readily attached itself to Puritan thought, only through his conviction that God's design in some sense included man's earthly as well as heavenly happiness, and consequently that the strictly human powers and pleasures were in themselves admirable.

The opinions of Calvin must be distinguished from the opinions of such Calvinists as Thomas Edwards. In spite of its emphatic assertion of man's powerlessness with regard to the things of the spirit, the *Institutes* is full of such references to man's reasonableness and to the legitimacy of temperate delights as might have come from the pen of any Christian humanist.[48] Yet in Calvin's strenuous effort to destroy the laxity which seemed to him to issue from the doctrine of justification by works, and the complacency which appeared to arise from the acceptance of classical philosophies, one recognizes a source of the distrust of human intelligence and the suspicion of earthly delights which displayed themselves throughout the Puritan revolution.

Calvin believed that "the corruption of nature is amended and healed" through divine grace; and that regeneration "hath no other mark whereunto it is directed but that the image of God, which was by Adam's offence foully defaced and in a manner utterly blotted out, may be renewed in us."[49] But his fear of pagan philosophies, his hatred of Rome, and his detestation of Antinomianism, caused him to insist at every point that this restoration was altogether above and beyond human capacities, and (in spite of his assertion that good works must flow from faith) that it issued from no strength in the naturally depraved individual but from the will and power of God alone.

Though the minds of the elect are illuminated, "faith is far above man's understanding"; indeed "it is so far above it, that man's wit must go beyond and surmount itself to come unto it, yea, and when it is come unto it, yet doth it not attain that which it feeleth, but while it is persuaded of that which it conceiveth not, it understandeth more by the very assuredness of persuasion that if it did with man's own capacity thoroughly perceive anything familiar to man."[50] And though their wills are "bent to good," "there is always sin in the holy ones until they be unclothed of the mortal body because there remaineth in their flesh the perverseness of lusting that fighteth against uprightness."[51] It is consequently only through the imputed righteousness of Christ, and through their submission to the divine will, not through any understanding or good endeavours within themselves, that those who are chosen according to God's secret will are justified and rescued for eternal salvation.[52]

Milton likewise believed that saving knowledge was not to be achieved "by our own unassisted judgment, but by means of that Holy Spirit promised to all believers"; and that without the divine grace which came through Christ's vicarious sacrifice, man's will must continue in its "innate perversity."[53] But in his handling of the effects produced by grace and the Spirit, one recognizes the forces which prevented him from accepting either the asceticism or the antinomianism which might variously be associated with the Calvinistic doctrine of redemption. The principles which must necessarily be included in any interpretation of Christian redemption are present alike in Calvin's treatment and in Milton's; but in Milton's one observes a heavy emphasis on the healing of man's natural corruption as well as on his spiritual enlightenment.

According to his definition, "the restoration of man is the act whereby man, being delivered from sin and death by God the Father through Jesus Christ, is raised to a far more excellent state of grace and glory than that from which he had fallen."[54] This restoration involves processes at once natural and supernatural.[55] The supernatural includes the removal of man's guilt and his justification before God through Christ. It chiefly concerns the glorification to be obtained only in another world, and has no direct bearing on the problems of the prose. But the natural is of profound importance since Milton's reading of its effect on the character of man is the key to his theory of liberty.

This natural renovation includes the general calling "whereby the natural mind and will of man being partially renewed by a divine impulse, are led to seek the knowledge of God, and for the time, at least, undergo an alteration for the better."[56] God thereby enlightens the minds of those in whom the change takes place, and "works in us the power of acting freely, of which, since our fall, we were incapable, except by means of a calling and renewal."[57] But this renewal is only partial, and, if not well employed, is forfeited. A full renewal belongs only to those who, having accepted the call, proceed in their regeneration and in the supernatural renovation which brings with it the renovation of nature.

The intent of supernatural renovation is not only to restore man more completely than before to the use of his natural faculties, as regards his power to form right judgment, and to exercise free will; but to create afresh, as it were, the inward man, and infuse from above new and supernatural faculties into the minds of the renovated.[58]

The sanctification which spritually creates man anew in the image of God, therefore includes his restoration to the original state of natural perfection from which he fell, and this in a real and substantial, not metaphorical or imputed, sense.

"For the new spiritual life and its increase bear the same relation to the restoration of man, which spiritual death and its progress (as described above, on the punishment of sin) bear to his Fall."[59] Though the regenerate man remains imperfect, he moves towards a perfection which includes the actual restoration of his natural faculties: "as the power of exercising these functions was weakened and in a manner destroyed by the spiritual death, so is the understanding restored in great part to its primitive clearness, and the will to its primitive liberty, by the new spiritual life in Christ."[60] There takes place in man both a new creation and a re-creation; and "this renewal of the will can mean nothing but a restoration to its former liberty."[61]

In his effort to undermine man's arrogant dependence upon himself, Calvin had insisted on the weakness of his depraved will, and on the fact that in regeneration "is all that which was of our own will taken away, and that which cometh in place thereof is all of God," that "all parts of good works, even from the first motion, are proper to God only."[62] It was this absolute dependence of good men, not on their own restored faculties, but on the will of God, which

Milton strove to avoid, for "if the will of the regenerate be not made free, then we are not renewed, but compelled to embrace salvation in an unregenerate state."[63]

Calvin was impressed by the laxity which issued from doctrines of self-dependence and works; Milton was impressed both by that danger and by the danger of repression which could spring from the exaggeration of man's dependence on God, more immediately demonstrated by the efforts of the Assembly to compel regenerate and unregenerate to embrace at least the outward forms of salvation. Driven to an extreme, the doctrines of imputed righteousness and regeneration through God's mere will, resulted either in the excesses of those antinomians who maintained that for the elect sin ceased to exist, or in the opposite excesses of those stern ascetics who maintained that man's corrupt nature must be rigorously repressed. Calvin had striven to avoid both these consequences; but his example, and the experience of revolution, drove English Presbyterianism to accept the first. The experience of Presbyterian repression drove some of the Calvinistic sectaries to accept the second. But Milton, with his idealistic individualism and his experience at once of the stultifying effects of repression and of the disintegrating effects of unbounded freedom, sought a formula which, more effectively than Calvin's, would free men for the prosecution of the good life. He found it in a doctrine of regeneration which involved not only a new spiritual creation but the re-creation of the natural man.

Because he could not accept either the Calvinistic condemnation of earthly good or the antinomian indulgence of the natural man, he refused to recognize the barrier which Puritanism erected between the spiritual and the natural. Though Calvin believed that God bestowed an inferior grace on all "for the common benefit of mankind," that "the world was made principally for mankind's sake," and that man should enjoy "the beauty of the world,"[64] the weight of his emphasis nevertheless fell on the need for "contempt of this present life" and of "the goods that be subject to mortality," so that, "despising the world, we may with all our hearts endeavour to the meditation of the life to come."[65] There are traces of this sense of the vanity of things in Milton's prose and more than traces (as one would expect) in his treatise on Christian doctrine; but the man who described the "delightful intermissions" and "the entertainment of wedded leisure,"[66] who wrote of the "divine harmonies of music,"[67] who said that God "pours out before us even to a profuseness all desirable things, and gives us minds that can wander beyond all limit and satiety,"[68] and who conceived the end of the revolution to be the achievement both of man's spiritual and temporal happiness, could not, even in 1660, accept the Calvinistic view without reservations.

4

Milton's theory of regeneration provided the basis for his interpretation of Christian liberty. According to Calvin, that was an exclusively spiritual privilege, not necessarily exercised "in the sight of men, but before God."[69] If the spiritual gifts of divine grace are to be "counted things coming from another to us, and beside nature,"[70] and if "there is in man as it were two worlds," it follows that "by this putting of difference shall come to pass that that which the Gospel teacheth of the spiritual liberty, we shall not wrongfully draw to civil order. . . ."[71]

Milton could accept Calvin's distinction between two sorts of government, "the one spiritual, whereby the conscience is framed to godliness and to the worship of God; the other civil, whereby man is trained to the duties of humanity and civility which are to be kept among men";[72] but he could recognize no such two worlds in himself or in man. He could not accept the common distinction between soul and body, as he could not accept the doctrine of particular election, because it did not suit with his view of human nature. Man was created in the image of God "not only as to his soul, but also as to his outward form."[73] The dualism which would separate these, and indeed set them in conflict, was unpalatable to one whose highest delight was the integration of form and substance in poetry. Man must therefore be regarded as an indivisible unit:

> Man having been created after this manner, it is said, as a consequence, that "man became a living soul"; whence it may be inferred . . . that man is a living being, intrinsically and properly one and individual, not compound or separable, not, according to the common opinion, made up and framed of two distinct and different natures, as of soul and body, but that the whole man is soul, and the soul man, that is to say, a body, or substance, individual, animated, sensitive, and rational. . . .[74]

It is ultimately to this conviction of the unity of soul and body in the human individual that one must trace the monism which issued in the several heresies of *De Doctrina Christiana*. It was because he could not accept any doctrine which involved a dualistic view of man or his world that Milton refused to believe that the universe "was formed from nothing," and insisted that "the original matter" was "intrinsically good, and the chief productive stock of every subsequent good," since it was "of God and in God";[75] that he argued at length concerning the union of the two natures in Christ to prove that he "was made flesh without thereby ceasing to be numerically the same as before," and died in his divine as well as human nature;[76] and that he accepted the mortalist doctrine that "the whole man dies," the soul with the body, to sleep until the final resurrection in the flesh.[77] But these abstruse matters are beyond the scope of this study. What is important here is the effect of Milton's monism on his interpretation of Christian liberty.

In Calvin and orthodox Puritanism Christian liberty defined the spiritual relationship between God and his elect by contrasting it with the legal relationship between God and his chosen people, the Jews. Throughout the prose this distinction between the old and new dispensations was the starting point for Milton's treatment, and it remained so in *De Doctrina Christiana*. The basic element in his interpretation is the freeing of the believer through grace from the guilt of sin imposed on all men by the rigorous Law.

The Law of Moses was a law demanding external works from fallen man, who was without the guidance of the law under which Adam lived in his perfection, and who was incapable of fulfilling its demands because of his depravity. It was "a written code," designed to lead the Jews "to an acknowledgment of the depravity of mankind," so that they "might have recourse to the righteousness of the promised saviour."[78] It was in itself a law of damnation rather than salvation, of death rather than life; and "Moses imposed the letter or external law even on those who were not willing to receive it."[79] It "constrains, because it is a law of bondage."

But as "constraint and bondage" were "inseparable from the dispensation of the Law," so is "liberty from the dispensation of the Gospel."[80]

> The Gospel is the new dispensation of the Covenant of Grace, far more excellent and perfect than the Law, announced first obscurely by Moses and the prophets, afterwards in the clearest terms by Christ himself, and his apostles and evangelists, written since by the Holy Spirit, in the hearts of believers. . . .[81]

The substitution of this "inward law" for the imposed Mosaic Law means that instead of being bound by an external code, believers are set free, since Christ "leads them as willing followers."[82]

This is an essentially orthodox exposition of the character of Christian liberty; but the Calvinist believed that, while the Gospel abrogated the ceremonial and judicial laws of the Jews, the moral law, as codified in the decalogue, remained in force as an external rule for Christians.[83] Milton's assertion of individual Christian liberty in divorce led him to insist in *Tetrachordon* on an interpretation of divine law which included the freedom of the Christian from all external rules, to follow the moral law in his heart; and that assertion was repeated with greater distinctness in his final ecclesiastical pamphlets. It marks his first significant divergence from orthodox opinion, and is fully expounded in *De Doctrina Christiana*.

Not a part, but "the whole of the preceding covenant, in other words, the entire Mosaic Law, was abolished," the decalogue, and the codification of the moral law, as well as the ceremonial and judicial directions.[84] The Law was "a law of works" in all its aspects, and gave place in its entirety to "the law of grace" which relieves men from all divine formulations to follow the law of the Spirit within themselves.[85]

This interpretation necessarily resulted in extreme Christian individualism since it removed even the external check provided by the ten commandments. It is clearly antinomian in this respect, for it made the individual Christian conscience the only sovereign rule. But it is important to observe that in Milton's interpretation "the sum and essence of the Law is not hereby abrogated," for "it is the tablet of the Law, so to speak, that is alone changed. . . ."[86] Moses wrote the Law "on tables of stone"; the Spirit writes it "in the fleshly tables of the heart."[87] But Christians still owe submission to the substance, though not to the letter, of the moral law. They will follow the Spirit rather than the letter when they are at variance, "namely, wherever by departing from the letter, we can more effectually consult the love of God and our neighbour."[88] Yet salvation is not to be achieved, nor liberty gained, without submission to God's law: "so far from a less degree of perfection being exacted from Christians, it is expected of them that they should be more perfect than those who were under the Law. . . ."[89]

This is the essence of Milton's doctrine of Christian liberty. It at once maintains true freedom and denounces licence. The weight of emphasis fell either on the first or the second of these consequences according to circumstances; but from the divorce tracts to the final pamphlets both were implicit in his doctrine at every point. The difference between his interpretation and the orthodox did not lie in any breaking down of the force of moral law which binds man, but in his description of its manifestation in the personalities of regenerate men. For those who are not regenerate, the works of the moral law, whether revealed by Moses or nature, are "matters of compulsion"; the regenerate "bring forth good works spontaneously and freely," under faith and through the Spirit.[90]

Regeneration therefore involves the abrogation of all external law in favour of the spiritual law of conscience; and this includes freedom from both divine and human impositions.

> Christian liberty is that whereby we are loosed as it were by enfranchisement, through Christ our deliverer, from the bondage of sin and consequently from the rule of the Law and of man; to the intent that, being made sons instead of servants, and perfect men instead of children, we may serve God in love through the guidance of the Spirit of Truth.[91]

It is from this liberty that all the aspects of individual freedom spring. It covers the whole life of man, and requires the individual's attendance merely on the light within him. In spite of Milton's continued insistence on the Scriptures as the essential rule of faith, even the restrictions of their letter are broken down for the regenerate by his emphasis on the superiority of the Spirit's teaching. "Hence, although the external ground which we possess for our belief at the present day in the written word is highly important . . ., that which is internal, and the peculiar possession of each believer, is far superior to all, namely, the Spirit itself."[92]

The first and most obvious consequence of this doctrine of Christian liberty—in its orthodox original a definition of the relationship between God and man—is the assertion of religious freedom. If Christians are freed from God's former ceremonial impositions, they are obviously "freed from the yoke of human judgments, much more of civil decrees and penalties in religious matters." For either the church or the state to enforce a particular interpretation of Scripture, is clearly "to impose a yoke, not on man, but on the Holy Spirit itself."[93]

Hence is derived Milton's assertion that, "although it is the duty of believers to join themselves, if possible, to a church duly constituted," yet individuals who "cannot do this conveniently, or with full satisfaction of conscience, are not to be considered as excluded from the blessing bestowed by God on the churches."[94] This is also the source of his extremely sectarian view of the visible church as consisting of altogether independent congregations, gathered according to mutual agreement under a particular covenant,[95] with a spiritual power in the whole church collectively,[96] which is to be distinguished from civil power and exercised only upon voluntary members (with excommunication as its most extreme penalty), by the whole congregation,[97] but through a ministry chosen by the people from among all believers without distinction and according to purely spiritual qualifications,[98] and maintained either by its own secular occupations or by free gifts, not by tithes or civil maintenance.[99] It is likewise his reason for insisting that, since faith cannot be forced but is achieved through the Spirit, it is "highly derogatory to the power of the church, as well as an utter want of faith, to suppose that her government cannot be properly administered without the intervention of the civil magistrate."[100]

This uncompromising emphasis on the inwardness of grace and the sovereignty of the revelation in the heart above all other laws, explains Milton's association with the sectaries of the left in whom Puritan individualism reached its extreme, and his opposition to the Puritan right with its belief in the necessity of submission to the letter of the moral law and the gospel precepts as interpreted by ecclesiastical authority. But his religious individualism had its moral counterpart, and this begot a further consequence of Christian liberty.

In spite of Calvin's insistence that faith must issue in good works, the Calvinistic emphasis on salvation through God's will and Christ's imputed righteousness, and on man's natural depravity, was linked with the belief that it was "rather to the guiltiness of sin than to the very matter of sin" that justification referred.[101] Though Calvin agreed that all things were sanctified to the use of the elect, the threat of antinomianism convinced him of the need for a continual moral discipline for both the elect and the reprobate;[102] and the pattern for such a discipline was obviously presented by the polity of the Jews.

Enforced morality seemed to Milton a contradiction in terms. "An accordance with faith, not with the decalogue," and "conformity, not with the written but with the unwritten law, that is with the law of the Spirit given by the Father to lead us into all truth, is to be accounted the true essential form of good works." Though such works issue from faith, they are not the works of the Law, nor can they be judged in accordance with its letter; for (as Ames himself had said), though "the reasons on which these precepts are founded apply equally to believers in general, and to all ages, . . . the precepts themselves are no longer obligatory."[103]

Consequently there is apparent in Milton's handling of works the antinomian tendency, denounced by Calvin, to say to the regenerate, "Take away vain fear . . . ; the Spirit will command thee no evil thing, so that thou boldly and without fear yield thee to the guiding thereof."[104] Since neither the love of God nor one's neighbour can be forced, laws must not be imposed either on the regenerate or the unregenerate to compel them to act in conformity with the scriptural letter. The function of the state is chiefly to restrain the evil from endangering the good of their fellows; but because the Spirit is the sovereign rule, men, especially the regenerate, must be free to obey the dictates of conscience.

It follows from Milton's theory of regeneration that restraint will apply merely to the unregenerate; the regenerate, willingly following the dictates of the Spirit, spontaneously act according to the love of God and their neighbours, and cannot possibly fall into the excesses of antinomianism. Because the effect of grace is the restoration of perfection, morality is thus not destroyed by Milton's interpretation. But because it is a spiritual and natural, not a legal, morality, the regenerate (and, according to the limits of civil power, the unregenerate) must be left free in such matters (like the Sabbath) as were imposed under the old Law, and in such ("usury, divorce, polygamy, and the like") as were not "conceded to the hard-heartedness of the Jews as venial infirmities, or as evils which were to be abated or regulated by law," but were permitted as indifferent according to conscience. "The Law can no more concede or tolerate the smallest degree of moral evil than a good man can voluntarily choose it."[105] In things private or indifferent, the evil must be left free to work their damnation, the good to exercise their Christian liberty in conformity with the conscientious morality of faith.[106]

But this second consequence of Christian liberty involved its transference from the spiritual relationship between God and believers to privileges exercised "in the sight of men"; and it was here that Milton's theory of regeneration had its radical effect. He rejected the doctrine of election according to divine pleasure and maintained that it depended on man's free choice because, "if this use of the will be not admitted, whatever worship or love we render to God is entirely vain and of no value; the acceptableness of duties done under a law of necessity is diminished, or rather is annihilated altogether, inasmuch as freedom can no longer be attributed to that will over which some fixed decree is inevitably suspended."[107] For precisely the same reasons, he rejected the doctrine of compulsion, either divine or human, to good works.

The restoration of the regenerate seemed to him necessarily to include the restoration of the will's freedom to choose in accordance with the law of morality and faith written in the heart by the Spirit; and that law was, in fact, the eternal law of divine morality under which Adam lived in his state of natural perfection.

> The unwritten law is no other than the law of nature given originally to Adam, and of which a certain remnant, or imperfect illumination, still dwells in the hearts of all mankind; which, in the regenerate, under the influence of the Holy Spirit, is daily tending towards a renewal of its primitive brightness.[108]

Because they are to live under this law alone, without even the single external prohibition imposed as a test, the regenerate are raised to a state far more excellent than Adam's.

Since redemption included the restoration of the whole man, not merely of the soul as distinct from the body, Milton applied the privileges of Christian liberty to the natural as well as the spiritual sphere, and so associated himself with the extreme Puritan revolutionaries. With moderate sectarians like William Dell, he believed that "not dead laws and orders, written by men, will do the church any good, but the living law of God, written in their hearts by the Spirit. . . ." But he applied this idea to the state as well as to the church because he carried even further than Dell the conclusion that "as the law of sin hath been written in our natures to corrupt us, so the law of the Spirit of Life must be written also in our natures, to reform us." If that reformation was really operative in man's nature, it must beget natural as well as spiritual privileges. Dell had been content to argue only for the spiritual equality of the true church: "For though according to our first nativity, whereby we are born of men, there is great inequality, some being born high, some low, some honourable, some mean, some kings, some subjects, &c.; yet according to our new and second birth, whereby we are born of God, there is exact equality, for here are none better or worse, higher or lower, but all have the same faith, . . . the same divine nature, the same precious promises. . . ."[109] But, since he believed that the second birth repaired the ruined nature which men inherit in the first, Milton argued for the natural equality of the regenerate in a true Christian Commonwealth.

For the same reason, he refused to deny the Christian magistrate a restrictive and defensive, as distinct from a compulsive, power in religion. As Sir Henry Vane observed, "the more illuminated the magistrate's conscience and judgment is, as to natural justice and right, by the knowledge of God and communication of light from Christ . . . , the better qualified is he to execute his office."[110] For this reason Milton could believe, like Calvin, that only "the observance of the divine commandments is the source of prosperity to nations."[111] Since these commands could, according to his interpretation, find their perfect expression only through the Spirit working in the hearts of believers, the magistrate could not attempt to reproduce the legalistic polity of the Jews. But it is nevertheless his duty to assist according to his powers in the development of the spirit of faith and goodness which alone produces the true liberty he must be careful not to limit. And because the laws of nature and of faith are essentially the same, "it is especially the duty of the magistrate to encourage religion and the service of God, public worship in particular, and to reverence the church."[112] Moreover, this association of natural and spiritual law was the principle on which Milton based his belief in the legitimacy of resistance to unjust magistrates, especially when compliance "would be incompatible with our duty towards God," and his rejection of the argument "that obedience is due to the commands not only of an upright magistrate, but of an usurper, and that in matters contrary to justice. . . ."[113]

Finally, it was because of this view of regeneration and Christian liberty that the reformation of the state according to the law of nature seemed to him to require the rule of the few rather than of the people. In spite of the liberating consequences for all men which followed from his reinterpretation of Christian doctrine, it remained his conviction that Christian liberty was the prerogative of the regenerate, and that the regenerate were few. All men have the gift of reason, "by which they may resist bad desires, so that no one can complain of, or allege in excuse, the depravity of his own nature." Thus all men are partially free, and the justice of God is vindicated. Yet "though all men be dead in sin and children of wrath, yet some are worse than others"; and though "some remnants of the divine image" remain in all, the union of these remnants "in one individual renders him more fit and disposed for the kingdom of God than another."[114] Moreover, though grace sufficient for the acceptance of calling is offered to all men, it is not offered to all "in equal measure." For God "claims to himself the right of determining concerning his own creatures according to his pleasure, nor can he be called to account for his decision, though, if he chose, he could give the best reasons for it. . . . That an equal portion of grace should not be extended to all, is attributable to the supreme will of

God alone; that there are none to whom he does not vouchsafe grace sufficient for their salvation, is attributable to his justice."[115]

Though Milton did his best to avoid the harsh consequences of the orthodox theory of predestination, there remained a place in his interpretation of Christian doctrine for an aristocracy of grace. That aristocracy coalesced in his mind with the natural aristocracy described by classical philosophers, and it formed the basis for his idea of government by those who are wise and good because they are God's saints. As all men do not achieve regeneration and cannot claim Christian liberty, so the full privileges of natural liberty are reserved for those in whom regeneration is progressing towards a renewal of man's primitive perfection.

It is therefore Milton's theory of regeneration which distinguishes him at once from the Puritans of the right, and from those who, like Williams, interpreted the doctrines of Puritanism in a manner which permitted the assertion of full Christian liberty for the saints and full natural liberty for men. The principle of segregation does not operate in his thinking as it does in Calvin's, to beget restriction, or in Williams', to beget liberation; for his ideal is a society at once truly Christian and truly human. The pattern of such a society he sought, with the Millenarians, in "that glorious reign of Christ on earth with his saints, so often promised in Scripture, even until all his enemies shall be subdued." That kingdom "will not commence till his second advent."[116] But on it the regenerate will model their endeavours until their resurrection in the flesh for that "perfect glorification" which "consists in eternal life and perfect happiness," and which "will be accompanied by the renovation of heaven and earth, and of all things therein adapted to our service or delight, to be possessed by us in perpetuity."[117]

## 5

Yet in Milton's interpretation of Christian doctrine one recognizes influences which, properly speaking, did not come from Puritanism at all, whether of the right or the left. His theory of regeneration and his interpretation of Christian liberty allowed free play to the predilections which he shared with some of the more liberal Puritans, but more especially with the Christian rationalists. The consequence of the rejection of the Calvinistic doctrine of predestination was to make possible, both in Goodwin and Milton, a faith which was an active humanizing force, and must have a real effect, not only on man as he stood before God, but on man in society. It helped to transform the Puritan idea of religion into a reasonable service and an ethical endeavour after the good life.

It is in Milton's view of the effects of regeneration that the influences from his Puritan and humanistic background find their peculiar and significant fusion. His refusal to segregate the spiritual from the natural resulted in principles which had their parallel in the doctrines of the Puritan sects, but only because his interpretation of divine grace differed from the typically Puritan interpretation. It is in the phrases of humanism rather than in those of "enthusiasm" that Milton speaks, for his God was one whose perfection consisted in a divine reasonableness and whose design for man could be described as the perfecting, not the destroying, of his humanity.

It was for men as saints that the Millenarians demanded liberty; Milton demanded it for men as truly men. That demand required their freedom even from the subjection to divine will which remained the keynote of Calvinism in all its forms, for their full and free development in the excellences of this life. In his repeated assertions that the rewards of faith are given, not to a passive dependence on the divine pleasure, but "to constant diligence, and to an unwearied search after truth"; that everyone must "persuade his reason into assent and faith";[118] that the essential of true religion "is the liberty not only of winnowing and sifting every doctrine, but also of thinking and even writing respecting it, according to our individual faith and persuasion";[119] that the perseverance of the saint does not depend solely on the divine pleasure, but on his endeavouring to fulfil the provision that he "purify himself to the utmost of his power, that he do righteousness, that he love his brother, that he remain himself in love, in order that God and his seed may also remain in him;"[120] one recognizes the note less of the energy which was released by the Puritan conviction of particular election than of the idealism which characterized the teaching of those rationalists, like Cudworth and Whichcote, whose voices were drowned in the clamour of the Puritan revolution, but who thought less of the privileges of the saints than of "whatsoever things are true, whatsoever things are honest, whatsoever things are just, whatsoever things are pure, whatsoever things are lovely, whatsoever things are of good report. . . ."[121]

Cudworth had protested in 1647 against the domineering contentiousness which seemed to him characteristic of a man "that builds all his comfort upon an ungrounded persuasion that God from all eternity hath loved him, and absolutely decreed him to life and happiness, and seeketh not for God really dwelling in his soul."[122] It appeared to him that such men, modelling God on themselves, made him "nothing but a blind, dark, impetuous self-will, running through the world"; and he based his doctrine on the conviction that "God is therefore God because he is the highest and most perfect Good; and good is not therefore good because God out of an arbitrary will of his would have it so."[123] Goodness then, not assurance, must be the test of man's condition before God; and consequently men must seek God's thoughts concerning them, not "in those hidden Records of Eternity," but "written in our own hearts."[124]

With Milton and Goodwin, he believed that "ink and paper" could never produce "a new nature, a living principle in us," that "the Gospel, that new law which Christ delivered to the world, is not merely a letter without us, but a quickening spirit within us." He therefore exhorted the nation, distracted by disputes over forms and opinions, to consider that "the end of the Gospel is life and perfection; 'tis a divine nature; 'tis a godlike frame and disposition of spirit, 'tis to make us partakers of the image of God in righteousness and true holiness, without which salvation itself were but a notion."[125] For he believed that "happiness is nothing but that inward sweet delight that will arise from the harmonious agreement between our wills and God's will"; and that it is only through the Spirit, issuing in "virtue and holiness" that "we shall find our wings to grow again, our plumes fairly spread, and ourselves raised aloft into the free air of perfect liberty, which is perfect happiness."[126]

Into Milton's conception of Christian faith as "a reasonable, manly, and in the highest sense free service," a service which raised believers "to the full strength of the new creature, and a manly liberty worthy the sons of God," there clearly entered much of the spirit of the Christian humanism which Cudworth's teaching represents.[127] It was because he sought freedom from depravity, through a grace which perfected human nature for the good life, that he was unable to accept either the doctrine of man's total natural depravity or of his equal natural freedom. He believed with Whichcote that "vice is contrary to the nature of man as man"; and that as "the practice of religion is the true use of those faculties with which God hath invested human nature," so "religion makes us live like men."[128]

The real and substantial liberty which he sought was therefore a liberty at once natural and Christian; and, because he perceived, with Cudworth, that if men were to "tune the world at last into better music," they must themselves "express this sweet harmonious affection,"[129] his writings on liberty had as their basic principle the ethical doctrine of Cudworth's final exhortation: "Last of all, if we desire a true reformation, as we seem to do, let us begin here in reforming our hearts and lives, in keeping Christ's commandments. All outward forms and models of reformation, though they be never so good in their kind, yet they are of little worth to us without this inward reformation of the heart."[130] Yet if that principle was constant in Milton's prose, its significance for him developed within the framework of Puritan thought and under the force of a bitter experience. The frustrations of twenty years deepened the tone of unyielding certainty and cold contempt in which the Lady had spoken in *Comus*. Throughout the prose period he sought the harmonious integration of the spiritual and the natural; but he could not echo the sweet affection of the Christian rationalists. The failure of the revolution concentrated his attention on the supine depravity of man rather than on his potential excellence. And his contempt for depraved nature was always threatening, as in *Comus*, to transform his musical chords into the jarring blast sounded by reforming Puritanism.

The prose is the record of the development not only of a mind, but of a character in which the dominating quality was a proud assurance. The sense of special illumination which Milton enjoyed as a poet could be expressed in the terms appropriate to the assurance of particular election according to the Calvinistic scheme of salvation. His confidence found satisfaction for a time in the effort to transform society, after the Puritan fashion, into a holy community in which the righteous individual should enjoy the privileges of Christ's kingdom. But because his illumination was the reward of "labour and intense study," and begot the "high reason" of a poetry useful "both in divine and human things,"[131] his version of the holy community was not an exactly Puritan version. And the Puritan experiment, its failure, his blindness, taught him to concentrate his attention upon his peculiar gift. The lesson of the prose, painfully learned and reluctantly accepted, was that Christian liberty as Milton defined it could not be fully exercised in the sight of depraved mankind since Christ's kingdom was not after all of this world. It was only after twenty years of effort that he recognized the profound significance of the belief, expressed by Cudworth, that "every true saint carrieth his Heaven about with him in his own heart; and Hell that is without him, can have no power over him."[132]

# *Conclusion*

MILTON'S treatment of the process of regeneration and its consequences was at once an exposition of the principles according to which his theory of liberty, religious, private, and civil, had been formulated, and a comment on the course of the revolution. The early 1640's had seemed to him to mark the calling of the English people; and the effect of God's offered grace had been to restore the nation, at least partially and for a time, to a sense of the freedom proper to a human and Christian society. Under the power of God's assisting spirit, it had appeared to rouse itself from its supine depravity; but the heroic strength which had manifested itself in the efforts of 1644 had not proved lasting. The triumphant vindication of divine justice in 1649 had been the achievement of the remnant in whom God's grace had worked effectively; but such was the wilful degeneracy of the many, and the weakness even of those who should have been God's champions, that the triumph was short-lived. The disintegration of the Commonwealth when the goal was within reach followed from a corrupt repudiation of divine grace and a wilful rejection of England's glorious destiny.

The failure of the efforts of good men left Milton with a painful problem. God seemed to have forsaken his servants and to have given them over to superstition and servitude. Yet the solution of that problem had all along been preparing itself in his mind. It was man who had rejected the divine guidance and had refused, as always, to strive for the establishment of God's kingdom.

According to Milton's reading, the revolution ought to have resulted in a society, imperfect but progressing, in which good men should have been free to achieve fulness of life and to meditate upon divine truth. One must not allow the energy he expended in "hoarse disputes" to cloud the significance of the repeated expressions of his desire for "a still time." His energy was bent towards the achievement of a holy community in which activity and contemplation should have been perfectly combined.

That ideal, in its various manifestations, the Puritan parties set out to achieve through reformation; and though it is necessary to consider the spirit of Christian humanism in order to define its peculiarities, Milton's interpretation of the ideal was developed according to principles accepted by his Puritan contemporaries. The growth of his mind reflects the growth of Puritanism. It took place under the same circumstances, it was confronted by the same problems, it was conditioned by personal experiences which intensified the significance of Puritan doctrines. There was, in fact, scarcely a point in Milton's prose which did not have its intimate connection with Puritan ideology.

That conclusion will be unpalatable only to such as suppose that Puritan thought was incapable of producing anything but the obscurantism of a Thomas Edwards or the hypocrisy of a Tribulation Wholesome. It could, and did, harden into a repressive code; yet that was but one of its manifestations through the personalities of its adherents. It could also give expression to the gentle tolerance of Lord Brooke, the revolutionary logic of Roger Williams, the democratic radicalism of John Lilburne, the mystical communism of Gerrard Winstanley, the enthusiastic idealism of Sir Henry Vane. It provided each of these with principles which could be modified according to his character and experience to formulate his view of human nature. It did the same for Milton.

Though he revised his theory of the one right discipline prescribed by God, Milton never abandoned his belief in the need for discipline according to absolute divine truth, nor his conviction that this alone begot admirable and heavenly privileges. Throughout the revolution he was closing up truth to truth as he found it revealed in experience and clarified by that intellectual ray and the voice of reason. Because experience seemed to show that the only trustworthy discipline must come from within, he became increasingly certain of the intimate connection between Christian and human liberty. He was confirmed in his belief that the end and good of a people free by nature could not be achieved otherwise than through the real and substantial liberty fully to be enjoyed in a commonwealth modelled on that only just and rightful kingdom. These convictions were sharpened by the far surpassing light which accompanied his blindness, so that Christian liberty became for him the main end of government.

That end was not to be achieved; but the knowledge in the making throughout the prose period was not wasted. His exposition of Christian doctrine was at once a record of his conclusions and a preparation for the extraordinary tasks of his later years. As he had feared, his hopes had "passed through the fire only to perish in the smoke";[1] but that tempering experience bore its fruit in his great poems. In them the ideal of Christian liberty was translated, by a process already under way in the prose, into a contemplation of the freedom to be obtained through obedience to eternal law, not in a temporal community which should make possible the achievement of something like the happiness enjoyed by Adam in his natural perfection and promised the saints in Christ's Kingdom, but in "a Paradise within thee happier far."[2]

# *Notes and Bibliography*

# Notes

In all quotations in the text and notes spelling and punctuation have been modernized. The original punctuation and spelling are preserved in titles. Dates of appearance of seventeenth-century pamphlets, given in brackets, are those assigned by the contemporary collector, George Thomason, and recorded in the *Catalogue* of the Thomason Collection in the British Museum.

All references for Milton's writings are to the volume and page of *The Works of John Milton*, edited by Frank Allen Patterson, Columbia University Press, 1931-1938.

## INTRODUCTION

[1]See Boswell, *Life of Johnson*, ed. Hill and Powell, Oxford, 1934, IV, 42; and Belloc, *Milton*, 31, 125.

[2]See Good, *Studies in the Milton Tradition*, 173-5, 222-9.

[3]See, for example, Brunner, *Milton's persönliche und ideele Welt in ihrer Beziehung zum Aristokratismus.*

[4]Liljegren, *Studies in Milton*, ix.

[5]Alexander Gill, *The Sacred Philosophie of the Holy Scripture*, 1635, "To the Reader."

[6]*Cross Currents in English Literature of the Seventeenth Century*, 274.

[7]*Defensio Secunda*, VIII, 125.

[8]The charges are refuted by B. A. Wright in "The Alleged Falsehoods in Milton's Account of His Continental Tour."

[9]Liljegren, *Studies in Milton*, xvi-xix.

[10]*Defensio Secunda*, VIII, 131.

[11]*Reason of Church Government*, III, 237.

[12]"The Pattern of Milton's *Nativity Ode*."

[13]Tillyard, *Milton*, 110.

[14]*Ibid.*, 110, and Pattison, *Milton*, 67.

[15]Hanford, "The Date of Milton's *De Doctrina Christiana*," 314.

[16]Tillyard, *Milton*, 108.

[17]Hanford, "The Chronology of Milton's Private Studies."

[18]Jordan, *The Development of Religious Toleration*, IV, 202; Liljegren, *Studies in Milton*, xl.

[19]See Saurat, *Milton, Man and Thinker*, especially Part II, "The System." Geoffroy's *Etude sur les pamphlets* and *Milton on Liberty* by Philo Buck, Jr., though excellent as brief surveys of Milton's controversial activity, present the same difficulty. The more recent and very illuminating study by Wolfe, *Milton in the Puritan Revolution*, which appeared after my text was complete, has a

topical arrangement which seems to me to obscure the details of Milton's development.

[20] *A Collection of Speeches Made by Sir Edward Dering . . .*, 1642, 112.

[21] *Milton and Wordsworth*, 37.

[22] Haller, *The Rise of Puritanism.*

[23] *The Judgement of Martin Bucer*, IV, 60.

[24] Agar, *Milton and Plato*; Bailey, *Milton and Jakob Boehme*; Fletcher, *Milton's Rabbinical Readings, Milton's Semitic Studies, The Use of the Bible in Milton's Prose*; Hartwell, *Lactantius and Milton.*

[25] Woodhouse, *Puritanism and Liberty*, [37].

[26] Some recent historians have elected roughly to equate Puritanism with Presbyterianism: see Miller, *Orthodoxy in Massachusetts*, 22; Jordan, *The Development of Religious Toleration*, I, 239-43, II, 199-206, III, 267-8. Others have given "Puritanism" a broader significance. For example, Trevelyan, *England under the Stuarts*, 60-71, and with him Knappen, *Tudor Puritanism*, 489, use it to mean the beliefs of all who wished to purify the Church of England, including some supporters of prelacy. Woodhouse, *Puritanism and Liberty*, [36-7], includes within the Puritan group Presbyterians, Congregationalists, Separatists, and Anabaptists, and argues that the active ideal of the holy community, whether spiritual or temporal, is "the only satisfactory basis for a working definition of Puritanism in its social and political aspects." Allen, *English Political Thought, 1603-1644*, 255-305, uses it to indicate only the Presbyterians and Congregationalists of the period before 1640, since he believes that after that date "it cannot be defined as a set of opinions upon any one subject." An examination of representative figures leads him to suggest that, "given the Puritan's attitude towards the Scriptures, Puritanism essentially consisted in a particular reaction to the belief in election or, simply, to the idea of Hell."

No definition of a movement so dynamic can be altogether satisfactory; and I shall not attempt here to add to the evidence produced by the authorities referred to. I have used "Puritanism" to signify all those who wished to purify the Church in accordance with directions divinely revealed, either in Scripture or by the Holy Spirit, so that it would become the holy community of the spirit and perhaps provide the basis for a holy state. Various as were their interpretations of this ideal, it was held by the Presbyterians or the party of the right, whose views were in general strict and reactionary and whose church government was to be founded on Scripture through a national authority; by the Independents or Congregationalists, the party of the centre, who were somewhat more liberal in their views and whose church government was founded in theory on the sovereignty of the particular congregation voluntarily formed by believers; and by the Separatists, including Baptists and Millenarians, the party of the left, who were in general radically individualistic. I have sometimes employed the phrase "orthodox Puritanism" to signify the thought of the Presbyterians and of the moderate Independents of the right centre. At the appropriate stage in my discussion of Milton's development I examine in detail the thought of each group.

[27] "Before Areopagitica," 875 ff.; *Tracts on Liberty*, I, 72 ff.

[28] "The Youth of Milton," 106. See also Bush, *The Renaissance and English Humanism*, 114.

[29] See Woodhouse, *Puritanism and Liberty*, [61-94].

[30]Barker, "Milton's Schoolmasters," 517; Parker, "Milton and Thomas Young."

[31]See Knappen, *Tudor Puritanism*, 218-19; John Peile, *Christ's College*, chaps. IV and V.

[32]Haller, *The Rise of Puritanism*, 318-19.

[33]*Of the Infallibility of the Church of Rome*, sig. C.

## CHAPTER I

[1]Life by Edward Phillips; *Early Lives of Milton*, ed. Darbishire, 62.

[2]*Defensio Secunda*, VIII, 127.

[3]See Gilbert, "The Cambridge Manuscript and Milton's Plans for Epic."

[4]*Defensio Secunda*, VIII, 125-7.

[5]See Hanford, "The Chronology of Milton's Private Studies"; and "The Youth of Milton," 155-7.

[6]*Reason of Church Government*, III, 241.

[7]*Ibid.*, 232-5.

[8]*Defensio Secunda*, VIII, 125.

[9]*Reason of Church Government*, III, 241.

[10]*Ibid.*, 240.

[11]See Hanford, "The Youth of Milton," 123-4; Tillyard, *Milton*, 40; Haller, *The Rise of Puritanism*, 312; Barker, "The Pattern of Milton's *Nativity Ode*"; and Milton's own account of his early development, *An Apology*, III, 302-6.

[12]*Second Prolusion*, XII, 157. See Tillyard, *Private Correspondence and Academic Exercises*, xxviii.

[13]See Tillyard, *Milton*, Appendix C; and Barker, "The Pattern of Milton's *Nativity Ode*."

[14]*Seventh Prolusion*, XII, 259.

[15]*Ibid.*, 255.

[16]The phrases quoted occur in the "retraction" which follows *Elegia Septima* in the *Poems* of 1645.

[17]*An Apology*, III, 303; *Elegia Sexta*, 55-80.

[18]See the "Letter to a Friend," probably written in 1632, XII, 322-5.

[19]*An Apology*, III, 304-5.

[20]*At a Solemn Music*, 14; *An Apology*, III, 306.

[21]Woodhouse, "The Argument of Milton's *Comus*." The following paragraph is based on Professor Woodhouse's discussion.

[22]The version of the debate in the Bridgewater Manuscript, which is thought to be the copy from which the masque was originally presented at Ludlow Castle, suggests some dissatisfaction on the part of the author or the producer with the argument. Lines 737-55 and 780-806 of the printed version do not appear in it. These lines include the whole of Comus's comment on virginity and the whole of the Lady's comment on chastity and virginity. What remains when these lines are omitted is a perfectly consistent debate in which Comus derides abstinence as the absurd alternative to his sensuality and the Lady neatly counters with her description of temperance. Chastity and virginity are not so much as mentioned.

[23]It is, I think, this note of repudiation which has led Professor Haller to

say that, on the ideal plane, "*Comus* and *Lycidas* are as authentic expressions of the Puritan spirit on the eve of the revolution as anything that came from the hand of Prynne" (*The Rise of Puritanism*, 317). Professor Haller has fully demonstrated the influence of the Puritan atmosphere on Milton's early development; but he seems to me to minimize the element of conflict in Milton; and, in the light of Professor Woodhouse's discussion of the masque, his view of its Puritanism seems too extreme.

[24]See *Arcades and Comus*, ed. A. W. Verity, xxxiii.

[25]Note prefixed in the *Poems* of 1645.

[26]See Tillyard, *Milton*, 81-5; Barker, "The Pattern of Milton's *Nativity Ode*," 171-2.

[27]*Epitaphium Damonis*, 212-19.

[28]*Ibid.*, 162-72; *Mansus*, 78-84.

[29]*Of Reformation*, III, 12, 73, 75.

[30]*Ibid.*, 35. The continued presence in Milton's mind of the Spenserian influence under which (among others) *Comus* and *Lycidas* were composed is indicated by his reference at this point to the Gospel as "a mirror of diamond" dazzling the opponents of reformation, and in *Animadversions* (III, 165) to "that false shepherd Palinode in the Eclogue of May."

[31]*Of Reformation*, III, 36.

[32]*Reason of Church Government*, III, 199.

[33]*Of Reformation*, III, 1-2.

[34]*Ibid.*, 25; *Reason of Church Government*, III, 188.

[35]*Reason of Church Government*, III, 184-5.

[36]*Animadversions*, III, 148.

[37]*Of Reformation*, III, 78.

[38]*Reason of Church Government*, III, 236; and see 237: "what K. or Knight before the Conquest might be chosen in whom to lay the pattern of a Christian hero."

[39]*Animadversions*, III, 142.

## CHAPTER II

[1]*Defensio Secunda*, VIII, 129. There follows a brief review of the five pamphlets forming the anti-episcopal group: *Of Reformation Touching Church-Discipline in England . . .*, (May) 1641; *Of Prelatical Episcopacy, and Whether it may be deduc'd from Apostolical times . . .*, (June-July) 1641; *Animadversions upon The Remonstrants Defence, against Smectymnuus . . .*, (July) 1641; *The Reason of Church-government Urg'd against Prelaty . . .*, (January-March) 1641/42; *An Apology Against . . . A Modest Confutation of the Animadversions . . .*, (March-April) 1642. For the dating of these, see Masson, II, 257, 361, 398.

[2]See *The Bloudy Tenent of Persecution*, *Hanserd Knollys Society Publications*, 30.

[3]Peloni Almoni, Cosmopolites, *A Compendious Discourse, Proving Episcopacy to be of Apostolical, And consequently of Divine Institution*, 1641; and the anonymous *Modest Confutation of . . . Animadversions upon the Remonstrants Defence*, 1642. See Whiting, *Milton's Literary Milieu*, 293-301; and for these and other briefer comments, Parker, *Milton's Contemporary Reputation*, 15, 71-2.

[4]In "The Preface" also Hooker examines the theory which established the rules of the church at Geneva "under that high commanding form which tendered them unto the people as things everlastingly required by the law of that Lord of lords against whose statutes there is no exception to be taken" (*Of the Lawes of Ecclesiastical Politie*, 1622, sig. B$^v$).

[5]The ministers from whose initials the pseudonym was formed were Stephen Marshall, Edmund Calamy, Thomas Young, Matthew Newcomen, and William Spurstowe. All subsequently became members of the Westminster Assembly. Calamy, who engaged in a pamphlet controversy with Henry Burton over Separatism, and Spurstowe, who became master of Catharine Hall, lived to accept, with some reservations, the Restoration. Marshall and Young signed with other ministers, both Presbyterian and Independent, *Certain Considerations to Dissuade Men from further gathering of Churches in this present juncture of Time*, (December 23) 1643, an exhortation to extreme Independents and Sectaries to be patient and not incontinently to set up unauthorized congregations, since "it is not to be doubted but the counsels of the Assembly of Divines and the care of Parliament will be not only to reform and set up religion throughout the nation, but will concur to preserve whatever shall appear to be the rights of particular congregations, according to the Word, and to bear with such whose conscience cannot in all things conform to the public rule, so far as the Word of God would have them born withal" (3). Young took no further part in ecclesiastical controversy. Marshall maintained the moderate position suggested by the above; see Jordan, *The Development of Religious Toleration*, III, 318, 328-30.

That Milton's former tutor was the leader in the controversy with Hall is indicated by Baillie's reference to him as "the author of *Dies Dominica* and of the Smectymnuus for the most part" (*Letters*, I, 366; Masson, II, 219). Masson (II, 238-44, 260) and after him Hale (*Of Reformation*, liii-liv) thought that Milton was drawn into the controversy to supply at least notes for the "Postscript" of *An Answer to . . . An Humble Remonstrance* in which the history of episcopacy in England is surveyed in the manner and with many of the references subsequently employed by Milton in *Of Reformation*. Whiting ("Milton and the Postscript") has cast doubt on this supposition, chiefly because the "Postscript" quotes a passage from Bucer's *De Regno Christi*, a book of which Milton professed ignorance until after the publication of *The Doctrine and Discipline of Divorce*; see *The Judgement of Martin Bucer concerning Divorce*, IV, 11. It would be possible to argue that this doubt is ill-founded since the Bucer passage in question appears to have been commonly known to the opponents of episcopacy, and might therefore have been ready to Milton's hand though he did not know the book from which it was taken or Bucer's treatment of divorce. The passage was used, for example, in *The Petition for the Prelates briefly examined*, 1641, and again in *Queene Elizabeths Bishops: or A Brief Declaration of the Wickednesse of the Generalitie of those Bishops . . . that lived in the purest times*, 1642. But even if this argument were pressed, and I see no reason for pressing it, the doubtfulness of Masson's assumption is increased by the fact that such historical reviews as the "Postscript" and *Of Reformation* present were popular with Puritan writers. Hall suggested, erroneously, that much of the "Postscript" had come from Alexander Leighton's *An Appeal to the Parliament, or, Sions Plea against the Prelacie*, 1628. The two pamphlets mentioned above make use of material similar to that used by the Smectymnuans and Milton, and often of identical examples of episcopal corruption. Much the same ground is covered in *A Speech of William Thomas, Esquire, in Parliament in May*, 1641; and examples could be multiplied. Many of the opponents of episcopacy were, like Milton, reading their Speeds, Holinsheds, and Foxes, in search of ammunition; and the Smectymnuans were perfectly capable of collecting their own. The fact remains, however, that while Milton cannot be said with certainty to have collaborated with the Smectymnuans, his interest in the controversy with Hall was lively. The pages which follow will establish the influence of Young's views on his.

[6]*A Defence of the Humble Remonstrance*, (April) 1641, 45; see also *An Humble Remonstrance to the High Court of Parliament*, (January) 1640/41, 17.

[7]*Of the Lawes of Ecclesiastical Politie*, 111-12: "If therefore we did seek to maintain that which most advantageth our own cause, the very best way for us and the strongest against them were to hold, even as they do, that in Scripture there must needs be found some particular form of church polity which God hath instituted, and which for that very cause belongeth to all churches, to all times. But with any such partial eye to respect ourselves, and by cunning to make those things seem the truest which are the fittest to serve our purpose, is a thing which we neither like nor mean to follow."

[8]*Episcopacie by Divine Right Asserted*, (February) 1640, I, 38, 27.

[9]*A Vindication of the Answer to the Humble Remonstrance*, (June) 1641, 113-14: "The best charter pleaded for episcopacy in former times was ecclesiastical constitution and the favour of princes. But our later bishops . . . have endeavoured to underpin it with some texts of Scripture that they might plead a *jus divinum* for it . . . ." The Smectymnuans asked "whether the three last books of Hooker's *Ecclesiastical Politie* be not suppressed by him that hath them because they give the prince too much power in ecclesiastical matters and are not for the divine right of bishops" (*ibid.*, 9). Milton makes a similar comment on the prelatical argument in *The Reason of Church Government* (III, 208-9).

[10]*An Answer to . . . An Humble Remonstrance*, (March) 1641, 70.

[11]*A Vindication*, 54.

[12]*Of Reformation*, III, 30.

[13]*Ibid.*, 28, 35; *Of Prelatical Episcopacy*, III, 101.

[14]*Of Reformation*, III, 21.

[15]*Ibid.*, 39-41.

[16]*Ibid.*, 69.

[17]*Reason of Church Government*, III, 184.

[18]*Ibid.*, 189-95.

[19]*Of Reformation*, III, 4.

[20]*Ibid.*, 5.

[21]*The Unlawfulnes and Danger of Limited Prelacie*, 1641, 7.

[22]*Reason of Church Government*, III, 193-5. Milton is considering 1 *Timothy* 4. 13, 14, a *locus classicus* on discipline discussed at some length by Hooker (*Of the Lawes of Ecclesiastical Politie*, 117-18). Hooker refutes the interpretation which would make St. Paul's directions to Timothy include the whole church after him, and so "exclude all liberty of changing the laws of Christ whether by abrogation, or addition, or howsoever." Milton must have had the *Lawes* beside him as he wrote. He does little more than adopt the argument there outlined for rebuttal, and concludes from the text "that the rules of church discipline are not only commanded but hedged about with such a terrible impalement

of commands as he that will break through wilfully to violate the least of them must hazard the wounding of his conscience even unto death."

[23]*Of Reformation*, III, 66.

[24]Whiting, *Milton's Literary Milieu*, 267-81, compares Milton's views on the church with Bacon's. As he notes, Milton refers to Bacon's *Certaine Considerations* in *Of Reformation*, III, 18; to his *Advertisement* (in connection with press-censorship) in *Animadversions*, III, 111-12, *An Apology*, III, 295, and in the *Areopagitica*, IV, 326, 333; and to the *New Atlantis* in *An Apology*, III, 294. Professor Hanford has remarked ("The Chronology of Milton's Private Studies," 301) that the recording of a note in the *Commonplace Book* (XVIII, 180) between 1641 and 1642 on Bacon's statement in the *Advertisement* about licensing "shows very clearly that the sources of Milton's defence of the freedom of the press (1644) lie deep in his early reading, and tends to minimize the merely personal and occasional element in the work." The force of Whiting's comparison and of Hanford's observation is somewhat reduced by the fact that Milton quotes from Bacon only what will support his party in the ecclesiastical dispute, and ignores what is against it, a fact which was noted by the author of *A Modest Confutation of . . . Animadversions*, 3-4. It is this charge which Milton attempted somewhat lamely to turn aside in *An Apology*, III, 320, by mentioning Bacon's contradiction of himself and his aspersions on Job. Bacon's motives, as my text shows, were fundamentally different from Milton's. His politic observations on the censorship of the press were designed merely to prove that it defeats its own end. They give little support to the argument of the *Areopagitica*. And the ecclesiastical position which Milton assumes in the early pamphlets is already firmly condemned in the *Considerations* and the *Advertisement*.

[25]*Certaine Considerations touching the better Pacification and Edification of the Church . . .*, 1640, sig. B3; first published 1604. Bacon gives an abstract of what is really Hooker's theory of the constitution of the church.

[26]*A Wise and Moderate Discourse, Concerning Church Affaires*, 1641, 22; written 1589, but not previously published.

[27]*Ibid.*, 30.

[28]See Marriott, *Life of . . . Falkland*, chap. III.

[29]*A Speech made to the House of Commons Concerning Episcopacy*, 1641, 7.

[30]*The Third Speech of the Lord George Digby . . . concerning Bishops and the Citie Petition, Febr. 9, 1640.* Whiting has shown (*Milton's Literary Milieu*, 282-92) that in some half-dozen pages at the end of *Of Reformation* (III, 65 ff.) Milton was refuting this speech point by point. The pages form a kind of appendix to the pamphlet, the main body of which is rather to be associated with the Smectymnuan controversy.

[31]*Of Reformation*, III, 66, 68.

[32]See Miller, *Orthodoxy in Massachusetts*, chaps. I-IV.

[33]*A Defence*, 135.

[34]*Episcopacie by Divine Right*, III, 25-6.

[35]*A Speech of the Honourable Nathanael Fiennes . . . in answer to the Third Speech of the Lord George Digby*, 1641, 16. Cromwell similarly answered a question put by Sir Philip Warwick: "I can tell you, sirs, what I would *not* have, though I cannot what I would" (Warwick, *Memoirs*, 177; quoted Miller, *Orthodoxy in Massachusetts*, 73).

[36]In 1644 the five dissenting members of the Assembly pointed out that

"the full strength and stream of our nonconformists' writings and others were spent rather in arguments against and for the overthrowing of episcopal government and the corruptions that cleave to our worship, and in maintaining those several officers in churches which Christ hath instituted," than in propounding any certain form of national church government to be substituted for the episcopal (*An Apologeticall Narration*, 1643, 15).

[37]"Table of Authorities," Young's *Dies Dominica*. For Ames's reputation, see Miller, *Orthodoxy in Massachusetts*, 77. Masson (II, 376) believed that Milton's anti-episcopal pamphlets were written in favour of the Scotch Presbyterian system, an opinion shared by Hale (*Of Reformation*, xlii) and Saurat (*Milton, Man and Thinker*, 30). Jordan (*The Development of Religious Toleration*, IV, 208) thinks that "his religious and intellectual position during these dark years was strikingly sympathetic" to moderate Presbyterianism. The line of demarcation between moderate Presbyterianism and Congregationalism is difficult to draw; and since Milton's early pamphlets contain no precise statements on the questions of discipline on which the two groups ultimately differed, it is impossible to link him positively with either. The phrase "Presbytery, if it must be so called" (*Of Reformation*, III, 73) suggests the tentative nature of his opinions.

[38]See Miller, *Orthodoxy in Massachusetts*, chap. IV. For Ames's theory of church government, see *Conscience* (first published 1631, translated 1639, 1643), chap. XXIV; and *Medulla Theologica* (1628, translated 1642 as *The Marrow of Sacred Divinity*), chaps. XXXII-XXXVII.

[39]The Smectymnuans were to be reminded of the liberal tendencies of their pamphlets when they later adopted the strict Presbyterian position in the toleration controversy. In March, 1644/45, John Saltmarsh published *Groanes for Liberty, Presented From the Presbyterian (formerly non-conforming) Brethren . . . in some Treatises called Smectymnuus, . . . now awakened and presented to themselves in the behalf of their now Non-conforming Brethren*. Seeing "occasion now of reminding the brethren of these because the strain of their preaching and printing seems to have forgotten these principles," he quotes passages from the *Answer* arguing against set forms of prayer, the enforcement of complete uniformity, the rigours which beget schism, the assumption that minor differences prejudice essential truth, and others implying that church organization should be in congregations rather than nationally.

[40]See *Of Reformation*, III, 77; *Animadversions*, III, 145-6.

[41]*An Answer*, 81: "Does not the root of these disorders proceed from the bishops . . . , whose practice has been according to that rule of Machiavill, *Divide et impera*?"

[42]*Reason of Church Government*, III, 211; see also 222 ff.

[43]The Smectymnuans pointed out that "our first reformation was only in doctrine" (*A Vindication*, 39), and that "it much concerns all those that desire the purity of the church to consider how near the discipline of the Church of England borders upon Antichrist, lest while they endeavour to keep out Antichrist from entering by the door of doctrine, they should suffer him secretly to creep in by the door of discipline" (*An Answer*, 85). This is Milton's point in *Of Reformation*: "albeit in purity of doctrine we agree with our brethren, yet in discipline we are no better than a schism from all the reformation" (III, 6). At this time he seems to have been perfectly orthodox in his theological beliefs. He accepted the Trinity (III, 76), censured Tertullian for making an imparity

between Father and Son (III, 97), denounced Arianism (III, 23), would not allow Arians and Pelagians to have been true martyrs (III, 10), and condemned the Arminians (III, 330).

[44]*Reason of Church Government*, III, 223-4.

[45]*Ibid.*, 216.

[46]"If the bounds of a kingdom must constitute the limits and bounds of a church, why are not England, Scotland, and Ireland all one church? . . . We read in Scripture of the churches of Judea, and the churches of Galatia; and why not the churches of England? Not that we deny the consociation or combination of churches into a provincial or national synod for the right ordering of them; but that there should be no church in England but a national church, this is what this author in his simplicity affirms . . ." (*An Answer*, 80).

[47]*Reason of Church Government*, III, 217.

[48]Hall repeated the common prelatical assertion (denied by Milton, *Of Reformation*, III, 36) that the Puritans would make "every parish minister and his eldership . . . a bishop and his consistory; yea, a pope and his conclave of cardinals within his own parish, not subject to controlment, not liable to superior censure" (*Episcopacie by Divine Right*, III, 34). He also insisted on the incapacity of a small village "to furnish forth an ecclesiastical consistory," and asked what would come of government by John a Nokes and John a Stiles and Smug the Smith: ". . . what a mad world it would be, that the ecclesiastical laws of such a company should be, like those of the Medes and Persians, irrevocable, that there should be no appeal from them; for as for classes and synods, they may advise in cases of doubt, but overrule they may not" (*ibid.*, 32).

[49]Francis Johnson's Separatist church at Amsterdam, for example, suffered a schism over the relative powers in excommunication of the minister with the elders and the whole body of church members. In this dispute Henry Ainsworth took the part of the members and maintained their complete power over the church executive in all matters of discipline. John Robinson, on the other hand, came from Leyden, where he was minister of a Separatist church, to attempt to mediate by arguing that, though power was originally in the congregation, the members must "of faith give their assent to their elders' holy and lawful administration" (*Works*, II, 43; and see Burgess, *John Robinson*, 200 ff.). Among the New England Congregationalists all power was virtually in the hands of the ministers and elders (Miller, *Orthodoxy in Massachusetts*, 181 ff.). John Cotton explained that "the Gospel alloweth no church authority or rule, properly so called, to the brethren, but reserveth that wholly to the elders; and yet preventeth the tyranny and oligarchy and exorbitancy of the elders by the large and firm establishment of the liberties of the brethren" (*The Keyes of the Kingdom of Heaven*, 12). This is typical of the Congregational effort to preserve a middle course, at least in theory. See Miller, *Orthodoxy in Massachusetts*, 148 ff., for an account of the administrative problems which inevitably arose. A somewhat more liberal interpretation of this "due-proportioned distribution" of power was given by Thomas Goodwin and Philip Nye in an introduction to Cotton's tract (Woodhouse, *Puritanism and Liberty*, 293-8). Robert Greville, Lord Brooke, who had Separatist sympathies, expressed a more radical view. He said that a representative parliament is desirable only because "no place can contain the whole body" of the people; that this would be unnecessary if "all the people could meet *in Campo Martio*"; and that similarly, "the whole church being present,

four or five shall not rule all." Though the execution of power is "ministerially" in the church officers, it is originally and fundamentally in the people, and the government of the church should therefore be "democratical" (*A Discourse opening the Nature of . . . Episcopacie*, 1641, 79-83). The political implications of these views will subsequently require attention.

[50]See Ames, *Marrow of Sacred Divinity*, 145; John Robinson, *A Justification of Separation*, 1610, 140; John Smith, *Parallels*, 416-17.

[51]*Of Reformation*, III, 63-4. It will be observed that the parallel is not perfectly clear. Milton does not mention an assembly or equate it with parliament, but compares the "knights and burgesses" to the ministers "in their several charges." The parallel was a common one. It was used by Nathaniel Fiennes against Digby (*A Speech*, 17). The Presbyterian John Paget, arguing against Ames, Ainsworth, and other Congregationalists and Separatists, asserted that it was false: "You seek to build the government upon unsure foundations . . . in that you argue from the example of civil government in the commonwealth to demonstrate the power of the people in the one by the authority exercised in the other" (*A Defence of Church Government, exercised in Presbyteriall, Classicall, & Synodall Assemblies*, 1641, 7).

[52]*Of Reformation*, III, 16; *An Answer*, 33. Both refer to the example of Cyprian.

[53]*Reason of Church Government*, III, 257, 258; *An Answer*, 41.

[54]*An Answer*, 73.

[55]*A Vindication*, 72: "You make yourselves the sole pastors, us but the curates; yourselves, chancellors, officials, the sole judges, us but the executors of your and their sentences, whether just or unjust."

[56]*Ibid.*, 72.

[57]*An Answer*, 12-13. The author of a reply to the Smectymnuans remarked that "it is apparent that that which our author drives at by his whole discourse is not that the people but the minister is to be left to his own liberty to use in public assemblies what form of prayer himself thinks fit" (*The Use of Daily Publick Prayers*, 1641, 13). The royalist Sir Thomas Aston likewise warned that the ministers "have no thought of the people's liberty, but to assume into their own hands the same power they cry down in bishops, not to qualify but to exalt it above all moderation" (*A Remonstrance, against Presbitery . . .*, (May) 1641, section VIII).

[58]*Sr. Henry Vane his Speech . . . at a Committee for the Bill against Episcopall-Government . . . June 11, 1641*, 3: "We should do with this government as we are done by in regeneration, in which all old things are to pass away and all things are to become new."

[59]*Of Reformation*, III, 11.

[60]*An Answer*, 63: cf. *An Apology*, III, 167-8, where Milton uses many of the arguments and references already used in the *Answer*.

[61]*Animadversions*, III, 163.

[62]Young was vicar of Stowmarket from 1628 till his death in 1655. Probably as a result of his share in the Smectymnuan pamphlets, he was appointed a member of the Westminster Assembly and to the parish of St. James, Duke Place. In 1644 he also became Master of Jesus College, Cambridge. He was removed from this post in 1650 because of his refusal to take the Engagement. Milton can hardly have avoided the thought of his former tutor when he commented in

the *History of Britain* (X, 322) on the apostacy of those members of the Assembly who, though in receipt of a public salary, were not unwilling to accept "(besides one, sometimes two or more, of the best livings) collegiate masterships in the universities, rich lectureships in the city, setting sail to all winds that might blow gain into their covetous bosoms." See David Laing, *Biographical Notices of Thomas Young*, and Barker, "Milton's Schoolmasters," 517-18.

[63]*An Answer*, 28, 45, 74. With reference to Constantine's enactment that "such as were to be tried before civil magistrates might have leave to appeal *ad judicium episcoporum*," the Smectymnuans remark that "this the historian [Zosimus] reckoneth as one argument of his reverend respect to religion" (*An Answer*, 45). Milton makes a very different use of Zosimus (*Of Reformation*, III, 23).

[64]*Of Reformation*, III, 22-6. The attack is repeated in *An Apology*, III, 359-60.

[65]*Of Reformation*, III, 23.

[66]*Ibid.*, 75; see also *Animadversions*, III, 159-67, 171-2, and *An Apology*, III, 359-64.

[67]*Of Reformation*, III, 18-19.

[68]*Reason of Church Government*, III, 257.

## CHAPTER III

[1]*Of Reformation*, III, 2-4; *Reason of Church Government*, III, 183.

[2]*Reason of Church Government*, III, 242. Milton here explains that he did not enter the church at the end of his college career because "he who would take orders must subscribe slave and take an oath withal which, unless he took with a conscience that would retch, must straight perjure or split his faith." This reminiscential statement must not be too heavily emphasized. In Milton's extant writings up to 1641 there are several attacks on ecclesiastical corruption; but there is no single passage before this one which suggests that his conscience prevented him from entering the ministry. He was not so scrupulous as to refuse, like the young Henry Vane, to take the oaths necessary for his academic degrees; in the letter to a friend (perhaps Young) in which he enclosed the sonnet *How soon hath Time* (1631 or 1632) he does not give conscience as a reason for not taking orders but defends his deliberate preference for private study; when he justifies his preoccupation with poetry in *Ad Patrem* (c. 1636), he does not tell his father that conscience prevented the fulfilment of the parental desire that he should enter the church; and over against the condemnation of corrupt priests in *Elegia Quarta* and *Lycidas* must be set his admiration for Young's ministry, his praise of King, and the formal but eulogistic elegies on Bishops Andrewes and Felton. Milton's choice of a career was conditioned by the literary ambitions which his conscience repeatedly made him justify.

[3]*Nativity Ode*, line 28; *Reason of Church Government*, III, 241: see Hanford, "That Shepherd, Who First Taught the Chosen Seed," and Barker, "The Pattern of Milton's *Nativity Ode*."

[4]*Reason of Church Government*, III, 258: "Origen, being yet a layman, expounded the Scriptures publicly, and was therein defended by Alexander of Jerusalem and Theoctistus of Caesarea, producing in his behalf divers examples,

that the privilege of teaching was anciently permitted to many worthy laymen . . . ."

[5]*Animadversions*, III, 156.

[6]*Reason of Church Government*, III, 228-42; *An Apology*, III, 302-6.

[7]Milton nowhere mentions Burton. He would have known of him because of his fame as a Puritan martyr, with Bastwicke and Prynne (see Haller, *Tracts on Liberty*, I, 9-11; Jordan, *The Development of Religious Toleration*, III, 19). When he said that the Parliament, "opening the prisons and dungeons, called out of darkness and bonds the elect martyrs and witnesses of the Redeemer" (*An Apology*, III, 338), he probably had expressly in mind the liberation of these three by the Long Parliament, amid much rejoicing, late in 1641. In the *Apology* he singles out as an example of the controversial methods of the enemies of Puritanism an answer to Burton's *Protestation Protested*, entitled *A Survay of that Foolish, Seditious, Scandalous, Prophane Libell, The Protestation Protested*, (May) 1641. Milton has apparently read this answer, which he thinks from Hall's pen (*An Apology*, III, 319-20). It seems likely that he had also read Burton's pamphlet, though I am suggesting its argument as an analogy not as a source.

[8]*Englands Bondage and Hope of Deliverance* (a sermon to the Parliament, June, 1641), 21, 26.

[9]*Ibid.*, 23.

[10]*The Protestation Protested*, sig. B3.

[11]*Ibid.*, sig. C3$^{v}$.

[12]Edwards was one of the most prolific of the Presbyterian apologists. In *Reasons against the Independant Government of Particular Congregations*, 1641, he had already begun his attack on Separatists like John Robinson and Burton and on Congregationalists like Ames.

[13]*The Justification of the Independant Churches of Christ*, 1641, 36: "though the Protestor declare what he would have for the church of the saints, yet he doth not take upon him to determine what government or rule shall be set up in the land to bring men out of darkness to light, but leaveth that to the judgment of them which have the power, even the King and Parliament."

[14]*Reasons against the Independant Government*, 32; *Justification of the Independant Churches*, 20.

[15]*Justification of the Independant Churches*, 79, 35.

[16]*Ibid.*, 38.

[17]*Ibid.*, 7.

[18]Henry Robinson, *Liberty of Conscience*, (March 24) 1643/44, "To every Christian Reader."

[19]*Reason of Church Government*, III, 256.

[20]*Ibid.*, 189 ff.

[21]*Ibid.*, 196, 198, 199.

[22]*A Justification of Separation*, 1610, 140 (reprinted 1639); cf. Luther, *Commentary upon Galatians* and *Concerning Christian Liberty*.

[23]*Reason of Church Government*, III, 260.

[24]*Ibid.*, 262; see also 257: the people "are not now any more to be separated in the church by veils and partitions, as laics and unclean, but admitted to wait upon the tabernacle as the rightful clergy of Christ, a chosen generation, a royal

priesthood, to offer up spiritual sacrifices in that meet place to which God and the congregation shall call and assign them."

[25]*An Apology*, III, 344.

[26]*Ibid.*, 338; *Reason of Church Government*, III, 258.

[27]*A Vindication*, 198, 113.

[28]*An Answer*, 88-9.

[29]*A Protestation of the Kings Supremacie*, 1605, 5.

[30]*English Puritanisme*, 1640, 4, 9, 14; written by William Bradshaw, first published 1605; ascribed to William Ames in the edition of 1640.

[31]*Of Reformation*, III, 12, 40 ff.; cf. *An Answer*, 95 ff.

[32]*Reason of Church Government*, III, 267; and see *Of Reformation*, III, 55-6.

[33]*Of Reformation*, III, 40, 65.

[34]*Reason of Church Government*, III, 254, 255.

[35]*Ibid.*, 256-7.

[36]*Ibid.*, 266; *Of Reformation*, III, 71-2.

[37]See *Of Reformation*, III, 40 ff.

[38]*A Discourse opening the Nature of that Episcopacie, which is exercised in England*, (November) 1641, 33.

[39]See *Reason of Church Government*, III, 254.

[40]*Ibid.*, 239.

[41]*Sr. Henry Vane his Speech . . . against Episcopall-Government*, (June 11) 1641, 9; Thomas Young, *Hopes Incouragement*, (sermon to Parliament, February 28) 1643, 26; Milton, *An Apology*, III, 340.

[42]*English Puritanisme*, 20.

[43]*Defensio Secunda*, VIII, 129.

[44]*Reason of Church Government*, III, 250; *Of Reformation*, III, 22-3.

[45]*Reason of Church Government*, III, 260.

## CHAPTER IV

[1]*Seventh Prolusion*, XII, 265.

[2]*For God and the King*, 1636, 82-3. It was this Fifth of November sermon which first brought Burton before the Star Chamber.

[3]In words which suggest the tone of the *Areopagitica*, Burton asserted that "if truth and error be both suppressed, truth by and by vanisheth, but error doth by necessary consequence come instead thereof and prevail. As if a man should be hoodwinked for the space of twenty-four hours, that he should see neither the day or the night; by this means all is night to him" (*For God and the King*, 114). For an account of Burton's later opposition to Presbyterianism, see Jordan, *The Development of Religious Toleration*, III, 358-61.

[4]*An Answer*, 20.

[5]Hooker is of course arguing in favour of a right use of reason: "Hereby it cometh to pass that custom, inuring the mind to long practice, and so leaving there a sensible impression, prevaileth more than reasonable persuasion what way soever. Reason therefore may rightly discern the thing which is good, and yet the will of man not incline itself thereunto, as oft as the prejudice of sensible experience doth oversway" (*Of the Lawes of Ecclesiastical Politie*, 1622, 16; and see 22). This is a position which Milton and the radicals are to develop po-

litically in defending the execution of Charles; but in 1641 Milton and the Smectymnuans are arguing against corrupt custom in favour of the divine prescript rather than in favour of the free activity of the reason.

[6]*An Answer*, 19. The quotation is from Epistle 73. A sentence from Epistle 74 is quoted marginally: "Frustra consuetudine nobis opponunt, quam si consuetudo major sit veritas, aut non id est in spiritualibus siquendum quod in melius fuerit a Spiritu Sancto revelatum."

[7]*Of Reformation*, III, 29. Milton gives in translation the sentence from Epistle 74 and the second part of the quotation from Epistle 73. He also quotes from Epistle 63.

[8]*Of the Lawes of Ecclesiastical Politie*, "The Preface," section IV.

[9]*A Vindication*, 114. Much space is nevertheless devoted by the Smectymnuans to the production of patristic authorities for the equality of ministers: "if this Remonstrant think to help himself by taking sanctuary in antiquity, though we would gladly rest in Scripture, the sanctuary of the Lord, yet we will follow him thither . . ." (*An Answer*, 23). This is also Milton's view in *Of Reformation* and *Of Prelatical Episcopacy*.

[10]*Of Reformation*, III, 29.

[11]*Reason of Church Government*, III, 183-4.

[12]*Ibid*., 211, 246.

[13]*Ibid*., 249.

[14]*An Apology*, III, 322-3.

[15]*Gangraena, or A Catalogue and Discovery of Many . . . Errours*, part II, 2.

[16]Young, *The Lords Day*, 1672, 408; first published as *Dies Dominica*, 1639. See Barker, "Milton's Schoolmasters," 518-21.

[17]The attitude of the establishment towards indifferent things is well represented by Bacon's complaint against the Puritans that "we contend about ceremonies and things indifferent, about the extern policy and government of the church" (*A Discourse*, 3-4), and by Hall's argument that "things indifferent or good" should not "upon light grounds be pulled up" (*Remonstrance*, 17). Fiennes stated the Puritan attitude: "Sir, if in things that are in their own nature indifferent, if in things disputable, it shall be as heinous to abet or maintain an opinion as in the most horrible heresies . . . , what liberty is left us as Christians? what liberty is left us as men?" (*A Second Speech*, 10.) This is the protest subsequently developed by the Puritan left against the authority of the Assembly.

[18]*Of Reformation*, III, 2, 50.

[19]*An Apology*, III, 338.

[20]*Areopagitica*, IV, 346-7. Milton refers to the appeal near the end of Brooke's *Discourse*. On Brooke see Haller, *Tracts on Liberty*, I, 15 ff., and *The Rise of Puritanism*, 332 ff.

[21]Whiting, *Milton's Literary Milieu*, 301-10, presents evidence, not, it is true, altogether conclusive, for believing that Brooke was indebted to Milton's *Of Prelatical Episcopacy* for his arguments against the antiquity of episcopacy, and that Milton was indebted to Brooke in his denunciation of episcopacy as itself a schism in *The Reason of Church Government*.

This relationship between Brooke and Milton is certainly possible; but it seems to me more likely that Milton's denunciation of episcopacy was suggested (if it needed to be suggested) by the Smectymnuans, who had devoted the whole of the seventeenth section of their *Answer* to an account of the confusion begotten by episcopacy in the state and the divisions fomented by it in the church. Certainly, whatever may have been true of Milton in this case, Brooke's debt to the Smectymnuans was very much greater than his possible debt to *Of Prelatical Episcopacy*. Whiting has not observed that the organization and much of the material of chapters II, III, and IV of Brooke's Second Book came from the *Answer*. Brooke makes no acknowledgement; but he refers specifically to Hall, "one of our own that offers to yield the cause for one example of lawful ordination by presbyters without a bishop" (*Discourse*, 72; cf. Hall's *Defence*, 71); and he remarks, "It hath been showed, and yet never answered (that I know) that some councils have intimated enough: presbyters were wont of old to ordain bishops." This reference to the Smectymnuan argument is followed by the list of authorities produced in the *Answer*.

Brooke's borrowing from the Smectymnuans indicates the importance of their pamphlets in the ecclesiastical controversy, and also suggests the complex community of Puritan ideas in 1641 which makes it difficult and dangerous to assign sources for Milton's arguments. It is not important enough to warrant the detailed production of evidence. A comparison of *An Answer*, 34-41, 61-2, and *A Discourse*, 70-3, 76-7, will show that Brooke followed the Smectymnuan argument closely, using some (though not all) of its scriptural and patristic evidence. His historical account of episcopacy (*A Discourse*, 41-3) came in part directly from the Smectymnuan "Postscript" to *An Answer*.

[22]*A Discourse*, second edition, 1642, 45.

[23]*Ibid.*, 71; and see 79-83. Brooke does not present the Separatists' opinions as his own, but the direction of his sympathies is clear.

[24]*A Discourse*, 107.

[25]*Ibid.*, 22.

[26]*Ibid.*, 22-5.

[27]See De Pauley, *The Candle of the Lord*, 1937.

[28]*A Discourse*, 27.

[29]*Ibid.*, 27-30.

[30]*A Discourse*, 118; *Areopagitica*, IV, 346-7.

[31]*A Discourse*, 13.

[32]*The Nature of Truth, its Union and Unity with the Soul*, 1640, 4: "the form of a reasonable soul is light, and therefore when the soul informeth and giveth life to animal rational, it enableth the creature to work according to light; and upon her accesses, the organs can entertain light, as the eye then beholds the light of the sun; upon her retirements, they are dark and useless. Thus while life is light, and light is truth, and truth is conformity to God, and the understanding . . . is this light to the soul, the understanding and truth can be but one."

[33]*Of Reformation*, III, 33.

[34]*Reason of Church Government*, III, 182.

[35]*An Answer*, 14; cf. *A Vindication*, 37-8: "It is a grief to see this distaste [of the liturgy] grow to such a height as tends to separation; and it is strange to us that this Remonstrant should have a heart so void of pity as that the yielding to the altering or removing of a thing indifferent . . . should be presented to public view under no better notion than the humouring of a company of ill-taught men."

[36]*Animadversions*, III, 126-7.

## CHAPTER V

[1]*Defensio Secunda*, VIII, 131. There follows a brief account of the pamphlets, of which the titles and dates are as follows: *The Doctrine and Discipline of Divorce . . .*, (August 1) 1643, first edition; *The Doctrine & Discipline of Divorce. . . . Now the second time revis'd and much augmented . . .*, (February 2) 1643/44; *To Samuel Hartlib*, registered June 4, 1644 (Masson, III, 255), dated June 5 by Thomason, reprinted as *Of Education* in *Poems*, 1673; *The Judgement of Martin Bucer concerning Divorce . . .*, 1644, registered July 15 (Masson, III, 255); *Areopagitica . . .*, (November 24) 1644; *Colasterion . . .*, (March 4) 1644/45; *Tetrachordon . . .*, (March 4) 1644/45. In "Christian Liberty in Milton's Divorce Pamphlets," I have given an account of some of the differences in argument between the two editions of *The Doctrine and Discipline.* Other editions and variants are extant, but they differ from the two listed only in typographical matters which do not affect the thought. See *Works*, III, 513-15; Parker, *Milton's Contemporary Reputation*, 230-3.

[2]Life by Edward Phillips, *Early Lives*, ed. Darbishire, 63; and see the anonymous life (*ibid.*, 22).

[3]See below, note 15.

[4]*An Apology*, III, 306. See also III, 342: ". . . I think with them who both in prudence and elegance of spirit would choose a virgin of mean fortunes, honestly bred, before the wealthiest widow."

[5]See the anonymous life and Phillips, *Early Lives*, ed. Darbishire, 22, 65. For the situation at the time of Milton's marriage, and for evidence proving that it must have taken place in 1642, not in 1643 as was formerly supposed, see Wright, "Milton's First Marriage." For the business relationship between Milton and Powell, see Hamilton, *Original Papers Illustrative of the Life and Writings of John Milton*, 75-134, and French, *Milton in Chancery*, 71-107, 291-6.

[6]In her deposition of June 4, 1656, in the case *Ashworth v. Milton*, Mistress Anne Powell, widow of Richard Powell, testifies that she "has known Milton 14 years"; i.e., since about June, 1642, the time of his marriage to Mary. Professor C. J. Sisson, of University College, London, discovered the document in the Record Office (C 24. 796/97), and has very kindly permitted me to refer to it. It has not been printed. For other documents in the case, see French, *Milton in Chancery*.

[7]Phillips, *Early Lives*, ed. Darbishire, 64.

[8]See, for example, *The Doctrine and Discipline*, III, 394.

[9]See *ibid.*, 400, 475.

[10]See Powell, *English Domestic Relations*, chap. III. On the Puritan acceptance of this view, see Knappen, *Tudor Puritanism*, 458.

[11]*Early Lives*, ed. Darbishire, 65. The fantastic theory that Mary refused to consummate the union has been propounded by Pattison, Raleigh, and Saurat. Evidence in support of it can only be presented by wresting from their context passages in which Milton argues that it is easier to moderate bodily than spiritual desires.

[12]*Defensio Secunda*, VIII, 133.

[13]*Doctrine and Discipline*, III, 388, and title-page.

[14]*Ibid.*, 384; and see 383, 393, 395, 486, 495-6, and *Tetrachordon*, IV, 89.

[15]*Early Lives*, ed. Darbishire, 23, 65.

According to Hanford's arrangement of the entries in the *Commonplace Book* ("The Chronology of Milton's Private Studies"), Milton set down only a few references to divorce before 1643. Before 1639 he noted that Valentinian permitted by law a second marriage after the death of a first wife; but this has only an indirect bearing on marriage after divorce (XVIII, 150). On two other occasions before 1639, he made notes on the legitimacy of marriage of the clergy (XVIII, 148, 149); and between 1639 and 1643 he set down three other notes on this subject (XVIII, 148). This was a question of great interest to all Protestants, but Milton's evident desire to prove the Roman Catholic view wrong is probably to be connected with his assertion in the *Apology* that marriage must not be called a defilement (III, 306). Between 1639 and 1643 he noted that the public rites of marriage were introduced many centuries after the Apostles (XVIII, 155); that matrimonial cases were originally dealt with by civil magistrates (XVIII, 155); that innumerable questions about divorce are treated with uncertain solutions (XVIII, 154); and that divorce cases were transferred to the courts when the canons learned how to profit from them (XVIII, 154). He also made three notes condemning marriage with a person of a different religion (XVIII, 150-1). Other references and examples which were used in the divorce tracts occur among the notes assigned by Hanford to 1643 or after. These were presumably made while Milton was considering the composition of his pamphlets. The earlier notes do not seem to me to indicate the unusual and academic interest in divorce which is sometimes assumed in the unmarried Milton. They do indicate an interest in marriage which one may justifiably connect with the personal problem of chastity suggested in *Comus* and other early poems. But the real bearing of all these notes, as of so much of Milton's early and unorganized thinking, is upon unjust eccclesiastical restraint.

[16]In *The Judgement of Martin Bucer*, IV, 11, Milton says that when he wrote the first edition of *The Doctrine and Discipline* he knew only that Grotius in his annotations on Matthew had "whispered rather than disputed" about divorce. There are three references to Grotius in this edition. There is no evidence of dependence on others. Part of the material added in the second edition consists of references to the opinions of Protestant divines; and Milton hoped that his translation of the relevant parts of Bucer's *The Kingdom of Christ* would show that his opinions were less unusual than his attackers maintained. But he remained proud of "being something first" (*Tetrachordon*, IV, 207; and see 230).

[17]These words were used of the author of *The Doctrine and Discipline* by Herbert Palmer in a sermon preached to Parliament on August 13, 1644, *The Glasse of Gods Providence*, 57; and by William Prynne in *Twelve Considerable Serious Questions . . .*, (September 16) 1644, 7. An order against Milton and others who had published without licences was issued by Parliament on a petition from the Stationers' Company on August 26, 1644. For other incidental attacks on Milton, and for the anonymous and worthless *Answer* to him, see Parker, *Milton's Contemporary Reputation*, 74-9. For Milton's replies, see *Colasterion*, IV, 233, and *Tetrachordon*, IV, 65, 69.

[18]Sonnets XI and XII. Of Prynne Milton said: "I stood awhile and wondered what we might do to a man's heart, or what anatomy use, to find in it sincerity; for all our wonted marks every day fail us, and where we thought it was, we see it not, for alter and change residence it cannot sure" (*Colasterion*, IV, 234).

This observation on the earless Puritan protagonist indicates the quality of Milton's growing disillusionment with Presbyterian reform. Another and different source of irritation was the use made of his opinions by "the common rout," such as that Mistress Attaway who, according to Edwards (*Gangraena*, part II, 113-15; Masson, III, 189-91), justified her desertion of her husband, who was "unsanctified" and did not "walk in the way of Sion nor speak the language of Canaan," by a reference to Milton's divorce argument. Such notoriety made Milton wish that he had written *The Doctrine and Discipline* in Latin (*Defensio Secunda*, VIII, 115). When he heard in 1655 that Leo Van Aizema meant to have the tract turned into Dutch, he wrote: "I would rather you had given it to be turned into Latin. For my experience in those books of mine has now been that the vulgar still receive according to their wont opinions not already common" (XII, 73). If the reception of his divorce tracts turned him away from the Presbyterians, it also confirmed that contempt for the vulgar which was to prevent him from identifying himself completely with the extreme radicals.

[19]See Daniel Featley, *The Dippers dipt*, (February) 1645, [xiii-xiv], and Ephraim Pagett, *Heresiography*, 1645, 142; Parker, *Milton's Contemporary Reputation*, 74-5. Baillie observed, "I do not know certainly whether this man professeth Independency (albeit all the heretics here whereof ever I heard avow themselves Independents)" (*A Dissuasive from the Errours of the Time*, 1645, 116).

[20]*Doctrine and Discipline*, III, 381.

[21]*Ibid.*, 368-9. The attack on custom is repeated in *The Judgement of Martin Bucer*, IV, 18, and in *Tetrachordon*, IV, 63.

[22]*Doctrine and Discipline*, III, 386.

[23]*Judgement of Martin Bucer*, IV, 11.

[24]*Deuteronomy* 24. 1: "When a man hath taken a wife, and married her, and it come to pass that she find no favour in his eyes, because he hath found some uncleanness in her; then let him write her a bill of divorcement, and give it in her hand, and send her out of his house." *Matthew* 5. 31, 32: "It hath been said, Whosoever shall put away his wife, let him give her a writing of divorcement. But I say unto you, that whosoever shall put away his wife, saving for the cause of fornication, causeth her to commit adultery; and whosoever shall marry her that is divorced committeth adultery."

[25]*Doctrine and Discipline*, III, 368.

[26]*Ibid.*, 494, 429.

[27]See Prolusions III and IV, and *Reason of Church Government*, III, 193.

[28]*Doctrine and Discipline*, III, 490-91.

[29]In a passage added in the second edition of *The Doctrine and Discipline*, III, 429, Milton asserted: "I want neither pall nor mitre, I stay neither for ordination or induction...." The title-page of both editions bore the text: "Matt. xiii, 52: Every scribe instructed in the kingdom of heaven is like the master of a house, which bringeth out of his treasury things new and old."

[30]*Doctrine and Discipline*, III, 375.

[31]*Ibid.*, 373-4.

[32]*Ibid.*, 467, 388.

[33]*Ibid.*, 444.

[34]*Ibid.*, 482-3.

[35]*A Discourse*, 24. See above, chap. IV, note 26.

[36]*Doctrine and Discipline*, III, 397.

[37]*Ibid.*, 494, 461.

[38]*Ibid.*, 495.

[39]*Ibid.*, 497-8.

[40]*Ibid.*, 500. The church is to instruct and admonish those who desire divorce; the state is to see to "the just and equal conditions" (*Doctrine and Discipline*, III, 504, 508). There is no need to consider here the vexed question of Milton's attitude towards the rights of women. See Gilbert, "Milton on the Position of Women."

[41]*Areopagitica*, IV, 350. In the anti-episcopal pamphlets Milton had asserted for himself, and against the bishops, "the honest liberty of free speech" (*Reason of Church Government*, III, 232), and, as we have seen, quoted Bacon against the prelatical restraint of the press. Whatever may have been his opinions on free printing, he did not react immediately and violently against the Parliamentary Ordinance for Printing of June 14, 1643, which required that books should be "first approved and licensed under the hands of such person or persons as both or either of the said Houses shall appoint" (Rushworth, V, 335-6; Masson, III, 269-71). The immediate and personal motive of the *Areopagitica* (November 24, 1644) is clearly indicated in the passage in *The Judgement of Martin Bucer* (registered July 15, 1644) in which, referring to the published opinions on divorce of Bucer and Erasmus, Milton says that, "if these their books . . . shall be published and republished, though against the received opinion . . . , and mine, containing but the same thing, shall in a time of reformation, a time of free speaking, free writing, *not find a permission to the press*, I refer me to wisest men whether truth be suffered to be truth, or liberty to be liberty now among us . . ." (IV, 61). The phrase which I have italicized seems to me to suggest that Milton had sought and been refused permission to print *The Doctrine and Discipline*, not that, as has sometimes been said, he purposely ignored the Ordinance because of the strength of his already-formed convictions. Neither edition of *The Doctrine and Discipline* (August 1, 1643; February 2,1644) was licensed or registered with the Stationers' Company by the printer, "M.S." The "Address" of the second edition was, however, signed. In his sermon to Parliament on August 13, 1644, Palmer remarked that "a wicked book is abroad and uncensured, though deserving to be burnt, whose author has been so impudent as to set his name to it, and dedicate it to yourselves" (see Parker, *Milton's Contemporary Reputation*, 74); and on August 24 the Stationers' Company petitioned the Parliament for the strict enforcement of the Ordinance, naming Milton among other offenders (Haller, *Tracts on Liberty*, I, 75). Two days later a Committee on Printing was instructed to find out and proceed against the author of the divorce tract; but nothing seems to have been done (Masson, III, 164-5). Meanwhile *To Samuel Hartlib* (June 4, 1644) had been duly licensed by James Cranford and registered by Thomas Underhill; and *The Judgement of Martin Bucer* (July 15, 1644) had likewise been licensed by John Downham and registered by Matthew Simmons, the "M.S." of the first tract. In December, 1644, Milton was again mentioned as an offender against the Ordinance (Masson, III, 293). *Areopagitica*, *Tetrachordon*, and *Colasterion* were all unlicensed and unregistered. That there was a considerable stir about the first unlicensed divorce tract is indicated by the address to the "Impartial Reader" which the licenser, John Bachiler, wrote in licensing John Goodwin's *Twelve Considerable Serious Cautions* in 1646: "*The Bloudy Tenent* and the treatise about divorce . . .

I have been so far from licensing that I have not so much as seen or heard of them till after they have been commonly sold abroad . . ." (Haller, *Tracts on Liberty*, I, 137). It was this stir, of which Bachiler's embarrassment at stories being told of his laxity was a by-product, which created in Milton's mind the conditions necessary for the *Areopagitica*. He had tried to have his first tract licensed and failed; he had obeyed the Ordinance in his next two publications; but the clamour from the Presbyterians and the Stationers proceeded; and he was thus angered into writing the *Areopagitica* which contains a violent attack on the Presbyterians and the fantastic charge that the Stationers wished to get power into their hands so that "malignant" or royalist and prelatical books might "the easier scape abroad" (IV, 354). For such books the *Areopagitica* asks no quarter.

[42]*Areopagitica*, IV, 338; *Judgement of Martin Bucer*, IV, 61.

[43]*Areopagitica*, IV, 318.

[44]*Ibid.*, 337.

[45]*Ibid.*, 337-8.

[46]The report was made by Edward Winslow; see Neal, *History of the Puritans*, II, 110-11; Burgess, *John Robinson*, 239. Jordan, *The Development of Religious Toleration*, II, 242, refuses to admit it as evidence of Robinson's opinions, and Allen, *English Political Thought, 1603-1644*, 151, thinks it "at least partially spurious." Yet the substance is perfectly characteristic of Robinson's published opinions.

[47]*An Apologeticall Narration*, (January) 1643, 24, 26.

[48]*Ibid.*, 10.

[49]*Queries of Highest Consideration*, (February) 1644; reprinted in *Publications of the Narragansett Club*, series I, volume II, 275, 253. See also *M.S. to A.S.* [Adam Steuart] *With A Plea for Libertie of Conscience in a Church Way*, (May 3, July 11) 1644, and *A Reply of two of the Brethren to A.S. wherein you have Observations on his Considerations . . . Upon the Apologetical Narration*, 1644. Both tracts have been attributed to John Goodwin, but they may have been written by others who shared his views (Haller, *Tracts on Liberty*, I, 52). One wonders if the "M.S." is the Matthew Simmons who printed Milton's unlicensed divorce tracts.

[50]*Liberty of Conscience*, (March) 1643/44, 49.

[51]*A Paraenetick . . . for (not loose but) Christian libertie*, (November) 1644, 12.

[52]*The Unlawfulnes and Danger of Limited Prelacie*, 1641, 2.

[53]*Ibid.*, 18; *Antapologia: Or A Full Answer to the Apologeticall Narration*, (July) 1644, 285.

[54]*Antapologia*, 85. Substantially the same view was expressed in Adam Steuart's *Some Observations . . . Upon the Apologeticall Narration*, (February 29) 1644; in Samuel Rutherford's *Due Right of Presbyteries*, 1644; and in William Prynne's *Twelve Considerable Serious Questions*, (September 16) 1644, and *Independency Examined*, (September 26) 1644. In his sonnet of 1646 *On the New Forcers of Conscience*, Milton attacked "mere A.S. and Rotherford," with "shallow Edwards and Scotch what d'ye call" (probably meaning Robert Baillie), and, in the first version, "marginal P[rynne]" (I, 71, 452).

[55]Burgess, *John Robinson*, 240.

[56]*An Apologeticall Narration*, 26.

[57]*Doctrine and Discipline*, III, 376.

[58]*Areopagitica*, IV, 348-9, 347.

[59]Title of Prynne's *A Fresh Discovery*, 1645.

[60]*Areopagitica*, IV, 340.

[61]*Ibid.*, 339, 350.

[62]*Ibid.*, 340. Milton's confidence in the English people expresses itself in such well-known passages as *Doctrine and Discipline*, III, 376-7, and *Areopagitica*, IV, 339-44. In 1645 he seems still to have been contemplating a poem in celebration of the freeing of England, for he tells the Parliament, "I have yet a store of gratitude laid up which cannot be exhausted; and such thanks perhaps they may live to be as shall more than whisper to the next ages" (*Tetrachordon*, IV, 64).

[63]*Areopagitica*, IV, 342-3.

## CHAPTER VI

[1]*Areopagitica*, IV, 341-2.

[2]*Ibid.*, 345.

[3]See Haller, *Tracts on Liberty*, I, chaps. VIII and IX.

[4]*Doctrine and Discipline*, III, 378.

[5]*Areopagitica*, IV, 343.

[6]*Ibid.*, 295-6, 310-11.

[7]*Of Reformation*, III, 5.

[8]*Areopagitica*, IV, 323, 351-2.

[9]See Bunyan, *Grace Abounding to the Chief of Sinners*; and on his conversion, Tindall, *John Bunyan, Mechanick Preacher*, chap. II; and Barker, "The Pattern of Milton's *Nativity Ode*," 167-9.

[10]*Areopagitica*, IV, 324.

[11]*Ibid.*, 298.

[12]*Ibid.*, 296; Gill, *The Sacred Philosophie of the Holy Scripture*, 2.

[13]See Marriott, *The Life of . . . Falkland*, chap. IV.

[14]Hales, "A Tract on . . . the Lord's Supper," *Works*, 1765, I, 69.

[15]*The Religion of Protestants a Safe Way to Salvation*, 1638, *Works*, 1838, I, 14.

[16]*The Lord of Falklands Reply* [to Thomas White's *Answer*]; written 1636; first published 1646; reprinted with *A Discourse of Infallibility*, 1660, 193.

[17]Falkland said, "I am confident that those who would know it [Scripture] by the Spirit run themselves into the same circle between Scripture and Spirit, out of which some of your side have but unsuccessfully laboured to get out between Scripture and Church" (*ibid.*, 54).

[18]*Ibid.*, 118-19.

[19]*The Religion of Protestants*, *Works*, I, 167; see also *Works*, III, 389, and II, 79.

[20]*The Lord of Falklands Reply*, 67.

[21]*Ibid.*, 138.

[22]Hales, "A Tract Concerning Schism," *Works*, I, 126.

[23]"Of Dealing with Erring Christians," *Works*, II, 94.

[24]*The Lord of Falklands Reply*, 262; see also 145.

[25]It was probably at St. Paul's School under Alexander Gill that Milton first felt the influence of Christian rationalism; see Barker, "Milton's Schoolmasters," 533-5.

[26]*Areopagitica*, IV, 319.

[27]*Ibid.*, 341.

[28]*Ibid.*, 345.

[29]*Doctrine and Discipline*, III, 495.

[30]*Areopagitica*, IV, 309, 318.

[31]*Tetrachordon*, IV, 127.

[32]*Areopagitica*, IV, 333.

[33]*Ibid.*, 310.

[34]*Gangraena*, Part I, 19.

[35]*Ibid.*, Part II, 2.

[36]De Pauley, *The Candle of the Lord*, 233 ff.

[37]See Lyon, *The Theory of Religious Liberty in England, 1603-1639*, 89 ff.

[38]*New Essays, or Observations Divine and Morall*, 1625, 1628, 1642; *Works*, I, 53. The significant influence of Bacon is apparent not only in the title but in the method.

[39]*Ibid.*, 67.

[40]*A Justification of Separation*, 1610, 48.

[41]*New Essays*, *Works*, I, 53-4.

[42]Henry Robinson, *Liberty of Conscience*, (March) 1644, sig. a; cf. William Walwyn, *The Compassionate Samaritane*, 1644.

[43]*The Ancient Bounds, or Liberty of Conscience*, (June) 1645, 26.

[44]No intimate connection between Milton and Goodwin has ever been established. Goodwin was, however, almost as notorious as Roger Williams as an opponent of Presbyterian intolerance, and Milton must have known of his writings. Many of them were printed by Matthew Simmons, the printer of Milton's *Doctrine and Discipline*, *The Judgement of Martin Bucer*, *The Tenure*, and *Eikonoklastes*. In his *Obstructours of Justice*, 1649, Goodwin included a number of passages from and references to Milton's *Tenure* (Parker, *Milton's Contemporary Reputation*, 80-2). On August 13, 1660, a royal proclamation called in Milton's *Defensio* and *Eikonoklastes* and Goodwin's *Obstructours*, and directed that the authors should be apprehended (Parker, *Milton's Contemporary Reputation*, 103). For accounts of Goodwin's career and thought see Haller, *Tracts on Liberty*, I, 30 ff.; *The Rise of Puritanism*, 199 ff.; and Jordan, *The Development of Religious Toleration*, III, 379-412.

[45]Goodwin's opinions on church government led to his ejection from St. Stephen's, Coleman Street, in May, 1645, whereupon he began to hold meetings in a house. For his views, see *Theomachia*, 21-31, and *An Apologeticall Account, of some Brethren of the Church, whereof Mr. John Goodwin is Pastor*, (February) 1647. Goodwin's Arminian tendencies became apparent very early. Before the war his disputes with the orthodox had caused Laud to command him and his opponents to avoid controverted points. He set forth his beliefs in *The Saints Interest*, 1640, *Impedit Ira*, 1641, and *Imputatio Fidei*, 1642.

[46]*Imputatio Fidei*, 1642, sig. b4$^{v}$.

[47]*Anti-Cavalierisme*, (October) 1642, 33.

[48]See *Theomachia; or The Grand Imprudence of men running the hazard of Fighting Against God*, (a sermon preached September 2) 1644, 21-31. For an account of the dispute, in which *Theomachia* and *The Bloudy Tenent* by Roger Williams were the most important radical publications, see Haller, *Tracts on Liberty*, I, chaps. VII-X.

[49]*Theomachia*, 30.

[50]*Ibid.*, 34; and see 51.

[51]*A Moderate Answer*, (January) 1645, 3; *Theomachia*, 11.

[52]*Theomachia*, 19; *Hagiomastix*, (February) 1646, 108.

[53]See Haller, *Tracts on Liberty*, I, 134, and Parker, *Milton's Contemporary Reputation*, 25.

[54]Williams had left Providence in June, 1643, to obtain a charter for the new colony from the Colonial Council, and was back in New England in September, 1644. He had published in London *The Bloudy Tenent, of Persecution, for cause of Conscience discussed*, in July, 1644. He was again in England in 1652 on a similar mission. There is no evidence for any connection between Williams and Milton during the first visit, but it is probable that they met. Ernst, *Roger Williams*, 233, has set forth the grounds of this probability. Both had been at Cambridge, though at different colleges; both had dealings with Gregory Dexter, the "G.D." who partly printed Milton's *Of Prelatical Episcopacy*; Milton was tutor to Cyriack Skinner, nephew of Mrs. Sadlier, the daughter of Coke (who had been Williams's patron) and a friend of Williams's, Skinner himself being Coke's grandson; and Milton was, or was shortly to be, acquainted with Vane, whose guest in Charing Cross Road Williams was. Milton nowhere refers to Williams; but in a letter to John Winthrop, written after his return to New England, in the summer of 1654, Williams said that "the Secretary of the Council (Mr. Milton) for my Dutch I read him, read me many more languages" (Straus, *Roger Williams*, 180). Milton became totally blind in 1652. But Williams was not given to prevarication, and there is no reason to doubt his positive statement. In a letter to Mrs. Sadlier written while he was in England, Williams recommended *Eikonoklastes* to her attention. The good lady replied with a reference to Milton's scandalous opinions on divorce. See Straus, *Roger Williams*, 183; and see also Ernst, *Roger Williams and the English Revolution.*

[55]Woodhouse, *Puritanism and Liberty*, [57-60]. Woodhouse points out that the development of radical political ideas among the Puritans of the left did not necessarily involve the undermining of Puritan dogma. It was possible, as in the case of Williams and Lilburne, to remain strictly orthodox in theology and at the same time to develop a radical theory of political organization and of the relationship between church and state because of the Puritan tendency "to distinguish sharply between religion and the rest of life, to segregate the spiritual from the secular, and to do this, in the first instance, for the sake of religion, though with momentous consequences for the life of the world." This tendency obviously runs counter to the Puritan desire "to carry the implications of dogma into secular life"; and it appears only in some of the Puritans, especially in the Independents and the parties of the left, excluding the Millenarians. Its source is, however, to be found in the basic Puritan distinction between the order of grace and the order of nature (already negatively apparent in the limitations imposed on Christian liberty by Luther and Calvin). The positive application of the distinction, or of this "principle of segregation," opens the way for a full development of secular liberty and equality, unrestricted by theological reservations.

[56]*The Casting Down of the last and strongest hold of Satan, or, A Treatise against Toleration*, (June) 1647, 5; see also *Antapologia*, 303.

[57]Baillie, *Letters*, II, 147; Edwards, *Antapologia*, 280-1.

[58]See Woodhouse, "Puritanism and Democracy," 10-11, for a succinct account of the secularizing of the state in Williams and other radicals as a result of their application of the principle of segregation.

[59]*The Bloudy Tenent,* (July) 1644; reprinted in *Hanserd Knollys Society Publications,* 1848, 175. Williams believed of course that "without search and trial no man attains this faith and right persuasion" (*ibid.*, 9).

[60]*Ibid.*, 82.

[61]*Ibid.*, 109; see also 97.

[62]*Ibid.*, 49, 100, 130, 200, 183-4.

[63]*Ibid.*, 218.

[64]*Ibid.*, 46-7.

[65]*Ibid.*, 66, 88, 145, 214-15, 355.

[66]*Ibid.*, 97; "the civil state, the world, being in a natural state, dead in sin," 214-15.

[67]*Ibid.*, 65-6.

[68]*Ibid.*, 124. For the Presbyterian view, see Edwards' *Antapologia*, 68 ff., and the Congregational *Model* quoted by Williams, 191 ff.

[69]*Antapologia*, 280-1; and the *Model* quoted by Williams, 268-9. See also Jordan, *The Development of Religious Toleration*, III, 282, 299-302, 318-21.

[70]*The Bloudy Tenent*, 62; and see 152, 179, 205, 245, 284.

[71]*Ibid.*, 130, 214-15, 305, 315, 340, 358.

[72]*Ibid.*, 64, 174.

[73]The *Model* quoted by Williams, 219.

[74]*Ibid.*, 221-2; and see 39, where Williams refuses to accept the common distinction between fundamentals and circumstantials.

[75]*Ibid.*, 69.

[76]See Woodhouse, *Puritanism and Liberty,* [16] ff., on the character of the centre or Independent party.

[77]In a letter written in 1670 Williams described Rhode Island as an "experiment whether civil government could consist with such liberty of conscience" (Ernst, *The Political Thought of Roger Williams*, 100).

[78]*Liberty of Conscience*, sig. A1$^{v}$. Cromwell, *Letters and Speeches*, I, 148: "The state, in choosing men to serve it, takes no notice of their opinions; if they be willing faithfully to serve it, that satisfies."

[79]*Liberty of Conscience,* sig. A3$^{v}$, and 34.

[80]*A Moderate Answer*, 45.

[81]*Theomachia*, 49 ff.

[82]*Ibid.*, 23; and see *A Moderate Answer*, 40.

[83]*The Ancient Bounds*, 2.

[84]*Ibid.*, 4.

[85]*Ibid.*, 5. The writer nevertheless makes the common distinction between the ecclesiastical and civil swords; 20.

[86]*An Apologeticall Narration*, 28-9.

[87]*Ibid.*, 8-9. Similarly the author of *A Paraenetick or humble address . . . for* (*not loose but*) *Christian libertie* emphasized the agreement in fundamentals, and said that what was desired was "liberty, not of another religion, but of this way of walking in your religion" (4-5). Even Brooke had been content to urge that it was sinful to make trouble about "those lower parts of discipline while we agree in doctrine" (*A Discourse*, 123).

[88] *Areopagitica*, IV, 320.

[89] *Ibid.*, 349.

[90] *Ibid.*, 349. Though the evidence is again chiefly negative, Milton's theological opinions appear to have been still orthodox in 1643 and 1644. The unorthodox application became apparent, as the following chapter will show, in *Tetrachordon*, though he insisted throughout the divorce tracts that his premises were orthodox (IV, 88). On the shifting of his opinions as a consequence of his development of the divorce argument, see Barker, "Christian Liberty in Milton's Divorce Pamphlets," 158-9. In *The Doctrine and Discipline* he deplores "Anabaptism, Familism, Antinomianism, and other fanatic dreams" (III, 426, 510); he repeats the orthodox argument against the Arminians, though he sees the force of their objection to predestination (III, 440 ff.); in *Areopagitica* he mentions the "acute and distinct Arminius" as "perverted" in trying to refute a book (IV, 313); and in *Tetrachordon* he remarks that the Socinians make Adam an idiot (IV, 95).

[91] *Areopagitica*, IV, 342, 350.

[92] *Ibid.*, 353-4. Milton did not object to the very sensible provision (already included in the earlier Ordinance of 1642) requiring the registration of "the printer's and the author's name, or at least the printer's"; but it is a curious conclusion to his magnificent argument to suggest that "those which otherwise come forth, if they be found mischievous or libellous, the fire and the executioner will be the timeliest and the most effectual remedy that man's prevention can use" (353). This suggestion must be taken into account in estimating Milton's position in the *Areopagitica*; and it can be made to consist with the arguments of the pamphlet only if one recognizes the distinction between fundamentals and circumstantials which is still present in his mind. Jordan (*The Development of Religious Toleration*, IV, 211-13) seems to me to over-emphasize Milton's "deep-seated scepticism concerning the possibility of knowing truth infallibly, or of determining with accuracy between truth and error." Scepticism of this kind was altogether foreign to Milton's personality, for it would have destroyed the conviction of truth which he required for action. Jordan notes the *Areopagitica's* exceptions of certain opinions from toleration; but he does not explain how these are compatible with the scepticism he sees. Since he does not take account of the passages concerning things indifferent which I am quoting, he assumes, with most of Milton's critics, that all the arguments are to be applied to fundamental and revealed truths. In these Milton has not lost his belief, nor will he ever; what he has come to see is the difficulty of determining with accuracy between truth and error in things indifferent or in matters concerning which there is no divine prescript.

[93] *Ibid.*, 310.

[94] *Ibid.*, 311.

[95] *Ibid.*, 310-11.

[96] *Ibid.*, 311.

[97] *Ibid.*, 341-2.

[98] *Ibid.*, 311.

[99] *Ibid.*, 308.

[100] *Ibid.*, 348.

[101] *The Ancient Bounds*, "A Light to the Work."

## CHAPTER VII

[1]In "Christian Liberty in Milton's Divorce Pamphlets," I have analysed the steps in this development by examining in detail the additions and changes in the second edition of *The Doctrine and Discipline* and the differences between its argument and *Tetrachordon*'s. The profound importance of the doctrine of Christian liberty in Milton and in radical Puritanism was strangely neglected until it was first pointed out by Woodhouse in "Milton, Puritanism and Liberty," 483-501. For a fuller account, see his *Puritanism and Liberty* [65-8], *et passim.*

[2]*An Apologeticall Narration*, 24.

[3]*A Paraenetick or humble address to the Parliament and Assembly for (not loose but) Christian libertie*, (November 30) 1644.

[4]*The Ancient Bounds*, 78.

[5]*Liberty of Conscience*, 40.

[6]*The Compassionate Samaritane*, (January 5) 1644/45, 56.

[7]See Calvin, *The Institution of Christian Religion*, book III, chap. XIX; Luther, *Concerning Christian Liberty*, and *Commentarie . . . upon the Epistle of S. Paul to the Galathians*, 1644.

[8]See Miller, *Orthodoxy in Massachusetts*, chap. VI.

[9]*Tetrachordon*, IV, 88.

[10]See Woodhouse, *Puritanism and Liberty*, [61] ff.

[11]The orthodox interpretation is to be found in Perkins, *A Discourse of Conscience, Works*, 1616, I, 538-9; Perkins, *A Godly and Learned Exposition upon the Whole Epistle of Jude, Works*, III, 501-2; Ames, *The Marrow of Sacred Divinity*, chap. 39; Usher, *A Body of Divinitie*, 1645, 134 ff.; and *The humble Advice of the Assembly*, 1646, chap. 20.

[12]*The Institution of Christian Religion*, translated by Thomas Norton, 1599, 224-5.

[13]*Ibid.*, 226; Luther, *Commentary upon Galatians*, in Woodhouse, *Puritanism and Liberty*, 225. The Presbyterians constantly produced this argument against the sects. For example, in a sermon full of zeal for reformation which he preached before Parliament on April 4, 1641/42, Thomas Wilson said: "In the external form and circumstances many superstitions be to be cast out, injunctions not of God, not good, after the doctrines and commandments of men, *Col.* 2.22, to which a Christian redeemed by Christ hath no reason to be subject; if ye be dead with Christ from the rudiments of the world, why as though living in the world are ye subject to ordinances, *Col.* 2.20?" Yet he was also able to assert that, as for the permission of differing opinions, "Christ will have no such toleration . . ." (*Davids Zeale for Zion*, 1641, 6-8). In the same way, Samuel Rutherford collected all the scriptural passages bearing on Christian liberty in chapter 19 of *A Free Disputation Against pretended Liberty of Conscience*, 1649, in order to show that no heretic has "a patent under the seal of the blood of the eternal covenant that he is freed from the magistrate's sword, though he destroy millions of souls" (233).

[14]*The Institution of Christian Religion*, 227.

[15]For a succinct account of this process see Woodhouse, *Puritanism and Liberty*, [65-9].

[16]*Tetrachordon*, IV, 88. In addition to the references to orthodox divines—Calvin, Beza, Paraeus, Fagius, Rivetus, Perkins, and others—in the second

edition of *The Doctrine and Discipline,* Milton appended a summary of their opinions to *Tetrachordon* to show his own orthodoxy.

[17]See Calvin, *The Institution of Christian Religion,* book II, chap. VII, sec. 14, and book IV, chap. XX, sec. 14; Ames, *The Marrow of Sacred Divinity,* 176, 193-4, 294, and *Conscience,* 108; and cf. Article VII of 1562: "Although the Law given from God by Moses, as touching Ceremonies and Rites, do not bind Christian men, nor the Civil precepts thereof ought of necessity to be received in any commonwealth; yet notwithstanding, no Christian man whatsoever is free from the obedience of the Commandments called Moral." The chief source of the unorthodox interpretation, on the other hand, was the belief, carefully limited in Luther's *Commentary upon Galatians,* that "the Moral Law or the Law of the Ten Commandments hath no power to accuse and terrify the conscience in which Jesus Christ reigneth by his grace, for he hath abolished the power thereof" (Woodhouse, *Puritanism and Liberty,* 224).

[18]*De Doctrina Christiana,* XVI, 125; Williams, *The Bloudy Tenent,* 307-13.

[19]*Doctrine and Discipline,* III, 430 ff. The argument is developed from *Matthew* 5.18, and Luke 16.17.

[20]*Ibid.,* 454.

[21]*Ibid.,* 443; see also *Tetrachordon,* IV, 157 ff. Even Williams accepted the view that the Jewish divorce was a permission to prevent evil (*The Bloudy Tenent,* 138).

[22]*Doctrine and Discipline,* III, 434.

[23]*Ibid.,* 434.

[24]*Ibid.,* 452.

[25]*Ibid.,* 444.

[26]*Ibid.,* 440.

[27]*Conscience,* 108.

[28]*Doctrine and Discipline,* III, 471, 473; *Tetrachordon,* IV, 160.

[29]*Doctrine and Discipline,* III, 468, 484.

[30]*Ibid.,* 430.

[31]*Ibid.,* 414.

[32]*Ibid.,* 410; *Tetrachordon,* IV, 153.

[33]*Doctrine and Discipline,* III, 452.

[34]*Ibid.,* 446.

[35]*Ibid.,* 482.

[36]*Tetrachordon,* IV, 140.

[37]*Doctrine and Discipline,* III, 428.

[38]*Ibid.,* 451; see also *Tetrachordon,* VI, 162.

[39]*Tetrachordon,* IV, 164.

[40]*Ibid.,* 136.

[41]*Ibid.,* 74-5.

[42]*Ibid.,* 135.

[43]*Ibid.,* 91.

[44]*A Moderate Answer,* (January) 1644/45, 46.

[45]*The necessity of Toleration,* (September) 1647, 10.

[46]*The Ancient Bounds,* 18.

[47]See Gierke, *Natural Law and the Theory of Society, 1500-1800,* trans. Barker; Allen, *English Political Thought, 1603-1644,* 456 ff.; Gooch, *English*

*Democratic Ideas in the Seventeenth Century*; Sabine, *History of Political Theory*, chap. XXI.

[48]*Tetrachordon*, IV, 318. Milton is referring to Palmer's attack on him in *The Glasse of Gods Providence.* He says he believes that *Scripture and Reason Pleaded for Defensive Armes; or, The whole Controversie about Subjects taking up Armes . . . , published by Divers Reverend and Learned Divines*, (ordered printed by the Commons, April) 1643, is chiefly Palmer's work. There is no evidence that this was so. Milton returned to *Scripture and Reason* in *The Tenure* in order to show that the logic of its arguments justified the execution of the King.

[49]If it were not that Milton specifically mentions *Scripture and Reason*, the ideas here discussed might better have been illustrated from such other parliamentary writings as Henry Parker's *Observations upon some of his Majesties Late Answers and Expresses*, (July) 1642, or Samuel Rutherford's *Lex Rex: The Law and the Prince. A Dispute for the just Prerogative of King and People*, (October 7) 1644. On Parker, Rutherford, and the parliamentary position, see Allen, *English Political Thought, 1603-1644*, 424 ff.; Haller, *Tracts on Liberty*, I, 24-8, and *The Rise of Puritanism*, 365 ff.; Woodhouse, *Puritanism and Liberty*, [61] ff. and 199-212.

[50]*Scripture and Reason*, 30, 42 ff.; cf. Parker, *Observations*, 3, and Rutherford, *Lex Rex*, 119.

[51]*Scripture and Reason*, 31. The marriage covenant was a favourite analogy among Puritan writers both for covenants with God and for political agreements. Baillie's use of it in connection with reformation has already been quoted. It is similarly used by Cornelius Burgess in *The First Sermon Preached to the Honorable House of Commons* on November 17, 1640, and by Stephen Marshall in the second sermon of the same day. Henry Parker, arguing that the contract between king and people does not involve the absolute subjection of the latter, observed: "In matrimony there is something of divine (the papist makes it sacramental beyond all royal inauguration); but is that any ground to infer that there is no human consent or concurrence in it? does the divine institution of marriage take away freedom of choice before or conclude either party under an absolute decree of subjection after the solemnization?" (*Jus Populi*, 4) John Goodwin, writing against Prynne, denied that the Independents could be regarded as guilty of separation when they had never agreed to join with the Presbyterians, and enforced his argument by an analogy curiously like one of Milton's arguments: "'Those whom God hath joined together, let no man separate, or put asunder.' That woman cannot be divorced nor forsake her husband, which never was married. No more can Independents be said . . . to separate from that government unto which they never were yet united" (*Innocency and Truth Triumphing*, 24). Samuel Rutherford, arguing that forms of government are variable and indifferent, though government is a moral act not "left indifferent to us," illustrated his point by saying that all forms of government, monarchical, aristocratic, democratic, "be from God, even as single life and marriage are both lawful ordinances of God, and the constitution and temper of the body is a calling to either of the two" (*Lex Rex*, in Woodhouse, *Puritanism and Liberty*, 202).

[52]*Doctrine and Discipline*, III, 457.

[53]*Scripture and Reason*, 46.

[54]*Ibid.*, 39-40; and see 60.

[55]*Anti-Cavalierisme, or, Truth Pleading As well the Necessity as the Lawfulness of this present War,* (October) 1643, 17. The other ideas illustrated from *Scripture and Reason* are also to be found in this pamphlet, which the divines mentioned with approval (*Scripture and Reason,* 50).

[56]*Lex Rex,* 57, 54; see also Parker, *Observations,* 29.

[57]*Doctrine and Discipline,* III, 390. The argument is repeated in *Tetrachordon,* IV, 118-19.

[58]*Doctrine and Discipline,* III, 374.

[59]*Defensio Secunda,* VIII, 135.

[60]*Doctrine and Discipline,* III, 429; *Of Reformation,* III, 53.

[61]*Doctrine and Discipline,* III, 423-4.

[62]*Tetrachordon,* IV, 75.

[63]*Ibid.,* 96.

[64]*Ibid.,* 117-18.

[65]Prolusion VII, XII, 255.

[66]*Scripture and Reason,* 28.

[67]*Tetrachordon,* IV, 75. Both examples are used for the same purpose in *Scripture and Reason,* 36.

[68]*Tetrachordon,* IV, 75.

[69]*Ibid.,* 115.

[70]*Ibid.,* 117.

[71]*Doctrine and Discipline,* III, 496.

[72]*Ibid.,* 419.

[73]*Ibid.,* 419.

[74]*Ibid.,* 427.

[75]*Tetrachordon,* IV, 134.

[76]*Doctrine and Discipline,* III, 445. Cf. Brooke on church government, expressing an opinion which has no place in Milton's anti-episcopal tracts: "God's law never appoints any standing law against the rules of nature" (*A Discourse,* 85).

[77]*Doctrine and Discipline,* III, 482.

[78]*Ibid.,* 467.

[79]*Ibid.,* 497, 505. Selden's review of the history of divorce is in *De Jure Naturali & Gentium, Juxta Disciplinam Ebraeorum,* 1640, lib. v, cap. vii.

[80]*Areopagitica,* IV, 298.

[81]*Doctrine and Discipline,* III, 451. This passage was added in the second edition of the tract, and the refutation of the argument illustrated from Paraeus was much revised; see III, 444-53, and notes, 554. As I have pointed out ("Christian Liberty in Milton's Divorce Pamphlets," 157-9), this revision, like the passage (also added in 1644) in which Milton considered the arguments of those who, "perhaps out of a vigilant and wary conscience, except against predestination" (III, 443), indicates how the divorce problem forced him to examine anew the fundamental points of Christian doctrine. In the first edition Milton attempted to dispose of the argument that Christians cannot divorce because they are expected to be more perfect than those living under the Law by arguing that, under the Gospel, "the nature of man is as weak, and yet as hard: and that weakness and hardness as unfit and as unteachable to be harshly dealt with as ever"; and also by emphasizing the charitable grace of the Gospel in contrast to the requirement of obedience by the Law. The latter argument

leads to the assertion of a radical Christian liberty; the former is essentially Puritan, though here used, through the accident of the Mosaic divorce law, in favour of greater liberty than the orthodox Puritan would allow. Its Puritan character is emphasized when Milton later says, "We find also by experience that the Spirit of God in the Gospel hath been always more effectual in the illumination of our minds to the gift of faith than in the moving of our wills to any excellence of virtue, either above the Jews or the heathen" (III, 554). I do not think that Milton ever again expressed this opinion; it contradicted his deepest convictions. But it is perfectly consistent with the demand of the anti-prelatical pamphlets for a divinely authorized discipline; and it is the belief which justified, in the eyes of the Presbyterians, the stern restraining hand of authority. The significance of the divorce problem in Milton's development is indicated by the fact that the entire passage was rewritten for the second edition and the quoted sentence dropped, its place being taken by a distinction between sin and natural affection or inclination: "We know it the work of the Spirit to mortify our corrupt desires and evil concupiscence; but not to root up our natural affections and disaffection . . ." (III, 451-2). This distinction is not made altogether clear in the divorce tracts; it becomes increasingly so as Milton's thought develops, until in *De Doctrina Christiana* the opinion here ascribed to Paraeus is firmly asserted and the implications of the 1643 statement denied (see below, chap. XVI, note 89). But the reason for the deletion of the statement in 1644 is obvious. Milton was not writing in defence of sin; and the antinomian implications of the original argument would have justified the attacks of Palmer and other Presbyterians. Moreover, the revision is a result of Milton's reaction against the rigorous Presbyterian position and against his own argument in the anti-episcopal tracts, and also of his return to and development of the doctrine expressed in *Comus* and the *Areopagitica* which involves precisely the belief that the process of regeneration both illuminates the mind and enables the will to progress in the virtue which makes it free.

[82]*Tetrachordon*, IV, 165-6.

[83]*Ibid.*, 165.

[84]*Doctrine and Discipline*, III, 396.

[85]*Ibid.*, 466.

[86]*Ibid.*, 451.

[87]*Ibid.*, 451.

[88]*Ibid.*, 477.

[89]*Ibid.*, 461.

[90]*Tetrachordon*, IV, 165. Cf. Samuel Rutherford, *Lex Rex*, 1644: "I judge . . . that princedom, empire, kingdom, or jurisdiction, hath its rise from a positive and secondary law of nations, and not from the law of pure nature" (Woodhouse, *Puritanism and Liberty*, 200-1).

[91]See Lyon, *The Theory of Religious Liberty in England, 1603-1639*, 111-12.

[92]See *The Works of Gerrard Winstanley*, ed. Sabine, "Introduction," 51-70.

[93]*Tetrachordon*, IV, 170-1. The fact that even in the political pamphlets (where the Law of Nations is sometimes invoked) Milton ignored the secondary law of nature and based his argument on the law of nature alone—meaning presumably the prime law of nature—presents a problem difficult to solve. I can find no satisfactory explanation for this dropping out of an idea so fully stated in the passages quoted. But it is certainly connected with the revision of

opinion discussed above in note 81. The unregenerate will of fallen man can act only in accordance with the secondary and imperfect law of nature; if the Spirit does not effectively influence the will of Christians, they also will act in accordance with this imperfect law, whatever their spiritual recognition of the perfect law. This is a view which justifies the reactionary political theory of Calvin, Luther, and most of the orthodox Puritans, and produces a state one of whose chief functions is the restraint of the imperfect will even of Christians. But if the Spirit works effectively on the will, then it will act in accordance with the prime law, spiritually renewed, and only the appeal to the prime law will have full validity for the Christian. This is the belief which underlies Milton's political argument.

[94]*Doctrine and Discipline*, III, 505.

[95]*Ibid.*, 494, 500, 509.

[96]*Tetrachordon*, IV, 134.

[97]*Conscience, with the Power and Cases Thereof*, 1643, 100. The subject is also handled in *The Marrow of Sacred Divinity*, book I, chaps. IX-X. Ames, who was a Christ's College man, is one of the divines mentioned by Phillips as a source of Milton's collections for his system of divinity after his return from Italy (Darbishire, *Early Lives*, 61). His definition of marriage is quoted and criticized in *Tetrachordon* (IV, 102-3). In *De Doctrina Christiana*, in discussing the Sabbath, Milton quotes *The Marrow*, book II, chap. XIII, to show that "that principle . . . 'that all those duties [of formal worship] are moral and immutable which are all bound up with moral and immutable reason,' is to be regarded as a rule of universal truth only where it is understood to imply that those duties follow upon those reasons without the interposition of a special commandment of God" (XVII, 173). The point is exactly the same as the one here being discussed in relation to divorce.

[98]*Tetrachordon*, IV, 92.

[99]*Conscience*, 108.

[100]*Tetrachordon*, IV, 80; *Conscience*, 107.

[101]*Conscience*, 108: "therefore is there nowhere found any true right practical reason, pure and complete in all its parts, but in the written law of God, Psalm 119.66."

[102]The vision of Peter and the sentence from *Titus* 1.15, used in *Areopagitica*, appear again in *Tetrachordon*, IV, 198.

[103]*Areopagitica*, IV, 314.

[104]*Ibid.*, 320.

[105]*Doctrine and Discipline*, III, 455.

[106]*Tetrachordon*, IV, 114; and see 129, 131, 142-3, 167.

[107]*Doctrine and Discipline*, III, 455.

[108]*Elegia quarta*, lines 29-32.

[109]See Samuel How, *The Sufficiencie of the Spirits Teaching without humane Learning. Or a treatise tending to prove Humane-learning to be no helpe to the spiritual understanding of the Word of God*, (January 22), 1645; first published in 1640.

[110]*The Advice of W. P. to Mr. Samuel Hartlib*, 1648; *Harleian Miscellany*, 1810, VI, 142, 157.

[111]*The Bloudy Tenent*, 263-4. The Digger, Gerrard Winstanley, likewise argued that all children should "be trained up in trades and some bodily employ-

ment," without any religious education (*Law of Freedom in A Platform*, 1652, chap. v). See *The Works of Gerrard Winstanley*, ed. Sabine, Introduction, 64-7. On the relationship between Puritanism and Baconianism, see Woodhouse, "Milton, Puritanism and Liberty," 505, and *Puritanism and Liberty* [84]; Jones, *Ancients and Moderns*.

[112]See Prolusions III and VII; *Animadversions*, III, 119; *Apology*, III, 359; *Of Education*, IV, 278; and Jones, *Ancients and Moderns*, 124ff.

[113]*Areopagitica*, IV, 295.

[114]*Of Education*, IV, 286.

[115]*Ibid.*, 280.

[116]*Ibid.*, 277.

[117]*The Ancient Bounds*, 36.

[118]*Tetrachordon*, IV, 74.

## CHAPTER VIII

[1]*Regii Sanguinis Clamor*, 1652, 10. I translate from the Latin.

[2]See chap. IX.

[3]*Defensio Secunda*, VIII, 135. There follows an account of the writing of the first three political pamphlets, to which must be added three others: *The Tenure of Kings and Magistrates: proving, That it is Lawfull, and hath been held so through all Ages, for any, who have the Power, to call to account a Tyrant, or wicked King, and after due conviction, to depose, and put him to death; if the ordinary Magistrate have neglected, or deny'd to doe it. And that they, who of late so much blame Deposing are the Men that did it themselves* . . . , (February 13) 1648/49; republished February 15, 1650, with additions of no importance for our purposes; *Observations on the Articles of Peace between James Earl of Ormond . . . and the Irish Rebels* . . . , (May 16) 1649; *Eikonoklastes in Answer to a Book Intitl'd Eikon Basilike, the Portraiture of his Sacred Majesty in his Solitudes and Sufferings* . . . , (October 6) 1649; republished in 1650 with additions of no importance for our purposes; *Joannis Miltoni Angli pro Populo Anglicano Defensio Contra Claudii . . . Salmasii, Defensionem Regiam* . . . , (April 6) 1650; frequently reprinted; corrected and enlarged 1658; *Joannis Miltoni Angli pro Populo Anglicano Defensio Secunda. Contra infamem libellum anonymum cui titulus, Regii sanguinis clamor ad coelum adversus parricidas Anglicanos* . . . , (May 30) 1654; *Joannis Miltoni Angli Pro Se Defensio contra Alexandrum Morum Ecclesiasten* . . . , (August 8) 1655. In what follows I quote from the translations of the Latin works in the Columbia *Works*.

[4]See Jesse F. Mack, "The Evolution of Milton's Political Thinking," 193.

[5]*Defensio Secunda*, VIII, 129.

[6]*The Readie and Easie Way*, VI, 116.

[7]*Animadversions*, III, 148.

[8]*An Humble Remonstrance*, 9. "Arbitrary" here means "according to discretion"; cf. *A Defence*, 4-5.

[9]*A Modest Confutation*, 15.

[10]See *An Answer*, 4; *A Vindication*, 6-7; the opening pages of *Of Reformation*, III, 39, 41; *Animadversions*, III, 114-15; *Apology*, III, 330-1.

[11]*A Short Answer*, 8.

[12]Browne, *A Treatise of Reformation without Tarying for Anie*, 1582. See

Knappen, *Tudor Puritanism*, 305: "but he too looked forward to the day when the magistrate should support and defend his system against all adversaries."

[13]*English Puritanisme*, 1, 19, 20.

[14]*A Protestation*, 18.

[15]*A Just and Necessarie Apologie*, 62; *A Justification of Separation*, 13, 31; *A Survey of the Confession of Faith Published by . . . Mr. Smyth's Company*, 1614, *Works*, III, 277.

[16]*The Institution of Christian Religion*, 1599, 412.

[17]Miller, *Orthodoxy in Massachusetts*, 61, 101.

[18]*Of Reformation*, III, 56, 47, 49; *Reason of Church Government*, III, 202; *Apology*, III, 338 ff.

[19]See Allen, *English Political Thought, 1603-1644*, 424-56; Kirby, *William Prynne*, 50-60.

[20]*Hopes Incouragement*, 26.

[21]*Apology*, III, 337.

[22]*Reason of Church Government*, III, 254.

[23]See above, chap. VI, note 55.

[24]*A Discourse*, 2.

[25]*Ibid.*, 48.

[26]*Of Reformation*, III, 70.

[27]*Reason of Church Government*, III, 203.

[28]*Of Reformation*, III, 47.

[29]*Ibid.*, 39-40.

[30]*Ibid.*, 57.

[31]*English Puritanisme*, 6.

[32]*Ibid.*, 6.

[33]*Ibid.*, 7.

[34]*Ibid.*, 6. See also Ames, *Conscience*, book V, 166, and book VI, 12; Bradshaw, *The Unreasonablenesse of the Separation*, 15; Henry Jacob, *A Christian And Modest Offer*, 3.

[35]*The Institution of Christian Religion*, 405-6; Milton quoted Sir Thomas Smith to this effect in the *Commonplace Book*, XVIII, 176.

[36]*The Marrow of Sacred Divinity*, 145; Robinson, *Works*, II, 140.

[37]*A Discourse*, 79-83. See above chap. II, note 49.

[38]*Counterpoyson Considerations touching the poynts in difference between the . . . Church of England, and the seduced brethren of the Separation*, 1642, 103.

[39]Cotton to Lord Saye and Sele; in Miller, *Orthodoxy in Massachusetts*, 229.

[40]*Of Reformation*, III, 63-4.

[41]*Ibid.*, 57.

[42]*Ibid.*, 63.

[43]*Ibid.*, 41.

[44]*Ibid.*, 41, 65.

[45]*Reasons Taken Out Of Gods Word*, 26; quoted Miller, *Orthodoxy in Massachusetts*, 240. See also Davenport, *Discourse about Civil Government*, 7-8.

[46]*Of Reformation*, III, 43-4, 57, 46-7; *Reason of Church Government*, III, 269 ff.; *Animadversions*, III, 175; *Apology*, III, 337.

[47]*Reason of Church Government*, III, 272.

[48]*Ibid.*, 184.

[49]*Of Reformation*, III, 53; *Reason of Church Government*, III, 239.

[50]*Of Reformation*, III, 53.

[51]*Apology*, III, 336.

[52]*Of Reformation*, III, 36, 38.

[53]*Ibid.*, 38-9.

[54]Note in the *Commonplace Book* from Camden, *Annales Rerum Anglicarum*; XVIII, 163.

## CHAPTER IX

[1]See Allen, *English Political Thought, 1603-1644*, 424-81; Haller, *The Rise of Puritanism*, chap. x; Pease, *The Leveller Movement*, chap. i; Woodhouse, *Puritanism and Liberty*, "Introduction"; Petegorsky, *Left-Wing Democracy in the English Civil War*, 71 ff.

[2]*Doctrine and Discipline*, III, 374; *Tetrachordon*, IV, 68.

[3]The *Commonplace Book* contains a number of notes from Milton's historical reading which concern the relationship between a king and his people; but they cannot be dated accurately and many of them belong to the period of his political writings. See Hanford, "The Chronology of Milton's Private Studies."

[4]See French, *Milton in Chancery*, chap. viii. Milton expressed his annoyance over these legal difficulties in his bitter indictment of the sequestrators in his *History of Britain*, X, 320-1.

[5]Letter to Charles Dati, XII, 47.

[6]Letter to Leonard Philaris, September 28, 1654, XII, 67. Milton writes, "It is ten years, I think, more or less, since I felt my sight getting weak and dull. . . ."

[7]My attention was drawn to this point by a graduate student, Miss Jean MacLaurin. The two psalms are the eighty-sixth and eighty-eighth.

[8]*An Apology*, III, 305.

[9]Four books of the *History* were finished by the beginning of 1649; *Defensio Secunda*, VIII, 137. See Hanford, *A Milton Handbook*, 89.

[10]Letter to Charles Dati, XII, 51.

[11]*Ad Joannem Rousium*, Strophe ii, I, 319.

[12]*Defensio*, VII, 409.

[13]*Doctrine and Discipline*, III, 473.

[14]*Ibid.*, 464.

[15]*Tetrachordon*, IV, 137.

[16]See above, chap. vii, note 47.

[17]See Agar, *Milton and Plato*.

[18]John Lilburne, *A Worke of the Beast or A Relation of a most unchristian Censure, Executed upon John Lilburne*, 1638.

[19]Knappen, *Tudor Puritanism*, 402, shows that the political thought of the early English Puritans was essentially conservative. They condemned the excesses of the continental Anabaptists as vigorously as their prelatical opponents.

[20]*A Short Answer*, 8.

[21]*A Short History of the Anabaptists Of High And Low Germany*, 1642, 53-4: "I am afraid that Anabaptism is very rife in England; though not perhaps of one entire body, but scattered in pieces . . . , yet not so scattered that they meet in one head, which is the hatred of all rule. Mark the end of the present dis-

tempers. . . ." See Brown, *The Political Activities of the Baptists and Fifth Monarchy Men*, 6 ff.

[22]*Animadversions*, III, 111; *Apology*, III, 319.

[23]*The Epistle Congratulatorie of Lysimachus Nicanor . . . to the Covenanters in Scotland*, 1640. The pamphlet draws a lengthy parallel between the opinions of the Papists and those of Knox, Cartwright, Buchanan, Christopher Goodman, Alexander Leighton, and others, to show that the Puritans, like the Jesuits, teach the power of the people, the right of resistance, the legitimacy of tyrannicide.

[24]*A Remonstrance, against Presbitery*, (May) 1641, section 13.

[25]Lindsay, *The Essentials of Democracy*, 11-24; Gough, *The Social Contract*, 82-4.

[26]See Miller, *Orthodoxy in Massachusetts*, 168-73.

[27]See Woodhouse, *Puritanism and Liberty*, [72-6].

[28]*Englands Bondage and Hope of Deliverance*, 23; *Tenure*, V, 11.

[29]*Spiritual Whordome*, (May 26) 1647, 34.

[30]The *Representation* was dated by Thomason January 18, 1649, almost a month before *The Tenure*. In *Defensio Secunda*, VIII, 135, Milton said that he wrote *The Tenure* when "certain Presbyterian ministers . . . , unable to endure that the Independent party should now be preferred to them, and that it should have greater influence in the senate, began to clamour against the sentence which the Parliament had pronounced upon the King. . . ." In *The Tenure* he also refers to *A Vindication of the Ministers of the Gospel in, and about London, from the unjust Aspersions upon their former Actings for the Parliament*, (January 27) 1648/49, and to Prynne's *Briefe Memento to the Present Unparliamentary Iunto*, (January 4) 1648/49 (*Tenure*, V, 45, 5). The *Representation*, the most important Presbyterian statement at this time, called forth a number of replies, among them *An Answer*, (January 27) 1648/49, by Samuel Richardson, author of *The necessity of Toleration*, and *Obstructors of Justice*, (May 30) 1649, by John Goodwin.

[31]*Representation*, 1-3. The ministers refer chiefly to the *Remonstrance and Declaration of the Army* of November 16, 1648.

[32]*Ibid.*, 4, 6. "The constant judgment and doctrine of Protestant divines" condemn "the opposing of lawful magistrates by private persons and the murdering of kings by any" (11). It is to this assertion that Milton offers an answer, *The Tenure*, V, 45 ff.

[33]*Ibid.*, 3, 11.

[34]*Ibid.*, 13.

[35]Quoted by Marriott, *Life . . . of Lucius Cary*, 141.

[36]*Tenure*, title-page.

[37]*Right and Might*, (January 2) 1648/49, 2.

[38]*Defensio*, VII, 31-3; and see 269.

[39]*Tenure*, V, 28, 8-10; *Eikonoklastes*, V, 202-3; *Defensio*, VII, 269. In the political pamphlets Milton makes no use of the analogy between the marriage contract and the contract between a king and his people to which he had referred in the divorce tracts. This is the more curious since the analogy was frequently employed in defence of tyrannicide, just as it had been employed in justification of resistance to the King. Thus *The Armies Vindication*, (January 11) 1649—a pamphlet which defended the action being taken against the King by arguments

very like those of *The Tenure* a month later—observes that "as Christ, in the controversy between him and the Pharisees touching divorce, sends them back to the original and first institution of marriage and to the fathers of the first age of the world, as being the first and best pattern . . . , so there is no better way to have a commonwealth settled in peace and righteousness than to look back at the beginning when men walked by the exact and even rules of equity, justice, and conscience, and kept the clear and plain principles of reason and nature. This is the land-measure and standard whereby the faulty measures coming after are to be corrected and mended" (sig. A3). Later in the pamphlet the author asserts that, as the "very bond and knot of marriage" is broken by adultery either in man or wife, so "a subject breaking his covenant with a king" and "the king breaking his covenant with the people" are alike punishable (47-8). The same analogy between a "bill of divorce" and the rejection of a king by his people appears in John Redingstone's *Plain English To The Parliament and Army*, (January 12) 1649. In his *Obstructours of Justice*, 1649, John Goodwin compares parliament and king to man and woman, the former in each case being first in origin and superior to the latter (11); and he remarks that "a king and tyrant are as specifically distinct as a lawful husband and an adulterer" (31). Earlier, in the Putney debates, Rainborough had illustrated his view of the legitimacy of breaking engagements by saying, "No man takes a wife but there is an engagement, and I think that a man ought to keep it; yet if another man that had married her before claims her, he ought to let him have her and so break the engagement" (Woodhouse, *Puritanism and Liberty*, 32-3).

40 *Tenure*, V, 8, 10. Cf. Parker, *Observations*, 1-2; Rutherford, *Lex Rex*, in Woodhouse, *Puritanism and Liberty*, 202-3; Lilburne, *The Free-mans Freedome Vindicated*, 11-12. On the contract theory during the revolution, see Gough, *The Social Contract*, chap. VII.

41 *Leviathan*, 90-1, 96. Cf. Salmasius, quoted by Milton in *Defensio*, VII, 283.

42 Parker, *Observations*, 8, 14. Cf. *Scripture and Reason*, 29, 39-40, 44; and *A serious and faithful Representation*, 6-7.

43 *Defensio*, VII, 361-3.

44 *Tenure*, V, 14, and see 18; *Defensio*, VII, 193. See also *Defensio*, VII, 177, 359, and *Eikonoklastes*, V, 130.

45 *The Compassionate Samaritane* is ascribed to Walwyn by Haller, *Tracts on Liberty*, I, 123. See also Pease, *The Leveller Movement*, 104; and Lilburne, *Englands Birth-right Justified*, (October 10) 1645, and *Innocency and Truth Justified*, (January 6) 1645/46.

46 *The Compassionate Samaritane*, 67.

47 *Englands Lamentable Slaverie, Proceeding from the Arbitrarie will, severitie, and Injustnes of Kings, Negligence, corruption, and unfaithfulnesse of Parliaments, Coveteousness, ambition, and Variablenesse of Priests, and simplicitie, Carelesnesse, and cowardlinesse of People*, (October 11) 1645, 3-4. Pease, *The Leveller Movement*, 116, tentatively assigns this pamphlet to Walwyn. Cf. Lilburne, *Englands Birth-right*, 3; the power of parliaments is "limited by those that betrust them" so that they will "not do what they list, but what they ought, namely, to provide for the people's good."

48 *A Remonstrance of Many Thousand Citizens*, 4-5. See Haller, *Tracts on Liberty*, I, 111.

49 See *Innocency and Truth Justified*, and Pease, *The Leveller Movement*, 115 ff.

[50]*Tenure,* V, 53. There follows a review of *Scripture and Reason* to demonstrate the truth of this statement.

[51]*Right and Might well met,* 3-10; *Defensio,* VII, 357, 507-9.

[52]*Defensio,* VII, 427. See also *Defensio,* VII, 99, 361, and *Eikonoklastes,* V, 129, 237.

[53]*Tenure,* V, 41.

[54]*Defensio,* VII, 291.

[55]*Eikonoklastes,* V, 183; and see 281.

[56]*Ibid.,* 271.

[57]*Ibid.,* 128, 121.

[58]*Defensio,* VII, 445.

[59]*Right and Might well met,* 34. Cf. *Defensio,* VII, 427.

[60]*Right and Might well met,* 15. "Yea, many of the laws of God themselves think it no disparagement to give place to their elder sister, the law of necessity. . . ."

[61]*Londons Liberty In Chains,* (October) 1646, 41.

[62]For the disputes between Prynne and Lilburne and Walwyn, see Pease, *The Leveller Movement,* 101 ff., and Haller, *Tracts on Liberty,* I, 164 ff. Milton attacked Prynne in *Colasterion,* IV, 233-4, in the sonnet *On the New Forcers of Conscience,* and in *The Likeliest Means,* VI, 65.

[63]*A Helpe to the right understanding of a Discourse Concerning Independency. Lately published by William Pryn,* (February 6), 1644/45, 2-3.

[64]*Englands Birth-right Justified Against all Arbitrary Usurpation, whether Regall or Parliamentary,* (October) 1645, 8.

[65]*Ibid.,* 2.

[66]*Tenure,* V, 3. See also *Commonplace Book,* XVIII, 166, 191, for similar remarks. French, *Milton in Chancery,* has recently shown that Milton was involved in a complicated suit with Sir Robert Pye from 1647 to 1649. No doubt this and the following outburst were partly produced by his experience.

[67]*Defensio,* VII, 33.

[68]*Tenure,* V, 4; *Eikonoklastes,* V, 298.

[69]*Tenure,* V, 35. The reference here is to the Solemn League and Covenant.

[70]*Eikonoklastes,* V, 300; and see *Defensio,* VII, 267.

[71]*Defensio,* VII, 359-61.

[72]Rutherford, *Lex Rex,* 54, 57; see *Scripture and Reason,* 39-40.

[73]*Leviathan,* 70-1, 74.

[74]Woodhouse, *Puritanism and Liberty,* "The Putney Debates," 10.

[75]*Ibid.,* 11.

[76]*Ibid.,* 26.

[77]*Ibid.,* 26.

[78]*Ibid.,* 57-8.

[79]*Ibid.,* 27.

[80]*Ibid.,* 13.

[81]*Ibid.,* 24.

[82]*Ibid.,* 34.

[83]Thus Thomas Edwards wrote of the Levellers: "As they do in matters of religion and conscience fly from the Scriptures and from supernatural truths revealed there, that a man may not be questioned for going against them, but only for errors against the light of nature and right reason; so they do also in

civil government and things of this world. They go from the laws and constitutions of kingdoms, and will be governed by rules according to nature and right reason: and though the laws and customs of a kingdom be never so clear and plain against their ways, yet they will not submit, but cry out for natural rights derived from Adam and right reason" (*Gangraena*, part III, 20).

[84]*Tenure*, V, 19; *Eikonoklastes*, V, 120; *Defensio*, VII, 427.

[85]*Right and Might well met*, 31.

[86]*Ibid.*, 20.

[87]*Observations concerning the Originall of Government*, 19.

[88]*An Arrow Against All Tyrants*, 1646, 3-4.

[89]Woodhouse, *Puritanism and Liberty*, [69].

[90]*Ibid.*, 55, 56.

[91]*Ibid.*, 122; and see 65-6.

[92]*Tenure*, V, 11, 46.

[93]*Eikonoklastes*, V, 131; *Defensio*, VII, 73; *Eikonoklastes*, V, 202.

[94]*Defensio*, VII, 151-3.

[95]*Ibid.*, 305; *Defensio Secunda*, VIII, 239.

[96]*Tenure*, V, 57.

## CHAPTER X

[1]*Reason of Church Government*, III, 225; *Areopagitica*, IV, 334.

[2]*Eikonoklastes*, V, 69, 71.

[3]*Eikonoklastes*, V, 143, 309, 68.

[4]*Defensio*, VII, 63. See Lilburne, *Englands New Chains*; and Needham, *A Plea for the King and Kingdom.*

[5]*Defensio Secunda*, VIII, 67.

[6]See the attack of Liljegren, *Studies in Milton*, xl.

[7]*Defensio*, VII, 35, 497.

[8]*Ibid.*, 393.

[9]See Woodhouse, *Puritanism and Liberty*, [16-17].

[10]*Ibid.*, 127.

[11]*Defensio*, VII, 379.

[12]*Tenure*, V, 25; *Eikonoklastes*, V, 283; and see 180 ff., and *Defensio*, VII, 427.

[13]*Eikonoklastes*, V, 83, 168.

[14]*Ibid.*, 202; *Defensio*, VII, 349-59.

[15]*Tenure*, V, 58.

[16]Especially chaps. I to V. For Milton's use in *Eikonoklastes* of Thomas May's *History of the Parliament of England*, 1647, written by order of the Houses, and of various parliamentary declarations, see Whiting, *Milton's Literary Milieu*, 324-53.

[17]See Gardiner, *Commonwealth and Protectorate*, I, 3 ff.

[18]*Defensio*, VII, 489; *Tenure*, V, 7.

[19]*Observations*, VI, 265.

[20]*Ibid.*, 253, 254.

[21]See Pease, *The Leveller Movement*, 278 ff.

[22]*Defensio*, VII, 357; *Defensio Secunda*, VIII, 179. See *Right and Might well met*, 3-10.

[23]*Tenure*, V, 41; *Eikonoklastes*, V, 270. See Gardiner, *Civil War*, chaps. XLVII–IX, on the conflict between Parliament and Army.

[24]*Defensio*, VII, 51, 491, 495.

[25]*Ibid.*, 55.

[26]*Ibid.*, 31, 507; *Defensio Secunda*, VIII, 139.

[27]*Defensio Secunda*, VIII, 151-3. Cf. Goodwin, *Right and Might*, 15: "Besides, it is a ruled case amongst wise men, 'that if a people be depraved and corrupt, so as to confer places of power and trust upon wicked and undeserving men, they forfeit their power in this behalf unto those that are good, though but a few.' So that nothing pretended from a nonconcurrence of the people with the Army will hold water."

[28]See Gardiner, *Commonwealth and Protectorate*, II, 209, 221-95.

[29]*Defensio Secunda*, VIII, 221-3.

[30]*Defensio Secunda*, VIII, 157.

[31]See Pease, *The Leveller Movement*, 310 ff. and Woodhouse, *Puritanism and Liberty*, 31 ff.

[32]See Pease, *The Leveller Movement*, chap. XI.

[33]*Ibid.*, 348.

[34]*The Leveller*, 1659, 4.

[35]Woodhouse, *Puritanism and Liberty*, "The Putney Debates," 53, 59.

[36]*Ibid.*, 58.

[37]*Ibid.*, 55.

[38]*Ibid.*, 26; cf. Hobbes, *Leviathan*, 70-4.

[39]*Ibid.*, 67; *Defensio*, VII, 393.

[40]*Letters and Speeches*, II, 353.

[41]Woodhouse, *Puritanism and Liberty*, "The Putney Debates," 8.

[42]*Ibid.*, "The Reading Debates," 420.

[43]*Tenure*, V, 8. Italics mine.

[44]*Eikonoklastes*, V, 73-4.

[45]*Leviathan*, 64.

[46]*Observations*, 13. See Rutherford, *Lex Rex*, in Woodhouse, *Puritanism and Liberty*, 206-7.

[47]*Defensio*, VII, 175; see also *Tenure*, V, 8.

[48]*Lex Rex*, in Woodhouse, *Puritanism and Liberty*, 206-7.

[49]*Leviathan*, 114; and see 63.

[50]*The Free-mans Freedome Vindicated*, (June 16) 1646, 11-12.

[51]Wildman, at Putney, in Woodhouse, *Puritanism and Liberty*, 66.

[52]*Leviathan*, 63, 67.

[53]*Ibid.*, 83, 172.

[54]*Ibid.*, 89, 92-3, 143, 172, 372.

[55]*Ibid.*, 90-6, 143, 172.

[56]*Ibid.*, 386.

[57]*Ibid.*, 373-4.

[58]*Tenure*, V, 9.

[59]*Defensio*, VII, 291.

[60]See especially *Tenure*, V, 19-20, 39; *Defensio*, VII, 143.

[61]*Lex Rex*, in Woodhouse, *Puritanism and Liberty*, 210.

[62]*Leviathan*, chap. XXXI

[63]*The Free-mans Freedome Vindicated*, 11.

[64]*Defensio*, VII, 233; and see *Tenure*, V, 22, 20.

[65]*Defensio*, VII, 191-3, 77.

[66]*Tenure*, V, 41.

[67]Overton, *An Appeale from the Degenerate Representative Body the Commons . . . To the Body Represented. The Free People . . .*, (July 17) 1647; in Woodhouse, *Puritanism and Liberty*, 323.

[68]It is curious that Milton nowhere mentions by name the Agreements of the People or the Levellers. He was certainly familiar with their proposals. When he was appointed Secretary for Foreign Tongues to the Council of State of the Commonwealth, March 15, 1649, the government was engaged in consolidating its position; and its activities were chiefly directed not against the Royalists but against the Levellers; see Pease, *The Leveller Movement*, chaps. VIII and IX. On March 26, Milton was appointed "to make some observations" upon one of Lilburne's anti-Commonwealth tracts, *Englands New Chains discovered*; see the Order Book of the Council, quoted by Masson, IV, 87. So far as we know, he did not compose his observations. On March 28 he was ordered to compose his *Observations* on the Irish peace. On the same day, Lilburne, Overton, Walwyn, and Prince, the leading Levellers, were brought before the Council and committed to prison. It is possible that Milton was then present; see Masson, IV, 87. Subsequently, on October 24, he was appointed with Mr. Sergeant Denby to examine the papers of Clement Walker, whose *History of Independency*, (December) 1648, and its second part, *Anarchia Anglicana*, (September) 1649, constituted at once a defence of the royalist Presbyterians and of the Levellers, and indicated the beginning of the co-operation between these two ill-sorted groups against the Commonwealth and, later, the Protectorate. Wolfe, "Lilburne's Note on Milton," suggests that Milton did not write against the Levellers either because they were known to him personally or because he disapproved Cromwell's treatment of them. This suggestion he supports by his interesting discovery of a passage in Lilburne's *As You Were*, 1653, 15-16, quoting Milton's exhortation in the *Defensio* to the English people to refute their adversaries with their just deeds. This quotation seems to Wolfe to indicate "a closer ideological and perhaps personal bond with the Levellers than scholars have hitherto assumed." Actually, Lilburne's quotation—a skilful turning of one of their own guns on his enemies—tells us nothing of Milton's view of the Levellers. An explanation of his failure to write against them, more consistent with their ideological differences, is to be found in his work on *Observations* (May 16) and *Eikonoklastes* (October 6) throughout the larger part of 1649, and in his approaching blindness. Moreover, the need for a written refutation of the Leveller arguments passed with the defeat of the Army Levellers at Burford on May 14 by a force sent by Fairfax and Cromwell. June 6 and 7 were appointed "days of public thanksgiving for the seasonable and happy reducing of the Levellers." See Petegorsky, *Left-Wing Democracy*, 154-60.

[69]In the argument about the need for acting in accordance with previous engagements which occupied a large part of the Putney debates (Woodhouse, *Puritanism and Liberty*, 24-30), Wildman and Ireton disputed the extent to which obedience must be given to Parliament if it acted unjustly. Ireton used the argument for submission previously employed by the Royalists in defence of the king's prerogative, that anarchy would result if Parliament's authority were questioned. Wildman pushed forward to an extreme the former parliamentary argument for obedience only according to principles of justice.

[70]Liljegren, *Studies in Milton*, xix; see *Defensio*, chap. III, and *Tenure*, V,

16-17. Milton gave the same interpretation in 1660: *Brief Notes upon a Late Sermon*, VI, 155.

[71]Woodhouse, *Puritanism and Liberty*, [33-4]. As Goodwin observed, "undue compliance with any faction or party whatsoever, whether prevailing or failing, hath been none of my least visible sins" (*Right and Might*, 102).

[72]*Right and Might*, 31.

[73]*Obstructours of Justice*, 40. In this pamphlet Goodwin refers to or quotes from Milton's *Tenure* six times; see Parker, *Milton's Contemporary Reputation*, 80-2. Except in the case of one historical comment, the references occur in passages in which Goodwin is dealing with the *Serious and faithful Representation* of the Presbyterian ministers. He did not need to borrow from Milton for his political theory. That had already been expressed before *The Tenure* in such pamphlets as *Anti-Cavalierisme* and *Right and Might*.

[74]*Ibid.*, 40; *Right and Might*, 14-15.

[75]*Right and Might*, 40; see also *Obstructours*, 110-11.

[76]*Obstructours of Justice*, 22. Goodwin is here dealing with Hammond's assertion in his *Humble Address* that the appeal to nature means that "God gave all men freedom, either to do what they list or to live without all government." Goodwin denies that it means this. Nor does it mean that "any particular man" may refuse subjection to a "lawfully established" government, "so far as it is lawful," but only that an unlawful government may be resisted (22-3).

[77]*Ibid.*, 40. John Canne, *The Golden Rule, Or, Justice Advanced*, (February 16) 1649, 21, interprets Romans 13 in the same way in justifying the execution of the King. The higher powers are to be obeyed "so far as they govern according to reason and just laws, preserve the people's liberties, persons and estates." For a comparison of *The Tenure* and *The Golden Rule*, see Whiting, *Milton's Literary Milieu*, 309-23. Whiting would like to believe that Canne owed something to Milton. This is improbable; but the similarity between their arguments does show that the ideas of *The Tenure* were those "of a party, of which Milton was not the only self-appointed spokesman."

[78]*Defensio*, VII, 173.

[79]*Tenure*, V, 16.

[80]*Eikonoklastes*, V, 241-2.

[81]*Defensio*, VII, 161-75.

[82]*Defensio Secunda*, VIII, 213-15, 219, 223.

[83]*The Institution of Christian Religion*, 413.

[84]*Leviathan*, 74, 146, 172; *De Corpore Politico*, 139.

[85]*Eikonoklastes*, V, 292.

[86]*Ibid.*, 212.

[87]*Tenure*, V, 4-5.

## CHAPTER XI

[1]*Defensio Secunda*, VIII, 185; *Eikonoklastes*, V, 307; and see also 272.

[2]*Eikonoklastes*, V, 145.

[3]*Letters and Speeches*, I, 350. See Buchan, *Oliver Cromwell*, 147, 290, for a discussion of Cromwell's tendency to read "God's providence less by the inner light than in events—a scarcely less dangerous method."

[4]Woodhouse, *Puritanism and Liberty*, "The Putney Debates," 103.

[5]*The Declaration of His Excellency The Lord General Fairfax and his General Councel of Officers, shewing the grounds of the Armies advance towards the City of London*, 1648; in Woodhouse, *Puritanism and Liberty*, 467.

[6]*Defensio*, VII, 7.

[7]*Eikonoklastes*, V, 266.

[8]*Tenure*, V, 3, 7.

[9]*Observations*, VI, 252.

[10]*Defensio*, VII, 267; and see 31, 427.

[11]*Eikonoklastes*, V, 203.

[12]*An Appeale from . . . the Commons . . . To the Body Represented;* in Woodhouse, *Puritanism and Liberty*, 324.

[13]*Innocency and Truth Justified*, (January) 1645/46, 28, 37; *Regall Tyrannie discovered*, (January 6) 1647, 9.

[14]*The Law of Freedom in a Platform; Or, True Magistracy Restored*, (February 20), 1652, 25, 32-3, 78-80. For the religious origins of Winstanley's communism, see his *Works*, edited by G. H. Sabine, "Introduction," 21-51. Petegorsky seems to me to over-emphasize the materialistic elements in Winstanley's interpretation of the law of nature; see *Left-Wing Democracy*, 180-3, 211. See also Patrick "The Literature of the Diggers."

[15]*The Perfect Weekly Account*, July 18-25, 1649; quoted in Petegorsky, *Left-Wing Democracy*, 172.

[16]*Observations*, VI, 268.

[17]*Defensio*, VII, 391.

[18]*Ibid.*, 63, 357, 389.

[19]Woodhouse, *Puritanism and Liberty*, "The Putney Debates," 27, 82.

[20]*Defensio Secunda*, VIII, 247.

[21]*Tenure*, V, 1.

[22]*Eikonoklastes*, V, 289-90; see also *Defensio*, VII, 543-5.

[23]*Eikonoklastes*, V, 177; *Tenure*, V, 3.

[24]*Tenure*, V, 2; *Defensio Secunda*, VIII, 249.

[25]*Defensio*, VII, 75.

[26]*Defensio Secunda*, VIII, 245.

[27]*Tenure*, V, 1.

[28]*Ibid.*, 7.

[29]*Defensio Secunda*, VIII, 153-5; *Defensio*, VII, 273.

[30]*Defensio Secunda*, VIII, 251.

[31]*Defensio*, VII, 357, 389.

[32]*Ibid.*, 547.

[33]*Tetrachordon*, IV, 74.

[34]*Defensio Secunda*, VIII, 239-41.

[35]*Ibid.*, 249-51.

[36]*Ibid.*, 129-37, 235-9.

[37]*Areopagitica*, IV, 320.

[38]*Defensio Secunda*, VIII, 249, 251.

[39]*Ibid.*, 215, 223-5, 229.

[40]*Observations concerning the Originall of Government*, 13.

[41]*De Corpore Politico*, in *The Elements of Law*, ed. Tonnies, 88; *Leviathan*, 79-80.

[42]*Ibid.*, 19; and see *De Corpore Politico*, 188.

[43]*Defensio Secunda*, VIII, 241.

[44]*Ibid.*, 129, 236-7.

[45]*Ibid.*, 115, 133.

[46]*Ibid.*, 135, 237-9.

[47]*Ibid.*, 237.

[48]*Ibid.*, 237, 131.

[49]*Ibid.*, 237.

[50]Woodhouse observes that the consequence of Milton's view of Christian liberty is that the state acts merely as a restraint upon those who do not have the law written in the heart and is denied any power over those who do (*Puritanism and Liberty* [93], and "Milton, Puritanism and Liberty," 494). This is true of his extreme statements; but it would only be completely true if Milton applied with rigorous logic the doctrine of Christian liberty, religious and political, developed by the Millenarians. As it is, the humanistic ideal of a progressive development under a discipline which is self-imposed, but in which the individual has the assistance of the educative and religious function of the state, remains a part, though a decreasing part, of his thinking. The failure of the Puritan experiment went far to destroy it, and produced the exclusively spiritual discipline of *Paradise Regained.* But in the works under discussion, and even in *The Readie and Easie Way,* traces of the ideal remain in the directions for a religious education to which I am about to refer. And even in 1672, after *Paradise Regained*, Milton could publish an *Artis Logicae* which is essentially humanistic in its method.

[51]*Defensio Secunda*, VIII, 237.

[52]*Ibid.*, 251.

[53]*Leviathan*, 114.

[54]Aubrey's "Minutes," *Early Lives of Milton*, ed. Darbishire, 7. On the contrast between the views of Hobbes and the later Milton, see Nicolson, "Milton and Hobbes."

[55]*Of Reformation*, III, 49, 38.

[56]*Areopagitica*, IV, 318; *Tetrachordon*, IV, 75.

[57]*Tenure*, V, 12; *Eikonoklastes*, V, 84; *Defensio*, VII, 87, 163.

[58]*Defensio*, VII, 351, 167.

[59]*Ibid.*, 427, 169.

[60]See Woodhouse, "Milton, Puritanism, and Liberty," 511-13, on Milton's inability to apply the principle of segregation completely, because of the crossing of Puritanism and Humanism in him; and Bush, *The Renaissance and English Humanism*, 115.

[61]See Jordan, *The Development of Religious Toleration*, III, 402 ff.

[62]See Woodhouse, *Puritanism and Liberty*, [56-7].

[63]*The Bloudy Tenent*, 307, 313.

[64]*Ibid.*, 130.

[65]*Ibid.*, 214-15; see also 304-5, 315, 343.

[66]*Ibid.*, 341.

[67]*Ibid.*, 132.

[68]*Ibid.*, 46.

[69]*Ibid.*, 121-2.

[70]Williams was no Antinomian. Indeed, so consistent was his segregation of the spiritual and natural that he repudiated the political argument from Chris-

tian liberty which was employed (in different ways) by Overton and the Millenarians: "If any should preach or write that there ought to be no commanders because all are equal in Christ, I say I never denied but in such cases, whatever is pretended, the commander or commanders may judge, resist, compel, and punish such transgressors according to their deserts and merits" (Letter to Winthrop, 1637; quoted by Ernst, *Roger Williams*, 136).

[71]*The Bloudy Tenent*, 193, 211-12.

[72]*Ibid.*, 142, 200.

[73]Quoted by Ernst, *Roger Williams*, 99-100.

[74]*Defensio Secunda*, VIII, 97.

[75]*Cross Currents*, 25.

[76]*The Bloudy Tenent*, 193.

[77]*Pro Se Defensio*, IX, 203.

[78]*Eikonoklastes*, V, 301.

[79]*Ibid.*, 250.

[80]*Ibid.*, 226, 286. The Presbyterians had now, of course, taken the place of the bishops in Milton's eyes; see *ibid.*, 69.

[81]*Tenure*, V, 24.

[82]*Ibid.*, 27.

[83]*The Ancient Bounds*, 1.

[84]*Defensio*, VII, 149.

[85]*Eikonoklastes*, V, 226.

[86]*Defensio*, VII, 145.

[87]*Tenure*, V, 23; *Defensio*, VII, 145.

[88]*Defensio*, VII, 155-7; *Tenure*, V, 23.

[89]*Defensio*, VII, 145.

[90]*Ibid.*, 161-3; *Tenure*, V, 16-17.

[91]*Defensio*, VII, 145.

[92]The orthodox fear is well expressed in *Christophilos. The True Christian Subject* (from which the quotation comes, p. 9), a sermon against Anabaptism preached at St. Paul's by Benjamin Spencer, August 7, 1642.

[93]*Defensio Secunda*, VIII, 147.

[94]*Defensio*, VII, 13.

[95]*Ibid.*, 555.

[96]*Antapologia*, 301.

[97]Woodhouse, *Puritanism and Liberty*, 174, 225.

[98]*Defensio*, VII, 67.

[99]*Eikonoklastes*, V, 74.

[100]*Defensio*, VII, 211.

## CHAPTER XII

[1]See Woodhouse, *Puritanism and Liberty*, [82] ff.; Brown, *The Political Activities of the Baptists and Fifth Monarchy Men*, 44 ff., 201 ff.

[2]*The Peasants Price of Spirituall Liberty*, 1642, 15.

[3]*Ibid.*, 14-15, 17, 34.

[4]*Ibid.*, 30.

[5]See especially Homes's "Epistolar Preface" to Walter Cradock's *Gospel-*

*libertie*, (July 24) 1648; *The New World; or The New Reformed Church*, 1651. After the Restoration Homes published several other chiliastic pamphlets.

[6]*A Glimpse of Sions Glory*, 1641, in Woodhouse, *Puritanism and Liberty*, 237.

[7]Joseph Mede, *Clavis Apocalyptica ex innatis et insitis visionum characteribus* . . . , 1627; reprinted 1632, 1642; translated 1643. See also Henry Archer, *The personall Reign of Christ upon Earth*, 1642; Brown, *The Political Activities of the Baptists*, 12 ff.; and Haller, *The Rise of Puritanism*, 269-72.

[8]*A Glimpse of Sions Glory*, in Woodhouse, *Puritanism and Liberty*, 237, 233, 234, 238.

[9]*Of Reformation*, III, 78. See above, chap. I, p. 17.

[10]*Animadversions*, III, 148.

[11]Sonnet XII, I, 63.

[12]*Areopagitica*, IV, 318.

[13]*Ibid.*, 311, 338.

[14]See Brown, *The Political Activities of the Baptists*, 23.

[15]*Ibid.*, 41 ff.

[16]In the *Pro Se Defensio*, 1655, Cromwell is mentioned only twice, and then incidentally; IX, 13, 47. On the personal controversy between Milton and More, see Hanford, *Handbook*, 111-15.

From 1655 till 1659, Milton was living in comparative retirement. He had gone totally blind early in 1652; see French, "The Date of Milton's Blindness." His official work for the Council was not however reduced till 1655, though he had actually been doing little; see Masson, V, 176-7. In April, 1655, his salary was commuted to a life pension, and though he continued to translate letters for Oliver and for Richard, the burden of his work was taken over by others. Edward Phillips says that after the composition of *Pro Se Defensio*, 1655, "being now quiet from state adversaries and public contests, he had leisure for his own studies and private designs." Phillips then mentions the *History of Britain*, of which the last two books were now written, the Latin Thesaurus, and *Paradise Lost*. To these must be added *De Doctrina Christiana*. The comparative calm of these years is indicated by such letters as that to Emeric Bigot of March 24, 1656, XII, 86.

[17]*Defensio Secunda*, VIII, 221; see Brown, *The Political Activities of the Baptists*, 30 ff.

[18]*Letters and Speeches*, II, 298.

[19]See Brown, *The Political Activities of the Baptists*, 41-3; Jordan, *The Development of Religious Toleration*, III, 149-52.

[20]*Republic*, IX, 592.

[21]*Leviathan*, 219.

[22]*Ibid.*, 241-2.

[23]*Ibid.*, 262-3; and see also 332-3, 377.

[24]*The Bloudy Tenent*, 2; and see also 87, 124, 130, 138.

[25]*Ibid.*, 303.

[26]*A Brief Description of the Fifth Monarchy*, 1653, 10; Woodhouse, *Puritanism and Liberty*, [40].

[27]*The Bloudy Tenent*, 307, 313.

[28]*Innocency and Truth Justified*, (January 6) 1645/46, 62; *Regall Tyrannie discovered*, (January 6) 1647, 9.

[29]Woodhouse, *Puritanism and Liberty*, "The Putney Debates," 146.

[30]*Defensio*, VII, 91.

[31]*Ibid.*, 77; and see 157.

[32]*Tenure*, V, 39.

[33]*Defensio Secunda*, VIII, 249.

[34]See *An Agreement of the People*, in Woodhouse, *Puritanism and Liberty*, 357.

[35]*Certain Quaeres humbly presented . . . to . . . the Lord General . . . . Together with an humble advice for the settling of the kingdom*, (February 19) 1648/49; in Woodhouse, *Puritanism and Liberty*, 241-7. As Woodhouse notes, the advice repudiates the method of settlement by an Agreement of the People. See also Brown, *The Political Activities of the Baptists*, 54, on the similar proposals of *A Declaration Of several of the Churches of Christ*, (September 2) 1654.

[36]*Certain Quaeres*, in Woodhouse, *Puritanism and Liberty*, 241, 242.

[37]*Ibid.*, 246, 244.

[38]Brown, *The Political Activities of the Baptists*, 15-16.

[39]*Eikonoklastes*, V, 226.

[40]*Defensio*, VII, 115.

[41]*Eikonoklastes*, V, 306.

[42]In the *Defensio Secunda* and the *Pro Se Defensio* there is a singular absence of reference to the kingdom of Christ, to the activities of the Millenarians at this time, to God's displeasure at the desire of the Jews for a king, and to the superiority of a republic to a monarchy. Of the passages mentioning the kingdom of Christ, to which I refer in the text, two occur in *The Tenure*, two in *Eikonoklastes*, and four in the *Defensio*. The idea did not, of course, disappear from Milton's thought at this point; it is strongly emphasized in *The Readie and Easie Way* of 1660. The omission of it in the last two defences may perhaps be explained by a desire to avoid any suggestion that the Commonwealth was inspired by ideas which had contributed to the excesses of the continental Anabaptists. It is to the examples of Greece and Rome that Milton would have his European audience turn. But the *Defensio Secunda* is addressed to the audience which had received the *Defensio*. That pamphlet not only contains four references to the kingdom of Christ but (in addition to several vaguer remarks) four specific assertions of the superiority of a commonwealth to a monarchy, the point made in each case being that God was displeased with the Jews for desiring a king, because "monarchy slips aptest into tyranny." Only the most naïve could assume that the absence of such ideas in *Defensio Secunda* resulted from the reported commendation of the *Defensio* by a Scandinavian queen. The reason lies closer home. After the expulsion of the Parliament in April, 1653, it appeared that the establishment of the Protectorate might be the prelude to an assumption of the crown by Cromwell. The Levellers were strong in their denunciation of such a possibility; but, especially after the failure of the Nominated Parliament in 1653, they were far outdone by the Millenarians. The absence of references to the disadvantages of monarchy in the last two defences can only be explained by the possibility that Oliver might yet become king. The absence of references to the kingdom of Christ must similarly be explained by the dangerous activities of the Millenarians and the measures taken against them. Henry Vane, who was in retirement in Lincolnshire, was more and more suspected, after his refusal to sit in Cromwell's new parliament in July, of going "up and down amongst these people [the Millenarians] and others, endeavouring to withdraw them from their subjection to the present government" (Henry Cromwell to Thurloe, *Thurloe State Papers*,

IV, 509; Willcock, *Vane*, 253); and he was destined to be imprisoned in the Isle of Wight in April, 1656. References to the kingdom of Christ at such a time might have been misunderstood. This is, I think, the only instance in which Milton appears to have suppressed ideas for politic reasons; and it is to be observed that, if he did not comment on the disadvantages of monarchy, he made his opinion clear by urging Cromwell in *Defensio Secunda* to associate with him in the government those who had distinguished themselves in the service of the cause; and that if he did not mention the kingdom of Christ, neither did he join with Cromwell's supporters in condemning the Millenarians.

[43]Brown, *The Political Activities of the Baptists*, 44 ff. See Cromwell's speech to the first Protectorate Parliament, in which the Millenarians are castigated, September 4, 1654; *ibid.*, 62. It is worth noting that Milton nowhere refers to these events, or indeed to anything which occurred between 1654 and 1659.

[44]*Ibid.*, 46, note 8, *et passim.*

[45]*Anti-Cavalierisme*, 32-3.

[46]*Hagiomastix: Or The Scourge Of The Saints*, (February 5) 1646, "To the Reader."

[47]*Dis-satisfaction Satisfied*, (November 22) 1653, 16. The passage is followed by quotations from Millenarian pamphlets and an examination of their arguments. See also *Peace Protected, And Discontent Dis-armed*, 1654.

[48]Woodhouse, *Puritanism and Liberty*, 396.

[49]On Collier's thought, see Jordan, *The Development of Religious Toleration*, III, 526-31.

[50]Woodhouse, *Puritanism and Liberty*, 390-1.

[51]*Ibid.*, 392-3.

[52]*Ibid.*, 394-5.

[53]Sonnet XVII, I, 65.

[54]See Willcock, *The Life of Sir Henry Vane*, 253 ff.

[55]*Sr. Henry Vane his Speech . . . at a Committee for the Bill against Espicopall-Government*, (June 11) 1643.

[56]See Woodhouse, *Puritanism and Liberty*, [45-7].

[57]*The Retired Mans Meditations*, (July 2), 1655, 383.

[58]*Ibid.*, 391.

[59]As Woodhouse has noted ("Puritanism and Liberty," 400), this difference between Vane's view of magistracy as useful even to unfallen man and Milton's view of it as chiefly designed to restrain the sinful effects of the Fall is striking. But the point in question here is the function of magistracy in a world of fallen men, in which some are redeemed. In spite of their real differences in temper, Vane and Milton are in close agreement on that subject. See above, chap. XI, note 50.

[60]*An Epistle General, to the Mystical Body of Christ on Earth*, 1662, 3.

[61]*Ibid.*, 3.

[62]*The Retired Mans Meditations*, 60.

[63]*Ibid.*, 75.

[64]*An Epistle General*, 21, 31; *The Retired Mans Meditations*, 144.

[65]*The Retired Mans Meditations*, 154-5.

[66]See Hosmer, *Sir Henry Vane*, 429 ff.; and on Milton, Allen, *English Political Thought, 1603-1644*, 337.

[67]*A Healing Question propounded and resolved, upon occasion of the late*

*publique and seasonable Call to Humiliation,* (May 12) 1656. On March 14 Cromwell issued a proclamation calling for a fast and referring to possible faults in his government in a way which seemed to suggest that he wished (in Ludlow's words) "that the people would apply themselves to the Lord to discover that Achan which had so long obstructed the settlement of these distracted nations." See Willcock, *The Life of Sir Henry Vane,* 259.

[68]*The Retired Mans Meditations,* 393.

[69]*Ibid.,* 387, 393.

[70]*Ibid.,* 393-4.

[71]*Ibid.,* 395.

[72]*A Healing Question,* 3.

[73]*Ibid.,* 17.

[74]*An Epistle General,* 11.

[75]*A Healing Question,* 17.

[76]*Ibid.,* 15.

[77]*Ibid.,* 13.

[78]*Ibid.,* 19.

[79]*Ibid.,* 9.

[80]*Ibid.,* 19.

[81]*Ibid.,* 19.

[82]The sonnets to Fairfax (1648) and to Cromwell (1652), like the *Defensio Secunda,* contain warnings as well as commendations.

[83]*An Epistle,* 2.

[84]*The Retired Mans Meditations,* 394-5.

[85]*An Epistle,* 36.

[86]*Defensio,* VII, 29.

[87]*Ibid.,* 279.

[88]*The Tenure,* V, 57.

[89]*Defensio,* VII, 127-9.

[90]Woodhouse, *Puritanism and Liberty,* [36].

[91]*The Substance of what Sir Henry Vane Intended to have Spoken upon the Scaffold,* 1662, 4.

[92]*Defensio,* VII, 543.

## CHAPTER XIII

[1]*Defensio,* VII, 559.

[2]*De Doctrina Christiana,* XIV, 3, 9. Masson assumed that in the addition to the revised *Defensio* Milton was "thinking of his progress in *Paradise Lost*" (V, 574). Tillyard (*Milton,* 207) suggests that the remarks from the *De Doctrina* which I have quoted in the text indicate that the reference is to the theological treatise. Parker (*Milton's Contemporary Reputation,* 41) has recently complicated the question by arguing that Milton had in mind the subject matter of his next two pamphlets, *Of Civil Power* and *The Likeliest Means.* Since, as Parker notes, the situation which called forth Milton's brief treatments of religious liberty and of tithes arose *after* his promise of "yet greater things," it is difficult to understand how he could have foreseen the composition of the two pamphlets. That he had in mind their subject matter is certainly true; but the treatment of which he was thinking was the treatment in those chapters of *De Doctrina*

in which liberty and tithes are discussed in Latin, the universal language. Parker begs the question of tongue which invalidates both his and Masson's assumption. Milton was giving his hint in a Latin work which (as Parker says, 35) was more read abroad than in England. He consistently and naturally preferred Latin to English when writing for "men of all nations," as in *De Doctrina*. When he said in *Of Civil Power* (VI, 1) that the treatise belonged "to all Christian magistrates equally" and ought "to have been written in the common language of Christendom," he was not thinking of the *Defensio*'s promise but of its fulfilment in the Latin treatise in which the subject of the pamphlet was dealt with at length. In the pamphlets of 1659 he was hurrying to do for England what the *De Doctrina*, already largely written, was meant to do for religion throughout the world. This question is intimately connected with the date of the theological treatise; see below, chap. XVI, note 8.

[3]See above, chap. XII, note 16; and Tillyard, *Milton*, 192 ff.

[4]See above chap. VI, note 90.

[5]*A Treatise of Civil power in Ecclesiastical causes: shewing that it is not lawful for any power on earth to compell in matters of Religion*, 1659, registered February 16; *Considerations touching The likeliest means to remove Hirelings out of the church. Wherein is also discourc'd of {Tithes, Church-fees, Church-revenues; and whether any maintenance of ministers can be settl'd by law*, (August) 1659.

[6]Milton apologizes for the brevity of his discussion at the end of *Of Civil Power*, VI, 41.

[7]*The Likeliest Means*, VI, 44.

[8]*Of Civil Power*, VI, 1; and see *The Likeliest Means*, VI, 44.

[9]See below, chap. XV, note 1.

[10]Hanford, "The Date of Milton's *De Doctrina Christiana*," 315.

[11]On the ordinance see Jordan, *The Development of Religious Toleration*, III, 80. No enabling legislation was passed.

[12]Sonnet XVI. See Jordan, *The Development of Religious Toleration*, III, 140 ff.; Gardiner, *Commonwealth and Protectorate*, II, 28-35.

[13]Sonnet XVII.

[14]*The Tenure*, V, 42.

[15]See for example *Observations*, VI, 264; *Eikonoklastes*, V, 208, where Milton denounces the attempt of the Scots to impose their government on the English, "not Presbytery, but arch-presbytery, classical, provincial, and diocesan presbytery, claiming to itself a lordly power and superintendency both over flocks and pastors, over persons and congregations no way their own"; *Eikonoklastes*, V, 183, where he rejects "all antiquity that adds or varies from the Scripture."

[16]*Eikonoklastes*, V, 279; *Observations*, VI, 256.

[17]*Eikonoklastes*, V, 295-6; *Observations*, VI, 249-50, 264; *Defensio*, VII, 35, 463.

[18]*Observations*, VI, 251, 256.

[19]*Defensio Secunda*, VIII, 161, 236-7, 161-3; and see 179, 183.

[20]See Jordan, *The Development of Religious Toleration*, III, 353-8.

[21]See, for example, John Owen, *A Short Defensative about Church Government, Toleration*, 1646; and *Righteous Zeal Encouraged by Divine Protection; With a Discourse about Toleration*, 1648.

[22]See *The Humble Proposals . . . for the . . . Propagation of the. Gospel*, (December 2) 1652, and *A Declaration of The Faith and Order Owned and prac-*

*tised in the Congregational Churches In England; Agreed upon and consented unto By their Elders and Messengers In Their Meeting at the Savoy. October 12. 1658*; and also Gardiner, *Commonwealth and Protectorate*, II, 28-32, and Jordan, *The Development of Religious Toleration*, 140-3, 435-6.

[23]See Gardiner, *Commonwealth and Protectorate*, II, 290, 318-26, III, 61; Jordan, *The Development of Religious Toleration*, III, 152, 160; Gardiner, *Constitutional Documents*, 314 ff.; *Acts and Ordinances of the Interregnum*, ed. Firth and Rait, II, 821-2.

[24]Jordan, *The Development of Religious Toleration*, III, chap. II.

[25]See Kirby, *William Prynne*, 112 ff.

[26]Jordan, *The Development of Religious Toleration*, III, 140-3, 164-5.

[27]*An Apology for the Present Government*, 1654.

[28]Jordan, *The Development of Religious Toleration*, III, 406.

[29]Brown, *The Political Activities of the Baptists and Fifth Monarchy Men*, chap. III.

[30]*Ibid.*, 20, 34.

[31]*Of Civil Power* was addressed to Richard's Parliament; *The Likeliest Means* to the remnant of the Long Parliament, restored May 7, 1659. Both bodies debated the vexed ecclesiastical questions and received numerous petitions. To these discussions Milton refers in *The Likeliest Means*, VI, 44, 47. Among the many pamphlets written on the subject at this time may be mentioned Prynne's *Ten Considerable Queries concerning Tithes*, parts of which Milton refutes (VI, 65). For accounts of the situation see Brown, *The Political Activities of the Baptists*, 183, and Jordan, *The Development of Religious Toleration*, III, 253 ff.

[32]*Of Civil Power*, VI, 2; and see *The Likeliest Means*, VI, 45.

[33]*The Vanity of the Present Churches*, 34.

[34]*The Likeliest Means*, VI, 96.

[35]*Of Civil Power*, VI, 2.

[36]*Of Civil Power*, VI, 10, 18; *The Likeliest Means*, VI, 64, and see 83. See William Dell, *The Way Of True Peace*, 1649, in Woodhouse, *Puritanism and Liberty*, 303 ff., for an exposition of the extreme sectarian theory of church government; and Brown, *The Political Activities of the Baptists*, 4 ff.

[37]*Of Civil Power*, VI, 6.

[38]*Ibid.*, 6-7.

[39]Adam Steuart, *The Second Part of the Duply to M.S.*, 1644, 17; Samuel Rutherford, *A Free Disputation Against pretended Liberty of Conscience*, 1649; Thomas Hobbes, *De Corpore Politico*, 1650, in *The Elements of Law*, ed. Tönnies, 146, 164.

[40]Steuart, *The Second Part*, 166; Rutherford, *A Free Disputation*, 61; Hobbes, *Leviathan*, 269.

[41]*Of Civil Power*, VI, 5.

[42]*Of Civil Power*, VI, 5, 20, 29.

[43]*Ibid.*, 20.

[44]*Ibid.*, 36.

[45]*Ibid.*, 10.

[46]*Ibid.*, 27-8.

[47]*Ibid.*, 22.

[48]*Ibid.*, 10.

[49]*Ibid.*, 18.

[50]*Ibid.*, 20, 15-16.

[51]*Ibid.*, 39-40, 37; and see 22.

[52]*Ibid.*, 17.

[53]*Ibid.*, 39, 7; and see 17.

[54]*The Likeliest Means*, VI, 82.

[55]*Ibid.*, 82-3; and see 96.

[56]*Ibid.*, 89.

[57]*Ibid.*, 64, 74, 75-8.

[58]*Ibid.*, 80.

[59]Dell, *The Way of True Peace and Unity*, 1649, in Woodhouse, *Puritanism and Liberty*, 312; *The Likeliest Means*, VI, 99.

[60]*Ibid.*, 98. Cf. Dell, *The Way of True Peace*, 313.

[61]*The Likeliest Means*, VI, 93.

[62]*Ibid.*, 75.

[63]*Ibid.*, 95.

[64]*Ibid.*, 93.

[65]*Ibid.*, 96.

[66]*The Lord of Falklands Reply*, 95; Chillingworth, *The Religion of Protestants*, 12; Taylor, *Ductor Dubitantium*, *Works*, XI, 353, and see *The Liberty of Prophesying*, *Works*, V, 410.

[67]*A Sermon Preached before the Honourable House of Commons*, March 31, 1647, 14, 39.

[68]*Ibid.*, sig. A1.

[69]See the argument of Hewitt in the Whitehall Debates, Woodhouse, *Puritanism and Liberty*, 27; and of Dell, *The Way of True Peace*, 313.

[70]For an account of these disputes, see Jones, *Ancients and Moderns*, 119, and Brown, *The Political Activities of the Baptists*, 36.

[71]Webster, *Academiarum Examen*, 1654, 16, quotes the *De Augmentis* on the separation of theology and natural philosophy. See Jones, *Ancients and Moderns*, 105.

[72]*Academiarum Examen*, 16, 2, 13, 7.

[73]William Dell, *The Stumbling-Stone*, (April 20) 1653, 24, 39. See also Dell, *The Way of True Peace*, 1649, in Woodhouse, *Puritanism and Liberty*, 310; *The Right Reformation of Learning, Schooles and Universities according to the State of the Gospel and the True Light that Shines Therein*, 1653, 30 (ascribed to Dell by Jones, *Ancients and Moderns*, 311); *The Tryal of Spirits Both in Teachers & Hearers*, 1653.

[74]*The Hireling Ministry None of Christs*, (April 8) 1652, 15, 3-4.

[75]*Ibid.*, 14, 15. Williams censures the "sacriligious and superstitious degrees" and the "vain and superstitious studies" through which the universities make "a trade of selling God himself" (16-17).

[76]*The Likeliest Means*, VI, 96, 93.

[77]*Ibid.*, 75.

[78]*Ibid.*, 75, 98.

[79]*Ibid.*, 94, 80-1.

[80]*The Vanity of the Present Churches*, 1649, 2. Like Milton, the author of this pamphlet attacks the wealth and luxury of the clergy, episcopal, Presbyterian, and Independent, insists that Scripture is the only source of truth, and that "for how long work soever ministers and pretended preachers make of it, to

maintain themselves and families in wealth, plenty and honour, necessary doctrines are not at all hard to be understood, nor require long time to learn them" (7-8).

[81]*Church-Levellers, or Vanity of Vanities and Certainty of Delusion discovered in the late pamphlet called The Vanity of the Present Churches*, (June 22) 1649, 3.

[82]*The Likeliest Means*, VI, 78.

[83]Hanford, "The Date of Milton's De Doctrina Christiana," 315-16; see *De Doctrina Christiana*, XIV, 7.

[84]*Defensio Secunda*, VIII, 73.

[85]*Ibid.*, 71, 11. On the effects of Milton's blindness on his spirit, expressed in the two sonnets on it and in *Defensio Secunda*, see Tillyard, *Milton*, 187-91, 202-5, and Brown, *Milton's Blindness*.

[86]Letter to Emeric Bigot, XII, 87.

[87]*The Likeliest Means*, VI, 75.

## CHAPTER XIV

[1]Woodhouse, *Puritanism and Liberty*, "The Whitehall Debates," 136. The debate arose from the proposed Agreement of the People, and concerned the questions, "Whether the magistrate have, or ought to have, any compulsive and restrictive power in matters of religion?" and "Whether to have [in the Agreement] any reserve to except religious things, or only to give power in natural and civil things and to say nothing of religion?" (*ibid.*, 125).

[2]The Agreement had been drawn up by a committee of Levellers and sectaries under Lilburne, who had included a provision against the magistrate's power "in or about matters of faith, religion, or God's worship" (Woodhouse, *Puritanism and Liberty*, 362). In the debate which followed the presentation of this original draft to the Council of Officers of the Army, John Goodwin, Collier, Sprigge, Peter, Wildman, Lilburne, Overton, supported the above provision, while Ireton, Nye, and other Independents opposed it. The Independent ministers and officers succeeded in revising the provision before the Agreement was presented to Parliament, January 20, 1649, to permit the public support of the ministry but no compulsion and no restraint upon "any person professing Christianity." Lilburne drew public attention to the debates by publishing the original version of the Agreement in *Foundations of Freedom*, (December 15) 1648. See Woodhouse, *Puritanism and Liberty*, [32-5], 361-2.

[3]*Of Civil Power*, VI, 2.

[4]*Ibid.*, 25.

[5]*The Likeliest Means*, VI, 50-1.

[6]*Ibid.*, 53-4, 57.

[7]*Ibid.*, 57.

[8]*Ibid.*, 51, 74, 82.

[9]Woodhouse, *Puritanism and Liberty*, 130-1.

[10]*Ibid.*, 153-4; 140, 150-2.

[11]*Ibid.*, 155-6. For the Presbyterian argument from the Old Testament, see Adam Steuart, *Some Observations . . . Upon the Apologeticall Narration*, 1644, 62; Thomas Edwards, *Antapologia*, 1644, 68; and Rutherford, *A Free Disputation*, 1649, 233.

[12]See Jordan, *The Development of Religious Toleration*, III, 329, 433.

[13]Chap. XXIII, sec. III: "The civil magistrate may not assume to himself the administration of the word and sacraments, or the power of the keys of the kingdom of heaven; yet he hath authority, and it is his duty, to take order that unity and peace be preserved in the church, that the truth of God be kept pure and entire, that all blasphemies and heresies be suppressed, all corruptions and abuses in worship and discipline prevented or reformed, and all the ordinances of God duly settled, administered, and observed."

[14]Woodhouse, *Puritanism and Liberty*, 157-8.

[15]*Ibid.*, 160-1, 163, 164-5. The same argument is set forth in Collier's *The Decision and Clearing of the Great Point now in Controversie, about the interest of Christ and the Civil Magistrate, in the rule of Government in this world*, 1659. See Jordan, *The Development of Religious Toleration*, III, 526-31. Williams again emphasized the difference between the Jewish and Christian churches in *The Hireling Ministry*, 1652, 10, and in *The Bloudy Tenent Yet More Bloody*, (April 28) 1652.

[16]Woodhouse, *Puritanism and Liberty*, 141, 145.

[17]*The Leveller*, 1659, 12-13: ". . . there are two parts of true religion: the first consists in the right conceptions or receptions of God, as he is revealed by Christ, and sincere adoration of him in the heart or spirit, and the expressions or declarations of that worship outwardly, in and by the use of those ordinances that are appointed by Christ for that purpose. The second part of it consists in works of righteousness and mercy towards all men. . . . The first part, being wholly built upon the foundation of revealed truths, doth in its own nature absolutely exclude all possibility of man's being lord of his brother's faith. . . . But the second part falls under the cognisance or judgment of man and the law-maker's or magistrate's power" (*ibid.*, 11-12).

[18]*Of Civil Power*, VI, 25, 16, 26; Williams, *The Hireling Ministry*, 1652, 10.

[19]*Of Civil Power*, VI, 40.

[20]*Ibid.*, 24.

[21]*Ibid.*, 26.

[22]See *The Likeliest Means*, VI, 50-1, 67, for the argument against those who maintain that tithes and the Sabbath are commanded by the perpetual moral law; and VI, 72, for the argument that marriage is "of itself a civil ordinance, a household contract, a thing indifferent and free to the whole race of mankind, not as religious, but as men. . . ." On August 24, 1653, Cromwell's Nominated Parliament had passed an act declaring that the state would recognize only marriages performed by a Justice of the Peace; see Gardiner, *Commonwealth and Protectorate*, II, 242.

[23]*Of Civil Power*, VI, 23-4. At this point Milton criticizes those ministers who would "give to the state in their settling petition that command of our implicit belief which they deny in their settled confession both to the state and to the church." The reference seems to be to the Savoy *Declaration* of the Independents.

[24]*The Casting Down of the last and strongest hold of Satan, or, A Treatise against Toleration*, (June 28) 1647, 149.

[25]*A Declaration of the Faith and Order . . . in the Congregational Churches*, 1658; in Walker, *Creeds and Platforms*, 393.

[26]*Conscience*, 9-10.

[27] *Of Civil Power*, VI, 11, 12.

[28] *The Bloudy Tenent*, 59.

[29] See Gardiner, *Civil War*, III, 139, and Jordan, *The Development of Religious Toleration*, III, 91-3.

[30] *Some Modest and Humble Queries Concerning . . . An Ordinance Presented to the Honourable House of Commons*, 1646, 5; Jordan, *The Development of Religious Toleration*, III, 389.

[31] *Thirty Queries*, (March 1) 1653, 5; *The Hireling Ministry*, "Epistle Dedicatory," and 24.

[32] *Of Civil Power*, VI, 12.

[33] *The Institution of Christian Religion*, 17.

[34] *Of Civil Power*, VI, 12.

[35] Orders for the regulation of printing, chiefly directed against news-sheets, had been issued in 1649, 1653, and 1655. See *Acts and Ordinances*, ed. Firth and Rait, II, 696, 245.

[36] *Of Civil Power*, VI, 13. Milton presented the same argument for the equal liberty of all Protestants in *Of True Religion, Haeresie, Schism, Toleration And what best means may be us'd against the growth of Popery*, published early in 1673 in the controversy which followed the Declaration of Indulgence (March 15, 1672). Because it lies outside the period with which I am concerned, I have not analysed the pamphlet in the text. In general it repeats the main arguments of *Of Civil Power*, though it is far less doctrinaire in tone. References are given below to passages which confirm my interpretation of *Of Civil Power*. For the argument for the toleration of all who accept Scripture as the rule of their consciences, see VI, 166, 170.

[37] *Ibid.*, 12-13, 14, 16. This definition is repeated in *Of True Religion*: "Heresy therefore is a religion taken up and believed from the traditions of men and additions to the word of God" (VI, 167); "Heresy is in the will and choice profestly against Scripture; error is against the will in misunderstanding Scripture" (VI, 168).

[38] Woodhouse, *Puritanism and Liberty*, 144.

[39] *Of Civil Power*, VI, 14.

[40] *Ibid.*, 16. See also *Defensio*, VII, 35: "It is for the church to expel them from the company of the faithful, not for the magistrate to banish them the country, provided they break no civil law."

[41] *The Religion of Protestants*, 23.

[42] Woodhouse, *Puritanism and Liberty*, 143.

[43] *Ibid.*, 153-4.

[44] *Anapologesiates Antapologias, Or, The inexcusablenesse of that Grand Accusation of the Brethren called Antapologia*, 1646, "Preface"; Jordan, *The Development of Religious Toleration*, III, 397.

[45] *Innocency and Truth Triumphing together*, (January 8) 1645, 5.

[46] *Of Civil Power*, VI, 1.

[47] *Ibid.*, 4.

[48] *Ibid.*, 2.

[49] *The Institution of Christian Religion*, 408.

[50] Woodhouse, *Puritanism and Liberty*, 155-6; and see 146, 167.

[51] *Ibid.*, 161.

[52] *Ibid.*, 157.

[53]*Hagiomastix: Or The Scourge Of The Saints Displayed*, (Feb. 5) 1646, 47.

[54]*Thirty Queries*, (March 1) 1653, 16, 3. Cf. Williams, *The Hireling Ministry*, 25-6: "opinions offensive are of two sorts, some savouring of impiety and some of incivility"; the magistrate has no power over the first; "opinions of incivility, doubtless the opinions as well as practices, are the proper object of the civil sword . . . ." It will be observed that the admission of uncivil opinions destroys the simple division between the power of the church over the inward man and of the state over the outward man.

[55]*A Healing Question*, (May 12), 1656, 6.

[56]*Of Civil Power*, VI, 5.

[57]*Ibid.*, 40-1. Sewell, "Milton's *De Doctrina Christiana*," 547, thinks this passage indicates that Milton himself had not yet made up his mind on the relationship of the laws. I cannot share this view. See below, chap. XVI, note 7.

[58]*The Bloudy Tenent*, 122-3, 307: "it is true the second table contains the law of nature, the law moral and civil, yet . . . ."

[59]*The Ancient Bounds*, 1645, 7.

[60]*Ibid.*, 5.

[61]*Of Civil Power*, VI, 24; see also 39: "the settlement of religion belongs only to each particular church by persuasive and spiritual means within itself, . . . the defence only of the church belongs to the magistrate."

[62]*Ibid.*, 22-3.

[63]*Ibid.*, 3.

[64]*The Bloudy Tenent*, 301; and see 183, 266. Cf. Dell, *The Tryal of Spirits*, 1653, on those who "would have the secular magistrate to have right and power to enforce men to such a religion as himself judges true, by the help and counsel of those ministers which himself judges orthodox." See Jordan, *The Development of Religious Toleration*, III, 510; and also Dell, *The Way of True Peace*, in Woodhouse, *Puritanism and Liberty*, 314-15.

[65]*Thirty Queries*, 5, 9.

[66]*Of Civil Power*, VI, 46.

[67]*Observations*, VI, 263, 251.

[68]*Of Civil Power*, VI, 11.

[69]This act announced the Parliament's determination to punish, first with imprisonment and then with banishment, those holding "atheistical, blasphemous or execrable opinions," particularly those of an antinomian kind. It deplored "the growth of the aforesaid . . . opinions and practices, tending to the dishonouring of God, the scandal of Christian religion and the professors thereof, and destructive to human society" (Scobell, *A Collection of Acts and Ordinances . . .*, 1640 . . . 1656, 124-6). On its passing, see Jordan, *The Development of Religious Toleration*, III, 133-5; Gardiner, *Commonwealth and Protectorate*, I, 395. It was, of course, much less severe than the Presbyterian act of May 2, 1648; see Jordan, *The Development of Religious Toleration*, III, 111-15.

[70]*Of Civil Power*, VI, 20.

[71]*The Bloudy Tenent*, 174. On the attitude towards Roman Catholics, see Jordan, *The Development of Religious Toleration*, III, 179-94.

[72]*Observations*, VI, 254; and see 251.

[73]*Of Civil Power*, VI, 14, 19. In *Of True Religion* Milton was still arguing against the public or private toleration of papists because their "state activities"

were dangerous and their idolatry was offensive to God, who had "declared against all idolatry" (VI, 172). He also urged again that "popery is the only or the greatest heresy" (VI, 167), and distinguished between the true Protestant conscience and the corrupt popish conscience: "we have no warrant to regard conscience which is not grounded on Scripture . . ." (VI, 173).

[74]*Eikonoklastes*, V, 216; *Of Civil Power*, VI, 19.

[75]*Of Civil Power*, VI, 24.

[76]Woodhouse, *Puritanism and Liberty*, 159-60.

[77]*The Institution of Christian Religion*, 406, 404: "that idolatry, sacrileges against the name of God, blasphemies against his truth, and other offences of religion, may not rise up and be scattered among the people" (*ibid.*, 403).

[78]*A Healing Question*, 5.

[79]*Ibid.*, 6.

[80]See *Observations*, VI, 251, 263; and *Of Civil Power*, VI, 24.

[81]Quoted by Firth, *Oliver Cromwell*, 267.

[82]*Observations*, VI, 249.

[83]*Ibid.*, 263.

[84]*The Leveller*, 1659, 11.

[85]*Of Civil Power*, VI, 21-2; and see 37.

[86]*Ibid.*, 33, 35-6.

[87]*Ibid.*, 34.

[88]*Ibid.*, 38-9.

[89]*Innocencies Triumph*, 1644, 8.

[90]Woodhouse, *Puritanism and Liberty*, 143.

[91]*Of Civil Power*, VI, 28.

[92]*Ibid.*, 28-31.

[93]*Ibid.*, 30, 32.

[94]*Ibid.*, 39.

[95]*Ibid.*, 39; *The Likeliest Means*, VI, 48; *Of Civil Power*, VI, 28.

[96]*The Likeliest Means*, VI, 47.

[97]*Of Civil Power*, VI, 31-2.

[98]*The Way of True Peace*, in Woodhouse, *Puritanism and Liberty*, 316. Cf. Calvin, *The Institution of Christian Religion*, 147, 153.

[99]*An Apology for the . . . Quakers*, 3, 92.

[100]*Of Civil Power*, VI, 6.

[101]*Ibid.*, 26.

[102]*Ibid.*, 21.

## CHAPTER XV

[1]*A Letter to a Friend, concerning the Ruptures of the Commonwealth*, dated October 20, 1659, first published from a manuscript in Toland's edition of Milton's *Prose Works*, 1698 (Masson, V, 617). *Proposals of Certaine Expedients for the Preventing of a Civil War now feard, & the settling of a Firme Government by J. M.*, first published from the Columbia Manuscript in the Columbia *Works* (XVIII, 501). *The Readie & Easie Way to Establish A Free Commonwealth, and the Excellence thereof Compar'd with The inconveniences and dangers of re-admitting kingship in this nation*, (March 3) 1660. *The Present Means and Brief Delineation of a Free Commonwealth . . .; In a Letter to General Monk*; undated,

but probably sent to Monk with a copy of the above; first published by Toland in 1698 (Masson, V, 656). *Brief Notes upon a Late Sermon, Titl'd, The Fear of God and the King; Preachd and since Publishd, by Matthew Griffith, D.D. . . . , 1660* between March 31 (registration of Griffith's sermon) and April 20 (Thomason's date for L'Estrange's reply, *No Blinde Guides*). *The Readie and Easie Way to Establish A Free Commonwealth. . . . The second edition revis'd and augmented . . . .* 1660, about April 25, when the Convention Parliament met (Masson, V, 689).

[2]*A Letter to a Friend*, VI, 101. See above, chap. XII, note 16. In a letter to Peter Heimbach of December 18, 1657, Milton mentions, "my very few intimacies with the men of influence, almost shut up at home, as I prefer to be . . . ." (XII, 103).

[3]*The Readie and Easie Way*, VI, 134.

[4]Milton was imprisoned for a time, and released on December 15, 1660. See Masson, VI, 192-5.

[5]See *Proposals*, XVIII, 4-5, and *A Letter*, VI, 104.

[6]See Gardiner, *Commonwealth and Protectorate*, I, 271, II, 198.

[7]*A Letter*, VI, 102. The letter was written while Vane and some other members of the Rump were discussing the establishment of a new government with the Army officers. On the events of these months see Firth, "Anarchy and the Restoration," and Davies, "The Army and the Downfall of Richard Cromwell."

[8]*A Letter*, VI, 102, 104-5.

[9]Milton proposed that either the Rump should be recalled or the Army should choose a Council of State including those members of the Rump who accepted his two conditions, both Council of State and Army to be kept "during life." This was in line with Vane's efforts, and suggests that the letter may have been written to him. See Firth, "Anarchy and the Restoration," 546.

[10]*Readie and Easie Way*, first edition, VI, 360.

[11]*Proposals*, XVIII, 4.

[12]*Readie and Easie Way*, first edition, VI, 363-4, second edition, VI, 126.

[13]*A Declaration of the General Council of the Officers of the Army: Agreed upon at Wallingford-house, 27 October, 1659*, 1.

[14]*Readie and Easie Way*, VI, 149, 117.

[15]*Brief Notes*, VI, 159.

[16]*Ibid.*, 158; see also *Readie and Easie Way*, VI, 146.

[17]*Readie and Easie Way*, VI, 113, 117.

[18]*Proposals*, XVIII, 3; *Readie and Easie Way*, VI, 126.

[19]See Roger L'Estrange, *No Blinde Guides*, April 20, 1660; *The Censure of the Rota Upon . . . The Ready and Easie way . . .* (March 30) 1660, an anonymous royalist pamphlet in which James Harrington and his associates are represented as criticizing Milton's proposals; and G.S., *The Dignity of Kingship Asserted: In Answer to Mr. Milton's Ready and Easie way . . .*, 1660. On these and other attacks, see Masson, V, 658-66, 689-94; and Parker, *Milton's Contemporary Reputation*.

[20]See above, chap. XII; and *The Ready and Easy Way*, ed. Clark, xxix-xxxi.

[21]See Firth, "Anarchy and the Restoration"; and Jordan, *The Development of Religious Toleration*, III, 253-66. *The Dignity of Kingship Asserted*, 1660, an answer to *The Readie and Easie Way* recently ascribed to George Starkey by W. R. Parker, is a good example of Presbyterian royalism.

[22]Woodhouse, *Puritanism and Liberty*, [18], [53-60], [82-6].

[23]Brown, *Political Activities of the Baptists*, chap. III.

[24]Vane's *Healing Question* was reprinted in 1659. It was attacked by Baxter in *A Key for Catholics* and in *A Holy Commonwealth*, 1659, and defended by John Rogers in *A Vindication of . . . Sir Henry Vane*, (June 7) 1659, and *A Christian Concertation with Mr. Prin, Mr. Baxter, Mr. Harrington*, (September 20) 1659, and by Henry Stubbe in *Malice Rebuked, Or A Character of Mr. Richard Baxters Abilities*, (September) 1659.

[25]Some of the Levellers, among them Wildman, were members of the Rota Club; see Pease, *The Leveller Movement*, 352, and Smith, *Harrington and his Oceana*, 111.

[26]Aubrey, *Brief Lives*, I, 289; *The Ready and Easy Way*, ed. Clark, xlix-l; Parker, *Milton's Contemporary Reputation*, 280.

[27]*Readie and Easie Way*, first edition, VI, 363, second edition, VI, 147. In the first edition (perhaps partly following Vane's proposals for a perpetual council in *A Healing Question*), Milton suggests that the third should be elected by lot or suffrage of the rest, not by the people as in Harrington's system. In the longer discussion in the second edition, which probably resulted from the attack of *The Censure of the Rota*, the choice is left to the people.

[28]*Readie and Easie Way*, VI, 127-8.

[29]*Oceana*, in *The Oceana and Other Works*, 1737, 45; see also on Hobbes, 37-8.

[30]*Ibid.*, 40, 54, 48; and see Smith, *Harrington and his Oceana*, 36-52.

[31]*The Prerogative of Popular Government*, 1658; *Works*, 241.

[32]*Oceana*, *Works*, 75-6; and see *A Discourse upon this Saying, The Spirit of the Nation is not yet to be trusted with Liberty*, 1659 (a reply to Stubbe), *Works*, 602: "The spirit of the people is in no wise to be trusted with their liberty, but by stated laws or orders; so the trust is not in the spirit of the people, but in the frame of those orders . . . ."

[33]*The Leveller*, 1659, approved Harrington's proposal for two houses (7). Harrington criticized *The Agreement of the People* in *The Art of Lawgiving*, 1659 (*Works*, 430-1); but his objection is not to its principles but to the machinery which makes for anarchy because it leaves the ultimate decision to the people under arms.

[34]*Readie and Easie Way*, VI, 130.

[35]*Ibid.*, 127, 130.

[36]*Ibid.*, 125.

[37]*Ibid.*, first edition, VI, 360.

[38]*Ibid.*, 133-4.

[39]*Aphorisms Political*, 1659, *Works*, 515; see also *Oceana*, *Works*, 193.

[40]*Likeliest Means*, VI, 45. The Harringtonian petition was published as *The Humble Petition of divers Well-affected Persons, delivered The 6th day of July, 1659. To the supreme authority, the Parliament of the Commonwealth*, (July 7), 1659. See *The Ready and Easy Way*, ed. Clark, 112.

[41]*Of Civil Power*, VI, 2.

[42]See Brown, *Political Activities of the Baptists*, chap. VII.

[43]*Ibid.*, 187-9; Jordan, *The Development of Religious Toleration*, IV, 335-6.

[44]*A Holy Commonwealth*, 226, 224.

[45]*A Christian Concertation*, 75. Like Milton, Baxter and Rogers objected that

the system of rotation would prevent good men from being re-elected; *A Holy Commonwealth*, 233; *A Christian Concertation*, 81; *Readie and Easie Way*, VI, 128.

[46]*Oceana, Works*, 74.

[47]Baxter, *Holy Commonwealth*, 227, 92.

[48]*The Humble Petition of divers Well-affected Persons, delivered The 6th day of July, 1659*, 8.

[49]*Lilburns Ghost, With a Whip in one hand, to scourge Tyrants out of Authority; And Balme in the other* . . . (June 22), 1659, 5.

[50]*The Fifth Monarchy; or Kingdom of Christ, In opposition to the Beasts' Asserted* . . . , (August 23) 1659, 51. *The Declaration and Proclamation of the Army of God, owned by the Lord of Hosts in many Victories* . . . , (June 9) 1659, 4.

[51]Baxter, *Holy Commonwealth*, sig. a3; Harrington, *A Parallel of the Spirit of the People, with the Spirit of Mr Rogers; A sufficient Answer to Mr Stubs, Works*, 618.

[52]*A Letter*, VI, 105.

[53]*Readie and Easie Way*, VI, 114.

[54]*Ibid.*, 114-15.

[55]*Ibid.*, 140-1.

[56]*The Censure of the Rota*, 13, 15.

[57]Lambert, who had been committed to the Tower March 6, escaped on April 9; but his attempted insurrection was easily overcome on the twenty-second. See Masson, V, 565, and Firth, "Anarchy and the Restoration," 557.

[58]*Readie and Easie Way*, first edition, VI, 361.

[59]*A Christian Concertation*, 73; *M. Harrington's Parallel Unparallel'd* . . . , (September 22) 1659, 3.

[60]*A Christian Concertation*, 60.

[61]*Malice Rebuked, Or A Character of Mr. Richard Baxters Abilities*, 16. In support of his scheme Harrington argued that the Apostles "intended the government of the church to be democratical or popular" (*Oceana, Works*, 49).

[62]*An Essay In Defence of the Good Old Cause* . . . , (September) 1659; Preface.

[63]*A Letter to An Officer of the Army concerning A Select Senate* . . . , (October 26) 1659, 1, 73; *The Common-wealth of Oceana Put into the Ballance and found too light* . . . , 1659. 10.

[64]*An Essay In Defence of the Good Old Cause*, Preface; *A Letter to An Officer*, 5.

[65]*A Letter to An Officer*, 49.

[66]*Readie and Easie Way*, VI, 145.

[67]*Ibid.*, 160.

[68]*Ibid.*, 123, 147-8.

[69]*Ibid.*, 123.

[70]*A Letter*, VI, 106.

[71]*Readie and Easie Way*, VI, 131-2.

[72]*The Substance of what Sir Henry Vane Intended to have Spoken upon the Scaffold* . . . , 1662, 7.

[73]*Readie and Easie Way*, VI, 119, 116.

[74]*Ibid.*, 116.

[75]*A Letter to An Officer*, 10.

[76]*A Discourse upon this Saying, The Spirit of the Nation is not yet to be*

*trusted with Liberty, lest it introduce Monarchy, or invade the Liberty of Conscience*, 1659, *Works*, 601.

[77]*Aphorisms Political*, 1659, *Works*, 516.

[78]*A Light Shining out of Darkness*, 1659, 174-5, in reference to *Of Reformation* (see Parker, *Milton's Contemporary Reputation*, 97-8); *An Essay In Defence of the Good Old Cause*, 20-1.

[79]*Readie and Easie Way*, first edition, VI, 365-6.

[80]*Ibid.*, second edition, VI, 142-3.

[81]*Proposals of Certaine Expedients*, XVIII, 4.

[82]*Ibid.*, 5.

[83]*A Christian Concertation*, 48; *A Vindication of that Prudent and Honourable Knight, Sir Henry Vane*, 14.

[84]*Readie and Easie Way*, VI, 143, 138.

[85]*Ibid.*, 142.

[86]*Proposals*, XVIII, 6-7.

[87]*Readie and Easie Way*, VI, 129.

[88]*Holy Commonwealth*, 208.

[89]*Ibid.*, 214.

[90]*Readie and Easie Way*, VI, 137-8; *Brief Notes*, VI, 156.

[91]*Holy Commonwealth*, sig. d2$^{v}$.

[92]*Ibid.*, sig. d3.

[93]*Ibid.*, 246. Baxter proposed that civil rights be refused such men as the Jews were commanded by the Law of Moses to cut off from their commonwealth (175-9, 249-51).

[94]*The Fifth Monarchy*, 50.

[95]*The Christian Commonwealth: or, The Civil Policy of The Rising Kingdom of Jesus Christ. Written Before the Interruption of the Government*..., (October 26) 1659, Preface, and 3.

[96]*The Declaration and Proclamation of the Army of God*, 4.

[97]*A Christian Concertation*, 31.

[98]*The Dignity of Kingship Asserted*, 1660, 65-6.

[99]*Readie and Easie Way*, VI, 113.

[100]*Brief Notes*, VI, 158.

[101]*Aphorisms Political, Works*, 522.

[102]*A Christian Concertation*, 31, 47.

[103]*Ibid.*, 59-60. Rogers' effort to reconcile the conflicting arguments of the republicans and Millenarians is worth quoting at length: "There be two extremes men have a mighty propension to in the stating of the Cause; both which are wisely avoided in the *Healing Question*. 1. That wherein men do give up our Cause to merely natural right, without respect at all to the forfeitures of them that have warred, fought against it, betrayed it, and given up their interest in it to the King or single person; putting all unto a like capacity, (viz.) the cavaliers, common enemies to this right, and the faithful adherents to the Cause, the conquered and the conquerors, upon such grounds too [as] are very dangerous and destructive to the Cause. (Mr. Harrington and others go that way.) 2. That wherein (upon the single account of our conquests) others go to the challenging of their rights and liberties and stating of the Cause without any consideration at all of the natural rights and freedom which people have to choose their representatives in the commonwealth. (This way Mr. Feake and others

go.) But these extremes are very excellently waived, and yet the substance of both as admirably and amiably comprehended in the *Healing Question*, wherein the Cause is set upon both its feet."

[104]Edward Bagshaw, *Saintship No Ground of Soveraignty: or A Treatise Tending to prove That the Saints, barely considered as such, ought not to Govern*, 1660, 14. Cf. Harrington, *Oceana*, *Works*, 75. Baxter (*Holy Commonwealth*, sig. a3 ff.) repudiated the claims of the saints while arguing that, "though godliness give men no authority, yet as freemen we have a certain liberty, and wickedness may forfeit this liberty; and therefore I shall thus far close with you, that the church and commonwealth should be very near commensurate, and that proved ungodly persons should neither choose nor be chosen."

[105]*Readie and Easie Way*, VI, 119-20.

[106]*Ibid.*, 119.

[107]*The Censure of the Rota*, 10. A somewhat similar refutation was developed by G. S.: see *The Dignity of Kingship Asserted*, 88.

[108]*Readie and Easie Way*, VI, 119.

[109]*Ibid.*, 122, 143.

[110]*The Censure of the Rota*, 12.

[111]*No Blinde Guides*, 8.

[112]*Readie and Easie Way*, VI, 119, 124.

[113]*Ibid.*, 132.

[114]*Ibid.*, 133.

[115]*Ibid.*, 148.

[116]*Holy Commonwealth*, 491.

[117]*Readie and Easie Way*, VI, 148.

## CHAPTER XVI

[1]*Humane Nature*, 1; *Leviathan*, 2.

[2]Woodhouse, *Puritanism and Liberty*, [37]: "It is unnecessary to posit a unity in all Puritan thought; it is sufficient to recognize a continuity."

[3]Life of Milton by Edward Phillips, *Early Lives*, ed. Darbishire, 61.

[4]*De Doctrina Christiana*, XIV, 5.

[5]*Defensio Secunda*, VIII, 137.

[6]Anonymous life of Milton, *Early Lives*, ed. Darbishire, 29.

[7]The question of the period of Milton's life with which the *De Doctrina Christiana* (as it now stands) should be associated seems to me to have been settled by Kelley's recent volume, *This Great Argument. A Study of Milton's "De Doctrina Christiana" as a Gloss upon "Paradise Lost."* He is concerned to establish an intimate relationship between the theological treatise and the epic, and so refers only incidentally to the connection between the treatise and the prose works; but his admirably developed argument for believing that the treatise as we now have it expresses Milton's beliefs in the period in which *Paradise Lost* was being composed—in the years immediately preceding and immediately following the Restoration—also provides a justification for my use of the treatise as the record of the opinions at which Milton finally arrived in consequence of the development of his thought in the controversial period. There is no need to present here even a summary of the argument whereby Kelley disposes of the contention of Sewell, that the state of the manuscript now in the Record Office and the relationship of its ideas to those of *Paradise Lost* require us to regard the

treatise as expressive of Milton's opinions at a time subsequent to the composition of that poem. In the second and third chapters of Kelley's study, the reader will find a full and exact account of the manuscript and a detailed examination of the revisions made by Milton in the version copied out by an amanuensis between 1658 and 1661. Kelley has shown that these revisions modify Milton's opinions in no significant degree. Since this examination exists, I have thought it unnecessary to complicate my exposition of Milton's ideas at the end of the revolution by noting which of the passages quoted from the *De Doctrina Christiana* occur in the 1658-61 draught and which are revisions. The doubtful reader may be referred to the notes of the Columbia *Works*. To Kelley's discussion of the revisions I have nothing of importance to add; but perhaps I may be allowed to observe that it fully supports the reasoning and the conclusions, based on an examination of the manuscript, which I embodied in the thesis deposited in the Library of the University of London in 1937.

[8]*De Doctrina Christiana*, XIV, 5, 7.

[9]*Ibid.*, 9.

[10]Chap. II.

[11]Chap. III, sec. 1.

[12]*Ibid.*, sec. 2.

[13]Chap. IV.

[14]Chap. V.

[15]Chap. VII, secs. 1-2.

[16]*Ibid.*, secs. 3-4.

[17]Chap. VI.

[18]Chap. VII, sec. 5.

[19]Chaps. VIII and IX.

[20]Chap. X.

[21]Chap. XI.

[22]Chap. XII.

[23]Chap. XIII, secs. 1-4.

[24]Chap. XIV.

[25]Chap. XIII, sec. 5.

[26]Chap. XIV.

[27]Chap. XV, secs. 1-3.

[28]*Ibid.*, secs. 4-5.

## CHAPTER XVII

[1]*De Doctrina Christiana*, XIV, 5, 3.

[2]*Ibid.*, XV, 113, 179-81; Calvin, *The Institution of Christian Religion*, 45, 59.

[3]*De Doctrina Christiana*, XV, 113, 115.

[4]*Ibid.*, 113.

[5]*Conscience*, 100.

[6]*De Doctrina Christiana*, XV, 181.

[7]*Ibid.*, 205, 193.

[8]*Ibid.*, 209, 211; XIV, 131.

[9]*Ibid.*, XV, 213.

[10]*The Institution of Christian Religion*, 65, 66.

[11]*Ibid.*, 69-70.

[12]*The Marrow of Sacred Divinity*, 62-3.

[13]*The Institution of Christian Religion*, 72.

[14]*De Doctrina Christiana*, XV, 205.

[15]*Ibid.*, 207.

[16]*Ibid.*, 209, 211.

[17]See Calvin, *The Institution of Christian Religion*, book III, chap. 21; and Prynne, *Anti-Arminianisme*, 1630, in Woodhouse, *Puritanism and Liberty*, 232.

[18]*De Doctrina Christiana*, XV, 213-15. This is, of course, the Arminian objection which Milton set aside in *The Doctrine and Discipline of Divorce*, III, 440-2; see Barker, "Christian Liberty in Milton's Divorce Pamphlets," 158.

[19]*De Doctrina Christiana*, XIV, 109.

[20]*Ibid.*, 105.

[21]*Ibid.*, 103, 107.

[22]*The Institution of Christian Religion*, book III, chap. 22, sec. 10; Prynne, *Anti-Arminianisme*, in Woodhouse, *Puritanism and Liberty*, 232.

[23]*De Doctrina Christiana*, XIV, 147.

[24]*Ibid.*, 107.

[25]*Ibid.*, XV, 213.

[26]See Barker, "Christian Liberty in Milton's Divorce Pamphlets."

[27]*The Divine Authority Of The Scriptures Asserted*, 1648, 169. See also *Sion-Colledg Visited. Or, Some brief Animadversions upon a Pamphlet . . . A Testimonie to the Truth of Jesus Christ*, 1648; *The Remedie of Unreasonableness*, 1650; *Redemption Redeemed*, 1651; *The Pagans Debt, and Dowry*, 1651; and Jordan, *The Development of Religious Toleration*, III, 402-10.

[28]*The Pagans Debt, and Dowry*, 1651, 35.

[29]*Ibid.*, 10.

[30]*Ibid.*, 13.

[31]*De Doctrina Christiana*, XV, 349, 403-5. Cf. Goodwin, *The Divine Authority Of The Scriptures*, 18.

[32]Barker, "Milton's Schoolmasters," 530.

[33]Jordan, *The Development of Religious Toleration*, III, 403, seems to me somewhat to exaggerate the sceptical and humanitarian elements in Goodwin's thought, especially when he says that Goodwin evolved "an almost unlimited doctrine of general redemption." The doctrine of general "calling" must be sharply distinguished from the doctrine of general redemption. The first is compatible with both liberalism and a realistic view of human nature; the second only with sentimentalism.

[34]*The Divine Authority Of The Scriptures*, 169: "To conceive that God applieth himself with such moving and melting expressions of mercy, tenderness . . . towards his creature man as the Scripture emphatically asserts that he doth, promising them life and glory if they will believe and turn to him, and yet to suppose that these men . . . are destitute of all power to do what he requires of them, is to represent the glorious God . . . rather as laughing the world to scorn . . . than as a God truly desirous and intending to relieve it."

[35]See *A Fresh Discovery Of The High-Presbyterian Spirit*, 1655.

[36]*The Pagans Debt, and Dowry*, 22; and see 30 ff.

[37]*Ibid.*, 42.

[38]*De Doctrina Christiana*, XVI, 109.

[39]*The Divine Authority Of The Scriptures*, 26.

[40]*De Doctrina Christiana*, XV, 405.

[41]*The Divine Authority Of The Scriptures*, sig. a2.

[42]*De Doctrina Christiana*, XIV, 117.

[43]*The Institution of Christian Religion*, 13.

[44]*History of Britain*, X, 324. The remark occurs in Milton's review of "the late civil broils." It expresses the essence of his comment on the failure of the revolution.

[45]*Ibid.*

[46]*De Doctrina Christiana*, XIV, 71.

[47]*Ibid.*, 73.

[48]De Pauley, *The Candle of the Lord*, 242-3.

[49]*The Institution of Christian Religion*, 72, 159.

[50]*Ibid.*, 153, 147.

[51]*Ibid.*, 73, 159.

[52]See *ibid.*, book III, chap. 11.

[53]*De Doctrina Christiana*, XVI, 259-61.

[54]*Ibid.*, XV, 251.

[55]*Ibid.*, 343-5.

[56]*Ibid.*, 353-7.

[57]*Ibid.*, 357.

[58]*Ibid.*, 367.

[59]*Ibid.*, XVI, 5.

[60]*Ibid.*, 5.

[61]*Ibid.*, XV, 371; and see 205.

[62]*The Institution of Christian Religion*, 73.

[63]*De Doctrina Christiana*, XV, 373.

[64]*The Institution of Christian Religion*, 66, 48, 29.

[65]*Ibid.*, 190.

[66]*Tetrachordon*, IV, 86.

[67]*Of Education*, IV, 288.

[68]*Areopagitica*, IV, 320.

[69]*The Institution of Christian Religion*, 226.

[70]*Ibid.*, 227.

[71]*Ibid.*, 228.

[72]*Ibid.*, 227.

[73]*De Doctrina Christiana*, XIV, 35.

[74]*Ibid.*, XV, 39-41.

[75]*Ibid.*, 17-27.

[76]*Ibid.*, 263, 307.

[77]*Ibid.*, 219.

[78]*Ibid.*, XVI, 103-5.

[79]*Ibid.*, 151.

[80]*Ibid.*, 149-51.

[81]*Ibid.*, 113.

[82]*Ibid.*, 151.

[83]*The Institution of Christian Religion*, 408; Ames, *Conscience*, 108.

[84]*De Doctrina Christiana*, XVI, 125.

[85]*Ibid.*, 133.

[86]*Ibid.*, 141-3.

[87]*Ibid.*, 119.

[88]*Ibid.*, 143.

[89]*Ibid.*, 151. The contrast between this statement and the refutation of the same contention, expressed by Paraeus, in *The Doctrine and Discipline of Divorce*, III, 451, indicates the extent to which Milton had to revise his ideas under the Commonwealth.

[90]*Ibid.*, 153, 9.

[91]*Ibid.*, 153-5.

[92]*Ibid.*, 275. Cf. Goodwin, *The Divine Authority Of The Scriptures*, 17: "the true and proper foundation of Christian religion is not ink and paper, not any book or books, not any writing or writings whatsoever, whether translations or originals; but that substance of matter, those gracious counsels of God, concerning the salvation of the world by Jesus Christ, which indeed are presented and declared both in translations and originals, but are essentially and really distinct from both . . . ."

[93]*De Doctrina Christiana*, XVI, 157, 267, 281.

[94]*Ibid.*, 233-5.

[95]*Ibid.*, 309-11, 321-3.

[96]*Ibid.*, 327.

[97]*Ibid.*, 333-5.

[98]*Ibid.*, 241-9.

[99]*Ibid.*, 293-9, 301-3.

[100]*Ibid.*, 337; and see XVII, 393-5.

[101]*The Institution of Christian Religion*, 159.

[102]See especially book III, chap. 3, sec. 14.

[103]*De Doctrina Christiana*, XVII, 7-9, 173.

[104]*The Institution of Christian Religion*, 160.

[105]*De Doctrina Christiana*, XVII, 39.

[106]On the indifferency of the Sabbath, see *De Doctrina Christiana*, XV, 117, XVII, 173; on marriage and divorce, see XV, 121-79, where the essential arguments of the divorce tracts are repeated; on polygamy, XV, 123-51.

[107]*Ibid.*, XIV, 139-41.

[108]*Ibid.*, XVI, 101.

[109]*The Way of True Peace*, in Woodhouse, *Puritanism and Liberty*, 310-11, 312-13.

[110]*The Retired Mans Meditations*, 388-9.

[111]*De Doctrina Christiana*, XVII, 413.

[112]*Ibid.*, 393. The argument of *Of Civil Power* on the relationship between church and state is here repeated.

[113]*Ibid.*, 401-3.

[114]*Ibid.*, XIV, 129.

[115]*Ibid.*, 147-9.

[116]*Ibid.*, XVI, 359.

[117]*Ibid.*, 353, 375, 379.

[118]*Ibid.*, XIV, 9, 11.

[119]*Ibid.*, 11-13.

[120]*Ibid.*, XVI, 93.

[121]*Philippians* 4.8. See Cudworth, *A Sermon Preached before the Honourable House of Commons*, March 31, 1647, "To the Honourable House of Commons."

[122]*A Sermon*, 8.

[123]*Ibid.*, 26-7.

[124]*Ibid.*, 11.

[125]*Ibid.*, 5, 46.

[126]*Ibid.*, 19, 26, 20.

[127]*De Doctrina Christiana*, XVI, 179, 105.

[128]Whichcote, *Aphorisms*, 212, 983, 87.

[129]*A Sermon*, 61.

[130]*Ibid.*, 81.

[131]*Reason of Church Government*, III, 236; *Of Education*, IV, 286.

[132]*A Sermon*, 51.

## CONCLUSION

[1]*Defensio Secunda*, VIII, 245.

[2]*Paradise Lost*, bk. XII, 587.

# *Bibliography*

Part I lists only works to which reference has been made in the text or notes. Part II includes some works not mentioned in the text or notes.

## I. PRIMARY SOURCES

### A. MILTON


The Works of John Milton. General editor, Frank Allen Patterson, New York, Columbia University Press. 1931-1940.

Of Reformation Touching Church-Discipline in England: And the Causes that hither-to have hindered it. Two Bookes, Written to a Freind. Printed for Thomas Underhill, 1641.

Of Reformation. . . . Edited with introduction, notes, and glossary by W. T. Hale. Yale Studies in English, No. 54. New Haven, 1916.

Of Prelatical Episcopacy, and Whether it may be deduc'd from the Apostolical times . . . . London, Printed by R. O. & G. D. for Thomas Underhill . . . , 1641.

Animadversions upon The Remonstrants Defence, against Smectymnuus. London, Printed for Thomas Underhill . . . , 1641.

The Reason of Church-government Urg'd against Prelaty By Mr. John Milton. In two Books. London, Printed by E. G. for Iohn Rothwell . . . . 1641.

An Apology Against a Pamphlet call'd A Modest Confutation of the Animadversions upon the Remonstrant against Smectymnuus. London, Printed by E. G. for Iohn Rothwell . . . . 1642.

The Doctrine and Discipline of Divorce: restored to the good of both sexes, From the bondage of Canon Law, and other mistakes to Christian freedom, guided by the Rule of Charity . . . . London, Printed by T. P. and M. S. . . . 1643.

The Doctrine & Discipline of Divorce: Restor'd to the good of both Sexes, From the bondage of Canon Law, and other mistakes, to the true meaning of Scripture in the Law and Gospel compar'd . . . . Now the second time revis'd and much augmented . . . . The Author J. M. . . . London, 1644.

To Samuel Hartlib. [1644.]

Milton on Education. The Tractate of Education with supplementary extracts from the other writings of Milton. Edited with an introduction and notes by O. M. Ainsworth. Cornell Studies in English, volume 12. New Haven, 1928.

The Iudgement of Martin Bucer concerning Divorce. Writt'n to Edward the sixt, in his second Book of the Kingdom of Christ. And now Englisht. Wherin a late Book restoring the Doctrine and Discipline of Divorce, is heer confirm'd and justify'd by the authoritie of Martin Bucer .... London, Printed by Matthew Simmons, 1644.

Areopagitica: A Speech of Mr. John Milton For the Liberty of Unlicenc'd Printing, To the Parliament of England .... London ..., 1644.

Areopagitica .... Edited with introduction and notes by J. W. Hales .... Oxford, 1898.

Tetrachordon: Expositions upon The foure chief places in Scripture, which treat of Mariage, or nullities in Mariage .... By the former Author J. M.... London ..., 1645.

Colasterion: A Reply to A Nameless Answer against The Doctrine and Discipline of Divorce .... By the former Author, J. M.... 1645.

The Tenure of Kings and Magistrates: proving, That it is Lawfull, and hath been held so through all Ages, for any, who have the Power, to call to account a Tyrant, or wicked King, and after due conviction, to depose, and put him to death; if the ordinary Magistrate have neglected, or deny'd to doe it .... The author, J. M. London, Printed by Matthew Simmons ..., 1649.

The Tenure of Kings and Magistrates .... Published now the second time with some additions .... London. Printed by Matthew Simmons ..., 1650.

The Tenure of Kings and Magistrates .... Edited with introduction and notes by W. T. Allison. Yale Studies in English, No. 40. New Haven, 1911.

Articles of Peace, made and concluded with the Irish Rebels, and Papists, by James Earle of Ormond ..., also a Letter sent by Ormond to Col. Jones, Governor of Dublin ..., and A Representation of the Scotch Presbytery at Belfast in Ireland, upon all which are added Observations. London: Printed by Matthew Simmons ..., 1649.

Εἰκονοκλάστης in Answer to a Book Intitl'd Εἰκὼν Βασιλική, The Portraiture of his Sacred Majesty in his Solitudes and Sufferings. The Author I. M.... London, Printed by Matthew Simmons .... 1649.

Εἰκονοκλάστης .... Publish'd now the second time, and much enlarg'd .... Printed by T. N ..., 1650.

Joannis Miltoni Angli Pro Populo Anglicano Defensio Contra Claudii Anonymi, alias Salmasii, Defensionem Regiam. Londini, Typis Du Gardianis ... 1651.

Joannis Miltoni Angli Pro Populo Anglicano Defensio .... Editio correctior & auctior, ab Autore denuo recognita. Londini, Typis Neucomianis, 1658.

Joannis Miltoni Angli Pro Populo Anglicano Defensio Secunda. Contra infamen libellum anonymum cui titulus, Regii sanguinis clamor ad coelum adversus parricidas Anglicanos. Londini, Typis Neucomianis, 1654.

Joannis Miltoni Angli Pro Se Defensio contra Alexandrum Morum Ecclesiasten, Libelli famosi, cui titulus, Regii sanguinis clamor adversus Parricidas Anglicanos, authorem recte dictum. Londini, Typis Neucomianis, 1655.

A Treatise of Civil power in Ecclesiastical causes: shewing that it is not lawful for any power on earth to compell in matters of Religion. The author J. M. London, Printed by Tho. Newcomb, ... 1659.

Considerations touching The likeliest means to remove Hirelings out of the church. Wherein is also discourc'd of {Tithes, Church-fees, Church-revenues; And whether any maintenance of ministers can be settl'd by law. The author J. M. London. Printed by T. N. for L. Chapman .... 1659.

The Readie & Easie Way to Establish A Free Commonwealth, and the Excellence thereof Compar'd with The inconveniences and dangers of readmitting kingship in this nation. The author J. M. London. Printed by T. N. [for] Livewell Chapman . . . 1660.

The Readie and Easie Way to Establish A Free Commonwealth . . . . The second edition revis'd and augmented. Printed for the Author. 1660.

The Ready and Easy Way to establish a Free Commonwealth . . . . Edited with introduction, notes and glossary by E. M. Clark. Yale Studies in English, No. 51. New Haven, 1915.

Brief Notes upon a Late Sermon, Titl'd, The Fear of God and the King: Preachd and since Publishd, by Matthew Griffith, D.D. . . . Wherin many Notorious Wrestings of Scripture and other Falsities are observed by J. M. London, 1660.

Of True Religion, Haeresie, Schism, Toleration, And what best means may be us'd against the growth of Popery. The Author I. M. London . . . 1673.

Poems of Mr. John Milton, both English and Latin, Compos'd at several times . . . . London, Printed by Ruth Raworth for Humphrey Mosely . . . . 1645.

The Sonnets of John Milton. Edited by J. S. Smart. Glasgow, 1921.

Private Correspondence and Academic Exercises. Translated by P. B. Tillyard, with an introduction by E. M. W. Tillyard. Cambridge, 1932.

### B. THE BACKGROUND

Acts and Ordinances of the Interregnum, 1642-1660. Edited by C. H. Firth and R. S. Rait. London, 1911.

Ainsworth, Henry. Counterpoyson Considerations touching the poynts in difference between the Godly Ministers and people of the Church of England, and the seduced brethren of the Separation . . . . 1642. [First published 1608.]

Almoni, Peloni (*pseud.*). A Compendious Discourse, proving Episcopacy to be of Apostolical, And consequently of Divine Institution, by a clear and weighty testimony of St. Irenaeus . . . . Printed by E. G. for Richard Whitaker: London, 1641.

Ames, William. Guiliel. Amesii Medulla Theologica . . . . Apud I. Ianssonium: Amstelod., 1628.

The Marrow of Sacred Divinity . . . . Translated out of the Latine . . . . Published by order . . . from the House of Commons. London, Printed by E. Griffin for H. Overton. 1642.

Guiljelmi Amesij, De Conscientia et ejus jure, vel casibus, libri quinque . . . . Apud I. Ianssonium: Amstelodami, 1631.

Conscience, with The Power and Cases Thereof . . . . Translated out of Latine . . . . London, 1639. [Selections in Woodhouse, *Puritanism and Liberty.*]

Conscience, with the Power and Cases Thereof . . . . London, Printed by Edw. Griffen for John Rothwell. 1643.

The Substance of Christian Religion: or, a plain and easie Draught of the Christian Catechisme in LII lectures. London: Printed by T. Mabb for Thomas Davies. 1659.

The Ancient Bounds, or Liberty of Conscience tenderly stated, modestly asserted, and mildly vindicated .... London, Printed by M. S. for Henry Overton ... 1645. [Selections in Woodhouse, *Puritanism and Liberty.*]

An Answer to a Book, Intituled, The Doctrine and Discipline of Divorce, or, A Plea for Ladies and Gentlewomen, and all other Married Women against Divorce .... London, Printed by G. M. for W. Lee .... 1644. [Reproduced in Parker, *Milton's Contemporary Reputation.*]

An Apologeticall Account, of some Brethren of the Church, whereof Mr. John Goodwin is Pastor. (On the behalfe of the Church.) Why they cannot execute that Unchristian and passionate Charge, viz. of delivering up Their said Pastor unto Sathan. London, Printed by I. D. and R. I. for Henry Overton, 1647.

Archer, Henry. The personall Reign of Christ upon Earth. Printed ... by B. Allen. 1642. [First published 1641.]

Aspinwal, William. A Brief Description of the Fifth Monarchy, or Kingdome, that shortly is to come into the World. Printed by Matthew Simmons .... 1653.

Aston, Sir Thomas. A Remonstrance, against Presbitery. Exhibited by divers of the Nobilitie, Gentrie, Ministers, and Inhabitants of the County Palatine of Chester .... London, Printed for John Aston: 1641.

Bacon, Francis. Certaine Considerations touching the better Pacification and Edification of the Church of England .... 1640. [Reprinted in *Works*, ed. Spedding, VII.]

A Wise and Moderate Discourse, concerning Church Affaires. As it was written, long since, by the famous authour of those Considerations, which seem to have some reference to this .... 1641. [Reprinted in *Works*, VII, with variations, as An Advertisement touching the Controversies of the Church of England.]

Bagshaw, Edward. Saintship No Ground of Soveraignty: or A Treatise Tending to prove That the Saints, barely considered as such, ought not to Govern. Oxford. Printed by H. Hall .... 1660.

Baillie, Robert. The Unlawfulnes and Danger of Limited Prelacie or Perpetual Precidence in the Church briefly discovered .... London. 1641.

A Dissuasive from the Errours of the Time: wherein the tenets of the principal sects, especially the Independents, are drawn together in one map .... London. For Samuel Gellibrand. 1645.

Letters and Journals. Edited by David Laing. Edinburgh, 1841-1842.

Barclay, Robert. An Apology for the True Christian Divinity, as the same is held forth, and preached by the People, Called, in Scorn, Quakers .... 1678.

Baxter, Richard. A Holy Commonwealth, or Political Aphorisms, Opening The true Principles of Government: for The Healing of the Mistakes, and Resolving the Doubts, that most endanger and trouble England .... London, Printed for Thomas Underhill and Francis Tyton .... 1659.

The Beauty of Godly Government in a Church Reformed: or a Platforme of Government consonant to the Word of Truth and the present reformed Churches .... 1641.

Bradshaw, William. A Protestation of the Kings Supremacie. Made in the name of the afflicted ministers .... 1605.

English Puritanisme. Containing the maine Opinions of the rigidest sort of those that are called Puritanes in the Realme of England .... 1640. [First published 1605, and ascribed to William Ames in 1640.]

The Unreasonablenesse of the Separation; Made apparent by an Examination of Mr. Johnsons pretended reasons .... Dort, 1614. [Reprinted 1640.]

Browne, Robert. A Treatise of Reformation without Tarying for Anie, and of the wickedness of those preachers which will not reforme till the magistrate commande or compell them. Middleburgh, 1582.

Burges, Cornelius. The First Sermon Preached to the Honorable House of Commons ... at their Publique Fast, November 17. 1640. London, Printed by I. L. for Philemon Stephens and Christopher Meredeth. 1641.

Burton, Henry. For God and the King. The Summe of Two Sermons Preached on the fifth of November last in St. Matthewes Friday Streete. 1636. Printed Anno Dom. 1636.

Englands Bondage and Hope of Deliverance. A Sermon preached before the Honourable House of Parliament ... Iune 20, 1641. London, 1641.

The Protestation Protested: or a short Remonstrance, shewing what is principally required of all those that have or doe take the last Parliamentary Protestation. 1641.

Calvin, John. The Institution of Christian Religion, written in Latine by M. John Calvin, and translated into English ... by Thomas Norton. Printed at London by Arnold Hatfield, for Bonham Norton. 1599. [Selections in Woodhouse, *Puritanism and Liberty.*]

Institutes of the Christian Religion. Translated by H. Beveridge. Edinburgh, 1875.

Canne, John. The Golden Rule, Or, Justice Advanced, wherein is shewed that the Commons assembled in Parliament have a lawfull power to Arraign the King for Tyranny .... Printed by Peter Cole. 1649.

A Seasonable Word To the Parliament-Men, To take with them when they go into the House .... London. Printed by J. C. for L. Chapman. 1659.

Cary, Lucius, Viscount Falkland. A Speech made to the House of Commons Concerning Episcopacy. London, Printed for Thomas Walkley, 1641.

A Discourse of Infallibility, with Mr. T. White's Answer to it .... The Second Edition. To which are now added, two discourses of Episcopacy by the said Viscount Falkland.... London. Printed for William Nealand. 1660.

Case, Thomas. Spiritual Whordome discovered in a Sermon Preach'd before the Honourable House of Commons ... May 26, 1647. London, Printed by J. Macock, for Luke Fawne. 1647.

The Censure of the Rota Upon Mr Miltons Book, Entituled, The Ready and Easie way to Establish A Free Common-wealth .... London .... 1660. [Reproduced in Parker, *Milton's Contemporary Reputation.*]

Certain Considerations to Dissuade Men from further gathering of Churches in this present juncture of time .... 1643.

Certain Quaeres humbly presented in way of petition, By many Christian people dispersed abroad throughout the county of Norfolk and city of Norwich, to the serious and grave consideration and debate of his Excellency the Lord General and of the General Councel of War .... Together with an humble advice for the settling of the kingdom, according to such a model hinted therein, offered as the sence of many Christians .... London, Printed for Giles Calvert .... 1648. [Selections in Woodhouse, *Puritanism and Liberty.*]

Chidley, Katherine. The Justification of the Independent Churches of Christ; being an answer to Mr. Edwards his Booke ... against the Government of Christs Church and Toleration of Christs Publike Worship .... London. Printed for William Larnar. 1641.

Chillingworth, William. The Religion of Protestants a Safe Way to Salvation, or An Answer to a book entituled, Mercy and Truth, or, Charity maintain'd by Catholiques .... Oxford, Printed by Leonard Lichfield. MDCXXXVIII.

The Works .... Oxford, 1838.

Church-Levellers, or Vanity of Vanities and Certainty of Delusion discovered in the late pamphlet called The Vanity of the Present Churches .... London, Printed for Thos. Underhill. 1649.

The Clarke Papers. Edited by C. H. Firth. Camden Society Publications, N.S., XLIX. London, 1891.

Collier, Thomas. A Discovery of the New Creation. In a Sermon Preached at the Head-Quarters at Putney Sept. 29. 1647. London. Printed for Giles Calvert. 1647. [Selections in Woodhouse, *Puritanism and Liberty.*]

The Decision and Clearing of the Great Point now in Controversie, about the interest of Christ and the Civil Magistrate, in the rule of Government in this world. London, 1659.

The Constitutional Documents of the Puritan Revolution, 1625-1660. Edited by S. R. Gardiner. Oxford, 1906.

Cotton, John. The True Constitution of A Particular visible Church, proved by Scripture .... London: Printed for Samuel Satterthwaite. 1642.

The Keyes of the Kingdom of Heaven, and Power thereof, according to the Word of God ..., tending to reconcile some present differences about Discipline .... London. Printed by M. Simmons for Henry Overton, 1644. [Selections in Woodhouse, *Puritanism and Liberty.*]

The Way of the Churches of Christ in New-England. Or, The Way of Churches walking in Brotherly equalitie, or co-ordination, without Subjection of one Church to another. London. Printed by Matthew Simmons. 1645.

The Bloudy Tenent, washed, And made white in the bloud of the Lambe. London, Printed by Matthew Simmons for Hannah Allen, 1647.

The Way of Congregational Churches Cleered .... London, Printed by Matthew Simmons for John Bellamie. 1648.

Cradock, Walter. Gospel-libertie, in the {Extensions Limitations} of it. Wherein is laid down an exact way to end the present dissentions, and to preserve future peace among the Saints. London, Printed by Matthew Simmons for Henry Overton. 1648.

Cromwell, Oliver. Letters and Speeches. Edited by S. C. Lomas. London, 1904.

Cudworth, Ralph. A Sermon Preached before the Honourable House of Commons At Westminster, March 31. 1647. Cambridge. Printed by Roger Daniel .... 1647.

Davenport, John. A Discourse about Civil Government in a new Plantation whose design is religion. Cambridge, 1663. [First published 1643.]

The Declaration and Proclamation of the Army of God, owned by the Lord of Hosts in many Victories .... The second eddition enlarged with new Additions. London. Printed by J. Clowes for The Author. 1659.

The Declaration of His Excellency The Lord General Fairfax and his General Councel of Officers, shewing the grounds of the Armies advance toward the City of London. London. Printed by John Field for John Partridge, Novemb. 1. 1648. [Selections in Woodhouse, *Puritanism and Liberty*.]

A Declaration Of several of the Churches of Christ, And Godly People In and about the Citie of London; Concerning The Kingly Interest Of Christ, And the present suffrings Of His Cause and Saints in England. London, Printed for Livewel Chapman .... 1654.

A Declaration of the Christian-Free-Born Subjects of the once Flourishing Kingdom of England. Making Out the Principles relating both to their Spiritual and Civil Liberties .... 1659.

A Declaration of The Faith and Order Owned and practised in the Congregational Churches In England; Agreed upon and consented unto By their Elders and Messengers In Their Meeting at the Savoy. October 12. 1658. London, Printed for D. L. ..., 1658. [Reprinted in *Creeds and Platforms of Congregationalism*, edited by W. Walker, New York, 1893.]

A Declaration of the General Council of the Officers of the Army: Agreed upon at Wallingford-house, 27 October. 1659 .... London, Printed by Henry Hills .... 1659.

Dell, William. The Way Of True Peace and Unity Among The Faithful and Churches of Christ, In all humility and bowels of love presented to them. London, Printed for Giles Calvert. 1649. [Selections in Woodhouse, *Puritanism and Liberty*.]

The Stumbling-Stone, Or, A Discourse touching that offence which the World and Worldly Church do take against {1. Christ Himself. 2. His true Word. 3. His True Worship .... London, Printed by R. W. for Giles Calvert .... 1653.

The Right Reformation of Learning, Schooles and Universities according to the State of the Gospel and the True Light that Shines therein. London, 1653.

The Tryal of Spirits Both in Teachers & Hearers. Wherein is held forth The clear Discovery and certain Downfal Of The Carnal and Antichristian Clergie of These Nations .... London, Printed for Giles Calvert ..., 1653.

Dering, Sir Edward. A Collection of Speeches made by Sir Edward Dering Knight and Baronet in matter of Religion. London. Printed by E. G. for F. Eglesfield and Jo. Stafford. 1642.

Digby, Lord George. The Third Speech of the Lord George Digby to the House of Commons, concerning Bishops and the Citie Petition, Febr. 9, 1640. 1640.

Du Moulin, Pierre, the younger. Regii Sanguinis Clamor Ad Coelum Adversus

Parricidas Anglicanos. Hagae-Comitum. Ex Typographia Adriani Vlac. MDCLII.

Edwards, Thomas. Reasons against the Independant Government of Particular Congregations: As also against the Toleration of such Churches to be erected in this Kingdome. London, Printed by Richard Cotes for Jo. Bellamie & Ralph Smith. 1641.

Antapologia: Or A Full Answer to the Apologeticall Narration .... London, Printed by G. M. for Ralph Smith. 1644.

Gangraena, or a Catalogue and Discovery of many of the Errours, Heresies, Blasphemies and Pernicious Practices of the Sectaries of this time .... London, Printed for Ralph Smith. MDCXLVI.

The Second Part of Gangraena. London, Printed by T. R. and E. M. for Ralph Smith. 1646.

The Third Part of Gangraena. London, Printed for Ralph Smith. 1646.

The Casting Down of the last and strongest hold of Satan, or, A Treatise against Toleration and pretended liberty of conscience. London, Printed by T. R. and E. M. for George Calvert. 1647.

Eliot, John. The Christian Commonwealth: or, The Civil Policy of The Rising Kingdom of Jesus Christ. Written Before the Interruption of the Government, by Mr. John Eliot, Teacher of the Church of Christ at Roxbury in New England .... London, Printed for Livewell Chapman. 1659.

Feake, Christopher. A Beam of Light, shining In the midst of much Darkness and Confusion: Being ... An Essay towards the stating ... The Best Cause under Heaven: viz. The Cause of God, of Christ, of his People, of the whole Creation, that groans and waits for the manifestation of the Sons of God. London, Printed by J. C. for Livewell Chapman. 1659.

Featley, Daniel. *Κατα-βαπτισται κατάπτυστοι.* The Dippers dipt. Or, The Anabaptists duck'd and plung'd Over Head and Eares, at a Disputation in Southwark. London, Printed for N. Bourne and R. Royston. 1645.

Ferne, Henry. The Resolving of Conscience, Upon this Question. Whether upon such a Supposition or Case, as is now usually made ... Subjects may take Arms and resist? ... Cambridge, Printed by Roger Daniel. 1642.

Fiennes, Nathaniel. A Speech of the Honourable Nathanael Fiennes ... in answer to the Third Speech of the Lord George Digby. Concerning Bishops and the City of Londons Petition ... the 9th of Feb. 1640, in the hon. house of Commons .... 1641.

A Second Speech of the Honourable Nathanael Fiennes ... in the Commons House of Parliament. Touching the Subjects Liberty against the late Canons, and the New Oath. 1641.

The Fifth Monarchy; or Kingdom of Christ, In opposition to the Beasts', Asserted, By the Solemn League and Covenant, several learned divines, the late General and Army .... London: Printed for Livewell Chapman. 1659.

Filmer, Sir Robert. Observations concerning the Originall of Government, Upon Mr. Hobs Leviathan. Mr. Milton against Salmasius. H. Grotius De Jure Belli. Mr. Huntons Treatise of Monarchy. London: Printed for R. Royston ..., 1652. [Reproduced in part in Parker, *Milton's Contemporary Reputation.*]

Gill, Alexander. The Sacred Philosophie of the Holy Scripture: laid downe as Conclusions On the Articles of our Faith, commonly called the Apostles' Creed. Proved by the Principles or rules taught and received in the light of Understanding .... Imprinted at London by Anne Griffin for Ioyce Norton and Rich. Whitaker, 1635.

Goodwin, John. The Saints Interest In God: Opened In Severall Sermons .... London, Printed by M. F. for Henry Overton .... 1640.

Impedit ira animum, Or Animadversions Upon Some Of The Looser And Fouler Passages In A Written Pamphlet Intituled, A Defence of the True Sence And meaning of the words of the holy Apostle . . . by George Walker .... 1641.

Imputatio Fidei. Or A Treatise of Justification wherein ye imputation of faith for righteousnes . . . is explained & also yt great Question largely handled, Whether ye active obedience of Christ performed to ye morall law, be imputed in Justification, or noe .... London, Printed by R. O. and G. D. 1642.

Anti-Cavalierisme, or, Truth Pleading As well the Necessity, as the Lawfulness of this present War .... London. Printed by G. B. and R. W. for Henry Overton .... [1642.] [Reproduced in Haller, *Tracts on Liberty*.]

Θεομαχια; or The Grand Imprudence of men running the hazard of Fighting Against God, In suppressing any Way, Doctrine, or Practice, concerning which they know not certainly whether it be from God or no .... London; Printed for Henry Overton .... 1644. [Reproduced in Haller, *Tracts on Liberty*.]

Innocencies Triumph, or, An Answer to the Back-Part of a Discourse lately published by W. Prynne, Esquire, intituled, A Full Reply, &c .... London, Printed for Henry Overton. 1644.

A Moderate Answer to Mr. Prins full Reply to certaine Observations on his first Twelve Questions. London, Printed for Benjamin Allen. 1645.

Innocency and Truth Triumphing together; Or The latter part of an Answer to the back-part of a Discourse, lately published by William Prynne, Esquire, called A Full Reply, &c .... London; Printed by Matthew Simmons for Henry Overton .... 1645.

Anapologesiates Antapologias. Or, The inexcusablenesse of that Grand Accusation of the Brethren, called Antapologia .... Printed by Matthew Simmons for H: Overton: London, 1646.

Some Modest and Humble Queries Concerning a Printed Paper, intituled, An Ordinance Presented to the Honourable House of Commons, &c. for the preventing of the growing and spreading of Heresies .... London, Printed by Matthew Simmons for Henry Overton .... 1646.

Hagiomastix: Or The Scourge Of The Saints Displayed In his colours of Ignorance & Blood: Or, A vindication of some printed Queries published . . . by Authority, in . . . Answer to certaine Anti-papers of Syllogismes, entitled A Vindication of a Printed paper. London. Printed by Matthew Simmons for Henry Overton. 1646.

Right and Might well met, Or, A Brief and unpartiall enquiry into the late and present proceedings of the Army under the Command of . . . the Lord Fairfax. Wherein the equity and regularnesse of the said proceedings are demonstratively vindicated upon undeniable Principles, as well of Reason, as Religion. London. Printed by Matthew Simmons for Henry Overton. 1648. [Selections in Woodhouse, *Puritanism and Liberty*.]

The Divine Authority Of The Scriptures Asserted, Or The Great Charter of the worlds Blessedness vindicated .... London, Printed by A. M. for Henry Overton. 1648.

Sion-colledg visited. Or, Some brief Animadversions upon a Pamphlet lately published, under the title of, A Testimonie to the Truth of Jesus Christ, and to our Solemne League and Covenant .... London, Printed by M. S. for Henry Overton ..., 1648.

*'Υβριστοδίκαι*, The Obstructours of Justice. Or, A Defence of the Honourable Sentence passed upon the late King, by the High Court of Justice, opposed chiefly to the Serious and Faithful Representation and Vindication of some of the ministers of London, as also to the Humble Address of Dr. Hammond. London. Printed for Henry Cripps and Lodowick Lloyd. 1649.

The Remedie of Unreasonableness, Or The Substance of a Speech Intended at a Conference or Dispute, in Al-hallows the Great, London. Feb. 11. 1649. Exhibiting the brief Heads of Mr. John Goodwin's Judgement, concerning the Freeness, Fulness, Effectualnes of the Grace of God. As also concerning the Bondage or Servility of the Will of Man. London. Printed by John Macock for Lodowick Lloyd and Henry Cripps. 1650.

*'Απολύτρωσις 'Απολυτρώσεως*. Or, Redemption Redeemed. Wherein the Most Glorious Work of the Redemption Of The World by Jesus Christ, is by Expressness of Scripture, clearnes of Argument, countenance of the best Authority, as well Ancient as Modern, Vindicated and Asserted in the Just Latitude and Extent of it .... London, Printed by John Macock, for Lodowick Lloyd and Henry Cripps. MDCLI.

The Pagans Debt, and Dowry. Or A Brief Discussion of these Questions, Whether, How far, and in what Sence, such Persons of Mankinde amongst whom the Letter of the Gospel never came, are notwithstanding bound to Believe on Jesus Christ .... London, Printed by J. Macock for H. Cripps .... 1651.

Thirty Queries, Modestly propounded in order to a Discovery of the Truth, and Mind of God, in that Question, or Case of Conscience; Whether the Civil Magistrate stands bound by way of Duty to interpose his Power or Authority, in matter of Religion, or Worship of God. London. Printed by J. M. for Henry Cripps and Lodowick Lloyd. 1653.

*Συγκρητισμός*. Or Dis-satisfaction Satisfied. In seventeen sober and serious Queries, Tending to allay the Discontents, and satisfie the Scruples of persons Dis-satisfied about the late Revolution of government in the Common-wealth .... London. Printed by J. Macock, for H. Cripps and L. Lloyd. 1654.

Peace Protected, And Discontent Dis-armed, Wherein the Seventeen Queries (with the addition of three more, Postscript-wise) lately published ... are reinforced. ... London. Printed by I. Macock for H. Cripps & L. Lloyd. 1654.

A Fresh Discovery Of The High-Presbyterian Spirit. Or The Quenching of the second Beacon fired .... London, Printed for the Author .... 1654.

Βασανισταὶ, or The Triers, (or Tormentors) Tryed and Cast, by the Laws both of God and of Men.... London. Printed for Henry Eversden. ... 1657.

Goodwin, Thomas, and Philip Nye, Sidrach Simpson, Jeremiah Burroughs, William Bridge. An Apologeticall Narration, Humbly Submitted to the Honourable Houses of Parliament. London, Printed for Robert Dawlman. MDCXLIII. [Reproduced in Haller, *Tracts on Liberty.*]

Greville, Robert, Lord Brooke. The Nature of Truth, its Union and Unity with the Soule, which is one in its essence, faculties, acts; one with truth. London, Printed by R. Bishop for Sam. Cartwright. 1640.

A Discourse opening the Nature of that Episcopacie, which is exercised in England. Wherein, with all Humility, are represented some Considerations tending to the much-desired Peace, and long expected Reformation, of This our Mother Church. The Second Edition, Corrected and Enlarged. London, Printed by R. C. for Samuel Cartwright, 1642. [First published 1641. Reproduced in Haller, *Tracts on Liberty.*]

Hales, John. The Works.... Glasgow, 1765.

Hall, Joseph. Episcopacie by Divine Right Asserted. London, Printed by R. B. for Nathanael Butter. 1640.

An Humble Remonstrance to the High Court of Parliament by a dutifull Sonne of the Church. London, Printed for Nathaniel Butter. 1640.

A Defence of the Humble Remonstrance, Against the frivolous and false exceptions of Smectymnuus .... London, Printed for Nathaniel Butter. 1641.

A Short Answer to the Tedious Vindication of Smectymnuus.... London. Printed for Nathaniel Butter. 1641.

Harrington, James. The Commonwealth of Oceana. London, Printed by J. Streater for Livewell Chapman. 1656.

James Harrington's Oceana. Edited by S. B. Liljegren. Lund, 1924.

The Art of Law-giving. London, Printed by J. C. for H. Fletcher. 1659.

Aphorisms Political. London, Printed by J. C. for Henry Fletcher. [1659.]

The Oceana and Other Works. London: Printed for A. Millar.... MDCCXXXVII.

Hobbes, Thomas. Humane Nature: Or, The fundamental Elements of Policie... London, Printed by T. Newcomb, for Fra: Bowman of Oxon. 1650.

De Corpore Politico. Or The Elements of Law, Moral & Politic. London, Printed for J. Martin and J. Ridley. 1650.

The Elements of Law Natural and Politic. Edited by F. Tönnies. London, 1889.

Leviathan, or the Matter, Forme and Power of a Common-wealth Ecclesiastical and Civil. London, Printed for Andrew Crooke. 1651.

Leviathan. Edited by A. D. Lindsay. London, 1914.

Homes, Nathaniel. The New World; or The New Reformed Church. London, Printed by T. P. and M. S. for William Adderton. 1641.

The Peasants Price of Spirituall Liberty. London, Printed by R. O. and G. D. for Benjamin Allen. 1642.

The Ressurection-Revealed .... London, Printed for the Author. 1661.

Miscellanea: Consisting of Three Treatises; Exercitations Extracted; resolving Ten Questions, Touching the Glorious Kingdom of Christ on Earth, yet to come .... London, Printed for the Author. [1666.]

Hooker, Richard. Of the Lawes of Ecclesiastical Politie, Eight Bookes .... London, Printed by William Stansbye. 1622.

How, Samuel. The Sufficiencie of the Spirits Teaching without humane Learning. Or a treatise tending to prove Humane-learning to be no helpe to the spiritual understanding of the Word of God. London, 1645. [First published 1640.]

The humble Advice of the Assembly of Divines ..., Concerning a Confession of Faith, Presented by them lately to both Houses of Parliament. London, Printed for the Company of Stationers. [1646].

The Humble Petition of divers Well-affected Persons, delivered The 6th day of July, 1659. To the supreme authority, the Parliament of the Commonwealth .... London, Printed for Thomas Brewster .... 1659.

Jacob, Henry. Reasons Taken Out Of Gods Word And The Best Humane Testimonies Proving A Necessitie Of Reforming Our Churches In England. 1604.

A Christian And Modest Offer Of A Most Indifferent Conference, Or Disputation, About the maine and principall Controversies betwixt the Prelats, and the late silenced and deprived ministers in England .... 1606.

A Declaration And Plainer Opening Of Certain Points, With A Sound Confirmation Of Some Other, Contained In A Treatise Intituled, The Divine Beginning ... Of Christes True ... Church .... 1612.

Knollys, Hanserd. A Glimpse of Sions Glory: Or The Churches Beautie specified. Published for the Good and Benefit of all those whose Hearts are raised up in the expectation of the glorious Liberties of the Saints. London. Printed for William Larnar. MDCXLI. [Selections in Woodhouse, *Puritanism and Liberty*.]

Leighton, Alexander. An Appeal to the Parliament, or, Sions Plea against the Prelacie. The summe whereoff is delivered in a decade of positions .... [1628.]

L'Estrange, Roger. No Blinde Guides, In Answer To a seditious Pamphlet of J. Milton's, intituled Brief Notes upon a late Sermon .... London, Printed for Henry Brome April 20. 1660. [Reproduced in Parker, *Milton's Contemporary Reputation*.]

The Leveller: or, The Principles & Maxims Concerning Government and Religion, Which are Asserted by those that are commonly called Levellers. London, Printed for Thomas Brewster. 1659. [Reprinted in *The Harleian Miscellany*, VII, 1810.]

Lilburne, John. A Worke of the Beast or A Relation of a most unchristian Censure, Executed upon Iohn Lilburne, (Now prisoner in the fleet) the 18 of Aprill 1638. With the heavenly speech uttered by him at the time of his suffering .... 1638. [Reproduced in Haller, *Tracts on Liberty*.]

The Christian Mans Triall: or, A True Relation of the first apprehension and several examinations of John Lilburne .... London, Printed for William Larner .... 1641.

Englands Birth-right Justified Against all Arbitrary Usurpation, whether Regall or Parliamentary, or under what Vizor soever. [1645.] [Reproduced in Haller, *Tracts on Liberty.*]

Innocency and Truth Justified. First against the unjust aspertions of W. Prinn, affirmed in ... A Fresh Discovery of Prodigious New wandering blazing Stars and Fire Brands .... 1645.

The Free-mans Freedome Vindicated. Or A true relation of the cause and manner of Lieut. Col. Iohn Lilburns present imprisonment in Newgate. [1646.] [Selections in Woodhouse, *Puritanism and Liberty.*]

Londons Liberty In Chains Discovered. And, Published by Lieutenant Colonell John Lilburn, prisoner in the Tower of London, Octob. 1646. [1646.]

Regall Tyrannie discovered: or, A Discourse, shewing that all lawfull (approbational) instituted power by God amongst men, is by common agreement, and mutual consent .... In which is also punctually declared, The Tyrannie of the Kings of England, from the dayes of William the Invader ... to this present king Charles. London .... 1647.

An Agreement Of The People For A firme and present Peace, upon grounds of common-right and freedom .... 1647.

Englands New Chains discovered: or, The serious apprehensions of a part of the People in behalf of the Commonwealth .... February 26, 1648. [1649.]

Foundations of Freedom or an Agreement of the People: Proposed as a rule for future government in the establishment of a firm and lasting peace. Drawn up by several well-affected persons, and tendered to the consideration of the General Councel of the Army; and now offered to the consideration of all persons .... 1648. [Selections in Woodhouse, *Puritanism and Liberty.*]

An Agreement of the Free People of England. Tendered as a Peace Offering to this distressed Nation. By Lieutenant Colonel John Lilburne, Master William Walwyn, Master Thomas Prince, and Master Richard Overton .... May the 1. 1649.

The second Part of Englands New-Chaines Discovered: Or a sad Representation of the uncertain and dangerous condition of the Commonwealth ... as it is avowed by Lieutenant Colonel John Lilburn, Mr. Richard Overton, and Mr. Tho. Prince .... London ... 1649. [Reprinted in Wolfe, *Milton in the Puritan Revolution.*]

The Legall Fundamentall Liberties of the People of England Revived, Asserted, and Vindicated. London ... 1649. [Selections in Woodhouse, *Puritanism and Liberty.*]

As You Were; Or, Lord General Cromwel and the Grand Officers of the Armie their Remembrancer .... 1652.

Lilburns Ghost, With a Whip in one hand, to scourge Tyrants out of Authority; And Balme in the other, to heal the sores of our (as yet) Corrupt State; Or, Some of the late dying principles of freedom, revived, and unvailed, for the Lovers of Freedome and Liberty, peace & righteousness to behold. Printed for Livewell Chapman .... 1659.

Luther, Martin. A Commentarie of Master Doctor Martin Luther upon the Epistle of S. Paul to the Galathians .... London, Printed by George Miller .... 1644. [Selections in Woodhouse, *Puritanism and Liberty.*]

Luther's Primary Works. Translated by Wace and Buckheim. London, 1896.

Marshall, Stephen. A Sermon preached before the Honourable House of Commons, at their Publicke Fast, Nov. 17, 1640. London, Printed by J. Okes for Samuel Man, 1641.

May, Thomas. The History of the Parliament of England, which began Nov. the third, 1640 .... London, Printed by M. Bell for G. Thomason. 1647.

Mede, Joseph. The Works of the Pious and Profoundly-Learned Joseph Mede. London, Printed by James Flesher for Richard Royston. MDCLXIV.

A Modest Confutation of A Slanderous and Scurrilous Libell, entituled, Animadversions upon the Remonstrants Defense against Smectymnuus .... MDCXLII. [Reproduced in Parker, *Milton's Contemporary Reputation.*]

Nicanor, Lysimachus (*pseud.*). The Epistle Congratulatorie of Lysimachus Nicanor of the Societie of Jesu, to the Covenanters in Scotland: wherin is paralleled our sweet Harmony and correspondency in . . . Doctrine and Practice. 1640.

Overton, Richard. The Araignment of Mr. Persecution Presented to the consideration of the House of Commons and to all the Common People of England .... 1645. [Reproduced in Haller, *Tracts on Liberty.*]

A Remonstrance of Many Thousand Citizens, and other Free-born People of England, To their owne House of Commons. Occasioned through the Illegal and Barbarous imprisonment of . . . John Lilburne. 1646. [Ascribed by Haller, I, 111, and reproduced in *Tracts on Liberty.*]

An Arrow Against All Tyrants And Tyrany, shot from the Prison of Newgate, into the Prerogative Bowels of the arbitrary House of Lords, and all . . . tyrants whatsoever .... 1646.

An Appeale from the Degenerate Representative Body the Commons of England assembled at Westminster: To the Body Represented. The free people in general of the several counties, cities, townes, burroughs, and places within this Kingdome of England .... London, 1647. [Selections in Woodhouse, *Puritanism and Liberty.*]

Owen, John. A Short Defensative about Church Government, Toleration, and Petitions about these things .... London, 1646.

Righteous Zeal Encouraged by Divine Protection: With a Discourse about Toleration .... London, 1649.

Owen, John, and others. The Humble Proposals of Mr. Owen, Mr. Tho. Goodwin, Mr. Nye, Mr. Sympson, and other Ministers, who presented the Petition to the Parliament, and other Persons, Febr. 11. under debate . . . for the furtherance and Propagation of the Gospel in this nation. Printed at London for Robert Ibbitson. 1652.

Paget, John. A Defense of Church Government, exercised in Presbyteriall Classicall & Synodall Assemblies according to the practice of the Reformed Churches. London, Printed for Thomas Underhill, 1641.

Pagitt, Ephraim. Heresiography: or A description of the Heretickes and Sectaries of these latter times. London, Printed by M. Okes [for] Robert Trot. 1645.

Palmer, Herbert. The Glasse of Gods Providence towards His Faithfull Ones. Held forth in a Sermon preached to the two Houses of Parliament . . . Aug. 13, 1644. London, Printed by G. M. for Thomas Underhill. 1644.

A Paraenetick or humble address to the Parliament and Assembly for (not loose but) Christian libertie. London, Printed by Matthew Simmons for Henry Overton. 1644.

Parker, Henry. The Question Concerning The Divine Right of Episcopacie truly stated. London, Printed for Robert Bostock, 1641.

Observations upon some of his Majesties Late Answers and Expresses. [1642.] [Reproduced in Haller, *Tracts on Liberty*.]

Jus Populi. Or, A Discourse Wherein clear satisfaction is given, as well concerning the Right of Subiects, as the Right of Princes. London: Printed for Robert Bostock, 1644.

Perkins, William. The Works of . . . . London, Printed for J. Legatt, 1616-1618.

The Petition for the Prelates Briefly Examined . . . . MDCXLI.

Petty, William. The Advice of W. P. to Mr. Samuel Hartlib, for the advancement of some particular parts of learning. London, 1648. [Reprinted in *The Harleian Miscellany*, VI, 1810.]

Philodemius, Eleutherius (*pseud.*). The Armies Vindication . . . . Printed for Peter Cole, 1649.

Prynne, William. Anti-Arminianisme. Or The Church of Englands Old Antithesis to New Arminianisme. Wherein seven Anti-Arminian Orthodox Tenets, are evidently proved . . . to be the ancient, established, undoubted Doctrine of the primitive and modern Church of England . . . . The second Edition much enlarged. 1630. [First edition 1630. Selections in Woodhouse, *Puritanism and Liberty*.]

Independency Examined, Unmasked, Refuted, By twelve new particular Interrogatories. Printed by F. L. for Michael Sparks, 1644.

Twelve Considerable Serious Questions touching Church government. . . . London, Printed by F. L. for Michael Sparke. 1644.

A Fresh Discovery of some Prodigious New Wandering-Blasing-Stars, & Firebrands, Stiling themselves New-Lights, Firing our Church and State into New Combustions. London, Printed by John Macock for Michael Spark. 1645.

A Briefe Memento to the Present Unparliamentary Iunto Touching their present Intentions and Proceedings to Depose and Execute, Charles Steward, their lawfull King. London, 1648.

Ten Considerable Quaeries concerning Tithes. London, Printed for Edward Thomas. 1659.

The Putney Debates: General Council of the Army, 1647: ed. A. S. P. Woodhouse, *Puritanism and Liberty*, 1-124. London, 1938.

Queene Elizabeths Bishops: or A Brief Declaration of the Wickednesse of the Generalitie of those Bishops of England that lived in the purest times . . . . London, 1642.

Redingstone, John. Plain English To The Parliament and Army, and to the rest of the People . . . . London, Printed by Henry Hils . . . . 1649.

A Reply of two of the Brethren to A. S. wherein you have Observations on his

Considerations, Annotations, &c. Upon the Apologetical Narration. With A Plea for Libertie of Conscience for the Apologists Church way; Against the Cavils of the Said A. S. Formerly called M. S. to A. S. London, Printed by M. Simmons for Henry Overton. 1644.

Richardson, Samuel. The necessity of Toleration In Matters of Religion, Or, Certain Questions propounded to the Synod, tending to prove that Corporal punishments ought not to be inflicted upon such as hold Errors in Religion .... London, 1647.

An Answer to the London Ministers Letter: From them To his Excellency & his Counsel of War; as also an Answer to John Geeree's Book, entituled, Might overcomming Right .... London, Printed by I. C. for Hanah Alin, 1649.

An Apology for the Present Government and Governour. Printed ... by Gyles Calvert. 1654.

Robinson, Henry. Liberty of Conscience: or the Sole means to obtaine Peace and Truth .... 1643. [Reproduced in Haller, *Tracts on Liberty.*]

Robinson, John. A Justification of Separation from the church of England: against Mr. Richard Bernard his Invective, intituled The Separatists Schism. 1610.

A Just and Necessarie Apologie of certaine Christians, no less contumeliously than commonly called Brownists or Barrowists. 1625.

New Essays, or Observations Divine and Morall. Collected out of the holy Scriptures, ancient and moderne Writers, both Divine and Humane. ... 1628. [First published 1625.]

The Works of .... With a memoir and annotations by Robert Ashton. London, 1851.

Rogers, John. *Διαπολιτεία.* A Christian Concertation With Mr. Prin, Mr. Baxter, Mr. Harrington. For the True Cause of the Commonwealth. Or, An Answer to Mr. Prin's (Perditory) Anatomy of the Republick, and his True and Perfect Narrative, &c. To Mr. Baxter's (Purgatory) Pills for the Army: and his Wounding Answer to the Healing Question .... London, Printed for Livewell Chapman .... 1659.

A Vindication of that Prudent and Honourable Knight, Sir Henry Vane, From the Lyes and Calumnies of Mr. Richard Baxter .... London, Printed for Livewell Chapman .... 1659.

M. Harrington's Parallel Unparallel'd: or A Demonstration upon it .... Wherein it appears that neither the Spirit of the People, nor the Spirit of men like Mr. R. but the Spirit of God, of Christ, of his people in Parliament and Adherents to the Cause, is the fittest for the Government of the Commonwealth. 1659.

Mr. Pryn's Good Old Cause Stated and Stunted 10. years ago .... London, Printed by J. C. for L. Chapman. 1659.

Rutherford, Samuel. Lex Rex: The Law and the Prince. A Dispute for the just Prerogative of King and People. London; Printed for Iohn Field. Octob. 7. 1644. [Selections in Woodhouse, *Puritanism and Liberty.*]

The Due Right of Presbyteries; or, A Peaceable Plea for the Government of the Church of Scotland. London, Printed by E. Griffin for R. Whittaker and A. Crook. 1644.

A Free Disputation Against pretended Liberty of Conscience Tending to Resolve Doubts moved by Mr. John Goodwin, John Baptist, Dr. Jer. Taylor . . . and other Authors . . . . London, Printed by R. I. for Andrew Crook. MDCIL.

S., G. The Dignity of Kingship Asserted: In Answer to Mr. Milton's Ready and Easie way to establish a Free Common-wealth. London, Printed by E. C. for H. Seile and W. Palmer, 1660. [Reproduced, and ascribed to George Starkey in an introduction by W. R. Parker; the Facsimile Text Society, New York, 1942.]

S., M. M.S. to A.S. With A Plea for Libertie of Conscience in a Church Way, Against the Cavils of A.S. And Observations of his considerations, and Annotations Upon the Apologetical Narration . . . . London, Printed by F. N. for H. Overton. 1644.

Saltmarsh, John. Groanes for Liberty. Presented From the Presbyterian (formerly non-conforming) Brethren, reputed the ablest and most learned among them, in some Treatises called Smectymnuus . . . in the yeare 1641, by reason of the Prelates Tyranny. Now awakened and presented to themselves in the behalf of their now Non-conforming Brethren . . . . London, Printed for Giles Calfert, 1645.

Saumaise (Salmasius), Claude. Defensio Regia Pro Carolo I ad Serenissimum Magnae Britannia Regem Carolum II Filium natu majorem, Heredem & Successorem legitimum, Sumptibus Regiis. 1649.

Scobell, Henry. A Collection of Acts and Ordinances . . . made in the Parliament begun and held at Westminster the third day of November, anno 1640, and since, unto the Adjournment of the Parliament begun and holden the 17th of September, anno 1656 . . . . London, Printed by Henry Hills and John Field. 1658.

Scripture and Reason Pleaded for Defensive Armes: or The whole Controversie about Subjects taking up Armes. Published by Divers Reverend and Learned Divines. London, Printed for John Bellamy and Ralph Smith, MDCXLIII.

Selden, John. Ioannis Seldeni De Jure Naturali & Gentium, Juxta Disciplinam Ebraeorum, Libri Septem. Londini, Excudebat Richardus Bishopius. 1640.

A serious and faithful Representation of the Judgements of Ministers of the Gospell Within the Province of London. Contained In a Letter from them to the Generall and his Councell of Warre . . . Jan. 18, 1648. Imprinted at London by M. B. for Samuel Gellibrand and Ralph Smith. 1649.

A Short History Of The Anabaptists Of High And Low Germany. London, Printed by T. Badger, for Samuel Brown. MDCXLII.

Smith, Sir Thomas. De Republica Anglorum, A Discourse on the Commonwealth of England. Edited by L. Alston. Cambridge, 1906. [First published 1583.]

Spencer, Benjamin. Christophilos. The True Christian Subject Decyphered in a Sermon preached at Saint Pauls London, on the seventh of August, Anno 1642. London, Printed for Thomas Paybody. 1642.

Steuart, Adam. Some Observations And Annotations Upon the Apologeticall Narration . . . . London, Printed for Christopher Meredith . . . . 1643.

The Second Part of the Duply to M. S. alias Two Brethren . . . . With

A brief Epitome and Refutation of all the whole Independent-Government. . . . Printed for Iohn Field. 1644.

Stubbe, Henry. The Common-Wealth of Israel, or a brief Account of Mr. Prynnes Anatomy of the Good Old Cause. London, Printed for Tho. Brewster . . . . 1659.

An Essay In Defence of the Good Old Cause, or A Discourse concerning the Rise and Extent of the power of the Civil Magistrate in reference to Spiritual Affairs. With A Praeface Concerning {The Name of the Good Old Cause. An Equal Common-wealth. A Co-ordinate Synod. The Holy Common-wealth . . . by Mr. Richard Baxter. And A Vindication Of The Honourable Sir Henry Vane from the false aspersions of Mr. Baxter. London . . . . 1659.

A Light Shining out of Darkness: Or Occasional Queries Submitted To the Judgment of such as would enquire into the true State of things in our Times . . . . London . . . , MDCLIX.

Malice Rebuked, Or A Character of Mr. Richard Baxters Abilities. And A Vindication of the Honourable Sr. Henry Vane From His Aspersions in his Key for Catholicks . . . . London . . . MDCLIX.

A Letter to An Officer of the Army concerning A Select Senate mentioned by them in their Proposals to the late Parliament. The Necessity and Prudentialness of such a Senate is here asserted by Reason and History . . . . London, Printed for T. B. . . . 1659.

The Common-wealth of Oceana Put into the Ballance, and found too light. Or An Account of the Republic of Sparta, with occasional Animadversions upon Mr. James Harrington and the Oceanistical Model. London. Printed for Giles Calvert . . . . 1660.

A Survay of that Foolish, Seditious, Scandalous, Prophane Libell, The Protestation Protested. London, 1641.

Taylor, Jeremy. The Whole Works of . . . . With a life . . . and a critical examination . . . by Reginald Heber. London, 1822.

Thomas, William. A Speech of William Thomas, Esquire, in Parliament, in May, 1641, Being a short View and Examination of the Actions of Bishops in Parliament, from A.D. 1116 to this present of 1641 . . . . Printed at London by Tho. Harper. 1641.

The Use of Daily Publick Prayers, in three Positions. London, Printed for Iohn Maynard. 1641.

Usher, John. A Body of Divinitie, or the Summe and Substance of Christian Religion, Catechestically propounded, and explained . . . . London, Printed by M. F. for Tho: Downes and Geo: Badger. MDCXLV.

Vane, Sir Henry, the younger. Sr. Henry Vane his Speech in the House of Commons, at a Committee for the Bill against Episcopall-Government . . . June 11, 1641. London, Printed for Francis Constable, 1641.

The Retired Mans Meditations, or the Mysterie and Power of Godlines Shining forth in the Living Word, to the unmasking of the Mysterie of Iniquity in the most Refined and Purest Forms. London, Printed by R. W. [for] T. Brewster. 1655.

A Healing Question propounded and resolved upon occasion of the late publique and seasonable Call to Humiliation, in order to love and union amongst the honest party, and with a desire to apply Balsome to the wound, before it becomes incurable. [1656.]

An Epistle General to the Mystical Body of Christ on Earth, the Church Universal in Babylon, who are Pilgrims and strangers on the Earth, desiring and seeking after the Heavenly Country. Written by Sir Henry Vane, Knight, in the time of his Imprisonment. 1662.

The Substance of what Sir Henry Vane Intended to have Spoken upon the Scaffold on Tower-Hill, at the Time of his execution, Being the 14th of June 1662. London, 1662.

The Vanity of the Present Churches and uncertainty of their Preaching Discovered, wherein the pretended immediate teaching of the spirit is denied, and the all-sufficiencie of the Scriptures teaching is maintained. London, Printed for J. Clows, 1649.

A Vindication of the Ministers of the Gospel in, and about London, from the unjust Aspersions upon their former Actings for the Parliament, as if they had promoted the bringing of the King to Capitall punishment. London, Printed by A. M. for Th. Underhill, 1648.

Walker, Clement. The History Of Independency, With The Rise, Growth, and Practices of that powerful and restlesse Faction. 1648.

Anarchia Anglicana Or, The History of Independency. The Second Part. MDCXLIX.

Walwyn, William. The Compassionate Samaritane Unbinding The Conscience, and powring Oyle into the wounds which have been made upon the Separation. The Second Edition, corrected and enlarged .... 1644. [First published 1644. Ascribed by Haller, I, 123, and reproduced in *Tracts on Liberty*.]

A Helpe to the right understanding of a Discourse Concerning Independency. Lately published by William Pryn .... 1644. [Reproduced in Haller, *Tracts on Liberty*.]

Englands Lamentable Slaverie, Proceeding from the Arbitrarie will, severitie, and Injustnes of Kings, Negligence, corruption, and unfaithfulnesse of Parliaments, Coveteousness, ambition, and Variablenesse of Priests, and simplicitie, Carelesnesse, and cowardlinesse of People. [1645.] [Ascribed by Pease, *The Leveller Movement*, 116.]

Webster, John. Academiarum Examen, Or The Examination Of Academies. Wherein is discussed and examined the Matter, Method, And Customes of Academick and Scholastick Learning, and the insufficiency thereof discovered and laid open .... London, Printed for Giles Calvert .... MDCLIV.

Whichcote, Benjamin. Moral and Religious Aphorisms. London, 1930. [First published 1703.]

The Whitehall Debates: Council of Officers, 1648-1649: ed. A. S. P. Woodhouse, *Puritanism and Liberty*, 125-178. London, 1938.

Williams, Roger. Queries of Highest Consideration Proposed to Mr. Tho. Goodwin, Mr. Philip Nye, Mr. Wil Bridges, Mr. Jer. Burroughs, Mr. Sidr. Simpson and to the Commissioners from the General Assembly (so called) of the Church of Scotland, upon occasion of their late Printed Apologies .... MDCXLIV. [Edited by R. A. Guild and reprinted in *Publications of the Narragansett Club*, Series I, volume II, Providence, 1867.]

The Bloudy Tenent, of Persecution, for cause of Conscience discussed, in A Conference betweene Truth and Peace. 1644. [Edited by E. B. Underhill and reprinted in *Hanserd Knollys Society Publications*, IV, London, 1848. Selections in Woodhouse, *Puritanism and Liberty.*]

The Bloudy Tenent Yet More Bloody: by Mr Cottons endeavour to wash it white in the Blood of the Lambe .... London, Printed for Giles Calvert ..., 1652.

The Hireling Ministry None of Christs or A Discourse touching the Propagating the Gospel of Christ Jesus. London, Printed in the second Moneth, 1652.

Wilson, Thomas. Davids Zeale for Zion. A Sermon Preached before sundri of the Honourable House of Commons ... April 4. London, Printed for Iohn Bartlet, 1641.

Winstanley, Gerrard. The Law of Freedom in a Platform: Or, True Magistracy Restored .... Wherein is Declared, What is Kingly Government, and what is Commonwealths Government. London, Printed for the Author, and are to be sold by Giles Calvert, 1652.

The Works of .... Edited by G. H. Sabine. Ithaca, 1941.

Young, Thomas. Dies Dominica sive Succincta narratio ex S. Scriptuarum, & venerandae antiquitatis Patrem testimoniis concinnata, et Duobus Libris distincta .... 1639.

The Lords Day, or a Succinct Narration Compiled Out of the Testimonies of H. Scripture, and the Reverend Ancient Fathers: and Divided into Two Books .... Lately translated out of the Latin. London, Printed by E. Leach [for] Nevil Symmons. 1672.

Hopes Incouragement pointed at in a Sermon preached in St. Margarets Westminster, before the Honourable House of Commons .... At the last Solemn Fast February 28, 1643. Printed at London for Ralph Smith, 1644.

Young, Thomas, and Stephen Marshall, Edmund Calamy, Matthew Newcomen, William Spurstowe. An Answer to a Book entituled An Humble Remonstrance In which the Original of {Liturgy, Episcopacy is discussed. Written by Smectymnuus. London, Printed for I. Rothwell. 1641.

A Vindication of the Answer to the Humble Remonstrance, from the unjust imputations of frivolousnesse and falsehood: Wherein the cause of {Liturgy and Episcopacy is farther debated, By the same Smectymnuus. London, Printed for John Rothwell, 1641.

## II. SECONDARY SOURCES

The following abbreviations have been used: *MLN, Modern Language Notes; MLR, Modern Language Review; PMLA, Publications of the Modern Language Association of America; PQ, Philological Quarterly; RES, Review of English Studies; SP, Studies in Philology; UTQ, University of Toronto Quarterly.*

### A. MILTON

Agar, H. Milton and Plato. Princeton, 1928.

Bailey, M. L. Milton and Jacob Boehme. New York, 1914.

Barker, A. E. Milton's Schoolmasters. MLR, XXXII (1937), 517-36.
Christian Liberty in Milton's Divorce Pamphlets. MLR, XXXV (1940), 153-61.
The Pattern of Milton's *Nativity Ode*. UTQ, X (1941), 167-81.

Belloc, H. Milton. Philadelphia, 1935.

Benn, A. W. Milton's Ethics. International Journal of Ethics, XXI (1911), 422-47.

Brown, E. G. Milton's Blindness. New York, 1935.

Brunner, H. Milton's Persönliche und Ideele Welt in ihrer Beziehung zum Aristokratismus. Bonn, 1933.

Buck, P. Milton on Liberty. University Studies, University of Nebraska, XXV, 1925.

Chauvet, Paul. La religion de Milton. Paris, 1909.

Darbishire, H., editor. Early Lives of Milton. London, 1932.

Fay, C. R. The Political Philosophy of Milton. Christ's College Magazine, XXIII (1908), 81-92.

Fletcher, H. F. Milton's Semitic Studies. Chicago, 1926.
The Use of the Bible in Milton's Prose. University of Illinois Studies in Language and Literature, XIV, no. 3, Urbana, 1929.
Milton's Rabbinical Readings. Urbana, 1930.

French, J. M. The Date of Milton's Blindness. PQ, XV (1936), 93-4.
Milton, Needham, and *Mercurius Politicus*. SP, XXXIII (1936), 236-52.
Milton in Chancery. New York, 1939.

Geoffroy, A. Étude sur les pamphlets politiques et religieux de Milton. Paris, 1848.

Gilbert, A. H. The Cambridge Manuscript and Milton's Plans for Epic. SP, XVI (1919), 172-6.
Milton on the Position of Women. MLR, XV (1920), 7-27, 240-64.

Gilman, W. E. Milton's Rhetoric: Studies in his Defence of Liberty. University of Missouri Studies, XIV, no. 3, Columbia, 1939.

Good, J. W. Studies in the Milton Tradition. University of Illinois Studies in Language and Literature, I, nos. 3 and 4, Urbana, 1913.

Grierson, Sir H. J. C. Milton and Wordsworth: Poets and Prophets. Cambridge, 1937.

Hamilton, W. D. Original Papers Illustrative of the Life and Writings of John Milton. Camden Society Transactions, LXXV, London, 1859.

Hanford, J. H. Milton and the Return to Humanism. SP, XVI (1919), 126-38.
The Date of Milton's *De Doctrina Christiana*. SP, XVII (1920), 309-19.
The Chronology of Milton's Private Studies. PMLA, XXXVI (1921), 251-314.
The Rosenbach Milton Documents. PMLA, XXXVIII (1923), 290-6.

The Youth of Milton. Studies in Shakespeare, Milton, and Donne. University of Michigan Publications in Language and Literature. New York, 1925.

That Shepherd, Who First Taught the Chosen Seed. UTQ, VIII (1939), 403-19.

A Milton Handbook. New York, 1941.

Hartwell, K. E. Lactantius and Milton. Cambridge, Mass., 1929.

Kelley, Maurice. This Great Argument: A Study of Milton's *De Doctrina Christiana* as a Gloss upon *Paradise Lost.* Princeton, 1941.

Liljegren, S. B. Studies in Milton. Lund, 1918.

Looten, C. Les débuts de Milton pamphlétaire. Études Anglais, I (1937), 297-313.

Lowenhaupt, W. H. The Writing of Milton's *Eikonoklastes.* SP, XX (1923), 29-51.

Mack, J. F. The Evolution of Milton's Political Thinking. Sewanee Review, XXX (1922), 193-205.

Martin, B. The Date of Milton's First Marriage. SP, XXV (1928), 457-61.

Masson, D. The Life of John Milton: Narrated in Connexion with the ... History of his Time. London, 1859-94.

Nicolson, M. H. Milton and Hobbes. SP, XXIII (1926), 405-33.

Parker, W. R. Milton and Thomas Young. MLN, (1938), 399-407.

Milton's Contemporary Reputation. An Essay together with A Tentative List of Printed Allusions to Milton, 1641-1674, and facsimile reproductions of five contemporary pamphlets written in answer to Milton. Columbus, 1940.

Patterson, F. A. An Index to the Columbia Edition of the Works of John Milton. New York, 1940.

Pattison, M. Milton. London, 1879.

Raymond, D. N. Oliver's Secretary: John Milton in an Era of Revolt. New York, 1932.

Saurat, D. Milton, Man and Thinker. New York, 1925.

Seeley, J. R. Milton's Political Opinions. Lectures and Essays. London, 1870.

Sewell, A. Milton's *De Doctrina Christiana.* Essays and Studies by Members of the English Association, XIX (1934), 40-66.

Milton and the Mosaic Law. MLR, XXX (1935), 13-18, 218.

A Study in Milton's Christian Doctrine. London, 1939.

Smart, J. S. Milton and the King's Prayer. RES, I (1925), 385-91.

Stern, A. Milton und seine Zeit. Leipzig, 1877-9.

Thompson, E. N. S. Milton's *Of Education.* SP, XV (1918), 159-75.

Tillyard, E. M. W. Milton. London, 1930.

Whiting, G. W. Milton and the Postscript. MLR, XXX (1935), 506-8.

Milton's Literary Milieu. Chapel Hill, 1939.

Wolfe, D. M. Milton in the Puritan Revolution. New York, 1941.

Lilburne's Note on Milton. MLN, LVI (1941), 360-3.

Wolff, S. L. Milton's "Advocatum Nescio Quem": Milton, Salmasius and John Cook. Modern Language Quarterly, II (1941), 559-600.

Woodhouse, A. S. P. Milton and His Age. UTQ, V (1935), 130-9.

Milton, Puritanism, and Liberty. UTQ, IV (1935), 483-513.

The Argument of Milton's *Comus*. UTQ, XI (1941), 46-71.
Wright, B. A. Milton's First Marriage. MLR, XXVI (1931), 383-400; XXVII (1932), 6-23.
The Alleged Falsehoods in Milton's Account of His Continental Tour. MLR, XXVIII (1933), 308-14.

**B. THE BACKGROUND**

Allen, J. W. English Political Thought, 1603-1644. London, 1938.
Berens, L. N. The Digger Movement. London, 1906.
Bernstein, E. Cromwell and Communism. London, 1930.
Brown, L. F. The Political Activities of the Baptists and Fifth Monarchy Men. Oxford, 1912.
Buchan, John. Oliver Cromwell. London, 1934.
Burgess, W. H. John Robinson, Pastor of the Pilgrim Fathers. London, 1920.
Bush, D. The Renaissance and English Humanism. Toronto, 1939.
Two Roads to Truth: Science and Religion in the Early Seventeenth Century. English Literary History, VIII (1941), 81-102.
Clark, G. N. The Seventeenth Century. Oxford, 1929.
Clyde, W. M. The Struggle for the Freedom of the Press from Caxton to Cromwell. Oxford, 1934.
Davies, G. The Army and the Downfall of Richard Cromwell. Huntington Library Bulletin, VII (1935), 131-67.
De Pauley, W. C. The Candle of the Lord: Studies in the Cambridge Platonists. London, 1937.
Dunning, W. A. A History of Political Theories from Luther to Montesquieu. London, 1905.
Ernst, J. E. The Political Thought of Roger Williams. University of Washington Publications in Language and Literature, VI, no. 1, Seattle, 1929.
Roger Williams and the English Revolution. Rhode Island Historical Society Collections, XXIV (1931), 1-58.
Roger Williams, New England Firebrand. New York, 1932.
Fink, Z. S. Venice and English Political Thought in the Seventeenth Century. Modern Philology, XXXVIII (1940), 155-72.
Firth, Sir C. H. Oliver Cromwell and the Rule of the Puritans in England. New York, 1900.
Anarchy and the Restoration (1659-1660). The Cambridge Modern History, IV, 539-59, Cambridge, 1906.
The Last Years of the Protectorate, 1656-1658. London, 1909.
Freund, M. Die Idee der Toleranz im England der grossen Revolution. Halle, 1927.
Gardiner, S. R. History of the Great Civil War. London, 1886-91.
History of the Commonwealth and Protectorate. London, 1894.
Gierke, O. Natural Law and the Theory of Society, 1500-1800. Translated by E. Barker. Cambridge, 1934.
Gooch, G. P. Political Thought in England from Bacon to Halifax. London, 1923.
Gooch, G. P. and Laski, H. J. English Democratic Ideas in the Seventeenth Century. Cambridge, 1927.
Gough, J. W. The Social Contract: A Critical Study of Its Development. Oxford, 1936.

Grierson, Sir H. J. C. Cross Currents in English Literature of the Seventeenth Century. London, 1929.

Haller, W. Before *Areopagitica*. PMLA, XLII (1927), 875-900.

Tracts on Liberty in the Puritan Revolution, 1638-1647. New York, 1934.

The Rise of Puritanism . . . , 1570-1643. New York, 1938.

Haller, W. and M. The Puritan Art of Love. Huntington Library Quarterly, V (1942), 235-72.

Hosmer, J. K. The Life of Young Sir Henry Vane. Boston, 1889.

James, M. Social Problems and Policy during the Puritan Revolution. London, 1930.

Janet, P. Histoire de la science politique dans ses rapports avec la morale. Paris, 1887.

Jones, R. F. Ancients and Moderns: A Study of the Background of *The Battle of the Books*. Washington University Studies, New Series, Language and Literature, VI, St. Louis, 1936.

Jordan, W. K. The Development of Religious Toleration in England. London and Cambridge, Mass., 1932, 1935, 1938, 1940.

Kirby, E. W. William Prynne: A Study in Puritanism. Cambridge, Mass., 1931.

Knappen, M. M. Tudor Puritanism: A Chapter in the History of Idealism. Chicago, 1939.

Laing, D. Biographical Notices of Thomas Young. Edinburgh, 1870.

Lindsay, A. D. The Essentials of Democracy. Oxford, 1930.

Lyon, T. The Theory of Religious Liberty in England, 1603-1639. Cambridge, 1937.

McIlwain, C. H. The High Court of Parliament. New Haven, 1910.

Marriott, Sir J. A. R. The Life and Times of Lucius Cary, Viscount Falkland. London, 1907.

Miller, P. Orthodoxy in Massachusetts, 1630-1650. Cambridge, Mass., 1933.

Neal, D. History of the Puritans. London, 1822.

Patrick, J. M. The Literature of the Diggers. UTQ, XII (1942), 95-110.

Pease, T. C. The Leveller Movement. Oxford, 1916.

Peile, J. Christ's College. London, 1900.

Petegorsky, D. W. Left-Wing Democracy in the English Civil War: A Study of the Social Philosophy of Gerrard Winstanley. London, 1940.

Powell, C. L. English Domestic Relations, 1487-1653. New York, 1917.

Powicke, F. J. The Cambridge Platonists. Cambridge, Mass., 1926.

Quintana, R. Notes on English Educational Opinion in the Seventeenth Century. SP, XXVII (1930), 265-92.

Sabine, G. H. A History of Political Theory. New York, 1937.

Schneider, H. W. The Puritan Mind. New York, 1930.

Seaton, A. A. The Theory of Toleration under the Later Stuarts. Cambridge, 1911.

Sisson, C. J. The Judicious Marriage of Mr. Hooker and the Birth of *The Laws of Ecclesiastical Polity*. Cambridge, 1940.

Smith, H. F. R. Harrington and his *Oceana*. Cambridge, 1914.

Smith, P. A History of Modern Culture. London, 1930.

Straus, O. S. Roger Williams: The Pioneer of Religious Liberty. London, 1894.

Tawney, R. H. Religion and the Rise of Capitalism. London, 1936.
Tindall, W. Y. John Bunyan, Mechanick Preacher. New York, 1934.
Trevelyan, G. M. England under the Stuarts. London, 1933.
Troeltsch, E. The Social Teaching of the Christian Churches. London, 1931.
Tulloch, J. English Puritanism and its Leaders. London, 1861.
Rational Theology in England in the Seventeenth Century. London, 1874.
Willcock, J. The Life of Sir Henry Vane the Younger. London, 1913.
Woodhouse, A. S. P. Puritanism and Liberty. UTQ, IV (1935), 395-404.
Puritanism and Democracy. Canadian Journal of Economics and Political Science, IV (1938), 1-21.
Puritanism and Liberty. Being the Army Debates (1647-9) from the Clarke Manuscripts with Supplementary Documents. London, 1938.

*Index*

# Index

PR
3592
P985
B255
12518
Barker
Milton and the Puritan dil-
emma, 1641-1660